# Qualitative Spatio-Temporal Representation and Reasoning:

## Trends and Future Directions

Shyamanta M. Hazarika
*Tezpur University, India*

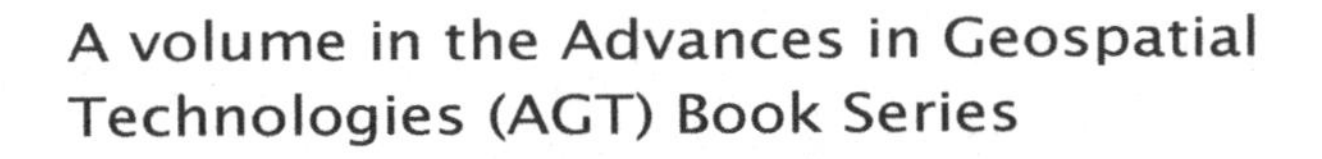
A volume in the Advances in Geospatial Technologies (AGT) Book Series

Managing Director: Lindsay Johnston
Senior Editorial Director: Heather A. Probst
Book Production Manager: Sean Woznicki
Development Manager: Joel Gamon
Acquisitions Editor: Erika Gallagher
Cover Design: Nick Newcomer

Published in the United States of America by
Information Science Reference (an imprint of IGI Global)
701 E. Chocolate Avenue
Hershey PA 17033
Tel: 717-533-8845
Fax: 717-533-8661
E-mail: cust@igi-global.com
Web site: http://www.igi-global.com



Library of Congress Cataloging-in-Publication Data

Qualitative spatio-temporal representation and reasoning: trends and future directions / Shyamanta M. Hazarika, editor.
p. cm.
Includes bibliographical references and index.
Summary: This book is a contribution to the emerging discipline of qualitative spatial information theory within artificial intelligence, covering both theory and application-centric research and providing a comprehensive perspective on the emerging area of qualitative spatio-temporal representation and reasoning -- Provided by publisher.
ISBN 978-1-61692-868-1 (hardcover) -- ISBN 978-1-61692-870-4 (ebook) -- ISBN 978-1-4666-1654-7 (print & perpetual access) 1. Qualitative reasoning. 2. Spatial analysis (Statistics) 3. Space and time--Mathematical models. 4. Logic, Symbolic and mathematical. I. Hazarika, Shyamanta M.
Q339.25.Q84 2012
006.3'33--dc23

2011050504

This book is published in the IGI Global book series Advances in Geospatial Technologies (AGT) (ISSN: 2327-5715; eISSN: 2327-5723)

British Cataloguing in Publication Data
A Cataloguing in Publication record for this book is available from the British Library.

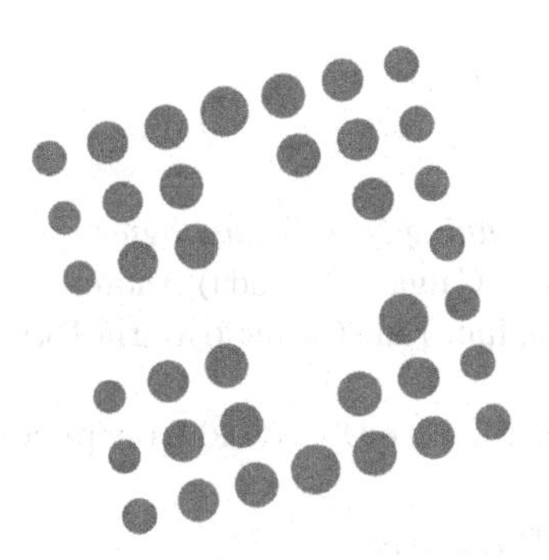

# Advances in Geospatial Technologies (AGT) Book Series

ISSN: 2327-5715
EISSN: 2327-5723

Mission

The geospatial technology field is a fast-paced, high growth industry that is involved in a variety of fields, including military planning, public health, land use, environmental protection, and Google Earth mapping. With such a diverse body of applications, the research in geospatial technologies is always evolving and new theories, methodologies, tools, and applications are being developed. **Advances in Geospatial Technologies (AGT) Book Series** is a reference source and outlet for research that discusses all aspects of geographic information, including areas such as geomatics, geodesy, GIS, cartography, remote sensing, and other areas. Because geospatial technologies are so pervasive in such a variety of areas, AGT also includes books that address interdisciplinary applications of the technologies.

Coverage

- Cartography
- Digital Terrain Modeling
- Environmental Monitoring
- Geospatial Analysis
- Geovisualization
- Global Positioning Systems
- Land Surveying
- Public Sector Use of Geospatial Technologies
- Remote Systems
- Spatial Reference Systems

IGI Global is currently accepting manuscripts for publication within this series. To submit a proposal for a volume in this series, please contact our Acquisition Editors at Acquisitions@igi-global.com or visit: http://www.igi-global.com/publish/.

The Advances in Geospatial Technologies (AGT) Book Series (ISSN 2327-5715) is published by IGI Global, 701 E. Chocolate Avenue, Hershey, PA 17033-1240, USA, www.igi-global.com. This series is composed of titles available for purchase individually; each title is edited to be contextually exclusive from any other title within the series. For pricing and ordering information please visit http://www.igi-global.com/book-series/advances-geospatial-technologies-agt-book/73686. Postmaster: Send all address changes to above address. 

## Titles in this Series

*For a list of additional titles in this series, please visit: www.igi-global.com*

*Geographic Information Analysis for Sustainable Development and Economic Planning New Technologies*
Giuseppe Borruso (University of Trieste, Italy) Stefania Bertazzon (University of Calgary, Canada) Andrea Favretto (University of Trieste, Italy) Beniamino Murgante (University of Basilicata, Italy) and Carmelo Maria Torre (Polytechnic of Bari, Italy)
Information Science Reference • copyright 2013 • 434pp • H/C (ISBN: 9781466619241) • US $180.00 (our price)

*Qualitative Spatio-Temporal Representation and Reasoning Trends and Future Directions*
Shyamanta M. Hazarika (Tezpur University, India)
Information Science Reference • copyright 2012 • 381pp • H/C (ISBN: 9781616928681) • US $195.00 (our price)

*Universal Ontology of Geographic Space Semantic Enrichment for Spatial Data*
Tomaž Podobnikar (Scientific Research Centre of the Slovenian Academy of Sciences and Arts, Slovenia & University of Ljubljana, Slovenia) and Marjan Čeh (University of Ljubljana, Slovenia)
Information Science Reference • copyright 2012 • 304pp • H/C (ISBN: 9781466603271) • US $180.00 (our price)

*Geospatial Web Services Advances in Information Interoperability*
Peisheng Zhao (George Mason University, USA) and Liping Di (George Mason University, USA)
Information Science Reference • copyright 2011 • 552pp • H/C (ISBN: 9781609601928) • US $180.00 (our price)

www.igi-global.com

701 E. Chocolate Ave., Hershey, PA 17033
Order online at www.igi-global.com or call 717-533-8845 x100
To place a standing order for titles released in this series, contact: cust@igi-global.com
Mon-Fri 8:00 am - 5:00 pm (est) or fax 24 hours a day 717-533-8661

# Editorial Advisory Board

# Table of Contents

# Detailed Table of Contents



This chapter focuses on the topological and mereological relations, contact, and parthood, between spatio-temporal regions as axiomatized in so-called mereotopologies. Despite, or because of, their simplicity, a variety of different first-order axiomatizations have been proposed. This chapter discusses their underlying ontological choices and different ways of systematically looking at them. The chapter further gives an overview of the algebraic, topological, and graph-theoretic representations of mereotopological models which help to better understand the model-theoretic consequences of the various ontological choices. While much work on mereotopologies has been primarily theoretical, the focus started shifting towards applications and domain-specific extensions of mereotopology. These aspects will most likely guide the future direction of the field: How can mereotopologies be extended or otherwise adjusted to better suit practical needs? Moreover, the integration of mereotopology into more comprehensive and maybe more pragmatic ontologies of space and time remains another challenge in the field of region-based space.



This chapter describes a framework called PLCA for Qualitative Spatial Reasoning (QSR) based on the connection patterns of regions. The goal of this chapter is to provide a simple but expressive and feasible representation for qualitative data with sufficient reasoning ability. PLCA provides a symbolic representation for spatial data using simple objects. The authors of this chapter define its expression and operations on it, and show the correspondance between the expression and a figure. PLCA also provides semantical reasoning incorporated with spatial reasoning. Moreover, it can be extended to handle shapes of regions. Throughout the study, the authors discovered many topics that relate QSR to other research areas such as topology, graph theory, and computational geometry, while achieving the research goals. This indicates that QSR is a very fruitful research area.

This chapter discusses the use of transition graphs for reasoning about continuous spatial change over time. The chapter first presents a general definition of a transition graph for a partition of a topological space. Then it defines the path-connected and the homogeneous refinements of such a partition. The qualitative behavior of paths through the space corresponds to the structure of paths through the associated transition graphs, and of associated interval label sequences, and the authors prove a number of metalogical theorems that characterize these correspondences in terms of the expressivity of associated first-order languages. They then turn to specific real-world problems and show how this theory can be applied to domains such as rigid objects, strings, and liquids.



A number of qualitative calculi have been developed in order to reason about space and time. A recent trend has been the emergence of integrated spatiotemporal calculi in order to deal with dynamic phenomena such as motion. In 2004, Van de Weghe introduced the Qualitative Trajectory Calculus (QTC) as a qualitative calculus to represent and reason about moving objects. This chapter presents a general overview of the principal theoretical aspects of QTC, focusing on the two most fundamental types of QTC. It shows how QTC deals with important reasoning concepts and how calculus can be employed in order to represent raw moving object data.



Although a wide range of sophisticated Qualitative Spatial and Temporal Reasoning (QSTR) formalisms have now been developed, there are relatively few applications that apply these commonsense methods. To address this problem, the authors of this chapter developed methodologies that support QSTR application design. They established a theoretical foundation for QSTR applications that includes the roles of application designers and users. The authors adapted formal software requirements that allow a designer to specify the customer's operational requirements and the functional requirements of a QSTR application. The chapter presents design patterns for organising the components of QSTR applications, and a methodology for defining high-level neighbourhoods that are derived from the system structure. Finally, the authors develop a methodology for QSTR application validation by defining a complexity metric called H-complexity that is used in test coverage analysis for assessing the quality of unit and integration test sets.

**Chapter 6**
Enriching the Qualitative Spatial Reasoning System RCC8 ........................................................ 203
*Ahed Alboody, Université Paul Sabatier (UPS), France*
*Florence Sedes, Université Paul Sabatier (UPS), France*
*Jordi Inglada, Centre National d'Etudes Spatiales (CNES), France*

GIS and image databases are often based on the description of relations between spatial regions. One kind of these relations is the topological relations, where the general description of region-region topological relations in detail is still an unsolved issue although much effort has been done. The eight basic topological relations between two spatial regions are written without any details in the classical form of the spatial reasoning system RCC8. In this chapter, multi-level topological relations are introduced by using two concepts: Separation Number and the Type of Spatial Elements (Points and Lines) of the Boundary-Boundary Intersection Spatial Set (BBISS) to enrich the RCC8 system. The chapter focuses on the four relations EC, PO, TPP, and TPPi, which can be detailed and enriched at two levels. At the first detailed level, these four relations are written in general detailed forms by using the concept of Separation Number of Spatial Elements of BBISS. At the second detailed level, the same relations are expressed in other general forms more detailed by using the concept of Types of Spatial Elements of BBISS. In this context, definitions for the generalization of these detailed topological relations at these two levels are developed. Examples for GIS applications are provided to illustrate the determination of the detailed topological relations studied in this chapter

**Chapter 7**
A Region-Based Ontology of the Brain Ventricular System and Its Relation to Schizophrenia ........ 255
*Paulo E. Santos, Centro Universitário da FEI, Brazil*
*Rodolpho Freire, Centro Universitário da FEI, Brazil*
*Danilo N. dos Santos, Centro Universitário da FEI, Brazil*
*Carlos E. Thomaz, Centro Universitário da FEI, Brazil*
*Paulo C. Sallet, Universidade de São Paulo, Brazil*
*Mario Louzã, Universidade de São Paulo, Brazil*
*Anthony G. Cohn, University of Leeds, UK*

This chapter describes an initial region-based formalisation of some concepts about neuroanatomy into ontological and epistemic terms, as part of a major effort into the formalisation of the knowledge contained in neuroimages of patients with schizophrenia. The long-term goal is to build an ontology that is a formal basis for the expectations generated from statistical data analysis. To this end, the chapter presents an example of applying this ontology to interpret the results of image-based analysis of neuroimages from schizophrenic patients.

**Chapter 8**
Explanation Generation over Temporal Interval Algebra ............................................................ 273
*Debasis Mitra, Florida Institute of Technology, USA*
*Florent Launay, Florida Institute of Technology, USA*

Temporal interval algebra has generated strong interest for both theoretical and practical reasons. All its Maximal Tractable Subalgebras (MTS) have been identified. Now is the time to make the transition toward their practical applications. In this chapter, the authors have proposed a formalism on how to classify an input temporal network in one of these MTSs or decide its intractability. They have also proposed a linear algorithm for checking consistency when the input belongs to one of the seventeen MTSs, and for finding the constraints responsible for inconsistency in case the network is unsatisfiable.

Qualitative spatial conceptualizations provide a relational abstraction and interface to the metrical realities of the physical world. Humans, robots, and systems that act and interact, are embedded in space. The space itself undergoes change all the time, typically as a result of volitional actions performed by an agent, and events, both deterministic and otherwise, which occur in the environment. Both categories of occurrences are a critical link to the external world, in a predictive as well as an explanatory sense: anticipations of spatial reality conform to commonsense knowledge of the effects of actions and events on material entities. Similarly, explanations of the perceived reality too are established on the basis of such apriori established commonsense notions. The author reasons about space, actions, and change in an integrated manner, either without being able to clearly demarcate the boundaries of each type of reasoning, or because such boundaries do not exist per se. This chapter is an attempt to position such integrated reasoning as a useful paradigm for the utilization of qualitative spatial representation and reasoning techniques in relevant application domains. From a logical perspective, the author notes that formalisms already exist and that effort need only be directed at specific integration tasks at a commonsense conceptual, formal representational, and computational level.



Scene descriptions are typically expressed in natural language texts and are integrated within Web pages, books, newspapers, and other means of content dissemination. The capabilities of such means can be enhanced to support automated content processing and communication between people or machines by allowing the scene contents to be extracted and expressed in ontologies, a formal syntax rich in semantics interpretable by both people and machines. Ontologies enable more effective querying, reasoning, and general use of content and allow for standardizing the quality and delivery of information across communicating information sources. Ontologies are defined using the well-established standards of the Semantic Web for expressing scene descriptions in application fields such as Geographic Information Systems, medicine, and the World Wide Web (WWW). Ontologies are not only suitable for describing static scenes with static objects (e.g., in photographs) but also enable representation of dynamic events with objects and properties changing in time (e.g., moving objects in a video). Representation of both static and dynamic scenes by ontologies, as well as querying and reasoning over static and dynamic ontologies are important issues for further research. These are exactly the problems this chapter is dealing with.



About two decades ago, the field of Qualitative Spatial and Temporal Reasoning (QSTR) emerged as a new area of AI research that set out to grasp human-level understanding and reasoning about spatial and temporal entities, linking formal approaches to cognitive theories. Empowering artificial agents with QSTR capabilities is claimed to facilitate manifold applications, including robot navigation, Geographic Information Systems (GIS), natural language understanding, and computer-aided design. QSTR is an active field of research that has developed many representation and reasoning approaches so far, but only comparatively; few applications exist that actually build on these QSTR techniques. This chapter

# Preface

## INTRODUCTION

*Qualitative Spatio-Temporal Representation and Reasoning: Trends and Future Directions* is a contribution to the emerging discipline of Qualitative Spatial Information Theory within Artificial Intelligence (AI). The research reported in this collection covers both theory and application-centric work in the area of qualitative spatial and temporal reasoning and provides a comprehensive perspective on the emerging area of Qualitative Spatio-Temporal Representation and Reasoning (QSTR).

## WHAT IS QSTR?

Moving around the environment is one of the primary tasks, which human beings and animals accomplish equally well. In the animal kingdom as a whole, reasoning about space is probably the most common and basic form of intelligence (Davis, 1990). For human beings, spatial reasoning, the representation and reasoning about space, is a particularly powerful and accessible mode of cognition (Piaget & Inhelder, 1967; Davis, 1990). Our every day interaction with the physical world is through spatial reasoning which appears to be driven by qualitative abstractions rather than complete quantitative knowledge a priori (Escrig & Toledo, 1998). *Qualitative Reasoning* holds promise for developing formal theories for reasoning about space (Freksa, 1991).

The desire to reason about space more akin to the cognitive process led to the birth of *Qualitative Spatial Reasoning* (QSR) within Knowledge Representation and Reasoning (KR & R). One of the central topics within AI, in general, and KR & R, in particular, is our ability to represent and reason with common-sense knowledge (McCarthy, 1959). Of our commonsensical abilities, those involving space and spatial attributes are perhaps the most basic ones. The physical world in which we live has a spatial extent and all physical objects are located in space. Space is an important part of common-sense reasoning. Driven by the motivation for a qualitative approach for the embodiment of commonsense spatial knowledge in intelligent systems, Qualitative Spatial Information Theory has emerged as a discipline within AI. Work within this discipline is designed to formulate formal frameworks to represent and reason about space, time, action, and change (Cohn & Hazarika, 2001; Cohn & Renz, 2008).

Space and time are inextricably linked. Spatial configurations change over time. Reasoning about space often involves reasoning about change in spatial configurations. Actions and events form the crucial connecting link between space, time, and spatial change, i.e., spatial configurations change as a result of actions and events within the environment. Spatial change is spatio-temporal.

Spatio-temporal reasoning is so common in our daily life that we rarely notice it as a particular concept of spatial analysis. When applied to computer information systems, spatio-temporal reasoning attempts to solve problems that deal with objects that occupy space and change over time (Egenhofer & Golledge, 1998).

Taking time into account is a central issue for GIS (Egenhofer & Golledge, 1998) and spatial databases (Peuquet, 1999). A lot of effort is devoted to providing useful and well-grounded models to be used as high-level qualitative description of spatio-temporal change (Hornsby & Egenhofer, 2000). Driven by cognitive approaches that characterize the processing of spatial information in QSR, there has been considerable influx of people from other areas within AI such as computer vision, robotics, etc. working on spatial change and spatial interactions (Fernyhough, et al., 2000; Galata, et al., 2002; Stock, 1997; Bhatt, et al., 2011). QSTR encompasses all such techniques.

Ambient Intelligence, Ubiquitous Computing, Intelligent Assistive Systems, and many other emerging fields will benefit immensely from the vast body of representation and reasoning tools that have been developed in QSR, in general, and the sub-field of QSTR, specifically. QSTR is increasingly becoming a core issue within Mobile Computing, GIS / Spatial Information Systems, Databases, and Computer Vision, as well as Knowledge Discovery and Data Mining. Attempts are already underway to explicitly utilize qualitative spatial calculi pertaining to different spatial domains for modeling the spatial aspect of an ambient environment (e.g., smart homes and offices); as well as to utilize a formal basis for representing and reasoning about space, change, and occurrences within such environments.

*Qualitative Spatio-Temporal Representation and Reasoning: Trends and Future Directions* covers both theory and applications with QSTR. The thrust is on research that focuses on formalizing commonsense spatial and temporal knowledge and directs the integration of qualitative spatial reasoning with general approaches for reasoning about spatio-temporal change. Applications that demonstrate the utility of well-established qualitative spatial and temporal calculi are also covered.

## THE INSIDE STORY

Formal region based theories of space date back to the early part of the 20th century. Whitehead, in his book *The Concept of Nature* proposed the construction of a geometry in which spatial regions rather than points would be basic entities (Whitehead, 1920). In *Process and Reality* he suggested that a general theory of objects, events, and processes could be developed based on the primitive relation of connectedness (Whitehead, 1929). The book begins with a chapter on region-based theories of space. Hahmann and Grüninger gathered and organized the knowledge about ontological commitments for the wealth of region-based theories that have been proposed for representing space qualitatively. The chapter discusses the underlying ontological choices of a variety of first-order axiomatizations proposed and different ways of systematically looking at them. This gives a broader picture of mereotopology and how the different theories fit into this bigger picture regardless of their concrete axiomatization. It is made clear that the actual differences between the various mereotopologies are usually only minor and that there are only a handful of substantially different approaches.

Takahashi put forwards a framework called PLCA for QSR based on the connection patterns of regions. PLCA provides a simple but expressive and feasible representation for qualitative data with sufficient reasoning ability. PLCA also provides semantical reasoning incorporated with spatial reasoning and can be extended to handle shapes of regions.

Continuity of change is the perception of being seamless and is dependent on the granularity. What seems as continuous at some level of granularity may be discontinuous at a finer level. Nevertheless, continuity may be thought of as the intuitive idea of a gradual variation with no abrupt jumps or gaps. Characterization of such an intuitive notion of continuity for a qualitative theory of motion is referred to as qualitative spatio-temporal continuity (Hazarika, 2005). In his chapter on "Qualitative Reasoning and Spatio-Temporal Continuity," Davis discusses the use of transition graphs for reasoning about continuous spatial change over time. Putting forward a general definition of a transition graph for a partition of a topological space, path-connected and homogeneous refinements of such a partition is defined. The qualitative behavior of paths through the space corresponds to the structure of paths through the associated transition graphs, and of associated interval label sequences; and a number of metalogical theorems that characterize these correspondences in terms of the expressivity of associated first-order languages are proved. The chapter then turns to specific real-world problems and shows how this theory can be applied to domains such as rigid objects, strings, and liquids.

The field of QSTR started with Allen's Interval Calculus (Allen, 1983) introduced some 25 years. Thereafter, a number of calculi have been developed to encapsulate commonsense knowledge about space and time. New research aims at combining existing qualitative calculi for improving the expressiveness; bringing with it an increasing complexity. Further, there is a trend towards emergence of integrated spatiotemporal calculi in order to deal with dynamic phenomena such as motion. Van de Weghe (2004) introduced the Qualitative Trajectory Calculus (QTC) as a qualitative calculus to represent and reason about moving objects. Delafontaine et al. present a general overview of the principal theoretical aspects of QTC, focusing on the two most fundamental types of QTC. It is shown how QTC deals with important reasoning concepts, and how the calculus can be employed in order to represent raw moving object data.

QSTR is an active field of research that has developed many representation and reasoning approaches so far, but only comparatively few applications exist that actually build on these QSTR techniques. For QSTR application development, a number of critical barriers to QSTR application development must be addressed, including methodologies for developing or analysing QSTR applications. Schultz, Amor, and Guesgen develop methodologies for QSTR application design. A theoretical foundation for QSTR applications that includes the roles of application designers and users is established. Their chapter adapts formal software requirements that allow a designer to specify the customer's operational requirements and the functional requirements of a QSTR application. Design patterns for organising the components of QSTR applications and a methodology for defining high-level neighbourhoods that are derived from the system structure is presented.

Alboody, Sedes, and Inglada enrich RCC-8, the set of base relations for the spatial representation language Region Connection Calculus (Randell, et al., 1992). In their chapter, multi-level topological relations are introduced by using concepts such as separation number and the type of spatial elements of the boundary-boundary intersection spatial set to enrich RCC-8. Definitions for the generalization of the detailed topological relations are developed. Examples for GIS applications are provided to illustrate concepts developed in this chapter.

Santos et al. describe an initial region-based formalisation of some concepts about neuroanatomy into ontological and epistemic terms, as part of a major effort into the formalisation of the knowledge contained in neuroimages of patients with schizophrenia.

Temporal interval algebra has generated strong interest for both theoretical and practical reasons. All its Maximal Tractable Subalgebras (MTS) have been identified. Formalism on how to classify an input temporal network in one of these MTSs, or decide its intractability, has been proposed. Mitra and Launay present a linear algorithm for checking consistency when the input belongs to one of the seventeen MTS, and for finding out the constraints responsible for inconsistency in case the network is unsatisfiable.

Application of QSTR in realistic (relevant) domains, e.g., in the form of spatial control and spatial planning in cognitive robotics, for spatial decision-support in intelligent systems and as explanatory models in a wide-range of systems requiring the formulation of hypothesis, e.g., diagnosis requires integration of QSTR techniques within general commonsense reasoning frameworks in AI. The chapter by Bhatt is an attempt to position such integrated reasoning as a useful paradigm for the utilization of QSTR in relevant application domains.

Ontologies are not only suitable for describing static scenes with static objects (e.g., in photographs) but also enable representation of dynamic events with objects and properties changing in time (e.g., moving objects in a video). Representation of both static and dynamic scenes by ontologies, as well as querying and reasoning over static and dynamic ontologies are dealt with by Batsakis and Petrakis. Different types of temporal and spatial representations are all integrated into a unique spatio-temporal ontology representation capable of representing temporal and spatio-temporal information.

Wolter and Wallgrun approach QSTR from an application perspective. According to them, considering the exemplary application domains of robot navigation, GIS, and computer-aided design, reasoning must be interpreted in a broader sense than the often-considered constraint-based reasoning and that supporting tools must become available. Their chapter discusses these newly identified reasoning tasks and how they can be supported by QSTR toolboxes to foster the dissemination of QSTR in applications. Furthermore, the chapter explains the aim to overcome the lack-of-tools dilemma through the development of the QSTR toolbox SparQ.

Mastrogiovannet et al. introduce a framework for enabling context-aware behaviors in smart environment applications, with a special emphasis on smart homes and similar scenarios. The chapter describes an ontology-based architecture that allows system designers to specify non-trivial situations the system must be able to detect on the basis of available sensory data. The ontology encodes temporal operators that, once applied to sensory information, allow efficient recognition and correlation to different human activities and other events whose temporal relationships are contextually important. Special emphasis is devoted to actual representation and recognition of temporally distributed situations and the proof of concept is validated through a thoroughly described example of system usage.

Web databases evolve over time. Therefore, it is important that the database content summaries remain fresh so that they are able to serve all user queries. Database content summary construction need to take a step further so that content summaries do not pertain only to the topics covered in the database records but also represent the spatial and the temporal orientation of the database contents. Domain-specific ontologies can be utilized for deducing the thematic, the spatial, and the temporal orientations of the database contents. Zotos and Stamou propose a novel framework for the support of multi-faceted searches over distributed web-accessible databases. A method for analyzing and processing a sample of the database contents in order to deduce the topical, the geographic and the temporal orientation of the entire database contents is introduced.

## FINAL COMMENTS

The QSTR approaches presented in the above chapters are by no means exhaustive and prescriptive, but rather they provide examples of various frameworks. The chapters in this book are thus intended as an invitation to further exploration of relevant theories to study QSTR within KR & R. While much of the work discussed above or work very close to what is reported here has individually received attention in prior QSTR literature, they have not been collectively brought together into a single book. We believe that each of the chapters in this book offers its own focus and explanation, and distinctive framework for the study and understanding of QSTR from multiple perspectives.

*Shyamanta M Hazarika*
*Tezpur University, India*

## REFERENCES

Allen, J. F. (1983). Maintaining knowledge about temporal intervals. *Communications of the ACM, 26*(11), 832–843. doi:10.1145/182.358434

Bhatt, M., Guesgen, H., Woelfl, S., & Hazarika, S. (2011). Qualitative spatial and temporal reasoning: Emerging applications, trends, and directions. *Spatial Cognition & Computation: An Interdisciplinary Journal, 11*(1), 1–14. doi:10.1080/13875868.2010.548568

Cohn, A. G., & Hazarika, S. M. (2001). Qualitative spatial representation and reasoning: An overview. *Fundamenta Informaticae, 46*(1-2), 1–29.

Cohn, A. G., & Renz, J. (2008). Qualitative spatial representation and reasoning. In van Harmelen, F., Lifschitz, V., & Porter, B. (Eds.), *Handbook of Knowledge Representation*. London, UK: Elsevier.

Davis, E. (1990). *Representations of commonsense knowledge*. San Mateo, CA: Morgan Kaufmann.

Egenhofer, M. J., & Golledge, R. G. (1998). *Spatial and temporal reasoning in geographic information systems*. Oxford, UK: Oxford University Press.

Escrig, M. T., & Toledo, F. (1998). *Qualitative spatial reasoning: Theory and practice - Application to robot navigation: Frontiers in AI and applications*. Amsterdam, The Netherlands: IOS Press.

Fernyhough, J. H., Cohn, A. G., & Hogg, D. (2000). Constructing qualitative event models automatically from video input. *Image and Vision Computing, 18*(2), 81–103. doi:10.1016/S0262-8856(99)00023-2

Freksa, C. (1991). Qualitative Spatial Reasoning. In D.M. Mark & A.U. Frank (eds.), *Cognitive and Linguistic Aspects of Geographic Space*, p. 361-372. Dordrecht: Kluwer Academic Publishers.

Galata, A., Cohn, A. G., Magee, D., & Hogg, D. (2002). Modeling interaction using learnt qualitative spatio-temporal relations and variable length Markov models. In F. van Harmelen (Ed.), *Proceedings of the 15th European Conference on AI (ECAI 2002)*, (pp. 741–745). ECAI.

Hazarika, S. M. (2005). *Qualitative spatial change: Space time histories and continuity*. PhD Thesis. Leeds, UK: University of Leeds.

Hornsby, K., & Egenhofer, M. J. (2000). Identity-based changes: A foundation for spatio-temporal knowledge representation. *International Journal of Geographical Information Science, 14*(3), 207–224. doi:10.1080/136588100240813

McCarthy, J. (1959). Programs with common senses. In *Proceedings of Symposium on Mechanization of Thought Processes*. Retrieved from http: //www-formal. stanford. edu/ jmc/ mcc59.pdf.

Peuquet, D. J. (1999). Making space for time: Issues in space-time data representation. In *Proceedings of the 10th International Workshop on Database and Expert Systems Applications*, (pp. 404–408). DEXA.

Piaget, J., & Inhelder, B. (1967). *The child's conception of space*. New York, NY: Basic Books.

Randell, D. A., Cui, Z., & Cohn, A. G. (1992). A spatial logic based on regions and connection. In B. Nebel, C. Rich, & W. Swartout (Eds.), *Proceedings of 3rd International Conference on Knowledge Representation and Reasoning (KR 1992)*, (pp. 165–176). San Mateo, CA: Morgan Kaufmann.

Stock, O. (Ed.). (1997). *Spatial and temporal reasoning*. London, UK: Kluwer Academic Publishers. doi:10.1007/978-0-585-28322-7

Van de Weghe, N. (2004). *Representing and reasoning about moving objects: A qualitative approach.* PhD Thesis. Ghent, Belgium: Ghent University.

Whitehead, A. N. (1920). *The concept of nature*. Cambridge, UK: Cambridge University Press.

Whitehead, A. N. (1929). *Process and reality*. New York, NY: The MacMillan Company.

Whitehead, A. N. (1978). *Process and reality: Corrected edition*. New York, NY: MacMillan.

# Chapter 1
# Region-Based Theories of Space:
## Mereotopology and Beyond

**Torsten Hahmann**
*University of Toronto, Canada*

**Michael Grüninger**
*University of Toronto, Canada*

## ABSTRACT

*This chapter focuses on the topological and mereological relations, contact, and parthood, between spatio-temporal regions as axiomatized in so-called mereotopologies. Despite, or because of, their simplicity, a variety of different first-order axiomatizations have been proposed. This chapter discusses their underlying ontological choices and different ways of systematically looking at them. The chapter further gives an overview of the algebraic, topological, and graph-theoretic representations of mereotopological models which help to better understand the model-theoretic consequences of the various ontological choices. While much work on mereotopologies has been primarily theoretical, the focus started shifting towards applications and domain-specific extensions of mereotopology. These aspects will most likely guide the future direction of the field: How can mereotopologies be extended or otherwise adjusted to better suit practical needs? Moreover, the integration of mereotopology into more comprehensive and maybe more pragmatic ontologies of space and time remains another challenge in the field of region-based space.*

DOI: 10.4018/978-1-61692-868-1.ch001

## 1. INTRODUCTION

The very nature of topology and its close relation to how humans perceive space and time make mereotopology an indispensable part of any comprehensive framework for Qualitative Spatial and Temporal Reasoning (QSTR). Within QSTR, it has by far the longest history, dating back to descriptions of phenomenological processes in nature (Husserl, 1913; Whitehead, 1920, 1929)—what we call today 'commonsensical' in Artificial Intelligence. There have been plenty of other motivations to study the topological and mereological relations of space—as an appealing alternative to set theory or point-set topology, or as an region-based alternative to Euclidean geometry. Even beyond QSTR, mereotopology is fairly universal and can be applied to various other fields, where the spatial or temporal character is not its primary purpose.

Mereotopology also often serves for testing and exploring techniques of building qualitative spatial reasoning frameworks. Likewise, central issues of knowledge representation can be tested within it—building reusable, generic ontologies, constructing *upper ontologies*, testing specification and validation of formal semantics for ontologies and not least, coming up with general mathematical frameworks to systematically compare ontologies model-theoretically or axiomatically.

Without doubt, we can say that within QSTR mereotopology encompasses some of the most advanced and best understood spatial theories. This chapter gives a high-level overview of the early and more recent advances in the field, what mathematical tools and techniques are successful, how the theories vary, and what are the challenges remaining within and beyond the field.

The quest for region-based theories of space as alternatives to classical point-based geometry is often driven by the human cognition: how humans perceive their spatial and spatio-temporal environment. An urge for common-sense representations and reasoning systems is given by work on naïve physics (Hayes, 1978; Hayes, 1985b; Smith & Casati, 1994) and naïve geography (Egenhofer & Mark, 1995b). Theories of space and time will be a major component of any common-sense representation of geographic or physical space. For common-sense reasoning, region-based theories of space (and time) are more promising than point-based theories since they are able to draw commonsensical topological or mereological conclusions even in the absence of exact data, or as Egenhofer and Mark (1995b, p. 9) put it: "topology matters, metric refines." Not least, the study of region-based theories contributes towards the understanding of the nature of points—they actually have structure that is not evident in Euclidean geometry (Eschenbach, 1994). Through the inclusion of qualitative models of space, common-sense reasoning but also the next generation of Geographic Information Systems (GIS) and other spatial reasoning software can at least partially bridge the gap between rigid computational models of space and less rigid users that freely navigate between quantitative and qualitative and between low-level and high-level conceptions of space.

### 1.1. Scope and Structure

Upfront a few words on the scope of this chapter. There have been a few overviews of mereotopology in the context of qualitative spatial reasoning (Bennett, 1997; Casati & Varzi, 1999; Cohn & Hazarika, 2001; Cohn & Renz, 2008; Cohn & Varzi, 2003; Donnelly, 2001; Eschenbach, 2007; Vieu, 1997). We do not simply aim to extend these summaries with more recent work, but we hope to compile a more comprehensive account of mereotopology paying respect to the whole breadth of the field. Overviews covering mereotopology just as one amongst many qualitative spatial reasoning frameworks (Cohn & Hazarika, 2001; Cohn & Renz, 2008) have been unable to allocate sufficient space to cover the many different approaches towards mereotopology. More technical accounts (Casati & Varzi, 1999; Cohn & Varzi, 2003; Eschenbach, 2007) compare axioms and assumptions of different theories, but tend to lose the big picture. Moreover, these accounts focus on a few select theories, leaving out others that do not fit well into the respective frameworks. In particular, work on algebraic theories of region-based space, systematically covered by Vakarelov (2007) as well as topological models and theories are largely left aside. The same defect holds for the summaries given in (Bennett, 1997; Donnelly, 2001; Vieu, 1997). Furthermore, there is often a certain bias towards a particular class of region-based theories: either considering exclusively Whiteheadean space, only RCC-style axiomatizations, only relation calculi (which we admittedly only briefly cover), or only algebraic approaches. We shall attempt here to give a synthesis of the different mathematical formulations used to axiomatize region-based space. We try to guide through the various mereotopologies, their ontological choices, and their mathematical representations. Throughout, parallels between the approaches (despite their differences in the choice of mathematical tools) and their historic development are sketched out. The picture we give relies solely on known results from the literature, however they tend to be spread in various publications and sometimes well hidden by the technical details. We hope the chapter to be accessible to a broad audience, but occasionally we point out technical results of interest to the versed reader in the particular context. However, readers new to the field can safely skip these results without losing the big picture. In general, our presentations are fairly high-level and refrain from using axioms unless absolutely necessary.

After giving a bit of background on topology and mereology, Section 3 constitutes the first of two parts of the chapter. It introduces the wealth of ontological commitments relevant for mereotopology. We follow along the lines of the commitments discussed by Eschenbach (2007) and give examples how the many different mereotopological theories fit into this space of potential mereotopologies. After reviewing some known systematic frameworks of mereotopologies (Section 4), we proceed to the second part of the chapter which presents different mathematical accounts—logical, algebraic, and topological—of mereotopology. In Section 5, three main families of logical theories of mereotopologies are presented: Whiteheadean theories, boundary-tolerant theories, and mereogeometries. Within each family the ontological commitments vary only marginally; they guide the exploration of the space of logical accounts of mereotopologies while commitments manifested in each of the families are pointed out. It turns out that the ontological commitments of Whiteheadean theories have been studied most widely; most other theories lack a comprehensive analysis of ontological commitments. Often it is not trivial to extract the ontological decisions implicit in a particular region-based theory of space. For Whiteheadean space, their algebraic counterparts, contact algebras, treated in Section 6 are well-suited for mapping out the space of possible theories. In general, we believe that ontological commitments of other theories would become more obvious if we study their algebraic representations. Apart from contact algebras, very little work has been done on algebraic representations of logical theories of mereotopologies. The topological models and embeddings in Section 7 once more show the interrelation between the various mereotopologies. As comparison, we review region-based theories directly built from point-set topology. Not surprisingly, it turns out that despite their different mathematical foundations, the resulting region-based theories of space are remarkably close to the axiomatic and algebraic theories. The comparison with the topological models of the latter shows the parallels clearly.

Finally, we point to some work on mereotopology and mereogeometry used in specific application domains. Some specific applications are presented, while for other areas only the necessary expressivity with respect to the ontological commitments is discussed. To complete the chapter, we highlight points that we consider most important for future research in the field. Theoretical and practical challenges within the field as well as challenges in the broad scope of spatial and spatio-temporal qualitative ontologies are briefly discussed.

Of course, we cannot cover the complete literature in the area, but we hope to give the interested reader sufficient starting points where to continue in-depth reading. We see this chapter as a reader's guide to mereotopology accompanied by a comprehensive bibliography useful to start further reading. The chapter shall give a general AI-centered overview of representations of region-based space and its current state and future work. The field of mereotopology and its formal treatise seems to be clustered into separate fields with little awareness and interaction between them. We hope that this chapter helps reconnect the different views on region-based space. Additionally, we hope to point more experienced researchers to some related work, discovering alternative perspectives on methods, tools, and applications of mereotopology and mereogeometry.

## 2. BACKGROUND

This section prepares the reader for the material in this chapter. Specifically, we briefly cover relevant background on point-set topology and mereology, before giving a short introduction to mereotopology and how it is intrinsically linked to both. This is more of a historical introduction to mereotopology; a more axiomatic overview will be given in Section 5.1. The reader familiar with topology and mereology can easily skip this section, for those who need more background references are given. Although we will make use of lattice theory in Section 6, only little lattice-theoretic background is assumed; it can be found in standard references (Birkhoff, 1967; Grätzer, 1998).

### 2.1. Point-Set Topology

Point-set topology (from Greek *topos*, "place") is traditionally based on set theory. Open and closed sets of points are distinguished and standard set intersection and union are assumed. A *topological space* $(\mathrm{X},\tau)$ can be defined over a set of *open* (or *closed*) sets τ (the topology) where $\varnothing, X \in \tau$ and every set in τ is a subset of *X*. Moreover, τ is closed under arbitrary unions (finite unions) and finite intersections (arbitrary intersections). If *A* is an open set, $(X \setminus A)$ is a closed set. If no confusion can arise, the topological space is identified by its base set *X*. In a topological space the sets $\varnothing, X$ are *clopen* sets, i.e. they are open and closed. In general, there are sets that are neither open nor closed. The interior int(*x*) of a set *x* is the union of all open sets contained in it, which is necessarily open (the union and the intersection of open sets is open). Equally, the closure cl(*x*) of a set *x* is the intersection of all closed sets that contain the set. In other words, the interior of *A* is the largest open set contained in *A*, while the closure of *A* is the smallest closed set containing *A*.

The study of topological spaces of regular sets is a distinctive feature of point-free topology, which in traditional topology is not of much relevance. An open set x is called *regular open* iff $x = \mathrm{int}(\mathrm{cl}(x))$ and a closed set *x* is called regular closed iff $x = \mathrm{cl}(\mathrm{int}(x))$. The set complement of a regular open set is regular closed. It is well known that the regular open sets form a Boolean algebra under the operations $x + y := \mathrm{int}(\mathrm{cl}(x \cup y))$, $x \cdot y := x \cap y$, and $-x := \mathrm{int}(X \setminus x)$, see (Halmos, 1963). Algebras over regular sets have been defined by McKinsey and Tarski (1944). They used the term *closure algebra* (dually *interior algebra*) for a Boolean algebra equipped with a closure operation cl satisfying $\mathrm{cl}(x) \geq x$, $\mathrm{cl}(\mathrm{cl}(x)) = \mathrm{cl}(x)$, $\mathrm{cl}(x) + \mathrm{cl}(y) = \mathrm{cl}(x + y)$, and $\mathrm{cl}(0) = 0$. Such closure algebra can be constructed from a topological space: Let $(X,\tau)$ be a topological space, then $(2^X, \mathrm{cl})$ is a closure algebra (McKinsey & Tarski, 1944). For more background on point-set topology, we invite the reader to consult standard references (Engelking, 1977; Munkres, 2000). Specific topological concepts, in particular separation axioms, are introduced in Section 7 as needed.

## 2.2. Mereology

The origins of mereology (from Greek *méros*, "part") date back to the beginning of the 20th century and the work of Husserl (1901). It received formal treatment by Leśniewski (1931), an English translation appeared in Luschei (1962). Leśniewski is credited with the first development of an extensional part-whole theory, soon Leonard and Goodman (1940) followed with an alternative. We only introduce key concepts that help enable the reader to understand the role mereology plays within mereotopology. For further reading, we refer to Simons (1987) and Varzi (2009). Additionally, Casati and Varzi (1999) give a systematic overview of mereologies deemed relevant for mereotopology.

Common to all mereological theories is a primitive binary relation of *parthood* relating parts to wholes (of which they are part of). Parthood is an anti-symmetric relation that is either reflexive or irreflexive (*proper parthood*). Such basic Mereology (**M**) can be axiomatized as following. We include the definition of proper parthood.

(P1) $\forall x\left[P(x,x)\right]$ (Reflexivity)

(P2) $\forall x,y\left[\left(P(x,y)\wedge P(y,x)\right)\rightarrow x=y\right]$
(Anti-symmetry)

(P3) $\forall x,y\left[\left(P(x,y)\wedge P(y,z)\right)\rightarrow P(x,z)\right]$
(Transitivity)

(P4) $PP(x,y)\equiv_{def} P(x,y)\wedge\neg P(y,x)$
(Proper parthood)

While parthood is usually the only primitive, overlap is the next most important concept. Further relations and operations such as union (or fusion), and intersection are also definable in terms of parthood alone.

(P-O) $O(x,y)\equiv_{def}\exists z\left(P(z,x)\wedge P(z,y)\right)$
(Overlap)

To build extensional mereology (**EM**), strong supplementation is required.

(P5) $\forall x,y\left[\neg P(y,x)\rightarrow\exists z\left(P(z,y)\wedge\neg O(z,x)\right)\right]$
(Strong supplementation)

In the presence of this axiom, the proper parthood relation is rendered extensional, meaning that two distinct entities differ in at least one part.

(P6) $\forall x,y\left[\forall z\left(O(z,x)\leftrightarrow O(z,y)\right)\rightarrow x=y\right]$
(Extensionality of O)

Assuming weak supplementation alone does not renders proper parthood extensional.

(P5') $\forall x,y\left[PP(x,y)\rightarrow\exists z\left(P(z,y)\wedge\neg O(z,x)\right)\right]$
(Weak supplementation)

A further restriction of **EM** to Closure Extensional Mereology (**CEM**) assumes the existence of sums and intersections, the latter conditional on overlap. These closure principles lead in the presence of mereological extensionality to unique sums and intersections.

(P7) $\forall x,y\left[\exists z\forall u\left(O(u,z)\leftrightarrow O(u,x)\vee O(u,y)\right)\right]$
(Sum $z=x+y$)

(P8)
$\forall x, y\left[O(x,y) \rightarrow \exists z \forall u\left(P(u,z) \leftrightarrow P(u,x) \wedge P(u,y)\right)\right]$
(Intersection $z = x \cdot y$)

Opinions differ on whether mereological theories may consist of *atoms*, i.e. individuals without proper parts. This issue is discussed for mereotopologies in Section 3.6.

It is well-known that mereology can be built from algebraic structures. The close relationship between Boolean algebras and mereological structures was first pointed out by Leonard and Goodman (1940), while Grzegorczyk (1955, 1960) coined the term *mereological field*—a complete Boolean algebra with the zero element removed (a *quasi-Boolean algebra*). Grzegorczyk also stressed that the close relationship between mereology and Boolean algebras can be readily exploited for a better understanding of mereology. Extending this argument to mereotopology, we will see in Section 6 how the mereological component of mereotopologies can be regarded as an algebraic structure.

## 2.3. Origins of Mereotopology

Mereotopology is not only by name intrinsically linked to mereology and topology. From mereology, it inherits the desire to talk about parthood relations amongst entities, while it also aims to capture topological relations between entities. Originally, it has been proposed as a point-free alternative to standard point-set topology which is criticized for countering the human conception of space. Set-theoretic notions are often believed to be at the root of the problem, being an overly complicated abstraction when we deal with commonsense spatial relations. The idea of using regions as primitive entities instead of points was first explored by Whitehead (1920, 1929) and de Laguna (1922). Whitehead proposed *extensive connection* as topological relation between regions of space, though strictly speaking he also formalized mereological relations. However, de Laguna and Whitehead did not eliminate points altogether, they just wanted to replace the unnatural primitive of a point by a more natural one, such as *solid* or *region*. Albeit considering regions as primitive entities, Whitehead suggested the method of *extensive abstraction* to define *abstractive sets*, i.e. infinite sets of regions that are totally ordered with respect to containment. In the limit case, such abstractive sets converge to points. Hence, points were reconstructed as abstract, infinitesimally small regions. We may analogously define other lower-dimensional entities such as lines, surfaces, etc.

Mereotopology is tightly coupled with the idea of region-based space since both mereology and the topological relation of connection rely on the relations between regions. If we accept regions as primitives, mereotopology is a mere combination of mereological concepts of parthood with topological concepts of contact or connection (we use them synonym). Although in principle so simple, it turns out that this combination leaves manifold options to build mereotopological theories. We will study the rich space of these theories in this chapter. First of all, let us summarize what is common to all mereotopologies. This is indeed a rather small core (Varzi, 1998): a reflexive, anti-symmetric, and transitive parthood relation for its mereological component and a reflexive, symmetric connection or contact relation for its topological component. As relation between them, monotonicity shall be obeyed.

(Mon) $\forall x, y\left[P(x,y) \rightarrow \forall z\left(C(x,z) \rightarrow C(y,z)\right)\right]$
(Monotonicity)

Moreover, it is undisputed that in mereotopology, there should be a distinction between (topological) connection and (mereological) overlap. This difference is usually reflected in a relation of external connection, defined as following:

(EC) $EC(x,y) \equiv_{def} C(x,y) \wedge \neg O(x,y)$
(External connection)

Apart from these basic requirements for mereotopological theories, we can choose freely amongst many ontological commitments discussed in the following section.

## 3. ONTOLOGICAL CHOICES IN MEREOTOPOLOGY

A major motivation for region-based theories of space is the argument that regions are more parsimonious than points in logical formalizations of commonsense spatial knowledge. From the philosophical perspective, this is an important justification. However, from a model-theoretic view where theories with identical models are considered interchangeable, such an argument is only superficial if semantic mappings between a point-based and a point-free theory can be given. Indeed, many so-called mereogeometrical theories equipped with regions as primitive entities have equally expressive point-based counterparts (Borgo & Masolo, 2009; Pratt & Schoop, 1997). Then it becomes a matter of ontological preference which theory to choose.

This section covers some of the core ontological issues that all mereotopologies and mereogeometries have to address—even if only by stating explicitly that certain concepts are simply not definable in a particular mereotopology or class of mereotopologies. Though most mereotopological theories agree on basic terminology and definitions, there is a strong disagreement over these ontological decisions. Eschenbach (2007) systematically studies the axioms, which characterize these ontological decisions for selected theories. To make mereotopology more accessible to readers not familiar with the field, we discuss the controversies and decisions from a more high-level perspective. Hereby no specific order of treatment is intended; instead, we try to follow a natural flow between the issues. Most importantly, none of the issues are independent of one another. When comparing theories of mereotopology, we have to be aware of some unavoidable tradeoffs. If one theory shall encompass all the features discussed (if that is even possible), it would be overly complex for humans and unacceptably inefficient for automated reasoning. There are many other choices we must make when building or choosing a theory of mereotopology. Amongst others, the choice of language or formalism is critical. We leave these questions largely aside, focusing instead on ontological issues that are of concern irrespective of the choice of language. We mostly discuss first-order theories of mereotopology, but this does not mean that the many ontological choices do not apply to other theories as well.

Many ontological decisions e.g. extensionality, identity, and dimensionality are, moreover, influenced by discussions of their commonsensical, cognitive, and philosophical adequacy. Per se, we avoid taking any particular stance on these adequacy issues. Instead, we raise awareness of these ontological commitments to equip readers with sufficient understanding to make acceptable choices in their domain of interest.

### 3.1. Mereology vs. Topology as Foundation

One of the earliest systematic studies of mereotopologies (Casati & Varzi, 1999; Varzi, 1996a) classified theories by the interaction between mereology and topology within them. Three main ways of building mereotopology from a topological and a mereological component have been identified. Extending mereology by an additional topological primitive is one way, pursued in (Eschenbach, 1999; Pratt & Schoop, 1997; Smith, 1996). Smith employs a reflexive parthood relation for mereology, extended by the mereotopological primitive of interior parthood (comparable to non-tangential parthood in other mereotopologies). Pratt and Schoop (1997) use a Boolean language which implicitly defines parthood, extended by a primitive contact relation. Eschenbach (1997) uses for her 'Closed Region Calculus' (CRC) a standard mereology (based on parthood) equipped with a topological notion of disconnection.

Mereology and topology can also be merged by treating topology as more fundamental and defining mereology in terms of topological primitives. De Laguna (1922) and Whitehead (1929), intrigued by its formal economy, chose this paradigm. It is the most common approach in QSTR. Clarke (1981) chose connection as only primitive for his 'Calculus of Individuals,' while most later work stuck to this choice, e.g. the system $RT_0$ of Asher and Vieu (1995), the *Region Connection Calculus* (RCC: Cohn, et al., 1997a, 1997b; Randell, et al., 1992; Gotts, 1994). Parthood is expressed in terms of connection alone, i.e. parthood and the topological notion of *enclosure* (Varzi, 1996a) coincide. All sentences in such theories are limited to the expressiveness of contact. The *n-intersection model* (Egenhofer, 1989, 1991) uses likewise only (point-set) topological primitives: interior, boundary, and complement. Mereological relations are then solely defined in terms of these topological concepts.

A third way to combine topology and mereology was employed by Eschenbach and Heydrich (1995). They extend the mereological framework of Leonard and Goodman (1940) by a primitive unary relation 'of being a region.' However, the latter primitive captures a topological idea. Hence, it is questionable whether the theory is purely mereological. Analogously, many mereogeometries (Bennett, 2001; Bennett, et al., 2000; Borgo, et al., 1996; Tarski, 1956a) use a combination of a mereological primitive together with the primitive of 'being a region.' More recently, the algebraic representations of Clarke (1985) and Asher and Vieu (1995) give rise to mereotopologies definable from a single mereological primitive of parthood (compare Section 6.2). The later in particular is either definable from connection or from parthood alone. Hence, it becomes clear that Casati and Varzi's framework is not a real partitioning of mereotopologies.

This classification of mereotopologies distinguishes principles of how to fuse mereology and topology into a common theory. This is a coarse classification; many mereotopologies do not fit well into this framework. For example theories that employ very powerful predicates that are neither strictly of mereological nor topological nature, e.g. (Gotts, 1996b) with a single primitive *INCH(x,y)* meaning '*x includes a chunk of y*,' or some of the mereogeometries (de Laguna, 1922; Donnelly, 2001; Nicod, 1924) cannot be easily classified in this way. In particular, notions of convexity are usually expressive enough to recover the topological structure as demonstrated by Borgo and Masolo (2009).

## 3.2. Extensionality and Identity

Different strengths of extensionality are a core distinction between mereotopological theories. The following generic axiom captures extensionality of a binary, symmetric predicate *Q*.

(Ext-Q)
$$\forall x, y \Big(\forall z \big[(Q(x,z) \leftrightarrow Q(y,z)) \rightarrow x = y\big]\Big)$$
(Generic extensionality)

If a theory is extensional with respect to Q, we say that two elements in the theory are indistinguishable with respect to *Q*. If exactly one of the primitives of a theory is extensional, this provides an intuitive notion of identity. Not surprisingly, Whiteheadean theories with a single primitive *C* are extensional with respect to *C* (cf. Section 5.1.1). Other theories require extensionality with respect to the mereological relation of 'overlap' (Eschenbach, 1999; Gotts, 1996b; Randell, et al., 1992; Roeper, 1997). This is equivalent to requiring extensionality with respect to proper parthood

*PP*, although the axiomatization of extensionality for *PP* would need to accommodate the asymmetry of PP. Any such mereologically extensional theory satisfies the strong supplementation axiom (P5). If *C* and *O* are extensional in a mereotopology, *EC* is also extensional.

Mereotopology allows various weaker assumptions, e.g. weak supplementation (Casati & Varzi, 1999; Varzi, 1996a) where mereological extensionality is not required as in the theories of Asher and Vieu (1995), Clarke (1981), and Roy and Stell (2002). Therein parts of a region *r* do not uniquely identify *r*. There can be multiple, possibly infinitely many, regions $r_1$, $r_2$, ... consisting of the same parts, but distinguishable by their connection relation to other regions. This occurs in theories where regions are distinguished from their closure and/or interior with contact depending on this distinction. In contrast, the *Closed Region Calculus* (CRC: Eschenbach, 1999) is mereologically extensional, but not topologically. Instead, Eschenbach (1999) points out that the CRC is extensional with respect to external connection. The RCC is in fact extensional with respect to *C*, *O*, and *EC*. For more discussions on extensionality in different theories see Eschenbach (2007).

### 3.3. Sums and Fusions

Within mereology, there is a controversy over whether arbitrary (unrestricted) sums of entities should be allowed or even required. From an algebraic perspective, such requirement yields in complete lattices more elegant structures. However, from a philosophical or cognitive perspective, such requirement seems stringent. Abundant examples of irrelevant arbitrary fusions have been given. But most mereotopologies at least assume the existence of binary sums—either mereological sums, denoted here by $\oplus$, or topological sums preserving contact, denoted here by +.

(Sum-M)
$$x \oplus y = z \leftrightarrow \forall u \big(O(u,z) \leftrightarrow \big(O(u,x) \vee O(u,y)\big)\big)$$
(Mereological sum)

(Sum-T)
$$x + y = z \leftrightarrow \forall u \big(C(u,z) \leftrightarrow \big(C(u,x) \vee C(u,y)\big)\big)$$
(Topological sum)

Either sum is unique if the relation within the definition (overlap or contact, respectively) is extensional. Mereological sums are found in theories with a mereological primitive while topological sums are standard for theories with a topological primitive, e.g. Whiteheadean theories (Asher & Vieu, 1995; Bennett, 2001; Clarke, 1981; Gotts, 1994; Randell, et al., 1992). Equivalently, binary sums are expressed as upper bounds in lattices, see Section 6 for details. Therefore, we mainly deal with bounded lattices for representing the mereological component of mereotopologies. The existence of *lowest upper bounds* in the lattices indicates the existence of mereological sums. Non-distributive lattices can contain non-unique relative complements and therefore are representative of theories where mereological extensionality is not guaranteed to hold.

Theories (e.g. Clarke, 1981) that go beyond binary, i.e. finite, sums define what Casati and Varzi (1999) call *unrestricted fusion* or what is also known as *infinitary* or *universal fusion*. Notice that unrestricted fusion of arbitrary—possibly infinite sets—of entities is not first-order axiomatizable. Similarly, algebraic or topological theories of region-based space employ either a set-theoretic definition of unrestricted fusion or use complete algebras as basis, e.g. complete Boolean algebras have been considered by Roeper (1997) and used for representing models of Clarke' theory (cf. Biacino & Gerla, 1991).

## 3.4. Self-Connectedness

*Self-connectedness of a region*, written as *SelfCon(x)*, is an intuitive property that expresses that a region does not consist of several disconnected, i.e. scattered, parts. *Self-connectedness of the space* (the universe), expressed as *SelfCon(u)* or through the following sentence, means that every region is connected to its complement.

(SC)
$\forall x, y\left[\forall z\left(C(x,z) \vee C(y,z)\right) \rightarrow SelfCon(x+y)\right]$
(Self-connectedness)

Depending on the intended (regular) regions we want to capture, two main approaches to enforce self-connectedness are available. If we allow any kind of regular regions in a theory, the topological complement of a regular closed region is regular open. We then obtain a space where every element is not connected to its complement, i.e. $\forall x\left[\neg C(x,-x)\right]$ when using the intuitive definition of Self-Connectedness (SC-S).

(SC-S)
$SelfCon(x) \equiv_{def} \forall y, z\left(y+z=x \rightarrow C(y,z)\right)$
(Strong self-connectedness)

The models of such a theory can never be self-connected. To avoid this problem, weaker axioms for self-connectedness have been proposed, in particular the following.

(SC-W)
$SelfCon'(x) \equiv_{def} \forall y, z\left(y+z=x \rightarrow C(cl(y), cl(z))\right)$
(Weak self-connectedness)

In the presence of SC-W, a regular closed set and its regular open complement are indeed self-connected. If a theory only allows regular open regions and contact is defined as $C(x,y) \Leftrightarrow x \cap y \neq \varnothing$ (compare C-Weak in Section 5.1.1), then SC-S also results in disconnection between a region and its complement while SC-W would not. For theories that only consider regular closed sets, both definitions of self-connectedness coincide. In such theory, the universe is only not self-connected if there are true disconnected partitions in the universe. Of course, then self-connectedness of the universe can be postulated as an axiom (cf. Egenhofer, 1991; Egenhofer & Franzosa, 1991; Roeper, 1997). There are few theories using an intermediate notion of (self-) connectedness with an open region and its closed complement being connected (Grzegorczyk, 1960; Pratt & Schoop, 1997), compare the discussion of (Cohn & Varzi, 2003) in Section 4.

In atomistic mereotopologies, self-connectedness is trickier to achieve. While it is a widely held view that connectedness between an atom and its complement is desirable to enforce self-connectedness of space, in the context of Whiteheadean space this would lead to the fact that an atom is also part of its complement. Roy and Stell (2002) argue that this is not a defect because discrete space can be seen as approximation of continuous space where extensionality of *P* does not necessarily hold any longer (due to the approximation loss). Hence, we might need to abandon extensionality of *P* in discrete mereotopology. Apart from that, extensionality of *C* conflicts with atomistic mereotopology if connectedness is defined in the weak form, i.e. if atoms are connected to their complement. As Eschenbach (1999, p. 163) notes: "[*C*-extensionality] means to exclude the coexistence of the universe and the complement of an atom because both would be connected to all regions." This problem does not apply to theories with the open/closed distinction and the stronger form of self-connectedness. However, other options such as a relaxed version of self-connectedness (similar to the second version above, while accommodating atoms, which are usually open) could help overcome the problem.

## 3.5. Dimensionality

One of the most common simplifications amongst axiomatic theories of mereotopology is the restriction that only entities of equal dimensions can co-exist in a single model. The theories in the Whiteheadean conception of space (Asher & Vieu, 1995; Casati & Varzi, 1994; Clarke, 1981; de Laguna, 1922; Eschenbach, 1999; Nicod, 1924; Randell, et al., 1992; Smith, 1996; Tarski, 1956a; Whitehead, 1920, 1929; Pratt & Schoop, 1997; Galton, 1999) all rely on a single class (sort) of entities. Though all regions must be of equal dimension, this dimension can be chosen freely for each domain except within the theory of Pratt and Schoop (1997). Lower dimensional can only be defined using higher-order constructs, e.g. in a three-dimensional domain, lower dimensional entities such as points, lines, and surfaces can be reconstructed through *extensive abstraction* (de Laguna, 1922; Whitehead, 1929), an idea dating back to Lobačevskij (1834). Indeed, most region-based theories define so-called *abstract points* as limits of infinitely many nested regions or sets of regions (cf. Clarke, 1985; Eschenbach, 1994; Menger, 1940; Tarski, 1956b). Equally, points can be recovered as prime ideals, ultrafilters (maximal filters), or generalizations thereof from many classes of lattices in a second-order way (cf. Asher & Vieu, 1995; Roeper, 1997).

Galton (1996) argues that we should neither assume regions nor points, nor any other kind of spatial entities as more fundamental than the other. In this spirit and irrespective of the philosophical or cognitive adequacy of regions or points, Galton (1996) and Gotts et al. (1996) have proposed frameworks that accommodate entities of any kind of dimension (in particular points, lines, surfaces) through a binary predicate of *equi-dimensionality* and separate parthood relations between equi-dimensional and non-equi-dimensional entities. This comes close to what Hayes (1985a) envisioned for commonsense reasoning in physics. Points and indivisible atomic regions can then theoretically co-exist (Galton, 1996). This also lets us define boundaries elegantly: boundaries are defined as entities of a dimension one lower than the entities they bound. Key to the axiomatization of Galton (1996) is the insight that entities of a lower dimension cannot be part of a higher-dimensional entity, but can only lie within such. In the result, two separate parthood relations are distinguished: one exclusively between equi-dimensional regions, whereas a separate relation *IN(x,y)* relates a lower-dimensional entity x to a higher-dimensional y. We would say 'a point lies in a region' instead of 'a point is part of a region.' In a similar framework, Gotts (1996b) uses the *INCH(x,y)* primitive to state that '*x includes a chunk of y*' whereas the overlap relation *OV(x,y)* only applies to objects of equal dimensions. The use of cell complexes, i.e. collections of discrete objects of different dimensions, is another solution, which can accommodate objects of different dimensions (cf. Winter & Frank, 2000; Roy & Stell, 2002). Cell complexes are frequently used in GIS (cf. Burrough & Frank, 1995; Frank, 2005).

In strictly topological theories of region-based space (Egenhofer, 1989, 1991; Egenhofer & Herring, 1991; Egenhofer & Sharma, 1993b; McKenney, et al., 2005), a natural topological distinction between points, lines (and hence boundaries), and regions exists. However, these frameworks employ full point-set topology avoided by the previously mentioned theories. This trade-off is characteristic for region-based space: we can either resort to classical point-set-theoretic axiomatizations allowing entities of any dimension and relations between them, or chose a cognitively or ontologically more appropriate approach without points as primitives, but then need to overcome inherent difficulties when defining entities of different dimensions and their relation to one another.

### 3.6. Atoms and Continuous vs. Discrete Mereotopologies

While points can be defined as abstract entities, explicit definitions of so-called *concrete points* (Eschenbach, 1994) are also common. Concrete points—to prevent confusion usually referred to as *atoms*—are the smallest, indivisible regions without proper parts. They are found in the mereotopologies of Nicod (1924) and Smith (1996) and in the point-free geometry (mereogeometry) proposed by Huntington (1913). Atoms are extended—contrary to the definition of points as limits, which have no extension.

(PT) $Pt(x) \equiv_{def} \forall y \left(P(y,x) \rightarrow y = x\right)$
(Concrete points)

Historically, de Laguna and Whitehead implicitly required hat every region has a proper part, defining extensionless abstract points through higher-order constructs. Their understanding of *atomless*, i.e. *continuous*, mereotopology was adopted by Tarski (1956a), Menger (1940), Clarke (1981, 1985), and the RCC. E.g. in the RCC space is required to be Atomless (AL) because AL is a theorem of the remaining axioms. In AL, the relation *NTPP* (Non-Tangential Proper Part) is a specialization of proper parthood in which boundaries are not shared.

(AL) $\forall x \exists y \left[NTPP(y,x)\right]$ (Atomless)

Hence, we immediately conclude $\forall x \exists y \left[PP(x,y)\right]$ and with *O* being extensional, we can derive the principle of infinite divisibility (see also Masolo & Vieu, 1999).

(Div) $\forall x \exists y,z \left[PP(y,x) \wedge PP(z,x) \wedge \neg O(y,z)\right]$
(Infinite divisibility)

Though the original RCC theory is atomless, changes to the RCC axioms to allow models with atoms (*atom-tolerant*) have been proposed (Roy & Stell, 2002; Dong, 2008). The other extreme—requiring the existence of atomic parts for each region—results in *atomistic* (or *discrete*) mereotopologies (Galton, 1999; Masolo & Vieu, 1999; Nicod, 1924; Smith, 1996). Notice that atomicity does not imply that all models are finite since such restriction cannot be expressed in first-order logic.

(AT) $\forall x \exists y \left[P(y,x) \wedge \neg \exists z PP(z,y)\right]$
(Atomicity)

There are a number of arguments in favor of non-continuous theories of region-based space (and time). For example, the data recorded in geospatial applications is always of limited granularity so that we have some smallest set of entities that we can treat as atoms. These might be parcels of land when modeling land use or counties or municipalities within GIS, or molecules, atoms, or smaller elements in physics—whatever is appropriate for the domain. Here the choice of atoms is always dependant on the particular domain, however for most domains we can come up with some set of atoms. This view matches early ideas of atomism in space, e.g. as Masolo and Vieu (1999) remark: "Aristotle held that one can always divide a magnitude any finite number of times but that infinite divisibility is only potential" (p. 236). For any particular domain, the potential is barely relevant; however, for a general qualitative theory of space, it must be taken into account. We can also build discrete mereotopologies using graph-theoretic concepts and their relationships to (discrete) tessellations of space (cf. Section 8).

Other theories (Asher & Vieu, 1995; Li & Ying, 2004) allow atomistic and atomless models. These *atom-tolerant* theories generalize both atomistic and atom-less theories. For an in-depth discussion of the relationship between atomicity, divisibility, and density in mereologies and mereotopologies, we invite the reader to consult Masolo and Vieu (1999). Moreover, Masolo and Vieu (1999) have surveyed several mereotopologies from Casati and Varzi (1999) and Varzi (1996a) with respect to their consistency with axioms of atomicity and axioms of divisibility and atomicity.

## 3.7. Boundaries

Associated to the issue of dimensionality and the reconstruction of lower-dimensional entities is the treatment of boundaries. One of the criticisms of mereotopology raised by Breysse and De Glas (2007) and within the field itself is that point-set topological interpretations of regions leaves us with three unsatisfying options of how to treat boundaries. See also Fleck (1996) for a discussion of the problematic topological nature of boundaries. Restricting ourselves to closed regions, we have to accept that there are points of a region and its complement that overlap which seems discomforting. Retreating to an option where the complement of a closed region is open and vice versa (cf. Asher & Vieu, 1995) seems arbitrary. E.g. cutting a region then leaves one part of it with a boundary at the cut, while the other part does not have that boundary. Many more examples have been given to demonstrate the problematic nature of boundaries, e.g. for a black area on a sheet of white paper, is the boundary between the black area and the remainder of the paper black or white? When restricting ourselves to open regions, there remain points that belong to neither region. Fleck (1996) suggested deleting these points to obtain a more intuitive topological structure and to make a proper distinction between real contact and touching (so-called *weak contact*).

An axiomatic theory incorporating boundaries as special kind of extended but dependent (depending on the region they bound) entities has been proposed by Smith (1996). With an appropriate definition of boundaries and by allowing both open and closed regions, a boundary of a region is also a boundary of its complement. Most importantly, boundaries are not part of the bounded region itself. In this way, Smith (1996) provides for one of the rare accounts of boundaries within mereotopology while abstaining from the arbitrary choice of to which region the boundary actually belongs. Contact can then be defined as two regions sharing a boundary. The discrete version of the RCC of Roy and Stell (2002) resembles Smith's theory in that boundaries are defined as regions without interiors. Other theories (Galton, 1996; Gotts, 1996b) treat boundaries as separate sort of entities. From an abstract view, this makes perfect sense, although arguments treating boundaries as thin layers of space instead have their justifications especially for modeling physical objects. Similarly, Eschenbach (1994) handles topological entities such as boundaries and points separately from the mereological regions.

In general, the nature of boundaries is philosophically disputed. It is questionable what kind of entity a boundary is—either spatial object or abstract entity (cf. Varzi, 2008). Another philosophical distinction has been made between natural (*bona fide*) and artificial (*fiat*) boundaries (Smith, 1996; Smith & Varzi, 1997). Fiat boundaries seem to always be perceived as lower-dimensional artifacts, while bona fide boundaries are more appropriately modeled as 'thin layers.' Following the serious doubts of the existence of bona fide boundaries, we could argue that the abstraction of all boundaries as lower-dimensional entities seems indeed the most viable option for commonsense space.

## 3.8. Holes, Discontinuities, and Superficialities

Mereotopology is able to express self-connectedness of solids through the connectedness of its parts in a first-order way (Section 3.4) while topology can express self-connectedness only by quantifying over all subsets of a set (a region): set A is self-connected if for all $B, C \subset A$ $A = B \cup C \Rightarrow cl(B) \cap C \neq \varnothing \vee B \cap cl(C) \neq \varnothing$ (Masolo & Vieu, 1999). The question arises to what extent mereotopology can define concepts such as holes and other discontinuities. Casati and Varzi (1994) give a remarkably fine-grained, though informal, classification of different kinds of discontinuities: cavities, tunnels, hollows, ridges, cracks, fissures, and every imaginable combination thereof, but only the appendix of Casati and Varzi (1994) gives an axiomatic treatment of these discontinuities, also found in Varzi (1996b). Unfortunately, a primitive notion *H(x,y)* meaning '*x is a hole in (or through) y*' is assumed. No attempt to define holes in terms of connection and parthood is made. (Gotts, 1994) tested the definability of holes using the RCC notions (basically connection) with the example of a 'doughnut' (a torus) and derivations thereof. Similarly, the definability of holes in the n-intersection model was researched in Egenhofer et al. (1994). Critical to Gott's investigations is the definition of *finger-connectivity* and *separation numbers*, which depends on the actual dimensions and is not dimension independent. In particular, a theory of the natural numbers is required while the separation number can only be defined recursively. More limiting is that the RCC and other Whiteheadean axiomatization of space can capture only holes of the same dimension as the regions, inhibiting the definition of lower-dimensional superficialities (Hahmann & Gruninger, 2009). Again, mereotopologies allowing entities of different dimensions are necessary in such cases, emphasizing the argument in Section 3.5. A more general definition of holes within RCC can be found in Mormann (2001), where *ECN(x,y)* is the external connection relation of *x* without the complement of *y*, i.e.

$$ECN = \{(x,y) \mid EC(x,y), x \neq y'\}.$$

(ECN)

$$ECN(x,y) \equiv_{def} EC(x,y) \wedge \exists z[\neg C(x+y,z)]$$

(H) $H(x,y) \equiv_{def} EC(x,y) \wedge \exists z[PP(x+y,z)] \wedge \forall v[ECN(v,x) \rightarrow O(v,y)]$

(Hole)

This definition of a hole in RCC has been useful in constructing non-standard (Düntsch & Winter, 2004a) and maybe even undesirable (cf. Li & Ying, 2003) models of the RCC.

Occasionally, proposals to restrict the intended semantics of mereotopology so that all regions are hole-less have been made (Egenhofer, 1991; Egenhofer & Franzosa, 1991).

## 3.9. Convexity and Mereogeometries

So far, we have been chiefly concerned with purely mereotopological theories and their ontological commitments. However, analogous ideas also apply to theories that define geometrical notions in addition to mereological and topological ones, but what exactly distinguishes mereotopology from mereogeometry? Both are classes of region-based theories of space. The name mereogeometry suggests the inclusion some geometrical relation. Indeed, Gerla (1995) proposes the ability to reconstruct points as criteria for a region-based theory to be geometrical. Such theories are usually called *pointless geometries*, or nowadays, *point-free geometries* (Gerla, 1995); similar approaches can be found in the early works by Lobačevsky (1934) and Huntington (1913) trying to build Euclidean geometry from regions or solids. In contrast, Borgo and Masolo (2009) take the sheer inclusion of a geometrical primitive such as convexity, e.g. *Conv(x)*, *Congr(x,y)*, *SPH(x)*, or relative size, e.g. *CanConnect(x,y,z)*, as distinctive feature lifting a mereotopology to the geometrical level (though not necessarily to Euclidean geometry). Here we follow the later interpretation. While (mereo-)topological relations are required to be invariant under all continuous transformation, (mereo-)geometrical relations are required to be invariant to the strength of the desired geometry. Usually this is elementary geometry, but can also be weaker forms thereof such as affine geometry (invariant under affine transformations) or projective geometry (invariant under transformations of the projective group). From Borgo and Masolo (2009) we learn that the mereogeometrical theories of Bennett et al. (2000), Borgo et al. (1996), de Laguna (1922), Donnelly (2001), Nicod (1924), and Tarski (1956a) all have equivalent standard topological model in $\mathbb{R}^n$. Borgo and Masolo (2009) introduce the term *full mereogeometries* for these theories. However, the non-standard models have not been systematically studied; it remains open whether the models without topological interpretation are also equivalent for the full mereogeometries.

With Tarski's two primitives *sphere* and *parthood* (Tarski, 1956a; see Gruszczyński & Pietruszczak, 2008 for a full development of his theory), we can define a ternary relation of co-linear points with equal distances between them. Thus, defining the predicate of *betweenness* between three points, it is easy to reconstruct elementary geometry as axiomatized in Tarski (1959). Indeed, Tarski (1956a) states the equivalence between his geometry of solids and three-dimensional Euclidean geometry as a theorem. Hence, all full mereogeometries are region-based equivalents of Euclidean geometry.

The only theory including a notion of convexity but not constructing a full mereogeometry that we know of is the RCC extended by a convex hull primitive (cf. Cohn, 1995; Cohn, et al., 1994, 1997b; Randell, et al., 1992). Borgo and Masolo (2009) conjectured and Cohn and Renz (2008) confirmed that this theory is strictly weaker than full mereogeometries. It is suspected that the RCC together with a convex hull (or convexity) primitive is a point-free equivalent of affine geometry. For possible future work in this direction, see Section 10.3.

Within topological theories of mereotopology, it is even possible to define convexity in Boolean terms, compare the discussion of Roeper (1997) in Section 7.3. This however relies on points as smallest entities. It remains an open question whether such a convexity notion can be defined without using points. Separately, it remains a challenge to build theories in between mereotopology and mereogeometry that can express basic morphological distinctions without constructing a full mereogeometry—if any such theories exist.

## 3.10. Vagueness, Location, and Granularity

Beyond the analysis of ontological commitments within mereotopologies, several other aspects are of practical relevance when constructing such theories of space. In particular, vagueness has to be dealt with in reality, since information is often incomplete. Input data is usually not perfect (e.g. from satellite pictures, maps, descriptions, etc.) or the exact outlines of regions and boundaries are unclear for other reasons. Furthermore, our world is very dynamic in the large and small scale, e.g. gravitational effects and winds let shorelines vary, while also atoms and molecules are constantly in movement and, physically speaking, constantly alter the surface of any physical object. Finally, available information about spatial configurations usually comes in a wide range of granularity—especially in the realm of geographic information. We have high-level maps such as political maps but also very detailed maps such as topographical maps of small areas. Integrating mereotopological information of diverse granularity is far from obvious. These three aspects, namely vagueness, the distinction between objects and their location, and granularity, are crucial in real-world applications. However, there are not specific to mereotopology. Nevertheless, we cover them briefly in this subsection. For the sake of brevity, we will not address these issues in later sections.

Within QSTR, there is an abundance of work on notions of vagueness using *vague* or *rough sets*, i.e. approximations of crisp sets (cf. Pawlak,

1991), in so-called *rough relation algebras* (cf. Düntsch, 1994; Düntsch, et al., 2001b; Düntsch & Winter, 2006), algebras of approximate regions (Düntsch, et al., 2001*a*), approximate topological relations (Clementini & Di Felice, 1997b), fuzzy relations/set (Burrough, 1996), or more recently used for the definition of the fuzzy region connection calculus (Schockaert, et al., 2009). One specific way to look at vagueness in regions is the use of indeterminate boundaries. Regions with indeterminate boundaries commonly occur when dealing with geographic features (lakes, mountains, mountain ranges, deserts, etc.) as well as rapidly changing objects such as clouds, crowds, swarms, etc. The groundwork for objects with indeterminate boundaries was laid by Burrough and Frank (1995, 1996) distinguishing the region an object certainly occupies from its maximal possible extent, the vague region. A classification of boundaries and their properties has been attempted by Galton (2003), while more philosophical discussions are found in Varzi (2008). The *egg-yolk calculus* (Cohn & Gotts, 1996b) is the most prominent logical theory of vague regions. The yolk represents the certain region ('*definitely in*'), while the whole egg represents the maximal possible extent ('*possibly in*'). There is a direct relation to spatio-temporal reasoning, where the yolk represents the area an object is always in, while the remainder of the egg represents the spatial region where the objects is sometimes located (Stell, 2003). Guesgen (2002) extended the egg-yolk theory to spatio-temporal regions by using fuzzy sets, resulting in the *scrambled-egg calculus*. Ibrahim and Tawfik (2004) apply a similar fuzzy-logical approach to Muller's qualitative spatio-temporal framework (Muller, 1998a, 1998b, 2002). In general, vagueness is orthogonal to other ontological commitments within mereotopological theories.

In reality, humans distinguish physical objects and the location, i.e. the space they occupy. Many mereotopological theories assume that either only regions of space or only physical objects are in the domain of discourse. To incorporate both within one theory, we need to define a theory of space (ground) and one of physical objects (figure) while additionally axiomatizing the relationships between them (*figure-ground relations*). Such theory of localization is discussed in Casati and Varzi (1996), presenting the idea of a topological theory of space combined with a mereological theory of physical objects—therefore redefining the interaction between topology and mereology in a rather unorthodox way. *Rough locations* have been studied extensively, e.g. by Bittner (1999, 2004). Later, a series of papers extended the RCC with notions of vagueness and rough locations (Bittner & Stell, 1998, 2000a, 2000b, 2002). For space occupied by physical objects, Schmolze (1996) considers a topological account of space extended by axioms governing the interrelation between space and objects.

Dealing with spatial information of different granularity is closely related to vagueness in the following way: less fine-grained information leads to a higher degree of vagueness. For that reason, granularity, granular partitions, and hierarchical theories of mereotopology have been usually studied in the context of vagueness (Bittner, 2002; Bittner & Smith, 2001, 2003; Bittner & Stell, 2003). Major aspects of granularity and location influenced the design of the *Basic Formal Ontology* (BFO: Grenon, 2003). Another hierarchical approach integrating discrete and continuous mereotopology using Generalized Boolean Contact algebras (see Section 6.1) has been presented by Li and Nebel (2007). Cohn and Gotts (1996a) use 'crisping' as a way to capture granularity for dealing with spatial vagueness while Cohn (1995) presents another hierarchical theory based on the RCC and convexity. Finally, a congruence primitive has been combined with the RCC by Cristani et al. (2000) which in turn allows defining spheres and four JEPD relations of congruence defining the MC-4 calculus (cf. Cristani, 1999). Location is expressed in terms of parthood, but the essential new idea is the definition of *mobile parts*, which

*Table 1. Set of ontological commitments and their choices for mereotopology*

| Ontological aspect | Set of possible choices |
|---|---|
| Foundation | · Mereology<br>· Topology<br>· Mereology and Topology |
| Extensionality | · Choice of one or many extensional primitives, e.g. *C*, *O*, *P*, and/or *EC* |
| Sums | · Mereological sum<br>· Topological sum<br>· Mereological and topological sum |
| Fusion (restriction of sums) | · Restricted to finite fusions<br>· Allows infinite (unrestricted) fusions |
| Connectedness of space | · Regions and their complements connected<br>· Regions and their complements disconnected |
| Dimensionality and Boundaries | · Only equi-dimensional regions (as in Whiteheadean space)<br>· Inclusion of one sort of entities, but allowing regions without interiors as boundaries (boundary-tolerant theories)<br>· Multiple sorts of entities (Multi-dimensional mereotopology) |
| Atomicity | · Atomless (continuous)<br>· Atomic (discrete)<br>· Atom-tolerant theories |
| Dimensionality of holes | · No holes<br>· Only equi-dimensional holes (same dimension as the host)<br>· Equi-dimensional holes and holes of one dimension lower than the host ('cracks')<br>· Any kind of holes (missing points, etc.) |
| Types of holes | · No holes<br>· Only interior holes (cavities)<br>· Only superficialities<br>· Both cavities and superficialities acceptable |
| Geometric expressivity | · No geometric notion such as convexity (pure mereotopology)<br>· Full mereogeometry (restoration of Euclidean geometry possible) |

can move freely within their host body. In this light, the proposed theory is an egg-yolk theory where the maximal extent is the location extent of a mobile part. However, with the ability to define spheres in the tradition of Tarski, the resulting theory is just another full mereogeometry (see Sections 3.9 and 5.2).

### 3.11. Summary of Ontological Choices

The ontological choices we presented in this section are summarized in Table 1. Each aspect is presented as a partitioning of the available choices with the exception of the aspect of geometric expressivity and the aspect of the foundation as explained in Section 3.1. We use the aspects to discuss ontological choices within families of mereotopology, especially of Whiteheadean space and their algebraic counterparts in later sections of this chapter. Notice although dimensionality and boundaries were discussed separately, they are both related choices of a single ontological decision. The aspect of geometric expressivity is quite different from the remaining commitments in that we only name two extremes of a scale of possible choices. At the lower end of the scale of geometric expressivity, which have pure mereotopologies that cannot express any convexity or other geometric notions, while on the other extreme full mereogeometries are able to express anything that can be expressed in Euclidean geometry without reference to points. Filling the other potential choices in between pure mereotopology and full mereogeometry remains one of the tasks for future research (compare Section 10.3).

Not surprisingly, the ontological aspects summarized in the table resemble those discussed by Eschenbach (2007) for a set of five mereotopological theories. One aspect we have not treated separately is the possible distinction of open and closed regions. Though it is important especially for understanding the difference between some of the Whiteheadean theories of space, it is more a technical than an ontological distinction. Practically what matters is whether we can explicitly model boundaries and the connectedness of elements to their complements. Both distinctions are covered by the set of ontological commitments extracted here. For the remaining chapter, the aspect of holes will be discussed only marginally. Whiteheadean mereotopologies allow all types of equi-dimensional holes, with some theories requiring the intended regions to be hole-free. However, many theories have not been explicitly analyzed in that respect.

## 4. SYSTEMATIC TREATMENTS OF MEREOTOPOLOGY

Beyond the more informal analysis of ontological commitments of mereotopologies, categorizing the various theories in more formal ways helps us understand the theories, their limitations, and their relations to one another. For mereotopology, simple classification methods as well as more complex, partially-ordered hierarchies of theories with respect to certain ontological aspects (e.g. extensionality, connectedness of complements, existence of atoms, etc.) have been used to organize the wealth of theories. This section gives an overview of four different ways of systematically comparing mereotopological theories. These differ on what they compare—logical statements such as axioms and theorems, the models of theories, the semantics of key predicates, or the set of primitives. Apart from these frameworks, algebraic representations have been prolific in systematically analyzing mereotopologies. These representations are covered in-depth in Section 6. Equally, comparisons of topological models of Whiteheadean theories of space are given in Section 7, relating them also to purely topological theories of region-based space.

### 4.1. Logical Statements

A first systematic study of axiomatic systems of mereology and topology has been conducted in Casati and Varzi (1999) and Varzi (1996a). The space of theories is divided into mereology-based and topology-based theories of space as outlined in Section 3.1. The theories are further analyzed with respect to their strength of extensionality. Following up on these results, a purely axiomatic study of the relationship between Whiteheadean theories, in particular the theories of Asher and Vieu (1995), Clarke (1981), Eschenbach (1999), Randell et al. (1992), and Roeper (1997), has been conducted by Eschenbach (2007). In her work, the space of (Whiteheadean) mereotopological theories is mapped out according to several ontological aspects which significantly influenced our discussions in Section 3 and the comparison of axiomatic theories of Whiteheadean space in Section 5.1.1. Amongst the ontological commitments considered by Eschenbach (2007) varying degrees of extensionality, kinds of universal regions, self-connectedness of space, and open/closed distinctions are explored. Moreover, different kinds of complement and sum/fusion operators are used to chart the investigated mereotopologies.

### 4.2. Models

The comparative framework of Borgo and Masolo (2009) studies axiomatic theories with respect to their standard topological models. Though their work is limited to mereogeometry, the approach has a much wider applicability as we will see in Section 7.1. Borgo and Masolo (2009) utilize the interdefinability of primitives of several so-called *full mereogeometries* (Bennett, et al., 2000; Borgo, et al., 1996; de Laguna, 1922; Donnelly, 2001; Nicod, 1924; Tarski, 1956a) to prove the equivalence of their standard topological models in $\mathbb{R}^n$ when limited to only regular closed subsets or to only regular open subsets. The theories presented in Borgo et al. (1996), de Laguna (1922), and Donnelly (2001) are further restricted to those subsets with finite diameter. As a consequence of Borgo and Masolo's (2009) work, we can freely pick amongst these theories depending on our preferred primitives. For example the sphere primitive *SPH(x)* from Tarski (1956a) and congruence *CG(x,y)* from Borgo et al. (1996) are equally express in the presence of the parthood relation, while the primitives *CCon(x,y,z)*—'*x can connect y and z*'—from de Laguna (1922) and Donnelly (2001) or Conjugate *Conj(x,y,z,w)* from Nicod (1924) are alone sufficient to construct full mereogeometry. That allows us in Section 5.2 to discuss a single axiomatic theory representative for all full mereogeometries. However, the possible non-standard models, i.e. the models without interpretation in traditional point-set topology, of these mereogeometries might still differ. Further follow-up work is required to investigate this possibility.

## 4.3. Semantics of Connection and Parthood

A very different framework by Cohn and Varzi (1998, 2003) explores mereotopologies with respect to a three-dimensional space of the type of their connection relation, parthood relations, and fusion operation. This focuses on a select set of ontological commitments from the larger set covered in Section 3, but treats them within a formal framework. It allows us to better understand what combinations of distinct connection and parthood relations are feasible in mereotopological theories. However, some ontological choices such as, for instance multi-dimensionality, are incompatible with this framework, while choices such as atomism, holes, and self-connectedness of space are compatible, but independent from the dimensions of Cohn and Varzi's framework. Cohn and Varzi (2003) shows the difference between boundary-tolerant (they refer to them as boundary-based) and boundary-free theories. Boundary-free ones are all uniformly typed, e.g. their connection and parthood relations are based on the same notion of 'contact.' Of course, Whiteheadean theories (see Section 5.1.1) must be uniformly typed since they are only equipped with a single connection primitive and parthood is defined in terms of that. On the contrast, boundary-based theories are not uniformly typed. In other words, the boundary-based theories use a different notion of connection for their parthood relation than what is assumed for their own connection relation. In addition, Cohn and Varzi (1999, 2003) investigate the strength of the connection as an orthogonal dimension in their framework. It refines the coarse separation of weak and strong self-connectedness found in Section 3.4 and in Asher and Vieu (1995) to allow more fine-grained notions of connectedness. A mereotopology incorporating several different notions of connection could resolve the implausibility of several boundary-based theories that Cohn and Varzi (2003) and Breysse and De Glas (2007) mention. For instance, an interior can be in weak contact (adjacent) to its exterior in the presence of boundaries, compare also Fleck (1996) if a definition of weak contact independent of the standard contact relation (implying the sharing of a point) exists.

## 4.4. Sets of Primitives

Finally, we devise a categorization based upon the set of primitives of mereotopologies. Although being highly informal, it contributes to a deeper understanding of different kinds of mereotopological theories. As already observed by Robinson (1959), a single binary relation is insufficient to construct a theory of elementary geometry, such as Tarski's theory (Tarski, 1959). With the establishment of equivalences of a large set of mereogeometrical theories (Borgo & Masolo, 2009), it becomes clear why these theories either use some ternary relation (de Laguna, 1922; Donnelly, 2001; Nicod, 1924) or a combination of two relations of which at least one is binary (Bennett, et al., 2000; Borgo, et al., 1996; Nicod, 1924; Tarski, 1956a). As demonstrated by Clarke (1981) and others, if we are willing to stay within certain restrictions, a single binary primitive is sufficient to construct a mereotopology: Whiteheadean mereotopology (compare Section 5.1.1).

Mereotopology can be extended with additional geometric primitives without necessarily obtaining a full mereogeometry. For example, the RCC has been extended in with a binary predicate *convex hull, conv(x)* (cf. Cohn, 1995; Cohn, et al., 1997b) which gives a theory strictly weaker than full mereogeometry, conjectured by Borgo and Masolo (2009) and verified by Cohn and Renz (2008) using earlier results from Davis et al. (1999). It remains open whether mereotopological theories more expressive then the ones currently known, but strictly weaker than full mereogeometry, exist. This is especially important, since unary functions or predicates such as 'convex hull of *x*' or '*x* is convex' seem to be difficult to extract from real-world applications (e.g. a computer vision system) and should be replaced by notions that are more primitive. Furthermore, it is unclear whether we can define such a theory using a single binary predicate or whether some additional predicate is necessary.

As Smith (1996) remarks, formal ontology is no longer primarily concerned with devising spatial ontologies with minimal sets of non-logical primitives of low arity (ternary relations proposed to build mereogeometry seem in general less intuitive in comparison with a combination of unary/binary predicates). Nevertheless, thinking about minimal sets of primitives is still useful when studying and comparing different axiomatizations of common real-world information, e.g. of qualitative space. For practical applications, it might well be the case that the number of primitives will increase.

## 5. LOGICAL AXIOMATIZATIONS OF MEREOTOPOLOGY

After identifying the set of choices for different ontological commitments in mereotopology and after reviewing earlier comparative studies of mereotopology, we are now in a position to take a closer look at some specific axiom sets for mereotopology and mereogeometry. Based on earlier studies about mereotopological theories and their assumptions, we present three main families of logical axiomatizations of mereotopology and mereogeometry. Many theories from the literature fall within one of these families. We present axiomatizations in first-order logic, outlining alternative sets of primitives, definitions, and axioms where appropriate. Most importantly, for each family we identify the common ontological commitments on the one hand and explore the differing ontological choices on the other hand. In the subsequent sections, we study alternative ways (alternative to logical axiomatizations) of treating mereotopology: Section 6 the algebraic counterparts of some mereotopology are interrelated, before turning in Section 7 to topological interpretations and topological specifications of mereotopologies. It is followed by a short section on graph theoretic ways of building mereotopology—especially discrete mereotopology. Altogether, we hope to give the reader an overview of the different styles of axiomatizations and what kinds of theories exist in the space of possible theories (along the ontological commitments). At the same time, we hope to convince the reader that studying the different mathematical frameworks (logic, algebra, topology, and graph theory) for

*Figure 1. Examples of non-regular regions: in the first a point is missing while the others have so-called 'cracks'—positive or negative*

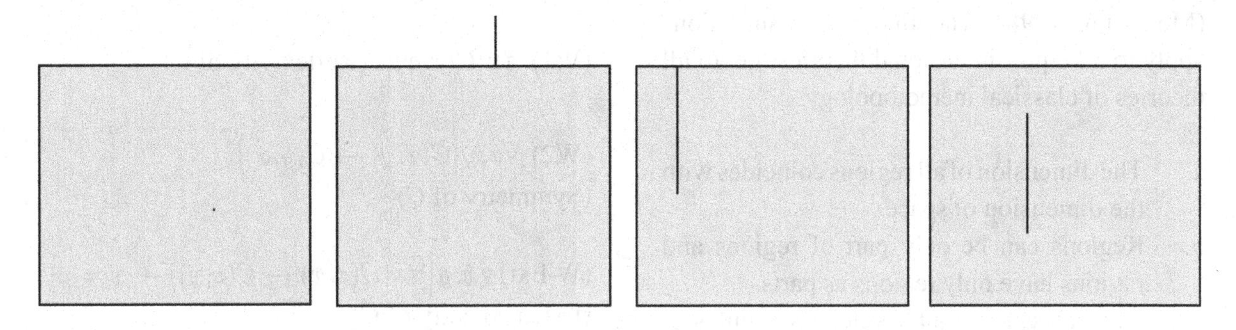

specifying mereotopologies allows us to fully understanding the rich space of mereotopologies.

In this section, we will first look at two families of what we call *classical mereotopology*—Whiteheadean and boundary-based accounts of region-based space. Both families have been studied quite exhaustively (Casati & Varzi, 1999; Cohn & Varzi, 1998, 1999, 2003; Eschenbach, 2007; Varzi, 1996a). Though the immediate results are related directly only to continuous mereotopology, most of the results readily extend to discrete theories as Section 6.1 will demonstrate. In the subsequent Section 5.2, we give an overview of full mereogeometry using the axiomatization of Borgo et al. (1996) in combination with Tarski's 'Geometry of Solids' (Tarski, 1956a). Due to the results of Borgo and Masolo (2009) other mereogeometries can be reformulated using his primitives and axioms. The first subsections are formulated in first-order logic, while the last subsection discusses alternative, logical approaches with their differences, advantages, and disadvantages.

## 5.1. Classical Mereotopology

What we call classical mereotopology comprises pure mereotopological theories restricted to regular, equi-dimensional regions (see Figure 1 for examples of non-regular regions). This means three of our ontological aspects are fixed: the dimensionality of entities, indirectly also the dimensionality of holes, and the geometric expressivity. Notice that there is no restriction to any particular dimension, but instead each model is restricted to regions of equal dimensions. For instance, if a model contains three-dimensional entities like spatial regions, it cannot contain entities of any other dimension, e.g. two-dimensional surfaces, one-dimensional lines, or zero-dimensional points. Consequently, all entities must be regular. That means the domain of discourse is either a set of regular closed regions, i.e. regions that satisfy $x = \mathrm{cl}(x) = \mathrm{cl}(\mathrm{int}(x))$, a set of regular open regions, i.e. regions that satisfy $x = \mathrm{int}(x) = \mathrm{int}(\mathrm{cl}(x))$ ), or a set of regular regions (not necessarily open or closed) that satisfy both $\mathrm{int}(\mathrm{cl}(x)) = \mathrm{int}(x)$ and $\mathrm{cl}(\mathrm{int}(x)) = \mathrm{cl}(x)$.

### 5.1.1. The Whiteheadean Approach

Whitehead (1920, 1929) and de Laguna (1922) pioneered mereotopology by proposing the relation *extensive connection* to qualitatively describe the topological relations between regions of space. Extensive connection is what we call today *connection* or *contact*, or more generally *proximity*. Such an economical framework built around a single topological primitive distinguishes their work from the mereological approach of their contemporaries (Husserl, 1913; Leonard & Goodman, 1940; Leśniewski, 1927, 1931). Apart from regions being primitives instead of points, assumptions of Whiteheadean theories include the following (Mormann, 1998). The first two assumptions apply to all equi-dimensional theories, i.e. to all theories of classical mereotopology.

a. The dimension of all regions coincides with the dimension of space
b. Regions can be only part of regions and regions have only regions as parts
c. Regions can be interpreted as point sets (topological representability)
d. The theory is based on a single connection primitive

We now concentrate on assumption d) while the interpretation of regions as point sets is discussed in more detail in Section 7.3. Notice that often another assumption is added restricting the topological representability to representability by regular regions, which follows from a) and b). Because of assumption d), Whiteheadean theories are extensional with respect to the contact relation *C*. In fact, Whiteheadean theories are extensions of Strong Mereotopology (**SMT**) (Casati & Varzi, 1999). Other ontological commitments vary across the different Whiteheadean theories; we will discuss them as appropriate. Notice that some theories appearing as Whiteheadean do not satisfy d), for example, the theory of Roeper (1997) uses an additional mereological primitive hidden in the Boolean structure. However, it can be redefined as shown in (W-P') below.

Interest in Whiteheadean space was sparked by the axiomatic treatment presented by Clarke (1981, 1985). Now, perhaps most prominently the Region Connection Calculus (RCC: Cohn, et al., 1997a, 1997b; Gotts, 1994; Gotts, et al., 1996; Randell, et al., 1992), but also Asher and Vieu (1995) and Roeper (1997) give axiomatizations of region-based space based on the Whiteheadean assumption of extensionality of *C* as required by W-Ext. Notice that W1 and W2 are common to all mereotopologies characterizing contact as reflexive and symmetric relation.

(W1) $\forall x\left[C(x,x)\right]$ (Reflexivity of *C*)

(W2) $\forall x,y\left[C(x,y)\rightarrow C(y,x)\right]$
(Symmetry of *C*)

(W-Ext) $\forall x,y\left[\forall z\left(C(z,x)\leftrightarrow C(z,y)\right)\rightarrow x=y\right]$
(Extensionality of *C*)

Alternative to W3, the axiom W-P can be posited (Masolo & Vieu, 1999). This is indeed the common definition of parthood for Whiteheadean space.

(W-P) $\forall x,y\left[\forall z\left(C(z,x)\rightarrow C(z,y)\right)\leftrightarrow P(x,y)\right]$
(Definition of *P*)

Notice that despite the similarities between the theory of Roeper (1997) and other Whiteheadean theories, the former is a purely topological account using a topologically inspired complement $-x:=\bigcup_{y}\neg C(x,y)$ inspired by Clarke's definition. This complement is not necessarily a mereological complement as in the RCC. The complement itself serves to define the relation of proper parthood.

(W-P') $PP(x,y)\equiv_{def}\neg C(x,-y)$
(Roeper's definition of *PP*)

In algebraic terms, this is equivalent to $\neg C(x,-y)\Leftrightarrow x<y$ which holds in the RCC. Similarly, $\neg C(x,-y)\Leftrightarrow x\leq y$ induces the contact relation from parthood for Clarke (1981) and Asher and Vieu (1995) (cf. Biacino & Gerla, 1991; Hahmann, et al., 2009). Notice the $\leq$ in the second equivalence; this is caused by a definition of complements (interpretable as true set complements) in the theories of Clarke and Asher and Vieu that differs from complements in RCC.

The work of Roeper (1997) will be discussed in more detail in Section 7.3. For now, we concentrate on the purely logical theories of Whiteheadean space. For the other theories, overlap $O$ and external connection $EC$ are defined as following.

(W-O) $O(x, y) \equiv_{def} \exists z(P(z, x) \wedge P(z, y))$
(Definition of $O$)

(W-EC) $EC(x, y) \equiv_{def} C(x, y) \wedge \neg O(x, y)$
(Definition of $EC$)

In addition, Whiteheadean theories define binary topological sums and intersection of regions, as well as complements. Additionally, concepts such as tangential (proper) part and non-tangential (proper) part can be defined. Most importantly, the notion of self-connectedness is definable through axiom SC-S, compare Section 3.4 and Randell et al. (1992). For Asher and Vieu (1995), self-connectedness is defined using the weaker variant SC-W—accommodating the fact that the space is not self-connected.

The theories differ in their axiomatization. Clarke (1981) utilizes second-order notions (set-theory or definite descriptions) to describe infinitary fusions, while Asher and Vieu (1995) and the RCC are first-order theories limited to finite sums. Thus, the latter two are first-order axiomatizable. Both the RCC and Clarke (1981, 1985) are atomless, while the account of Asher and Vieu (1995) is atom-tolerant. The Generalized Region Connection Calculus (GRCC: Li & Ying, 2004) has been proposed as atom-tolerant generalization of the RCC theory.

The main difference between these theories lies in the domain of discourse. Clarke (1981) and Asher and Vieu (1995) allow any kind of regular regions, while the RCC and (Roeper, 1997) only deal with regular closed regions. This in turn is reflected in the definition of the contact relation and thus in the self-connectedness of space. Either kind of theory defines the Whiteheadean contact relation as following.

(C-Weak) $C(x, y) \Leftrightarrow x \cap y \neq \varnothing$
(Weak contact)

Notice that even for theories over regular closed regions the standard topological interpretation comes closer to that of (C-Strong) if we consider regular closed regions as equivalence classes of all elements that have the same closure. For instance in the system of Roeper (1997), C-Strong is a theorem. In theories over regular open regions, contact is also characterized by C-Strong.

(C-Strong) $C(x, y) \Leftrightarrow cl(x) \cap cl(y) \neq \varnothing$
(Strong contact)

In theories allowing all kinds of regular regions, C-Strong could be used to ensure that a region and its complement are connected and thus self-connected spaces are possible.

The algebraic structure and extensionality also depend on the accepted type of regular regions. If only regular closed regions are considered, the models are quasi-Boolean algebras. The algebraic structure is more general if all kinds of regular regions are acceptable (see Section 6). With regard to extensionality, the algebraic representations show that theories concerned only with regular closed regions are $O$-extensional, while others are not necessarily, e.g. Asher and Vieu (1995) is not $O$-extensional.

*Theories related to Whiteheadean space.* The RCC, the most studied Whiteheadean theory, has been modified with regard to several ontological commitments resulting in new theories. Many of these modifications are studied in the algebraic counterparts of the RCC, see Section 6.1. These include mainly weakening of the atomless and extensional nature of RCC. Another modification of interest pertains to the dimensionality restriction. The INCH calculus (Gotts, 1996b) absorbs most of RCC's ontological commitments, but relaxes the limitation to a single primitive to accommodate entities of diverse dimensions in single model. Thus, the INCH calculus violates the assumptions a) and b); hence, we do not call the resulting theory Whiteheadean. In fact, the algebraic representation most likely consists of a set of contact algebras with each of the contact algebras captures the entities of a single dimension and their topological contact.

To a limited extend, Pratt and Schoop (1997) also uses Whitehead's style but is restricted to polygonal regions. The theory employs a single, unary primitive of self-connectedness, but their first-order logic comes equipped with the Boolean operations meet $\cdot$ and join $+$ which are equivalent to a partial order $\leq$ defined in the following way: $x \leq y \Leftrightarrow x \cdot y = x$ . However, this partial order can be directly used to define a mereological primitive. Therefore, implicitly a mereological and a topological primitive are used.

In many respects similar to Whiteheadean spatial theories, the CRC (Eschenbach, 1999) differentiates itself in one important ontological choice. Though based on a mereological primitive of parthood and a topological primitive of disconnection, the CRC could be axiomatized using parthood and connection. However, Eschenbach (2007) showed that in the CRC the mereological relation *CoveredBy* can have a different extension than the topological relation of enclosure, Encl. In contrast, in Whiteheadean theories enclosure and parthood coincide, compare axiom W-P.

(Encl) $Encl(x,y) \equiv_{def} \forall z\left[C(z,x) \rightarrow C(z,y)\right]$ (Enclosure)

### 5.1.2. Boundary-Tolerant Approaches

Within Whiteheadean and any other classical, i.e. equi-dimensional axiomatizations of region-based space, regions are the only entities considered in the domain of interest. Moreover, all regions are of the same dimension; hence, boundary elements cannot be in the domain of discourse. For instance, Clarke (1981) and Asher and Vieu (1995) require that all regions have non-empty interiors which must be regions themselves. Hence, boundaries are excluded. In theories restricted to regular closed regions, there is no difference between a regions' interior and closure, i.e. boundary elements cannot be modeled either. This is a fundamental ontological commitment. Since boundaries often play an important role, other authors (Casati & Varzi, 1999; Galton, 1996, 2004; Gotts, 1996b; Smith, 1996; Smith & Varzi, 1997) incorporate them into their theories. Two different approaches have been pursued. Either boundaries are considered as being of the same dimension as regions (Smith, 1996). Other authors go a step further and treat boundaries as entities of a lower dimension (Galton, 1996, 2004; Gotts, 1996b), hence dismissing the Whiteheadean assumptions a) and b) altogether. In particular, these fall outside the scope of classical mereotopology and are not further treated in this section. We refer to Section 3.5 for a brief discussion of these theories.

Smith's (1996) theory combines a mereological primitive of parthood *P* and a topological primitive of interior parthood *IP* which together define the contact relation *C*. Within Smith's theory, points are defined as regions without proper parts using axiom (PT) from Section 3.6. Unrestricted fusions and the topological operations sum, intersection, complement, and difference are defined using definite descriptions; thereby avoiding second-order notions but not really giving a first-order axiomatization either. What makes it unique amongst the logical region-based theories of space is that in addition to regions, Smith allows boundaries as special regions without interior. Every boundary region is part of the region they bound. Moreover, boundaries are self-bounding. Using fusion, a maximal boundary *bdy(x)* can be defined.

Although Smith (1996) sticks to regions as only entities in the domain, it is clear that boundaries have special properties that distinguish themselves from other regions. However, no topological interpretation or algebraic representation of the models has been given. Without formal semantics it is, however, far from obvious what the whole set of ontological commitments are.

In an attempt to capture the notion of boundaries using only standard topological notions, Fleck (1996) comes to an understanding similar to that of Smith. However, no axiomatization is proposed by Fleck (1996) that allows an explicit comparison.

## 5.2. First-Order Full Mereogeometry

Classical mereotopology does not deal with any geometric notions at all. On the other end of the scale of the ontological aspect of geometric expressivity, we have several theories classified as full mereogeometries. As noted before, these theories share a common topological interpretation, which allows the reconstruction of points. Hence, we present only one set of axioms for full mereogeometry. All of the full mereogeometry consider only regions of a single dimension.

Tarski's categorical Geometry of Solids (Tarski, 1956a) is probably the best known mereogeometry, later incorporated into the *Region-based Geometry* (RBG: Bennett, 2001; Bennett, et al., 2000), a categorical first-order theory. Borgo et al. (1996) have proposed an alternative first-order theory (we refer to the theory as *BGM*) using three primitives: parthood *P* for the mereological part, the unary, quasi-topological predicate 'simple region' *SR*, and the morphological primitive of congruence *CG*. In style, the axiomatization of BGM is closer to the axiomatizations of Whiteheadean space we saw before, so we use this theory to exemplify constructing a mereogeometry from mereology, topology, and morphology. Nevertheless, we will be able to outline Tarski's theory within the scope of these axioms. The primitives of other full mereogeometries can be expressed as definitions reusing the axiomatization we present here.

The mereological part of BGM consists of a standard **CEM** (compare Section 2.2) without infinitary fusion operation (cf. Section 3.3). The topological definition of connection relies on the primitive notion of *simple regions*, *SR*.

(G-C)

$$C(x,y) \equiv_{def} \exists z[SR(z) \wedge O(z,x) \wedge O(z,y) \wedge \forall u\left(P(u,z) \rightarrow O(u,x) \vee O(u,y)\right)]$$

In addition, the concepts of interior part *IP* (compares to *NTPP*), maximally connected part *MCP*, and strong connection *SC* are defined in BGM. Strong connection only holds between two regions if a simple region exists that consists of parts of each region.

(G-IP)

$$IP(x,y) \equiv_{def} PP(x,y) \wedge \forall z\left(SR(z) \wedge PO(z,x) \rightarrow O(z,y-x)\right)$$

(Interior part)

(G-MCP)

$$MCP(x,y) \equiv_{def} P(x,y) \wedge SR(x) \wedge \neg\exists z\left[P(z,y) \wedge SR(z) \wedge PP(x,z)\right]$$

(Maximally connected part)

(G-SC)

$$SC(x,y) \equiv_{def} \exists uv\left[P(u,x) \wedge P(v,y) \wedge SR(u+v)\right]$$

(Strong connection)

The following axioms complete the topological structure of the full mereogeometry. They force the existence of simple regions with interiors that are simple regions as well and the existence of a maximal connected part. (G3) requires all regions to be an interior part of some simple region. Thus no universal region can exist, hence excluding atomistic models.

(G1)
$$\forall x,y,z[SR(z) \wedge z = x + y \rightarrow \exists u\big(SR(u) \wedge O(u,x) \wedge O(u,y) \wedge IP(u,z)\big)]$$

(G2) $\forall x \exists y\big[MCP(y,x)\big]$

(G3) $\forall x \exists y\big[SR(y) \wedge IP(x,y)\big]$

In the presence of a definition of complementation the topological primitive *SR* can be defined using connection. *C*, in turn, can be defined in terms of overlap and congruence *CG* (Borgo & Masolo, 2009).

(G-Comp)
$$Compl(x,y) \equiv_{def} \forall z\big[C(z,y) \leftrightarrow \neg IP(z,x)\big]$$
(Complement)

(G-SR)
$$SR(x) \equiv_{def} \forall y,z,w\big[(y + z = x \wedge Compl(w,x)) \rightarrow \exists v\big(SC(v) \wedge O(v,y) \wedge O(v,z) \wedge \neg C(v,w)\big)\big]$$
(Simple region)

(G-C')
$$C(x,y) \equiv_{def} \forall z \exists z'\big[CG(z',z) \wedge O(z',x) \wedge O(z',y)\big]$$

On the geometrical (or morphological) part, BGM uses the primitive relation *congruence, CG,* to define spheres as special kinds of simple regions. Notice that without a notion of congruence, BGM is closely related to Whiteheadean theories of space, although two primitives are necessary, e.g. parthood and connection or parthood and simple region. For its place relative to other Whiteheadean theories, see Eschenbach (2007).

(G-SPH)
$$SPH(x) \equiv_{def} SR(x) \wedge \forall y\big[CG(x,y) \wedge PO(x,y) \rightarrow SR(x - y)\big]$$
(Sphere)

This enables the theory to reuse Tarski's definition of spheres (cf. Tarski, 1956a), such as *externally tangent, internally tangent, externally diametrical,* and *internally diametrical*. That leads to a definition of two spheres being *concentric*, which in turn allows defining the ternary relation of '*sphere x is in between the spheres y and z,*' *BTW(x,y,z)*. The core notion of equidistance of two points to a third can then be defined by two pair of congruent spheres having equidistance centers (Tarski, 1956a). Assume *x* and *x'* congruent and *y* and *y'* congruent. The spheres *x* and *y* have the same center, and so do *x'* and *y,'* i.e. the centers of *x, y* and *x, 'y'* are equidistant as follows (Borgo & Masolo, 2009). Since the first-order BGM does not reconstruct points, Tarski's notion of equidistance (cf. also Bennett, 2001; Bennett, et al., 2000) of two points from a third is not definable.

(G-SCG)
$$SCG(x,y) \equiv SPH(x) \wedge SPH(y) \wedge CG(x,y)$$
(Congruent spheres)

(G-EqD)
$$EqD(x,y,x',y') \equiv_{def} SCG(x,x') \wedge SCG(y,y') \wedge \neg P(x,y) \wedge \neg P(y,x) \wedge \neg P(x',y') \wedge \neg P(y',x') \wedge \exists z,z'\big[ID(z,x,y) \wedge ID(z',x',y') \wedge SCG(z,z')\big]$$
(Equidistance)

Now it is easy to imagine how the *between* or the *equidistance* relation can be used to define a metric system, therefore reconstructing elementary geometry (cf. Tarski, 1959). For more details on the full mereogeometries we refer to Bennett (2001), Bennett et al. (2000), Borgo et al. (1996), and Tarski (1956a). A comprehensive algebraic/topological analysis of Tarski's geometry of solid can be found in Gruszczyński and Pietruszczak (2008).

For the other mereogeometries, e.g. the primitive *CCon(x,y,z)* meaning '*x can connect y and z*' of de Laguna (1922) and Donnelly (2001) can be defined in terms of *CG* and *P*. Vice versa, *CCon* is sufficient to define *C, P,* and *CG*. For details see Borgo and Masolo (2009).

(G-C'') $C(x,y) \equiv_{def} \forall z[CCon(z,x,y)]$

## 5.3. Beyond First-Order Theories

So far, we have focused our discussion on ontological commitments of mereotopologies axiomatized in first-order logics and compared them amongst each other. For actual reasoning applications, concerns about the computational complexity of first-order mereotopologies have been raised. In general, we know that the language of first-order logic is undecidable, while reasoning with specific first-order theories might be decidable but is in most cases still highly intractable. A core issue here is the tradeoff between expressivity and tractability: a theory might be able to express a large variety of concepts, but reasoning with it is intractable, while another theory with a more limited expressiveness might be tractable with respect to the fewer sentences it can express. Hence, the development of less expressive, but more tractable theories is of great interest. This section showcases constraint calculi and modal logics as widespread approaches to build computationally more efficient mereotopological systems. First of all, we summarize the complexity results obtained for some of the first-order theories previously mentioned.

### 5.3.1. Computational Complexity and Decidability

Amongst the classical mereotopologies, the RCC has perhaps received the widest attention. Computational properties have been explored in much detail, especially when using the RCC as a relation calculus and reasoning with composition tables (Düntsch, et al., 2001*b*; Li & Ying, 2003; Li, et al., 2005; Renz, 1999, 2002, 2007; Renz & Li, 2008; Renz & Nebel, 1998, 1999; Xia & Li, 2006). Similarly, Smith and Park (1992) investigated the complexity of reasoning with the topological relations from Egenhofer's n-intersection. Although the full first-order theory of RCC is undecidable (cf. Dornheim, 1998; Gotts, 1996c; Grzegorczyk, 1951), tractable segments of the compositional calculi of the RCC have been identified (Renz, 1999; Renz & Li, 2008; Renz & Nebel, 1999). Approaches based on the RCC but using languages such as constraint calculi or propositional/modal logics (cf. Section 5.3.3) also yield more efficient reasoning frameworks.

If we go beyond pure mereotopology, Davis (2006) showed that a region-based theory consisting of a connection primitive extended by a primitive of convexity is already able to express any analytical relation (which contains a very broad class of relations) invariant under affine transformations. Loosely speaking, a Whiteheadean theory of space extended by a notion of convexity is equally expressive as affine geometry. Then it is only small step to elementary/Euclidean geometry (Borgo & Masolo, 2009). However, if our only concern is the definability of concepts within an ontology (cf. Hahmann & Gruninger, 2009), we can resort to Euclidean geometry which is quite expressive and decidable (cf. Tarski, 1959), though intractable. However, elementary geometry is more a geometric than a qualitative spatial framework. On the other side if we feel mereotopology to be too restrictive for some applications, theories in between mereotopology and full mereogeometry might be a solution (cf. Section 10.3). Besides the RCC with a convexity primitive *convex hull* (Cohn, 1995; Cohn, et al., 1994, 1997b; Randell, et al, 1992), we do not know of any theory filling this gap on the expressiveness scale.

### 5.3.2. Composition Tables and Constraint Calculi

A common alternative to axiomatizations of mereotopology in first-order logic are qualitative spatial frameworks using *composition tables* or *Binary Constraint Networks* (BCN), short *constraint calculi,* as representation. Composition tables might be most familiar from work on the temporal interval calculus (Allen, 1983), but have also been used for spatial reasoning, for instance with the RCC (cf. Renz & Ligozat, 2004; Renz & Nebel, 2007) and the n-intersection model of Egenhofer and colleagues (see Section 7.3.2). Any set of binary relations complete with respect to composition can be compactly represented by composition tables (cf. Düntsch, 1999; Düntsch, et al., 1999; Ligozat, 2001). Composition tables and their representations as BCNs are especially well-suited for reasoning with constraint propagation mechanisms. As prerequisite, the logical theory must consist of a set of Jointly Exhaustive and Pairwise Disjoint (JEPD) binary relations. For example, the relations of RCC-8 form a JEPD lattice (Li & Ying, 2003, Randell, et al., 1992) from which we can construct a composition table. We have to be careful here to distinguish between weak and proper composition. The latter is required to obtain a relation algebra (cf. Düntsch, 1999; Renz & Ligozat, 2004, 2005) while the former is commonly used to define a composition table. Composition-based reasoning methods, e.g. determining path consistency for constraint networks or algebraic closure for relation algebras, are usually more tractable than reasoning with a full first-order language.

For representational purposes, it is easy to translate a composition table into an axiomatic theory (Eschenbach, 2001). Conversely, for many first-order mereotopology the composition table can be easily constructed from a first-order theory if we can identify a set of binary base relations. In that respect, composition tables are just compact representations of axiomatic theories. Hence, it is usually sufficient to consider (first-order) axiom systems of mereotopologies and mereogeometries for a study of ontological commitments of related constraint calculi. We do not cover relation algebraic and composition-based representations, since they can be transformed into axiomatic theories with identical ontological commitments if we follow the straightforward methods of Düntsch (1999) and Eschenbach (2001). As Schlieder (1996, p. 124) argues:

*"Even though it is not always practicable to give a spatial representation formalism in this strict logical form, the idea of axiomatization is generally thought of as the ideal to achieve because it is a prerequisite for any further analysis of the formalism's properties."*

Notice that the known tractable (or at least decidable) relational calculi for region-based reasoning are incapable of expressing self-connectedness (Bennett & Düntsch, 2007), a core concept when bringing mereology and topology together, but theories unable to express self-connectedness can be barely recognized as full-fledged mereotopologies.

### 5.3.3. Modal Logics

Undecidability of first-order logic has sparked interest in other logics for spatio-temporal reasoning. Amongst them encodings of spatial theories in terms of propositional modal logics (Bennett, 1997; Wolter & Zakharyaschev, 2000, 2002; Balbiani, et al., 2008) seem to be most popular. Balbiani et al. (2008) summarize the modal logic approaches towards mereotopology, giving topological and relational semantics for several decidable propositional theories, for example for the modal theory BRCC-8 (Wolter & Zakharyaschev, 2000, 2002), a propositional version of RCC and GRCC. This work implicitly establishes the relationship between the propositional versions of continuous and discrete RCC theories. Computational aspects of these and various other propositional spatial and temporal logics have also been analyzed by Gabelaia et al. (2005).

The accessibility relations of modal operators have also been directly employed as spatial relations in modal logics (Cohn, 1993; Lutz & Wolter, 2004) and multi-modal logics (Bennett, et al., 2002). More generally, every spatial logic is just a logic interpreted over spatial, i.e. geometrical, metric, or topological, structures. However, spatial logics—even those employing regions as primitive entities—are beyond the scope of this chapter. The interested reader may consult (Aiello, et al., 2007). In this chapter, we focus on first-order theories of space, whereas some of these ontological decisions are representative for a much larger set of region-based theories of space.

Algebraic logic (cf. Andréka, et al., 2001) has been prolific in researching the interpretation of algebraic structures within logical systems. Best known for establishing algebraic representations of sentential logic (as two-element Boolean algebra) or first-order logic (as cyclindric algebras or as relation algebras with quasi-projections), similar relationships can be exploited to construct spatio-temporal logics from algebraic structures, i.e. by giving a modal logic a topological interpretation. We, however, continue by focusing on the algebraic representation of logical theories of region-based space.

## 6. ALGEBRAIC REPRESENTATIONS OF MEREOTOPOLOGY

While lattice theory was still in its early development Menger (1940) realized that lattice concepts as developed by Birkhoff can be readily used for constructing pointless point-free topology. Algebraic theories share an important aspect with the logical theories discussed so far: they directly yield axiomatic theories—sometimes even equational theories (so-called lattice varieties). It has been long known that certain mereological theories have a quasi-Boolean algebraic structure (cf. Leonard & Goodman, 1940; Tarski, 1935). Tarski (1935, 1956b) showed that General Extensional Mereology (**GEM**)—a CEM with an unrestricted fusion operation added—is isomorphic to a mereological field, another name for a quasi-Boolean algebra. In that sense, mereological fields are probably the earliest algebraic structures associated with mereology and mereotopology.

In AI, many mereotopological theories are known to be representable by so-called (Boolean) contact algebras—algebraic structures consisting of a lattice and a contact relation. As we will see shortly, these are closely related to the logical system of RCC and to proximity spaces known from topology. We present different classes of contact algebras, their axiomatizations, and their relations to logical theories of mereotopology. Topological representations of contact algebras and the relationship between contact algebras and proximity spaces are discussed subsequently in Section 7.2. In both sections, we follow the terminology and axiomatizations of Vakarelov (2007).

A great benefit of algebraic theories is that they overcome a criticism by Smith (1996) that in Whiteheadean space "the mereological and topological components [...] are difficult or impossible to separate formally" (p. 288). In contact algebras the lattice structure defines the mereological component while the topological component is captured by the contact relation. Apart from this achievement, algebraic representations of logical theories of mereotopologies help to relate mereotopological structures to more established mathematical structures. Eventually, algebraic representations can help us to rewrite axioms for mereotopological systems and create more computationally efficient theories, for instance equational theories of region-based space.

One comment in order concerns relation algebras (cf. Düntsch, 1999, 2005). Though applicable to compositional spatio-temporal reasoning (Egenhofer, 1994; Egenhofer & Sharma, 1993), relation algebras are distinct from the algebraic representations used in this section. The former are concerned with the algebra of relations of a theory, while we just treat the models of a theory algebraically. In this chapter, relation algebras are not in the focus; we solely concentrate on algebraic representations of models of logically specified mereotopologies.

## 6.1. (Boolean) Contact Algebras

Contact algebras of the form $\langle A, C \rangle$ are algebraic structures consisting of a lattice $\langle A; 0; 1; +; \cdot \rangle$ defining a partial order $\leq$ and a contact relation $C$. They are the algebraic counterparts of logical theories of Whiteheadean space and are also closely related to proximity spaces (cf. Section 7.2.3) known from topology. Here, we present different strengths of contact algebras and show their relationship to logical theories of mereotopology. Boolean connection algebras first appeared in Stell (2000) as counterpart of (strict) RCC models. Later, the term *Boolean Contact Algebra* (BCA) has been established instead. In a series of papers (Düntsch, 2005; Düntsch & Winter, 2004a, 2004b, 2005b), Düntsch and Winter examined contact algebras with axiomatic extensions guaranteeing extensionality, interpolation/normality/density, and connectivity of space. They also studied the relationships between contact algebras and RCC theories which led to indirect topological representations of RCC models through the topological representtation of their corresponding algebraic structures (Düntsch, et al., 2006). BCAs have been generalized to classes of contact algebras that correspond to other mereotopologies. Amongst others, *weak contact structures* (cf. Düntsch & Winter, 2005b), *contact algebras* (CA: Roy & Stell, 2002), *Generalized Boolean Contact Algebras* (GBCA: Li & Ying, 2004), *Distributive Contact Algebras* (DCA: Düntsch, et al., 2008), and *Precontact Algebras* (PCA: Dimov & Vakarelov, 2005; Düntsch & Vakarelov, 2007) have been defined and their properties studied.

The lattice within a contact algebra can be seen as algebraic description of its mereological component. The overlap relation between two regions can be defined as non-empty meet, thus expressing $O(x,y) \Leftrightarrow x \cdot y \neq \varnothing$ in algebraic terms:

$$O(x,y) \equiv_{def} \exists z[z \neq 0 \wedge z \leq x \wedge z \leq y]$$

Different strengths of mereologies correspond to various classes of lattices, e.g. pseudocomplemented lattices, distributive lattices, or Boolean lattices. Unless otherwise stated, we restrict ourselves to non-trivial (non-degenerate) lattices, i.e. lattices that contain at least another element besides 0 and 1. Moreover, we consider only bounded lattices. A contact algebra is called *complete* if the underlying lattice is complete, i.e. for arbitrary, possibly infinite, sets of lattice elements there exists a *supremum* (lowest upper bound) and an *infimum* (greatest lower bound). Completeness of lattices directly corresponds to the existence of unrestricted fusions in the logical axiomatizations, (cf. Section 3.3, Biacino & Gerla, 1991; Mormann, 1998) but is not first-order definable. Finite bounded lattices are always complete. We use general lattice theory as found in standard literature. We mainly follow Blyth (2005); more background can be found in Birkhoff (1967) and Grätzer (1998). The purely axiomatic treatment of lattices and Boolean algebras in Padmanabhan and Rudeanu (2008) is also a helpful guide.

For the remainder of this subsection we consider the following axioms. Many alternative notations and alternative sets of axioms occur throughout the literature.

(C0) $\forall x[\neg C(0,x)]$ (Null disconnectedness)

(C1) $\forall x[x \neq 0 \rightarrow C(x,x)]$ (Reflexivity)

(C2) $\forall x,y[C(x,y) \rightarrow C(y,x)]$ (Symmetry)

(C3) $\forall x,y,z[C(x,y) \wedge y \leq z \rightarrow C(x,z)]$ (Closure/Monotonicity)

(C3') $\forall y,z[y \leq z \rightarrow \forall x(C(x,y) \rightarrow C(x,z))]$

(C4) $\forall x, y, z\left[C(x, y+z) \rightarrow C(x, y) \vee C(x, z)\right]$
(Topological sum)

(C4') $\forall x, y, z\left[C(x+z, y) \rightarrow C(x, y) \vee C(z, y)\right]$
(Symmetric topological sum)

(Ext) $\forall x\left[x \neq 1 \rightarrow \exists y\left(y \neq 0 \wedge \neg C(x, y)\right)\right]$
(Disconnection)

(Ext') $\forall x, y\left[\forall z\left(C(x, z) \leftrightarrow C(y, z)\right) \leftrightarrow x=y\right]$
(Extensionality)

(Ext") $\forall x, y\left[\forall z\left(C(x, z) \rightarrow C(y, z)\right) \rightarrow x \leq y\right]$
(Compatibility)

Notice that C0–C3 are satisfied by all mereotopologies according to our definition in Section 2.3. Moreover, axioms C1, C2, and Ext' correspond to the logical axioms W-1, W-2, and W-Ext of Whiteheadean mereotopology introduced in Section 5.1.1.

Obviously, C3 and C3' are equivalent. In the presence of C0–C4, all of Ext, Ext', and Ext" are equivalent (Vakarelov, 2007). In general, Ext" implies Ext' which implies Ext but none of the reverse directions hold in general; more such implications are studied in Düntsch and Winter (2005b). Alternatively, Ext can be stated as '$C$ is anti-symmetric.' Then, because C3 establishes the reverse direction of the implication in C4, i.e. $\forall x, y, z\left[C(x, y) \vee C(x, z) \rightarrow C(x, y+z)\right]$, a partial order can be defined on $C$ (Düntsch & Winter, 2004b), which is usually the parthood relation $P$ used in many Whiteheadean mereotopologies.

Now we define different strengths of contact structures that arise from mereotopological theories. Where appropriate, we reference the corresponding logical theories of mereotopology from Section 5.1.1. Irrespective whether such correspondences exist, all the classes of lattices used here are first-order definable—indeed they are definable as equational theories. Thus, the algebraic definitions directly lead to axiomatic theories.

**Definition 1.** (Düntsch & Winter, 2005b) A weak contact algebra $\langle A, C\rangle$ is a bounded distributive lattice $\langle A; 0; 1; +; \cdot\rangle$ equipped with a binary relation $C$ satisfying C0–C3.

**Definition 2.** (Düntsch, et al., 2008; Düntsch & Vakarelov, 2007) A distributive contact algebra $\langle A, C\rangle$ satisfying C4.

**Definition 3.** (Roy & Stell, 2002) A contact algebra $\langle A, C\rangle$ is a distributive contact algebra where the lattice is equipped with a dual pseudocomplementation * operator, i.e. the lattice is a structure $\langle A; 0; 1;^{*}; +; \cdot\rangle$.

Notice that because of the duality of lattices, a contact algebra can also be obtained from a pseudocomplemented distributive lattice. If $\langle A, C\rangle$ is a contact algebra where the dual pseudocomplementation * is indeed a unique complementation operation, denoted by $'$, the lattice $\langle A; 0; 1;^{*}; +; \cdot\rangle = \langle A; 0; 1;'; +; \cdot\rangle$ must be Boolean. If the lattice is Boolean and satisfies C0–C4, it is a GBCA. If it additionally satisfies Ext, we obtain a BCA.

**Definition 4.** (Li & Ying, 2004) A generalized Boolean contact algebra is a Boolean algebra $\langle A; 0; 1;'; +; \cdot\rangle$ equipped with a binary relation $C$ satisfying C0–C4.

**Definition 5.** (Vakarelov, 2007) A Boolean contact algebra is a generalized Boolean contact algebra satisfying Ext.

Notice that we deviate from the common definition of a Boolean Connection Algebra which needs to satisfy Con, e.g. in Stell (2000). We stick to the naming of Düntsch and Winter (2004b) and Vakarelov (2007) by referring to the BCA that satisfy Con as RBCAs, compare Definition 7 below. Notice further that the class of BCAs as we define them here allows overlap as only contact relation if the underlying Boolean algebra is finite-cofinite (Düntsch & Winter, 2005a). Therefore, BCAs are unsuited to construct discrete mereotopology because BCAs cannot adequately capture external connection. The more general classes of contact algebras yield mereotopologies that are not necessarily atomless (cf. Li & Ying, 2004, Stell & Roy, 2002). In general, since lattices describe only the mereological component of a contact algebra, more than a single contact relation can be defined—in particular for Boolean lattices (Düntsch & Winter, 2008).

Definition 5 generalizes to arbitrary distributive (dually) pseudocomplemented lattices: In the presence of Ext, Ext', or Ext" the lattice must be Boolean (cf. Düntsch, et al., 2006; Düntsch & Winter, 2005b).

Finally, the precontact algebras were introduced to further generalize BCAs to adjacency spaces useful for discrete mereotopology (Galton, 1999). PCAs need both axioms C4 and C4' since symmetry of $C$ as required by C2 is not assumed.

**Definition 6.** (Dimov & Vakarelov, 2005) A precontact algebra $\langle A, C\rangle$ is a Boolean algebra $\langle A; 0; 1; '; +; \cdot\rangle$ equipped with a binary relation $C$ satisfying C0, C4, and C4'.

For bounded lattices $\langle A; 0; 1; +; \cdot\rangle$ with some unary operation $'$, such as (dual) pseudocomplementation, orthocomplementation, or unique complementation (as in Boolean lattices), the following additional axioms are of importance:

(Con) $\forall x\left[(x \neq 0 \wedge x \neq 1) \rightarrow C(x, x')\right]$
(Connection)

(Nor)
$\forall x, y\left[\neg C(x, y) \rightarrow \exists u, v\left(\neg C(x, u) \wedge \neg C(y, v) \wedge u + v = 1\right)\right]$
(Normality)

(Nor')
$\forall x, y\left[PP(x, y) \rightarrow \exists z\left(PP(x, z) \wedge PP(z, y)\right)\right]$
(Density)

(Int)
$\forall x, y\left[\neg C(x, y) \rightarrow \exists z\left(\neg C(x, z) \wedge \neg C(y, z')\right)\right]$
(Interpolation)

(Int') $\forall x, y\left[\forall z\left(C(x, z) \vee C(y, z')\right) \rightarrow C(x, y)\right]$
(Complement. interpolation)

Assuming C0–C4, it can be easily verified that Int and Int' are equivalent, while Nor and Int are only equivalent if Con is also present; it suffices to choose $z = u$ and $z' = v$ so that $z + z' = 1$ follows. Notice, however, that in the presence of Con, $C \neq O$ must hold.

Indeed, strict RCC models correspond to the BCAs satisfying Con (Düntsch & Winter, 2004b; Stell, 2000). Algebraic variants of RCC can then be defined as *RCC BCAs* (RBCA) and *Proximity BCAs* (PBCA), compare (Düntsch & Winter, 2004b; Vakarelov, et al., 2002). The notion of a *proximity BCA* establishes the close relationship to the proximity spaces which relax the notion of contact to that of *proximity*. Notice that PBCAs are always compact, or dense, since they satisfy Nor. Contact algebras involving Heyting lattices were used by to represent the non-strict models of RCC by the complete, regular, connected Heyting algebras (Stell & Worboys, 1997). Heyting algebras are more general than Boolean algebras but more restricted than distributive pseudocomplemented lattices.

**Definition 7.** (Düntsch & Winter, 2004b) An RCC algebra is a BCA satisfying Con.

**Definition 8.** (Düntsch & Winter, 2004b) A proximity BCA is a BCA satisfying Int.

The algebraic representations in this section are often favored for their elegance over the corresponding logical theories—in particular as a way to separate mereology (the lattice structure) from topology (the contact relation) clearly, thereby addressing the criticism of Smith (1996). Moreover, studying these algebraic structures seems more manageable than studying large sets of entangled axioms.

## 6.2. Other Algebraic Representations

While in contact algebras, a lattice represents the mereological component and some contact relations represents the topological component of a mereotopology, in some special cases the contact relation is completely defined by the algebraic structure. The theories of Clarke (1981) and Asher and Vieu (1995) have representations where contact $C$ can be solely defined in terms of the partial order of the lattices as $\neg C(x, y) \Leftrightarrow x \leq y^{\perp}$. Hence, either theory can be completely reconstructed using mereology alone. In contrast, the choice of a contact relation in contact algebras is only limited by the underlying algebra but is not completely eliminated (Düntsch & Winter, 2008).

The results from Biacino and Gerla (1991) and Hahmann et al. (2009) construct the relevant representations and prove the definition of the contact relation. The first one represents the *connection structures* of Clarke (1981)—satisfying C1, C2, Ext, and an unrestricted fusion variant of C4—as complete orthocomplemented lattices (cf. Kalmbach, 1983). The contact relation defined as mentioned together with orthocomplementation allow deriving C3 as theorem. The connection structure are complete because Clarke's use of unrestricted fusion. No assumption about atomicity is made; the structures are atom-tolerant. For Clarke's complete theory with points (Clarke, 1981, 1985) the orthocomplemented lattice is in fact a complete atomless Boolean algebra. Then the connection relation collapses to overlap, so no external connection can exist—something that Clarke was most likely unaware of. Similarly, Hahmann et al. (2009) represents a generalized theory $RT^-$ of Asher and Vieu (1995)—itself a continuation of Clarke's work, but fully axiomatized in first-order logics—by Stonean portholattices, i.e. lattices that are orthocomplemented and (dual) pseudocomplemented while satisfying the Stone identity $(x{\cdot}y)^* = x^*{\cdot}y^*$. While the latter identity holds in Boolean algebras, Stonean p-ortholattices are modestly weaker than Boolean algebras; in fact, any of modularity, distributivity, unique complementation, or non-existence of external connection (as in Clarke's theory) immediately requires the lattice to be Boolean (Hahmann, et al., 2009). Therefore, $RT^-$ exhibits all desired algebraic properties of the similar RCC, except for distributivity. The failure of distributivity is owed to the inclusion of regular open and regular closed sets in the theory, which prevents mereological extensionality. With $RT^-$ making no assumption about continuity, it can be seen as open-closed variant of GBCAs. The precise relationship between RCC and $RT^-$ via the skeleton has been established in Winter et al. (2009). A theory such as $RT^-$ directly gives an equational theory which might lend itself to answer certain queries more efficiently. It needs to be further investigated whether even some standard first-order theorem proves provide an advantage when reasoning with such an equational theory compared that an equivalent non-equational theory such as the original axioms of $RT^-$. In addition, the question whether certain other contact algebras can be expressed in terms of equational theories remains open.

## 6.3. Map of Algebraic Theories of Whiteheadean Space

Figure 2 maps the algebraic theories into a two-dimensional space. The first dimension measures the strength of the contact relation (the topological component), while the second dimension displays the strength of the underlying lattice (the mereological component). The latter is further divided into distributivity, a property often assumed but not further discussed, and the existence of different strengths of unary complementation operations on the lattices (orthocomplemented, pseudocomplemented, uniquely complemented). Interestingly enough not so much distributivity seems essential for the large set of contact algebras,

Figure 2. Map of the algebraic theories of Whiteheadean space within several dimensions

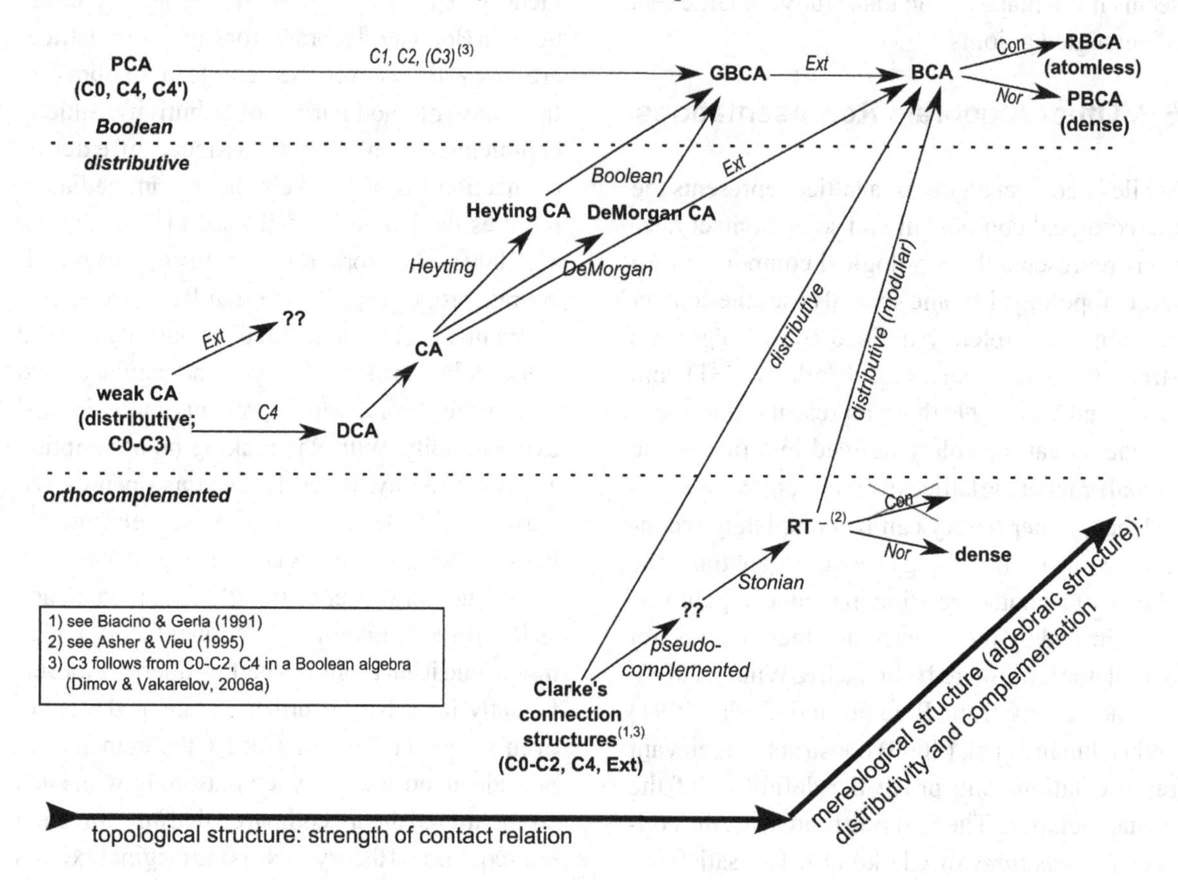


but instead pseudocomplementation. For finite lattices, pseudocomplementation follows directly from distributivity. More generally, it forces the existence of topologically closed complements. Notice that as soon as the connection relation satisfies either of Con or Int, all the models are infinite. All other theories allow atomistic variants by adding axiom AT from Section 3.6.

The map exhibits the relationship between the few non-distributive theories (at the bottom) and the large set of distributive theories. It makes explicit that lattices with a unique contact relation are no more than a special case of other contact algebras; the contact relation is just directly dependent upon the lattice structure. As another benefit, this map highlights few 'missing' theories such as p-ortholattices (a weaker variant of RT$^-$), extensional weak contact algebras, and Heyting, DeMorgan, or Ockham contact algebras (all weaker variants of GBCAs where the complementation is not unique). These theories have to our knowledge not yet been fully analyzed. Further analysis might reveal that these either collapse to one of the stronger theories or that they are inadequate for construction mereotopological theories for other reasons. Devising similar maps of other region-based theories will also be of interest for future work (compare the discussion in Section 10.2). Notice further the close relationship between the extensionality of the contact relation and the mereological structure, e.g. extensionality forces a CA and anything stronger to be Boolean. Notice further the inconsistency of RT$^-$ with Con.

All the contact algebras could be also interpreted as proximity algebras by changing the interpretation of *C*. In that way, proximity algebras are not special compared to contact algebras and there is no reason to assume that all proximity algebras must be Boolean, as often found in the literature.

## 7. TOPOLOGY FOR MEREOTOPOLOGY

Recall one of the original motivations of mereotopology: finding a suitable, cognitive adequate formalization of space using regions instead of points as primitives. In that light, point-set topological models of space seem inadequate—although they might use sets of points as primitives, standard operations such as interior, boundary, complement, neighborhood, etc. are still defined using points (cf. Roeper, 1997). Additionally, the use of any set theory raises suspicion in parts of the ontology community given its second-order nature. Though we might restrict ourselves to the first-order definable fragment of set theory, a great benefit of mereotopology would be an adequate theory of space that can replace point-wise and set-theoretic axiomatizations. In that regard, topological theories of mereotopology are only of limited use for QSTR. Moreover, unlike algebraic formalisms, topological theories do not directly yield efficient axiomatic theories.

Nevertheless, there is a need for (point-set) topological models within the study of mereotopologies. Topological representations help to understand the models of mereotopology. Often we think about mereotopological models in the traditional topological sense and judge a theory based on their topological interpretation. Oddly enough, such an argument implies that we actually understand point-based topological models better than mereotopological models. Though possibly true for mathematicians, it does not apply to a broader audience, or do humans tend to conceive space in a point-based way since most of us are taught classical Euclidean geometry? However, it is naïve to assume that the point-based models can give us a complete understanding of a mereotopology. We have no proof that only the topological models are relevant. Non-standard models are often forgotten. Only through a careful investigation of these models, can we understand whether there are intuitive mereotopological models without corresponding point-set interpretations. As far as we know, only few studies of the non-standard models of mereotopologies have been conducted, identifying some counter-intuitive models such as space-filling curves or 'completely holed regions' (Düntsch & Winter, 2004a), but obtaining topological representation does not guarantee the existence of corresponding spatial interpretations. Indeed, we can construct 'abstract' topological spaces from algebraic structures without a meaningful spatial interpretation (Johnstone, 1983). Since the topological representation of Boolean algebras by Stone (1936), the duality between topological spaces and algebraic structures has been known—leading to the fact that topological representations are just another way of looking at algebraic structures. On the other side, such representations emphasize that topology does not depend on points (Mormann, 1998). Nevertheless, topological representations can assist us in finding meaningful spatial interpretation of all models of a mereotopology. However, it is only one of the tools available.

This section discusses some of the key ideas in using topology for mereotopology. First, work on topological models of mereotopologies is presented in Section 7.1, while so-called embeddings are discussed in Section 7.2. Both sections focus on the role of topological models in comparing mereotopologies. In particular, the relationship between axiomatic theories of Whiteheadean space (cf. Section 5.1.1), contact algebras (cf. Section 6.1), and point-set topological models is outlined. Subsequently, Section 7.3 briefly introduces work on purely topological accounts of mereotopology.

## 7.1. Topological Models

When thinking about topological interpretations of region-based theories of space, there are two main directions pursued. The easier way constructs standard point set models, i.e. showing that a certain logical or algebraic system admits a classical interpretation of regions as point sets (*satisfiability*). Most commonly, models in Euclidean (vector) spaces $\mathbb{R}^n$, in spaces of rational numbers $\mathbb{Q}^n$, or in $\mathbb{Z}^n$ (for discrete mereotopologies) are given. We discuss these so-called *standard models* of region-based theories in this subsection, while the next subsection concentrates on the generally more challenging task of giving a full representation for all the models of a region-based theory.

Constructing models, i.e. showing satisfiability, for a certain logical or algebraic theory helps us verify that some intuitive class of (intended) models are covered by the theory. For mereotopological theories, these intended models usually rely on point sets where contact means either $\mathrm{cl}(x) \cap \mathrm{cl}(y) \neq \varnothing$ for theories limited to regular open sets or $x \cap y \neq \varnothing$ for theories allowing arbitrary regular sets or theories limited to regular closed sets (where $x \cap y = \mathrm{cl}(x) \cap \mathrm{cl}(y) \neq \varnothing$). For logical axiomatizations such topological models in $\mathbb{R}^2$ have been considered for Whitehead's theory (Gerla & Miranda, 2009), for polygonal mereotopology (Pratt & Schoop, 1997), and for the RCC (Gotts, 1996a). For algebraic theories it is usually shown that the set of all regular closed (or open) sets of some (restricted) topological space is in fact a model of a mereotopology of interest (cf. Stell, 2000; Vakarelov, 2007). This argument dates back to the famous construction of a Boolean algebra over the regular open sets of a topological space (cf. Halmos, 1963). For discrete mereotopologies and their algebraic counterparts, discrete (raster) models of GBCAs and the theory of Galton (1999) have been constructed in the digital plane $\mathbb{Z}^2$ (Li & Ying, 2004). Likewise, the full mereogeometries have been compared with respect to their models in $\mathbb{R}^n$ (Borgo & Masolo, 2009), see Section 5.2 for details. However, Fleck (1996) investigated boundaries of topological models of mereotopology and concludes that $\mathbb{R}^n$ interpretations fail to provide intuitive models.

Unintended models are more challenging to find, we often have to think outside the box of standard spatial models. For example completely holed regions (all regions have infinitely many holes) as RCC algebras (Düntsch & Winter, 2004a) seems counter-intuitive, prompting (Li & Ying, 2003) to recommend disallowing holed regions in RCC altogether. An interpretation of the RCC contact relation as 'distance-less-than-or-zero-meter' is given in Dong (2008). This interpretation reminds us of proximity relations as defined in Section 7.2.3. However, it is unclear whether such proximity interpretation can be avoided without referring to points or set-theoretic notions explicitly.

## 7.2. Topological Representations

It is well known that the open subsets $\tau$ of a topological space form a complete lattice. If the lattice is distributive it is called a *frame* or *local* (cf. Gerla, 1995; Johnstone, 1983). In distributive lattices, points may be defined in terms of maximal ideals (or ultrafilters), as shown in Stone's representation theorem for Boolean algebras (Stone, 1936), extended to distributive lattices (Priestley, 1970; Stone, 1937) and complete lattices (Urquhart, 1978). Already, earlier, it was earlier known that algebraic structures give rise to topological spaces (McKinsey & Tarski, 1944; Wallman, 1938). Studying these topological representations gives insight into the corresponding algebraic structures. Equally, we can study the topological spaces arising from algebraic counterparts of mereotopologies to understand the mereotopological theories better, e.g. Grzegorczyk (1960) was interested in the topological spaces of his theory of a mereological field (quasi-Boolean algebra) with a contact relation—a predecessor of today's BCAs. Here we give a taste of more recent results that focus on the different classes of contact algebras and their equivalent logical theories. First, we introduce some terminology for topological spaces necessary for the remainder of the section.

### 7.2.1. Properties of Topological Spaces

Classical point-set topology often characterizes topological spaces by their adherence to separation axioms. We restate the ones necessary for our discussions, for more background see Munkres (2000).

**(Axiom $T_0$)** Given two points of a topological space, at least one of them is contained in an open set not containing the other.

**(Axiom $T_1$)** Of any two points one lies in an open sets not containing the other.

**(Axiom $T_2$)** For any two points, there are disjoint open sets, each containing just one of the two points.

**(Axiom $T_3$)** For a closed set S and a point p not in S, there are disjoint open sets, one containing S and the other containing p.

**(Axiom $T_4$)** For any two disjoint closed sets, there are two disjoint open sets each of which contains one of the closed sets.

A topological space satisfies $T_1$ if all finite point sets are closed. In point-free topology, this axiom is tricky considering that arbitrarily many points could be in a region. A space satisfying $T_2$ ($T_1$ and $T_3$; $T_4$) is called *Hausdorff* (*regular*; *normal*). A regular and normal space is called a *$T_4$-space*. Assuming $T_1$, a normal space is always regular. If a space has a basis of regular open sets, it is called *semi-regular*.

Topological representations of region-based theories of space often use weaker properties unfamiliar to traditional topologists. This is owed to the fact that separation is point-based, while point-free topological representations need to be more general. A topological space is *weakly regular*, a point-free version of regularity, if it is semi-regular and for each non-empty set *S*, there is a non-empty set $S'$ with $cl(S') \subseteq S$. Restricting $T_4$ to the regular closed sets yields a special kind of normal space, called *κ-normal*. From Düntsch and Winter (2004b), we know the following implications:

X is normal → X is κ-normal → X is regular
→ X is weakly regular → X is semi-regular

Moreover, a space *X* is *connected* if it is not representable as the sum of two non-open disjoint empty sets. *X* is *compact* if for every non-empty family of closed sets $\{A_i \mid i \in I\}$ with every finite subset $J \subseteq I$ having a non-empty intersection $\bigcap\{A_i \mid i \in J\}$, the intersection $\bigcap\{A_i \mid i \in I\}$ is also non-empty (*finite intersection property*, cf. Düntsch, et al., 2008). *X* is *locally compact at a point P* if there exists a compact subspace $S \subseteq X$ that contains an open neighborhood of *P*. If *X* is locally compact at every point, it is simply called *locally compact*. Compact spaces are always locally compact (Munkres, 2000).

### 7.2.2. Topological Embeddings of Contact Algebras

Several variants of contact algebras have been embedded into topological spaces with the standard topological contact relation defined on the set of regular closed regions. We give some of these results, but refer for details to Dimov and Vakarelov (2006a, 2006b) and Vakarelov (2007). We only want to demonstrate how logical and algebraic theories can be grounded in topological interpretations in principle.

**Theorem 1.** (Düntsch & Winter, 2004a) Let $\langle X, \tau \rangle$ be a topological space with the contact relation *C* defined on $B = \mathrm{RegCl}(X)$. Then,

a. If X is semi-regular, X is weakly regular if and only of B satisfies Ext.
b. X is κ-normal if and only if B satisfies Nor.
c. X is connected if and only if B satisfies Con.
d. If X is compact and Hausdorff $T_2$, then B satisfies Ext and Nor.
e. If X is Hausdorff $T_2$ and normal, then $\bar{B} = \text{RegOp}(X)$ satisfies Nor.

These results let us deduce topological representations of classes of contact algebras as in f) to i), while j) and k) give embeddings into more restricted spaces.

**Theorem 2.** (Düntsch & Winter, 2004a, 2004b) Let $\langle X,\tau\rangle$ be a topological space with the contact relation *C* defined on $B = \text{RegCl}(X)$. Then,

f. B is a GBCA if and only if X is any such topological space.
g. B is a BCA if and only if X is weakly regular.
h. B is an RBCA if and only if X is weakly regular and connected.
i. B is a PBCA if and only if X is weakly regular and κ-normal.
j. Every BCA is isomorphic to a dense substructure of some $\langle \text{RegCl}(X), C_\tau\rangle$ for a weakly regular $T_1$-space.
k. Each RCC model (or alternatively RBCA model) is isomorphic to a substructure of some $\langle \text{RegCl}(X), C_\tau\rangle$ for a connected weakly regular $T_1$-space.

However, not every model of RBCA is directly embeddable into a regular $T_1$-space (Düntsch & Winter, 2004b). Instead, weak regularity is necessary and sufficient, compare Theorem 2k). In general, the separation axioms are not applicable to topological representations of BCAs. Though every BCA might be embeddable in a certain $T_1$-space, there are embeddings into spaces that are not $T_1$ or even $T_0$ (cf. Eschenbach, 1994). Results for weaker, but still distributive CAs show that U-extensional (underlap $U(x,y) \Leftrightarrow x + y \neq 1$, a dual to overlap, is extensional) distributive contact algebras are embeddable in BCAs over a semi-regular $T_0$-space (Düntsch, et al., 2006, 2008). Notice that not all distributive CAs are topologically representable. This hints that distributivity alone is too weak to build classical mereotopology. Only the combination with pseudocomplementation ensures representability. For all finite models, pseudocomplementation automatically follows from distributivity. Topological embeddings of precontact algebras have been studied by Düntsch and Vakarelov (2007).

### 7.2.3. Proximity Spaces

Proximity relations appeared independently from point-free topology in work by Efremovič (1952); see also Naimpally and Warrack (1970). Proximity spaces are constructed from a set and a binary relation expressing that two entities are 'close' to each other. Proximity spaces are intermediates to topological spaces and contact algebras as we outline here. We follow the account of Vakarelov (2007) on the use of proximity spaces for mereotopologies and contact algebras.

A *proximity* (or *nearness*) relation δ as defined by Efremovič (sometimes called an *Efremovič proximity*) must satisfy the condition Prox'. The relation δ is only used in the context of proximity spaces; we rewrite the axioms in terms of the familiar relation *C*, e.g. Prox' can be easily rewritten as Prox using the lattice terms and *C*.

(Prox') $A \cap B \neq \varnothing \Rightarrow A\delta B$

(Prox) $x \cdot y \neq 0 \Rightarrow C(x,y)$

The contact relations we considered as part of contact algebras trivially satisfy Prox. However, the reverse implication as common for the standard topological contact relation is not required here. All proximity spaces must further satisfy the axioms C0–C4 defining contact relations in the previous section.

Such a system $\langle X, C\rangle$ with $X$ being a non-empty set and a binary relation $C$ satisfying C0–C4 and Prox is a *Čech proximity space* (cf. Čech, 1966). The relation between CAs and Čech proximity spaces has been pointed out by Vakarelov (2007). If a Čech space additionally satisfies E', we obtain an *Efremovič proximity space*. We can rewrite it as the first-order sentence E. This is equivalent to the interpolation axiom Int considered in the context of CAs. Int, Int', or Nor are equivalently sufficient to turn a Čech proximity space into an Efremovič proximity space.

(E') $A\bar{\delta}B \Rightarrow \exists C\left[A\bar{\delta}C \wedge (X-C)\bar{\delta}B\right]$

(E)
$\forall x, y\left[\neg C(x,y) \rightarrow \exists z\left(\neg C(x,z) \wedge \neg C(y,z')\right)\right]$

We can give semantics to contact algebras by constructing proximity spaces that do not define a traditional contact relation, i.e. not both directions of $A \cap B \neq \varnothing \Leftrightarrow C(A,B)$ are satisfied, as shown in Vakarelov (2007). A proximity spaces induces a topology when using the topological closure $Cl(A) = \{x \in X \mid \{x\}\delta A\}$ of the proximity relation. If we consider the subset of regular closed sets thereof, the regular closed sets not only satisfy the axioms C0–C4 of contact algebras, but also Nor and Ext (cf. Vakarelov, 2007). Thus, we obtain a model of a Proximity BCA (PBCA) defined earlier. A proximity space is called separated if and only if $A\delta B$ implies $A = B$. In a separated proximity space, the topology induced by the closure $Cl(A) = \{x \in X \mid \{x\}\delta A\}$ is in fact Tychonoff (completely regular Hausdorff), and if the space is not separated, the space induced by the closure is still completely regular—a stronger notion than regularity.

The relationship between (separated) proximity spaces and contact algebras has been investigated in great detail in Vakarelov et al. (2001). In principle, proximity spaces behave like contact algebras, only their intended topological interpretation differ. Although typically Boolean lattices are considered in combination with proximity relations, proximity algebras can be built from bounded lattices in combination with a proximity relation that satisfies a subset of all the axioms considered for contact algebras.

## 7.3. Purely Topological Theories

After our treatise of topological models and representations of mereotopology, we now shift the attention even further to consider frameworks that define mereotopological relations using topology alone. Stone (1936) fostered an interest in point-free topology based on the insight that topology does not depend on points (Mormann, 1998). Equally, Menger (1940) anticipated the development of point-free topology early on. Johnstone (1983) interest in point-free (he calls it—pun intended—pointless) topology was motivated by an attempt to obtain a generalization of point-set topology to a point-free theory of *locales* (see Gerla, 1995 for a detailed introduction). Within locales, points may be defined as prime ideals (or dually as filters) very similar to the construction used by Stone (1936) and to the topological representations of contact algebras in Section 7.2. However, these ideas have not resonated much in the mereotopological community. Instead, besides logical and algebraic theories of mereotopology, the main purely topological theories in the field are based on traditional point-set topology. We will review two of them here. First, we go into more depth of Roeper's theory (Roeper, 1997) as topological alternative of building Whiteheadean mereotopology. Not only are its ontological assumptions very similar to those of the RCC, but it can also be considered as a proximity space. We follow this idea (due to Vakarelov, 2007) in the next subsection. Subsequently, we present the n-intersection model, a topological theory created by Egenhofer and colleagues. Some variations thereof as well as an extension to multi-dimensional mereotopology by the Dimension Extended Method (DEM) are outlined. Again, this is a topological formulation adhering to the ontological commitments of Whiteheadean space. Another point-set topological account of mereotopological relation (Schmolze, 1996) is based on regular open sets, similar in the idea to Tarski's work (Tarski showed that regular open sets are models of his theory).

### 7.3.1. Roeper's Region-Based Topology

A purely topological, but first-order axiomatizable (without the infinite join and meet operations) theory of region-based space was presented by Roeper (1997). Despite being built from topology, there is a close resemblance to the algebraic and logical theories of Whiteheadean space, cf. Section 5.1.1. It is based on a primitive contact relation, denoted by $\infty$, and a primitive unary predicate of *limitedness*. The underlying mereological structure is a Boolean algebra of regions—indeed the first five axioms, i.e. A1–A5 of Roeper (1997) correspond to C0–C4 from Section 6.1. For that reason, we omit them here and use C0–C4 instead. Given the intended interpretation of $x \infty y$ as '*x and y are at least infinitesimally close*,' the similarity to proximity spaces which satisfy exactly the same axioms comes at no surprise. Indeed, postulate Prox should always hold in the intended interpretation of $\infty$. In addition to the contact relation, all regions are *limited*, i.e. bounded. We use the following axiomatization, using $C$ instead of $\infty$.

(B1) $Lim(0)$

(B2) $\forall x, y\left[Lim(x) \wedge y \leq x \rightarrow Lim(y)\right]$

(B3) $\forall x, y\left[Lim(x) \wedge Lim(y) \rightarrow Lim(x+y)\right]$

Contact and limitedness are closely related in Roeper (1997) by the following two axioms. B4 states that contact between regions requires contact between limited regions (interpolation), while B5' is some sort of compactness condition, as we will see shortly.

(B4)
$\forall x, y\left[C(x,y) \rightarrow \exists z\left(Lim(z) \wedge z \leq y \wedge C(x,z)\right)\right]$

(B5') $\forall x, y[\left(Lim(x) \wedge y \neq 0 \wedge x < y\right)$
$\rightarrow \exists z\left(Lim(z) \wedge z \neq 0 \wedge x < z < y\right)]$

So-called *local proximity spaces* (Leader, 1967) satisfy besides B1-B4 also B5 and E (see Vakarelov, 2007 for details).

(B5) $\forall x\left[Lim(x) \rightarrow \exists y\left(Lim(y) \wedge \neg C(x, y')\right)\right]$

In algebraic terms, Vakarelov (2007) defined a *Local Contact Algebra* (LCA) as a CA with a predicate of boundedness, *Lim(x)*, where the extension of *Lim* contains a subset of regions satisfying B1–B5. If a LCA additionally satisfies Ext and Nor, we obtain Roeper's axiom B5' as theorem. Hence the axioms B1–B5 together with Ext and Nor give and equivalent definition of Roeper's region-based topology.

The notion of limitedness allows defining points as limit of sets; in particular, points are *collocated ultrafilters* (Roeper, 1997). Besides this marginal difference to the usual use of arbitrary ultrafilters, his construction of points resembles the previously discussed ones for logical and algebraic theories. An important part of Roeper's work is establishing a one-to-one correspondence between the *limited regions* in his region-based topology and *compact regular closed sets* in traditional point-based topology. That leads to a grounding of Roeper's theory of region-based space in the locally compact $T_2$-spaces. The theory can be extended by requiring infinite divisibility, simply postulated by:

(B6) $\forall x\left[x \neq 0 \rightarrow \exists y\left(y \neq 0 \wedge y < x\right)\right]$

In addition, Roeper (1997) defines what it means for a region to be *coherent* (self-connected) and *convex* in terms of the primitives. We restate them in algebraic terms. These definitions go beyond what is usually found in Whiteheadean mereotopology.

(B-SC)

$$Coherent(x) \equiv_{def} \forall y,z[(y \neq 0 \wedge z \neq 0 \wedge y + z = x) \rightarrow C(y,z)]$$

(B-Conv)

$$Convex(x) \equiv_{def} \forall y,z[y + z = x \rightarrow \exists v\left(v < x \wedge C(v \cdot y, v \cdot z)\right)]$$

Obviously, a convex region must be coherent (self-connected). Roeper's theory is accompanied by two simple existential axioms. B7 requires the mereology being a non-degenerate Boolean algebra as in most of the region-based theories of space, while B8 demands the universal region to be self-connected.

(B7) $\exists x\left[x \neq 0 \wedge x \neq 1\right]$

(B8) $Coherent(1)$

In the presence of these two axioms, B6 is in fact a theorem. Roeper (1997) further explores continuity and the restriction of region-based topologies to continua. Unfortunately, continuity, standard contact, and boundaries seem do not seem to fit well together in a single theory, compare the discussion of Breysse and De Glas (2007) and Fleck (1996).

As a side note, the primitive notion of limitedness can be substituted by the topological notion *compactness*, reducing Roeper's theory to a mereology where the contact relation can be expressed in terms of the Boolean algebra as $\neg C(x,-y) \Leftrightarrow x < y$ (Mormann, 1998). This relates the topological theories to the algebras in Section 6.

For LCAs embeddings in locally compact semi-regular $T_0$-spaces exist (for details see Vakarelov, 2007). Topological properties for the additional axioms Con, Ext, and Nor are analogue to Theorem 1 from Section 7.2.2. Hence, Roeper's region-based topology is accounted for by the *locally compact Hausdorff* spaces (Roeper, 1997).

### 7.3.2. Models of n-Intersection

GIS has been traditionally a major force in the advancement of region-based theories of space. Long before the majority of work in QSR, Egenhofer (1989) and Egenhofer and Franzosa (1991) proposed the *4-intersection* model based on the set intersections of regions interior, A°, and region boundaries, δA, resulting in four feasible topological relations between two regions. However, this turned out to be insufficient to capture all possible topological relations of $\mathbb{R}^n$ with complements being especially difficult to define. However, Egenhofer (1991) extended this model to *9-intersections* taking the set intersection of region interiors, boundaries, and complements, $A^{-1}$, into account. Then, it is easily verified that indeed all topological relations are expressible in these terms—for each point set A the sets A°, δA, and $A^{-1}$ partition the underlying space completely. Of the theoretically possible 81 combinations, with some additional restrictions these can be reduced to eight topological relations that are directly mappable to the JEPD relations *EQ*, ¬*C*, *O*, *EC*, *TP*, *TP*$^{-1}$, *NTP*, *NTP*$^{-1}$ of RCC-8 and RT$^{-}$. Notice that indeed the 4-intersection model is already sufficient to describe the five RCC-5 relations (Cohn & Renz, 2008). Three of the restrictions imposed on the 9-intersection model are similar to those in Whiteheadean space: equi-dimensionality of all regions (and space), regions are always non-empty, and only regular closed regions are considered (Egenhofer, 1991). The fourth condition requires each of the interiors, boundaries, and complements to be self-connected, going beyond what Whiteheadean space demands. This last assumption excludes holed objects; holes have only been considered within the scope of the 4-intersection model in Egenhofer et al. (1994). Contrary to Whiteheadean space, regions assumed primitive, instead standard point-set topology is used as underlying formalism, with an assumed interpretation in $\mathbb{R}^n$. Therefore, we can see the n-intersection model as a mereological framework build from topology. The necessary changes to obtain a discrete version of the 9-intersection model have been discussed in Egenhofer and Sharma (1993b). In the discrete version, adjacency needs to be accounted for separately (compare the use of adjacency by Galton, 1999), whereas boundaries need to have some 'thickness.' This results in a total of 16 relations, while a discrete 4-intersection model contains only five JEPD relations.

The set intersection approach has been transferred to include points, lines, and regions in Egenhofer and Herring (1991). It results in groups of possible topological relations between elements of different dimensionality. However, this set of possible relations is prohibitively large. In the *Dimension Extended Method* (DEM: Clementini, et al., 1993), instead of only distinguishing between empty and non-empty intersection, the dimension of the intersection is also taken into account, resulting in a more fine grained classification of possible relations while also reducing the number of feasible relations to 52 consisting of 9 area/area, 17 line/area, 3 point/area, 18 line/line, 3 point/line, and 2 point/point relations. A three-dimensional framework disregarding points would therefore be limited to 44 relations—still quite complex and most likely an important factor why many theories restrict themselves to equi-dimensional entities. Line/line (Clementini & Di Felice, 1998) and region/line relations (Egenhofer & Mark, 1991, 1994, 1995a) received special attention. This again relates to the idea of a boundary-toleration theory (cf. Section 5.1.2) as compromise between the simplicity of classical mereotopology and complexity of multi-dimensional mereotopology.

Clementini and Di Felice (1995) compared the point-based n-intersection model to an alternative calculus based model, proposed in Clementini et al. (1993). The calculus-based model is indeed very similar to the RCC-5. It builds on the five relations 'touch,' 'in,' 'cross,' 'overlap,' and 'disjoint,' but allows lines and/or points for the relations where they make sense, e.g. overlap is applicable to area/area and line/line relations only. Clementini et al. (1993) show that their calculus is expressive enough to represent all relations of the 9-intersection model combined with the DEM.

## 8. GRAPHS FOR MEREOTOPOLOGY

For certain applications such as route finding, route optimization, etc. graph-based representations of space have been proven to be of great help. Tessellations of space such as raster, triangulations, and Voronoi diagrams are of widespread use within GIS (see Chen, et al., 2001; Li, et al., 2002). In this context, the basic entities are *cells* (usually thought of as smallest elements in the sense of indivisible regions) and *cell complexes* (cf. Frank & Kuhn, 1986). The concepts are borrowed from algebraic topology (cf. Faltings, 1995), which defines *simplices* (the n-dimensional equivalent of triangles) and *(simplicial) complexes* (triangulations of space as collections of simplices (Frank, 2005). Modeling discrete space based on such tessellations of space is common in the GIS community. We refrain from covering this large area of research; instead, we just outline the relationship to axiomatic theories of continuous and discrete mereotopology. In particular, the graph representations of such tessellations shall be of interest here, since they exhibit interesting properties that might be helpful for building intuitive theories of discrete mereotopology that avoid the paradoxical nature of atoms experienced in discrete axiomatic theories of Whiteheadean space.

Tessellations of space are directly representable as graphs where every cell is a vertex in the corresponding graph while adjacency of cells is modeled by edges. Such graph representations are independent of the particular kind of adjacency or contact relation between cells. To keep the graph simple, adjacency shall only be modeled on the cell level. Arbitrary (non-atomic) regions made up of cells can then be thought of as subgraphs. For a grid/raster interpretation, the use of either 4-adjacency, 6-adjacency, or 8-adjacency is most common and natural (cf. Roy & Stell, 2002).

A mereotopological theory along these lines has been proposed by Galton (1999) using two sorts: one for cells (vertices) and one for regions (subgraphs) including a null region (the empty set), atomic regions (singletons), the universal region (the full graph), and arbitrary subgraphs. Not considering cells, the algebraic structures of regions are specialized GBCAs (cf. Section 6.1; Galton, 1999; Lin & Ying, 2004). Galton (1999) also constructs standard topological concepts for his theory of cell adjacency. However, the properties of the interior and closure operations differ significantly from their topological counterparts, i.e. $cl(x) \subseteq y \Leftrightarrow x \subseteq \mathrm{int}(y)$ holds—an impossible theorem for point-set topology (consider the example $\mathrm{int}(y) < y = x = cl(x)$ in a topological space). Problems arise because Galton (1999) wants to ensure atoms are connected to their complements. Then the Whiteheadean definition of parthood in terms of connection fails unless we allow atoms to be part of their complements. It would be interesting to see whether we can alter the theory to differentiate two notions of self-connectedness: a weak (using adjacency, indeed an atom and its complement should be adjacent) and a strong one (using connection in the sense of sharing a point; an atom would then not be strongly self-connected). Galton's so-called *adjacency spaces* resemble the distinction between connection and weak contact in the theory of Asher and Vieu (1995). Moreover, they are captured by the precontact algebras mentioned briefly at the end of Section 7.2.2.

## 9. APPLICATION DOMAINS OF MEREOTOPOLOGY

Though theoretical work on mereotopology is often motivated by practical applications, these applications remain sparse. Only recently, more work on specific applications of mereotopology and mereogeometry emerged. Most of the work known chooses a set of ontological commitments reasonable in the domain and then customizes the ontologies to fit the envisaged applications. The benefits of studying practical applications do not only lie in proofs of the usefulness of the theoretic work, but more importantly, we can gain more insight into the ontological choices relevant in real world. In practice, it has turned out that mereotopology by itself is rarely useful; instead integration into larger ontologies or reasoning frameworks is necessary.

Amongst the main areas for applications of mereotopologies GIS, navigation, computer vision applications, biological and medical ontologies, and applications in (computational) linguistics, e.g. for language understanding, are widely recognized. Less known is the work using mereotopologies for product engineering and product modeling.

Apart from these specific areas of applications, it is undisputed that upper ontologies need to incorporate spatial and spatio-temporal concepts. Most proposals use some mereotopological component, e.g. the BFO (Grenon, 2003), DOLCE, SUMO, and openCyc. However, it is often not clear what kind of ontological assumptions are made in the respective mereotopologies—the relation to earlier theoretical work is usually vague while the actual axiomatizations are rarely scrutinized with respect to their models. More recently, the OntoSpace project surveyed the spatial ontologies of the previously mentioned upper ontologies in Bateman and Farrar (2005).

## 9.1. GIS and CAD

Traditionally, the GIS community has been a driving force in the advancement of qualitative theories of space with the objective of expressing topological relations that humans use and of applying high-level reasoning to it. For a discussion of the role of ontologies—including spatial ontologies—in GIS we refer to Fonseca et al. (2000, 2002). In the context of built structures/ environments, Bittner (2000) used a mereotopological theory with rough location relations to model parking lots. He explored the necessity of boundaries in general, but also the necessary distinction of different kinds (bona fide and fiat) of boundaries to capture the space naturally.

One particularly promising field for applications of mereotopologies are ontologies for CAD (Computer-Aided Design) software. Not only are many representations of space in such software systems region-based, but there is further a need to exchange models between different CAD systems. For such a model exchange, meaning of terms must be preserved and translations between different ontological commitments must be bridged while avoided much loss of information, e.g. one software system treating all regions as open but having lines as separate entities and another system supporting lines only as boundaries of regions must overcome their ontological differences to enable data exchange. On a higher level, we want to know when a lossless translation is possible or what specific data will be lost.

## 9.2. Bio-Ontologies

Biological, biomedical, and medical research has shown considerable interest in ontologies to represent various relations, e.g. anatomical, genetical, or simple spatial and spatio-temporal relations for describing medical images (X-rays, tomographic images, etc.). Not surprisingly, many relations occurring in these fields are of mereological and mereotopological nature. The ontologies in the Open Biomedical Repository (OBO) use basic spatial and spatio-temporal relationships defined in the BFO and the OBO *relation ontology*. The mereotopological and mereogeometrical concepts of the OBO relation ontology have been explored in Smith et al. (2005) and Bittner (2009). The relation ontology framework for general biological and medical ontologies also contains location relations, while an explicit distinction between contact and adjacency (external connection) is made. Moreover, all mereotopological and mereogeometrical relations are temporal, thus allowing for change over time. Bittner (2009) gives an example how anatomical relations can be expressed in this framework. Body parts are also considered by Donnelly (2004) from a mereotopological perspective where holes play an important role. A comprehensive ontology of anatomy based on mereological, topological, and orientation relations also exists (Rosse & Mejino, 2003). Related works in Description Logics includes the clinical GALEN ontology (Rector, et al., 1996; Rogers & Rector, 2000; Schulz & Hahn, 2001a, 2001b; Schulz, et al., 2005). However, most of the literature dedicates most of their research energy on taxonomical relations. First-order logical axiomatizations are rare with BFO being a notable exception.

## 9.3. Robot Navigation and Linguistics

Robot navigation through unknown or partially known territory can profit from (mereo-)topological representations of space. Examples are exploring the connectivity of rooms in an unknown building to learn which rooms/hallways/staircases are connected (Kuipers & Byun, 1991; Kuipers & Levitt, 1988; Levitt & Lawton, 1990; Remolina & Kuipers, 2004) or which rooms belong to certain floors, etc. This provides a high-level spatial model for a robot to search for things in a building (e.g. search-and-rescue robots), find their way out again, or backtrack once trapped in a dead end. Learning topological maps directly from the environment can be achieved used mereotopological representations where the maps usually consist of entities of multiple dimensions including regions, lines, and points, supplemented by orientation information about the robot. After learning topological maps, these can be refined by geometrical information. More recent work in that direction additionally uses landmarks to define fiat boundaries demarcating regions. However, the amount of mereotopology used is often marginal; complex qualitative reasoning on the topological maps is rarely done. Instead, most of the work uses graph-based approaches such as Voronoi diagrams or connectivity graphs, sometimes in connection with region partitioning (Thrun, 1998), while reasoning is usually algorithmic and not symbolic. It is interesting to see that work on robot navigation using topological maps predates the growth of interest in qualitative representations of space in AI. There still seems little work that actually uses mereotopological or mereogeometrical theories discussed in this chapter in practical navigation applications.

Interesting problems in a similar direction include qualitative route finding where traditional graph-based route finding is combined with region properties, e.g. instead of finding the shortest or fastest route between some points, we might be interested in the most scenic route (going through forests, along a like, outside a city) where the different properties are represented as regions (from geographic maps) instead of assigning each link in the network an individual value for such properties. Other navigation problems such as translating a route description into a map are directly linked to natural language processing of spatio-temporal relations. Because of the variability and ambiguity of language in expressing mereological and topological relations, understanding of mereotopological relations or spatio-temporal relations in general is more of an extraction challenge. We need to identify the proper interpretation of terms such as 'is a part of,' 'adjacent,' etc. to build mereotopological models. This has been done for temporal relations (Verhagen, et al., 2005), but the methodology is applicable to spatial relations as well. For instance the language presented in Chaudet (2004)—an extension of event calculus with mereotopological relations—can help track epidemics by capturing and understanding the language of epidemic outbreak reports.

## 9.4. Product Modeling, Design, and Engineering

Mereotopology has been customized to a so-called *Design Mereotopology* (DMT) by Salustri (2002). He believes that regions are perfect because engineers tend to take them as primitive anyways. The DMT is an atomistic mereotopology based on CRC (Eschenbach, 1999) and Smith's mereotopology (Smith, 1996). DMT uses a mereological and a topological primitive, $P$ and $C$, and postulates mereological extensionality. Though not directly an applications, Salustri mentions many possible applications of DMT: CAD, semantic knowledge bases of materials to distinguish between matter (steel, lubricants, etc.) and objects and provide properties of different materials, and configuration, function, and system modeling (cf. Salustri, 2002; Yang & Salustri, 1999).

In engineering, mereotopological and mereogeometrical relations can also be used for representing the assembly of parts. Kim et al. (2006, 2008, 2009) have developed an ontology using the Semantic Web Rule Language (SWRL) to distinguish different kinds of assembly joints obtained by welding, gluing, brazing, fastening, soldering, stitching/stapling, etc. common product design and manufacturing. As basis, they use the boundary-tolerant mereotopology of Smith (1996), but introduce additional geometrical predicates such as angles and offsets of the joined objects. The basic mereotopological definitions are translated into SWRL rules. The contact is further refined to distinguish the morphology of the contact. This documents that for practical applications, mereotopology is usually only a basis and needs to be extended by domain-specific terminology.

## 10. REMAINING CHALLENGES

As we previously emphasized, testing region-based theories of space in real-world domains is an essential task that needs to be undertaken. Only feedback from practice will spur the development of new theories that can cope with the peculiarities of individual domains and applications. We just outlined some research addressing this 'practice challenge.' Apart from that ongoing work, there is theoretical work left in the field. We briefly explain some directions of future research and discuss how these could help to advance the field of mereotopology. However, we do not discuss the many computational issues in need for future research. Amongst them, the question of decidability or the nature of tractable fragments is still of unanswered for many theories. Equational theories (Bennett, 1997) could be of great help in that pursuit. To our knowledge, there has been little work on equational theories for region-based spatial reasoning despite the fact that contact algebras are naturally equational theories. It needs to be explored whether specific equational theories have more efficient reasoning behaviors than comparable first-order theories. Even if complexity is not reduced, efficient equational solvers and theorem provers likely fare better in practice compared to first-order theorem provers.

Now, we will look at representational challenges, first within the scope of mereotopology before proceeding to the integration challenge for spatial ontologies at large.

### 10.1. Dimensionality and Boundaries

The discussion of the ontological commitments made it quite clear that still only little is known of how to integrate boundaries and entities of varying dimensions in a region-based mereotopology/-geometry. Though we pointed out the existing work in this direction, these can be only seen as starting points. Their models and formal semantics are often not yet completely captured, thus preventing the adaptation of these ontologies for applications or larger, more generic ontologies. The complexity of these mereotopological systems goes way beyond those of Whiteheadean space, but because of this complexity, there is an even greater urgency to capture the models thereof in a more familiar mathematical framework (cf. Section 10.2). This could also spur the development of new mereotopologies that integrate multi-dimensional mereotopologies with other aspects, e.g. holes, other discontinuities, or geometric properties such as convexity.

### 10.2. Formal Semantics

As outlined in Section 7, there is a need for identifying all the models of mereotopological and mereogeometrical theories. Even though the standard models are equivalent for large set of theories, the non-standard models are decisive to select an appropriate theory. Out of two theories with equivalent standard models, one could still be the preferable one because it is more restricted and allows fewer unintended models. A model-theoretic study of all the region-based theories along the lines of the algebraic/topological representations of Whiteheadean theories as contact algebras is necessary. A starting point could be the study of other mereotopologies as algebraic systems.

## 10.3. Region-Based Equivalents of Geometry

It is suspected that the RCC together with a convex hull (or convexity) primitive is a point-free equivalent of affine geometry, thus being strictly weaker than the full mereogeometries. This analogue to point-based geometry provokes questions whether region-based equivalents of other point-based geometries, e.g. projective or ordered geometry, can be constructed. The idea of such research in the style of Klein's *Erlanger programm*' is discussed by Clementini and Di Felice (1997a) who propose an approach combining topological, projective, and metric properties to describe shapes. A survey on algebraic representations of projective geometries building on the work of Menger, Birkhoff, and Faltings can be found in Greferath and Schmidt (1998) while Wehrung (1998) considers algebraic representations of von-Neumann's continuous geometries. Both representations rely on orthocomplementation and modularity properties of the underlying algebras.

Of particular interest is the question whether other theories exist in between mereotopology and mereogeometries. The RCC with convexity is so far the weakest theory extending pure mereotopology with some morphological predicate, but perhaps, other predicates such as relative size can be used to extend mereotopology without reaching full mereogeometry or even the equivalent of affine geometry. This question remains unexplored as far as we know and needs to be looked at more carefully in the future.

## 10.4. Integrated Ontologies

### 10.4.1. Integrated Ontologies of Qualitative Space

Recently, combinations of qualitative properties have received increased attention. Amongst them, one of the most challenging qualities of spatial objects and regions is their shape. In this chapter, we limited ourselves to convexity as only shape attribute. It extends purely mereotopological theories rather naturally. The equally important concept of relative size turns out to be only superficially different from convexity. Relative size has been integrated into mereogeometries, in particular the RBG, in Bittner and Donnelly (2007). Relative size is linked to parthood: proper parts must always be smaller (cf. Gerevini & Renz, 2002). Relative distances (cf. Bittner, 2009; Bittner & Donnelly, 2007; Gahegan, 1995) are another aspect of qualitative space that seems to seamlessly integrate with region-based space, but as in the case of the mereogeometry of Donnelly (2001) with a ternary '*can connect*' relation, it might result in a full mereogeometry.

Qualitative theories about relative positions, directions and orientation have been the focus of the work on cardinal directions (Frank, 1996; Hernández, et al., 1995; Renz & Mitra, 2004), the single and double cross calculus (SCC, DCS: Freksa, 1992; Schockaert, et al., 2008). Their combination with regions would present a more powerful and practical framework. Two examples thereof are a combination of cardinal directions with RCC-5 (Chen, et al., 2007b) and a rectangular cardinal direction calculus (Navarrete, 2006; Skiadopoulos & Koubarakis, 2004, 2005). Relative positions of extended objects are tricky to apply since they either rely on some center of regions (centre of mass, geometrical centre, etc.), or are expressed in terms of minimal bounding objects, such as rectangles, blocks, cubes (Balbiani, et al., 1998; Chen, et al., 2007a), or spheres.

The main challenge here is to use only primitives of very limited expressiveness to avoid the definition of a full mereogeometry. In that way, integrating region-based theories of space with other qualitative properties is a challenge that goes hand in hand with the exploration of theories between mereotopology and mereogeometry, compare Section 10.3.

### 10.4.2. Integration of Qualitative and Quantitative Space

The misfit of continuous mereotopologies for representing discrete data from the real-world has been singled out as a major shortcoming limiting the applicability of continuous mereotopologies in practice. However, discrete mereotopologies have been proposed to overcome this problem in principle. However, there is a broad scale of possible discreteness, i.e. data from different sources has different granularity. Hierarchical approaches of qualitative spatial reasoning with mereotopological relations might be of great help (cf. Li & Nebel, 2007). Nevertheless, there is still some distance to go to fully integrate qualitative approaches towards space with quantitative models, i.e. integrating region-based theories with point-based theories of space. In one direction, mereotopological relations have been extracted from metric representations of space or directly from the environment (cf. Galata, et al., 2002; they learn Markov models from the environment; it should in principle be possible to obtain logical predicates of qualitative spatial relations instead), while reconstructing metric space from qualitative space is still open. Of course, since full mereogeometries are able to reconstruct Euclidean space, their models are implicitly translated into metric models. However, for general mereotopology, this is not as straightforward. The framework outlined by Clementini and Di Felice (1997a) proposes to incorporate varying levels of granularity for such integration. However, extensions thereof need to overcome its agnosticism towards connection relations. Alternatively, we can construct minimal point-based embeddings of mereotopological models. For this task, the experience with topological embeddings comes handy, since these are usually embeddings into intuitive point-based topological models.

### 10.4.3. Integration into Upper Ontologies

From a broader perspective, upper ontologies able to express common-sense knowledge need to incorporate qualitative and quantitative spatial and spatio-temporal predicates. However, many of today's upper ontologies (compare the introduction in Section 9) have on informal formulations of their spatial relations. A study of their ontological commitments and considering replacement by stronger or weaker theories is necessary to foster reuse of these ontologies. Otherwise, their reliability is doubted, resulting in limited reuse.

## 11. SUMMARY

This chapter gives an overview of the main ontological commitments in mereotopological and mereogeometrical theories. We gathered and organized the knowledge about ontological commitments for the wealth of region-based theories that have been proposed for representing space qualitatively. Further, we reviewed the methods and formalisms that have proven useful for analyzing and comparing mereotopologies. Altogether, we hope that this gives a broader picture of mereotopology and how the different theories fit into this bigger picture regardless of their concrete axiomatization. In particular, we mapped out the space of algebraic theories corresponding to the logical theories of Whiteheadean space. Despite the overwhelmingly disperse set of theories, we hope to have made it clear that the actual differences are usually only minor and that there are only a handful of substantially different approaches. We hope this chapter inspires more work on mathematical representations of mereotopological theories not yet fully understood. Moreover, we hope the chapter provides sufficient information for choosing and integrating a mereotopological theory into applications or more general ontologies.

## ACKNOWLEDGMENT

This chapter would not have been possible with the systematic overviews of Cohn and Renz (2008), Vakarelov (2007), Eschenbach (2007), and Borgo and Masolo (2009). We gratefully acknowledge that many ideas of structuring the wide field originate in their work. Cohn and Renz (2008) provided a rich resource for pointers to applications and related QSTR work. Moreover, we are indebted to Michael Winter for his valuable suggestions on how to improve the chapter. A preliminary version of Section 6 has been presented at the Doctorial Consortium at RelMiCS 2009 in Doha, Qatar. We are grateful for the helpful feedback given and the fruitful discussions that arose.

## REFERENCES

Allen, J. F. (1983). Maintaining knowledge about temporal intervals. *Communications of the ACM*, *26*(11), 832–823. doi:10.1145/182.358434

Andréka, H., Németi, I., & Sain, I. (2001). Algebraic logic. In Gabbay, D. M., & Guenthner, F. (Eds.), *Handbook of Philosophical Logic* (2nd ed., *Vol. 2*, pp. 133–147). Dordrecht, The Netherlands: Kluwer.

Asher, N., & Vieu, L. (1995). Toward a geometry of common sense: A semantics and a complete axiomatization for mereotopology. In *Proceedings of the International Joint Conference on Artificial Intelligence (IJCAI-95)*, (pp. 846–852). IJCAI.

Balbiani, P., Condotta, J., & del Cerro, L. F. (1998). A model for reasoning about bidimsional temporal relations. In *Proceedings of KR98: Principles of Knowledge Representation and Reasoning* (pp. 124–130). Morgan Kaufmann.

Balbiani, P., Tinchev, T., & Vakarelov, D. (2008). Modal logics for region-based theories of space. *Fundamenta Informaticae*, *81*(1-3), 29–82.

Bateman, J., & Farrar, S. (2005). *OntoSpace project report: Spatial ontology baseline deliverable D2 I1, version: 1.6. Technical Report*. Bremen, Germany: University of Bremen.

Bennett, B. (1994). Spatial reasoning with propositional logic. In *Proceedings of KR94: Principles of Knowledge Representation and Reasoning* (pp. 51–62). Morgan Kaufmann.

Bennett, B. (1997). *Logical relations for automated reasoning about spatial relationships*. Unpublished Doctoral Dissertation. Leeds, UK: University of Leeds.

Bennett, B. (2001). A categorical axiomatisation of region-based geometry. *Fundamenta Informaticae*, *46*(1-2), 145–158.

Bennett, B., Cohn, A. G., Torrini, P., & Hazarika, S. M. (2000). A foundation for region-based qualitative geometry. In *Proceedings of the European Conference on Artificial Intelligence (ECAI-2000)*, (pp. 204–208). ECAI.

Bennett, B., Cohn, A. G., Wolter, F., & Zakharyaschev, M. (2002). Multi-dimensional modal logic as a framework for spatio-temporal reasoning. *Applied Intelligence*, *17*(3), 239–251. doi:10.1023/A:1020083231504

Bennett, B., & Düntsch, I. (2007). Axioms, algebras and topology. In *Handbook of Spatial Logics* (pp. 99–159). London, UK: Springer. doi:10.1007/978-1-4020-5587-4_3

Biacino, L., & Gerla, G. (1991). Connection structures. *Notre Dame Journal of Formal Logic*, *32*(3), 242–247. doi:10.1305/ndjfl/1093635748

Birkhoff, G. (1967). *Lattice theory* (3rd ed.). New York, NY: American Mathematical Society.

Bittner, T. (1999). *Rough location*. Unpublished Doctoral Dissertation. Vienna, Austria: Vienna Technical University.

Bittner, T. (2000). A qualitative formalization of built environments. In *Proceedings of the Conference on Database and Expert Systems Applications (DEXA-2000)*, (pp. 959–969). London, UK: Springer.

Bittner, T. (2002). Granularity in reference to spatio-temporal location and relations. In *Proceedings of the Florida Artificial Intelligence Research Society Conference (FLAIRS-15)*, (pp. 466–470). FLAIRS.

Bittner, T. (2004). A mereological theory of frames of reference. *International Journal of Artificial Intelligence Tools, 13*(1), 171–198. doi:10.1142/S0218213004001478

Bittner, T. (2009). Logical properties of foundational mereogeometrical relations in bio-ontologies. *Applied Ontology, 4*.

Bittner, T., & Donnelly, M. (2007). A formal theory of qualitative size and distance relations between regions. In *Proceedings of the Workshop on Qualitative Reasoning (QR07)*. QR.

Bittner, T., & Smith, B. (2001). Vagueness and granular partitions. In *Proceedings of the Conference on Formal Ontology in Information Systems (FOIS-01)*, (pp. 309–320). FOIS.

Bittner, T., & Smith, B. (2003). *Foundations of geographic information science: A theory of granular partitions*. New York, NY: Taylor & Francis.

Bittner, T., & Stell, J. G. (1998). A boundary-sensitive approach to qualitative location. *Annals of Mathematics and Artificial Intelligence, 24*(1-4), 93–114. doi:10.1023/A:1018945131135

Bittner, T., & Stell, J. G. (2000a). Approximate qualitative spatial reasoning. *Spatial Cognition and Computation, 2*(4), 435–466. doi:10.1023/A:1015598320584

Bittner, T., & Stell, J. G. (2000b). Rough sets in approximate spatial reasoning. In *Proceedings of the Conference on Rough Sets and Current Trends in Computing (RSCTC-2000)*, (pp. 445–453). Springer.

Bittner, T., & Stell, J. G. (2002). Vagueness and rough location. *GeoInformatica, 6*(2), 99–121. doi:10.1023/A:1015291525685

Bittner, T., & Stell, J. G. (2003). Stratified rough sets and vagueness. In *Proceedings of the Conference on Spatial Information Theory (COSIT-03)*, (pp. 270–286). Springer.

Blyth, T. S. (2005). *Lattices and ordered algebraic structures*. London, UK: Springer.

Borgo, S., Guarino, N., & Masolo, C. (1996). A pointless theory of space based on strong connection and congruence. In *Proceedings of KR96: Principles of Knowledge Representation and Reasoning*, (pp. 220–229). KR.

Borgo, S., & Masolo, C. (2009). Full mereogeometries. *The Review of Symbolic Logic*. Retrieved from http://citeseerx.ist.psu.edu/viewdoc/similar?doi=10.1.1.98.2266&type=ab.

Breysse, O., & De Glas, M. (2007). A new approach to the concepts of boundary and contact: Toward an alternative to mereotopology. *Fundamenta Informaticae, 78*(2), 217–238.

Burrough, A. (1996). Natural objects with indeterminate boundaries. In Burrough, A., & Frank, A. U. (Eds.), *Geographic Objects with Indeterminate Boundaries* (pp. 171–188). Taylor & Francis.

Burrough, A., & Frank, A. U. (1995). Concepts and paradigms in spatial information: Are current geographic information systems truly generic? *International Journal of Geographical Information Science, 9*(2), 101–116. doi:10.1080/02693799508902028

Burrough, A., & Frank, A. U. (1996). *Geographic objects with indeterminate boundaries*. New York, NY: Taylor & Francis.

Casati, R., & Varzi, A. C. (1994). *Holes and other superficialities*. Cambridge, MA: MIT Press.

Casati, R., & Varzi, A. C. (1996). The structure of spatial localization. *Philosophical Studies, 82*, 205–239. doi:10.1007/BF00364776

Casati, R., & Varzi, A. C. (1999). *Parts and places*. Cambridge, MA: MIT Press.

Čech, E. (1966). *Topological spaces*. Berlin, Germany: Interscience.

Chaudet, H. (2004). STEEL: A spatio-temporal extended event language for tracking epidemic spread from outbreak reports. In *Proceedings of the CEUR Workshop on Formal Biomedical Knowledge Representation (KR-MED-04)*. KR-MED.

Chen, J., Li, C., Li, Z., & Gold, C. (2001). A Voronoi-based 9-intersection model for spatial relations. *International Journal of Geographical Information Science, 15*(3), 201–220. doi:10.1080/13658810151072831

Chen, J., Liu, D., Zhang, C., & Xie, Q. (2007a). Cardinal direction relations in 3D space. In *Proceedings of the Conference on Knowledge Science, Engineering and Management (KSEM-07)*, (pp. 623–629). Springer.

Chen, J., Liu, D., Zhang, C., & Xie, Q. (2007b). Combinative reasoning with RCC5 and cardinal direction relations. In *Proceedings of the Conference on Knowledge Science, Engineering and Management (KSEM-07)*, (pp. 92–102). Springer.

Clarke, B. (1981). A calculus of individuals based on connection. *Notre Dame Journal of Formal Logic, 22*(3), 204–218. doi:10.1305/ndjfl/1093883455

Clarke, B. (1985). Individuals and points. *Notre Dame Journal of Formal Logic, 26*(1), 61–75. doi:10.1305/ndjfl/1093870761

Clementini, E., & Di Felice, P. (1997a). A global framework for qualitative shape description. *GeoInformatica, 1*(1), 11–27. doi:10.1023/A:1009790715467

Clementini, E., & Di Felice, P. (1997b). Approximate topological relations. *International Journal of Approximate Reasoning, 16*(2), 173–204. doi:10.1016/S0888-613X(96)00127-2

Clementini, E., & Di Felice, P. (1998). Topological invariants for lines. *IEEE Transactions on Knowledge and Data Engineering, 10*(1), 38–54. doi:10.1109/69.667085

Clementini, E., Di Felice, P., & Oosterom, P. (1993). A small set of formal topological relationships suitable for end user interaction. In *Proceedings of the Symposium on Spatial Databases (SSD93)*, (pp. 277–295). Springer.

Cohn, A. G. (1993). Modal and non-modal qualitative spatial logics. In *Proceedings of the Workshop on Spatial and Temporal Reasoning at IJCAI-93*, (pp. 93–100). IJCAI.

Cohn, A. G. (1995). A hierarchical representation of qualitative shape based on connection and convexity. In *Proceedings of the Conference on Spatial Information Theory (COSIT-95)*, (pp. 311–326). Springer.

Cohn, A. G., Bennett, B., Gooday, J. M., & Gotts, N. M. (1997a). RCC: A calculus for region based qualitative spatial reasoning. *GeoInformatica, 1*, 275–316. doi:10.1023/A:1009712514511

Cohn, A. G., Bennett, B., Gooday, J. M., & Gotts, N. M. (1997b). Representing and reasoning with qualitative spatial relations about regions. In Stock, O. (Ed.), *Spatial and Temporal Reasoning* (pp. 97–134). Kluwer. doi:10.1007/978-0-585-28322-7_4

Cohn, A. G., & Gotts, N. M. (1996a). A mereological approach to representing spatial vagueness. In *Proceedings of KR96: Principles of Knowledge Representation and Reasoning*, (pp. 230–241). KR.

Cohn, A. G., & Gotts, N. M. (1996b). The egg-yolk representation of regions with indeterminate boundaries. In Burrough, A., & Frank, A. U. (Eds.), *Geographic Objects with Indeterminate Boundaries* (pp. 171–188). Taylor & Francis.

Cohn, A. G., & Hazarika, S. M. (2001). Qualitative spatial representation and reasoning: An overview. *Fundamenta Informaticae*, *46*(1-2), 1–29.

Cohn, A. G., Randell, D. A., & Cui, Z. (1994). Taxonomies of logically defined qualitative spatial relations. In Guarino, N., & Poli, R. (Eds.), *Formal Ontology in Conceptual Analysis and Knowledge Representation*. Dordrecht, The Netherlands: Kluwer. doi:10.1006/ijhc.1995.1077

Cohn, A. G., & Renz, J. (2008). Qualitative spatial representation and reasoning. In van Harmelen, F., Lifschitz, V., & Porter, B. (Eds.), *Handbook of Knowledge Representation*. London, UK: Elsevier. doi:10.1016/S1574-6526(07)03013-1

Cohn, A. G., & Varzi, A. C. (1998). Connection relations in mereotopology. In *Proceedings of the European Conference on Artificial Intelligence (ECAI-98)*, (pp. 150–154). ECAI.

Cohn, A. G., & Varzi, A. C. (1999). Modes of connection. In *Proceedings of the Conference on Spatial Information Theory (COSIT-99)*, (pp. 299–314). Springer.

Cohn, A. G., & Varzi, A. C. (2003). Mereotopological connection. *Journal of Symbolic Logic*, *32*(4), 357–390.

Cristani, M. (1999). The complexity of reasoning about spatial congruence. *Journal of Artificial Intelligence Research*, *11*, 361–390.

Cristani, M., Cohn, A. G., & Bennett, B. (2000). Spatial locations via morpho-mereology. In *Proceedings of KR2000: Principles of knowledge representation and reasoning*, (pp. 15–25). KR.

Davis, E. (2006). The expressivity of quantifying over regions. *Journal of Logic and Computation*, *16*(6), 891–916. doi:10.1093/logcom/exl020

Davis, E., Gotts, N. M., & Cohn, A. G. (1999). Constraint networks of topological relations and convexity. *Constraints*, *4*(3), 241–280. doi:10.1023/A:1026401931919

de Laguna, T. (1922). Point, line, and surface, as sets of solids. *The Journal of Philosophy*, *19*(17), 449–461. doi:10.2307/2939504

Dimov, G., & Vakarelov, D. (2005). Topological representations of precontact lattices. In *Proceedings of the Conference on Relational Methods in Computer Science (RelMiCS-5)*, (pp. 1–16). Springer.

Dimov, G., & Vakarelov, D. (2006a). Contact algebras and region-based theory of space: A proximity approach - I. *Fundamenta Informaticae*, *74*(2-3), 209–249.

Dimov, G., & Vakarelov, D. (2006b). Contact algebras and region-based theory of space: A proximity approach - II. *Fundamenta Informaticae*, *74*(2-3), 250–282.

Dong, T. (2008). A comment on RCC: From RCC to *RCC*$^{++}$. *Journal of Philosophical Logic*, *37*(4), 319–352. doi:10.1007/s10992-007-9074-y

Donnelly, M. (2001). *An axiomatic theory of common-sense geometry*. Unpublished Doctoral Dissertation. Austin, TX: University of Texas.

Donnelly, M. (2004). On parts and holes: The spatial structure of the human body. In *Proceedings of MedInfo, 2004*, 351–356.

Dornheim, C. (1998). Undecidability of plane polygonal mereotopology. In *Proceedings of KR98: Principles of Knowledge Representation and Reasoning*, (pp. 342–353). KR.

Düntsch, I. (1994). Rough relation algebras. *Fundamenta Informaticae, 21*(4), 321–331.

Düntsch, I. (1999). *A tutorial on relation algebras and their application in spatial reasoning.*

Düntsch, I., & Winter. (2004a). Construction of Boolean contact algebras. *AI Communications, 17*(4), 235–246.

Düntsch, I. (2005). Relation algebras and their application in temporal and spatial reasoning. *Artificial Intelligence Review, 23*(4), 315–357. doi:10.1007/s10462-004-5899-8

Düntsch, I., MacCaull, W., Vakarelov, D., & Winter, M. (2006). Topological representations of contact lattices. In *Proceedings of the Conference on Relational Methods in Computer Science (RelMiCS-9)*, (pp. 135–147). Springer.

Düntsch, I., MacCaull, W., Vakarelov, D., & Winter, M. (2008). Distributive contact lattices: Topological representations. *Journal of Logic and Algebraic Programming, 76*(1), 18–34. doi:10.1016/j.jlap.2007.10.002

Düntsch, I., Orowska, E., & Wang, H. (2001a). Algebras of approximating regions. *Fundamenta Informaticae, 46*(1-2), 71–82.

Düntsch, I., Schmidt, G., & Winter, M. (2001b). A necessary relation algebra for mereotopology. *Studia Logica, 69*, 381–409. doi:10.1023/A:1013892110192

Düntsch, I., & Vakarelov, D. (2007). Region-based theory of discrete spaces: A proximity approach. *Annals of Mathematics and Artificial Intelligence, 49*(1-4), 5–14. doi:10.1007/s10472-007-9064-3

Düntsch, I., Wang, H., & McCloskey, S. (1999). Relation algebras in qualitative spatial reasoning. *Fundamenta Informaticae, 39*(3), 229–248.

Düntsch, I., & Winter, M. (2004b). Algebraization and representation of mereotopological structures. *Journal on Relational Methods in Computer Science, 1*, 161–180.

Düntsch, I., & Winter, M. (2005a). A representation theorem for Boolean contact algebras. *Theoretical Computer Science, 347*, 498–512. doi:10.1016/j.tcs.2005.06.030

Düntsch, I., & Winter, M. (2005b). Weak contact structures. In *Proceedings of the Conference on Relational Methods in Computer Science (RelMiCS-5)*, (pp. 73–82). Springer.

Düntsch, I., & Winter, M. (2006). Rough relation algebras revisited. *Fundamenta Informaticae, 74*(2-3), 283–300.

Düntsch, I., & Winter, M. (2008). The lattice of contact relations on a Boolean algebra. In *Proceedings of the Conference on Relational Methods in Computer Science (RelMiCS-10)*, (pp. 98–109). Springer.

Efremovič, V. A. (1952). The geometry of proximity I. *New Series, 31*, 189–200.

Egenhofer, M. J. (1989). A formal definition of binary topological relationships. In *Proceedings of the Conference on Foundations of Data Organization and Algorithms (FODO-89)*. Springer.

Egenhofer, M. J. (1991). Reasoning about binary topological relations. In *Proceedings of the Symposium on Spatial Databases (SSD91)*, (pp. 141–160). Springer.

Egenhofer, M. J. (1994). Deriving the composition of binary topological relations. *Journal of Visual Languages and Computing, 5*, 133–149. doi:10.1006/jvlc.1994.1007

Egenhofer, M. J., Clementini, E., & Di Felice, P. (1994). Topological relations between regions with holes. *International Journal of Geographical Information Science*, *8*(2), 129–144. doi:10.1080/02693799408901990

Egenhofer, M. J., & Franzosa, R. (1991). Point-set topological spatial relations. *International Journal of Geographical Information Science*, *5*(2), 161–174. doi:10.1080/02693799108927841

Egenhofer, M. J., & Herring, J. (1991). *Categorizing binary topological relations between regions, lines, and points in geographic databases. Technical Report*. Bangor, ME: University of Maine.

Egenhofer, M. J., & Mark, D. M. (1995a). Modeling conceptual neighborhoods of topological line-region relations. *International Journal of Geographical Information Science*, *9*(5), 555–565. doi:10.1080/02693799508902056

Egenhofer, M. J., & Mark, D. M. (1995b). Naive geography. In *Proceedings of the Conference on Spatial Information Theory (COSIT-95)*, (pp. 1–15). Springer.

Egenhofer, M. J., & Sharma, J. (1993a). Assessing the consistency of complete and incomplete topological information. *Geographical Systems*, *1*(1), 47–68.

Egenhofer, M. J., & Sharma, J. (1993b). Topological relations between regions in $R^2$ and $Z^2$. In *Proceedings of the Symposium on Spatial Databases (SSD93)*, (pp. 316–336). Springer.

Engelking, R. (1977). *General topology*. Warsaw, Poland: Polish Scientific Publishers.

Eschenbach, C. (1999). A predication calculus for qualitative spatial representations. In *Proceedings of the Conference on Spatial Information Theory (COSIT-99)*, (pp. 157–172). Springer.

Eschenbach, C. (2001). Viewing composition tables as axiomatic systems. In *Proceedings of the Conference on Formal Ontology in Information Systems (FOIS-01)*, (pp. 93–104). FOIS.

Eschenbach, C. (2007). *A comparison of calculi of mereotopology*. Draft manuscript.

Eschenbach, C., & Heydrich, W. (1995). Classical mereology and restricted domains. *International Journal of Human-Computer Studies*, *43*(5/6), 723–740. doi:10.1006/ijhc.1995.1071

Faltings, B. (1995). Qualitative spatial reasoning using algebraic topology. In *Proceedings of the Conference on Spatial Information Theory (COSIT-95)*, (pp. 17–30). Springer.

Fleck, M. M. (1996). The topology of boundaries. *Artificial Intelligence*, *80*, 1–27. doi:10.1016/0004-3702(94)00051-4

Fonseca, F., Egenhofer, M. J., Davis, C., & Borges, K. (2000). Ontologies and knowledge sharing in urban GIS. *Computers, Environment and Urban Systems*, *24*(3), 251–272. doi:10.1016/S0198-9715(00)00004-1

Fonseca, F. T., Egenhofer, M. J., Agouris, P., & Câmara, G. (2002). Using ontologies for integrated geographic information systems. *Transactions in GIS*, *6*(3), 231–257. doi:10.1111/1467-9671.00109

Frank, A. U. (1996). Qualitative spatial reasoning: Cardinal directions as an example. *International Journal of Geographical Information Science*, *10*(3), 269–290.

Frank, A. U. (2005). *Practical geometry-the mathematics for geographic information systems*. Unpublished.

Frank, A. U., & Kuhn, W. (1986). Cell graphs: A provable correct method for the storage of geometry. In *Proceedings of the International Symposium on Spatial Data Handling*. International Symposium.

Freksa, C. (1992). Using orientation information for qualitative spatial reasoning. In *Proceedings of the Conference on Advances in Geographic Information Systems (GIS-92)*, (pp. 162–178). Springer.

Gabelaia, D., Kontchakov, R., Kurucz, A., Wolter, F., & Zakharyaschev, M. (2005). Combining spatial and temporal logics: Expressiveness vs. complexity. *Journal of Artificial Intelligence Research, 23*, 167–243.

Gahegan, M. (1995). Proximity operators for qualitative spatial reasoning. In *Proceedings of the Conference on Spatial Information Theory (COSIT-95)*, (pp. 31–44). Springer.

Galata, A., Cohn, A. G., Magee, D., & Hogg, D. (2002). Modeling interaction using learnt qualitative spatio-temporal relations and variable lengths Markov models. In *Proceedings of the European Conference on Artificial Intelligence (ECAI-02)*, (pp. 741–745). ECAI.

Galton, A. (1996). Taking dimension seriously in qualitative spatial reasoning. In *Proceedings of the European Conference on Artificial Intelligence (ECAI-96)*, (pp. 501–505). ECAI.

Galton, A. (1999). The mereotopology of discrete space. In *Proceedings of the Conference on Spatial Information Theory (COSIT-99)*, (pp. 251–266). Springer.

Galton, A. (2003). *Foundations of geographic information science: On the ontological status of geographic boundaries*. Taylor & Francis.

Galton, A. (2004). Multidimensional mereotopology. In *Proceedings of KR04: Principles of Knowledge Representation and Reasoning*, (pp. 45–54). KR.

Gerevini, A., & Renz, J. (2002). Combining topological and size information for spatial reasoning. *Artificial Intelligence, 137*, 1–42. doi:10.1016/S0004-3702(02)00193-5

Gerla, G. (1995). Pointless geometries. In Buekenhout, F. (Ed.), *Handbook of Incidence Geometry* (pp. 1015–1031). Elsevier. doi:10.1016/B978-044488355-1/50020-7

Gerla, G., & Miranda, A. (2009). Inclusion and connection in Whiteheads point-free geometry. In M. Weber & W. Desmond (Eds.), *Handbook of Whiteheadian Process Thought*. Ontos Verlag.

Gotts, N. M. (1994). How far can we C? Defining a doughnut using connection alone. In *Proceedings of KR94: Principles of Knowledge Representation and Reasoning*, (pp. 246–257). KR.

Gotts, N. M. (1996a). *An axiomatic approach to topology for spatial information systems*. Technical Report 96.24. Leeds, UK: University of Leeds.

Gotts, N. M. (1996b). Formalizing commonsense topology: The INCH calculus. In *Proceedings of the International Symposium on Artificial Intelligence and Mathematics*, (pp. 72–75). International Symposium.

Gotts, N. M. (1996c). *Using the RCC formalism to describe the topology of spherical regions*. Technical Report 96.24. Leeds, UK: University of Leeds.

Gotts, N. M., Gooday, J. M., & Cohn, A. G. (1996). A connection based approach to commonsense topological description and reasoning. *The Monist, 79*(1), 51–75.

Grätzer, G. (1998). *General lattice theory* (2nd ed.). Birkhäuser.

Greferath, M., & Schmidt, S. E. (1998). *General lattice theory: Appendix E-projective lattice geometries* (2nd ed., pp. 539–553). Birkhäuser.

Grenon, P. (2003). *BFO in a nutshell: A bi-categorical axiomatization of BFO and comparison with Dolce. Technical Report*. Leipzig, Germany: Leipzig University.

Gruszczyński, R., & Pietruszczak, A. (2008). Full development of Tarskis geometry of solids. *The Bulletin of Symbolic Logic, 14*(4), 481–540. doi:10.2178/bsl/1231081462

Grzegorczyk, A. (1951). Undecidability of some topological theories. *Fundamenta Mathematicae, 38*, 109–127.

Grzegorczyk, A. (1955). The systems of Leśniewski in relation to contemporary logical research. *Studia Logic, 3*(1), 77–95. doi:10.1007/BF02067248

Grzegorczyk, A. (1960). Axiomatizability of geometry without points. *Synthese, 12*, 109–127. doi:10.1007/BF00485101

Guesgen, H. W. (2002). From the egg-yolk to the scrambled-egg theory. In *Proceedings of the Florida Artificial Intelligence Research Society Conference (FLAIRS-15)*. FLAIRS.

Hahmann, T., & Gruninger, M. (2009). Detecting physical defects: A practical 2D-study of cracks and holes. In *Proceedings of the AAAI-SS09: Benchmarking of Qualitative Spatial and Temporal Reasoning Systems,* (pp. 11–16). AAAI Press.

Hahmann, T., Gruninger, M., & Winter, M. (2009). Stonian p-ortholattices: A new approach to the mereotopology RT0. *Artificial Intelligence*. Retrieved from http://citeseerx.ist.psu.edu/viewdoc/summary?doi=10.1.1.149.8359.

Halmos, P. R. (1963). *Lectures on Boolean algebras*. Van Nostrand Reinhold.

Hayes, P. J. (1978). The naive physics manifesto. In Michie, D. (Ed.), *Expert Systems in the Microelectronic Age* (pp. 242–270). Edinburgh, UK: Edinburgh University Press.

Hayes, P. J. (1985a). Naive physics I: Ontology of liquids. In Hobbs, J., & Moore, R. (Eds.), *Formal Theories of the Commonsense World* (pp. 71–108). Ablex Publishing.

Hayes, P. J. (1985b). The second naive physics manifesto. In Hobbs, J., & Moore, R. (Eds.), *Formal Theories of the Commonsense World* (pp. 567–585). Ablex Publishing.

Hernández, D., Clementini, E., & Di Felice, P. (1995). Qualitative distances. In *Proceedings of the Conference on Spatial Information Theory (COSIT-95)*, (pp. 45–58). Springer.

Huntington, E. V. (1913). A set of postulates for abstract geometry, expressed in terms of the simple relation of inclusion. *Mathematische Annalen, 73*, 522–559. doi:10.1007/BF01455955

Husserl, E. (1913). *Logische untersuchungen: Zweiter band: Untersuchungen zur phänomenologie und theorie der erkenntnis (1. Teil)* (2nd ed.). Max Niemeyer.

Ibrahim, Z., & Tawfik, A. (2004). Spatio-temporal reasoning for vague regions. In *Proceedings of the Conference of the the Canadian Society for Computer Studies of Intelligence (Canadian AI)*, (pp. 308–321). Springer.

Johnstone, P. T. (1983). The point of pointless topology. *Bulletin of the American Mathematical Society, 8*(1), 41–53. doi:10.1090/S0273-0979-1983-15080-2

Kalmbach, G. (1983). *Orthomodular lattices*. Academic Press.

Kim, K.-Y., Chin, S., Kwon, O., & Ellis, R. D. (2009). Ontology-based modeling and integration of morphological characteristics of assembly joints for network-based collaborative assembly design. *Artificial Intelligence for Engineering Design, Analysis and Manufacturing, 23*, 71–88. doi:10.1017/S0890060409000110

Kim, K.-Y., Manley, D., & Yang, H. (2006). Ontology-based assembly design and information sharing for collaborative product development. *Computer Aided Design, 38*(12), 1233–1250. doi:10.1016/j.cad.2006.08.004

Kim, K.-Y., Yang, H.-J., & Kim, D.-W. (2008). Mereotopological assembly joint information representation for collaborative product design. *Robotics and Computer-integrated Manufacturing, 24*, 744–754. doi:10.1016/j.rcim.2008.03.010

Kuipers, B. J., & Byun, Y.-T. (1991). A robot exploration and mapping strategy based on a semantic hierarchy of spatial representation. *Journal of Robots and Autonomous Systems, 8*, 47–63. doi:10.1016/0921-8890(91)90014-C

Kuipers, B. J., & Levitt, T. (1988). Navigation and mapping in large-scale space. *AI Magazine, 9*, 25–43.

Leader, S. (1967). Local proximity spaces. *Mathematische Annalen, 169*.

Leonard, H. S., & Goodman, N. (1940). The calculus of individuals and its uses. *Journal of Symbolic Logic, 5*(2), 45–55. doi:10.2307/2266169

Leśniewski, S. (1927). O podstawack matematyki. In *Prezeglad Filosoficzny* (pp. 30–34). Academic Publisher.

Levitt, T., & Lawton, D. (1990). Qualitative navigation for mobile robots. *Artificial Intelligence, 44*, 305–360. doi:10.1016/0004-3702(90)90027-W

Li, S., & Nebel, B. (2007). Qualitative spatial representation and reasoning: A hierarchical approach. *The Computer Journal, 50*(4), 391–402. doi:10.1093/comjnl/bxl086

Li, S., & Ying, M. (2003). Region connection calculus: Its models and composition table. *Artificial Intelligence, 145*, 121–145. doi:10.1016/S0004-3702(02)00372-7

Li, S., & Ying, M. (2004). Generalized region connection calculus. *Artificial Intelligence, 160*, 1–34. doi:10.1016/j.artint.2004.05.012

Li, S., Ying, M., & Li, Y. (2005). On countable RCC models. *Fundamenta Informaticae, 64*(4), 329–351.

Li, Z., Zhao, R., & Chen, J. (2002). A Voronoi-based spatial algebra for spatial relations. *Progress in Natural Science, 12*(7), 528–536.

Ligozat, G. (2001). When tables tell it all: Qualitative spatial and temporal reasoning based on linear orderings. In *Proceedings of the Conference on Spatial Information Theory (COSIT-01)*, (pp. 60–75). Springer.

Lobačevskij, N. I. (1834). *New principles of geometry with complete theory of parallels* (*Vol. 2*). Gostexizdat.

Luschei, E. C. (1962). *The logical systems of Leśniewski*. Amsterdam, The Netherlands: North-Holland Publisher.

Lutz, C., & Wolter, F. (2004). *Modal logics of topological relations*. Technical Report LTCS-04-05. Dresden, Germany: Dresden University of Technology. Aiello, I., Pratt-Hartmann, E., & van Benthem, J. F. (Eds). (2007). *Handbook of spatial logics*. Springer.

Mark, D., & Egenhofer, M. J. (1994). Modeling spatial relations between lines and regions: Combining formal mathematical models and human subjects testing. *Cartography and Geographic Information Systems, 21*(3), 195–212.

Masolo, C., & Vieu, L. (1999). Atomicity vs. infinite divisibility of space. In *Proceedings of the Conference on Spatial Information Theory (COSIT-99)*, (pp. 235–250). Springer.

McKenney, M., Pauly, A., Praing, R., & Schneider, M. (2005). Dimension-refined topological predicates. In *Proceedings of the Conference on Advances in Geographic Information Systems (GIS-05)*, (pp. 240–249). ACM Press.

McKinsey, J. C. C., & Tarski, A. (1944). The algebra of topology. *The Annals of Mathematics*, *45*(1), 141–191. doi:10.2307/1969080

Menger, K. (1940). Topology without points. *Rice Institute Pamphlets*, *27*(1), 80–107.

Mormann, T. (1998). Continuous lattices and Whiteheadian theory of space. *Logic and Logical Philosophy*, *6*, 35–54.

Mormann, T. (2001). *Holes in the region connection calculus*. Preprint presented at RelMiCS-6.

Muller, P. (1998a). A qualitative theory of motion based on spatio-temporal primitives. In *Proceedings of KR98: Principles of Knowledge Representation and Reasoning*, (pp. 131–143). KR.

Muller, P. (1998b). Space-time as a primitive for space and motion. In *Proceedings of the Conference on Formal Ontology in Information Systems (FOIS-98)*, (pp. 3–15). FOIS.

Muller, P. (2002). Topological spatiotemporal reasoning and representation. *Computational Intelligence*, *18*(3), 420–450. doi:10.1111/1467-8640.00196

Munkres, J. R. (2000). *Topology* (2nd ed.). Prentice Hall.

Naimpally, S. A., & Warrack, B. D. (1970). *Proximity spaces*. Cambridge University Press.

Navarrete, I. S. G. (2006). Spatial reasoning with rectangular cardinal direction relations. In *Proceedings of the Workshop on Spatial and Temporal Reasoning at ECAI-06*, (pp. 1–9). ECAI.

Nicod, J. (1924). *Geometry in the sensible world*. Unpublished Doctoral Thesis. Paris, France: Sorbonne.

Padmanabhan, R., & Rudeanu, S. (2008). *Axioms for lattices and Boolean algebras*. World Scientific. doi:10.1142/9789812834553

Pawlak, Z. (1991). *Rough sets: Theoretical aspects of reasoning about data*. Dordrecht, The Netherlands: Kluwer.

Pratt, I., & Schoop, D. (1997). *A complete axiom system for polygonal mereotopology of the real plane. UMCS-97-2-2, Technical Report*. Manchester, UK: University of Manchester.

Priestley, H. A. (1970). Representation of distributive lattices by means of ordered stone spaces. *Bulletin of the London Mathematical Society*, *2*(2), 186–190. doi:10.1112/blms/2.2.186

Randell, D. A., Cui, Z., & Cohn, A. G. (1992). A spatial logic based on regions and connection. In *Proceedings of KR92: Principles of Knowledge Representation and Reasoning*, (pp. 165–176). KR.

Rector, A., Rogers, J., & Pole, P. (1996). The GALEN high level ontology. In *Medical Informatics Europe 96* (Part A), (pp. 174–178). IOS Press.

Remolina, E., & Kuipers, B. J. (2004). Towards a general theory of topological maps. *Artificial Intelligence*, *152*, 47–104. doi:10.1016/S0004-3702(03)00114-0

Renz, J. (1999). Maximal tractable fragments of the region connection calculus: A complete analysis. In *Proceedings of the International Joint Conference on Artificial Intelligence (IJCAI-99)*, (pp. 448–454). IJCAI.

Renz, J. (2002). *Qualitative spatial reasoning with topological information*. Springer. doi:10.1007/3-540-70736-0

Renz, J. (2007). Qualitative spatial and temporal reasoning: Efficient algorithms for everyone. In *International Joint Conference on Artificial Intelligence (IJCAI-07)*, (pp. 526–531). IJCAI.

Renz, J., & Li, J. J. (2008). Automated complexity proofs for qualitative spatial and temporal calculi. In *Proceedings of KR08: Principles of Knowledge Representation and Reasoning*, (pp. 715–723). KR.

Renz, J., & Ligozat, G. (2004). What is a qualitative calculus? A general framework. In *Proceedings of the Pacific Rim International Conference on Artificial Intelligence (PRICAI-04)*, (pp. 53–64). Springer.

Renz, J., & Ligozat, G. (2005). Weak composition for qualitative spatial and temporal reasoning. In *Proceedings of Principles and Practice of Constraint Programming (CP-05)* (pp. 534–548). Springer. doi:10.1007/11564751_40

Renz, J., & Mitra, D. (2004). Qualitative direction calculi with arbitrary granularity. In *Proceedings of the Pacific Rim International Conference on Artificial Intelligence (PRICAI-04)*, (pp. 65–74). PRICAI.

Renz, J., & Nebel, B. (1998). Efficient methods for qualitative spatial reasoning. In *Proceedings of the European Conference on Artificial Intelligence (ECAI-98)*, (pp. 562–566). ECAI.

Renz, J., & Nebel, B. (1999). On the complexity of qualitative spatial reasoning: A maximal tractable fragment of the region connection calculus. *Artificial Intelligence*, *108*, 69–123. doi:10.1016/S0004-3702(99)00002-8

Renz, J., & Nebel, B. (2007). Qualitative spatial reasoning using constraint calculi. In *Handbook of Spatial Logics* (pp. 161–216). Springer. doi:10.1007/978-1-4020-5587-4_4

Robinson, R. M. (1959). Binary relations as primitive notions in elementary geometry. In Henkin, L., Suppes, P., & Tarski, A. (Eds.), *The Axiomatic Method with Special Reference to Geometry and Physics* (pp. 68–85). Amsterdam, The Netherlands: North-Holland. doi:10.1016/S0049-237X(09)70020-5

Roeper, P. (1997). Region-based topology. *Journal of Philosophical Logic*, *26*(3), 251–309. doi:10.1023/A:1017904631349

Rogers, J., & Rector, A. (2000). GALENS model of parts and wholes: Experience and comparisons. In *Proceedings of the Symposium of the American Medical Informatics Association (AMIA-2000)*, (pp. 714–718). Hanley & Belfus.

Rosse, C., & Mejino, J. Jr. (2003). A reference ontology for bioinformatics: The foundational model of anatomy. *Journal of Biomedical Informatics*, *36*, 478–500. doi:10.1016/j.jbi.2003.11.007

Roy, A. J., & Stell, J. G. (2002). A qualitative account of discrete space. In *Proceedings of the Conference on Geographic Information Science (GIScience-02)*, (pp. 276–290). Springer.

Salustri, F. A. (2002). Mereotopology for product modeling. *Journal of Desert Research*, *2*(1).

Schlieder, C. (1996). Qualitative shape representation. In Burrough, A., & Frank, A. U. (Eds.), *Geographic Objects with Indeterminate Boundaries*. Taylor & Francis.

Schmolze, J. G. (1996). A topological account of the space occupied by physical objects. *The Monist*, *79*(1), 128–140.

Schockaert, S., De Cock, M., & Kerre, E. (2008). Modelling nearness and cardinal directions between fuzzy regions. In *Proceedings of the Conference on Fuzzy Systems (FUZZ 08)*, (pp. 1548–1555). FUZZ.

Schockaert, S., De Cock, M., & Kerre, E. (2009). Spatial reasoning in a fuzzy region connection calculus. *Artificial Intelligence*, *173*, 258–298. doi:10.1016/j.artint.2008.10.009

Schulz, S., Daumke, P., Smith, B., & Hahn, U. (2005). How to distinguish parthood from location in bio-ontologies. In *Proceedings of the Symposium of the American Medical Informatics Association (AMIA-05)*, (pp. 669–673). AMIA.

Schulz, S., & Hahn, U. (2001a). Mereotopological reasoning about parts and (w)holes in bio-ontologies. In *Proceedings of the Conference on Formal Ontology in Information Systems (FOIS-01)*, (pp. 210–221). FOIS.

Schulz, S., & Hahn, U. (2001b). Parts, locations, and holes-formal reasoning about anatomical structures. In *Proceedings of the Conference on Artificial Intelligence in Medicine in Europe (AIME-01)*. Springer.

Simons, P. (1987). *Parts-a study in ontology*. Clarendon Press.

Skiadopoulos, S., & Koubarakis, M. (2004). Composing cardinal direction relations. *Artificial Intelligence, 152*, 143–171. doi:10.1016/S0004-3702(03)00137-1

Skiadopoulos, S., & Koubarakis, M. (2005). On the consistency of cardinal directions constraints. *Artificial Intelligence, 163*, 91–135. doi:10.1016/j.artint.2004.10.010

Smith, B. (1996). Mereotopology: A theory of parts and boundaries. *Data & Knowledge Engineering, 20*(3), 287–303. doi:10.1016/S0169-023X(96)00015-8

Smith, B., & Casati, R. (1994). Naive physics: An essay in ontology. *Philosophical Psychology, 7*(2), 225–244.

Smith, B., Ceusters, W., Klagges, B., Kohler, J., Kumar, A., & Lomax, J. (2005). Relations in biomedical ontologies. *Genome Biology, 6*(5), 1–15. doi:10.1186/gb-2005-6-5-r46

Smith, B., & Varzi, A. (1997). Fiat and bona fide boundaries: Towards and ontology of spatially extended objects. In *Proceedings of the Conference on Spatial Information Theory (COSIT-97)*, (pp. 103–119). Springer.

Smith, T., & Park, K. (1992). Algebraic approach to spatial reasoning. *International Journal of Geographical Information Science, 6*(3), 177–192. doi:10.1080/02693799208901904

Stell, J. G. (2000). Boolean connection algebras: A new approach to the region-connection calculus. *Artificial Intelligence, 122*, 111–136. doi:10.1016/S0004-3702(00)00045-X

Stell, J. G. (2003). *Foundations of geographic information science: Granularity in change over time* (pp. 101–122). Taylor & Francis.

Stell, J. G., & Worboys, M. F. (1997). The algebraic structure of sets of regions. In *Proceedings of the Conference on Spatial Information Theory (COSIT-97)*, (pp. 163–174). Springer.

Stone, M. H. (1936). The theory of representations for Boolean algebra. *Transactions of the American Society, 40*(1), 37–111.

Stone, M. H. (1937). Topological representation of distributive lattices and Brouwerian logics. *Časopis pro Pěstování Matematiky a Fysiky, 67*, 1–25.

Tarski, A. (1935). Zur grundlegung der Booleschen algebra I. *Fundamenta Mathematicae, 24*, 177–198.

Tarski, A. (1956a). Foundations of the geometry of solids. In Tarski, A. (Ed.), *Logics, Semantics, Metamathematics: Papers from 1923-1938 by Alfred Tarski*. Clarendon Press.

Tarski, A. (1956b). On the foundation of Boolean algebra. In Tarski, A. (Ed.), *Logics, Semantics, Metamathematics: Papers from 1923-1938 by Alfred Tarski*. Clarendon Press.

Tarski, A. (1959). What is elementary geometry? In Henkin, L., Suppes, P., & Tarski, A. (Eds.), *The Axiomatic Method with Special Reference to Geometry and Physics* (pp. 16–29). North-Holland.

Thrun, S. (1998). Learning metric-topological maps for indoor mobile robot navigation. *Artificial Intelligence*, *99*, 21–71. doi:10.1016/S0004-3702(97)00078-7

Urquhart, A. (1978). A topological representation theory for lattices. *Algebra Universalis*, *8*, 45–58. doi:10.1007/BF02485369

Vakarelov, D. (2007). Region-based theory of space: Algebras of regions, representation theory, and logics. In Gabbay, D., Goncharov, S., & Zakharyaschev, M. (Eds.), *Mathematical Problems from Applied Logic II* (pp. 267–348). Springer. doi:10.1007/978-0-387-69245-6_6

Vakarelov, D., Dimov, G., Düntsch, I., & Bennett, B. (2002). A proximity approach to some region-based theories of space. *Journal of Applied Non-classical Logics*, *12*(3-4), 527–559. doi:10.3166/jancl.12.527-559

Vakarelov, D., Düntsch, I., & Bennett, B. (2001). A note on proximity spaces and connection based mereology. In *Proceedings of the Conference on Formal Ontology in Inf. Systems (FOIS-01)*, (pp. 139–150). FOIS.

Varzi, A. C. (1994). On the boundary between mereology and topology. In Casati, R., Smith, B., & White, G. (Eds.), *Philosophy and Cognitive Science* (pp. 423–442). Holder-Pichler-Tempsky.

Varzi, A. C. (1996a). Parts, wholes, and part-whole relations: The prospects of mereotopology. *Data & Knowledge Engineering*, *20*(3), 259–286. doi:10.1016/S0169-023X(96)00017-1

Varzi, A. C. (1996b). Reasoning about space: The hole story. *Logic and Logical Philosophy*, *4*, 3–39.

Varzi, A. C. (1998). Basic problems of mereotopology. In *Proceedings of the Conference on Formal Ontology in Information Systems (FOIS-98)*, (pp. 29–38). FOIS.

Varzi, A. C. (2008). Boundary. In *The Stanford Encyclopedia of Philosophy*. Palo Alto, CA: Stanford University Press.

Varzi, A. C. (2009). Mereology. In *The Stanford Encyclopedia of Philosophy*. Palo Alto, CA: Stanford University Press.

Verhagen, M., Mani, I., Sauri, R., Knippen, R., Jang, S. B., Littman, J., et al. (2005). Automating temporal annotation with TARSQI. In *Proceedings of the Association for Computational Linguistics (ACL-05)*, (pp. 81–84). ACL.

Vieu, L. (1997). Spatial representation and reasoning in artificial intelligence. In Stock, O. (Ed.), *Spatial and Temporal Reasoning* (pp. 5–42). Kluwer. doi:10.1007/978-0-585-28322-7_1

Wallman, H. (1938). Lattices and topological spaces. *The Annals of Mathematics*, *39*(2), 112–126. doi:10.2307/1968717

Wehrung, F. (1998). *General lattice theory: Appendix E-projective lattice geometries* (2nd ed.). Birkhäuser.

Whitehead, A. N. (1920). *Concept of nature*. Cambridge University Press.

Whitehead, A. N. (1929). *Process and reality*. MacMillan.

Winter, M., Hahmann, T., & Gruninger, M. (2009). On the skeleton of Stonian p-ortholattices. In *Proceedings of the Conference on Relational Methods in Computer Science (RelMiCS-11)*, (pp. 351–365). Springer.

Winter, S., & Frank, A. U. (2000). Topology in raster and vector representation. *GeoInformatica*, *4*, 35–65. doi:10.1023/A:1009828425380

Wolter, F., & Zakharyaschev, M. (2000). Spatial representation and reasoning in RCC-8 with Boolean region terms. In *Proceedings of the European Conference on Artificial Intelligence (ECAI-2000)*, (pp. 244–248). ECAI.

Wolter, F., & Zakharyaschev, M. (2002). Qualitative spatiotemporal representation and reasoning: A computational perspective. In Lakemeyer, G., & Nebel, B. (Eds.), *Exploring Artificial Intelligence in the New Millennium* (pp. 175–215). Morgan Kaufmann.

Xia, L., & Li, S. (2006). On mimimal models of the region connection calculus. *Fundamenta Informaticae*, *69*(4), 427–446.

Yang, B., & Salustri, F. (1999). Function modeling based on interactions of mass, energy and information. In *Proceedings of the Florida Artificial Intelligence Research Society Conference (FLAIRS-12)*, (pp. 384–388). FLAIRS.

## KEY TERMS AND DEFINITIONS

**Atom:** An indivisible region, i.e. a region that has no proper part.

**Algebraic Representation:** Representation of the models of a mereotopology by a class of algebraic structures, usually by some class of contact algebras or class of lattices.

**Boolean Contact Algebra:** A contact algebra where the underlying lattice is Boolean, i.e. is a complemented distributive lattice and the unique sums with respect to the extension of contact exist.

**Contact Algebra:** An algebraic structure consisting of a bounded lattice defining a partial order P and a binary reflexive and symmetric contact relation C that is monotone with respect to P. This is an algebraic representation of a Whiteheadean mereotopology.

**Extensionality:** A (binary) predicate is extensional in a logical theory if any two objects in the domain of the theory are distinct if and only if their extension of that particular predicate is different.

**Full Mereogeometry:** a region-based theory of space that is expressive enough to define every concept definable in Euclidean geometry.

**Regular Set:** A set x in a topological space is regular if and only if $cl(x) = cl(int(x))$ and $int(x) = int(cl(x))$. We distinguish regular closed sets which satisfy $x = cl(x) = cl(int(x))$ and regular open sets which satisfy $x = int(x) = int(cl(x))$.

**Topological Embedding:** The embedding of the models of an algebraic structure into the sets of some topological space. These sets must be closed at least under union and set intersection. An embedding theorem ensures that every model of a certain algebraic structure can be embedded into a topological space in such a way. A special case is that of a topological representation in which case the reverse also holds: from an arbitrary topological space from a certain class of topological spaces it is always possible to construct a model of the algebraic structure.

**Whiteheadean Mereotopology:** Region-based theories of space assuming regions as only elements in the domain of discourse, thus requiring that all regions are of the same dimension. Whiteheadean mereotopologies must be topologically representable, i.e. there must exist an embedding into some topological space. Usually this embedding must be into the regular sets of a topological space. The term 'Whiteheadean mereotopology' is used in a loose sense in this chapter; the more strict sense requires that such theory can be based on a single primitive (extensional) relation of contact, C.

# Chapter 2
# PLCA:
# A Framework for Qualitative Spatial Reasoning Based on Connection Patterns of Regions

**Kazuko Takahashi**
*Kwansei Gakuin University, Japan*

## ABSTRACT

*This chapter describes a framework called PLCA for Qualitative Spatial Reasoning (QSR) based on the connection patterns of regions. The goal of this chapter is to provide a simple but expressive and feasible representation for qualitative data with sufficient reasoning ability. PLCA provides a symbolic representation for spatial data using simple objects. The authors of this chapter define its expression and operations on it, and show the correspondance between the expression and a figure. PLCA also provides semantical reasoning incorporated with spatial reasoning. Moreover, it can be extended to handle shapes of regions. Throughout the study, the authors discovered many topics that relate QSR to other research areas such as topology, graph theory, and computational geometry, while achieving the research goals. This indicates that QSR is a very fruitful research area.*

DOI: 10.4018/978-1-61692-868-1.ch002

## 1. INTRODUCTION

Recent advances of computer performance and network infrastructure have increased the opportunities for various users to treat spatial data, such as figures and images. Compared to textual data, spatial data contains more abundant information and provides a representation that is easy to understand. But since spatial data are generally stored and processed as numerical data, their processing requires more memory and time. Therefore, an efficient mechanism for spatial data processing is desired. The more refined the data used are, the clearer and more precise the figure is. However, refined data are not always necessary unless a clear, precise figure is required. It is sometimes sufficient to know the number of objects or the positional relationships of the objects in a figure depending on a user's purpose.

Consider the following problem.

### Field and Tree Problem

We are planning to stage an event in a field and need to consider how to cope with rainy days. Although a big tree growing in the field provides a natural roof, it does not cover the entire field, and we are thus contemplating erecting shelters using tarpaulins to cover the areas exposed to rain. How many tarpaulins are required?

In this problem, what we need to know is not the exact position of the tree or the size of the field, but their relative positional relation.

Qualitative Spatial Reasoning (QSR) is a method that treats images or figures qualitatively, not quantitatively like numerical data, by extracting the information necessary for a user's purpose (Aliello, et al., 2007; Bailey-Kellog & Zhao; 2003, Cohn & Hazarika, 2001; Stock, 1997). It is condidered to be useful to many applications including Geographical Information Systems (GIS), physical simulation and image processing. Originally, qualitative reasoning is one of research areas in artificial intelligence which models and reasons about the recognition and analysis of physical phenomena, explanation of a causality, diagnosis, and so on (Forbus, 1981; Kuipers, 1994). QSR can be considered as a kind of qualitative reasoning which focuses the target on spatial data.

There are lots of formalizations and ontologies on QSR. Most of them use predicates on representing spatial properties. However, they are insufficient on the points of implementation and reasoning ability. We propose a novel framework PLCA which adopts an object-oriented concept (Takahashi & Sumitomo, 2005). PLCA provides a symbolic representation for spatial data using the simple objects: *points*($P$),*lines*($L$),*circuits*($C$) and *areas*($A$). No pair of areas has a part in common[1]. The entire space is covered with the areas. It can represent connected patterns of regions: e.g., two regions are connected by one line, or they are connected with two points, and distinguish figures depending on the patterns.

For a given figure in a two-dimensional plane, there exists a PLCA expression, that is unique in its pattern of connections among regions. On the other hand, we can generate a figure corresponsing to a given PLCA expression if it satisfies the condition that holds between the numbers of the objects contained in the expression. We give an algorithm for drawing the figure in a two-dimensional plane for a PLCA expression that satisfies this condition (Takahashi, et al., 2008). A part of the algorithm can be implemented using Genetic Algorithm to generate a ``good'' figure (Kumokawa & Takahashi, 2007).

We define operations on PLCA: area division and area integration, and others (Takahashi & Sumitomo, 2007). The operation on an expression corresponds that of a figure, and consistency is preserved on each operation. PLCA provides topological reasoning, such as obtaining the connected segments of the boundaries of regions and the number of pieces that constitute a region. In addition, we can perform semantical reasoning incorporated with spatial reasoning by adding an attribute to each object. The objects which have the same atttribute are classified into the same class using the operations. It corresponds to altering the classification level of objects.

Moreover, we extend PLCA to describe the convex hull of each area so that we can handle shapes (Kumokawa & Takahashi, 2008). The extended PLCA can represent not only the shape of the boundaries of a single object, but also the detailed connections between objects and the convexity of areas. We present an algorithm for generating an extended PLCA expression from a given figure in a two-dimensional plane, and discuss the properties the expression satisfies.

This chapter is organized as follows. In section 2, we describe the background and related works on this topic. In section 3, we describe the PLCA expressions. In section 4, we present operations on PLCA and show that they are well defined. In section 5, we add attributes to PLCA expressions and show reasoning on the attributed PLCA. In section 6, we discuss two-dimensional realizability of a PLCA expression and show the algorithm for drawing a figure corresponding to a PLCA expression. In section 7, we show the revision of the drawing algorithm to make a ``good'' figure. In section 8, we extend PLCA to handle shape representation. Finally, in section 9, we show the conclusion.

## 2. BACKGROUND

There are various frameworks for QSR depending on spatial aspects to be treated qualitatively, e.g. direction (Frank, 1992; Ligozat, 1998), orientation (Freska, 1992), size (Schmidtke & Woo, 2007), region, interval (Guesgen, 1989), distance (Hernandez, et al., 1995), and so on (Vieu, 1997).

A region-based formalization for a spatial data is the most relative formalization to ours. In this formalization, a space is usually represented as a set of relative positional relationships of objects such as regions or lines. RCC and 9-intersection model are the representatives of such formalization.

Clark presented an axiomatization for the region-based spatial calculus (Clarke, 1981,1985). He represents mereological and topological relationhsips of regions using a single predicate $C$ which means *connected*. Region Connection Calculus (RCC) is developed based on Clark's system (Randell, et al., 1992). RCC is the theory for qualitative spatial reasoning that considers a space as a set of regions paying attention only to their relative positions. Figure 1 shows the basic relations of RCC-8, a variant of RCC. These relations are pairwise disjoint and jointly exhaustive. Gotts examined the expressive power of RCC by defining topological notions inside RCC (Gotts 1994). RCC is a simple, elegant theory that is suitable for mereological reasoning, but the abstraction is rather coarse when treating realistic problems. Therefore, several extentions are proposed. Cohn and Gotts extended it to handle vagueness of the boundaries (Cohn & Gotts, 1996). Borgo et al. extended it by introducing morphological primitives (Borgo et al. 1996). Donnelly introduced the concept of *coincidence* which refines the relationship $PO$ (overlapping) relation (Donnely, 2003). Varzi extended it to handle regions with holes (Casati & Varzi, 1997; Cohn & Varzi, 1998). Cohn proposed another extention for representing shapes (Cohn, 1995). In these systems, the spatial relationships of objects are represented using predicates.

Egenhofer et al. proposed a framework in which regions, lines and points are taken as basic objects to describe topological relationships (Egenhofer & Herring, 1990). They divided each object $X$ into three parts: inner( $X^{\circ}$ ), border ( $\partial X$ ) and outer( $X^{-}$ ). Then, they distinguished the topological relationships between two objects by representing them as a $3 * 3$ matrix called the 9-intersection, the elements of which show whether the intersection of each part is empty or not. Line-line relationships and line-region rela-

*Figure 1. Fundamental relationships of RCC-8*

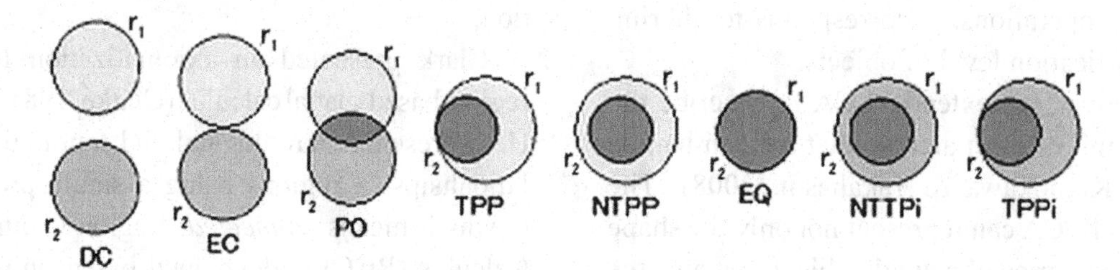


tionships are also expressed in this form. They also proposed a model that incorporates the concept involving orientations of lines (Egenhofer & Franzosa, 1995). Other studies have extended these models to handle regions with holes (Egenhofer, et al., 1994), splitting ratios (Nedas, et al., 2007), and so on. In these models, overlapping of primitive objects is allowed. Since there are many variations of overlapping patterns, different data structure is required in addition to 9-intersection to distinguish these patterns in these extended models.

In general, the abstracted representation should match human cognition and have enough power to express a practical problem in a QSR framework. Considering the example of the field and tree shown in Section 1, several situations can occur in which the relative positional relationships of the field and tree make and the number of tarpaulins differs depending on the case (Figure 2). In all cases, RCC regards the relation of a field region and a tree region as *overlapping*. This problem cannot be solved unless the information on the overlap/connection patterns of areas is given. In GIS or image processing applications, such discrimination of the connection patterns of regions is essential in many cases. On the other hand, if the abstraction is refined, many predicates and axioms are required to distinguish figures at the detail level if predicates are used in representation. Consequently, the system is not feasible and difficult to implement. Systems that involve a hierarchical treatment of abstraction have been proposed, but their implementation has not been fully discussed (Timpf, 1999).

PLCA can distinguish each pattern in Figure 2. It is based on simple objects and all the objects are handled in a unified manner. Symbolic representation enables compact information at a level suitable for the user's purpose and allows rapid processing. The completeness of the system is not a concern, since PLCA is not based on axiomatic systems. Its simple, clear data structure makes the system feasible and easy to implement. Moreover, if we add attributes such as size, shape or direction, or semantical properties (e.g. what an object stands for) to each object in PLCA, we can perform more fruitful reasoning.

The object-oriented concept of PLCA is close to a representation *doubly-connected edge list* used in computational geometry (de Berg, et al., 1997). In computational geometry, the expression of an

*Figure 2. Relationships between regions*

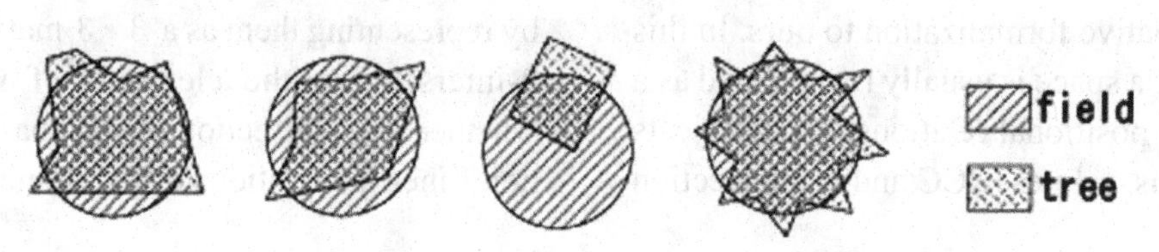

object is generally based on its precise position, while our purpose is a qualitative treatment of figures. In PLCA, the expression without coordinates and the operations on such an expression are both well-defined.

A major difference between PLCA and the other QSR systems is in representing the relationships of the objects. In the other approaches, the entire figure is represented in the form of a set of binary relations. If the figure data contain *n* objects, we have to assert ${}_nC_2$ relations, to avoid nondeterminacy. In contrast, with PLCA, the entire figure is represented in a form in which all of the objects are related. Another big difference is the intersection of primitive objects. In most of QSR systems, regions may share a part in common while we do not allow any pair of areas to cross, and consider a space to be covered with disjoint areas. This realizes the operations as well as a representation to distinguish connection patterns in a simple and unified manner. This is also suitbable for the treatment of a real problem on shapes. For example, to represent borders of countries, it is necessary to express not only the shape of each single border, but also the pattern of connections between borders. As the entire figure is treated as a partitioned regions in PLCA, shapes of a line viewed from both regions have to be handled, while only a single object is handled in the other QSR systems. PLCA can be considered to be upper compatible with the existing QSR frameworks.

Compared with the number of representation, fewer studies have been done on reasoning in QSR. The main idea of reasoning in most formalizations in which spatial relations are represented in the form of binary relations is a usage of composition table. It is a set of inference rules: for spatial entities *x*,*y*, and *z*, from binary relation between *x* and *y*, and that between *y* and *z*, derive that between *x* and *z*. In most cases, it is not determined uniquely. It is called a consistency problem that for a given set of binary relations on multiple regions, checking whether all the regions are realizable on some space satisfying the given relations. It is considered to be a Constraint Satisfaction Problem, which is generally NP-complete but tractable for some classes. A path-consistency method is proposed as an efficient algorithm to check consistency (Allen, 1983). Complexity and tractable set for various QSR formalizations are studied (Balbiani, et al., 1999; Liu, et al., 2009; Renz & Nebel, 1999, 2001; Renz, 2007). On the other hand, since relations between regions are not represented in the form of binary relations in PLCA, another method for determining the realizability for a given expression is required. We can check the realizability by counting the numbers of the objects contained in the expression based on well-known Euler's formula. Since it is not algorithmic but algebraiic, the computational complexity is lower.

## 3. PLCA EXPRESSION

### 3.1. Definition of Classes

PLCA has four basic classes of objects: *points*(*P*), *lines*(*L*), *circuits*(*C*), and *areas*(*A*).

*Point* is defined as a primitive class.

*Line* is defined as a class that satisfies the following condition: for an arbitrary instance *l* of *Line*, *l.points* is a pair $[p_1,p_2]$ where $p_1, p_2 \in Point$ A line has an inherent orientation. When $l=[p_1,p_2]$, $l^+$ and $l^-$ mean $[p_1,p_2]$ and $[p_2,p_1]$, respectively. $l^*$ denotes either $l^+$ or $l^-$, and $l^{*re}$ denotes the line with the inverse orientation of that of *line**. Intuitively, a line is the edge connecting two (not always different) points. No two lines are allowed to cross. We can distinguish (a) and (b) in Figure 3, by considering the orientation of the line. In Figure 4(a), the arrows denote the orientation of the lines. All of the lines $l_1$.*points*, $l_2$.*points* and $l_3$.*points* are defined to be $[p_1,p_2]$, but they are distinguished by the circuits to which they belong.

*Circuit* is defined as a class that satisfies the following condition: for an arbitrary instance *c*

*Figure 3. The distinct figures*

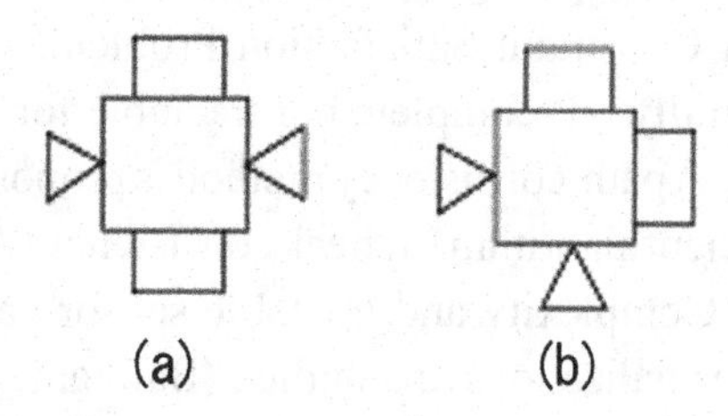


of *Circuit*, *c.lines* is a sequence $[l_0^*,\ldots,l_n^*]$ where $l_0,\ldots,l_n \in Line(n \geq 0)$, $l_i.points = [p_i, p_{i+1}](0 \leq i \leq n)$ and $p_{n+1} = p_0$. $[l_0^*,\ldots,l_n^*]$ and $[l_j^*,\ldots,l_n^*,l_0^*,\ldots,l_{j-1}^*]$ denote the same circuit for any $j$ $(0 \leq j \leq n)$. In Figure 4(b), we have three circuits: $c_1.lines = \{l_1^-, l_2^+\}$, $c_2.lines = \{l_2^-, l_3^+\}$, $c_3.lines = \{l_3^-, l_1^+\}$. For $c_1, c_2 \in Circuit$, we introduce two new predicates *lc* and *pc* to denote that two circuits share line(s) and point(s), respectively. $lc(c_1, c_2)$ is *true* iff there exists $l \in Line$ such that $(l^+ \in c_1.lines) \wedge (l^- \in c_2.lines)$. $pc(c_1, c_2)$ is *true* iff there exists $p \in Point$ such that $(p \in l_1.points) \wedge (p \in l_2.points) \wedge (l_1^* \in c_1.lines) \wedge (l_2^* \in c_2.lines)$. Intuitively, a circuit is the boundary between an area and its adjacent areas viewed from the side of that area. We say that *p is on c* if there exists *l* such that $p \in l.points \wedge l^* \in c.lines$.

*Area* is defined as a class that satisfies the following condition: for an arbitrary instance *a* of *Area*, *a.circuits* is a set $\{c_0,\ldots,c_n\}$ where $c_0,\ldots,c_n \in Circuit(n \geq 0)$, and

$$\forall c_i, c_j \in a.circuits; (i \neq j) \rightarrow (\neg pc(c_i, c_j) \wedge \neg lc(c_i, c_j)).$$

Intuitively, an area is a connected region which consists of exactly one piece. No two areas are allowed to cross. The final condition means that any pair of circuits that belong to the same area cannot share a point or a line.

The *PLCA expression e* is defined as a five tuple $e = \langle P, L, C, A, outermost\rangle$ where *P, L, C* and *A* are a set of points, lines, circuits and areas, respectively, and $outermost \in C$. An element of $P \cup L \cup C \cup A$ is called *a component of e*.

We assume that there exists a circuit in the outermost side of the figure that is called *outermost*. It means that the target figure is drawn in a finite space, and the space can be divided into a number of areas which do not overlap with each other.

In Figure 5, (a) shows an example of a target figure, (b) and (c) show the names of objects, and Table 1 gives a PLCA expression.

### 3.2. Consistency

**Definition: (PLCA consistency)** *For PLCA expression $e = \langle P, L, C, A, outermost\rangle$, if the following three constraints are satisfied, then it is said to be consistent.*

1. ***constraint on P-L:*** *For any $p \in Point$ there exists at least one line l such that $p \in l.points$.*
2. ***constraint on L-C:*** *For any $l \in Line$, there exist exactly two distinct circuits $c_1, c_2$ such that $l^+ \in c_1.lines, l^- \in c_2.lines$.*

*Figure 4. Multiple lines with the same direction and the associated circuits*

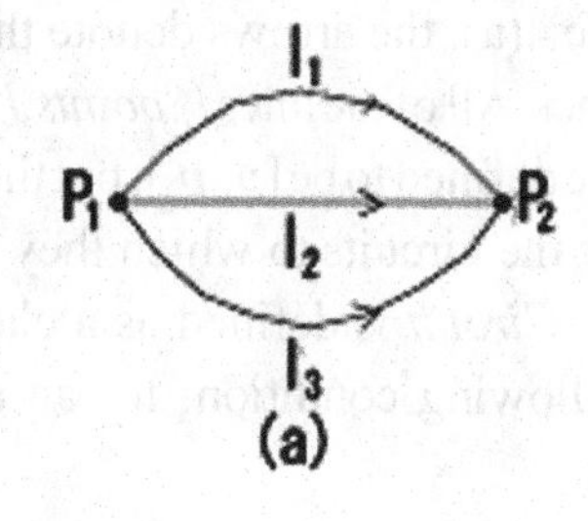


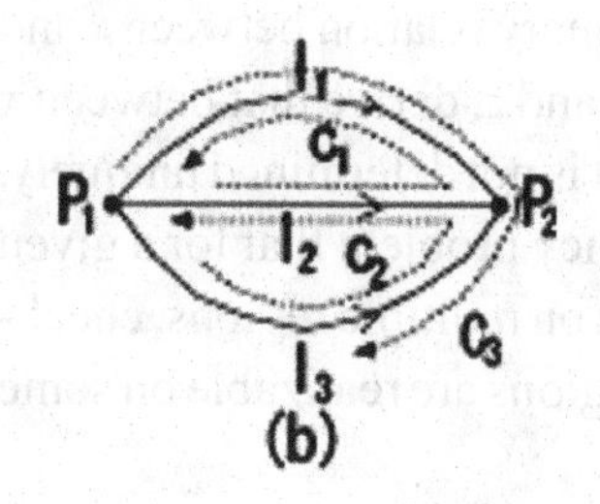

*Figure 5. Example of a target figure*

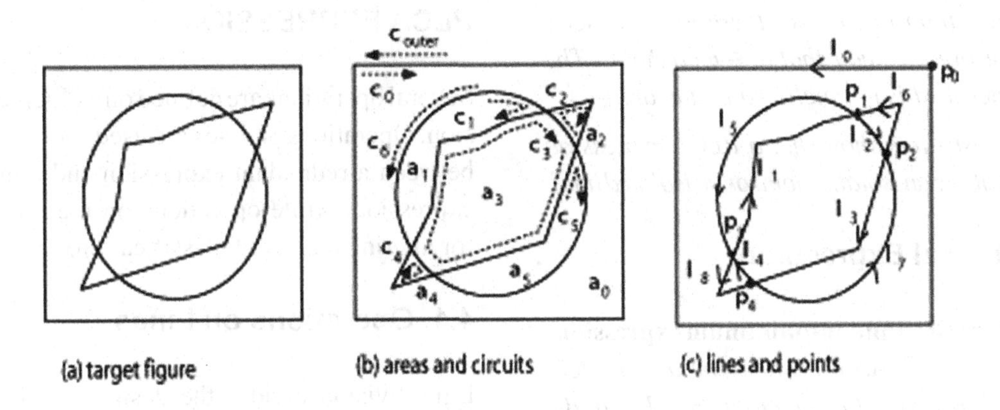


*Table 1. A PLCA expression corresponding to Figure 5*

| | |
|---|---|
| $e.points = \{p_0, p_1, p_2, p_3, p_4\}$ | $c_{outer}.lines = [l_0^+]$ |
| $e.lines = \{l_0, l_1, l_2, l_3, l_4, l_5, l_6, l_7, l_8\}$ | $c_0.lines = [l_0^-]$ |
| $e.circuits = \{c_{outer}, c_0, c_1, c_2, c_3, c_4, c_5, c_6\}$ | $c_1.lines = [l_1^-, l_5^-]$ |
| $e.areas = \{a_0, a_1, a_2, a_3, a_4, a_5\}$ | $c_2.lines = [l_2^-, l_6^-]$ |
| $e.outermost = c_{outer}$ | $c_3.lines = [l_1^+, l_2^+, l_3^+, l_4^+]$ |
| $l_0.points = [p_0, p_0]$ | $c_4.lines = [l_4^-, l_8^-]$ |
| $l_1.points = [p_4, p_1]$ | $c_5.lines = [l_3^-, l_7^-]$ |
| $l_2.points = [p_1, p_2]$ | $c_6.lines = [l_5^+, l_8^+, l_7^+, l_6^+]$ |
| $l_3.points = [p_2, p_3]$ | $a_0.circuits = \{c_6, c_0\}$ |
| $l_4.points = [p_3, p_4]$ | $a_1.circuits = \{c_1\}$ |
| $l_5.points = [p_1, p_4]$ | $a_2.circuits = \{c_2\}$ |
| $l_6.points = [p_2, p_1]$ | $a_3.circuits = \{c_3\}$ |
| $l_7.points = [p_3, p_2]$ | $a_4.circuits = \{c_4\}$ |
| $l_8.points = [p_4, p_3]$ | $a_5.circuits = \{c_5\}$ |

3. ***constraint on C-A:*** *For any* $c \in Circuit$ *other than outermost, there exists exactly one area a such that* $c \in a.circuits$. *The outermost is not included in any area.*

*These constraints show that a PLCA expression does not allow an isolated point or an isolated line*[2].

### 3.3. Minimal Expression

**Definition: (Redundant/minimum expression)** *Let* $e = \langle P, L, C, A, outermost \rangle$ *be a consistent PLCA expression. For a point* $p \in P$, *if the number of lines such that* $p \in l.points$ *is two, then p is said to be a redundant point. If e contains a redundant point, it is said to be a redundant expression; otherwise, it is said to be the minimum expression.*

### 3.4. PLCA Equivalence

For consistent PLCA expressions $e_1 = \langle P_1, L_1, C_1, A_1, outermost_1 \rangle$ and $e_2 = \langle P_2, L_2, C_2, A_2, outermost_2 \rangle$, if there exists a bijective mapping *f* from $e_1$ to $e_2$, that satisfies the following conditions, then $e_1$ and $e_2$ are said to be *PLCA-equivalent*.

For $\forall p \in P_1$, $f(p) \in P_2$

For $\forall l \in L_1$, $f(l) \in L_2$

For $\forall c \in C_1$, $f(c) \in C_2$

For $\forall a \in A_1$, $f(a) \in A_2$

For $\forall l \in L_1$, $f(l.points) = f(l).points$

For $\forall c \in C_1$, $f(c.lines) = f(c).lines$

For $\forall a \in A_1$, $f(a.circuits) = f(a).circuits$

## 4. OPERATIONS ON PLCA EXPRESSION

Several operations are defined on a PLCA expression. Operations on lines are used for conversion between a redundant expression and a minimal expression, while operations on areas are used for altering a level of classification.

### 4.1. Operations on Lines

Line division divides the designated line. It is defined as follows:

1. Select a line $l.points = [p_1, p_2]$ to be divided.
2. Assume that $c_1.lines = \{l_0^*, \ldots, l_{i-1}^*, l^+, l_i^*, \ldots, l_n^*\}$ and $c_2.lines = \{m_0^*, \ldots, m_{j-1}^*, l^-, m_j^*, \ldots, m_k^*\}$.
3. Set $l_1'.points = [p_1, p]$ and $l_2'.points = [p, p_2]$.
4. Set $L = L - \{l\} \cup \{l_1', l_2'\}$ and set $P = P \cup \{p\}$.
5. Replace $c_1.lines$ and $c_2.lines$ by $\{l_0^*, \ldots, l_{i-1}^*, l_1'^+, l_2'^+, l_i^*, \ldots, l_n^*\}$ and $\{m_0^*, \ldots, m_{j-1}^*, l_2'^-, l_1'^- m_j^*, \ldots, m_k^*\}$, respectively.

Line combination combines two adjacent lines that share a redundant point. The operation is the opposite of line division.

1. Select two lines $\{l_1', l_2'\}$ where $l_1'.points.= [p_1, p]$ and $l_2'.points = [p, p_2]$.
2. Assume that $c_1.lines = \{l_0^*, \ldots, l_{i-1}^*, l_1'^+, l_2'^+, l_i^*, \ldots, l_n^*\}$ and $c_2.lines = \{m_0^*, \ldots, m_{j-1}^*, l_2'^-, l_1'^-, m_j^*, \ldots, m_k^*\}$.

3. Set $l.points = [p_1, p_2]$.
4. Set $L = L - \{l_1', l_2'\} \cup \{l\}$ and set $P = P - \{p\}$.
5. Replace $c_1.lines$ and $c_2.lines$ by $\{l_0^*, \ldots, l_{i-1}^*, l^+, l_i^*, \ldots, l_n^*\}$ and $\{m_0^*, \ldots, m_{j-1}^*, l^-, m_j^*, \ldots, m_k^*\}$, respectively.

A redundant expression can be converted to the minimum expression by line division, and the minimum expression can be converted to a redundant one by line combination.

## 4.2. Operation on Areas

We define two operations *area integration* and *area division* on a consistent PLCA expression. Area integration corresponds to the deletion of an area, and area division corresponds to the addition of an area. When an area is added/deleted, the other objects that are attached to that area are modified simultaneously.

The action of area integration/division on a figure is realized as follows:

1. Extract all the relevant objects $O_1, \ldots, O_n$.
2. Ensure that $O_1, \ldots, O_n$ satisfy the specific condition.
3. Perform the operation on the PLCA expression.

The extracted objects are the arguments of the operations on the PLCA expression, and they are used to avoid nondeterminacy. The particular condition is required for preserving consistency. In this section, we describe the outline of the operations on a PLCA expression.

### 4.2.1. Area Integration

The operation *integrateAreas* is defined as follows.

*Figure 6. Area integration*

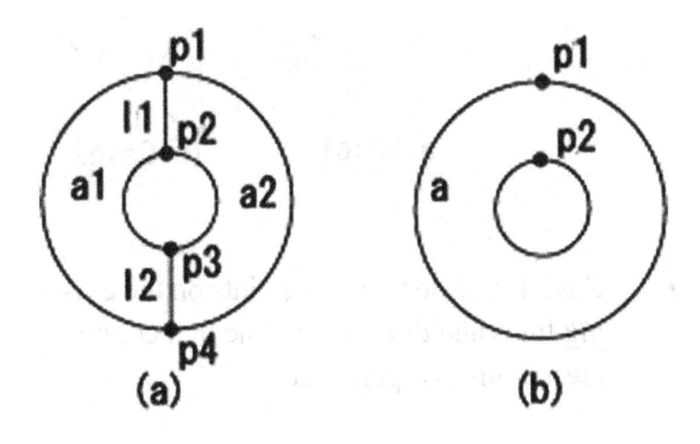


1. Choose two different areas $a_1$ and $a_2$ that share more than one line.
2. Delete all such shared lines, delete $a_1$ and $a_2$, and create a new area $a$ (In addition, modify the other relevant objects).

For example, if *integrateAreas* is performed on $a_1$ and $a_2$ in Figure 6(a), then we obtain Figure 6(b). In this operation, lines $l_1$ and $l_2$ shared by $a_1$ and $a_2$ are removed, and points $p_3$ and $p_4$ are also removed.

### 4.2.2. Area Division

The operation *divideArea* is more complicated than *integrateAreas*, since several conditions are required and many variations exist.

Since this operation adds lines to divide an area, we designate the position of these lines. There are four cases:

- Case 1: Draw a new line that does not share points or lines with the existing lines (Figure 7(a)).
- Case 2: Draw a new line that connects the existing points (Figure 7(b)).
- Case 3: Create a new point on the existing line and draw a new line that connects this point and an existing point (Figure 7(c)).

*Figure 7. Area division*

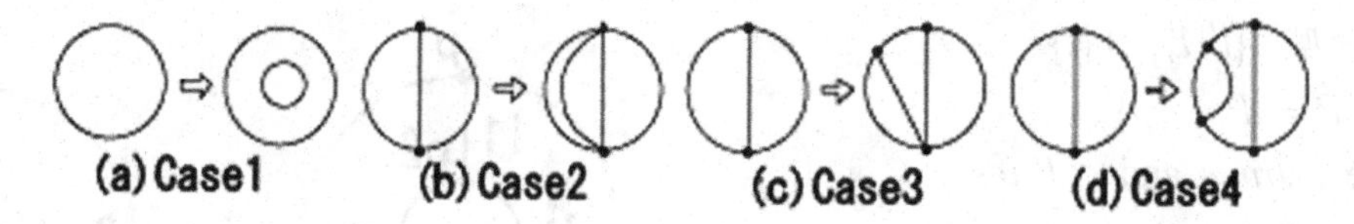


- Case 4: Create two new points on the existing lines and draw a new line that connects these points (Figure 7(d)).

In cases 2, 3, and 4, we cut the existing circuit and change its connection to the new line.

Moreover, even if the position of a line is determined, nondeterminacy occurs in drawing. Assume that an area $a$ is divided into $a_1$ and $a_2$. For example, in Figure 8, both (b) and (c) are obtained from (a) by *divideArea* operation with the same cutting points. They are not PLCA-equivalent, since $a_1$ and $b$ are line-connected in (b), while they are not in (c). To avoid this nondeterminacy, we have to designate that each area to which $a$ is connected be connected to either $a_1$ or $a_2$ after the division.

We show an outline of the algorithm below.

1. Choose an area $a$. Suppose that $a$ is divided into $a_1$ and $a_2$.
2. Create a new circuit, or choose a set of circuits $\{c_1,\ldots,c_k\}$ and determine the $k$ pairs of cutting points (the elements of a pair may be the same) $\langle p_{1a}, p_{1b}\rangle \ldots \langle p_{ka}, p_{kb}\rangle$ for $k$ cutting paths, respectively, in these circuits.
3. If the cutting point does not cut any existing line (i.e. the cutting point is the end of the line), then go to the next step. If the cutting point cuts an existing line, then create a new point that corresponds to the cutting point of the line, then go to the next step.
4. Determine the cutting path as follows: let $b_1,\ldots,b_n$ be areas to which $a$ is connected; set $BS_1, BS_2 \subset \{b_1,\ldots,b_n\}$ to the set of areas to which $a_1$ and $a_2$ are connected, respectively.
5. Create new lines so that they connect $p_{ib}$ and $p_{(i+1)a}$ ($i = 1,\ldots,k-1$), and a new line that connects $p_{(k+1)b}$ and $p_{1a}$, respectively. (In addition, modify all the relevant objects.)

A cutting point is given as a line if an existing line is cut, or as an array of two lines if a joint of two lines is cut. A cutting path is given as a set of the circuits of the areas to which the target area is connected.

Note that multiple lines may be created at one operation (from Figure 9(a) to (b)). If only one line is created (from Figure 9(a) to (c)), the PLCA expression for this figure is not consistent, since it violates the constraint on L-C.

*Figure 8. Nondeterminacy in area division*

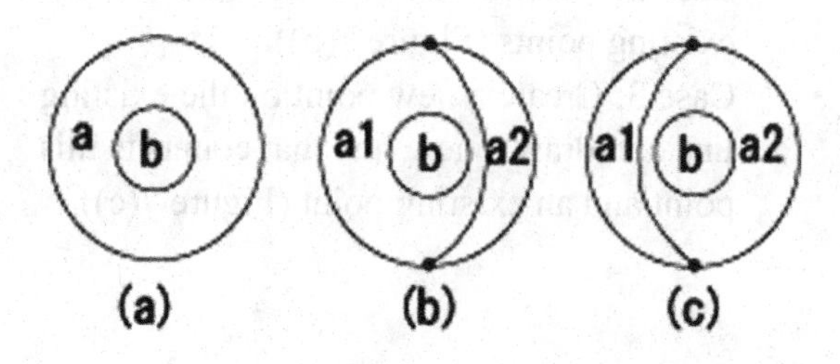


*Figure 9. A consistent PLCA and an inconsistent PLCA*

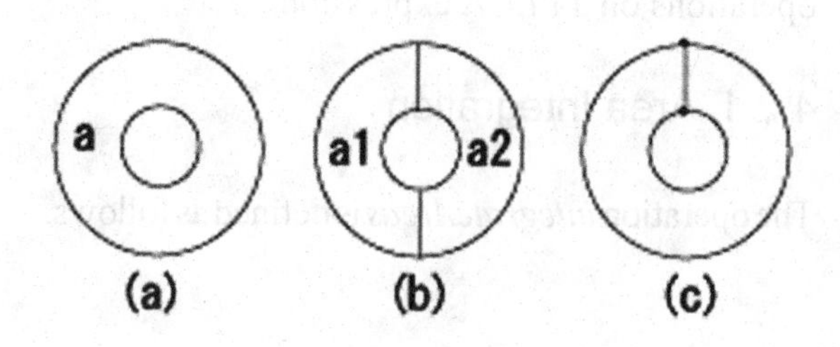

*Figure 10. Line shrink*

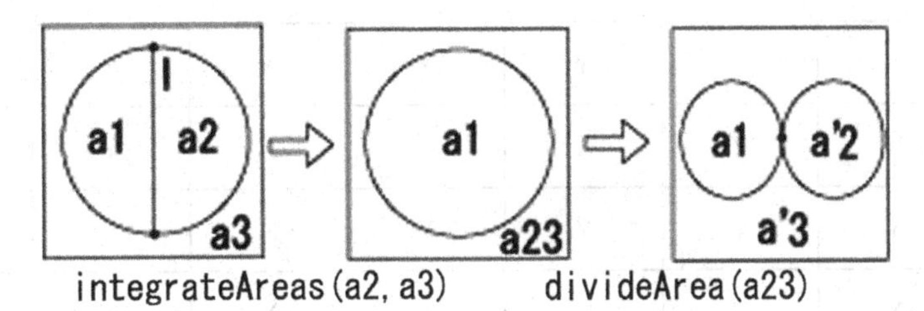


### 4.3. Combining Operations

An operation corresponding to another action on a figure can also be defined as a sequence of the above two operations. For example, shrinking a line *l* is defined as $\{integrateAreas(a2, a3), divideArea(a23)\}$ (Figure 10)[3].

## 5. REASONING ON ATTRIBUTED PLCA

### 5.1. Attributed PLCA

In most applications such as GIS, figure or image data include not only spatial information, such as shape, position and size, but also semantic information, such as what the object represents or which property holds on the area. Since PLCA itself provides only spatial information, we add regional attributes to each object so that semantic information can also be represented. Semantic spatial reasoning can be executed on an attributed PLCA, such as identifying the relative positional relationships between a region with some attribute and a region with another attribute, or determining whether multiple areas with the same attribute should be located to form a connected portion.

We define a *region* as a nonempty set of areas that have the same attribute. If an area belongs to some region, then all the circuits, lines and points that constitute that area also belong to the region. Note that a region may consist of multiple pieces.

Let *Region* be a class of region and $RA(r), RC(r), RL(r)$, and $RP(r)$ denote the set of areas, circuits, lines and points that belong to region $r \in Region$, respectively. In general, for a consistent PLCA expression *e*, the attributed PLCA expression can be constructed as follows. For each *r*, first, we assign a subset of *e.areas* to *r*, and then, we define $RA(r), RC(r), RL(r)$ and $RP(r)$.

$$RA(r) = \{a \mid a \in r.areas\}$$
$$RC(r) = \{c \mid c \in a.circuits \land a \in r.areas\}$$
$$RL(r) = \{l \mid l^* \in c.lines \land c \in a.circuits \land a \in r.areas\}$$
$$RP(r) = \left\{p \,\middle|\, \begin{array}{l} p \in l.points \land l^* \in c.lines \\ \land c \in a.circuits \land a \in r.areas \end{array}\right\}$$

The PLCA expression in which each object is attached to an attribute in this way is called an *attributed PLCA expression*.

*Region* in an attributed PLCA is the same concept as the 'region' in RCC. Table 2 shows the relationship between the attributed PLCA and RCC. In this table, Y/N mean that there exists an element in the corresponding part. Although the number of all the possible combination is $2^4$, the case that does not appear in this table is an inconsistent PLCA expression. This table shows that there exists a mapping from PLCA to RCC, and that PLCA provides mereological reasoning which is performed in RCC.

*Table 2. Attributed PLCA and RCC*

| $RA(r_1) \cup RA(r_2)$ | N | N | Y | Y | Y | Y | Y | Y |
|---|---|---|---|---|---|---|---|---|
| $RP(r_1) \cup RP(r_2)$ | N | Y | N | Y | N | Y | Y | Y |
| $RA(r_1) \setminus RA(r_2)$ | Y | Y | Y | Y | N | N | Y | N |
| $RA(r_2) \setminus RA(r_1)$ | Y | Y | N | N | Y | Y | Y | N |
| **RCC-8 relation** | DC | EC | NTPP | TPP | NTPPi | TPPi | PO | EQ |

## 5.2. Database Queries

If an attributed PLCA expression is a data form in the spatial database, the database can provide topological information about the regions. We define several database queries.

When two regions are connected, we can decide how these are connected:

$$isPointConnected(r_1, r_2) := (RP(r_1) \cap RP(r_2) \neq \phi) \wedge (RL(r_1) \cap RL(r_2) = \phi) \wedge (RA(r_1) \cap RA(r_2) = \phi)$$

$$isLineConnected(r_1, r_2) := (RL(r_1) \cap RL(r_2) \neq \phi) \wedge (RA(r_1) \cap RA(r_2) = \phi)$$

We can obtain the segments that are point-connected and line-connected in the boundaries of two regions:

$$getPointConnects(r_1, r_2) := \left\{ d \,\middle|\, \begin{array}{l} d \in RP(r_1) \cap RP(r_2) \wedge \\ \neg \exists l (d \in l.points \wedge l \in RL(r_1) \cap RL(r_2)) \end{array} \right\}$$

$$getLineConnects(r_1, r_2) := \{ l \,|\, l \in RL(r_1) \cap RL(r_2) \}$$

Furthermore, we can determine whether a region consists of one piece, and obtain the number of connected parts if it comprises several disconnected pieces:

$$isOnePiece(r) := \forall a_i \exists a_j \in RA(r); lc(a_i, a_j) \vee pc(a_i, a_j)$$

$$\begin{array}{l} getNumberOfParts(r) := k \text{ where} \\ \quad [\, r = \cup_i^k r_i \,] \wedge [\, \forall r_i;\, isOnePiece(r_i) \,] \wedge \\ \quad [\, \forall r_i \forall r_j; \neg isPointConnected(r_i, r_j) \wedge \neg isLineConnected(r_i, r_j) \,] \end{array}$$

Reconsider the Field and Tree problem shown in Section 1. We add the attributes of field($F$) and tree($T$) to each area. Then, the regions with the attribute field and that with tree are obtained as follows.

$$r_F.areas = \{a_1, a_3, a_5\}$$
$$r_T.areas = \{a_2, a_3, a_4\}$$

The part of the field that is not shaded by the tree is $r_{F \wedge \neg T}.areas = \{a_1, a_5\}$. On querying the database, we find that $isOnePiece(r_{F \wedge \neg T})$ does not hold and that

$$getNumberOfParts(r_{F \wedge \neg T}) = 2,$$

which indicates that two tarpaulins are necessary in this case.

*Figure 11. Making a figure viewed from the higher position*

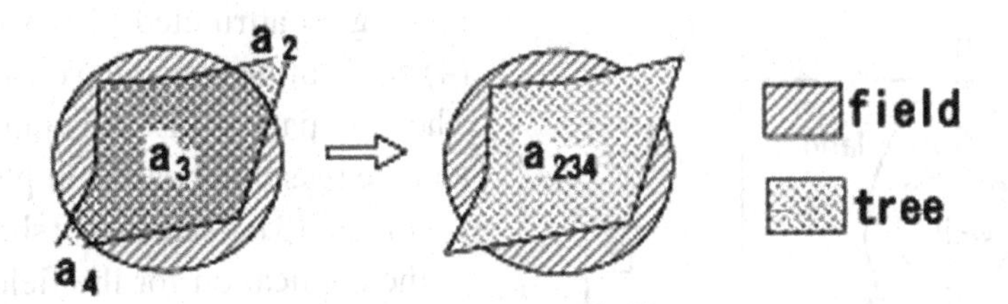


## 5.3. Applications

The operations of area integration/division on an attributed PLCA correspond to altering the classification level of objects. We classify the higher-level expression with the focal attributes by integrating the adjacent areas with the same attribute. Conversely, when an area with some attribute should be divided into two parts with different new attributes, then we divide the area to obtain the expression that represents the lower-level classification. We present some applications using these operations.

### 5.3.1. Figures from a Specific Viewpoint

Reconsider the example of the field and tree shown in Section 1.

Suppose that we draw the picture of Figure 2 viewed from the higher position. Then, the tree areas are drawn in the foreground, which might hide part of the field. This can be performed by repeatedly applying *integrateAreas* to areas $a_2, a_3, a_4$ (Figure 11). The modified part of the original PLCA expression is shown in Table 3.

### 5.3.2. Design Support

If you construct a fence to divide a piece of land, an important issue might arise in deciding which part of the land includes the well. The figures

*Table 3. Modified part of the original PLCA expression*

| **Deleted:** | **Added:** |
|---|---|
| $l_2.points = [p_1, p_2]$ | $c_{234}.lines = [l_6^+, l_1^-, l_8^+, l_3^-]$ |
| $l_3.points = [p_2, p_3]$ | $a_{234}.circuits = \{c_{234}\}$ |
| $l_4.points = [p_3, p_4]$ | |
| $c_2.lines = [l_2^-, l_6^-]$ | **Changed:** |
| $c_3.lines = [l_1^+, l_2^+, l_3^+, l_4^+]$ | $e.lines = \{l_0^+, l_1^+, l_3^+, l_5^+, l_6^+, l_7^+, l_8^+\}$ |
| $c_4.lines = [l_4^-, l_8^-]$ | $e.circuits = \{c_{outer}, c_0, c_1, c_{234}, c_5, c_6\}$ |
| $a_2.circuits = \{c_2\}$ | $e.areas = \{a_0, a_1, a_{234}, a_5\}$ |
| $a_3.circuits = \{c_3\}$ | |
| $a_4.circuits = \{c_4\}$ | |

Figure 12. Land division

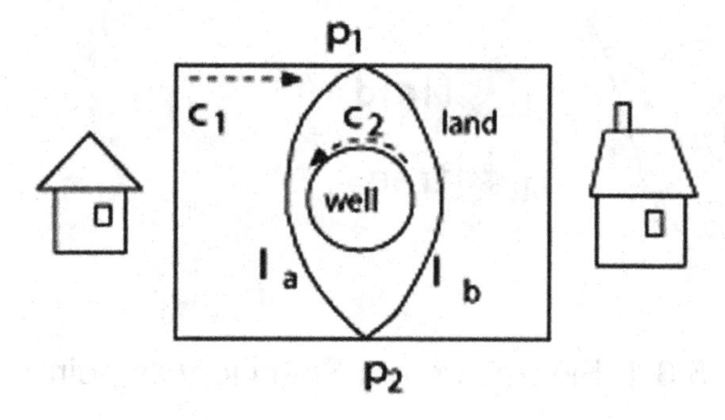


generated by the operation *divideArea* support such considerations (Figure 12). Choose *land*, $c_1$,$c_2$, and create cutting points $p_1$,$p_2$. If you designate *well* to be included in the area on the right, then line $l_a$ is drawn; while if it is to be included in the area on the left, then line $l_b$ is drawn.

## 5.4. Tool for Reasoning on PLCA Expression

We have developed a tool for reasoning on PLCA expression with a visual interface that supports: (1) generating a PLCA expression from a given figure, (2) updating the PLCA expression according to the operations performed on a figure, (3) making an attributed PLCA using a figure, and (4) performing reasoning on an attributed PLCA. The core part of PLCA is implemented in JAVA and the reasoning part is implemented in Prolog.

Figure 13 is a screenshot showing the reasoning in the application for the field and tree problem being performed on the prototype system. The user writes a query such as "how many parts does the region with the attribute *field* and without the attribute *tree* have?" or a declarative operation such as "integrate the areas with the attribute *tree*." Then the resulting figure and corresponding PLCA expression are obtained.

## 6. EMBEDDING PLCA IN A PLANE

For a given figure in a two-dimensional plane, there exists a PLCA expression, that is unique in its pattern of connections among regions. On the other hand, there are many figures for a PLCA expression, and it is difficult to generate a figure from a PLCA expression, since we have to supplement the missing part of the data. Moreover, it has not been clarified whether a figure can be

Figure 13. Screenshot of a reasoning with a tool

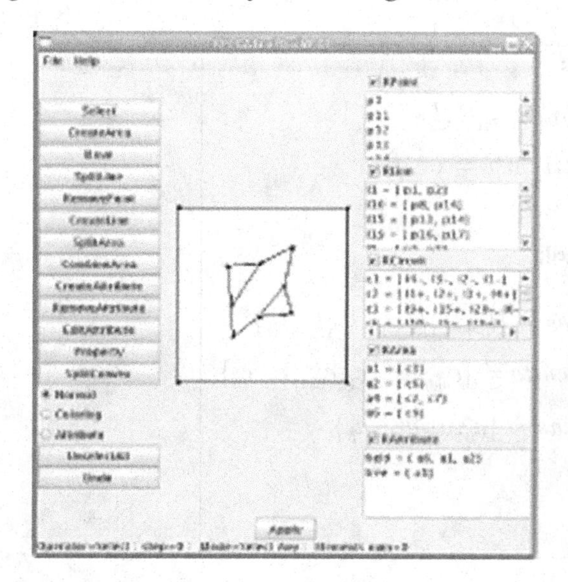

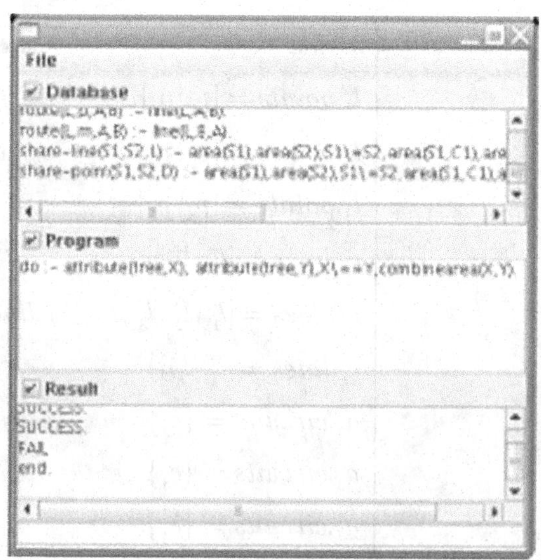

drawn in a two-dimensional plane. We investigate a condition in which a PLCA expression can be realized in a two-dimensional plane, and show an algorithm of drawing.

## 6.1. Concepts from Graph Theory

As a preparation, we introduce several concepts from graph theory.

*A (non-directed) graph* is defined to be $G = (V, E)$, where *V* is a set of vertices and *E* is a set of edges. An edge of *E* is defined as a pair of vertices of *V*. For graphs $G = (V, E)$ and $G' = (V', E')$, if $V' \subset V$ and $E' \subset E$, $G'$ is said to be *a subgraph* of *G*; if $V \cap V' = \phi$ and $E \cap E' = \phi$, it is said that *G* and $G'$ are *disjoint*. Here, when we consider more than one subgraph of *G*, we assume that they are disjoint. If there is no edge (*v*,*v*), and for any pair of different vertices, if there exists a unique edge that connects them, the graph is said to be *simple*. A graph that can be embedded in a plane so that no edges intersect is said to be *a planar graph*. If it is possible to move between any pair of vertices by moving along the edges of the graph, the graph is said to be *connected*; otherwise, it is said to be *disconnected*. A connected planar graph divides a plane into a number of regions, which are called *faces*. Note that faces include the outer infinitely large region. A sequence $(v_0, \dots, v_n)$ where $(v_i, v_{i+1})$ for each $i$ ($0 \le i \le n-1$) is an edge is said to be *a path*, and if $v_0 = v_n$, it is said to be *a cycle*. A cycle that is a border from the graph and the outer infinitely large region is said to be *an outer boundary cycle*.

For a connected planar graph, the following theorem holds.

**Theorem: (Euler's formula)** *Let G be a connected planar graph. Let* $V_G, E_G, F_G$ *be the numbers of the vertices, edges and faces of G. The following relation holds:* $V_G - E_G + F_G = 2$.

## 6.2. Mapping to Graph Expression

Let $e = \langle P, L, C, A, outermost \rangle$ be a consistent PLCA expression. We can define a non-directed graph $m(e) = (V, E)$ by relating *P* and *L* to *V* and *E*, respectively.

For $p \in P$, *m*(*p*) denotes the corresponding vertex, and for $l \in L$, *m*(*l*) denotes the corresponding edge. We extend *m* so that *c* is mapped to *m*(*c*). For each $l_i (i = 0, \dots, n), l_i^* \in c.lines$, if $m(l_i)$ is contained in a graph *G*, then we say that *m*(*c*) *is contained in G*.

## 6.3. PLCA Connectedness

We introduce the connectedness of the components of a PLCA expression.

**Definition: (D-pcon)** *Let* $e = \langle P, L, C, A, outermost \rangle$ *be a PLCA expression. For a pair of components of e, the predicate d-pcon is defined as follows.*

1. $d\text{-}pcon(p, l)$ *iff* $p \in l.points$.
2. $d\text{-}pcon(l, c)$ *iff* $l^* \in c.lines$.
3. $d\text{-}pcon(c, a)$ *iff* $c \in a.circuits$.

**Definition: (PLCA trail)** *A sequence* $(\alpha_0, \dots, \alpha_n)$ *where* $d\text{-}pcon(\alpha_i, \alpha_{i+1})$ *or* $d\text{-}pcon(\alpha_{i+1}, \alpha_i)$ *holds for each i* $(0 \le i \le n-1)$, *and* $\alpha_i \ne \alpha_j$ *for each* $i, j$ $(0 \le i < j \le n)$, *is said to be a PLCA trail from* $\alpha_0$ *to* $\alpha_n$.

**Definition: (Pcon)** *Let* $\alpha, \beta, \gamma$ *be components of a PLCA expression.*

1. *If* $d\text{-}pcon(\alpha, \beta)$, *then* $pcon(\alpha, \beta)$.
2. *If* $pcon(\alpha, \beta)$, *then* $pcon(\beta, \alpha)$.
3. *If* $pcon(\alpha, \beta)$ *and* $pcon(\beta, \gamma)$, *then* $pcon(\alpha, \gamma)$.

**Definition: (PLCA connected)** *A PLCA expression e is said to be PLCA connected iff* $pcon(\alpha, \beta)$ *holds for any pair of components of e,* $\alpha$ *and* $\beta$.

Intuitively, PLCA connectedness guarantees that all the components including the *outermost* are connected. That is, for any pair of components, there is a trail that can go from one component to the other by tracing components.

Let $e = \langle P, L, C, A, outermost \rangle$ be a consistent connected PLCA expression. For any pair of points $p_1, p_2 \in P$ $(p_1 \neq p_2)$, let $(\alpha_0, \ldots, \alpha_n)$ be a trail from $p_1$ to $p_2$. If $\alpha_1, \ldots, \alpha_{n-1}$ are not points, then this trail is one of the following three types. (Figure 14).

**[Trail Types between Points]**

[TType1] $(p_1, l, p_2)$

[TType2] $(p_1, l_0, c, l_1, c, l_2, \ldots, l_k, p_2)$

[TType3] $(p_1, l_1, c_0, a, c_1, a, c_2, \ldots, c_k, l_2, p_2)$

where $l, l_0, \ldots, l_k$ are lines, $l_i \neq l_j$ for each *i, j* $(0 \leq i < j \leq k)$, $c, c_0, \ldots, c_k$ are circuits, $c_i \neq c_j$ for each *i, j* $(0 \leq i < j \leq k)$, and *a* is an area.

Note that an area and a circuit do not appear in [TType1], and an area does not appear in [TType2]. If there exists a pair of points $p_1$ and $p_2$ such that the trail from $p_1$ to $p_2$ is [TType3], *m(e)* is disconnected.

## 6.4. Planar PLCA Expression

**Lemma:** *Let $e = \langle P, L, C, A, outermost \rangle$ be a consistent connected PLCA expression that satisfies $|a.circuits| = 1$ for any area $a \in A$, then m(e) is a connected graph.*

### Proof

For any pair of circuits $c_1$ and $c_2$ $(c_1 \neq c_2)$, there is no area *a* that satisfies $c_1, c_2 \in a.circuits$, since $|a.circuits| = 1$. That is, there is no area *a* that satisfies $d\text{-}pcon(c_1, a) \wedge d\text{-}pcon(c_2, a)$. Therefore, for any pair of $p_1$ and $p_2$ $(p_1 \neq p_2)$, trail type from $p_1$ to $p_2$ is either [TType1] or [TType2]. *m(e)* is a connected graph in both cases. ■

*Figure 14. A trail between points in PLCA*

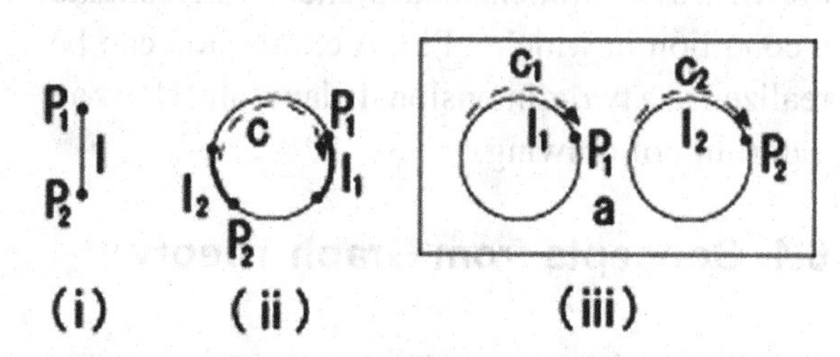


**Theorem:** *For a consistent connected PLCA expression $e = \langle P, L, C, A, outermost \rangle$, e can be realized in a two-dimensional plane iff $|P| - |L| - |C| + 2|A| = 0$ holds.*

### Proof

For a consistent connected PLCA expression *e*, if there exists an area *a* that satisfies $|a.circuits| \geq 2$, then we transform *e* by making lines between circuits so that any area contains only one circuit.

For an area *a* that satisfies $a.circuits = \{c_1, c_2\}$, let $p_1$ and $p_2$ be arbitrary points on $c_1$ and $c_2$, respectively. That is, for $c_1.lines = \{l_0^*, \ldots, l_n^*\}$, there exists $i (0 \leq i \leq n)$ such that $(p_1 \in l_{i-1}.points) \wedge (p_1 \in l_i.points)$, and for $c_2.lines = \{m_0^*, \ldots, m_k^*\}$, there exists $j (0 \leq j \leq k)$ such that $(p_2 \in l_{j-1}.points) \wedge (p_2 \in l_j.points)$.

Delete $c_1, c_2, a$ and add $l_1', l_2', c_1', c_2', a_1', a_2'$ that satisfy the following:

$$l_1'.points = [p_1, p_2]$$
$$l_2'.points = [p_2, p_1]$$
$$c_1'.lines = \{l_0^*, \ldots, l_{i-1}^*, l_1'^+, m_j^*, \ldots, m_k^*, m_0^*, \ldots, m_{j-1}^*, l_2'^+, l_i^*, \ldots, l_n^*\}$$
$$c_2'.lines = \{l_1'^-, l_2'^-\}$$
$$a_1'.circuits = \{c_1'\}$$
$$a_2'.circuits = \{c_2'\}$$

This operation is performed by an operation of area division by creating two lines between two existing points. The consistency is preserved by this operation. The number of lines is increased by 2, the number of areas is increased by 1, and that of the others is not changed in this operation.

If we repeat this operation for each area $a \in A$ such that $|a.circuits| \geq 2$, then we can obtain a consistent connected PLCA expression $e' = \langle P', L', C', A', outermost' \rangle$ that satisfies $|a'.circuits| = 1$ for any $a' \in A'$. Let $n$ be the repeated number of the operation. Then, $|P'| = |P|, |L'| = |L| + 2n, |C'| = |C|$ and $|A'| = |A| + n$.

$m(e')$ is a connected graph. Therefore, $|P'| - |L'| + |A'| = 1$ holds by Theorem 6., since $|A'|$ corresponds to the number of faces that does not include the outer infinitely large region. Therefore, $|P| - |L| - |A| = n + 1$ holds.

$n$ is equivalent to $\Sigma_{a \in A} |a.circuits|$, the number of the circuits excluding for *outermost*, since each circuit is contained in only one area. Therefore, $n = |C| - |A| - 1$. Hence, $|P| - |L| - |C| + 2|A| = 0$ holds.

On the other hand, if $|P| - |L| - |C| + 2|A| = 0$ holds, $e$ can be realized in a two-dimensional plane. It can be proved by induction on the structure of an expression. ■

Hereafter, for a PLCA expression $e = \langle P, L, C, A, outermost \rangle$, we denote the value of $|P| - |L| - |C| + 2|A|$ by $\varepsilon(e)$.

**Definition: (Planar PLCA expression)** *A consistent connected PLCA expression e that satisfies* $\varepsilon(e) = 0$ *is said to be planar.*

**Example: (Non-planar expression)** The following PLCA expression is consistent and PLCA connected, but not realizable in a two-dimensional plane (Figure 15). In this case, $\varepsilon(e) = -2$.

$e.points = \{p_0, p_1, p_2\}$
$e.lines = \{l_0, l_1, l_2\}$
$e.circuits = \{c_{outer}, c_0, c_1, c_2, c_3, c_4\}$
$e.areas = \{a_0, a_1\}$
$l_0.points = [p_0, p_0]$
$l_1.points = [p_1, p_1]$
$l_2.points = [p_2, p_2]$
$c_{outer}.lines = [l_0^+]$
$c_0.lines = [l_0^-]$
$c_1.lines = [l_1^+]$
$c_2.lines = [l_2^+]$
$c_3.lines = [l_1^-]$
$c_4.lines = [l_2^-]$
$a_0.circuits = \{c_0, c_3, c_4\}$
$a_1.circuits = \{c_1, c_2\}$

A consistent PLCA expression $e$ that satisfies $\varepsilon(e) = 0$ is not always PLCA connected.

**Example: (Non-connected expression)** The following PLCA expression is consistent and $\varepsilon(e) = 0$, but not PLCA connected. It can be divided into a plane part which consists of $p_0, l_0, c_{outer}, c_0, a_0$ and a floating part which consists of the other components. A component of the former is not *pcon* with that of the latter. (For example, $pcon(c_{outer}, c_1)$ does not hold.) This expression is not realizable in a two-dimensional plane.

$e.points = \{p_0, p_1\}$
$e.lines = \{l_0, l_1, l_2\}$
$e.circuits = \{c_{outer}, c_0, c_1, c_2, c_3\}$
$e.areas = \{a_0, a_1, a_2\}$
$l_0.points = [p_0, p_0]$
$l_1.points = [p_1, p_1]$
$l_2.points = [p_1, p_1]$
$c_{outer}.lines = \{l_0^+\}$

*Figure 15. PLCA expression unrealizable in a two-dimensional plane*

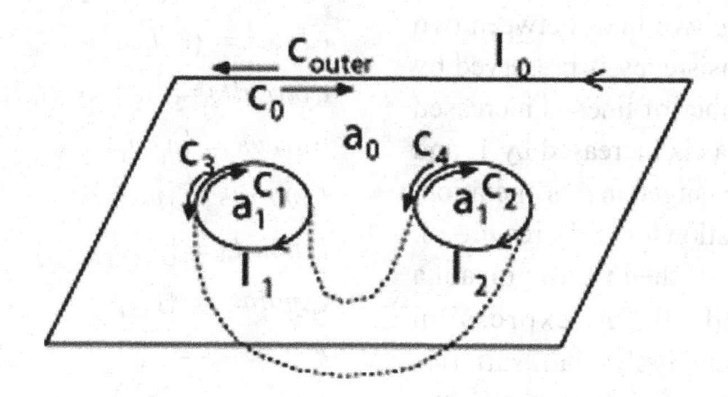


$c_0.lines = \{l_0^-\}$

$c_1.lines = \{l_1^+, l_2^+\}$

$c_2.lines = \{l_2^-\}$

$c_3.lines = \{l_1^-\}$

$a_0.circuits = \{c_0\}$

$a_1.circuits = \{c_1\}$

$a_2.circuits = \{c_2, c_3\}$

### 6.5. Orientation of a Circuit

Each circuit of a planar PLCA expression *e* has an orientation of *inner* or *outer*. If *m*(*e*) is a non-connected graph, then it can be decomposed into subgraphs. We determine the orientation of each circuit by considering the relations among these subgraphs, areas and circuits of *e*.

**[Algorithm: DCO (Determine Circuit's Orientation)]**

Let *e* be a consistent connected PLCA expression.

1. Set $c = outermost$.
2. Make a node $N_c$.
3. Set the orientation of *c* to be *outer*.
4. For a subgraph *g* such that $m(c) \in g$, make a node $N_g$ and draw an edge from $N_c$ to $N_g$.
5. For each $m(c') \in g$ such that $c' \neq c$, do the following:
   a. Set the orientation of $c'$ to be *inner*.
   b. Make a node $N_{c'}$ and draw an edge from $N_g$ to $N_{c'}$.
   c. For an area *a* such that $c' \in a.circuits$, make a node $N_a$ and draw an edge from $N_{c'}$ to $N_a$.
   d. If there is no circuit $c'' \in a.circuits$ such that $c'' \neq c'$, then terminate. Otherwise, for each $c''$, do the following:
      1. Make a node $N_{c''}$ and draw an edge from $N_a$ to $N_{c''}$.
      2. Set $c = c''$.
      3. Go to 3.

A diagram constructed in this way is called a *DCO diagram*. Each path in the diagram is a sequence of a pattern $N_{c_1} \rightarrow N_g \rightarrow N_{c_2} \rightarrow N_a$ where $c_1, c_2$ are circuits, *a* is an area of *e*, and *g* is a subgraph of *m*(*e*).

**Lemma:** *For a planar PLCA expression e, (1) the orientation of each circuit is decidable, (2) there exists the unique inner circuit in a.circuit for each area a, and (3) there exists an outer circuit c such that* $m(c) \in g$ *is an outer boundary cycle of g for each subgraph g.*

### Proof

Assume that the DCO algorithm does not terminate. There exists $c_1$,$c_2$ ($c_1 \neq c_2$) and $a$ such that both patterns $N_{c_1} \to N_a \to N_{c_2}$ and $N_{c_2} \to N_a \to N_{c_1}$ appear in the DCO diagram. It follows that there are trails

$(outermost,\ldots,c_1,a,c_2)$

and

$(outermost,\ldots,c_2,a,c_1)$,

since *e* is a planar PLCA expression. This means that $c_1$ is closer to the *outermost* than *a* and also that *a* is closer to the *outermost* than $c_1$, which is a contradiction. Therefore, the DCO algorithm terminates. Thus, each *a,c* of *e* and *g* of *m*(*e*) appears at most once in the DCO diagram. On the other hand, each appears at least once from the planarity of the PLCA expression. Therefore, they appear exactly once in the DCO diagram. For each pattern $N_{c_1} \to N_g \to N_{c_2} \to N_a$, $c_1$ and $c_2$ are determined as *outer* and *inner*, respectively. Therefore, the orientation of each circuit is decidable. There exists the unique *inner* circuit in *a.circuit* for each area *a*, since there exists only one $N_a$ such that $N_{c_2} \to N_a$. $m(c_1)$ in *g* is an outer boundary cycle of *g*, since there exists only one $N_g$ such that $N_{c_1} \to N_g$. ■

## 6.6. Drawing Algorithm

### 6.6.1 Outline

**Definition: (Module)** *Let e be a planar PLCA expression and* $\alpha$ *be either a point, a line or a circuit of e. If* $m(e)$ *is decomposed into n disjoint connected subgraphs* $g_1,\ldots,g_n$, *then we say that e has n modules. If* $m(\alpha)$ *is contained in gi, then* $\alpha$ *is contained in the module corresponding to gi. For an area a of e, a is contained in the module that contains the inner circuit c in* $a.circuits$.

Note that each component of the PLCA is contained only in one module.

**Definition: (E-circle)** *A unit circle in which each module of the PLCA is embedded in the second step of the algorithm is called an e-circle.*

**Definition: (Bridge)** *An area a such that* $|\, a.circuit \,| \geq 2$ *holds is said to be a bridge.*

We describe the algorithm for drawing a figure for a planar PLCA expression in a two-dimensional plane.

1. Make a redundant PLCA expression of a given planar PLCA expression using the line division operation, so that the corresponding graph expression of the result is a simple graph.
2. Decompose the graph into disjoint connected subgraphs, and determine the coordinates of nodes and edges in a unit circle for each subgraph independently. We utilize an existing graph-drawing algorithm using straight lines in this step.
3. Determine the location and the size of these subgraphs using the information on circuits and areas in the PLCA expression.
4. Substitute a curve for the pair of edges which are connected to the point added in the first step.

The final step, which avoids redundancy, can be omitted.

The third step of the algorithm is the most important since the location and the size of e-circles in a bridge are determined.

For each bridge $a \in A$, do the following: let $a.circuits = \{c_0, c_1, \ldots, c_n\}$, where the orientation of $c_0$ is *inner* and those of $c_1,\ldots,c_n$ are *outer*. Let $g_1,\ldots,g_n$ be the subgraphs whose e-circles are $ec_1,\ldots,ec_n$, respectively. For each $ec_i$

*Figure 16. Realization of a bridge*

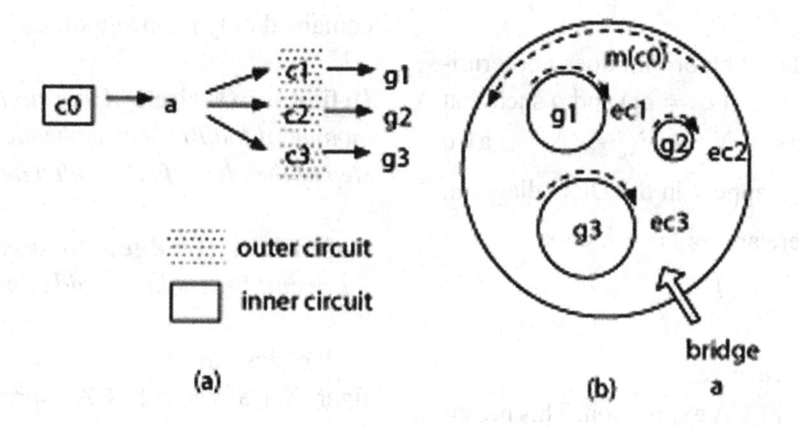


($i = 1, \ldots, n$), expand or reduce it and draw it in an appropriate location on the inner part of $m(c_0)$

Figure 16(a) shows a part of the DCO diagram that includes bridge *a*. Figure 16(b) is a realization of this part. A bridge is actually drawn as a polygon.

### 6.6.2. Details

**[Algorithm: DF(drawing a figure)]**
Let $e = \langle P, L, C, A, outermost \rangle$ be a planar PLCA expression.

**[STEP1]**

**[STEP1.1]** Elimination of edges that circulate the node itself.

1. Set $Lines = L, NewL = \{\}$.
2. If $Lines = \{\}$, terminate. Otherwise, extract an arbitrary $l \in Lines$ and set $Lines = Lines - \{l\}$.
3. If $l.points = [p, p]$, then divide $l$ to create new lines $l_1, l_2$ and set $NewL = NewL \cup \{l_1, l_2\}$. At the same time, update the other components of *e* according to the line division operation. Otherwise, set $NewL = NewL \cup \{l\}$.
4. Go to 2.

**[STEP1.2]** Elimination of multiple edges that connect the same pair of nodes, so that only one edge remains.

1. Set $L' = \{\}$.
2. If $NewL = \{\}$, terminate. Otherwise, extract an arbitrary $l \in NewL$ and set $NewL = NewL - \{l\}$.
3. If $l.points = [p_1, p_2]$ where $p_1 \neq p_2$ and there exists $l' = [p_1, p_2]$ or $l' = [p_2, p_1]$ such that $l' \in NewL$, do the following:
   a. Set $P = P \cup \{p'\}$.
   b. Set $L' = L' \cup \{l_1, l_2\}$ where $l_1, l_2$ are new lines.
   c. Set $l_1.points = [p_1, p'], l_2.points = [p', p_2]$.

   Otherwise, set $L' = L' \cup \{l\}$.
4. Go to 2.

As the result, $e' = \langle P', L', C', A, outermost \rangle$ is obtained where $P', C'$ are the updated set of $P, C$ by the line division operation, respectively.

**[STEP2]**
We utilize the existing graph drawing algorithm (e.g. (Ochiai 2004)) in this step.

**[STEP2.1]** Determine the orientation of circuits. For each circuit, determine the orientation using the DCO algorithm provided in the previous section.

**[STEP2.2]** Determine coordinates.
Let $m(e')$ be the graph corresponding to the PLCA expression obtained in STEP1.

1. Decompose $m(e')$ into the connected subgraphs that have no common elements.
2. For each connected subgraph, determine the coordinates that are used to draw a planar graph embedded in the unit circle of the center (0,0) by a straight line.

**[STEP3]**
We utilize the existing polygon triangulation algorithm (e.g.(Imai 2001)) in this step.
For each $a \in A$ where *a.circuits* contains more than one circuit, do the following:

1. Let $a.circuits = \{c_0, c_1, \ldots, c_n\}$, where the orientation of $c_0$ is *inner* and those of $c_1, \ldots, c_n$ are *outer*.
2. Decompose the polygon which has an edge $m(c_0)$ into triangles $t_1, \ldots, t_h$, where the size of $t_u$ is larger than or equal to $t_{u+1}$ ( $u = 1, \ldots, h-1$).
3. Let $g_1, \ldots, g_n$ be the subgraphs whose outer boundary cycle are $m(c_1), \ldots, m(c_n)$, respectively.
   a. Set *k=h*.
   b. While $k < n$ do the following:
      1. Decompose $t_1$ into two triangles $t_{11}$ and $t_{12}$.
      2. Sort $t_{11}, t_{12}, t_2, \ldots, t_k$ to make a new sequence $t'_1, \ldots, t'_{k+1}$ in the descending order of power.
      3. Set $k = k + 1$.
   c. For each *i* ( $i = 1, \ldots, n$ ), embed $g_i$ in $t_i$.

**[STEP4]**
Substitute a curve for the pair of edges and delete the node shared by the pair which corresponds to the points and lines added in STEP1.

### 6.6.3. Correctness

**Theorem:** *For a planar PLCA expression, a figure can be drawn in a two-dimensional plane by the algorithm DF.*

### Proof

The line division operation does not affect two-dimensional realizability, since consistency and connectedness are preserved, and the differences in the numbers of points and lines before and after the operation are equivalent. Thus, $m(e')$ which is obtained in STEP1 is a simple planar graph, as are the decomposed subgraphs.

A simple planar graph can be drawn in a two-dimensional plane using only straight lines (Chartland & Lesniak, 1996).

For a planar PLCA expression, the orientation of each circuit can be determined either as *inner* or *outer*. This also ensures that we can determine the outer boundary cycle for each subgraph and the positional relationships between subgraphs.

In STEP3, for an *a* such that
$a.cycles = \{c_0, c_1, \ldots, c_n\}$,
the polygon which has an edge $m(c_0)$ is decomposed into more than $n-1$ triangles and each subgraph is drawn in each triangle. Therefore, these subgraphs are embedded in the inner part of the polygon in such a manner that each pair does not intersect. Therefore, *a* is realized in this process.

Let $m(p)$ be a point to be deleted in STEP4. We can assume that there are exactly two lines $l_1.points = [p_1, p]$ and $l_2.points = [p, p_2]$, since $p$ is shared only by the lines added in STEP1. Edges $m(l_1)$ and $m(l_2)$ can be replaced by an approximating curve which connects nodes $m(p_1)$ and $m(p_2)$ without changing the connection patterns of areas.

Hence, a figure corresponding to a given PLCA expression can be drawn in a two-dimensional plane. ■

## 7. DRAWING ALGORITHM

### 7.1. Generation of a "Good" Figure

We have implemented a prototype system using JAVA for drawing a figure from a PLCA expression. The system checks whether a given PLCA expression is planar, and if it is, the corresponding figure is drawn in a two-dimensional plane[4]. However, the resulting figure was far from a "good" one. For example, many objects were drawn in a corner, leaving a large vacant space in the center. The main problem was embedding circles in part of another circle when related parts were combined. In STEP3 of *DF* algorithm, the challenge was to determine the location and the size of each unit circle to produce a "good" figure while preserving the relationships of objects described in the PLCA expression.

The problem of embedding is reduced to one of circle packing, putting $n$ circles of different sizes into a non-convex polygon so that they do not intersect. Circle packing is a well-known optimization problem that is NP-complete in general, and many studies have been undertaken. However, no algorithm has been proposed that covers the conditions in our problem. We address the problem using a Genetic Algorithm (GA) to determine the location and the size of each circle and produce an approximate solution to optimization, that gives a "good" figure. A "good" figure here means one in which the objects are drawn as large as possible, and a complex parts are drawn larger than the other parts.

### 7.2. Circle Packing

Circle packing is an arrangement of circles inside a given boundary such that no two of them overlap and some, or all, of them are mutually tangent (Williams, 1979; Stephanson, 2005). This is known as an NP-complete problem in general, but optimal solutions have been found in several cases. The studies on circle packing usually treat simple types: the area to be packed is a simple form such as a circle or a rectangle, and few constraints are imposed on the circles to be packed.

The realization of a bridge described in Subsection 6.6.1 is considered to be a type of circle packing problem which is formalized as follows:

**[Circle Packing Problem]** *Pack a non-convex polygon with a specified number n of circles with the constraints: (1) all the circles used for packing are as large as possible, and (2) the corresponding circle increases in size with the increasing number of areas in a module.*

This problem is a difficult one and none of the existing algorithms can be applied directly. Therefore, we use a Genetic Algorithm, as a more flexible solution.

### 7.3. Genetic Algorithm

A Genetic Algorithm (GA) is a search technique to find an optimal solution or an approximation to an optimal solution (Goldberg, 1989). It is inspired by evolutionary biology concept such as inheritance, mutation, selection and crossover.

In general, after creating the initial populations of chromosomes, each of which is represented by a bit string, the GA involves repeatedly computing the fitness of each chromosome, taking pairs of chromosomes and creating their offspring until a suitable solution is obtained. In creating offspring, crossover (exchanging selected bits between chromosome) and mutation (flipping chosen bits with a certain possibility) are used. Candidate optimal solutions evolve over time.

### 7.4. Implementation

#### 7.4.1. Gene Encoding

We implemented the above circle packing problem as follows. Let $(x_i, y_i)$ denote a coordinate of the center of an $i$-th circle ($1 \le i \le n$). In addition, let $M_1,\ldots,M_n$ be the set of modules obtained by decomposing the graph corresponding to a PLCA expression, and $n_i$ be the number of the areas in $M_i$ ($1 \le i \le n$).

Each chromosome corresponds to the locations of $n$ circles and it is denoted by an array of the coordinates of their centers $(x_1, y_1),\ldots,(x_n, y_n)$. Each coordinate $(x_i, y_i)$ is encoded as a sequence $a_{i1},\ldots,a_{iL}, b_{i1},\ldots,b_{iL}$, where each $a_{ij}(1 \le j \le L)$ and each $b_{ij}(1 \le j \le L)$ is a digit either of $0,\ldots,9$[5], and $L$ is a sufficiently large number. Let $x_{max}, x_{min}, y_{max}$ and $y_{min}$ be the coordinates defined as follows:

$x_{max}$: the largest $x$-coordinate of the drawn bridge
$x_{min}$: the smallest $x$-coordinate of the drawn bridge
$y_{max}$: the largest $y$-coordinate $y$ where $(x_i,y)$ is in the drawn bridge
$y_{min}$: the smallest $y$-coordinate $y$ where $(x_i,y)$ is in the drawn bridge

Then, $x_i$ and $y_i$ are calculated as follows so that there is no lethal gene[6].

$$\begin{cases} x_i = (x_{max} - x_{min})\sum_{j=1}^{n_i}\left(\frac{1}{10}\right)^j a_{ij} + x_{min} \\ y_i = (y_{max} - y_{min})\sum_{j=1}^{n_i}\left(\frac{1}{10}\right)^j b_{ij} + y_{min} \end{cases}$$

The radius of each circle is determined incrementally using distances between the centers of the circles and the boundary of the drawn bridge.

In addition, we use a local search method to compute the fitness for obtaining a better solution.

### 7.4.2. Parameter Setting

Let $S_{ij}$ ($j$=1,…,$n_i$) be the size of an area contained by $M_i$.

Let $S_{total}$, $N_{total}$ and $S_{av}$ denote the total size of the areas, the total number of all the areas, and the average size of an area contained in a PLCA expression, respectively. They are defined as follows:

$$S_{total} = \sum_{i=1}^{n}\sum_{j=1}^{n_i} S_{ij}, \quad N_{total} = \sum_{i=1}^{n} n_i, \quad S_{av} = \frac{S_{total}}{N_{total}}$$

Fitness is evaluated so that the total size of the circles used for packing an area is as large as possible, and the size of a circle is proportional to the total number of the areas that are recursively contained in the corresponding module. Therefore, it can be calculated as:

$$fitness = S_{total} - \sum_{i=1}^{n}\frac{1}{N_i}\cdot\sum_{j=1}^{n_i} | S_{av} - S_{ij} |$$

where $N_i$ is the total number of the areas that are recursively contained in module $M_i$.

Crossover takes place at $n$ randomly chosen points, and mutation at randomly chosen positions which in our case occurs when the digit is changed to any other digit.

We performed the simulation several times to find appropriate values for the crossover and mutation rates. As a result, the mutation rate is set at the fixed value 1.0, and the crossover rate is set at 0.4 for PLCA expressions with multiple bridges one inside another, and at 0.9 for PLCA expressions with a bridge in which multiple modules are embedded.

## 7.5. Experiment and Evaluation

Experiments are performed using three PLCA expressions corresponding to the figures shown in Figure 17.

1. Data1: This is a simple PLCA expression with one module and no bridge.

*Figure 17. Figures corresponding to given PLCA expression*

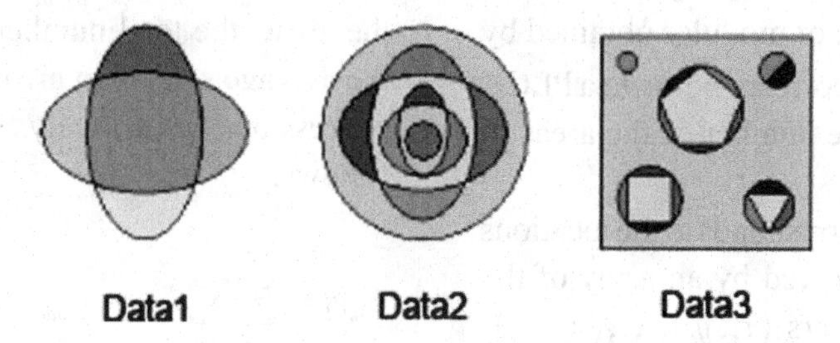


*Figure 18. Results of drawings*

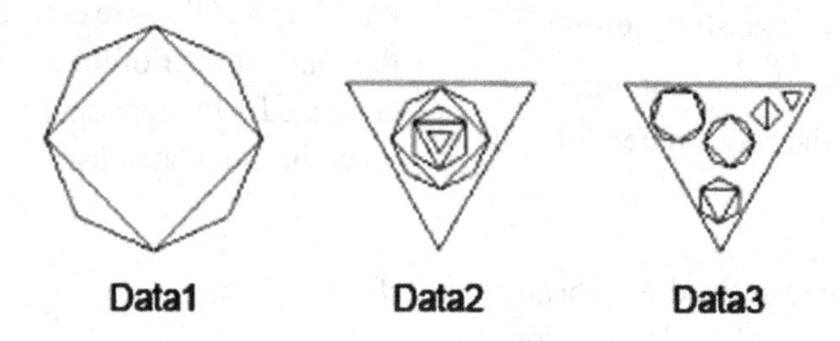


*Table 3. Numerical results of drawings*

| Data1 | | | Data2 | | | Data3 | | |
|---|---|---|---|---|---|---|---|---|
| module | radius | opt rad | module | radius | opt rad | module | size | no. of areas |
| 1 | 80.0 | 80.0 | 1 | 80.00 | 80.00 | 1 | 20066.00 | 18 |
| | | | 2 | 34.98 | 40.00 | 2.1 | 1219.97 | 6 |
| | | | 3 | 22.87 | 25.51 | 2.2 | 1068.04 | 5 |
| | | | 4 | 10.30 | 11.44 | 2.3 | 852.78 | 4 |
| | | | | | | 2.4 | 452.42 | 2 |
| | | | | | | 2.5 | 220.72 | 1 |

2. Data2: This has multiple bridges, one inside another, and is used to check that circles are drawn as large as possible.
3. Data3: This has a bridge in which multiple modules with varying numbers of areas are embedded. This is used to check that the size of a circle is proportional to the total number of areas recursively contained in the corresponding module.

We use a $160 * 160$ rectangle as a drawing field. Table 3 and Figure 18 show the results of drawings. It shows that all the relationships of the PLCA components are preserved. Above all, each module is embedded in the correct bridge.

For convenience, the number is given to each module depending on its level. The outermost module is numbered as 1. A module in the inner side of a module of level $n$ is numbered as $n$+1. If there are several modules of the same $n$ level, then they are numbered as $n.k$ where ($k$=1,2,...). In the table, *radius* is the radius of an e-circle and *opt rad* is the radius of an inscribed circle of a bridge, that is the biggest size of a module to be

*Figure 19. Cognition of "goodness"*

located there. And *size* is the total size of all the areas contained in that module, and *no.of areas* shows the total number of areas recursively contained in the corresponding module.

In evaluating the results, we ignore the shape of an *outermost*, which is always an inscribed polygon of an e-circle, and discuss the locations and the sizes of the e-circles.

For Data1, the radius is the biggest radius. It follows that a module is drawn as large as possible.

For Data2, the radii of e-circles are slightly smaller than the optimal ones, since the circle should not be tangent to the boundary of the bridge. It follows that the modules are drawn as large as possible.

For Data3, the size of an e-circle is proportional to the number of areas contained in the corresponding module. It is considered that a module containing the larger number of areas is more complex. Therefore, it follows that complex objects are drawn larger than non-complex objects.

We showed the three figures in Figure 19, equivalent according to PLCA, to twenty test subjects, and asked them to select the ``best" figure. Seventeen of them chose (c), the figure produced by our algorithm.

From these results, we conclude that we have obtained the "good figure."

## 8. EXTENSION TO SHAPE REPRESENTATION

### 8.1. Shape Representation

In PLCA, only the connection patterns between regions are represented, and shape information is ignored. However, shape representation is necessary in many fields: for example, in recognizing maps or geological changes, in designing and building objects, and in using GIS.

We extended PLCA so that it has the information of convex hull for each area. We represent qualitative convex shape of each object by its convex hull, and extract any concavity as the difference between the area and its convex hull, constructing the convex hulls of the remaining parts recursively. Using this approach, it is possible to express the detailed shapes of regions. Our goal is to represent not only the shape of the boundaries of a single object, but also the detailed connections between objects and the convexity of areas (Figure 20).

### 8.2. PLCA+ Expression

#### 8.2.1. Definition of Classes

PLCA has four basic classes of objects: *points*(*P*), *lines*(*L*), *circuits*(*C*), and *areas*(*A*). We add a new class *SubPLCA* to represent the convex shape of an area.

*Figure 20. Figures including multiple objects*

For PLCA expression $e = \langle P, L, C, A, outermost \rangle$, *SubPLCA* of an area $a \in A$ is defined as a class that satisfies several conditions: for an arbitrary instance *se* of *SubPLCA*, the following conditions are satisfied.

$$se.points = \{p_0, p_1, \cdots, p_{n-1}\} \quad where\ p_0, p_1, \cdots, p_{n-1} \in \text{Point}$$
$$se.lines = \{l_0, l_1, \cdots, l_{n-1}\} \quad where\ l_0, l_1, \cdots, l_{n-1} \in \text{Line}$$
$$se.circuits = \{c_0, c_1, \cdots, c_{n-1}\} \quad where\ c_0, c_1, \cdots, c_{n-1} \in \text{Circuit}$$
$$se.areas = \{a_0, a_1, \cdots, a_{n-1}\} \quad where\ a_0, a_1, \cdots, a_{n-1} \in \text{Area}$$
$$se.area = a \quad where\ a \in se.areas$$
$$se.som = c \quad where\ c \in se.circuits$$

Intuitively, a SubPLCA *se* represents a restricted region in which the extracted area *se.area* from the source figure is pasted. There exists a circuit along the outermost extremity of the frame, called *som*(*suboutermost*).

We also define three components of *se*: *se.iom* is the inner circuit of the frame, *se.ocs* is the outer circuit of the convex hull of the extracted area, and *se.oa*, which is called the *background area*, is the area between the convex-hull of the extracted area and the outer boundary of the whole region, the frame. Their formal definitions are given below.

**Definition: (The inner circuit of the frame)** *se.iom is a Circuit c that satisfies:*

$$\forall l^* \in se.som.lines(l^{*re} \in c.lines)$$
$$\wedge \quad \forall l^* \in c.lines(l^{*re} \in se.som.lines)$$
$$\wedge \quad c \in se.circuits$$

*For each line l* that belongs to the suboutermost circuit, the line oriented opposite to l* belongs to se.iom, and vice versa.*

**Definition: (The outer circuit of the convex-hull of the extracted area)** *se.oca is a Circuit c that satisfies:* $c \in se.oa.circuits \wedge c \neq se.iom$

**Definition: (The background area)** *se.oa is an Area a that satisfies:*

$$se.iom \in a.circuits$$
$$\wedge \quad |a.circuits| = 2$$
$$\wedge \quad a \in se.areas$$
$$\wedge \quad a \neq se.area$$

The only circuits belonging to the background area are the inner circuit of the frame and the outer circuit of the convex hull of the extracted area.

If the source figure contains *n* areas, then *n* SubPLCAs *se* are defined independently. Moreover, if a concave part of the source figure has concave sub-parts, we use hierarchical representation to capture its shape. Each SubPLCA is a PLCA+ expression that includes SubPLCA recursively. As a result, for a PLCA+ expression $e^+$, $e^+.ses$ has a tree structure. For a SubPLCA *se*, if $se.area = a \wedge se.areas = \{a, a_1, a_2, \cdots, a_n\}$, Area *a* is said to be *a parent Area* of Area $a_1, a_2, \cdots, a_n$, and $a_1, a_2, \cdots, a_n$ are said to be *child Areas* of Area *a*.

A *PLCA+ expression* is defined as a class that satisfies the following condition: for an arbitrary PLCA+ expression $e^+$, $e^+.points$, $e^+.lines$, $e^+.circuits$, $e^+.areas$ and $e^+.ses$ are sets of Points, Lines, Circuits, Areas and subPLCA expressions, respectively, and $e^+.om \in e^+.circuits$ is the outermost circuit of the whole figure.

**Definition: (Element)** *1) Let p, l, c and a be Point, Line, Circuit and Area, respectively. If* $p \in l.points$*, then p is said to be an element of l. If* $l \in c.lines$*, then l is said to be an element of c. If* $c \in a.lines$*, then c is said to be an element of a. 2) Let o1, o2 and o3 be each a Point, Line, Circuit or Area. If o1 is an element of o2 and o2 is an element of o3, then o1 is an element of o3.*

### 8.2.2. Consistency

**Definition: (PLCA+ consistency)** *A PLCA+ expression* $e^+$ *is said to be consistent iff the constraint on SubPLCA is satisfied in addition to the three conditions of PLCA consistency presented in Section 3.*

1. **constraint on P-L**
2. **constraint L-C**
3. **constraint C-A**
4. **constraint on SubPLCA:** *There exist a unique se.area, se.som, se.iom, se.oca, and se.oa for each SubPLCA. Moreover, the extracted area se.area and the background area se.oa should be line-connected.*

## 8.3. Planarity of PLCA+

The planarity condition for PLCA expressions is described in Section 6. For a PLCA+ expression, since $e^+$ and each SubPLCA *se* are also regarded as PLCA expressions, they satisfy this condition.

$$| e^+.points | - | e^+.lines | - | e^+.circuits | + 2 | e^+.areas | = 0$$

$$\forall se \in e^+.ses( | se.points | - | se.lines | - | se.circuits | + 2 | se.areas | = 0)$$

We require additional planarity constraints between Area and SubPLCA, and between SubPLCAs.

### 8.3.1. Constraint on Area-SubPLCA

For a consistent PLCA expression, an orientation of each Circuit is determined as either *inner* or *outer*. In this section, $iic(c)$ shows that a Circuit $c$ is an inner circuit, and $ioc(c)$ shows that a Circuit $c$ is an outer circuit. We define the notion of *inner object* using the orientation of a circuit. Let $o_1$ and $o_2$ be components of a PLCA expression. Intuitively, if $o_2$ is located in an inner side of $o_1$, then $o_2$ is an inner object of $o_1$, denoted by $io(o_1, o_2)$.

**Definition: (Inner object)**

$$io(o_1, o_2) = \begin{cases} o_1 \in As \wedge o_2 \in o_1.circuits \\ o_1 \in Cs \wedge o_2 \in o_1.lines \\ o_1 \in Ls \wedge o_2 \in o_1.points \\ iic(o_1) \wedge o_1 \in o_2.circuits \\ ioc(o_1) \wedge l^* \in o_1.lines \\ \quad \wedge \exists c \in o_2.circuits(l^{*re} \in c.lines) \\ io(o_1, o_3) \wedge io(o_3, o_2) \end{cases}$$

For each Area $a$ other than the background area in an $se$, there exists an Area in some $se'$ the parent Area of which is $a$. Background areas have no children. These constraints are formalized as follows.

Let $As_{se.oa} = \bigcup_{se \in e^+.ses} se.oa$.

$$\forall a \in As \setminus As_{se.oa}(| \{se \mid se.area = a\} | = 1)$$

$$\forall a \in As_{se.oa} \begin{pmatrix} | \{se \mid a \in se.areas\} | = 1 \\ \wedge a \notin \bigcup_{se \in e^+.ses} se.area \\ \wedge a \notin e^+.areas \end{pmatrix}$$

An Area $a$ and all of its *inner objects* are included in the interior of the background area of the SubPLCA of $a$. This constraint is formalized as follows.

$se.area = a$

$$se.points \supseteq \left\{ p \left| \begin{array}{l} (io(a,p) \wedge p \in Ps) \\ \vee \exists l \in \{l \mid l^* \in se.som.lines\}(p \in l.points) \end{array} \right. \right\}$$

$$se.lines \supseteq \{l \mid (io(a,l) \wedge l \in Ls) \vee l^* \in se.som.lines.\}$$

$$se.circuits \supseteq \left\{ c \left| \begin{array}{ll} & io(a,c) \wedge c \in Cs \\ \vee & c = se.som \\ \vee & c = se.iom \\ \vee & c = se.oca \end{array} \right. \right\}$$

$$se.areas \supseteq \left\{ a' \left| \begin{array}{ll} & io(a,a') \wedge a' \in As \\ \vee & c = se.oa \\ \vee & c = se.area \end{array} \right. \right\}$$

### 8.3.2. Constraint on SubPLCA-SubPLCA

Consider the SubPLCAs of areas that are line-connected. The line shared by these areas should not connect to the background areas of the SubPLCAs. This reflects the fact that when areas are line-connected, one is convex and the other is concave.

$$\forall l^* \in se_1.oca.lines(l^{*re} \notin se_2.oca.lines)$$
$$(se_1, se_2 \in e^+.ses \wedge se_1 \neq se_2)$$

## 8.4. Generation of PLCA+ Expression

### 8.4.1. Constructing PLCA+ from PLCA and Figure

For a given figure *F* in a two-dimensional plane, there exists the PLCA expression *e* for *F*. Here, we describe the generation of a PLCA+ expression $e^+$ from *F* and *e*. Note that *A* and $A'$ denote the parts in the figure *F* corresponding to the expression *a* and the convex hull of *A*. In this algorithm, for each area in *F*, we build a surrounding frame for that area's SubPLCA, construct expressions corresponding to the inside of *A* and to the background in the frame, and combine these expressions. If the extracted area has a concave part, this process is repeated recursively.

Here, we present the outline of the algorithm. Initially,

$e^+.points, e^+.lines, e^+.circuits, e^+.areas$ are set to be $\{\}$.

**function**: $generate(F, e)$

1. Set $e^+.points = e^+.points \cup e.points$, $e^+.lines = e^+.lines \cup e.lines$, $e^+.circuits = e^+.cps \cup e.circuits$ and $e^+.areas = e^+.areas \cup e.areas$.
2. Set $e^+.ses = \{\}$ and $Areas = e^+.areas$.
3. Repeat 4 until $Areas = \{\}$.
4. Select an arbitrary Area *a* from *Areas*, and proceed the followings.
   a. (The inside of the Area): Each element of *a* is added to *se.points*, *se.lines*, *se.circuits* and *se.areas*, depending on its class. In addition, set *se.area=a* (Figure 21(a)).
   b. (The outside of the Area): Make a SubPLCA expression *se*, which consists of the only one area $a'$ containing one Point, one Line, and two Circuits *se.som* and *se.iom* (Figure 21(b)).
   c. (Combining expressions): Make a new Circuit expression corresponding to the circuit that encircles the outer part of Area *a*, and add it to both *se.circuits* and *se.oa.circuits* (Figure 21(c)).
   d. (Generating expression for concavity): If the convex hull $A'$ is not filled by the area *A* in *F*, obtain the concave part of *A* by comparing *A* and $A'$ in *F*. To do this, we use the *line division* and *area division* operators shown in

*Figure 21. Generation of PLCA+ expression*

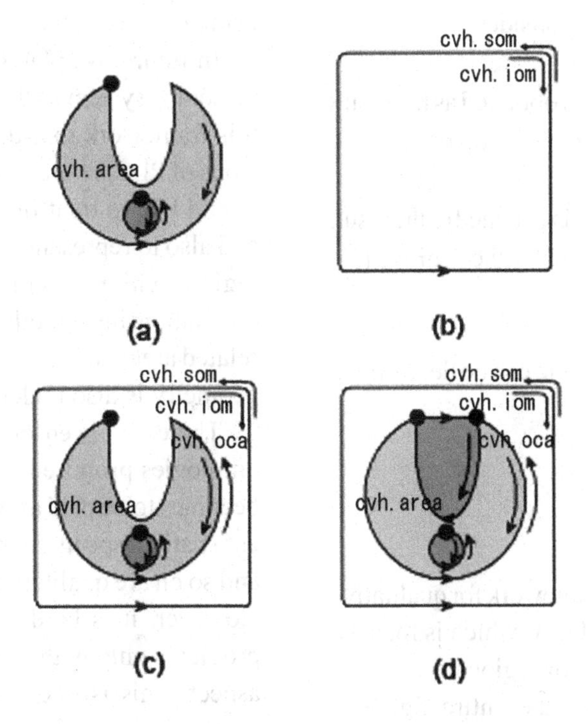


Section 4 (Figure 21(d)). Otherwise, do nothing.

e. (Updating Areas): Add *se* to $e^{+}.ses$, and add all Areas in *se.areas*, other than *se.area* and *se.oa*, to *Areas*.

## 8.5. Judgment of Line Convexity

For a given PLCA+ expression, say that *a* and $a'$ are the expressions corresponding to the Area *A* and its convex hull $A'$ in the figure. If *A* and $A'$ are matched, i.e., $A'$ is fully occupied by *A*, then *A* is said to be *convex*. Otherwise, it is *concave*.

The Line expression corresponding to the overlap between *A* and $A'$ when they are superimposed can be either *convex* or *concave*. Note that the convexity of a Line is defined with respect to the inside of *A* and it is inverted with respect to the outside of *A*. For a directed Line $l^{*}$, which is an element of an Area *a*, $convex(l^{*})$ denotes that Line *l* is convex with respect to an Area *a*; and $concave(l^{*})$ denotes that Line *l* is concave with respect to an Area *a*.

Each line in the figure is curved. Therefore, the Line in *se.oca* is concave, as *se.oca* corresponds to the outer circuit of the convex hull. Hence, the following properties hold.

$$convex(l^{*}) \leftrightarrow concave(l^{*re})$$

$$\forall se \in e^{+}.ses(\forall l^{*} \in se.oca.lines(concave(l^{*})))$$

### 8.5.1. An Algorithm for Judging the Convexity of a Line

We give an algorithm for determining the convexity of a Line which is not included in the outermost or sub-outermosts.

**function**: $getConvexity(l^{*})$

Consider SubPLCA *se* such that $l^{*} \in se.lines$ holds.

1. If $l^* \in se.oca.lines$, then $concave(l^*)$.
2. If $l^* \notin se.oca.lines$, consider $getConvexity(l^{*re})$.
   a. If $convex(l^{*re})$ is obtained as the result of $getConvexity(l^{*re})$, then $concave(l^*)$.
   b. If $concave(l^{*re})$ is obtained as the result of $getConvexity(l^{*re})$, then $convex(l^*)$.

The convexity of each Line can be determined by this algorithm.

## 9. CONCLUSION

We have proposed a new framework for qualitative spatial reasoning called PLCA, which is focused on the connection patterns of regions.

In a PLCA expression, the entire figure is represented in a form in which all the objects are related, and any figure in two-dimensional plane can be treated in a unified manner. Therefore, we can easily extend the system and the computational complexity for a complicated figure is rather small. Using simple objects such as points, lines, circuits and areas as primitives, it can easily distinguish the connection patterns, while it has sufficient reasoning power to deal with many realistic problems. The operations on PLCA expression correspond to real actions on figures and preserve the consistency of the expression. We add the attributes to each object so that semantical spatial reasoning can be performed. The correspondance of the expression and a figure is also discussed. We have only to check the numbers of the components for determining a planarity of PLCA expression. And if this condition is satisfied, we can draw the figure in a two-dimensional plane. The drawing algorithm can be implemented partly using Genetic Algorithm to generate a ``good'' figure. Moreover, we have shown an extended PLCA that can handle qualitative shape representation using convex hulls.

In future, we plan to construct a higher-level reasoning system on this framework, and to extend this framework to $n$-dimensional spaces. Extensions of PLCA+ are also under consideration. We would like to treat figures that use straight lines and also to represent other relationships between regions with respect to shapes. Further research on relationships of other QSR methods and other related areas such as topology and computational geometry is also under consideration.

There have been lots of QSR formalizations and ontologies proposed so far, and their integration becomes to be paid attention to. Currently, different spatial aspects such as region, direction, size and so on are qualitatively treated independently. However, it is hard to apply QSR to practical problems only with the formalization of a single aspect. This is one reason for the fact there is no good practical application so far, in spite of potential power of QSR. Therefore, it is necessary to make the unified formalization which can handle these aspects altogether, or to make some method to integrate independent formalizations. We believe that the approach of adding various aspects on the PLCA framework is one possibility. Corporation of PLCA and temporal reasoning is also an issue to be studied. Especiallly, if temporal change can be qualitatively treated, application to simulation will greatly contribute the reduction of computational complexity.

## ACKNOWLEDGMENT

The author would like to thank Takao Sumitomo, Shou Kumokawa, and Izumi Takeuti for their cooperation. This research was supported by KAKENHI19500134.

## REFERENCES


Aliello, M., Pratt-Hartmann, I. E., & Van Benthem, J. (2007). *Handbook of spatial logics*. Spinger-Verlag. doi:10.1007/978-1-4020-5587-4

Allen, J. (1983). Maintaining knowledge about temporal intervals. *Communications of the ACM*, *26*(11), 832–843. doi:10.1145/182.358434

Anderson, M., Meyer, N., & Olivier, P. (Eds.). (2002). *Diagrammatic representation and reasoning*. Springer-Verlag. doi:10.1007/978-1-4471-0109-3

Bailey-Kellog, C., & Zhao, F. (2003). Qualitative spatial reasoning: Extracting and reasoning with spatial aggregates. *AI Magazine*, *24*(4).

Balbiani, P., Condotta, J., & del Cerro, L. (1999). A new tractable subclass of the rectangle algebra. In *Proceedings of the Sixteenth International Joint Conference on Artificial Intelligence (IJCAI99)*, (pp. 442-447). IJCAI.

Bennett, B. (1994). Spatial reasoning with propositional logic. In *Proceedings of the Fourth International Conference on Principles of Knowledge Representation and Reasoning (KR94)*, (pp. 51-62). Morgan Kaufmann Publishers.

Borgo, S. (2009). Euclidean and mereological qualitative space: A study of SCC and DCC. In *Proceedings of the Twenty-First International Joint Conference on Artificial Intelligence (IJCAI 2009)*, (pp. 708-713). IJCAI.

Borgo, S., Guarino, N., & Masolo, C. (1996). A pointless theory of space based on strong connection and congruence. In *Proceedings of the Fifth International Conference on Principles of Knowledge Representation and Reasoning (KR96)*, (pp. 220-229). Morgan Kaufmann Publishers.

Casati, R., & Varzi, A. (1997). Spatial entities. In Stock, O. (Ed.), *Spaial and Temporal Reasoning* (pp. 73–96). Kluwer Academic Press. doi:10.1007/978-0-585-28322-7_3

Chartland, G., & Lesniak, L. (1996). *Graphs & digraphs* (3rd ed). Wadsworth & Brooks/Cole.

Clarke, B. L. (1981). A calculus of individuals based on connection. *Notre Dame Journal of Formal Logic*, *20*(3), 204–218. doi:10.1305/ndjfl/1093883455

Clarke, B. L. (1985). Individuals and points. *Notre Dame Journal of Formal Logic*, *268*(1), 61–75. doi:10.1305/ndjfl/1093870761

Cohn, A. G. (1995). A hierarchical representation of qualitative shape based on connection and convexity. In *Proceedings of the Spatial Information Theory: Cognitive and Computational Foundations of Geographic Information Science (COSIT95)*, (pp. 311-326). Springer-Verlag.

Cohn, A. G., & Gotts, N. (1996). A mereological approach to representing spatial vagueness. In *Proceedings of the Fifth International Conference on Principles of Knowledge Representation and Reasoning (KR96)*, (pp. 230-241). Morgan Kaufmann Publishers.

Cohn, A. G., & Hazarika, S. M. (2001). Qualitative spatial representation and reasoning: An overview. *Fundamental Informaticae*, *46*(1), 1–29.

Cohn, A. G., & Varzi, A. (1998). Connection relations in mereotopology. In *Proceedings of the European Conference on Artificial Intelligence (ECAI98)*, (pp. 150-154). ECAI.

de Berg, M., van Kreveld, M., Overmars, M., & Schwarzkopf, O. (1997). *Computational geometry*. Springer-Verlag.

Donnelly, M. (2003). Layered mereotopology. In *Proceedings of the Eighteenth International Joint Conference on Artificial Intelligence (IJCAI 2003)*, (pp. 1269-1274). IJCAI.

Egenhofer, M., Clementini, E., & di Felis, P. (1994). Topological relations between regions with holes. *International Journal of Geographical Information Systems*, *8*(2), 129–144. doi:10.1080/02693799408901990

Egenhofer, M. J. (1991). Reasoning about binary topological relations. In *Proceedings of the Second Symposium on Large Spatial Databases*, (pp. 143-160). Springer-Verlag.

Egenhofer, M. J., & Franzosa, R. D. (1991). Point-set topological relations. *International Journal of Geographical Information Systems*, *5*(2), 161–174. doi:10.1080/02693799108927841

Egenhofer, M. J., & Franzosa, R. D. (1995). On the equivalence of topological relations. *International Journal of Geographical Information Systems*, *9*(2), 133–152. doi:10.1080/02693799508902030

Egenhofer, M. J., & Herring, J. (1990). *Categorizing binary topological relations between regions, lines and points in geographic databases. Technical Report*. Bangor, ME: University of Maine.

Eschenbach, C. (1999). A predication calculus for qualitative spatial representations. In *Proceedings of the Spatial Information Theory: Cognitive and Computational Foundations of Geographic Information Science (COSIT99),* (pp. 157-172). Springer-Verlag.

Forbus, K. D. (1981). Qualitative reasoning about physical processes. In *Proceedings of the Seventh International Joint Conference on Artificial Intelligence*. IJCAI.

Frank, A. U. (1992). Qualitative spatial reasoning about distances and directions in geographic space. *Journal of Visual Languages and Computing, 3*, 343–371. doi:10.1016/1045-926X(92)90007-9

Freska, C. (1992). Using orientation information for qualitative spatial reasoning. In *Theories and Methods of Spatio-Temporal Reasoning in Geographic Space* (pp. 162–178). Springer-Verlag. doi:10.1007/3-540-55966-3_10

Gerevini, A., & Renz, J. (2002). Combining topological and size constraints for spatial reasoning. *Artificial Intelligence*, *137*(1-2), 1–42. doi:10.1016/S0004-3702(02)00193-5

Goldberg, D. E. (1989). *Genetic algorithms in search - Optimization and machine learning*. Kluwer Academic Publishers.

Gotts, N. (1994). How far can we C? Defining a doughnut using connection alone. In *Proceedings of the Fourth International Conference on Principles of Knowledge Representation and Reasoning (KR94),* (pp. 246-257). Morgan Kaufmann Publishers.

Grigni, M., Papadias, D., & Papadimitriou, C. (1995). Topological inference. In *Proceedings of the Fourteenth International Joint Conference on Artificial Intelligence (IJCAI95),* (pp. 901-906). IJCAI.

Guesgen, H. (1989). *Spatial reasoning based on Allen's temporal logic. Report ICSI TR89-049.* Berkeley, CA: International Computer Science Institute.

Hernandez, D., Clementini, E., & di Felice, P. (1995). Qualitative distances. In *Proceedings of the Spatial Information Theory: Cognitive and Computational Foundations of Geographic Information Science (COSIT95),* (pp. 45-57). Springer-Verlag.

Imai Labo. (2001). *Program.* Retrieved from http://www.ise.chuo-u.ac.jp/ise-labs/imai-lab/program/program.html.

Kuipers, B. (1994). *Qualitative reasoning: Modeling and simulation with incomplete knowledge.* Cambridge, MA: MIT Press.

Kumokawa, S., & Takahashi, K. (2007). Drawing a figure in a two-dimensional plane for a qualitative representation. In *Proceedings of the Conference on Spatial Information Theory (COSIT07),* (pp. 337-353). Springer-Verlag.

Kumokawa, S., & Takahashi, K. (2008). Qualitative spatial representation based on connection patterns and convexity. In *Proceedings of the AAAI-08 Workshop on Spatial and Temporal Reasoning*, (pp. 57-62). AAAI.

Ligozat, G. (1998). Reasoning about cardinal directions. *Journal of Visual Languages and Computing, 9*(1), 23–44. doi:10.1006/jvlc.1997.9999

Ligozat, G. (2005). Categorical methods in qualitative reasoning: The case for weak representations. In *Proceedings of the Spatial Information Theory: Cognitive and Computational Foundations of Geographic Information Science (COSIT05),* (pp. 265-282). COSIT.

Liu, W., Li, S., & Renz, J. (2009). Combining RCC-8 with qualitative direction calculi: Algorithms and complexity. In *Proceedings of the Twenty-First International Joint Conference on Artificial Intelligence (IJCAI 2009),* (pp. 854-869). IJCAI.

Museros, L., & Escrig, M. T. (2004). A qualitative theory for shape representation and matching. In *Proceedings of the Eighteenth International Workshop on Qualitative Reasoning*. Qualitative Reasoning.

Nedas, K., Egenhofer, M. J., & Wilmsen, D. (2007). Metric details of topological line-line relations. *International Journal of Geographical Information Science, 21*(1), 21–48. doi:10.1080/13658810600852164

Ochiai, N. (2004). *Introduction to graph theory: Application for plane graph.* Nihon-Hyouron-sha.

Pratt, I. (1999). Qualitative spatial representation languages with convexity. *Journal of Spatial Cognition and Computation, 1,* 181–204. doi:10.1023/A:1010037123582

Randell, D., Cui, Z., & Cohn, A. G. (1992). A spatial logic based on regions and connection. In *Proceedings of the Third International Conference on Principles of Knowledge Representation and Reasoning (KR92),* (pp. 165-176). Morgan Kaufmann Publishers.

Renz, J. (2002). *Qualitative spatial reasoning with topological information.* Springer-Verlag. doi:10.1007/3-540-70736-0

Renz, J. (2007). Qualitative spatial and temporal reasoning: Efficient algorithms for everyone. In *Proceedings of the Twentieth International Joint Conference on Artificial Intelligence (IJCAI 2007),* (pp. 526-531). IJCAI.

Renz, J., & Nebel, B. (1999). On the complexity of qualitative spatial reasoning: A maximal tractable fragment of the region connection calculus. *Artificial Intelligence, 108*(1-2), 69–123. doi:10.1016/S0004-3702(99)00002-8

Renz, J., & Nebel, B. (2001). Efficient methods for qualitative spatial reasoning. *Journal of Artificial Intelligence Research, 5,* 289–318.

Schlieder, C. (1996). Qualitative shape representation. In Frank, A. (Ed.), *Spatial Conceptual Models for Geographic Objects with Undetermined Boundaries* (pp. 123–140). London, UK: Taylor & Francis.

Schmidtke, H. R., & Woo, W. (2007). A size-based qualitative approach to the representation of spatial granularity. In *Proceedings of the Twentieth International Joint Conference on Artificial Intelligence (IJCAI 2007),* (pp. 563-568). IJCAI.

Stephenson, K. (2005). *Introduction to circle packing-the theory of discrete analytic functions.* Cambridge University Press.

Stock, O. (Ed.). (1997). *Spatial and temporal reasoning.* Kluwer Academic Press. doi:10.1007/978-0-585-28322-7

Takahashi, K., & Sumitomo, T. (2005). A framework for qualitative spatial reasoning based on connection patterns of regions. In *Proceedings of the IJCAI-05 Workshop on Spatial and Temporal Reasoning*, (pp. 57-62). IJCAI.

Takahashi, K., & Sumitomo, T. (2007). The qualitative treatment of spatial data. *International Journal of Artificial Intelligence Tools*, *16*(4), 661–682. doi:10.1142/S0218213007003497

Takahashi, K., Sumitomo, T., & Takeuti, I. (2008). On embedding a qualitative representation in a two-dimensional plane. *Spatial Cognition and Computation*, *8*(1-2), 4–26. doi:10.1080/13875860801944887

Timpf, S. (1999). Abstraction, levels of detail, and hierarchies in map series. In *Proceedings of the Spatial Information Theory: Cognitive and Computational Foundations of Geographic Information Science (COSIT99),* (pp. 125-139). Springer-Verlag.

Vieu, L. (1997). Spatial representation and reasoning. In Stock, O. (Ed.), *Spatial and Temporal Reasoning* (pp. 5–40). Kluwer Academic Press. doi:10.1007/978-0-585-28322-7_1

Williams, R. (1979). Circle packings, plane tessellations, and networks. In *The Geometrical Foundation of Natural Structure: A Source Book of Design* (pp. 34–47). New York, NY: Dover.

Wolter, F., & Zakharyaschev, M. (2000). Spatio-temporal representation and reasoning based on RCC-8. In *Proceedings of the Seventh International Conference on Principles of Knowledge Representation and Reasoning (KR2000),* (pp. 3-14). Morgan Kaufmann Publishers.

## KEY TERMS AND DEFINITIONS

**Attributed PLCA:** The PLCA expression in which each object is attached to an attribute so that the components that have the same property are unified.

**Planar PLCA Expression:** A PLCA expression that has the corresponding figure in a two-dimensional plane.

**PLCA Connected:** A PLCA expression of which all the components are connected.

**PLCA Consistent:** A PLCA expression that satisfies the constraints between the components: points, lines, circuits and areas.

**PLCA Expression:** A symbolic representation for spatial data using the simple objects: *points(P), lines(L), circuits(C)* and *areas(A).*

**PLCA+ Expression:** An extended PLCA so that convexity of an area can be represented.

**Qualitative Spatial Reasoning (QSR):** A method that treats images or figures qualitatively, by extracting the information necessary for a user's purpose.

## ENDNOTES

[1] We use the term *area* instead of *region*, since *area* used in this paper is a different entity from the *region* generally used in qualitative spatial reasoning.

[2] If an isolated point and an isolated line are regarded as a tiny area and a thin area, respectively, these constraints can be eliminated.

[3] We show only the main arguments in these operations here.

[4] In the prototype system, STEP4 has not yet been implemented.

[5] We used digits here for encoding whereas bits are used in general.

[6] This is the basic definition. The actual calculation of $y_i$ is more complicated.

# Chapter 3
# Qualitative Reasoning and Spatio-Temporal Continuity

**Ernest Davis**
*New York University, USA*

## ABSTRACT

*This chapter discusses the use of transition graphs for reasoning about continuous spatial change over time. The chapter first presents a general definition of a transition graph for a partition of a topological space. Then it defines the path-connected and the homogeneous refinements of such a partition. The qualitative behavior of paths through the space corresponds to the structure of paths through the associated transition graphs, and of associated interval label sequences, and the author proves a number of metalogical theorems that characterize these correspondences in terms of the expressivity of associated first-order languages. He then turns to specific real-world problems and shows how this theory can be applied to domains such as rigid objects, strings, and liquids.*

## 1. INTRODUCTION

Many spatial aspects of many persistent entities vary continuously over time: the direction of a weather vane, the length of a rubber band; the shape of a balloon and so on. Many others, of course, do not: the territory of the United States, the shape of a shadow on a surface, the shape of a tree when a limb is pruned. However, when it is known that a spatial entity does change continuously, that constraint can be very useful in reasoning about its behavior over time.

Consider the following inferences:

A. Two interlocked jigsaw puzzle pieces cannot be separated by a movement in the plane of the puzzle, but can be separated by lifting one perpendicular to the plane.
B. Consider a string loop of length $L$ wrapped once around the waist of an hourglass with

DOI: 10.4018/978-1-61692-868-1.ch003

spherical globes of circumference $C$. If $L>C$ then the loop can be removed from the hourglass without coming into contact with the hourglass and without ever being taut. If $L<C$, then the loop cannot be removed from the hourglass. If $L=C$, then the loop can be removed from the hourglass, but at some point it must be in contact with the hourglass, and it must be taut. It can be taken off either the upper or the lower globe.

If the globes of the hourglass are long cylinders, the circular cross section has circumference $C$, and $C=L$, then the string can be removed from the hourglass, but it will be taut and in contact with the hourglass over an extended interval of time.

If, instead of a string loop, we have a rubber band whose length is less than $C$ at rest but can be stretched to a length greater than $C$, then it can be removed from the hourglass without being in contact with the hourglass, but it must be stretched in order to do so.

C. A quantity of milk in a closed bottle remains in the bottle. If at time $T1$ there is milk sitting in cup A, and at a later time $T2$ this milk has moved to a cup B, and both cups are stationary, then the milk came out of the top of cup A and went in the top of cup B.

D. The dog can go from the dining room into the kitchen. However, if a chair is placed in the middle of the kitchen doorway, then the dog cannot go from the dining room to the kitchen. If the chair is placed at the edge of the doorway, then the dog can squeeze past and get into the kitchen.

E. A person who is in Canada at one time and in the United States at a later time must cross the U.S. border at some time in between. A person who is in Alaska at one time and in Idaho at a later time must cross the U.S. border at least twice in between. It is possible to travel from any point in Idaho to any point in Ohio without crossing the border of the United States. This seems like the simplest of these inferences; in fact, however, it is the example for which the theory we develop in this chapter is least adequate.

A number of points may be observed about these examples. First, both the givens and the conclusions are qualitative; no precise measurements or shape descriptions are given. Second, they depend on continuity: If Star Trek style teleportation were available, the inferences would not be valid. For that matter, analogous inference can fail if they involved entities that change discontinuously; for instance, when the Louisiana Purchase took effect in 1803, many objects went from being far from the United States to being deep inside the United States without ever being on the border. Third, many of the sample inferences above depend on further physical limitations on the dynamic spatial behaviors of the objects involved in addition to continuity.

Moreover, the well-known scheme for representing qualitative spatial change in terms of transitions between RCC relations is inadequate to justify or represent these inferences. In that theory, as we will discuss in greater detail in section 2, the relation between two regions is characterized in terms of eight possible mereotopological relations. Spatial change over time is characterized in terms of the sequence of the evolving sequence of these relations. Continuity is characterized in terms of possible and impossible transitions from one relation to another, as illustrated in the well known graph in Figure 1.

However, this representation is not expressive enough to deal with examples like those above, for a number of reasons. First, the set of states corresponding to a particular RCC relation is sometimes *disconnected* and we sometimes wish to distinguish different connected components. For instance, in example (A) we wish to distinguish the states where the jigsaw puzzle pieces are Externally Connected (EC) and interlocked from those where they are externally connected and

*Figure 1. Transition graph for RCC relations*

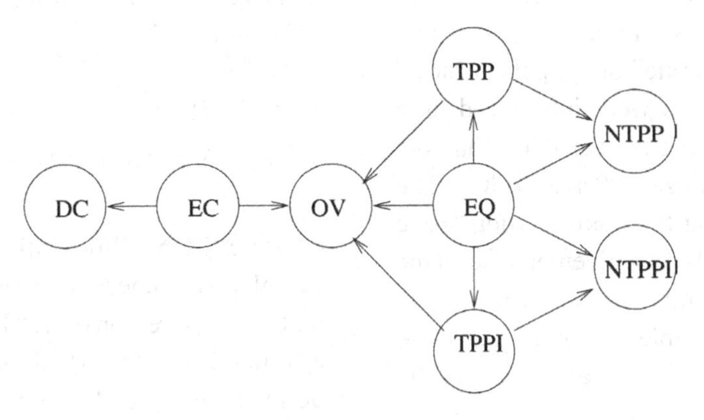


separable. Second, the set of states corresponding to a particular RCC relation is sometimes *non-uniform* with respect to the possible transitions. For instance, in example (B), there is a transition from the contact state to the non-contact state, but that transition cannot be executed immediately when the string is around the middle of the cylinder. Third, we sometimes wish to make qualitative distinctions other than the RCC relations. For instance, in example (B), we wish to distinguish states in which the rubber band is *relaxed* from those in which it is *stretched*.

The aim of this chapter is to present a generalization of the RCC transition graph that addresses these issues for a broad range of constraints on shapes, definitions of continuity, and qualitative relations. The essential idea is that, given a space of object configurations and a partition of that space into qualitative categories, we further subdivide each category into cells that are both connected and uniform with respect to transitions. That is, any two configurations in the same cell are connected by a path that remains within the cell and have the same possible transitions to other cells. This is called the *Qualitative Homogeneous Decomposition* (QHD) of the starting partition (section 3). The QHD can be viewed as a directed graph, called the QHD graph (section 3.1). We give a precise meta-logical characterization of the expressivity of QHD graphs as encodings of qualitative changes in dynamic systems (section 3.2). We then discuss the ways in which this representation can be applied to specific examples like those above (section 4).

## 2. RELATED WORK

Work on both qualitative and precise spatial reasoning using continuity constraints, including certainly the current chapter, has mostly been centered around the construction and use of transition graphs of various kinds. To the best of my knowledge, transition graphs were first introducted in the NEWTON program of de Kleer (1977) and the FROB program of Forbus (1980). These programs addressed the problem of qualitative reasoning about the motion of point objects in various physical environments. The transition graphs they generated combined spatial continuity constraints with dynamic constraints.

Transition graphs of this kind were likewise the chief output of so-called "qualitative reasoning" systems (Kuipers, 1986; Forbus, 1985; de Kleer & Brown, 1985). These constructed transition graphs that characterize the behavior of dynamic systems whose state is a tuple of real-valued parameters. Again, the transition graphs in these systems combine dynamic constraints with continuity constraints; the first analysis to separate these was in section 4.8 of (Davis, 1990). The most relevant aspect of this work to the current chapter is the analysis of the topological issues, particularly the "transition ordering rules" of Williams (1985), and the "epsilon transition rule" of Kuipers (1986).

Configuration spaces were introduced as a method of characterizing the feasible behaviors of jointed robots in Lozano-Perez (1983). The problem of calculating the configuration space for interacting solid objects, given precise shape specifications, is known as the "motion planning" or "piano movers" problem. There is a large literature on the subject; see Part II of LaValle (2006) for an overview.

The RCC-8 relations between spatial regions were introduced in Randell and Cohn (1989). Figure 1 (with undirected arcs) was presented in Randell, Cui, and Cohn (1992) as showing the possible "topological" transitions between RCC relations—that is, those that are consistent with continuity constraints.

Galton (1993) presented the undirected transition graphs for RCC relations between two spatial fluents that are rigid but may interpenetrate. There are six of these, depending on the shapes of the two objects. Galton (1995) changed the undirected arcs representing transitions in previous studies to directed arcs; there is a directed arc from relation R to relation S if it is possible for R to hold at time *t* and S to hold at an open interval with lower bound *t* (In Galton's terminology, R "dominates" S).

Recent knowledge representation research on continuous spatial change has mostly followed either an *axiomatic* or a *semantic* approach. In the axiomatic approach, the objective is to characterize continuous change in terms of axioms over regions in space-time. The first attempt at this was in Muller (1998a). Muller used a first-order language over "histories" (Hayes, 1979)—that is, 4-dimensional regular regions in space-time—with three primitives: "C*xy*," meaning that histories *x* and *y* are connected; "*x*<*y* " meaning that *x* strictly precedes *y* in time; and "$x \Diamond y$", meaning that *x* and *y* overlap in time. Using this language, he proposed the following definition of "continuity":

$$\mathrm{CONTINU}w \triangleq$$
$$\mathrm{CON}_t w \wedge \forall_x \forall_u (\mathrm{TS}xw \wedge x \Diamond u \wedge \mathrm{P}uw) \Rightarrow \mathrm{C}xu.$$

Here "$\mathrm{CON}_t w$" means that the temporal projection of *w* is a connected time interval. "P*uw*" means that *u* is a subregion of *w*. "TS*xw*" means that *x* is a "time-slice" of *w*. All of these predicates can be defined in terms of the primitives (Muller, 1998a). It can be shown that Muller's axiomatic definition of continuity corresponded to continuity relative to the Hausdorff distance (Davis, 2001). In Muller (1998b) Muller observed that the above definition allows a 4-dimensional region that shrinks to a point at an instant and then expand from there to be considered continuous; he therefore proposed an alternative, stronger definition[1] of transitions.

Muller (1998b) also proposed an analysis of the feasible transitions between spatial RCC relations. For each RCC-8 relation R, he defines a spatial equivalent $\mathrm{R}_{sp}xy$, meaning that *x* and *y* are coextensive in time and that they are related spatially by R throughout their lifetimes. He was able to prove axiomatically the impossibility of a number of transitions for continuous regions.

However, Muller's approach does not allow the analysis of transitions that involve spatial relations that hold only for an instant. The limitation was addressed in Davis (2000), which gives first-order constructions that in effect define the cross-section C of a history at a given time, a point x in space-time, and the relations x ∈ Interior(*C*), and x ∈ Bd(*C*). The spatial RCC relations can then be defined in terms of points in the usual way, and the transition rules can be stated. However, these definitions are very complex, and it is unlikely that the transition rules can be *proven* from any plausible set of simple RCC axioms.

A more principled approach is taken in Hazarika and Cohn (2011). Here, the spatial relation between histories *x* and *y* at time *t* is defined in terms of the connectivity relations of $x \cap y$, $x \cup y$, $x - y$, and $y - x$ restricted to an interval ending at *t* and an interval beginning at *t*. Remarkably, using these definitions, they have been able to generate automatic proofs of the impossibility of each of the 45 transitions excluded in Figure 1 using the first-order theorem prover SPASS (Weidenbach, 2001).

In the semantic approach, continuity is characterized by defining a topology (generally a metric) over the space of spatial configurations. This approach was first applied to the analysis of transitions of RCC relations, in which a configuration is a pair of regular regions, in Galton (2000a) and Davis (2001), which independently arrived at very similar results. Galton considered five metrics over regular regions: the Hausdorff distance, the Hausdorff distance between the boundaries (which, however, was found to be inadequate), the dual Hausdorff distance, the area of the symmetric distance, and the Fréchet distance between the boundaries. Davis considered four: the Hausdorff distance, the dual Hausdorff distance, the area of the symmetric difference, and the optimal-homeomorphism metric.

Galton's monograph "Qualitative Spatial Change" (Galton, 2000a) is an extensive and rich study, combining representational and philosophical analysis. Chapters 7 and 8 deal with continuity.

There has also been work on continuous change in discrete models of space. These, of course, require substantially different definitions, both of topological relations and of continuity (Galton, 2000b, 2003)

Finally, the concept of qualitative homogeneous decompositions introduced here is modelled on the concept of cylindrical algebraic decompositions in computational algebra (Collins, 1975), in the sense that a QHD, like a CAD, is a partition of the space into cells, each of which is connected and uniform with respect to specified properties.

## 3. QUALITATIVE HOMOGENEOUS DECOMPOSITIONS

In this section, we define QHD's and study their properties in an abstract and general setting. We will return to specific issues of geometric change in section 4.

The general problem we address here is to characterize a path through a general topological space **T** in terms of its transitions through "qualitatively different" subsets of **T**. For example **T** might be the space of all pairs of regular regions in the plane divided into eight subsets corresponding to one of the eight RCC relations. For the purposes of this section, we will treat the partition of **T** into "qualitatively different" subsets as externally given; that is, we are given a partition of **T** and told that this constitutes a qualitative discrimination. Our analysis below consists in subdividing this initial partition into a finer partition that characterizes points in terms of the qualitative characteristics of the paths that pass through them.

Throughout this section **T** will be a topological space; in some cases, we will impose stronger requirements. We will use boldface lower case letters, such as **x**, to denote points in **T**; boldface upper case letters, such as **P**, to denote subsets of **T**; and calligraphic letters such as $\mathcal{U}$ to denote sets of subsets of **T**.

**Definition 1** *A collection* $\mathcal{U}$ *of subsets of* **T** *is a* partition *of* **T**, *if for every point* $\mathbf{x} \in \mathbf{T}$ *there is exactly one* $\mathbf{U} \in \mathcal{U}$ *such that* $\mathbf{x} \in \mathbf{U}$. *This set* **U** *is called the "owner" of* **x** *in* $\mathcal{U}$, *denoted "*$\mathbf{O}(\mathbf{x}, \mathcal{U})$.*" The sets in* $\mathcal{U}$ *are called the cells of* $\mathcal{U}$.

**Definition 2** *Let* $\mathcal{U}$ *and* $\mathcal{V}$ *be partitions of* **T**. $\mathcal{V}$ *is a (non-strict) refinement of* $\mathcal{U}$, *if for every* $\mathbf{V} \in \mathcal{V}$ *there exists* $\mathbf{U} \in \mathcal{U}$ *such that* $\mathbf{V} \subset \mathbf{U}$.

**Definition 3** *A* path *through* **T** *is a continuous function from the closed real interval [0,1] to* **T**. *A subset* **U** *of* **T** *is path-connected if, for every* $\mathbf{x}, \mathbf{y} \in \mathbf{U}$, *there exists a path from* **x** *through* **U** *to* **y**.

Note that the image of a path in **T** is a compact set in **T**.

**Definition 4** *A partition* $\mathcal{U}$ of **T** *is locally finite if, for every point* $\mathbf{x} \in \mathbf{T}$ *there exists a neighborhood* **N** *of* $x$ *such that* **N** *intersects only finitely many cells of* $\mathcal{U}$.

**Definition 5** *Let* $\mathcal{U}$ *be a locally finite partition of* **T**. *The set of neighbors of* **x** *in* $\mathcal{U}$, *denoted "* $\mathbf{N}(\mathbf{x}, \mathcal{U})$ *" is defined as:*

$$\mathbf{N}(\mathbf{x}, \mathcal{U}) = \{\mathbf{U} \in \mathcal{U} \mid \mathbf{x} \in Cl_{\mathbf{T}}(\mathbf{U})\}$$

*where* $Cl_{\mathbf{T}}(\mathbf{U})$ *is the topological closure of* **U** *with respect to* **T**.

Note that the owner of **x** is always one of its neighbors. If **x** is in the interior of its owner, then its owner is the only neighbor. In particular, if **U** is open, then **U** is the only neighbor of any of the points in **U**. If **x** is on the boundary of its owner, then **x** has other neighbors in addition to its owner.

**Definition 6** *Let* $\mathcal{U}$ *be a locally finite partition of* **T**. *A cell* $\mathbf{U} \in \mathcal{U}$ *is uniform in its neighbors if, for every two points* $\mathbf{x}, \mathbf{y} \in \mathbf{U}$, $\mathbf{N}(\mathbf{x}, \mathcal{U}) = \mathbf{N}(\mathbf{y}, \mathcal{U})$

**Definition 7** *A path* $\pi$ *has a starting transition from point* **x** *to set* **V** *if* $\pi(0) = \mathbf{x}$, *and for all* $t \in (0,1]$, $\pi(t) \in \mathbf{V}$. $\pi$ *has an ending transition from set* **V** *to point* **x** *if* $\pi(1) = \mathbf{x}$, *and for all* $t \in [0,1)$, $\pi(t) \in \mathbf{V}$.

**Definition 8** *Let* $\mathcal{U}$ *be a locally finite partition of* **T**. $\mathcal{U}$ *allows simple transitions if, for every point* $\mathbf{x} \in \mathbf{T}$ *and for every neighbor* **V** *of* **x** *in* $\mathcal{U}$, *there exists a path* $\pi$ *with a starting transition from* **x** *to* **V**.

An example of a partition that is locally finite but does not allow simple transitions is as follows: Let **T** be the closed unit square. Let:

$$\mathbf{A} = ([0,1] \times [0,1/4]] \cup ([0,0] \times [0,3/4]) \cup \bigcup_{k=0}^{\infty} [1/4, 3/4] \times [2^{-(2k+1)}, 2^{-2k}]$$

$$\mathbf{B} = \mathbf{T} - \mathbf{A}.$$

*Figure 2. A locally finite partition that does not allow simple transitions*

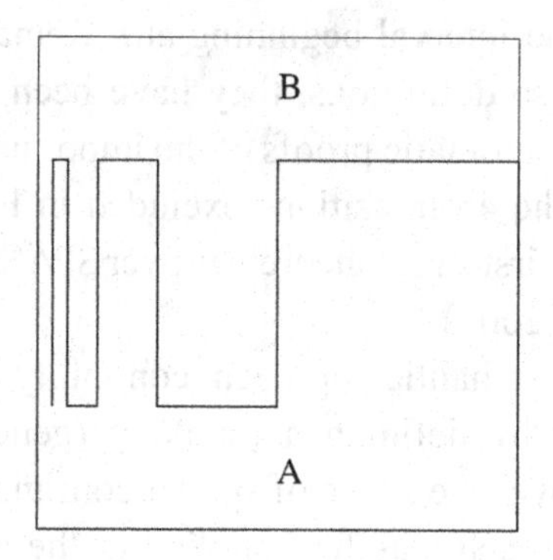


Thus **A** and **B** are alternating combs with infinitely many teeth (Figure 2). Note that **A** and **B** are both path-connected, **A** is closed regular, and **B** is open in **T**. The point $\langle 0, 1/2 \rangle$ is in **A** and is in the closure of **B**, but there is no starting transition from that point to **B**.

Another, more outré, example: Let **T** be the unit square [0,1] × [0,1]. Define **A** and **B** as follows:

$$\mathbf{A} = \{\langle x, y \rangle \mid y = 0 \lor (0 < y < 1 \land x \text{ is rational})\}$$

$$\mathbf{B} = \{\langle x, y \rangle \mid y = 1 \lor (0 < y < 1 \land x \text{ is irrational})\}$$

That is, **A** is the line at the bottom of the square plus all vertical lines with rational *x*-coordinates. **B** is the line at the top of the square plus all vertical lines with irrational *x*-coordinates. Then **A** and **B** are path-connected and uniform in their neighbors; every point has the neighbor set $\{\mathbf{A}, \mathbf{B}\}$. However, there cannot exist a path that has a starting transition from any point in **A** to **B**, or from any point in **B** to **A**, except where the starting point is at the boundary of the square.

**Definition 9** *A partition is* locally simple *if it is locally finite and allows simple transitions.*

**Definition 10** *Let* $\mathcal{U}$ *be a locally simple partition of* **T**. $\mathcal{U}$ *is a path-connected partition of* **T** *if every cell* $\mathbf{U} \in \mathcal{U}$ *is path-connected.* $\mathcal{U}$ *is a* *homogeneous partition of* $\mathbf{T}$ *if every cell* $\mathbf{U} \in \mathcal{U}$ *is path-connected and uniform in its neighbors.*

**Definition 11** *Let* $\mathcal{U}$ *and* $\mathcal{Q}$ *be partitions of* $\mathbf{T}$. $\mathcal{Q}$ *is the qualitative homogeneous decomposition (QHD) of* $\mathcal{U}$ *if the following are satisfied:*

a. $\mathcal{Q}$ *is a homogeneous refinement of* $\mathcal{U}$.
b. *Every homogeneous refinement of* $\mathcal{U}$ *is a refinement of* $\mathcal{Q}$.

*That is,* $\mathcal{Q}$ *is the coarsest homogeneous refinement of* $\mathcal{U}$.

It is clear from the definition that any partition $\mathcal{U}$ can have at most one QHD (if there were two, each would be a refinement of the other); hence the phrase "*the* QHD of $\mathcal{U}$" is justified. A partition $\mathcal{U}$ may have no QHD; for example, there may exists a point $\mathbf{x}$ that is in the closure of infinitely many connected components of $\mathcal{U}$. However, theorem 1 states that, if $\mathcal{U}$ has any homogeneous refinement, then it has a QHD.

**Theorem 1** *Let* $\mathcal{U}$ *be a partition of* $\mathbf{T}$. *If there exists a homogeneous refinement of* $\mathcal{U}$, *then there exists a* QHD *of* $\mathcal{U}$.

**Proof:** See Appendix.

Theorem 2 gives a "constructive" definition for the QHD using transfinite induction.

**Definition 12** *Let* $\mathcal{U}$ *be a locally simple partition of* $\mathbf{T}$. *Define the function* $\Phi(\mathcal{U})$ *to be the collection of all the path-connected components of* $\mathcal{U}$. *Define the equivalence relation* $\mathbf{x} \sim_U \mathbf{y}$ *as holding if* $\mathbf{x}$ *and* $\mathbf{y}$ *have the same owner and the same neighbors in* $\mathcal{U}$; *that is,* $\mathbf{O}(\mathbf{x},\mathcal{U}) = \mathbf{O}(\mathbf{y},\mathcal{U})$ *and* $N(\mathbf{x},\mathcal{U}) = N(\mathbf{y},\mathcal{U})$. *Define the function* $\Psi(\mathcal{U})$ *as the collection of equivalence classes of* $\mathbf{T}$ *under the relation* $\sim_U$.

A number of immediate consequences may be noted. First, $\Phi(\mathcal{U})$ and $\Psi(\mathcal{U})$ are refinements of $\mathcal{U}$. Second, $\Phi(\mathcal{U})$ is the coarsest path-connected refinement of $\mathcal{U}$; it is the set of *path-connected components* of $\mathcal{U}$. Third, a locally simple partition $\mathcal{V}$ is homogeneous if it is a fixed point under $\Phi$ and $\Psi$; that is, $\Phi(\mathcal{V}) = \Psi(\mathcal{V}) = \mathcal{V}$.

**Definition 13** *Let* $\mathcal{U}$ *be a locally simple partition of* $\mathbf{T}$. *The decompositional sequence corresponding to* $\mathcal{U}$ *is a sequence of refinements* $\mathcal{U}_\sigma$ *indexed by ordinals* $\sigma$ *as follows:*

- $\mathcal{U}_0 = \mathcal{U}$.
- *For each ordinal* $\sigma$, $\mathcal{U}_{\sigma+1} = \Psi(\Phi(\mathcal{U}_\sigma))$, where $\sigma + 1$ *is the successor to* $\sigma$.
- *For each limit ordinal* $\sigma$, *define the equivalence relation over* $\mathbf{T}$, $\mathbf{x} \sim_\sigma \mathbf{y}$ *if, for all* $i < \sigma$, $\mathbf{O}(\mathbf{x},\mathcal{U}_i) = \mathbf{O}(\mathbf{y},\mathcal{U}_i)$. *Define* $\mathcal{U}_\sigma$ to *be the equivalence classes of* $\mathbf{T}$ *under* $\sim_\sigma$.

**Theorem 2** *Let* $\mathcal{U}$ *be a locally simple partition of* $\mathbf{T}$. *Let* $\mathcal{U}_\sigma$ *be the decompositional sequence of* $\mathcal{U}$. *Then:*

- *The sequence reaches a fixed point. That is, there exists an ordinal* $\tau$ *such that, for all* $\sigma > \tau$, $\mathcal{U}_\sigma = \mathcal{U}_\tau$.
- *If* $\mathcal{U}_\tau$ *is locally simple, then it is the QHD of* $\mathcal{U}$.
- *If there exists a QHD of* $\mathcal{U}$, *then it is* $\mathcal{U}_\tau$.

**Proof:** See Appendix.

Tables 1 and 2 show simple examples of decompositional sequences, illustrated in Figures 3 and 4.

In both these examples, the final partition divides the points in $\mathbf{T}$ according to the local topological structure of the starting partition; that is, in the final QHD, any two points in the same cell have neighborhoods that are homeomorphic in terms of the original labels. That is not always the case: for instance, if $\mathbf{A}$ is the line from $\langle -1,0\rangle$ to $\langle 1,0\rangle$, and $\mathbf{B}$ is the complement of $\mathbf{A}$, then $\{\mathbf{A},\mathbf{B}\}$ is a homogeneous partition, even though the neighborhoods of the end points of the line are not homemorphic to the neighborhoods of the interior points of the line. The analysis in section 4.1 of the three-dimensional jigsaw puzzle will give another example of this.

## 3.1. Transition Graphs

The structure of a locally simple partition can be expressed as a graph. It should be noted that these "graphs" are not quite standard, in that they may have infinitely many vertices.

*Table 1. Decompositional sequence: example 1*

Let **T** be the plane, and let $\mathcal{U}$ consist of two cells:

**A**: The union of the solid disk of radius 1 centered at $\langle 1,0 \rangle$, the annulus with inner radius 1/2 and outer radius 1 centered at $\langle -1,0 \rangle$, and the solid disk of radius 1 centered at $\langle 0,2 \rangle$.
**B**: The complement of **A**.

The decompositional sequence proceeds as follows:

$\mathcal{U}_0 = \mathcal{U}$.

$\Phi(\mathcal{U}_0) = \{\mathbf{A1}, \mathbf{A2}, \mathbf{B1}, \mathbf{B2}\}$ where
$\mathbf{A1}$ is the disk centered at $\langle 0,2 \rangle$.
$\mathbf{A2} = \mathbf{A} - \mathbf{A1}$ is the union of the other disk and the annulus;
$\mathbf{B1}$ is the open disk of radius 1/2 centered at $\langle -1,0 \rangle$
$\mathbf{B2} = \mathbf{B} - \mathbf{B1}$ is the exterior of $\mathbf{A}$.
$\mathcal{U}_1 = \Psi(\Phi(\mathcal{U}_0)) = \{\mathbf{A1a}, \mathbf{A1b}, \mathbf{A2a}, \mathbf{A2b}, \mathbf{A2c}, \mathbf{B1}, \mathbf{B2}\}$ where
$\mathbf{A1a}$ is the boundary of $\mathbf{A1}$. Neighbor set: { $\mathbf{A1}, \mathbf{B2}$ }.
$\mathbf{A1b}$ is the interior of $\mathbf{A1}$. Neighbor set: { $\mathbf{A1}$ }.
$\mathbf{A2a}$ is the part of boundary of $\mathbf{A2}$ bordering $\mathbf{B2}$ (the Figure 8). Neighbor set: { $\mathbf{A2}, \mathbf{B2}$ }.
$\mathbf{A2b}$ is the interior of $\mathbf{A2}$. Neighbor set: $\mathbf{A2}$.
$\mathbf{A2c}$ is the part of the boundary of $\mathbf{A2}$ bordering $\mathbf{B1}$ (the inner circle). Neighbor set: { $\mathbf{A2}, \mathbf{B1}$ }.

$\Phi(\mathcal{U}_1) = \{\mathbf{A1a}, \mathbf{A1b}, \mathbf{A2a}, \mathbf{A2b1}, \mathbf{A2b2}, \mathbf{A2c}, \mathbf{B1}, \mathbf{B2}\}$ where
$\mathbf{A2b1}$ is the interior of the right-hand disk.
$\mathbf{A2b2}$ is the interior of the annulus.
$\mathcal{U}_2 = \Psi(\Phi(\mathcal{U}_1)) = \{\mathbf{A1a}, \mathbf{A1b}, \mathbf{A2a1}, \mathbf{A2a2}, \mathbf{A2a3}, \mathbf{A2b1}, \mathbf{A2b2}, \mathbf{A2c}, \mathbf{B1}, \mathbf{B2}\}$.
$\mathbf{A2a1}$ is the point $\langle 0,0 \rangle$. Neighbor set: $\{\mathbf{A2a}, \mathbf{A2b1}, \mathbf{A2b2}, \mathbf{B2}\}$.
$\mathbf{A2a2}$ is the right-hand circle except for $\langle 0,0 \rangle$. Neighbor set: $\{\mathbf{A2a}, \mathbf{A2b1}, \mathbf{B2}\}$.
$\mathbf{A2a3}$ is the left-hand circle except for $\langle 0,0 \rangle$. Neighbor set: $\{\mathbf{A2a}, \mathbf{A2b2}, \mathbf{B2}\}$.

$\Phi(\mathcal{U}_2) = \mathcal{U}_2$.
$\mathcal{U}_3 = \Psi(\Phi(\mathcal{U}_2)) = \mathcal{U}_2$, so a fixed point has been reached.

**Definition 14** *Let $\mathcal{U}$ be a partition of* **T**. *The corresponding transition graph G is defined as follows:*

- *The vertices of G are the cells in $\mathcal{U}$.*
- *For any $\mathbf{U}, \mathbf{V} \in \mathcal{U}$, there is an arc from* **U** *to* **V** *if $\mathbf{V} \neq \mathbf{U}$ and $\mathbf{U} \cap Cl_T(\mathbf{V})$ is non-empty. (That is,* **V** *is a neighbor of some point $\mathbf{x} \in \mathbf{U}$.)*

In the terminology of Galton (1995), there is an arc from **U** to **V** if **U** dominates **V**.

In general, a vertex in a transition graph may have infinite in-degree and infinite out-degree. If the partition is homogeneous, then since all points in the cell have the same neighbors and since a single point can have only finitely many neighbors, the out-degree of any vertex is finite, though the in-degree may still be infinite.

The direction of an arc in a transition graph does not indicate the allowable direction of a transition; a transition may occur either forward

*Table 2. Decompositional sequence: example 2*

Let **T** be the plane, and let $\mathcal{U}$ consist of two cells:

**A**: The upper half-disk, open on the bottom. That is, $\mathbf{A} = \{\langle x, y\rangle \mid x^2 + y^2 \le 1 \wedge y > 0\}$
**B**: The complement of **A**.

The decompositional sequence proceeds as follows:

$\mathcal{U}_0 = \mathcal{U}$.

$\Phi(\mathcal{U}_0) = \mathcal{U}_0$, since **A** and **B** are each path-connected.
$\mathcal{U}_1 = \Psi(\Phi(\mathcal{U}_0)) = \{\mathbf{A1}, \mathbf{A2}, \mathbf{B1}, \mathbf{B2}\}$ where
$\mathbf{A1}$ is the interior of the half-disk. Neighbor set $\{\mathbf{A}\}$
$\mathbf{A2}$ is the semi-circle $\mathbf{A} = \{\langle x, y\rangle \mid x^2 + y^2 = 1 \wedge y > 0\}$. Neighbor set $\{\mathbf{A}, \mathbf{B}\}$.
$\mathbf{B1}$ is the line from $\langle -1, 0\rangle$ to $\langle 1, 0\rangle$. Neighbor set $\{\mathbf{A}, \mathbf{B}\}$.
$\mathbf{B2} = \mathbf{B} - \mathbf{B1}$. Neighbor set $\{\mathbf{B}\}$.

$\Phi(\mathcal{U}_1) = \mathcal{U}_1$.
$\mathcal{U}_2 = \Psi(\Phi(\mathcal{U}_1)) = \{\mathbf{A1}, \mathbf{A2}, \mathbf{B1a}, \mathbf{B1b}, \mathbf{B2}\}$, where
$\mathbf{B1a}$ is the two endpoints of the line, $\{\langle -1, 0\rangle, \langle 1, 0\rangle\}$.
Neighbor set $\{\mathbf{A1}, \mathbf{A2}, \mathbf{B1}, \mathbf{B2}\}$
$\mathbf{B1b} = \mathbf{B1} - \mathbf{B1a}$ is the rest of the line. Neighbor set $\{\mathbf{A1}, \mathbf{B1}, \mathbf{B2}\}$.

$\Phi(\mathcal{U}_2) = \{\mathbf{A1}, \mathbf{A2}, \mathbf{B1a1}, \mathbf{B1a2}, \mathbf{B1b}, \mathbf{B2}\}$ where
$\mathbf{B1a1} = \{\langle -1, 0\rangle\}$, the left-hand end point.
$\mathbf{B1a2} = \{\langle 1, 0\rangle\}$, the right-hand end point.
$\mathcal{U}_3 = \Psi(\Phi(\mathcal{U}_2)) = \Phi(\mathcal{U}_2)$.

$\Phi(\mathcal{U}_3) = \mathcal{U}_3$.
$\mathcal{U}_4 = \Psi(\Phi(\mathcal{U}_3)) = \mathcal{U}_3$, so a fixed point has been reached.

or backward along an arc. Rather, the direction of the arc indicates the *topology* of a transition. If there is an arc from cell **U** to **V**, then a path $\pi$ carries out a forward transition along that arc at time $t$ if $\pi(t) \in \mathbf{U}$, and $\pi(t') \in \mathbf{V}$ for $t' \in (t, t1)$ for some $t1 > t$. The path $\pi$ carries out a backward transition along that arc at time $t$ if $\pi(t') \in \mathbf{V}$ for $t' \in (t1, t)$ for some $t1 < t$ and $\pi(t) \in \mathbf{U}$.

**Definition 15** *Let $\mathcal{U}$ be a partition of* **T**. *The Qualitative Homogeneous Decomposition graph (QHD graph) of $\mathcal{U}$ is the transition graph corresponding to the QHD of $\mathcal{U}$.*

There can exist partitions in which there are arcs in both directions between two cells. For instance, in the initial partition $\mathcal{U}$ in the example in Table 2, there is an arc from **A** to **B** and an arc from **B** to **A**. I do not know whether this can happen with a homogeneous partition over $\mathbb{R}^k$; it would certainly have to be highly pathological. It can happen with some kinds of partitions in some topological spaces of regions over $\mathbb{R}^k$; for instance, in the space of open regular regions in the plane, topologized by the area of the symmetric regions, it is possible to have closed transitions in either direction between DC and EC, or between TPP and NTTP (Davis, 2001, Figure 9).

In such cases, we must distinguish between going from **A** to **B** forward along the arc $\langle \mathbf{A}, \mathbf{B}\rangle$

*Figure 3. Decompositional sequence: example 1*

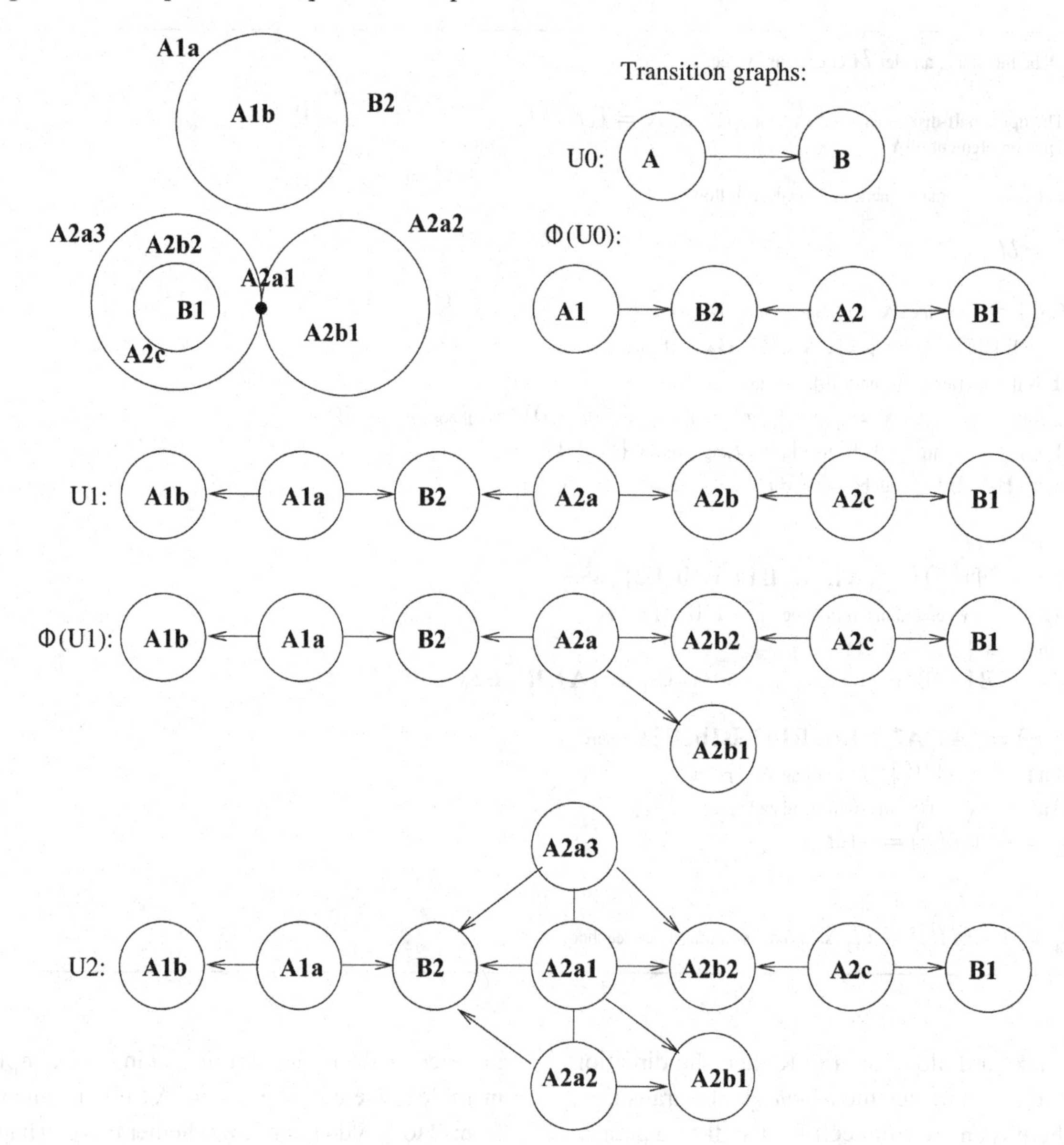


as opposed to going from **A** to **B** backward against the arc $\langle \mathbf{B}, \mathbf{A} \rangle$. In the first case, the path will be in **A** at the moment of transition, and in the second case it will be in **B**. Therefore, our definition of a path through the transition graph, which we will call a "gpath," is a little different from the usual:

**Definition 16** *Let G be a transition graph. A* gpath *is an alternating sequence of vertices and edges in G* $\langle \mathbf{V}_1, A_1, \mathbf{V}_2, A_2, \ldots A_{k-1}, \mathbf{V}_k \rangle$, *starting and ending with a vertex, such that* $A_i$ *is either the arc* $\langle \mathbf{V}_i, \mathbf{V}_{i+1} \rangle$ *or the arc* $\langle \mathbf{V}_{i+1}, \mathbf{V}_i \rangle$. *The sequence of a single vertex* $\langle \mathbf{V}_1 \rangle$ *is also considered a gpath.*

*Figure 4. Decompositional sequence: example 2*

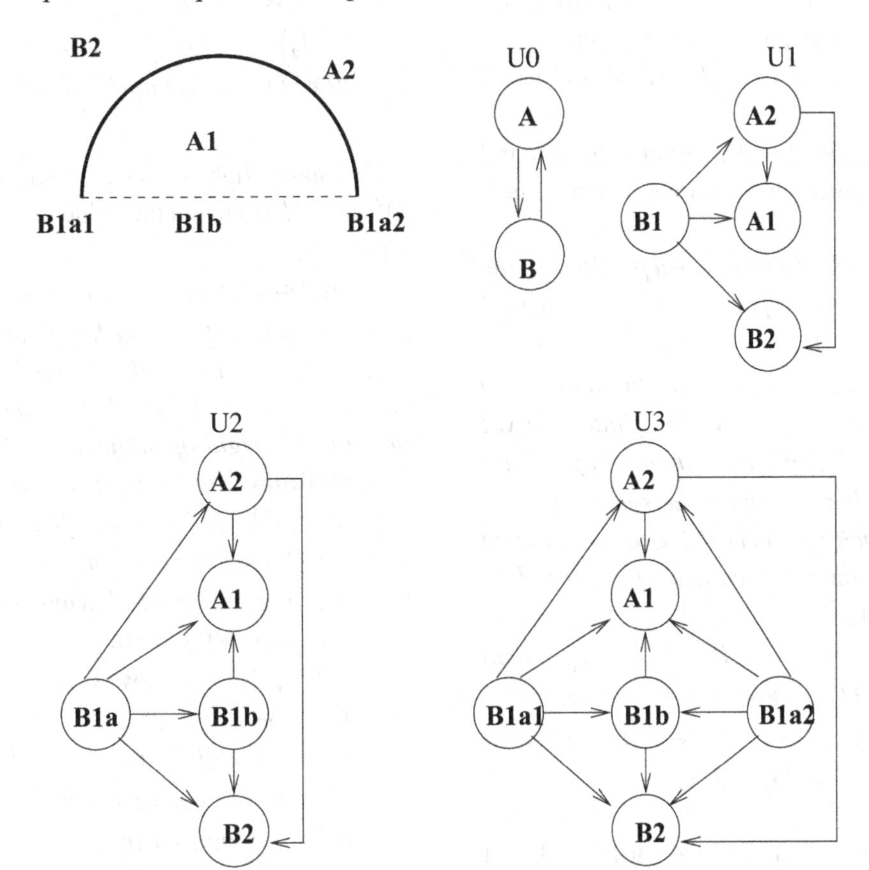


## 3.2. The Expressivity of QHD Graph

In this section, we study the relation between the paths through a partitioned space and the gpaths through the corresponding transition graph.

It will be convenient to define an intermediate structure, called an "Interval Label Sequence" (ILS). We will use $\pi$, $\phi$, and $\psi$, as variables over paths, $\alpha$ for interval label sequences, and $\beta$ for gpaths. We consider the vertices of the graph to be literally the cells of the partition; thus, we will use boldface letters for vertices of the graph.

We begin with a few definitions that describe how a path $\pi$ through **T** is characterized in terms of the sequence of qualitative states it passes through.

A path through a partitioned space divides the unit time interval into subintervals; in each subinterval, the path remains in one cell. We are interested in the topology of these intervals. We consider two ways of characterizing the topology of a real interval, called "interval label sets." The Z4 label set includes four labels: open ('O'), closed ('C'), closed on the left ('L'), and closed on the right ('R'). The Z5 label set includes five labels; it divides closed intervals into closed instantaneous ('CI') and closed extended ('CE'), together with 'O,' 'L,' and 'R.' The difference reflects the difference between characterizing the shape of successive *transitions,* in which case 'CI' and 'CE' are the same, versus characterizing the shape of the *intervals,* in which case they are different. As we shall see, the difference also corresponds to the difference between using a path-connected partition and a homogeneous partition.

**Definition 17** *Let Z be a interval label set; that is, either Z4 or Z5 as described above. The* shape *of an interval I in label set Z is denoted "shape(I, Z )."*

For any bounded real interval *I*, let *l*(*I*) and $u(I)$ be respectively the lower and upper bounds of *I*.

**Definition 18** *A finite interval partition of the interval [0,1] is a finite partition* $\langle I_1 \ldots I_k \rangle$ of [0,1] such that for $i = 1 \ldots k-1$, $u(I_i) = l(I_{i+1})$.

**Definition 19** *Let* $\mathcal{U}$ *be a partition of* **T** *and let* $\pi$ *be a path through* **T**. *The finite interval partition* $\langle I_1 \ldots I_k \rangle$ *of* [0,1] *is induced by* $\pi$ *with respect to* $\mathcal{U}$ *if* $\pi$ *occupies the same set in* $\mathcal{U}$ *throughout each subinterval* $I_i$ *and moves from one set to another in each transition from* $I_i$ *to* $I_{i+1}$. *Formally,*

- *For* $i = 1 \ldots k$, *if* $t_1, t_2 \in I_i$ *then* $\mathbf{O}(\pi(t_1), \mathcal{U}) = \mathbf{O}(\pi(t_2), \mathcal{U})$; *and*
- *For* $i = 1 \ldots k-1$, if $t_1 \in I_i, t_2 \in I_{i+1}$ *then* $\mathbf{O}(\pi(t_1), \mathcal{U}) \neq \mathbf{O}(\pi(t_2), \mathcal{U})$.

If $\pi$ induces a finite interval partition, then it is said to be *finitary*. Not all paths are finitary; a path that moves infinitely often between sets in $\mathcal{U}$ does not induce a finite interval partition. We will limit our discussion to finitary paths.

**Definition 20** *Let* $\mathcal{U}$ *be a locally simple partition of* **T** *and let* $Z$ *be an interval label set. An interval label pair is a pair of a cell of* $\mathcal{U}$ *and a label in* $Z$. *An Interval Label Sequence (ILS) is a finite sequence* $\langle\langle U_1, z_1 \rangle \ldots \langle U_k, z_k \rangle\rangle$ *of interval label pairs.*

**Definition 21** *Let* $\mathcal{U}$ *be a locally simple partition of* **T**, *let Z be an interval label set, and let* $\pi$ *be a finitary path. Let* $\langle I_1 \ldots I_k \rangle$ *be the interval partition induced by* $\pi$. *The interval trace of* $\pi$ *through* $\mathcal{U}$, *denoted* $\Gamma_{U,Z}(\pi)$, *is the interval label sequence:*

$$\langle\langle \mathbf{O}(\pi(I_1), \mathcal{U}), shape(I_1, Z)\rangle,\ \langle \mathbf{O}(\pi(I_2), \mathcal{U}), shape(I_2, Z)\rangle,\ \ldots \langle \mathbf{O}(\pi(I_k), \mathcal{U}), shape(I_k, Z)\rangle\rangle .$$

We have slightly abused notation in writing $\mathbf{O}(\pi(I_i), \mathcal{U})$ to mean the value of $\mathbf{O}(\pi(t), \mathcal{U})$ for all $t \in I_i$.

**Definition 22** *The closed labels are 'C,' 'CI,' and 'CE.' The left-closed labels are the closed labels and 'L.' The right-closed labels are the closed labels and 'R.' The left-open labels are 'R' and 'O.' The right-open labels are 'L' and 'O.'*

**Definition 23** *An interval label sequence* $\langle\langle \mathbf{U}_1, z_1 \rangle \ldots \langle \mathbf{U}_k, z_k \rangle\rangle$ *is coherent if either*

a. $k = 1$ *and* $z_1 =$ *'C' or 'CE'; or*

b. $k > 1$ *and all the following hold*:

*b.1* $z_1$ *is left-closed.*

*b.2* $z_k$ *is right-closed.*

*b.3* *for* $i = 1 \ldots k-1$, *either*:

*b.3.a* $z_i$ *is right-closed,* $z_{i+1}$ *is left-open, and* $\mathbf{U}_{i+1}$ *is a neighbor of* $\mathbf{U}_i$; *or*

*b.3.b* $z_i$ *is right-open,* $z_{i+1}$ *is left-closed, and* $\mathbf{U}_i$ *is a neighbor of* $\mathbf{U}_{i+1}$.

**Theorem 3** *The interval trace of any finitary path* $\pi$ *is a coherent* ILS.

**Proof:** Straightforward.

**Definition 24** *Let* $\mathcal{U}$ *be a locally simple partition of* **T**, *let G be the transition graph for* $\mathcal{U}$, *and let Z be a label set.*
*Let* $\alpha = \langle\langle \mathbf{U}_1, z_1 \rangle \ldots \langle \mathbf{U}_k, z_k \rangle\rangle$ *be a coherent ILS. The gpath through G corresponding to* $\alpha$, *denoted* $\Delta(\alpha)$, *is the gpath* $\beta = \langle \mathbf{U}_1, A_1, \ldots A_{k-1}, \mathbf{U}_k \rangle$ *where* $A_i = \langle \mathbf{U}_i, \mathbf{U}_{i+1} \rangle$ *if* $z_i$ *is right-closed and* $A_i = \langle \mathbf{U}_{i+1}, \mathbf{U}_i \rangle$ *if* $z_i$ *is right-open.*

**Example:** Consider the path $\pi$ shown in Figure 5, using the partition of Figure 4. The corresponding gpath is:

**⟨B2, ⟨B1a1, B2⟩, B1a1, ⟨B1a1, A1⟩, A1, ⟨B1b, A1⟩, B1b, ⟨B1b, A1⟩, A1, ⟨A2, A1⟩, A2, ⟨A2, B2⟩, B2⟩.**

The corresponding ILS is:

$\langle\langle \mathbf{B2}, `L'\rangle, \langle \mathbf{B1a1}, `CI'\rangle, \langle \mathbf{A1}, `O'\rangle, \langle \mathbf{B1b}, `CE'\rangle,$
$\quad \langle \mathbf{A1}, `O'\rangle, \langle \mathbf{A2}, `CI'\rangle, \langle \mathbf{B2}, `R'\rangle\rangle$

**Theorem 4** *Under the assumptions of definition 24, if $\alpha$ is a coherent ILS, then $\Delta(\alpha)$ is a gpath. Conversely, if $\beta$ is a gpath then for both Z4 and Z5, there exists a coherent ILS $\alpha$ such that $\Delta(\alpha) = \beta$ (For Z4, $\alpha$ is unique. In Z5, it may not be; if arc $A_{j-1}$ is traversed backward, and arc $A_j$ is traversed forward, then vertex $E_j$ may be labelled either 'CI' or 'CE.').*

**Proof:** Immediate from the definitions.

**Definition 25** *For any path $\pi$ through* **T**, *the start of $\pi$, $S(\pi) = \pi(0)$ and the end of $\pi$, $E(\pi) = \pi(1)$. For any interval label sequence $\alpha = \langle\langle \mathbf{V}_1, s_1\rangle \ldots \langle \mathbf{V}_k, s_k\rangle\rangle$, the start of $\alpha$, $S(\alpha) = \mathbf{V}_1$ and the end of $\alpha$, $E(\alpha) = \mathbf{V}_k$. For any gpath $\alpha = \langle \mathbf{V}_1, A_1, \ldots A_{k-1}, \mathbf{V}_k\rangle$, the start of $\alpha$, $S(\alpha) = \mathbf{V}_1$ and the end of $\alpha$, $E(\alpha) = \mathbf{V}_k$.*

We now show the converse of theorems 3 and 4: Any coherent ILS or coherent gpath is the trace of a finitary path. Moreover, one can choose the starting and ending points of the path to be any points in the starting and ending cell of the ILS/gpath.

**Theorem 5** *Let $\mathcal{U}$ be a path-connected partition of* **T**. *Let $\alpha$ be a coherent* Z4 ILS *for $\mathcal{U}$. Let* **x** *be a point in $S(\alpha)$ and let* **y** *be a point in $E(\alpha)$. Then there exists a finitary path $\pi$ through* **T** *such that $S(\pi) = \mathbf{x}$, $E(\pi) = \mathbf{y}$, and $\Gamma_{U,Z4}(\pi) = \alpha$.*

**Proof:** *If* $\alpha = \langle\langle \mathbf{U}, `C'\rangle\rangle$, then, since **U** is path-connected, let $\pi$ be a path through **U** connecting **x** and **y**.

Otherwise, let $\alpha = \langle\langle \mathbf{U}_1, z_1\rangle \ldots \langle \mathbf{U}_k, z_k\rangle\rangle$. For $i = 2 \ldots k-1$, let $\mathbf{a}_i$ be a point in $\mathbf{U}_i$; let $\mathbf{a}_1 = \mathbf{x}$ and let $\mathbf{a}_k = \mathbf{y}$. For $i = 1 \ldots k-1$ if $z_i$ is right-closed, let $\mathbf{b}_i$ be a point in $\mathbf{U}_i \cap \text{Cl}(\mathbf{U}_{i+1})$. Since $\mathbf{a}_i$ and $\mathbf{b}_i$ are in $\mathbf{U}_i$, which is path-connected, there is a path $\pi_i$ from $\mathbf{a}_i$ to $\mathbf{b}_i$. Since $\mathcal{U}$ is locally simple, there is a path $\phi_i$ that has a starting transition from $\mathbf{b}_i$ into $\mathbf{U}_{i+1}$. Since $\mathbf{U}_{i+1}$ is path-connected, there is a path $\psi_i$ from $\phi_i(1)$ to $\mathbf{a}_{i+1}$. If $z_i$ is right-open, let $\mathbf{b}_i$ be a point in $\text{Cl}(\mathbf{U}_i) \cap \mathbf{U}_{i+1}$. Since $\mathbf{a}_{i+1}$ and $\mathbf{b}_i$ are in $\mathbf{U}_i$, which is path-connected, there is a path $\psi_i$ from $\mathbf{b}_i$ to $\mathbf{a}_{i+1}$. Since $\mathcal{U}$ is locally simple, there is a path $\phi_i$ that has an ending transition from $\mathbf{U}_i$ to $\mathbf{b}_i$. Since $\mathbf{U}_i$ is path-connected, there is a path $\pi_i$ from $\mathbf{a}_i$ to $\phi_i(0)$. Then splicing all these together, the path $\pi_1 \mid \phi_1 \mid \psi_1 \mid \pi_2 \mid \phi_2 \mid \psi_2 \mid \ldots \pi_k \mid \phi_k \mid \psi_k$ is a path satisfying the conclusion of the lemma.

*Figure 5. Trace of a path*

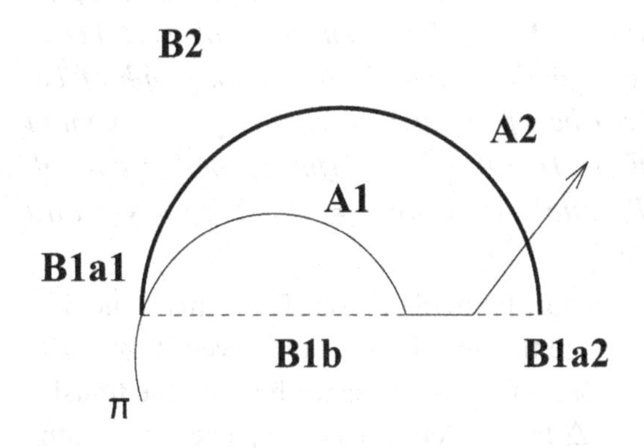


**Theorem 6** *Let $\mathcal{U}$ be a homogeneous partition of* **T**. *Let $\alpha$ be a coherent Z5 ILS through $\mathcal{U}$, let* **x** *be a point in $S(\alpha)$ and let* **y** *be a point in $E(\alpha)$ Then there exists a finitary path $\pi$ through* **T** *such that $S(\pi) = \mathbf{x}$, $E(\pi) = \mathbf{y}$, and $\Gamma_{U,Z5}(\pi) = \alpha$.*

**Proof:** The proof is the same as that of the previous theorem, with two changes. First, since cells are uniform in their neighbors, the point $\mathbf{b}_i$ can be identified with $\mathbf{a}_i$ if $z_i$ is right-closed, and with $\mathbf{a}_{i+1}$ if $z_i$ is right-open, so the paths from $\mathbf{a}_i$ to $\mathbf{b}_i$ and from $\mathbf{b}_i$ to $\mathbf{a}_{i+1}$ can be omitted. Second, for any $\mathbf{a}_i$ let $\psi_{i-1}$ be the path leading into $\mathbf{a}_i$ and let $\pi_i$ be the path leading out of $\mathbf{a}_i$, as constructed in the proof of the previous lemma. If $z_i$ is 'CI,' then splice $\pi_i$ directly onto $\psi_i$. If $z_i$ is 'CE,' then construct a path $\phi$ that remains at the point $\mathbf{a}_i$ for all of [0,1], and splice this between $\psi_i$ and $\pi_i$. ▪

**Corollary 7** *Let $\mathcal{U}$ be a path-connected partition of* **T**. *Let $Z$ be an interval label set. Let $\beta$ be a gpath through the transition graph of $\mathcal{U}$. Let* **x** *be a point in $S(\beta)$ and let* **y** *be a point in $E(\beta)$. Then there exists a finitary path $\pi$ through $T$ such that $S(\pi) = \mathbf{x}$, $E(\pi) = \mathbf{y}$, and $\Delta(\Gamma_{U,Z}(\pi)) = \beta$*

**Proof:** Immediate from Theorems 4 and 5.

Note that corollary 7 holds even if $Z = Z5$ and $\mathcal{U}$ is not homogeneous, because the translation $\Delta$ from interval label sequences to gpaths obliterates the distinction between Z4 and Z5 labels.

We next show that the condition in theorem 5 that $\mathcal{U}$ is path-connected and the condition in theorem 6 are necessary conditions; the conclusion holds only if the conditions are satisfied:

**Theorem 8** *Let $\mathcal{U}$ be a locally simple partition of* **T**. *Suppose it is true that, for every coherent Z4 ILS $\alpha$ through $\mathcal{U}$, and for any points* **x** *in $S(\alpha)$,* **y** *in $E(\alpha)$, there exists a path $\pi$ such that $S(\pi) = \mathbf{x}$, $E(\pi) = \mathbf{y}$, and $\Gamma_{U,Z4}(\pi) = \alpha$. Then $\mathcal{U}$ is path-connected.*

**Proof** of the contrapositive. Let **U** be a cell in $\mathcal{U}$ that is not path-connected, and let **x** and **y** be points in different path-connected components of **U**. Then the interval label sequence $\langle \mathbf{U}, C \rangle$ is coherent, but there is no path from **x** to **y** through **U**.

**Theorem 9** *Let $\mathcal{U}$ be a locally simple partition of* **T**. *Suppose it is true that for every coherent Z5 interval label sequence $\alpha$ through $\mathcal{U}$, and for any points* **x** *in $S(\alpha)$,* **y** *in $E(\alpha)$, there exists a path $\pi$ such that $S(\pi) = \mathbf{x}$, $E(\pi) = \mathbf{y}$, and $\Gamma_{U,Z5}(\pi) = \alpha$. Then $\mathcal{U}$ is homogeneous.*

**Proof** of the contrapositive. Suppose that $\mathcal{U}$ is not homogeneous. Then there exists a cell **U** in $\mathcal{U}$ which is either not path connected or not uniform in its neighbors. If it is not path-connected, then the proof proceeds as in theorem 8. If it is not uniform in its neighbors, then there exists $\mathbf{x} \in \mathbf{U}$ and a neighbor **V** of **U** such that **V** is not a neighbor of **x**. Then the Z5 interval label sequence $\langle\langle \mathbf{U}, \text{`CI'} \rangle, \langle \mathbf{V}, \text{`R'} \rangle\rangle$ is coherent, but there is no path starting in **x** with that trace.

A Z5 interval label sequence fully characterizes the topology of an interval partition:

**Definition 26** *Two interval partitions $\langle I_1 \ldots I_k \rangle$ and $\langle J_1 \ldots J_k \rangle$ are homeomorphic if and only if there is a direction-preserving automorphism $\mathcal{H}(t)$ from* [0,1] *to* [0,1] *such that $\mathcal{H}(I_i) = J_i$.*

**Theorem 10** *$\langle I_1 \ldots I_k \rangle$ and $\langle J_1 \ldots J_k \rangle$ are homeomorphic if shape $(I_i, Z5)$ = shape $(J_i, Z5)$ for $i = 1 \ldots k$.*

**Proof:** It is immediately clear topologically that if $J_i = \mathcal{H}(I_i)$ then shape($I_i, Z5$) = shape($J_i, Z5$). To prove the converse, we may construct $\mathcal{H}(t)$ as follows: For any $t$, let $I_i$ be the interval containing $t$. If $I_i$ is an instantaneous interval, define $\mathcal{H}(t) = l(J_i)$. Otherwise, let:

$$\mathcal{H}(t) = l(J_i) + \frac{(t - l(I_i)) * (u(J_i) - l(J_i))}{u(I_i) - l(I_i)}$$

It is easily shown that $\mathcal{H}$ satisfies the conditions of the theorem.

**Definition 27** *Paths $\pi$ and $\phi$ are $\mathcal{U}$-homeomorphic if there exists a direction-preserving automorphism $\mathcal{H}(t)$ from* [0,1] *to* [0,1] *such that, for all $t$, $\mathbf{O}(\pi(t), \mathcal{U}) = \mathbf{O}(\phi(\mathcal{H}(t)), \mathcal{U})$.*

**Theorem 11** *Paths $\pi$ and $\phi$ are $\mathcal{U}$-homeomorphic if and only if $\Gamma_{U,Z5}(\pi) = \Gamma_{U,Z5}(\phi)$.*

**Proof:** The implication left to right is immediate from theorem 10. For the implication right to left, let $\langle I_1 \ldots I_k \rangle$ and $\langle J_1 \ldots J_k \rangle$ be the interval partitions induced by $\pi$ and $\phi$ respectively, and let $\mathcal{H}$ be the function defined in the proof of theorem 10. It is immediate that this satisfies the conditions.

We now show that $\Gamma$ preserves the operation of splicing two paths, suitably defined.

**Definition 28** *Let $\pi$ and $\phi$ be paths such that $E(\pi) = S(\phi)$. The simple splice of $\pi$ and $\phi$, denoted $\pi \mid \phi$, is the path $\psi$ such that:*

*Table 3. Same interval label set*

| z1 / z2 | 'C' | 'CI' | 'CE' | 'L' |
|---|---|---|---|---|
| 'C' | 'C' | — | — | 'L' |
| 'CI' | — | 'CI' | 'CE' | 'L' |
| 'CE' | — | 'CE' | 'CE' | 'L' |
| 'R' | 'R' | 'R' | 'R' | 'O' |

$$\psi(t) = \begin{cases} \pi(2t) & for\ 0 \leq t \leq 1/2; \\ \phi(2t-1) & for\ 1/2 \leq t \leq 1. \end{cases}$$

**Definition 29** *Let $z_1$ and $z_2$ be labels from the same interval label set, where $z_1$ is closed-right, and $z_2$ is closed-left. The splice of $z_1$ and $z_2$ denoted $z_1 \mid z_2$ is defined as shown in Table 3.*

**Definition 30** *Let $\alpha_1 = \langle\langle \mathbf{V}_1, z_1\rangle \ldots \langle \mathbf{V}_k, z_k\rangle\rangle$ and $\alpha_2 = \langle\langle \mathbf{W}_1, y_1\rangle \ldots \langle \mathbf{W}_m, y_m\rangle\rangle$ be two coherent interval label sequences from the same label set. If $\mathbf{V}_k = \mathbf{W}_1$ then the splice of $\alpha_1$ and $\alpha_2$,*

$$\alpha_1 \mid \alpha_2 = \langle\langle \mathbf{V}_1, z_1\rangle \ldots \langle \mathbf{V}_{k-1}, z_{k-1}\rangle \ldots \langle \mathbf{V}_k = \mathbf{W}_1, z_k \mid y_1\rangle, \langle \mathbf{W}_2, y_2\rangle \ldots \langle \mathbf{W}_m, y_m\rangle\rangle$$

Note that since $\alpha_1$ and $\alpha_2$ are coherent, it follows that $z_k \mid y_1$ is defined.

**Theorem 12** *If $\pi$ and $\phi$ are paths such that $E(\pi) = S(\phi)$ then*
$\Gamma_{U,Z}(\pi \mid \phi) = \Gamma_{U,Z}(\pi) \mid \Gamma_{U,Z}(\phi)$.
*If $\alpha_1$ and $\alpha_2$ are interval label sequences such that $E(\alpha_1) = S(\alpha_2)$ then*
$\Delta(\alpha_1 \mid \alpha_2) = \Delta(\alpha_1) \mid \Delta(\alpha_2)$.

**Proof:** Immediate from the definitions.

## 3.3. Metalogical Theorems

Using the above semantic theorems, we can now prove metalogical results, showing that the decision problem for certain first-order languages over the domains of finitary paths can be reduced to a decision problem for corresponding languages over gpaths and ILS's.

There are a couple of issues to address at the outset. First, one has to be careful here not to make the language of paths too expressive. In particular, if the language supplies any way to express the relation that a point lies in the *middle* of a path, then the jig is up; there is no way to achieve this kind of reduction. The problem is that, in a one-dimensional cell **U**, like **B1b** of Table 2, it is a fact that there exist three distinct points **x, y, z** ∈ **U** such that any path from **x** to **y** that remains in **U** must go through **z.** In a language of points and paths with a predicate "On(x,p)," meaning point x lies on path p, this statement can be expressed in the formula

$\exists_{x,y,z}$ x ≠ z ≠ y ∧
$\forall_p$ [On(x, p) ∧ On(y, p) ∧
[$\forall_w$ On(w, p) ⇒ In(w, U)]] ⇒
On(z, p).

This kind of constraint is quite hopeless to capture in transition graphs or any reasonable extension of them. Since the relation "On(x,p)" can be defined in terms of the splice function, one likewise has to exclude the splice function. However, one needs something like splice so that there is some way to build up extended gpaths. The way out is that we will use relations "Z4Splice($\pi, \phi, \psi$)" and "Z5Splice($\pi, \phi, \psi$)," which hold if $\Gamma_{U,Z}(\psi) = \Gamma_{U,Z}(\pi) \mid \Gamma_{U,Z}(\phi)$ for $Z = Z4$ or $Z5$, respectively.

Second, even with this limited language, there is an inescapable logical distinction between a cell **U** with a single point, such as **A2a1** of Table 1, which satisfies the formula "$\forall_{x,y}$ In(x, u) ∧ In(y, u) ⇒ x = y" and a cell with infinitely many points, which does not. (In a Hausdorff topology,[2] any path-connected cell must be one or the other.) Therefore, the cells in a transition graph must be labelled as either "singleton cells" or "infinite cells."

We can now proceed to our formal construction. First, more typographical conventions. We will use symbols in block capitals for relations in the domains. We will use typewriter font, such as `Splice(a,b,c)` for symbols in the formal language, using lower-case symbols for variables and symbols beginning in upper-case for non-logical symbols. In defining domain relations, we will use curly angle brackets $\prec\succ$ for demarcating tuples, since we have rather overused the standard angle brackets $\langle\rangle$ already.

**Definition 31** *If* $\pi$ *is a path with one cell—that is,* $\Gamma_{U,Z5}(\pi) = \langle\langle \mathrm{U}, \text{`}CE'\rangle\rangle$ *—* $\pi$ *remains in cell* U *. If* $\pi$ *is a path with two cells, then let* $\Gamma_{U,Z5}(\pi) = \langle\langle \mathrm{U}, \mathrm{W}\rangle, \langle \mathrm{V}, \mathrm{X}\rangle\rangle$ *.* $\pi$ *has an open transition from cell* U *to cell* V *if* W *is open right and* X *is closed left.* $\pi$ *has a closed transition from cell* U *to cell* V *if* W *is closed right and* X *is open left.* $\pi$ *has a starting transition from cell* U *to cell* V *if* $X = \text{`}CI'$ *and* W *is open left.* $\pi$ has *a ending transition from cell* U *to cell* V *if* X *is open right and* W= $\text{`}CI'$ .

First we define a structure over the domain of finitary paths. We begin by defining two formal languages:

The language of paths for path-connected partitions, $\mathcal{L}^p$ , is the first-order language with the following predicate symbols (the arity is in parenthesis): `Point(1)`, `Cell(1)`, `Path(1)`, `Singleton(1)`, `In(2)`, `Start(2)`, `End(2)`, `Remains(2)`, `ClosedTrans(3)`, `OpenTrans(3)`, and `Z4Splice(3)`, together with a collection of constant symbols $\mathrm{U}_i$ for $i = 1 \ldots \infty$. The language of paths for homogeneous partitions, $\mathcal{L}^c = \mathcal{L}^p \cup \{$ `StartTrans(3)`, `EndTrans(3)`, `Z5Splice(3)` $\}$.

We next define the corresponding relations over the domains of points, cells, and paths. Let **T** be a topological space and let $\mathcal{U}$ be a path-connected partition over **T**. Define the relations shown in Box 1.

(In the definitions of Z4SPLICE and Z5SPLICE in Box 1, the first vertical bar is "such that" and the second is "splice.")

For any partition $\mathcal{U}$, let $\mathcal{I}^p_U$ and $\mathcal{I}^c_U$ be the interpretations of $\mathcal{L}^p$ and $\mathcal{L}^c$ respectively mapping each predicate symbol to the corresponding relation, and mapping each symbol $\mathrm{U}_i$ to a cell in $\mathcal{U}$.

Second, we define a structure over ILS's. Let $\mathcal{L}^l$ be the first-order language with the following predicate symbols: `Cell(1)`, `ILS(1)`, `Singleton(1)`, `IRemain(2)`, `IStartTrans(3)`, `IEndTrans(3)`, `ISplice(3)`, together with the constant symbols $\mathrm{U}_i$. It is easy to show that any coherent ILS can be formed by splicing together primitive ILS's that either remain in a cell, execute a starting transition, or execute an ending transition.

We define the corresponding relations as shown in Box 2.

Let $\mathcal{I}^l_U$ be the interpretation of $\mathcal{L}^l$ mapping each predicate symbol to the corresponding relation, and mapping each symbol $\mathrm{U}_i$ to a cell in $\mathcal{U}$.

Third, we define a structure over gpaths in the transition graph. Let $\mathcal{L}^g$ be the first-order language with the following predicate symbols: `Cell(1)`, `GPath(1)`, `GRemain(2)`, `ForwardArc(3)`, `BackwardArc(3)`, `GSplice(3)` together with the symbols $\mathrm{U}_i$.

For any graph $G$, define the following relations:

$$\mathrm{CELLS}_G = \{\prec U \succ \mid U \text{ is a vertex in } G\}$$

$$\mathrm{GPATHS}_G = \{\prec \beta \succ \mid \beta \textit{ is a gpath through } G\}.$$

$$\mathrm{DGRAPH}_G = \mathrm{CELLS}_G \cup \mathrm{GPATHS}_G.$$

$$\mathrm{GREMAIN}_G = \{\prec \beta, \mathrm{U} \succ \mid \beta \in \mathrm{GPATHS}_G \wedge \beta = \langle \mathrm{U} \rangle\}$$

*Box 1.*

$\text{POINTS}_U = \mathbf{T}$.
$\text{CELLS}_U = \mathcal{U}$
$\text{PATHS}_U = \{\pi \mid \pi \text{ is a path through } \mathbf{T} \text{ that is finitary over } \mathcal{U}.\}$
$\text{DPATH}_U$ (the domain of paths) $= \text{POINTS}_U \cup \text{CELLS}_U \cup \text{PATHS}_U$
$\text{SINGLETON}_U = \{V \mid V \in \text{CELLS}_U \wedge \exists x \in V\}$
$\text{IN}_U = \{\prec x, V \succ \mid V \in \text{CELLS}_U, x \in V\}$
$\text{START}_U = \{\prec \pi, \pi(0) \succ \mid \pi \in \text{PATHS}_U\}$
$\text{END}_U = \{\prec \pi, \pi(1) \succ \mid \pi \in \text{PATHS}_U\}$
$\text{REMAINS}_U = \{\prec \pi, V \succ \mid \pi \in \text{PATHS}_U \wedge V \in \text{CELLS}_U \wedge \Gamma_{U,Z5}(\pi) = \langle\langle V, \text{'CE'}\rangle\rangle\}$
$\text{CLOSEDTRANS}_U = \{\prec \pi, V, W \succ \mid \pi \in \text{PATHS}_U \wedge V, W \in \text{CELLS}_U \wedge \Gamma_{U,Z4}(\pi) = \langle\langle V, \text{'C'}\rangle, \langle W, \text{'}R\text{'}\rangle\rangle\}$
$\text{OPENTRANS}_U = \{\prec \pi, V, W \succ \mid \pi \in \text{PATHS}_U \wedge V, W \in \text{CELLS}_U \wedge \Gamma_{U,Z4}(\pi) = \langle\langle V, \text{'}L\text{'}\rangle, \langle W, \text{'}C\text{'}\rangle\rangle\}$
$\text{STARTTRANS}_U = \{\prec \pi, V, W \succ \mid \pi \in \text{PATHS}_U \wedge V, W \in \text{CELLS}_U \wedge \Gamma_{U,Z5}(\pi) = \langle\langle V, \text{'}CI\text{'}\rangle, \langle W, \text{'}R\text{'}\rangle\rangle\}$
$\text{ENDTRANS}_U = \{\prec \pi, V, W \succ \mid \pi \in \text{PATHS}_U \wedge V, W \in \text{CELLS}_U \wedge \Gamma_{U,Z5}(\pi) = \langle\langle V, \text{'}L\text{'}\rangle, \langle W, \text{'}CI\text{'}\rangle\rangle\}$
$\text{Z4SPLICE}_U = \{\prec \pi, \phi, \psi \succ \mid \pi, \phi, \psi \in \text{PATHS}_U \wedge \Gamma_{U,Z4}(\psi) = \Gamma_{U,Z4}(\pi) \mid \Gamma_{U,Z4}(\phi))\}$
$\text{Z5SPLICE}_U = \{\prec \pi, \phi, \psi \succ \mid \pi, \phi, \psi \in \text{PATHS}_U \wedge \Gamma_{U,Z5}(\psi) = \Gamma_{U,Z5}(\pi) \mid \Gamma_{U,Z5}(\phi))\}$

*Box 2.*

$\text{ILS}_U =$ the set of coherent Z5 ILS's over $\mathcal{U}$
$\text{IREMAIN}_U = \{\prec \alpha, V \succ \mid \alpha \in \text{ILS}_U \wedge \alpha = \langle\langle V, \text{'}CE\text{'}\rangle\rangle\}$
$\text{ISTARTTRANS}_U = \{\prec \alpha, V, W \succ \mid \alpha \in \text{ILS}_U \wedge \alpha = \langle\langle V, \text{'}CI\text{'}\rangle, \langle W, \text{'}R\text{'}\rangle\rangle\}$
$\text{IENDTRANS}_U = \{\prec \alpha, V, W \succ \mid \alpha \in \text{ILS}_U \wedge \alpha = \langle\langle V, \text{'}L\text{'}\rangle, \langle W, \text{'}CI\text{'}\rangle\rangle\}$
$\text{ISPLICE}_U = \{\prec \alpha_1, \alpha_2, \alpha_3 \succ \mid \alpha_1, \alpha_2, \alpha_3 \in \text{ILS}_U \wedge \alpha_3 = \alpha_1 \mid \alpha_2\}$

$\text{FORWARDARC}_G =$
$\{\prec \beta, \text{U}, \text{V} \succ \mid \beta \in \text{GPATHS}_G \wedge \beta = \langle \text{U}, \langle \text{U}, \text{V} \rangle, \text{V} \rangle\}$

$\text{BACKWARDARC}_G =$
$\{\prec \beta, \text{U}, \text{V} \succ \mid \beta \in \text{GPATHS}_G \wedge \beta = \langle \text{U}, \langle \text{V}, \text{U} \rangle, \text{V} \rangle\}$

$\text{GSPLICE}_G =$
$\{\prec \beta_1, \beta_2, \beta_3 \succ \mid \beta_1, \beta_2, \beta_3 \in \text{GPATHS}_G \wedge \beta_3 = \beta_1 \mid \beta_2\}$

Let $\mathcal{I}_G^g$ be the interpretation of $\mathcal{L}^g$ mapping each predicate symbol to the corresponding relation, and mapping each symbol $\text{U}_i$ to a cell in $\mathcal{U}$

We can now state two parallel metalogical theorems. Theorem 13 states that the decision problem of a sentence in $\mathcal{L}^p$ relative to a path-connected partition can be reduced to the decision of a corresponding sentence in $\mathcal{L}^g$ relative to the transition graph. Theorem 14 states that the decision problem of a sentence in $\mathcal{L}^c$ relative to a homogeneous partition can be reduced to the decision of a corresponding sentence in $\mathcal{L}^l$ relative to the set of Z5 ILS's. In both cases the translation from the language of paths to the language of the transition graph is independent of the particular partition involved, as long as it is path-connected or homogeneous, respectively.

**Theorem 13** *There exists a linear-time function $\mathcal{A}^p$ that maps every sentence in $\mathcal{L}^p$ to a sentence in $\mathcal{L}^g$ satisfying the following. Let* **T** *be a Hausdorff space, let $\mathcal{U}$ be a path-connected partition over* **T** *with at least 2 cells, and let $\mathcal{I}_U^p$ be the interpretation of $\mathcal{L}^p$ in* $\text{DPATHS}_U$ *defined above. Let G be the transition graph corresponding to $\mathcal{U}$ and let $\mathcal{I}_G^g$ be the interpretation of $\mathcal{L}^g$ in* $\text{DGRAPH}_G$ *defined above, such that for each symbol $U_i$. $\mathcal{I}_G^g(\text{U}_i) = \mathcal{I}_U^p(\text{U}_i)$. Let $\Phi$ be any sentence in $\mathcal{L}^p$. Then $\Phi$ holds in the structure* $\prec \text{DPATHS}_U, \mathcal{L}^p, \mathcal{I}_U^p \succ$ *if and only if $\mathcal{A}^p(\Phi)$ holds in the structure* $\prec \text{DGRAPH}_G, \mathcal{L}^g, \mathcal{I}_G^g \succ$.

**Theorem 14** *There exists a linear-time function $\mathcal{A}^c$ that maps every sentence in $\mathcal{L}^c$ to a sentence in $\mathcal{L}^l$ satisfying the following. Let* **T** *be a Hausdorff space, let $\mathcal{U}$ be a path-connected partition over* **T** *with at least 2 cells, and let $\mathcal{I}_U^c$ be the interpretation of $\mathcal{L}^c$ in* $\text{DPATHS}_U$ *defined above. Let $\mathcal{I}_U^l$ be the interpretation of $\mathcal{L}^l$ in* $\text{DILS}_U$ *defined above, such that for each symbol $U_i$, $\mathcal{I}_U^l(U_i) = \mathcal{I}_U^c(U_i)$. Let $\Phi$ be any sentence in $\mathcal{L}^c$. Then $\Phi$ holds in the structure* $\prec \text{DPATHS}_U, \mathcal{L}^c, \mathcal{I}_U^c \succ$ *if and only if $\mathcal{A}^c(\Phi)$ holds in the structure* $\prec \text{DILS}_U, \mathcal{L}^l, \mathcal{I}_U^l \succ$.

**Proofs:** See Appendix.

These results are not actually very surprising. We have carefully crafted the languages of paths so as to exclude the expression of any information not in the transition graph, so it is no great surprise that any sentence in these languages can be translated into a sentence about the transition graph. The point of the theorems is that they give a precise characterization of what kind of information about the paths is encoded in the graph.

From the point of view of worst-case computation theory this is not actually very encouraging, as the decision problem over the graph is in fact in general undecidable.[3] However, it does give us a decision procedure for the language of paths that sometimes gives an answer, and never gives a wrong answer.

The situation as regards existential sentences (i.e. sentences with no universal quantifiers in prenex form) is more promising. Both the mappings $\mathcal{A}^p$ and $\mathcal{A}^c$ map existential sentence to existential sentences. I conjecture that the decision problem for existential sentences over the ILS structure and the transition graph structure is of the same order of computational difficulty as the word equation problem of Makanin (1977), which is known to be in PSPACE though NP-hard (Plandowski, 1999).

## 4. TRANSITION GRAPHS FOR SOME SAMPLE PROBLEMS

We now return from the abstract and general discussion of paths through partitioned topological spaces to the specifics of continuous spatial change. In this section we will discuss the reasoning examples enumerated in section 1 and describe the associated transition graphs, path-connected graph, and homogeneous graphs.

For our purposes the specification of a "spatial continuity problem" involves the following elements:

1. There are a number of *spatial fluents:* that is, entities whose value at each moment of time is a geometric entity; equivalently, fuctions from time to some space of geometric entities. In this chapter, we consider only problems with 1 or 2 non-constant spatial fluents. The state of the system at a point in time, called a *configuration*, is the tuple of the values of these fluents.
2. For each fluent, there is a specification of the general category of values it attains, such as "the class of regular open regions," "the class of points," "the class of directions," and so on. The *general configuration space* is the cross-product of these categories.
3. For each fluent, there may be additionally be a restriction on the class of values it can attain, within the general category. For instance, the region occupied by rigid object at time $t$ is always congruent to the region it occupies at time 0. A quantity of liquid always occupies a constant volume. The *restricted configuration space* is the cross-product of these more limited classes of values.
4. There is a topology over the category of values in (2) that determines what changes are considered "continuous." Two different fluents may have values in the same category but be subject to different kinds of continuity constraints.
5. There is a JEPD (Jointly Exhaustive, Pairwise Disjoint) set of "qualitative" relations over the tuple of values of the fluents.

The space of spatial continuity problems is thus complex and diverse, and we have not found any systematic way to analyze or explore it as a whole. Lacking that, we will discuss the examples of section 1, and try to get insights into the issues involved.

Relating this to the abstract structure developed in section 3: Let $Q_1 \dots Q_k$ be the $k$ spatial fluents, and let $C_i$ be the range of values of $Q_1$. We assume that there is a topology defined on each $C_i$, as in (4) above. A point in the topological space $\mathbf{T}$ is a configuration, and the space $\mathbf{T}$ is either the general or the restricted configuration space. The topology on $\mathbf{T}$ is the cross-product of the topologies on the $C_i$. A path $\pi(t)$ is a tuple $\langle Q_1(t) \dots Q_k(t) \rangle$. The partition $\mathcal{U}$ is the JEPD set of qualitative relations in (5).

A general caveat about the discussion in this section: All of the transition graphs shown below are mathematical claims and should, in principle, be proven. For many of these (e.g. the path-connected transition graph for the three-dimensional jigsaw puzzle pieces) the proof would be long, difficult, boring, and quite pointless. A complete proof requires demonstrating that each cell is homogeneous; that no coarser refinement is homogeneous; that all the arcs in the graph are possible; and that none of the arcs omitted from the graph are possible. Rather, many of these claims are based on my personal geometric intuition, which is fallible. In cases where I do not feel fairly confident, I have labelled these "conjectural."

*Figure 6. Jigsaw puzzle pieces*

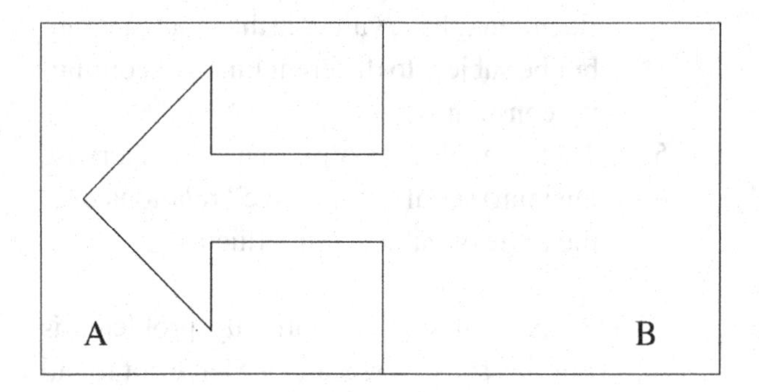


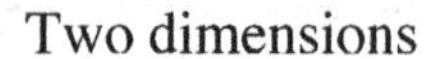

Two dimensions

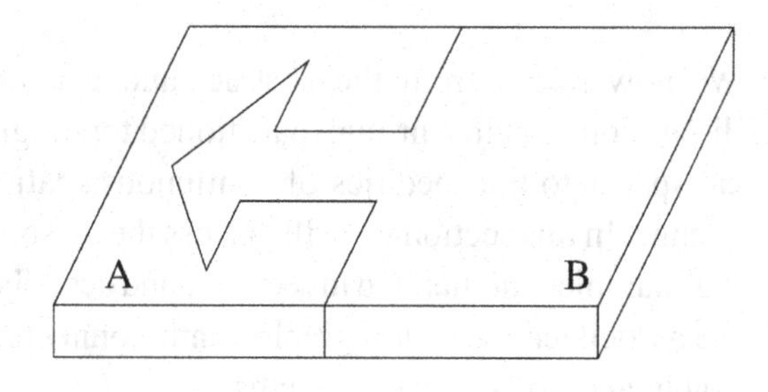


Three dimensions

### 4.1. Example A: Jigsaw Puzzle Pieces

Two interlocked jigsaw puzzle pieces cannot be separated by a movement in the plane of the puzzle, but can be separated by lifting one perpendicular to the plane (see Figure 6).

Here we have an interaction of two rigid solid objects. As discussed in Section 2, this is one of the two most extensively studied problem of continuous motion in the computer science literature (the other is the problem of jointed or linked objects), almost all considering the problem of computing the configuration space from precise shape specifications.

There are a number of different ways to formalize this problem. Specifically, there are three choices with two different options each:

**Two or three dimensions?** As indicated in the problem statement above, the problem can be viewed in two dimensions, in which case the pieces cannot be separated, or in three dimensions, in which case they can.

**Regions or placement?** A state of the system can be specified, either in terms of the *regions* occupied by the two objects or in terms of their *placements*. The placement of object $O$ at time $t$ is a rigid mapping from some standard position of $O$ to the position of $O$ at $t$. Each of these has its advantage.

One advantage of a region-based ontology is that it generalizes easily to non-rigid entities. The flip side of this, though, is that the rigidity constraint has to be added on as an additional constraint, whereas it is built into the placement ontology.

Another advantage of a region-based ontology is that the qualitative relations—feasible, excluded—are fixed and simple relations over regions. By contrast, as functions of the placements the qualitative relations must be indexed to the underlying shape of the objects. That is, in a region-based representation, one can use a simple relation "Feasible(x,y)"; in a placement-based representation, one must use the representation "$\text{Feasible}_{\alpha,\beta}(x,y)$" where $\alpha$ and $\beta$ are the base shapes of the objects. Viewed purely as a function of placement x and y, the latter is a strange and seemingly arbitrary region in the configuration space.

The major advantage of the placement ontology is that it gives rise to a much simpler configuration space. The configuration space of placements of a single rigid object is a three-dimensional manifold for a two-dimensional object in the plane, and a six-dimensional manifold for a three-dimensional object in three-space, and there is one standard topology. By contrast, the configuration space of regions is an strange, infinite dimensional space, with a number of different plausible topologies.

The configuration space of regions that are congruent (excluding reflection) to a reference region $R_0$ is isomorphic to the configuration space of placements, except when the object has some kind of symmetry, in which case multiple placements give the same region. For instance, if the three-dimensional jigsaw pieces are exactly symmetric, then the twelve homogeneous cells where the tab of B stick through the hole of A, as discussed below, reduce to 3; in the notation of Figure 10, the cells $\mathbf{A}i, \mathbf{B}i, \mathbf{C}i$ and $\mathbf{D}i$ are all identified, for each $i$. Though this simplifies the configuration space for symmetric objects, overall it actually tends to be an advantage of the placement ontology: the topological space of placements is constant regardless of the shape of the object, whereas the topological space of regions congruent to $R_0$ is isomorphic for all non-symmetric objects, but is different for symmetric objects, and each different kind of symmetry yields a different topological space. Moreover, small changes to shape that are irrelevant to the interaction—e.g. embossing the name of each jigsaw piece on its surface—will destroy the symmetry and thus alter the configuration space.

**Absolute or relative position?** For rigid objects, and only for rigid objects, one can view one of the objects as fixed, and characterize the position of the second relative to the first (i.e. its position in a coordinate system attached to the first).

The advantages here are closely related to those in the previous choice. A representation based on relative position does not generalize to non-rigid objects, and requires relations indexed on the shape of the fixed element or the shapes of both elements, depending on whether the ontology is region-based or placement-based. On the other hand, it reduces the dimensionality of the configuration space by a factor of 2.

In terms of our formulation of continuous spatial problems, then, this problem has the following characteristics:

**Fluents:** Either two fluents, for the absolute position of each object, or one fluent, for their relative position.

**Category:** Either the space of regular[4] bounded regions in $\mathbb{R}^k$, or the space in placements in $\mathbb{R}^k$.

**Additional restriction:** If the category is the space of regions, then there is the additional restriction that the region occupied by an object at any time is congruent to the region occupied at time $t_0$. If the category is the space of placements, then this is built in.

**Topology**. The state of placements has a single natural topology. The space of regions has several; however, they are all identical when restricted to the subspace of a rigidly moving object.

**Qualitative relations:** As discussed above, in a region-based representation, the starting set of qualitative relations is { **FEASIBLE, EXCLUDED** }; in a placement-based representation, it is { $\mathbf{FEASIBLE}_{\alpha,\beta}$, $\mathbf{EXCLUDED}_{\alpha,\beta}$ }, where $\alpha, \beta$ are the base shapes of the objects. Unlike Galton (1993), we will not distinguish between different categories of excluded placements, such as OV or TPP, as these make no difference in this application. If you want to categorize the relation between a solid object and an empty space which is defined by a rigid object, such as the inside of a suitcase, then OV and TPP are physically possible, and the distinction between them may be meaningful.

The simple transition graph is in Figure 7. This is the basic transition graph for the two relations {**FEASIBLE, EXCLUDED**} in almost all situations.

Whatever the shapes of the objects involved, the excluded space is always uniform in its neighbors, being open. It is generally path-connected. An exception is in the case of two-dimensional analysis of motions on a planar surface, where the horizontal cross-sections of the obstacles that rise above the level of the floor may be disconnected (see example D below).

*Figure 7. Basic transition graphs*

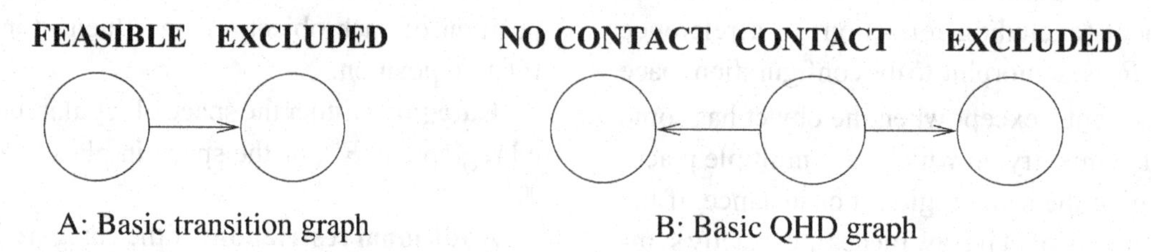


*Figure 8. Transition network for jigsaw puzzle pieces: two-dimensional motion*

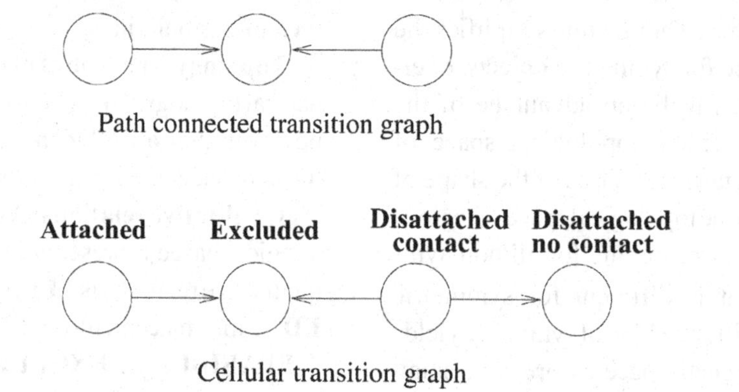


The feasible space for rigid objects may have multiple connected components, corresponding to different positions that cannot be attained one from another. There is always a single unbounded connected component, which includes all the configurations in which the two objects are fully separated. The remaining connected components are all bounded; there can be any number of these, or none. If object A has an interior cavity C which is large enough to hold object B, then the connected components of configuration space in which object B is in C are separate from those in which B is not in C.

In all cases, the homogeneous decomposition distinguishes between two kinds of feasible states: those that border the excluded region—i.e. those in which the two objects are in contact—and those that do not. It may also create additional distinctions, as we shall see below.

For the particular case of the jigsaw puzzle pieces: In the two dimensional case there are two connected components of feasible space: In one it is attached, and in the other it is not. The homogeneous decomposition creates the further distinction between feasible configurations where the two objects are in contact and configurations where they are separated (Figure 8)

In the three-dimensional case, the configurations where the two pieces are attached is connected in feasible space to the configurations where they are not, by sliding one of the pieces vertically. There are also configurations in which the tab of piece B goes through the hole in piece A, but I believe that, for the geometry pictured in Figure 8, these do not create additional connected components.

The homogeneous decomposition here distinguishes between configurations where the pieces are attached in the usual way but possibly with a

*Figure 9. Jigsaw piece B sticks through A*

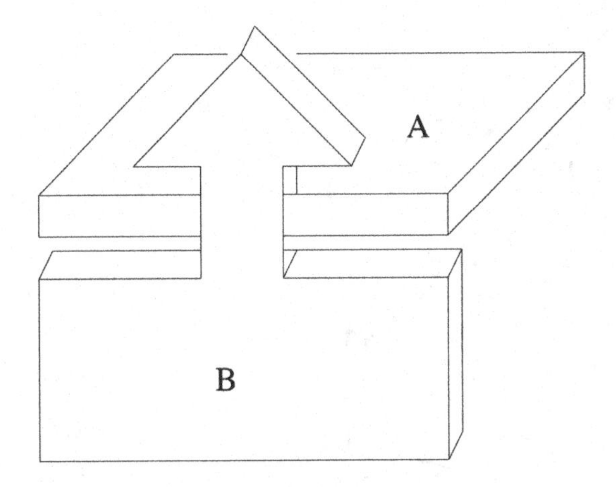


relative vertical displacement, and those where the pieces are separable and in contact in some other way. Even though these are connected in feasible space, they differ in terms of their neighbors. The latter border the configuration region where the two pieces are separated; the former do not. The homogeneous decomposition further subdivides this into three; two limit configurations, where the top plane of piece A is aligned with the bottom plane of piece B, or vice versa; and interior configurations. The homegenous configuration also distinguishes four regions where the tab of piece B sticks through the narrow neck of piece A, meeting it on both sides (Figure 9); four, because B may face forwards or backwards and may stick downward or upward. Each of these is likewise divided into three cells—two limit regions, and the interior. The (conjectural) QHT graph is shown in Figure 10 (and Table 4).

Though this appears like a fine partition, it does not actually make all possible topological distinctions among placements. For example, state A1 includes both the configurations where the bottom face of the triangle of B is in contact with the top surface of, and those where it is not. This is another illustration of the observation made above after theorem 2, that not all points in a cell necessarily have neighborhoods that are homeomorphic with respect to the initial partition.

## 4.2. Example B1: String Loop around an Hourglass

Consider a string loop of length $L$ around the waist of an hourglass with spherical globes of circumference $C$. If $L > C$ then the loop can be removed from the hourglass without coming into contact with the hourglass and without ever being taut. If $L < C$ then the loop cannot be removed from the hourglass. If $L = C$, then the loop can be removed from the hourglass, but at some point it must be in contact with the hourglass, and it must be taut. It can be taken off either the upper or the lower globe.

If the globes of the hourglass are long cylinders, the circular cross section has circumference $C$, and $C = L$, then the string can be removed from the hourglass, but it will be taut and in contact with the hourglass over an extended interval of time.

The hourglass is a rigid object, so the issues here are the same as in example A. For simplicity, we will view the hourglass as fixed, taking its shape to be a boundary condition of the problem, and characterize the configurations of the string.

We will model the string using an idealized model in which a configuration of the string is a continuous, arc-length preserving function from the circle of circumference $L$ into $\mathbb{R}^3$. We allow the string to cross itself, to overlay itself, or to pass through itself. A better model would additionally require that the configuration of the curve be a *simple curve*; i.e. a one-to-one function. We have not done this, because the analysis is much more complicated; the configuration space has infinitely many connected components, characterized by knot theory. If the string is taken to be of finite thickness $T$, then the number of connected components is exponential in $L / T$. Even in this simplified model, the analysis in this section should be considered conjectural.

In terms of our format for problem specification:

*Figure 10. QHT graph for jigsaw puzzle: three-dimensional motions*

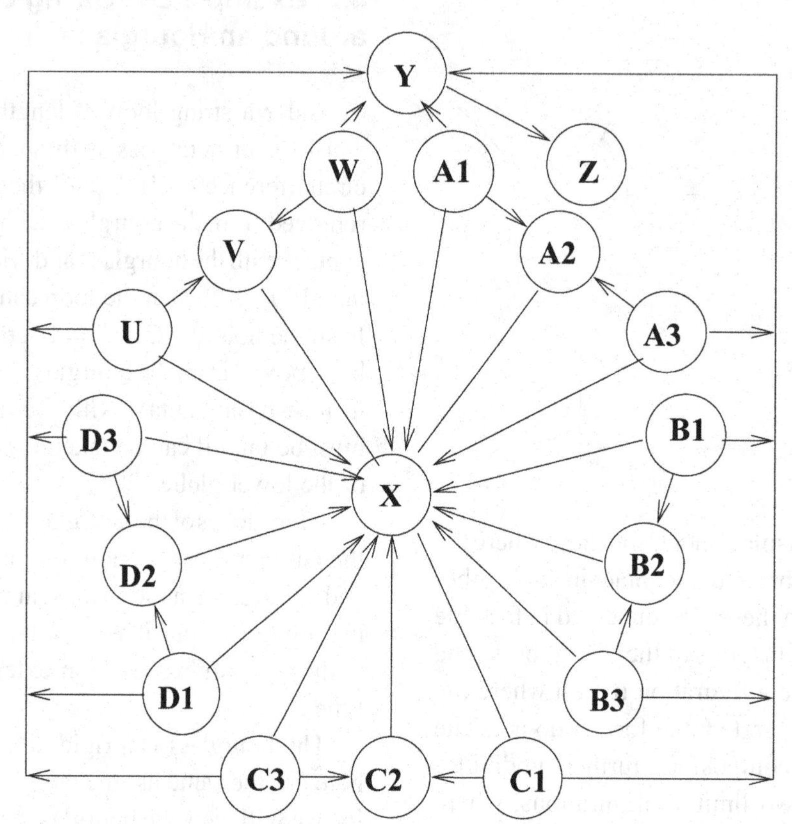


*Table 4. Cell labels for Figure 10*

| |
|---|
| **A1:** Tab of B upward through A; faces forward; borders outside. |
| **A2:** Tab of B upward through A; faces forward; interior. |
| **A3:** Tab of B upward through A; faces forward; borders inside. |
| **B1:** Tab of B upward through A; faces back; borders outside. |
| **B2:** Tab of B upward through A; faces back; interior. |
| **B3:** Tab of B upward through A; faces back; borders inside. |
| **C1:** Tab of B downward through A; faces forward; borders outside. |
| **C2:** Tab of B downward through A; faces forward; interior. |
| **C3:** Tab of B downward through A; faces forward; borders inside. |
| **D1:** Tab of B downward through A; faces back; borders outside. |
| **D2:** Tab of B downward through A; faces back; interior. |
| **D3:** Tab of B downward through A; faces back; borders inside. |
| **U:** Horizontal projections attached; top of A aligned with bottom of B. |
| **V:** Attached: no horizontal motions possible. |
| **W:** Horizontal projections attached; bottom of A aligned with top of B. |
| **X:** Excluded. |
| **Y:** Loose contact. |
| **Z:** No contact. |

**Fluents:** There is a single fluent, the position of the string relative to the hourglass.

**Category:** Let $S_L$ be the unit circle of radius $L / 2\pi$. The category is the set of all continuous function $\phi : S_L \rightarrow \mathbb{R}^3$.

**Topology:** The natural metric over configurations is $d_C(\phi, \psi) = \max_{x \in S_L} d(\phi(x), \psi(x))$ where $d(a,b)$ is the usual Euclidean distance in $\mathbb{R}^3$. This is similar to the Fréchet distance between the corresponding curves; the metric here is never less and may be greater.

**Additional restriction:** Let $A$ be a connected arc in $S_L$. Then $\phi(A)$ has a well-defined arc length, which is equal to the arc length of $A$.

**Qualitative Relations:** Let $\alpha$ be the region occupied by the hourglass. There are two starting qualitative regions of configuration space: **EXCLUDED**$_\alpha$, where the string penetrates the interior of $\alpha$, and **FEASIBLE**$_\alpha$, where it does not. The basic transition graph is always that shown in Figure 7a.

Let us assume that:

- The string has length $L$.
- The hourglass is solid; that is, we will not consider configuration in which the string lies inside the globes of the hourglass.
- The globes of the hourglass are identical spheres of radius $C / 2\pi$, with centers on the $z$-axis.
- The intersection of the surface of two spheres is a circle of radius $W / 2\pi$, and the hourglass is the union of the two spheres.

There are four cases to consider.

Case 1: $L < W$. The string will not go around the hourglass even at the waist. Hence, **FEASIBLE**$_\alpha$ has a single path-connected component. The path-connected transition graph is thus still Figure 7a. The homogeneous transition graph distinguishes configurations on the boundary between **FEASIBLE**$_\alpha$ and **EXCLUDED**$_\alpha$; i.e. configurations where the string has contact with the surface of $\alpha$ (Figure 7b).

Case 2: $W \leq L < C$. Let $k = \lfloor L / W \rfloor$. Here **FEASIBLE**$_\alpha$ has a $2k+1$ connected components, one component where it is separated from the hourglass, and $2k$ components where it is wrapped $i$ times around the neck of the hourglass, for $i = 1 \ldots k$, clockwise or counterclockwise. The homogeneous decomposition distinguishes configurations in which the string is in contact with the hourglass from those in which it is not. If $L > kW$ then there are thus $4k+2$ cells. If $L = kW$, then there does not exist a configuration in which the string wraps $k$ times around the hourglass and is not in contact, though there do exist two configurations in which it wraps $k$ times and is in contact; thus there are $4k$ homogeneous cells.

Case 3: $L > C$, $(L - C) / W$ is not an integer. Let $q = \lfloor (L - C) / W \rfloor$. If the string is wrapped $i$ times around the waist, where $q < i \leq \lfloor L / W \rfloor$, then it must remain so. As in Case 2, this gives $2(\lfloor L / W \rfloor - q)$ connected components, and either $4(\lfloor L / W \rfloor - q)$ or $4(\lfloor L / W \rfloor - q) - 2$ homogeneous cells, depending on whether $L / W$ is an integer. If the string is wrapped $q$ or fewer times around the waist, then it can be removed from the hourglass without coming into contact with it; all such situations form a single connected component with the disattached configurations, and form two homogeneous cells (contact and non-contact).

Case 4: $C + qW = L$ for integer $q \geq 0$. This is the same as Case 3, with the following change: If the string is wrapped $q+1$ times around the waist, then it is possible to separate the string from the hourglass, taking off one loop at a time; however, there is necessarily an instant at which the string is taut around both the globe and the waist. These configurations are thus also part of the connected component with the disattached configurations, but give rise to ten homogeneous cells: wrapped around the waist, contact or no

*Figure 11. Transition graphs for string and hourglass: cases 2 and 3*

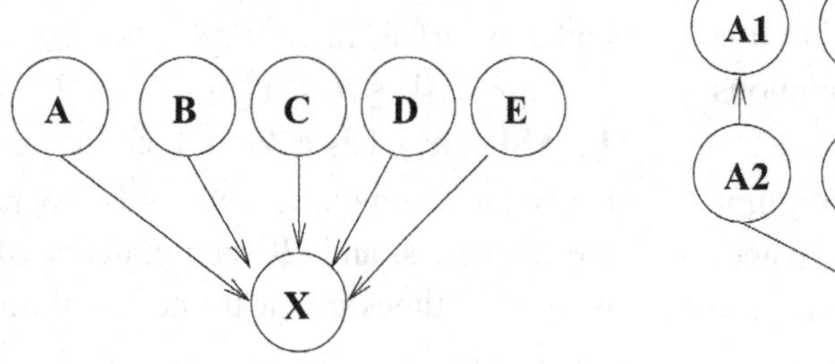


Path connected graph: Case 2–4

Homogeneous graph: Case 2,3

contact, clockwise or counter-clockwise (4 cells); taut around the upper/lower globe, clockwise and counter-clockwise (4 cells); and disattached, contact or no contact (2 cells).

If the globes of the hourglass are cylinders whose central axis is longer than $L / 2$ (the geometry for short cylinders is hairy), then the string can be removed at all from a position wrapped $i$ times around the waist if and only if $L \geq iC$. So, if $i > L / C$ it cannot be removed; this gives $2(\lfloor L / W \rfloor - \lfloor L / C \rfloor)$ connected components (each value of $i$, clockwise and counterclockwise) and $4(\lfloor L / W \rfloor - \lfloor L / C \rfloor)$ homogeneous cells (contact and no contact, unless $i = L / W$ is an integer, as in case 2). If $i < L / C$ then it can be removed without contact; these configurations are therefore all part of the same single component that includes disattached configurations. This component has two homogeneous cells. If $i = L / C$ is an integer, then this is also part of the disattached connected components, but gives rise to eighteen homogeneous cells: each of the taut cells of Case 4 above is split into three (at inner rim, at outer rim, in middle).

Figures 11 and 12 show the transition graphs for these four cases as explained in Table 5

## 4.3. Example B2: Rubber Band around an Hourglass

If, instead of a string loop, we have a rubber band whose length is less than $C$ at rest but can be stretched to a length greater than $C$, then it can be removed from the hourglass without being in contact with the hourglass, but it must be stretched in order to do so.

The problem specification for this example differs from Example B1 in two respects: First, the **Additional restrictions** becomes the following: Let $A$ be a connected arc in $S_L$. Then $\phi(A)$ has a well-defined arc length $|\phi(A)|$ and $|A| \leq \phi(A) \leq \gamma |A|$ where $\gamma$ is the ratio between the length of the band when maximally stretched and the length of the band when relaxed.

Second, the *Qualitative relations* involve a distinction between whether the band is relaxed or stretched . Thus, the basic set of qualitative relations has four elements:

$$\{\textbf{FEASIBLE}_{\alpha} \wedge \textbf{RELAXED},$$
$$\textbf{FEASIBLE}_{\alpha} \wedge \textbf{STRETCHED},$$
$$\textbf{EXCLUDED}_{\alpha} \wedge \textbf{RELAXED},$$
$$\textbf{EXCLUDED}_{\alpha} \wedge \textbf{STRETCHED}\}$$

The transition graphs are formed by combining the transition graph from Example B1 for a string whose length is the relaxed length of the rubber

*Figure 12. Transition graphs for string and hourglass: case 4 and cylinder*

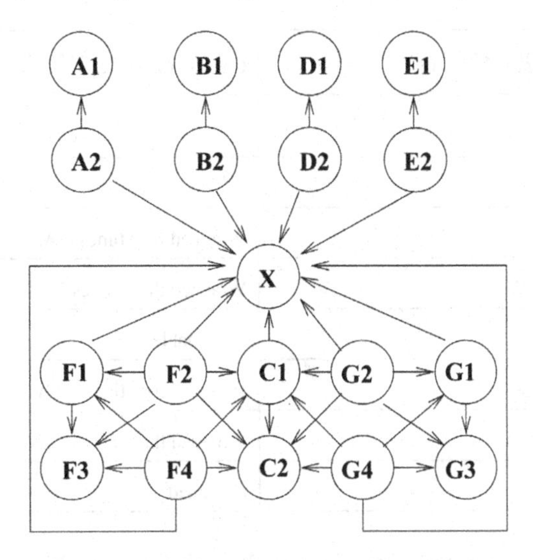


Homogeneous graph: Case 4: spheres

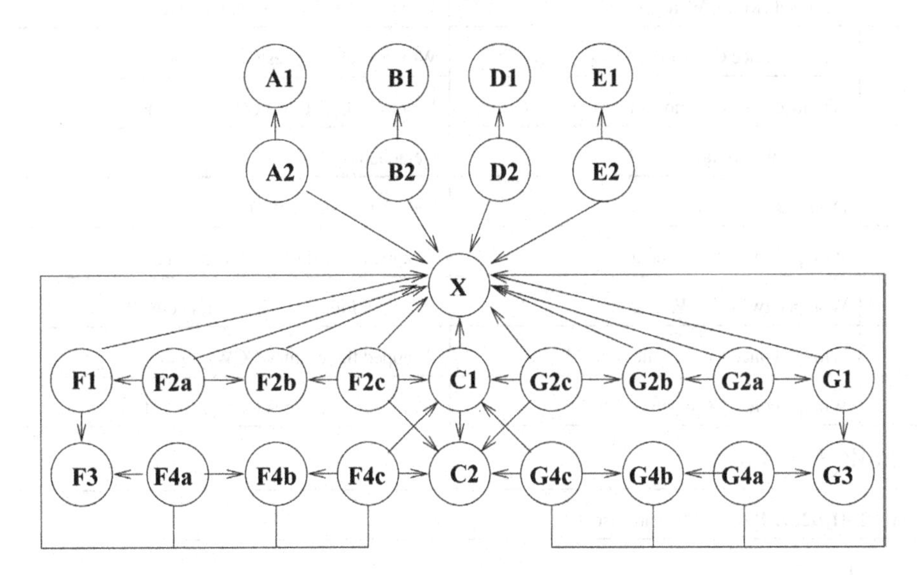


Homogeneous graph: cylinders

band, and the transition graph for a string whose length is the maximal length of the rubber band.

## 4.4. Example C: Milk in a Bottle

A quantity of milk in a closed bottle remains in the bottle.

There are a number of different ways to characterize the continuous motion of a liquid (Davis, 2008, 2009). For our purposes here, the simplest and most relevant is as follows: The fluent is the region occupied by the milk, which we take to be a regular region. Since liquid is incompressible—that is, a body of liquid occupies a constant

*Table 5. Transition graphs for string and hourglass: key*

| | Case 2: $L = 2.5W < C$ . | Case 3: $C = 2.5W, L = 4.2W$ . |
|---|---|---|
| | | |
| Path-connected graph | | |
| **A:** | Wrapped twice CW | Wrapped four times CW |
| **B:** | Wrapped once CW | Wrapped three times CW |
| **C:** | Detachable | Detachable |
| **D:** | Wrapped twice CCW | Wrapped four times CCW |
| **E:** | Wrapped once CCW | Wrapped three times CCW |
| **X:** | Excluded | Excluded |
| homogeneous graph | | |
| **A1:** | Wrapped twice CW, contact | Wrapped four times CW, contact |
| **A2:** | Wrapped twice CW, no contact | Wrapped four times CW, no contact |
| **B1:** | Wrapped once CW, contact | Wrapped three times CW, contact |
| **B2:** | Wrapped once CW, no contact | Wrapped three times CW, no contact |
| **C1:** | Detachable, contact | Detachable, contact |
| **C2:** | Detachable, no contact | Detachable, no contact |
| **D1:** | Wrapped twice CCW, contact | Wrapped four times CCW, contact |
| **D2:** | Wrapped twice CCW, no contact | Wrapped four times CCW, no contact |
| **E1:** | Wrapped once CCW, contact | Wrapped three times CCW, contact |
| **E2:** | Wrapped once CCW, no contact | Wrapped three times CCW, no contact |
| Case 4: $C = 2.5W, L = 4.5W$ . | | |
| **A,B,C,D,E,X,A1,A2,B1,B2,D1,D2,E1,E2:** as in case 3. | | |
| **C1:** Detached, contact. | | |
| **C2:** Detached, no contact. | | |
| **F1:** Wrapped twice around waist CW, contact. | | |
| **F2:** Taut around upper globe and waist, CW. | | |
| **F3:** Wrapped twice around waist CW, no contact. | | |
| **F4:** Taut around lower globe and waist, CW. | | |
| **G1:** Wrapped twice around waist CCW, contact. | | |
| **G2:** Taut around upper globe and waist, CCW. | | |
| **G3:** Wrapped twice around waist CCW, no contact. | | |

*continued on following page*

*Table 5. Continued*

| **G4:** Taut around lower globe and waist, CCW. |
|---|
| Cylindrical globes, $L = 4.5W = 2C$ . |
| **A,B,C,D,E,X,A1,A2,B1,B2,C1,C2,D1,D2,E1,E2,F1,F3,G1,G3**: as in case 4. |
| **F2a**: Taut around cylinder CW, at outer rim, upper cylinder. |
| **F2b**: Taut around cylinder CW, not at rim, upper cylinder. |
| **F2c**: Taut around cylinder CW, at inner rim, upper cylinder. |
| **F4a**: Taut around cylinder CW, at outer rim, lower cylinder. |
| **F4b**: Taut around cylinder CW, not at rim, lower cylinder. |
| **F4c**: Taut around cylinder CW, at inner rim, lower cylinder. |
| **G2a**: Taut around cylinder CCW, at outer rim, upper cylinder. |
| **G2b**: Taut around cylinder CCW, not at rim, upper cylinder. |
| **G2c**: Taut around cylinder CCW, at inner rim, upper cylinder. |
| **G4a**: Taut around cylinder CCW, at outer rim, lower cylinder. |
| **G4b**: Taut around cylinder CCW, not at rim, lower cylinder. |
| **G4c**: Taut around cylinder CCW, at inner rim, lower cylinder. |

volume—a natural metric to use is the following (original here, to the best of my knowledge):

**Definition 32** *Let $V(R)$ be the volume of region $R$. A function $\Phi$ over $R1$ is volume-preserving if, for every subset $R \subset R1$, $V(\Phi(R)) = V(R)$. The cost of $\Phi$ on $R1$, $C(\Phi, R1) = \sup_{p \in R} d(p, \Phi(p))$.*

*Let $R1$ and $R2$ be closed, bounded, regular regions such that $V(R1) = V(R2)$. The volume-preserving distance from $R1$ to $R2$, $d_{vp}(R1, R2)$ is the infimum of $C(\Phi, R1)$ for all volume-preserving $\Phi$ such that $Cl(\Phi(R1)) = R2$. (Note that $\Phi$ need not be continuous, and therefore $\Phi(R1)$ may not be closed).*

**Example (Figure 13a):** Let $R1$ be the unit square $[0,1] \times [0,1]$, and let $R2$ be the pair of rectangles $[0,1/2] \times [0,1] \cup [3/2,2] \times [0,1]$. Let $\Phi$ be the function:

$$\Phi(p) = \begin{cases} p & \text{if } p_x \leq 1/2 \\ p + \hat{x} & \text{if } p_x > 1/2 \end{cases}$$

Then $C(\Phi, R1) = 1$. It is easily shown that no volume-preserving function has lower cost, so $d_{vp}(R1, R2) = 1$.

It is easily shown that $d_{vp}$ is a metric over closed regular regions, and that it is always at least as large as the Hausdorff distance, and often greater. For instance in Figure13b, the Hausdorff distance from $R1$ to $R2$ is 1/16, since every point in $R1$ is within distance 1/16 of a point in $R2$ and vice versa. A volume-preserving function, however, must move one square unit of liquid from the left-hand side to the right hand side; it can be shown that $d_{vp}(R1, R2) = 1/2$. Taking this kind of example to the limit, it follows that the topology induced by $d_{vp}$ is stricly finer than that induced by the Hausdorff distance.

In terms of our format for problem specification:

**Fluent:** There is a single fluent, which is the region occupied by the milk. We take the region $\alpha$ occupied by the bottle to be a constant boundary condition.

**Category:** The value of the fluent is a regular region.

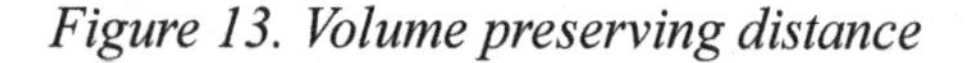

*Figure 13. Volume preserving distance*

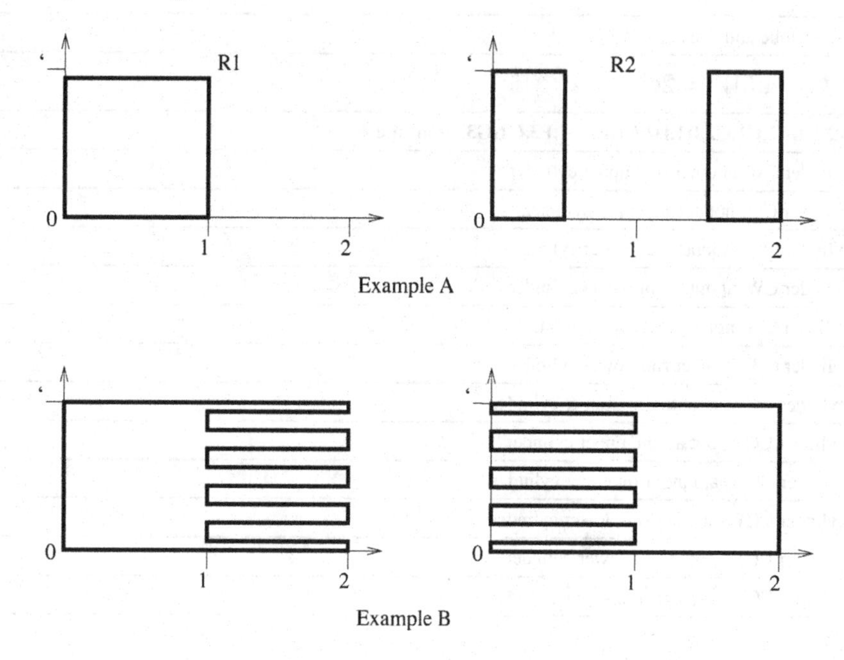


**Additional constraint:** The volume of the fluent is a constant value $V$.

**Topology:** The topology defined by the metric $d_{vp}$.

**Qualitative relation:** **EXCLUDED**$_\alpha$, in configurations where the milk penetrates the interior of the bottle, and **FEASIBLE**$_\alpha$ where it does not.

The basic transition graph is the standard one (Figure 7).

The feasible region actually has uncountably many connected components: for each $V1$ between 0 and $V$ inclusive, the set of configurations with volume $V1$ of milk inside the bottle and $V - V1$ outside is a separate connected component. The effect of a homogeneous decomposition is just to divide each of these connected components into two parts: configurations where the milk is in contact with the bottle (either on the inside or outside), and those where it is not (Figure 14).

Nonetheless, the partition is locally finite, so the theory developed in Section 3 still applies.

## 4.5. Example C2: Milk in Cups

If at time $T1$ there is milk sitting in open cup A, and at a later time $T2$ the milk has moved to a cup B, and both cups are stationary, then the milk came out of the top of cup A and went in the top of cup B.

The problem formulation is the same as in C1, except that the shape of the cups is different from the shape of the bottle, and that the basic qualitative relations are different. Specifically, we defined a region $RC$ as *cupped* by region $RO$ if the boundary of $RC$ is the union of two parts, $BO \cup BT$ where $BO$ is a subset of the boundary of $RO$, and $BT$ is a surface lying in a horizontal plane above $RC$ (Figure 15). We then consider a basic set of four possible qualitative relations:

- **EXCLUDED**: configurations where the milk penetrates the interior of the material of cup.
- **A** if all of the milk is in a region cupped by cup A.

*Figure 14. Transition network for milk and bottle*

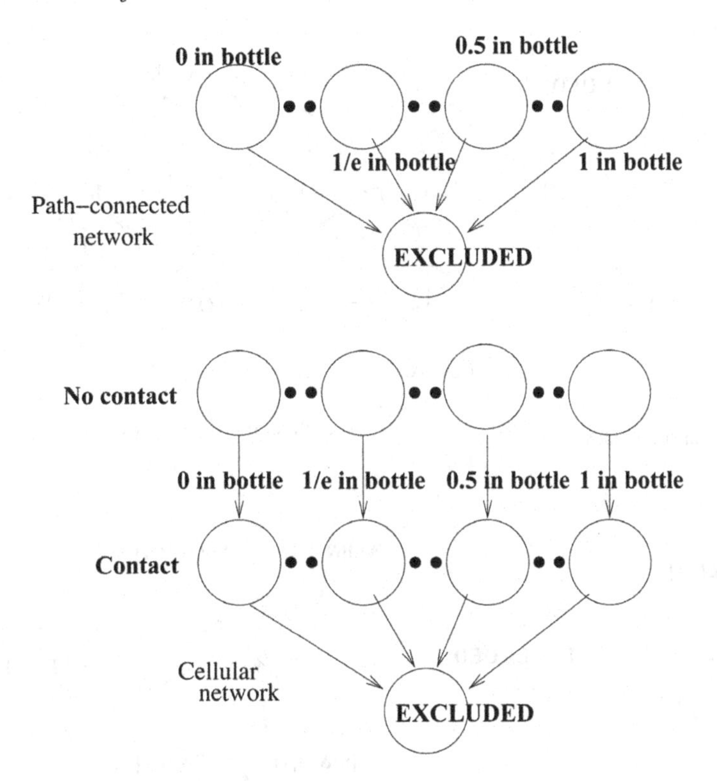


*Figure 15. Cupped region*

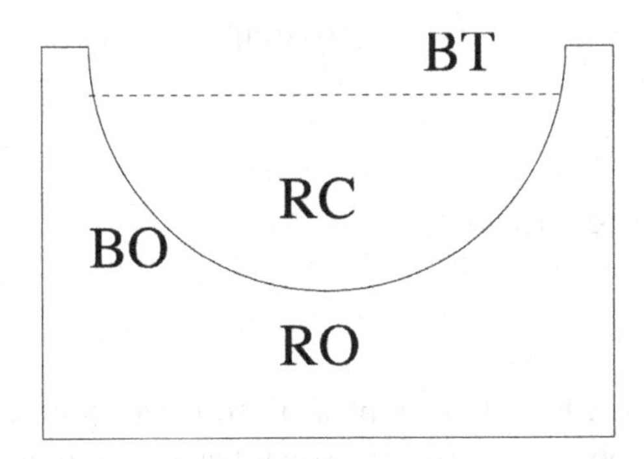


- **B** if all of the milk is in a region cupped by cup B.
- **OTHER** if the configuration is feasible, but neither **A** nor **B** holds.

Each of these cells is path-connected. A homogeneous decomposition divides cells **A** and **B** each into four subcells, according to whether the milk is (**A1**) in contact with the cup, (**A2**) with the opening at the top, (**A3**) both, or (**A4**) neither. It divides **OTHER** into two subcells, according to whether the milk is (**O1**) in contact with either cup or (**O2**) not (Figure 16a).

If we modify the problem to read that some but not all of the milk moves from cup A to cup B, then that can be formalized using a starting partition that has uncountably many cells, though it is locally finite:

- **EXCLUDED:** The milk penetrates the material of the cup.
- **A**[V1] & **B**[V − V1]: For any $V1$ between 0 and $V$, there is volume $V1$ in cup A and $V - V1$ in cup B.
- **OTHER**: The configuration is feasible and some of the milk is outside both cups.

Each of these is path-connected. The homogeneous decomposition divides the cupped com-

*Figure 16. Transition networks for milk in cups*

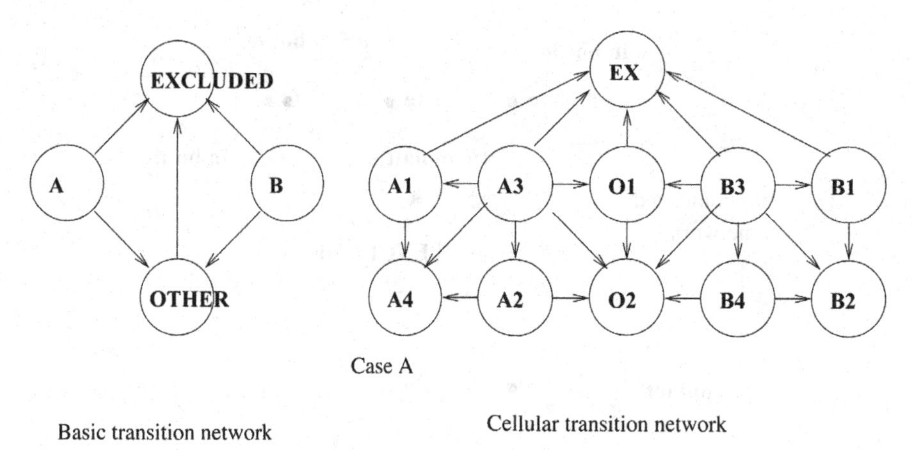




ponents into four, and the **OTHER** component into two, as in the earlier analysis (Figure 16b).

## 4.6. Example D: Blocking the Dog with a Chair

The dog can go from the dining room into the kitchen. However, if a chair is placed in the middle of the kitchen doorway, then the dog cannot go from the dining room to the kitchen. If the chair is placed at the edge of the doorway, then the dog can squeeze past and get into the kitchen.

The transition graph analysis of this problem is problematic. The problem is that if a configuration is taken to be the pair of the position of the chair and the position of the dog, then the class of paths includes any simultaneous motion of the dog and the chair. The transition graph over this set of paths cannot represent the above conclusions, which describe the possible motions of the dog in which the chair is static. In fact, the homogeneous transition graph just has the three states **NO CONTACT, CONTACT,** and **EXCLUDED** (Figure 7b).

*Figure 17. Dog and chair scenario*

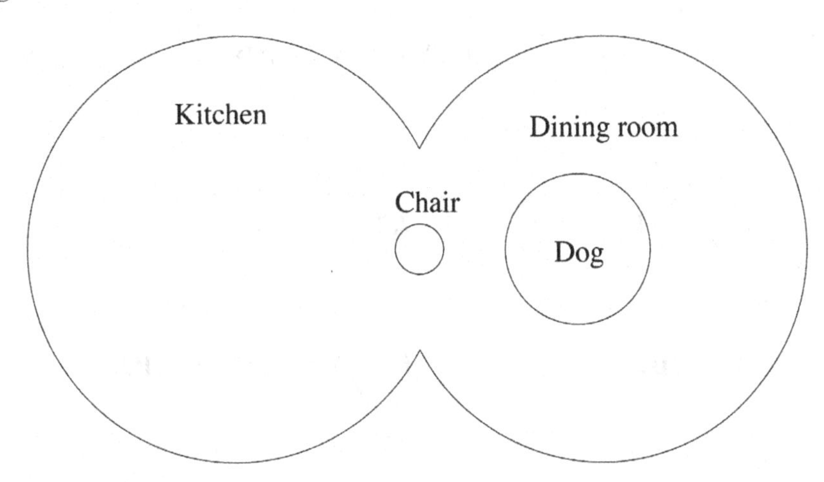


We can solve this problem by using a hierarchy of transition graphs, with two layers. The bottom layer of transition graphs describes the motions of the dog for possible fixed positions of the chair. The upper layer describes the motions of the chair, characterized by the the transition graphs of the lower level. That is, we take the starting qualitative relations over the position of the chair to be the transition graphs from the lower level (More precisely, equivalence classes of transition graphs under isomorphism; the graphs for any two positions of the chair are, strictly speaking, not equal because the corresponding cells created for the dog are not actually equal, just close.).

To simplify the analysis, I have taken the dog, the chair, and the walls of the two rooms to be circular, as shown in Figure 17; more realistic shapes will lead to both more complex transition graphs and more difficult analysis. Even with this simplification, the analysis here of the homogeneous case is somewhat conjectural. Let Dist(C,W) be the distance from the chair to the wall, and let Diam(D) be the diameter of the dog. The width of the doorway is equal to Dist(C,W)+Diam(D).

In a layered representation using path connected graphs, there are three lower-level transition graphs:

A. The chair does not block the dog, and Dist(C,W) $<$ Diam(D). In this case there are two cells: **(A1)** feasible and **(A2)** excluded.
B. The chair does not block the dog, and Dist(C,W) $\geq$ Diam(D). In this case, the excluded region has two connected components, so there are three cells: **(B1)** feasible; **(B2)** dog overlaps walls; **(B3)** dog overlaps chair.
C. The chair blocks the dog. In this case the feasible region has two connected components so there are three cells: **(C1)** dog in dining room; **(C2)** dog in kitchen; **(C3)** excluded.

The upper-level transition graph has four cells (Figure 18):

U1: The chair does not block the dog, and Dist(C,W) $<$ Diam(D). Lower-level graph A.
U2: The chair does not block the dog, Dist(C,W) $\geq$ Diam(D), and the chair is in the dining room. Lower-level graph B.
U3: The chair does not block the dog, Dist(C,W) $\geq$ Diam(D), and the chair is in the kitchen. Lower-level graph B.
U4: The chair blocks the dog. Lower-level graph C.

*Figure 18. Layered path-connected transition network for dog and chair*

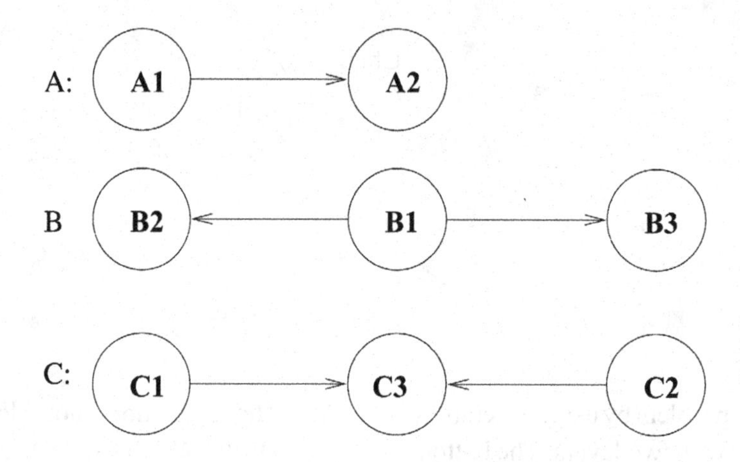


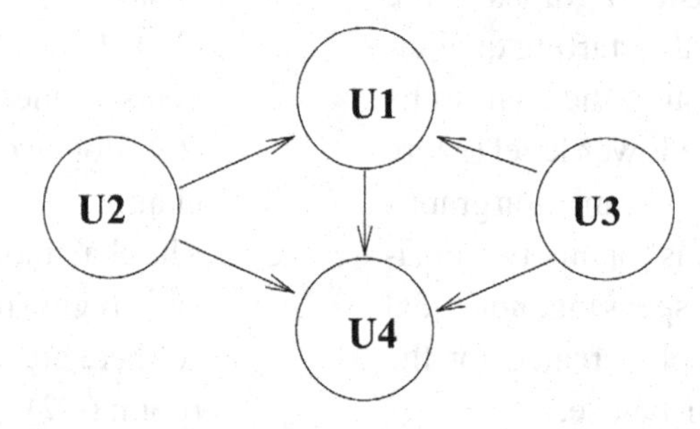


*Figure 19. Positions of chairs creating different low-level homogeneous graphs*

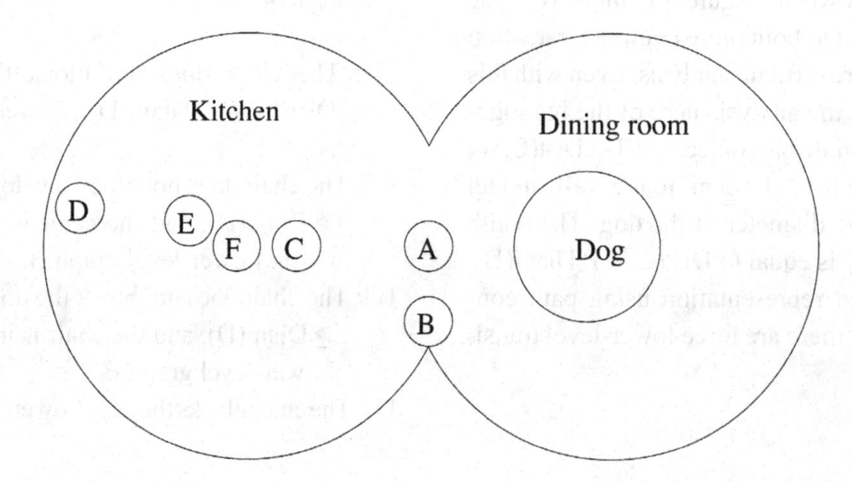

In a layered representation using homogeneous graphs, there are six transition lower-level transition graphs (Figures 19 and 20).

A. The chair blocks the dog. The homogeneous graph here has five cells: Dog in kitchen, (**A1**) with or (**A2**) without contact; dog in dining room,(**A3**) with or (**A4**) without contact; (**A5**) excluded.

B. The chair in the doorway allows the dog to squeeze by on one side. The homogeneous graph has six cells: Dog in kitchen, (**B1**) with or (**B2**) without contact; dog in dining room, (**B3**) with or (**B4**) without contact; (**B5**) dog squeezing by; (**B6**) excluded.

C. The chair is placed so as to allow the dog to squeeze by on either side. The homogeneous graph has ten cells: Dog in kitchen, (**C1**) with or (**C2**) without contact; dog in dining room, (**C3**) with or (**C4**) without contact; dog squeezing by (**C5**) on left or (**C6**) on right; dog in contact with chair (**C7**) on the kitchen side or (**C8**) on the dining room side; excluded because (**C9**) dog overlaps walls; (**C10**) dog overlaps chair.

D. The chair does not block the dog, and Dist(C,W) < Diam(D). The homogeneous graph has three states: (**D1**) dog not in contact, (**D2**) dog in contact, (**D3**) excluded.

E. The chair does not block the dog, and Dist(C,W)=Diam(D). The homogeneous graph has six states: (**E1**) dog not in contact, (**E2**) dog in contact with walls, (**E3**) dog in contact with chair, (**E4**) dog in contact with both walls and chair, (**E5**) dog overlaps walls, (**E6**) dog overlaps chair.

F. The chair does not block the dog, and Dist(C,W) > Diam(D). The homogeneous graph has five states: (**F1**) dog not in contact, (**F2**) dog in contact with walls, (**F3**) dog in contact with chair; (**F4**) dog overlaps walls, (**F5**) dogs overlaps chair.

The upper-level transition graph has eighteen cells (Figure 21):

U1a – U4b: Chair does not interfere with dog. Cross product of { Dist(C,W)=0 / Dist(C,W) < Diam(D) / Dist(C,W) = Diam(D) / Dist(C,W) > Diam(D) } times { Chair in kitchen, chair in dining room }. Lower-level graphs: D, D, D, D, E, E, F, F respectively.

U5: Chair blocks dog. Lower-level graph A.

U6: Dog can squeeze through on right. Chair is (**U6a**) in dining room, (**U6b**) in kitchen, (**U6c**) against the left wall. Lower-level graph B.

U7: Dog can squeeze through on left. Chair is (**U7a**) in dining room, (**U7b**) in kitchen, (**U7c**) against the right wall. Lower-level graph B.

U8: Dog can squeeze through on both sides. Chair is (**U8a**) in dining room, (**U8b**) in kitchen. Lower-level graph C.

U9: Excluded: Chair overlaps walls. Lower-level graph D.

In terms of our structure for problem specifications: At the lower level, the fluent is the position of the dog. The set of qualitative relations is { **EXCLUDED**$_\alpha$, **FEASIBLE**$_\alpha$} where $\alpha$ is the region occupied by the walls and by the chair. At the upper level, the fluent is the position of the chair. The starting set of qualitative relations is the set of transition networks from the lower level, plus the excluded state. The remainder of both problem is the same as in example A.

However, this analysis is not satisfactory, because it introduces a false assymetry between the chair and the dog. It is equally true, after all, that if the dog has settled down in the center of the doorway, then one cannot move the chair from one room to another, but this transition graph structure expresses that only very indirectly.

*Figure 20. Lower-level homogeneous graphs for dog and chair*

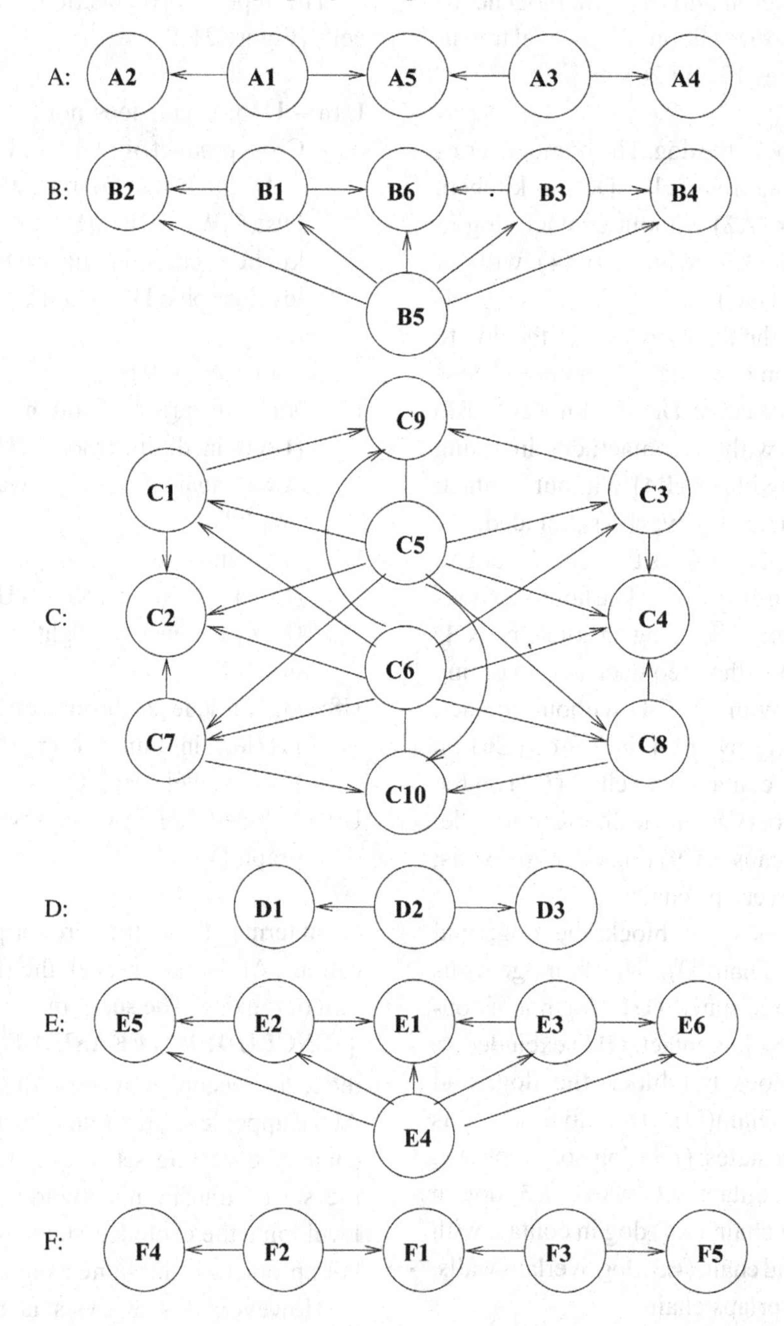


## 4.7. Example E: Travel from Alaska to Idaho

A person who is in Canada at one time and in the United States at a later time must cross the U.S. border at some time in between. A person who is in Alaska at one time and in Idaho at a later time must cross the U.S. border at least twice in between. It is possible to travel from any point in Idaho to any point in Ohio without crossing the border of the United States.

*Figure 21. Upper-level transition graph for dog and chair*

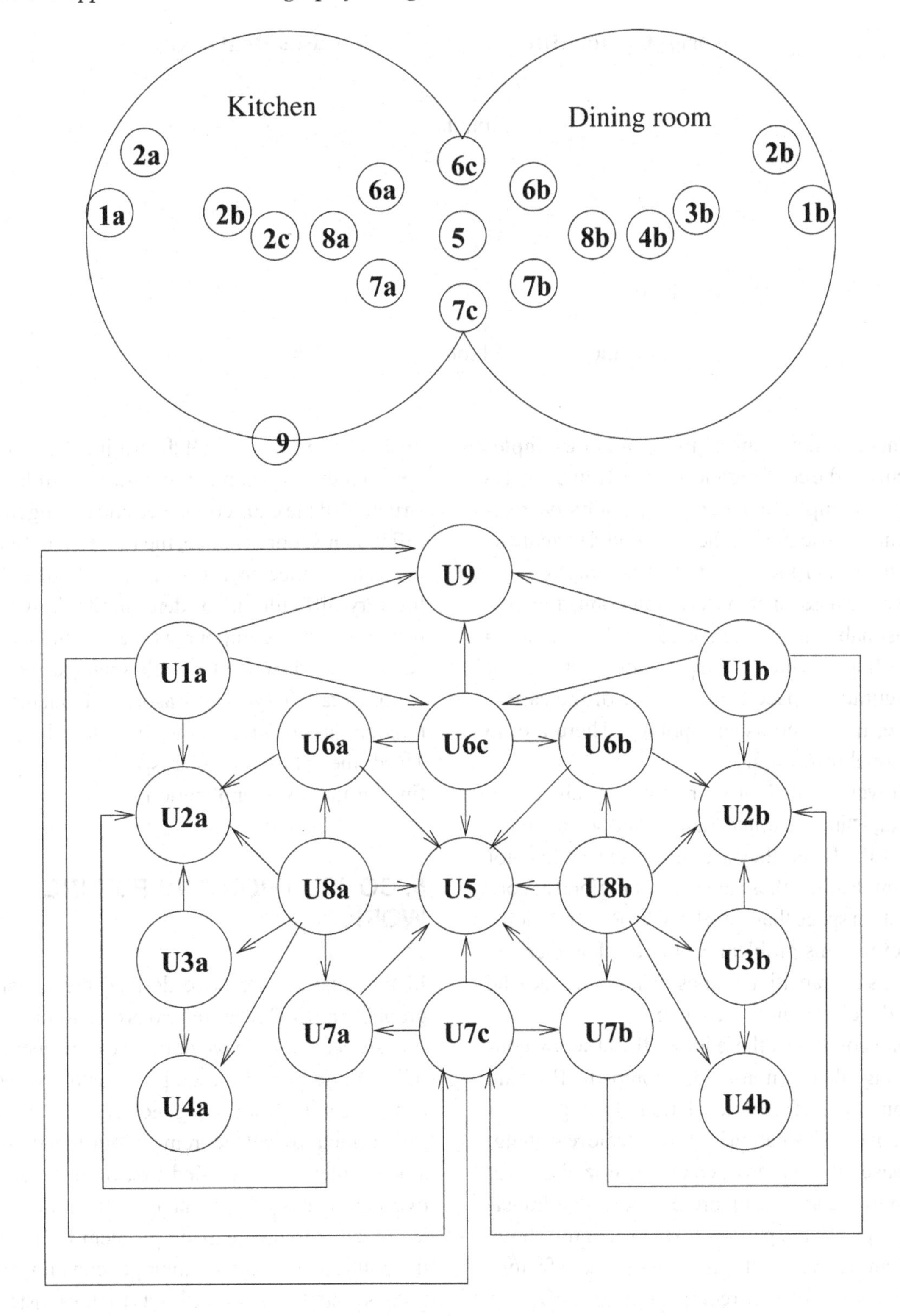

Figure 22. Transition network for traveller

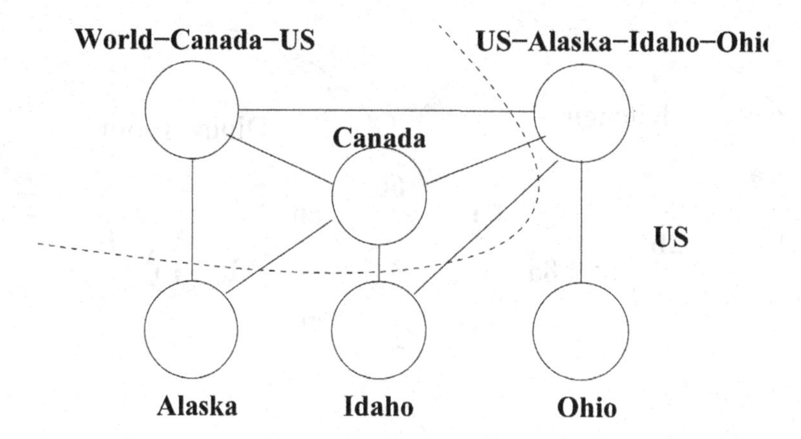


This is actually the simplest of our examples in terms of the configuration space. However, it is the most complex in terms of the qualitative relations and consequently the least suited to analysis in terms of our theory of transition graphs.

We idealize a person as a point object, which is reasonable in comparison to Alaska. There is a single fluent, which is the person's position. The configuration space is the surface of the earth's sphere, under the usual topology. There are no additional restrictions.

However, qualitative relations such as "in Alaska," "in the United States," and so on, do not form a JEPD set; they are neither exhaustive nor disjoint. Rather, these are a set of regions in configuration space that are related by RCC relations. Therefore, this problem cannot be characterized in terms of transition graphs in anything like the form developed in this chapter.

One could turn these into a JEPD set by constructing all the non-empty complete Boolean combinations of the base relations, analogous to a frame of discrimination in probabilistic reasoning. The base relations are then characterized as a set of atomic relations. Figure 22 shows the transition graph for the particular regions in the above problem. However, this is not a very satisfactory solution. First, even if a complete characterization of the RCC relations between the given regions is given, that does not at all determine the relations between the Boolean combinations, still less the structure of the path-connected and homogeneous refinements. For instance, the first step in finding the path-connected refinement of Figure 22 is the very difficult one of determining how many path-connected components the US and Canada have. Second, the set of relations can become exponentially large, and reasoning about the base relations involves reasoning about these large sets. Third, the set of relations is likely to be overly fine for the given application.

## 5. CONCLUSION AND FUTURE WORK

In this chapter, we have defined the transition graph for a JEPD set of relations over a configuration space, and we have defined two refinements of the basic graph: the graph of path-connected components and the homogeneous graph. We have proven metalogical theorems stating that the decision problem for specified first-order languages over continuous paths through configuration space is reducible to the decision problem for paths in the path-connected and homogeneous transition graphs; and that the same holds for the existential subset of those languages. We have shown how these techniques can be applied in a range of physical reasoning problems.

Many problems remain to be solved, however. The most important problem is the problem of deriving these transition networks from the problem specification. Currently, the only case where this is a well-developed theory for this is for the case of rigid objects with exact shape specification; this is the piano-movers problem. In a broader setting, such as the problems discussed in this chapter, we do not even have a reasonable representation language for problem specification, let alone an algorithm for deriving a transition network.

Other important problems include finding better techniques for solving problems like examples D and E of this chapter. In example D, there are several moving objects, and one wants to reason about moving one of these at a time. In example E, the qualitative relations involved are not JEPD; their topological relations are known, possibly incompletely.

In general, the examples in this paper suggest that qualitative homogeneous decompositions are not qualitative enough; they tend to introduce large number of distinctions that are of no actual value for the applications involved.

## REFERENCES


Collins, G. E. (1975). Lecture Notes in Computer Science: *Vol. 33. Quantifier elimination for real closed fields by cylindrical algebraic decomposition* (pp. 134–183). Berlin, Germany: Springer-Verlag.

Davis, E. (1990). *Representations of commonsense knowledge*. San Mateo, CA: Morgan Kaufmann.

Davis, E. (2000). *Describing spatial transitions using mereotopological relations over histories. Technical Report #2000-809*. New York, NY: New York University.

Davis, E. (2001). Continuous shape transformations and metrics on regions. *Fundamenta Informaticae, 46*(1-2), 31–54.

Davis, E. (2008). Pouring liquids: A study in commonsense physical reasoning. *Artificial Intelligence, 172*, 1540–1578. doi:10.1016/j.artint.2008.04.003

Davis, E. (2009). Ontologies and representations of matter. In *Proceedings of the Twenty-Fourth AAAI Conference on Artificial Intelligence (AAAI-10)*. AAAI.

de Kleer, J. (1977). Multiple representations of knowledge in a mechanics problem solver. In *Proceedings of the Fifth International Joint Conference on Artificial Intelligence (IJCAI-77)*, (pp. 299-304). IJCAI.

de Kleer, J., & Brown, J. S. (1985). A qualitative physics based on confluences. In Bobrow, D. (Ed.), *Qualitative Reasoning about Physical Systems* (pp. 7–83). Cambridge, MA: MIT Press.

Forbus, K. (1980). Spatial and qualitative aspects of reasoning about motion. In *Proceedings of the First National Conference on Artificial Intelligence, (AAAI-80)*, (pp. 170-173). AAAI.

Forbus, K. (1985). Qualitative process theory. In Bobrow, D. (Ed.), *Qualitative Reasoning about Physical Systems* (pp. 85–186). Cambridge, MA: MIT Press.

Galton, A. P. (1993). Towards an integrated logic of space, time, and motion. In *Proceedings of the Thirteenth International Joint Conference on Artificial Intelligence, (IJCAI-93)*, (pp. 1550-1555). San Mateo, CA: Morgan Kaufmann.

Galton, A. P. (1995). Towards a qualitative theory of motion. In *Proceedings of, COSIT-95*, 377–396.

Galton, A. P. (2000a). *Qualitative spatial change*. Oxford, UK: Oxford University Press.

Galton, A. P. (2000b). Continuous motion in discrete space. In *Proceedings of the Seventh International Conference on Principles of Knowledge Representation and Reasoning,* (pp. 26-37). Knowledge Representation and Reasoning.

Galton, A. P. (2003). A generalized topological view of motion in discrete space. *Theoretical Computer Science, 305*, 111–134. doi:10.1016/S0304-3975(02)00701-6

Hayes, P. (1979). The naive physics manifesto. In Michie, D. (Ed.), *Expert Systems in the Microelectronic Age* (pp. 242–270). Edinburgh, UK: Edinburgh University Press.

Hazarika, S., & Cohn, A. G. (2011). *Qualitative spatial change in a mereotopology*. Unpublished.

Kuipers, B. (1986). Qualitative simulation. *Artificial Intelligence, 29*, 289–338. doi:10.1016/0004-3702(86)90073-1

LaValle, S. (2006). *Planning algorithms*. Cambridge, UK: Cambridge University Press. doi:10.1017/CBO9780511546877

Lozano-Perez, T. (1983). Spatial planning: A configuration space approach. *IEEE Transactions on Computers, 32*(2), 108–120. doi:10.1109/TC.1983.1676196

Makanin, G. (1977). The problem of solvability of equations in a free semigroup. *Matematicheskii Sbornik, 32*, 129–198. doi:10.1070/SM1977v-032n02ABEH002376

Muller, P. (1998). A qualitative theory of motion based on spatio-temporal primitives. In *Proceedings of the Sixth International Conference on Principles of Knowledge Representation and Reasoning (KR-98),* (pp. 131-141). San Mateo, CA: Morgan Kaufmann.

Muller, P. (1998b). *Éléments d'une théorie du mouvement pour la modélisation du raisonnement spatio-temporel de sens commun.* Doctoral Dissertation. Toulouse, France: Université Paul Sabatier.

Plandowski, W. (1999). Satisfiability of word equations with constants is in PSPACE. In *Proceedings of the Annual Symposium on Foundations of Computer Science (FOCS '99),* (pp. 495-500). Los Alamitos, CA: IEEE Computer Society Press.

Randell, D. A., & Cohn, A. G. (1989). Modelling topological and metrical properites of physical processes. In *Proceedings of the First International Conference on Principles of Knowledge Representation and Reasoning, (KR-89),* (pp. 55-66). KR.

Randell, D. A., Cui, Z., & Cohn, A. G. (1992). A spatial logic based on regions and connection. In *Proceedings of the Third International Conference on Principles of Knowledge Representation and Reasoning, (KR-92),* (pp. 165-176). KR.

Weidenbach, C. (2001). SPASS: Combining superposition, sorts, and splitting. In Robinson, A., & Voronkov, A. (Eds.), *Handbook of Automated Reasoning* (*Vol. 2*, pp. 1965–2013). Amsterdam, The Netherlands: Elsevier.

Williams, B. (1985). Qualitative analysis of MOS circuits. In Bobrow, D. (Ed.), *Qualitative Reasoning about Physical Systems* (pp. 281–346). Cambridge, MA: MIT Press.

## KEY TERMS AND DEFINITIONS

**Configuration Space:** A point in a configuration space corresponds to one spatial arrangement of the objects under consideration.

**First-Order Definable:** Structure S is first-order definable in structure T if a collection of relations C isomorphic to the relations in S can be defined in the first-order language of T.

**First-Order Equivalent:** Two structures with the same language are first-order equivalent if the same first-order sentences are true in both.

**Partition:** P is a partition of T if P is a collection of subsets of T and every element of T is in exactly one set in P.

**Path:** A path in a space is a continuous function from a closed time interval into the space.

**Path-connected:** A region R is path-connected if every pair of points in R is connected by a path that remains in R.

**RCC-8: A exhaustive:** disjoint, collection of topological relations between pairs of regions in Euclidean space. Two regions may be equal (EQ), overlap (OV), externally connected (EC), disconnected (DC), one may be a tangential partial part of the other (TPP and $TPP^{-1}$), or one may be a non-tangential partial part of the other (NTPP and $NTPP^{-1}$) [Randell, Cui, and Cohn, 1992].

**Transition Graph:** A directed graphs whose vertices are regions of configuration space and whose edges represent a possible transition.

## ENDNOTES

1. It is not known whether this stronger definition corresponds to continuity relative to any topology over the space of regular regions. I would conjecture that it does not. It is certainly strictly stronger than continuity with respect to the Hausdorff distance and strictly weaker than continuity with respect to the dual-Hausdorff distance (Davis, 2001). Even if the conjecture is true, that does not indicate that the definition is flawed, just that standard results about continuity do not necessarily apply.
2. A Hausdorff topology satisfies the constraint that for any points **x,y** there exists disjoint open sets $U, V$ such that $\mathbf{x} \in U$ and $\mathbf{y} \in V$.
3. It is as hard as the decision problem for the first-order theory over the word problem discussed below, which is known to be undecidable (Martin Davis, personal communication).
4. A point set is *closed regular* if it is equal to the closure of its interior. It is *open regular* if it is equal to the interior of its closure. The two categories are isomorphic, so it does not matter which is used.

## APPENDIX: PROOFS

### Proof of Theorem 1

**Definition 33** *Let* $\mathbf{T}$ *be a topological space and let* $\Omega$ *be a collection of homogeneous partitions of* $\mathbf{T}$*. Let* $\Theta = \bigcup_{\mathcal{Q}\in\Omega}\mathcal{Q}$*; that is* $\Theta$ *is the set of all the cells that are in any partition in* $\Omega$*. A sequence* $\mathbf{U}_0 \ldots \mathbf{U}_k$ *of cells in* $\Theta$ *is a chain through* $\Omega$ *if* $\mathbf{U}_{i-1} \cap \mathbf{U}_i \neq \varnothing$ *for* $i = 1 \ldots k$*. If* $\mathbf{x} \in \mathbf{U}_0$ *and* $\mathbf{y} \in \mathbf{U}_k$*, then we say that the chain connects* $\mathbf{x}$ *and* $\mathbf{y}$*.*

**Lemma 15** *Let* $\mathbf{x}$ *be a point in* $\mathbf{T}$*, let* $\mathcal{U}$ *be a locally finite partition of* $\mathbf{T}$*, and let* $\mathbf{V}$ *be a subset of* $\mathbf{T}$ *such that* $\mathbf{x} \in Cl(\mathbf{V})$*. Then there exists a cell* $\mathbf{U} \in \mathcal{U}$ *such that* $\mathbf{U} \cap \mathbf{V} \neq \varnothing$ *and* $\mathbf{x} \in Cl(\mathbf{U})$*.*

**Proof:** Since $\mathcal{U}$ is locally finite, let $\mathbf{N}$ be a neighborhood of $\mathbf{X}$ that intersects only finitely many cells in $\mathcal{U}$; let these be $\mathbf{U}_1 \ldots \mathbf{U}_k$. Since $\mathcal{U}$ is a partition of $\mathbf{T}$, it follows that $\mathbf{N} \subset \mathbf{U}_1 \cup \ldots \cup \mathbf{U}_k$; hence $\mathbf{N} \cap \mathbf{V} \subset (\mathbf{U}_1 \cap \mathbf{V}) \cup \ldots \cup (\mathbf{U}_k \cap \mathbf{V})$. Since the right hand is a finite union, $Cl(\mathbf{N} \cap \mathbf{V}) \subset Cl(\mathbf{U}_1 \cap \mathbf{V}) \cup \ldots \cup Cl(\mathbf{U}_k \cap \mathbf{V})$. Since $\mathbf{x} \in Cl(\mathbf{N} \cap \mathbf{V})$, it must be the case that $\mathbf{x} \in Cl(\mathbf{U}_i \cap \mathbf{V})$ for at least one of the $\mathbf{U}_i$. It is immediate that $\mathbf{x} \in Cl(\mathbf{U}_i)$ and $\mathbf{U}_i \cap \mathbf{V} \neq \varnothing$. ▪

*Lemma 16 Let* $\mathbf{T}$ *be a topological space and let* $\Omega$ *be a non-empty collection of homogeneous partitions of* $\mathbf{T}$*. Let* $\Theta = \bigcup_{\mathcal{Q}\in\Omega}\mathcal{Q}$*. Define an equivalence relation over elements of* $\mathbf{T}$*,* $\mathbf{x} \sim_\Omega \mathbf{y}$ *if* $\mathbf{x}$ *and* $\mathbf{y}$ *are connected by a chain through* $\Omega$*. It is immediate that this is an equivalence relation. Let* $\mathcal{Q}$ *be the collection of equivalence classes of* $\mathbf{T}$ *under* $\sim_\Omega$*. Then* $\mathcal{Q}$ *is a homogeneous partition of* $\mathbf{T}$*.*

**Proof:** Since $\sim_\Omega$ is an equivalence relation, it is immediate that $\mathcal{Q}$ is a partition.

It is likewise immediate that, if $\mathbf{U}_0 \ldots \mathbf{U}_k$ is a chain through $\Omega$, then there exists a cell $\mathbf{U} \in \mathcal{Q}$ that contains their union. In particular, each of the partitions in $\Omega$ is a refinement of $\mathcal{Q}$.

We need to prove that $\mathcal{Q}$ satisfies four properties.

First, $\mathcal{Q}$ is locally finite. Let $\mathbf{x}$ be a point in $\mathbf{T}$. Let $\mathcal{U}$ be a partition in $\Omega$. Since $\mathcal{U}$ is locally finite, there is a neighborhood $\mathbf{N}$ of $\mathbf{x}$ that intersects only finitely many cells in $\mathcal{U}$. Since $\mathcal{U}$ is a refinement of $\mathcal{Q}$, it follows that $\mathbf{N}$ intersects only finitely many elements of $\mathcal{Q}$.

Second, $\mathcal{Q}$ allows simple transitions. Let $\mathbf{x}$ be any point in $\mathbf{T}$ and let $\mathbf{V}$ be a cell in $\mathcal{Q}$ such that $\mathbf{x} \in Cl(\mathbf{V})$. Let $\mathcal{U}$ be any partition in $\Omega$. By lemma 15, there exists a cell $\mathbf{U} \in \mathcal{U}$ such that $\mathbf{x} \in Cl(\mathbf{U})$ and $\mathbf{U} \cap \mathbf{V} \neq \varnothing$. Since $\mathcal{U}$ is a refinement of $\mathcal{Q}$, we must have $\mathbf{U} \subset \mathbf{V}$. Since $\mathcal{U}$ is locally simple, there is a path $\pi$ such that $\pi$ has a starting transition from $\mathbf{x}$ to $\mathbf{U}$. But then $\pi$ has a starting transition from $\mathbf{x}$ to $\mathbf{V}$. Thus $\mathcal{Q}$ allows simple transitions.

Third, $\mathcal{Q}$ is path-connected. Let $\mathbf{Q}$ be a cell in $\mathcal{Q}$ and let $\mathbf{x}$ and $\mathbf{y}$ be points in $\mathbf{Q}$. Then there is a chain $\mathbf{U}_0 \ldots \mathbf{U}_k$ through $\Omega$ connecting $\mathbf{x}$ and $\mathbf{y}$; as remarked above, all the $\mathbf{U}_i$ are subsets of $\mathbf{Q}$. For $i = 1 \ldots k-1$ let $\mathbf{z}_i$ be a point in $\mathbf{U}_i \cap \mathbf{U}_{i+1}$; let $\mathbf{z}_0 = \mathbf{x}$ and let $\mathbf{z}_k = \mathbf{x}$. Since $\mathbf{z}_i$ and $\mathbf{z}_{i+1}$ are in $\mathbf{U}_i$, which is path-connected, there is a path $\pi_i$ from $\mathbf{z}_i$ to $\mathbf{z}_{i+1}$ that stays in $\mathbf{U}_i$ and hence in $\mathbf{Q}$. Splicing the $\pi_i$ together gives a path from $\mathbf{x}$ to $\mathbf{y}$ that stays in $\mathbf{Q}$.

Fourth, $\mathcal{Q}$ is uniform in its neighbors. Let $\mathbf{Q}$ be a cell in $\mathcal{Q}$; let $\mathbf{x}$ and $\mathbf{y}$ be points in $\mathbf{Q}$, and let $\mathbf{V}$ be a cell in $\mathcal{Q}$ such that $\mathbf{x} \in Cl(\mathbf{V})$. We need to show that $\mathbf{y} \in Cl(\mathbf{V})$. Define the cells $\mathbf{U}_i$ and the points $\mathbf{z}_i$ as in the previous paragraph. Let $\mathcal{U}_i$ be the partition in $\Omega$ containing $\mathbf{U}_i$. By lemma 15, there is a cell $\mathbf{W}_1 \in \mathcal{U}_1$ such that $\mathbf{z}_0 \in Cl(\mathbf{W}_1)$, and $\mathbf{V} \cap \mathbf{W}_1 \neq \varnothing$. Since $\mathcal{U}_1$ is a refinement of $\mathcal{Q}$, $\mathbf{W}_1 \subset \mathbf{V}$. Again, there is a cell $\mathbf{W}_2 \in \mathcal{U}_2$ such that $\mathbf{z}_1 \in Cl(\mathbf{W}_2)$, and $\mathbf{W}_1 \cap \mathbf{W}_2 \neq \varnothing$; and again $\mathbf{W}_2 \subset \mathbf{V}$. Continuing on in this way, we can construct a chain $\mathbf{W}_1, \mathbf{W}_2 \ldots \mathbf{W}_k$ through $\Omega$ such that $\mathbf{W}_i \subset \mathbf{V}$ and $\mathbf{z}_i$ and $\mathbf{z}_{i+1}$ are in $Cl(\mathbf{W}_i)$. Thus $\mathbf{y} \in Cl(\mathbf{V})$. ▪

**Theorem 1** *Let* $\mathcal{U}$ be *a partition of* $\mathbf{T}$. *If there exists a homogeneous refinement of* $\mathcal{U}$, *then there exists a QHD of* $\mathcal{U}$.

**Proof:** Let $\Omega$ be the collection of all homogeneous refinements of $\mathcal{U}$, and construct $\mathcal{Q}$ as in lemma 16. By lemma 16, $\mathcal{Q}$ is a homogeneous partition of $\mathbf{T}$. It is immediate that $\mathcal{Q}$ is a refinement of $\mathcal{U}$ and that every homogeneous refinement of $\mathcal{U}$ is a refinement of $\mathcal{Q}$.

## Proof of Theorem 2

**Lemma 17** *Let* $\mathcal{U}$ *be a partition of* $\mathbf{T}$, *and let* $\mathcal{V}$ *be a homogeneous refinement of* $\mathcal{U}$. *Then* $\mathcal{V}$ *is a refinement of both* $\Phi(\mathcal{U})$ *and* $\Psi(\mathcal{U})$.

**Proof:** First, let $\mathbf{V}$ be a cell of $\mathcal{V}$ and let $\mathbf{x}$ and $\mathbf{y}$ be points in $\mathbf{V}$. Since $\mathbf{V}$ is path-connected, there is a path $\pi$ from $\mathbf{x}$ to $\mathbf{y}$ that remains in $\mathbf{V}$. Since $\mathcal{V}$ is a refinement of $\mathcal{U}$, there exists a cell $\mathbf{U} \in \mathcal{U}$ such that $\mathbf{V} \subset \mathbf{U}$. Then $\pi$ remains in $\mathbf{U}$; therefore $\mathbf{V}$ is a subset of one path-connected component of $\mathbf{U}$. Therefore $\mathcal{V}$ is a refinement of $\Phi(\mathcal{U})$.

Second, let $\mathbf{V}$, $\mathbf{x}$, $\mathbf{y}$, and $\mathbf{U}$ be as above. Let $\mathbf{W}$ be a cell of $\mathcal{U}$ such that $\mathbf{x} \in Cl(\mathbf{W})$; we wish to show that $\mathbf{y} \in Cl(\mathbf{W})$. Since $\mathcal{V}$ is a refinement of $\mathcal{U}$ and since both $\mathcal{V}$ and $\mathcal{U}$ are locally finite, there exists a cell $\mathbf{P} \in \mathcal{V}$ such that $\mathbf{P} \subset \mathbf{W}$ and $\mathbf{x} \in Cl(\mathbf{P})$. Since $\mathcal{V}$ is uniform in neighbors, $\mathbf{y} \in Cl(\mathbf{P})$; thus $\mathbf{y} \in Cl(\mathbf{W})$ as desired. Thus, by symmetry $\mathbf{N}(\mathbf{x}, \mathcal{U}) = \mathbf{N}(\mathbf{y}, \mathcal{U})$, so $\mathbf{x}$ and $\mathbf{y}$ are in the same cell of $\Psi(\mathcal{U})$. Hence $\mathcal{V}$ is a refinement of $\Psi(\mathcal{U})$.

**Theorem 2** *Let* $\mathcal{U}$ *be a locally simple partition of* $\mathbf{T}$. *Let* $\mathcal{U}_\sigma$ *be the decompositional sequence of* $\mathcal{U}$. *Then:*

a. *The sequence reaches a fixed point. That is, there exists an ordinal* $\tau$ *such that, for all* $\sigma > \tau$, $\mathcal{U}_\sigma = \mathcal{U}_\tau$.
b. *If* $\mathcal{U}_\tau$ *is locally simple, then it is the QHD of* $\mathcal{U}$.
c. *If there exists a QHD of* $\mathcal{U}$, *then it is* $\mathcal{U}_\tau$.

**Proof:** First, we prove by transfinite induction that, if $\sigma > \nu$ then $\mathcal{U}_\sigma$ is a refinement of $\mathcal{U}_\nu$. Assume that the statement holds for all $\eta < \sigma$. If $\sigma$ is the successor of $\mu$, and $\nu < \sigma$ then $\nu \le \mu$ so $\mathcal{U}_\mu$ is a refinement of $\mathcal{U}_\nu$ by the inductive hypothesis. Since $\Phi(\mathcal{V})$ and $\Psi(\mathcal{V})$ are refinements of $\mathcal{V}$ for any $\mathcal{V}$, it follows that $\mathcal{U}_\sigma = \Psi(\Phi(\mathcal{U}_\mu))$ is a refinement of $\mathcal{U}_\mu$ and hence of $\mathcal{U}_\mu$.

If $\sigma$ is a limit ordinal, then the conclusion is immediate from the definition.

Second, since each partition of $\mathbf{T}$ is a set of subsets of $\mathbf{T}$, the cardinality of the set of partitions of $\mathbf{T}$ is certainly no more than $2^{2^{|\mathbf{T}|}}$. Since refinement is a partial ordering over partitions, a chain of refinements cannot have cycles, and consequently cannot have more than more than $2^{2^{|\mathbf{T}|}}$ different values. (It can easily be shown that the true bound is actually $|\mathbf{T}|$, but we do not need that here.) Hence a fixed point must be reached for ordinals corresponding to that cardinality. This establishes part (a).

Third, since $\mathcal{U}_\tau$ is a fixed point of $\Psi(\Phi(\cdot))$, if it is also locally simple, then it is homogeneous, by definition. By a simple transfinite induction using lemma 17, it follows that, if $\mathcal{V}$ is any homogeneous refinement of $\mathcal{U}$, then it is a refinement of $\mathcal{U}_\tau$. Hence, if $\mathcal{U}$ is locally simple, then it is the QHD of $\mathcal{U}$

. This establishes (b). Conversely, if there exists a QHD $\mathcal{W}$ of $\mathcal{U}$, then it is a refinement of $\mathcal{U}_T$. Thus $\mathcal{U}_T$ must be locally simple; hence it is a homogeneous refinement of $\mathcal{U}$; hence it must be equal to $\mathcal{W}$. This establishes (c).

## Proof of Theorems 13 and 14

The construction in this proof is a little involved, so we will begin with a general overview and some motivation. Throughout this section, $\mathcal{U}$ is a path-connected partition of $\mathbf{T}$ and $G$ is the corresponding transition graph.

The proof proceeds in two steps. First, we slightly extend the domain of transition graphs and gpaths, and we define a structure over this extension that is first-order equivalent to the structure $\prec \text{DPATH}_U, \mathcal{L}^p, \mathcal{I}^p_U \succ$ over domain of paths in $\mathbf{T}$. Second, we show that this extension can be modelled in the unextended structure $\prec \text{DGRAPH}_G, \mathcal{L}^g, \mathcal{I}^g_G \succ$ over the domain of gpaths through the transition graph.

The obvious difference between the DPATH domain and the DGRAPH domain is that the former has points and the latter does not. So we will need to extend the latter to have something corresponding to points; we will call these "gpoints."

Moreover, if a cell has infinitely many points, then, in a first-order language with equality, it can be stated that it has at least $k$ points for any finite $k$, and this must be true of the gpoints as well. Therefore, for any cell with infinitely many points, there must exist infinitely many gpoints. For a cell with a single point, such as cell **B1a1** of Table 2, there must exists a single gpoint. Therefore, we adopt the following definition:

**Definition 34** *Let $\Omega$ be an arbitrary infinite set. A gpoint of $\mathbf{U}$ is any pair $\langle \mathbf{U}, \omega \rangle$ where $\omega \in \Omega$. If $\mathbf{U}$ is an infinite cell, then every such pair is a gpoint of $\mathbf{U}$. If $\mathbf{U}$ is a singleton cell, then there is one such pair that is a gpoint of $\mathbf{U}$. The set of gpoints of $\mathbf{U}$ is denoted "GPS($\mathbf{U}$)." If $\mathbf{x}$ is a gpoint of $\mathbf{U}$, then we say that $\mathbf{U}$ is the owner of $\mathbf{x}$, written $\mathbf{U} = \mathbf{O}(\mathbf{x})$.*

Typographically, we will use boldface, lower case symbols for gpoints as well as points.

We also need to construct extended gpaths, called "egpaths" to deal with two issues. First, a path starts and ends in a point; so a egpath must start and end in a gpoint. Second, there is again an issue with the number of paths. For any starting point $\mathbf{x} \in \mathbf{U}$, ending point $\mathbf{y} \in \mathbf{V}$ and gpath $\beta$ from $\mathbf{U}$ to $\mathbf{V}$, there normally exist infinitely many paths $\pi$ that start at $\mathbf{x}$, end at $\mathbf{y}$, and have trace $\beta$; so there must exist infinitely many egpaths of this kind as well. There is one exception: if $\mathbf{U}$ is a singleton cell, then there is a single path that stays in $\mathbf{U}$.

**Definition 35** *A* singleton path *is a path that remains in a single singleton cell.*

Let $\Omega$ and $\omega_0$ be as above. Let $\beta$ be a gpath. An *egpath corresponding to* $\beta$ is a quadruple $\langle \beta, \mathbf{x}, \mathbf{y}, \omega \rangle$ where $\mathbf{x} \in GPS(S(\beta))$, $\mathbf{y} \in GPS(E(\beta))$, and $\omega \in \Omega$. If $\beta$ is not a singleton path, then any such quadruple is a egpath for $\beta$. If $\beta$ is a singleton path, then there is one such quadruple that is the unique egpath for $\beta$. The set of all egpaths corresponding to $\beta$ is written "EGPATHS($\beta$)." If $\gamma \in$ EGPATHS($\beta$) we will write $\beta = \mathbf{O}(\gamma)$.

The only properties of gpoints and egpaths that matter are (a) that a gpoint is in a cell; (b) that a gpoint is the start or end of an egpath; (c) that there are the right number (one or infinite) of gpoints and egpaths for each cell or gpath respectively.

We now define a collection of relations on the space of gpoints, cells, and egpaths.

EGPOINTS$_G$ = the union of GPS( **V** ) for **V** $\in CELLS_G$.

EGPATHS$_G$ = the union of EGPATHS( $\beta$ ) for $\beta$ $\in$GPATHS$_G$

DEGPATHS$_G$=GPOINTS$_G$$\cup$CELLS$_G$$\cup$EGPATHS$_G$.

EGIN$_G$= $\{\prec \mathbf{x}, \mathbf{V} \succ \mid \mathbf{x} \in \text{GPS}(\mathbf{V})\}$.

EGSTART$_G$= $\{\prec \gamma, \mathbf{V} \succ \mid \mathbf{O}(\gamma) \in \text{GPATHS}_G \wedge \mathbf{V} = S(\mathbf{O}(\gamma))\}$.

EGEND$_G$= $\{\prec \gamma, \mathbf{V} \succ \mid \mathbf{O}(\gamma) \in \text{GPATHS}_G \wedge \mathbf{V} = S(\mathbf{O}(\gamma))\}$.

EGREMAINS$_G$= $\{\prec \gamma, \mathbf{V} \succ \mid \mathbf{O}(\gamma) = \langle \mathbf{V} \rangle\}$

EGCLOSEDTRANS$_G$= $\{\prec \gamma, \mathbf{V}, \mathbf{W} \succ \mid \prec \mathbf{O}(\gamma), \mathbf{V}, \mathbf{W} \succ \in \text{FORWARDARC}_G\}$

EGOPENTRANS$_G$= $\{\prec \gamma, \mathbf{V}, \mathbf{W} \succ \mid \prec \mathbf{O}(\gamma), \mathbf{V}, \mathbf{W} \succ \in \text{BACKWARDARC}_G\}$

EGSPLICE$_G$= $\{\prec \gamma_1, \gamma_2, \gamma_3 \succ \mid \mathbf{O}(\gamma_1) \mid \mathbf{O}(\gamma_2) = \mathbf{O}(\gamma_3)\}$.

Define the interpretation $\mathcal{I}^e$ of $\mathcal{L}^p$ as mapping each symbol onto the corresponding relation over $DEGPATH_U$ and as mapping the constant symbols $U_i$ onto the same cells as $\mathcal{I}^p$. Let $\mathcal{S}^p$ be the structure $\prec$DPATHS$_U$, $\mathcal{L}^p$, $\mathcal{I}^p_U \succ$ and let $\mathcal{S}^e$ be the structure $\prec$DEGPATHS$_G$, $\mathcal{L}^p$, $\mathcal{I}^e_G \succ$

**Definition 36** *A subset* $MP$ of $DPATHS_U$ is matchable *if it satisfies the following:*

- *MP is the union of* $CELLS_U$ *with a finite (possibly empty) set of points and a finite set of paths.*
- *If path* $\pi \in MP$, *then* $S(\pi) \in MP$ *and* $E(\pi) \in$ MP.

*A subset* $ME$ of $DEGPATHS_G$ *is* matchable *if it satisfies the following:*

- *MP is the union of* $CELLS_G$ *with a finite (possibly empty) set of gpoints and a finite set of egpaths.*
- *If egpath* $\gamma = \langle \beta, \mathbf{x}, \mathbf{y}, \omega \rangle \in ME$ *then* $\mathbf{x} \in ME$ *and* $\mathbf{y} \in ME$.

**Definition 37** *Let* $MP$ *be a matchable subset of* $DPATHS_U$ *and let* $ME$ *be a matchable subset of* $DEGPATHS_U$. *A bijection* $\zeta$ *from* $MP$ *to* $ME$ *is a correspondence if for all* $m, n \in MP$:

- *If* $m \in CELLS_U$ *then* $\zeta(m) = m$.
- *If* $m \in POINTS_U$ *then* $\zeta(m) \in EGPOINTS_G$ *and* $\mathbf{O}(m,\mathcal{U}) = \mathbf{O}(\zeta(m))$.
- *If* $m \in PATHS_U$ *then* $\zeta(m) \in EGPATHS_G$ *and* $\mathbf{O}(\zeta(m)) = \Delta(\Gamma_{U,Z4}(m))$.
- *If* $m \in PATHS_U$ *and* $n \in POINTS_U$ *then*

*[*$n = S(m)$ *if and only if* $\prec \zeta(m), \zeta(n) \succ \in EGSTART_G$*] and*
*[*$n = E(m)$ *if and only if* $\prec \zeta(m), \zeta(n) \succ \in EGEND_G$*].*

**Definition 38** *Let* $\mu_1 \ldots \mu_k$ *be variable symbols. Let* $\sigma$ *be a valuation of the* $\mu_i$ *in* $DPATHS_U$ *and let* $\tau$ *be a valuation of the* $\mu_i$ *in* $DEGPATHS_G$. *We say that* $\sigma$ *and* $\tau$ *correspond if there exist set* $MP$ *and* $ME$ *and a correspondence* $\zeta$ *such that for each variable* $\mu_i$, $\sigma(\mu_i) \in MP$, $\tau(\mu_i) \in ME$, *and* $\tau(\mu_i) = \zeta(\sigma(\mu_i))$

From here the proof proceeds along standard lines for proof of first-order equivalence. We show that any matching valuations have extensions that are still matching; we show that atomic formulas are equivalent under matching valuations; and we show inductively that complex formulas are equivalent under matching valuations.

**Lemma 18** *Let* $\sigma$ *and* $\tau$ *be corresponding valuations, and let* $\phi$ *be an atomic formula in* $\mathcal{I}^p$. *Then* $\mathcal{S}_U^p, \sigma \models \phi$ *if and only if* $\mathcal{S}_U^e, \tau \models \phi$.

**Proof:** Straightforward from the definitions, though lengthy. Check each predicate and equality in turn.

**Corollary 19** *Let* $\sigma$ *and* $\tau$ *be corresponding valuations, and let* $\phi$ *be a quantifier-free formula in* $\mathcal{I}^p$. *Then* $\mathcal{S}_U^p, \sigma \models \phi$ *if and only if* $\mathcal{S}_U^e, \tau \models \phi$.

**Proof:** Immediate from lemma 18.

**Definition 39** *If* $\sigma$ *is a valuation and* $\mu$ *is a variable not in the domain of* $\sigma$, *then an extension of* $\sigma$ *to* $\mu$ *is a valuation that agrees with* $\sigma$ *on all the variables in the domain of* $\sigma$ *and assigns a domain value to* $\mu$.

**Lemma 20** *Let* $\sigma$ *and* $\tau$ *be corresponding valuations. Let* $\sigma'$ *be an extension of* $\sigma$ *to a new variable* $\mu$. *Then there exists an extension* $\tau'$ *of* $\tau$ *to* $\mu$ *such that* $\tau'$ *corresponds to* $\sigma'$.

*Conversely, if* $\tau'$ *is an extension of* $\tau$ *to* $\mu$ *then there exists an extension* $\sigma'$ to $\mu$ that corresponds to $\tau$.

**Proof** of the first implication: Let $\zeta$ be a correspondence matching $\sigma$ and $\tau$ and let $MP$ and $ME$ be the associated matchable sets. If $\sigma'(\mu) \in MP$, then define $\tau'(\mu) = \zeta(\sigma'(\mu))$.

Otherwise, let $m = \sigma'(\mu)$.

If $m$ is a point, define $\zeta'(m)$ to be $\zeta(m)$ if $m \in MP$; otherwise, to be a gpoint $n$ such that $\mathbf{O}(n) = \mathbf{O}(m,\mathcal{U})$ and $n \notin ME$. Let $\tau'$ be the extension of $\tau$ with $\tau'(\mu) = n$.

If $m$ is a path, define $\zeta'(m)$ to be $\zeta(m)$ if $m \in MP$; otherwise, to be a egpath $n$ such that $\mathbf{O}(n) = \Delta(\Gamma_{U,Z4}(m))$ and $n \notin ME$. Define $\zeta'(S(m))$ and $\zeta'(E(m))$ as above. Let $\tau'(\mu) = n$.

It is immediate that $\zeta'$ is a correspondence and that $\sigma'$ and $\tau'$ are corresponding valuations. Note that this construction relies, first, on the fact that there are infinitely many gpoints for every infinite cell and infinitely many egpaths for every gpath and every starting and ending gpoint; and, second, that it relies on theorem 4 that there exists a gpath corresponding to every path.

The proof of the second implication has exactly the same structure. Here, in going from egpaths to paths, we rely on corollary 7 to be sure that there is a path corresponding to every gpath and starting and ending point. ▪

**Lemma 21** *Let $\sigma$ and $\tau$ be corresponding valuations, and let $\phi$ be a formula in $\mathcal{I}^p$. Then $\mathcal{S}^p_U, \sigma \vDash \phi$ if and only if $\mathcal{S}^e_G, \tau \vDash \phi$.*

**Proof** by induction on the number $k$ of quantifiers in $\phi$. Assume that $\phi$ has been placed in prenex form. The case $k = 0$ is just corollary 19.

Suppose that $\phi$ has the form $\exists_\mu \psi$. Let free variables $\mu_1 \ldots \mu_q$ be the free variables of $\phi$. If $\mathcal{S}^p_U, \sigma \vDash \phi$ then let $m$ be an entity in $\text{DPATHS}_U$ such that the extension of $\sigma$, $\sigma' = \sigma \cup \{\mu \rightarrow m\}$ satisfies $\mathcal{S}^p_U, \sigma' \vDash \psi$. By lemma 20 there exists a valuation $\tau'$ extending $\tau$ corresponding to $\sigma'$. By the inductive hypothesis, $\mathcal{S}^e_G, \tau' \vDash \psi$. Therefore $\mathcal{S}^e_G, \tau \vDash \phi$.

The converse — if $\mathcal{S}^e_G, \tau \vDash \phi$ then $\mathcal{S}^p_U, \sigma \vDash \phi$ — is exactly analogous.

Suppose that $\phi$ has the form $\forall_\mu \psi$. Then $\mathcal{S}^p_U, \sigma \vDash \phi$ if and only if $\mathcal{S}^p_U, \sigma \vDash \exists_\mu \neg \psi$ which by the contrapositive to the previous paragraph holds if and only if $\mathcal{S}^e_G, \tau \vDash \exists_\mu \neg \psi$, which holds if and only if $\mathcal{S}^e_G, \tau \vDash \phi$

**Corollary 22** *The structures $\mathcal{S}^p_U$ and $\mathcal{S}^e_G$ are first-order equivalent; i.e, for any sentence $\phi \in \mathcal{L}^p$, $\mathcal{S}^p_U \vDash \phi$ if and only if $\mathcal{S}^e_G \vDash \phi$.*

**Proof:** This is just the special case of lemma 21 for formulas with no free variables. ▪

We now show that the structure $\mathcal{S}^e_G$ is definable in $\mathcal{S}^g_G$, using a definitional mapping that is independent of $G$. To do this, we will have to model gpoints and egpaths in terms of cells and gpaths, which are all we have in $\mathcal{S}^g_G$, and we have to translate the predicates (including equality and the universal relation) of $\mathcal{L}^p$ into corresponding formulas in $\mathcal{L}^g$. Neither of these is very difficult.

First, we need to model $\Omega$. Since all we need out of $\Omega$ is that it should be infinite and that we can determine equality and inequality, we can just use $\text{GPATHS}_G$ itself, since there are always infinitely many gpaths (This is why we require that $\mathcal{U}$ has at least two cells).

If $\mathbf{x} = \langle \mathbf{U}, \omega \rangle$ is a singleton gpoint—i.e. the unique gpoint in singleton cell $\mathbf{U}$—then we choose $\omega$ to be the gpath $\langle \mathbf{U} \rangle$. If $\gamma = \langle \beta, \mathbf{x}, \mathbf{x}, \omega \rangle$ is a singleton path—i.e the unique path that remains in a singleton cell $\mathbf{U}$—then again then we choose $\omega$ to be the gpath $\langle \mathbf{U} \rangle$.

We map any entity $m \in \text{DEGPATHS}_G$ to a quadruple over $\text{DGPATHS}_G$.

**Definition 40** *Define the mapping $\Theta : DEGPATHS_G \rightarrow (DGPATHS_G)^4$ as follows:*

- *If $m$ is the cell $\mathbf{U}$ then $\Theta(m) = \prec \mathbf{U}, \mathbf{U}, \mathbf{U}, \mathbf{U} \succ$.*
- *If $m$ is the gpoint $\langle \mathbf{U}, \omega \rangle$ then $\Theta(m) = \prec \mathbf{U}, \omega, \mathbf{U}, \mathbf{U} \succ$.*
- *If $m$ is the egpath $\langle \beta, \mathbf{x}, \mathbf{y}, \omega_1 \rangle$ where $\mathbf{x} = \langle S(\beta), \omega_2 \rangle$ and $\mathbf{y} = \langle E(\beta), \omega_3 \rangle$*

*then $\Theta(m) = \prec \beta, \omega_1, \omega_2, \omega_3 \succ$.*

Note that if $m$ is a singleton gpoint, then $m_1$ is a singleton cell, Remains($m_2, m_1$) and $m_1 = m_3 = m_4$ If $m$ is a singleton egpath, then there exists a singleton cell $\mathbf{U}$ such that Remains($m_1, \mathbf{U}$), and $m_1 = m_2 = m_3 = m_4$.

The following rules specify the translation of each relation of $\mathcal{S}^e_G$ into a first-order definable relation in $(\mathcal{S}^g_G)^4$. We will write $\vec{m}$ as an abbreviation for the tuple $\prec m_1, m_2, m_3, m_4 \succ$. For readability, we will omit the subscript G, which applies to all the relations below.

$\Theta(\mathbf{U}_i) = \prec \mathbf{U}_i, \mathbf{U}_i, \mathbf{U}_i, \mathbf{U}_i \succ$

$\Theta(\text{CELLS}) = \{\vec{m} \mid m_1 \in \text{CELLS} \wedge m_1 = m_2 = m_3 = m_4\}$

$\Theta(\text{SINGLETON}) = \{\vec{m} \mid \vec{m} \in \Theta(\text{CELLS}) \wedge m_1 \in \text{SINGLETON})\}$

$\Theta(\text{GPOINTS}) =$

$\{\vec{m} \mid [m_1 \in \text{SINGLETON} \wedge \prec m_1, m_2 \succ \in \text{REMAINS} \wedge m_1 = m_3 = m_4] \vee$

$[m_1 \in \text{CELLS} - \text{SINGLETON} \wedge m_2 \in \text{GPATHS} \wedge m_1 = m_3 = m_4]$

$\}$

The definition of Θ (EGPATHS) is rather complicated, because we have to deal, both with singleton egpaths and with the cases of non-singleton egpaths that begin or end at a singleton point. Moveover, we have structured this definition to be purely existential, so as to support a translation of an existential formula in $\mathcal{L}^p$ into an existential formula in $\mathcal{L}^g$; the translation could be somewhat simpler if we allowed the use of universal quantifiers. We begin by defining some relations over DGPATHS.

$\text{SINGLETONPATH} = \{\gamma \mid \exists_{\text{U}} \mathbf{U} \in \text{SINGLETON} \wedge \prec \gamma, \mathbf{U} \succ \in \text{GREMAINS}\}$

$\text{NONSINGLETONPATH} =$

$\{\gamma \mid \exists_{\text{U}} \prec \gamma, \mathbf{U} \succ \in \text{GSTART} \wedge [\mathbf{U} \not\in \text{SINGLETON} \vee \prec \gamma, \mathbf{U} \succ \not\in \text{GREMAINS}]\}$

$\text{SINGLETONSTART} = \{\prec \gamma, \mathbf{U} \succ \mid \prec \gamma, \mathbf{U} \succ \in \text{GSTART} \wedge \mathbf{U} \in \text{SINGLETON}\}$

$\text{NONSINGLETONSTART} = \{\gamma \mid \exists_{\text{U}} \prec \gamma, \mathbf{U} \succ \in \text{GSTART} \wedge \mathbf{U} \not\in \text{SINGLETON}\}$

$\text{SINGLETONEND} = \{\prec \gamma, \mathbf{U} \succ \mid \prec \gamma, \mathbf{U} \succ \in \text{GEND} \wedge \mathbf{U} \in \text{SINGLETON}\}$

$\text{NONSINGLETONEND} = \{\gamma \mid \exists_{\text{U}} \prec \gamma, \mathbf{U} \succ \in \text{GEND} \wedge \mathbf{U} \not\in \text{SINGLETON}\}$

$\Theta(\text{EGPATHS}) =$
$\{\vec{m} \mid [m_1 \in \text{SINGLETONPATH} \wedge m_1 = m_2 = m_3 = m_4] \vee$
$[m_1, m_2, m_3, m_4 \in \text{GPATHS} \wedge m_1 \in \text{NONSINGLETONPATH} \wedge$
$[m_1 \in \text{NONSINGLETONSTART} \vee$
$[\exists_{\mathbf{U}} \prec m_1, \mathbf{U} \succ \in \text{SINGLETONSTART} \wedge \prec m_3, \mathbf{U} \succ \in \text{GREMAINS}]] \wedge$
$[m_1 \in \text{NONSINGLETONEND} \vee$
$[\exists_{\mathbf{U}} \prec m_1, \mathbf{U} \succ \in \text{SINGLETONEND} \wedge \prec m_4, \mathbf{U} \succ \in \text{GREMAINS}]]$
$]$
$\}$

$\Theta(\text{DEGPATHS}) = \Theta(\text{CELLS}) \cup \Theta(\text{GPOINTS}) \cup \Theta(\text{EGPATHS})$.

$\Theta\,(\text{EGIN}) = \{ \prec \vec{m}, \vec{n} \succ \mid \vec{m} \in \Theta\,(\text{GPOINTS}) \wedge \vec{n} \in \Theta(\text{CELLS}) \wedge m_1 = n_1 \}$.

$\Theta\,(\text{EGSTART}) = \{ \prec \vec{m}, \vec{n} \succ \mid \vec{m} \in \Theta\,(\text{EGPATHS}) \wedge \vec{n} \in \Theta\,(\text{GPOINTS}) \wedge \prec m_1, n_1 \succ \in \text{GSTART} \}$.

$\Theta\,(\text{EGEND}) = \{ \prec \vec{m}, \vec{n} \succ \mid \vec{m} \in \Theta\,(\text{EGPATHS}) \wedge \vec{n} \in \Theta\,(\text{GPOINTS}) \wedge \prec m_1, n_1 \succ \in \text{GEND} \}$.

$\Theta\,(\text{EGREMAINS}) =$

$\{ \prec \vec{m}, \vec{n} \succ \mid \vec{m} \in \Theta\,(\text{EGPATHS}) \wedge \vec{n} \in \Theta\,(\text{GPOINTS}) \wedge \prec m_1, n_1 \succ \in \text{GREMAINS} \}$.

$\Theta\,(\text{EGCLOSEDTRANS}) =$

$\{ \prec \vec{m}, \vec{n}, \vec{p} \succ \mid \vec{m} \in \Theta\,(\text{EGPATHS}) \wedge \vec{n}, \vec{p} \in \Theta\,(\text{CELLS}) \wedge \prec m_1, n_1, p_1 \succ \in \text{FORWARDARC} \}$.

$\Theta\,(\text{EGOPENTRANS}) =$

$\{ \prec \vec{m}, \vec{n}, \vec{p} \succ \mid \vec{m} \in \Theta\,(\text{EGPATHS}) \wedge \vec{n}, \vec{p} \in \Theta\,(\text{CELLS}) \wedge \prec m_1, n_1, p_1 \succ \in \text{BACKWARDARC} \}$.

$\Theta\,(\text{EGSPLICE}) = \{ \prec \vec{m}, \vec{n}, \vec{p} \succ \mid \vec{m}, \vec{n}, \vec{p} \in \Theta\,(\text{EGPATHS}) \wedge \prec m_1, n_1, p_1 \succ \in \text{GSPLICE} \}$.

$\Theta\,(=) = \{ \prec \vec{m}, \vec{n} \succ \mid \vec{m}, \vec{n} \in \Theta\,(\text{DEGPATHS}) \wedge \vec{m} = \vec{n} \}$.

That completes the definition of $\Theta$.
**Lemma 23** *For any relation* $\Phi$ *in* $S^e_G$ *and entities* $x_1 \ldots x_k \in DEGPATHS_G$, $\prec x_1 \ldots x_k \succ \in \Phi$ *if and only if* $\prec \Theta(x_1) \ldots \Theta(x_k) \succ \in \Theta(\Phi)$.
**Proof:** Long but straightforward case analysis. Each case follows immediately from the definition.

**Lemma 24** *The structure* $\mathcal{S}^e_G$ *is first-order definable in terms of* $\mathcal{S}^g_G$. *Moreover, the form of the definition is independent of* $G$.

**Proof:** Immedate from lemma 23.

**Theorem 10** *There exists a linear-time function* $\mathcal{A}^p$ *that maps every sentence in* $\mathcal{L}^p$ *to a sentence in* $\mathcal{L}^g$ *satisfying the following. Let* **T** *be a Hausdorff space, let* $\mathcal{U}$ *be a path-connected partition over* **T** *with at least 2 cells, and let* $\mathcal{I}^p_U$ *be the interpretation of* $\mathcal{L}^p$ *in* $DPATHS_U$ *defined above. Let* $G$ *be the transition graph corresponding to* $\mathcal{U}$ *and let* $\mathcal{I}^g_G$ *be the interpretation of* $\mathcal{L}^g$ *in* $DGRAPH_G$ *defined above, such that for each symbol* $U_i$, $\mathcal{I}^g_G(U_i) = \mathcal{I}^p_U(U_i)$. *Let* $\Phi$ *be any sentence in* $\mathcal{L}^p$. *Then* $\Phi$ *holds in the structure* $\prec DPATH_U, \mathcal{L}^p, \mathcal{I}^p_U \succ$ *if and only if* $\mathcal{A}^p(\Phi)$ *holds in the structure* $\prec DGRAPH_G, \mathcal{L}^g, \mathcal{I}^g_G \succ$.

**Proof:** Immediate from corollary 22 and lemma 24. ▪

The proof of theorem 14 is exactly analogous. Extended ILS's are defined analogously to extended gpaths. One can then prove that the structure over extended ILS's is elementary equivalent to the Z5 structure of paths, and is definable in the structure of unextended ILS's.

# Chapter 4
# A Qualitative Trajectory Calculus to Reason about Moving Point Objects

**Matthias Delafontaine**
*Ghent University, Belgium*

**Seyed Hossein Chavoshi**
*Ghent University, Belgium*

**Anthony G. Cohn**
*University of Leeds, UK*

**Nico Van de Weghe**
*Ghent University, Belgium*

## ABSTRACT

*A number of qualitative calculi have been developed in order to reason about space and time. A recent trend has been the emergence of integrated spatiotemporal calculi in order to deal with dynamic phenomena such as motion. In 2004, Van de Weghe introduced the Qualitative Trajectory Calculus (QTC) as a qualitative calculus to represent and reason about moving objects. This chapter presents a general overview of the principal theoretical aspects of QTC, focusing on the two most fundamental types of QTC. It shows how QTC deals with important reasoning concepts and how calculus can be employed in order to represent raw moving object data.*

## INTRODUCTION

Reasoning about spatial and temporal information takes a central place in human daily life. A number of qualitative calculi have been developed to represent and reason about spatial or temporal configurations. Most of them focus on one of the two domains, whereas a few are true spatio-temporal calculi that deal with spatiotemporal phenomena. One such is the Qualitative Trajectory Calculus, which in the remainder of this chapter will be referred to as QTC. QTC is a qualitative calculus to reason about a specific spatiotemporal phenomenon: moving objects.

DOI: 10.4018/978-1-61692-868-1.ch004

The remainder of this chapter is structured as follows. First, relevant background issues are discussed. Second, some general characteristics of QTC are explained and a brief overview of all QTC calculi that have been elaborated so far is given. The two most fundamental QTC calculi, $QTC_B$ and $QTC_C$, are then presented in detail. The following sections discuss representing and reasoning with QTC, as well as how QTC can be extended. An application section follows in order to highlight the potential of implementing QTC in information systems. The final sections mention opportunities for further research and conclusions.

## BACKGROUND

In Artificial Intelligence, several qualitative calculi exist to reason about either spatial or temporal information, the most well-known being Allen's Interval Calculus (Allen, 1983), which has about 1200 citations in the ISI Web of Science by the time of writing. According to Wolter and Zakharyaschev (2000), an apparent and natural step is to combine both spatial and temporal formalisms in order to reason about spatiotemporal phenomena. A crucial and fundamental phenomenon at this cross-pollination of space and time is motion. Note that motion is an inherently spatiotemporal phenomenon (Peuquet, 2001). Dealing with motion is essential to spatial and geographical information systems, where an evolution from static to dynamic formalisms and representations has been made. A specific type of motion is associated with moving objects, i.e. objects whose position moves through space in time.

In the past decade, the modelling of moving objects has been a hot topic in fields such as GIScience, Artificial Intelligence and Information Systems (Bitterlich, Sack, Sester, & Weibel, 2008). In qualitative reasoning, however, considerable work has focused on the formalisation of motion, or moving objects in particular. Some examples are Muller (2002), Ibrahim (2007), Hallot and Billen (2008), and Kurata and Egenhofer (2009). These approaches have in common that they rely on topological models such as the Region Connection Calculus (Randell, Cui, & Cohn, 1992) or the 9-Intersection model (Egenhofer & Franzosa, 1991). However, a general shortfall of topological models is their inability to further differentiate between *disjoint* relations. This makes their applicability to represent and reason about continuously moving objects questionable, as in many cases moving objects remain disjoint for most of the time. For instance, cars in a traffic situation are usually disjoint, apart from the exceptional case of an accident.

In order to overcome this inability, the Qualitative Trajectory Calculus (QTC), was proposed by Van de Weghe (2004). QTC provides a qualitative framework to represent and reason about moving objects which enables the differentiation of groups of disconnected objects. The development of QTC has been inspired by some major qualitative calculi: the Region Connection Calculus (Randell, et al., 1992), the temporal Semi-Interval Calculus (Freksa, 1992a), and the spatial Double Cross Calculus (Freksa, 1992b; Zimmerman & Freksa, 1996).

## THE QUALITATIVE TRAJECTORY CALCULUS

### Simplifications

Information systems usually represent knowledge according to an underlying model of the real world, making simplifications in order to abstract away from the mass of details that would otherwise obscure essential aspects. To this end, QTC makes four simplifications (Figure 1). First and foremost, QTC considers the relation between two objects, i.e. binary relations (*relational simplification*, Figure 1b), as is common in spatial and temporal reasoning (Cohn & Renz, 2007). Second, moving objects are spatially simplified into moving point

*Figure 1. Simplification in QTC of a real-life situation (a) by taking cumulatively account of the relational simplification (b), the object simplification (c), and the temporal simplification (d) (simple arrows for trajectories, double arrows for instantaneous velocity vectors)*

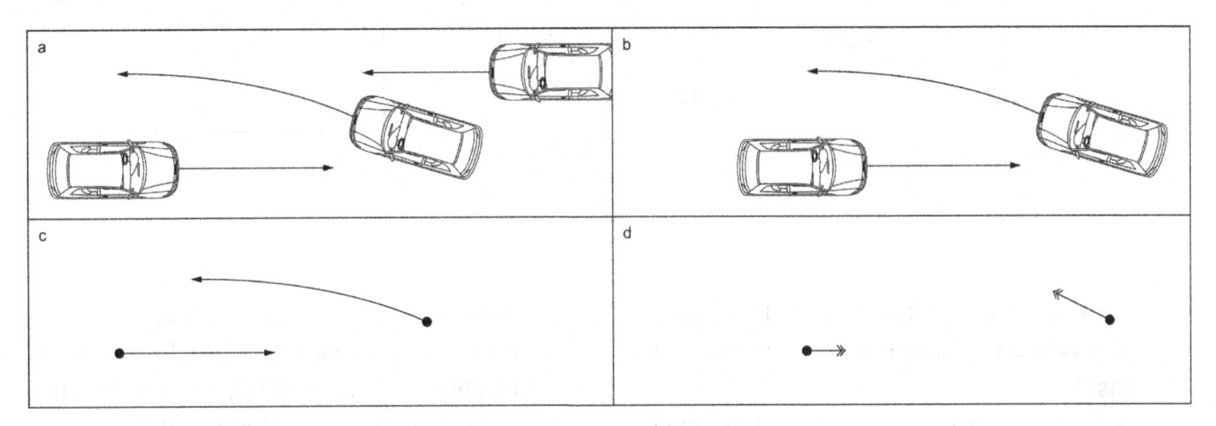


objects or MPOs (*object simplification*, Figure 1c), as is common in GIScience and geoinformatics (Gudmundsson, van Kreveld, & Speckmann, 2004; Guting, et al., 2000; Laube, 2005; Noyon, Claramunt, & Devogele, 2007). There are only two topological relations (*disjoint* and *equal*) between two MPOs. Since the relation between two *equal* MPOs is trivial, the third simplification in QTC is the restriction to *disjoint* MPOs (*topological simplification*). Finally, in order to understand the temporal dimension in depth, it is important to find out what happens at one time point. Hence, QTC relations are relations that hold at a particular time point (*temporal simplification*, Figure 1d).

## Continuity, Conceptual Neighbours, and Transitions

QTC assumes space and time, and thus the motion of objects, to be continuous. As a consequence, QTC relations change in time according to the laws of continuity. Along with continuity comes the important concept of conceptual neighbourhood as introduced by Freksa (1992b). Two QTC relations between the same pair of MPOs are *conceptual neighbours* if and only if these relations can directly follow each other through continuous motion of the MPOs, without the necessity for a third relation to hold at an intermediate point in time. A *transition* then denotes the continuous change of one relation into a conceptual neighbouring relation. Each transition thereby happens at a certain instant or point in time, which we will term a *transition instant*. A conceptual neighbourhood can be represented by a *Conceptual Neighbourhood Diagram* (CND), i.e. a visualisation of a graph which nodes represent relations, and where two nodes are connected if they are conceptual neighbours of each other.

All QTC calculi are associated with a set of Jointly Exhaustive and Pairwise Disjoint (JEPD) base relations. Consequently, there is one and only one relation for each pair of coexisting MPOs at each time instant. In addition, due to continuity, the concurrent movement of two MPOs over a given time interval is uniquely mapped to a sequence of conceptually neighbouring base relations.

All QTC relations are formed by a tuple of labels (representing different primitive qualitative relations) that all have the same three-valued qualitative domain $\{-, 0, +\}$, which we will denote as $U$ in the remainder of this chapter. A '0' symbol corresponds to a landmark value, and as Galton (2001) points out, this value always *dominates* both '−' and '+' values. Hence:

*Figure 2. Two MPOs represented in a typical two-dimensional $QTC_B$ (a), $QTC_C$ (b), and $QTC_N$ (c) setting. The frame of spatial reference is represented by the dashed line.*

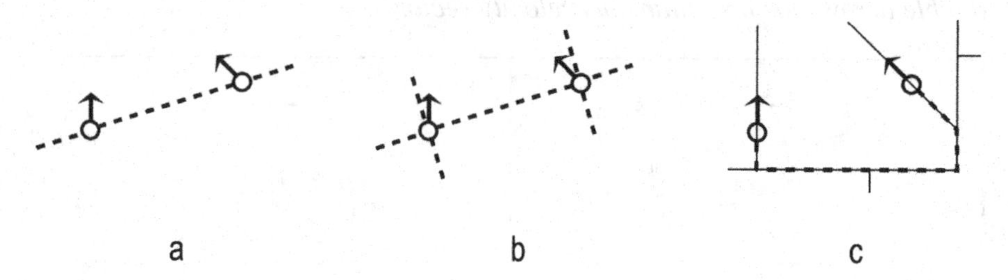


- A '0' must always last over a closed time interval (of which a time instant is a special case);
- A '–' / '+' must always last over an open time interval;
- Only transitions to or from '0' are possible (transitions from '–' / '+' to '+' / '–' are impossible) and transition instants always correspond with a '0' value.

Based on the notion of topological distance introduced by Egenhofer and Al-Taha (1992), the *conceptual distance* can be defined as a measure for the closeness of QTC relations (Van de Weghe & De Maeyer, 2005). We take the conceptual distance between '0' and another symbol to be one. This is the smallest conceptual distance, apart from zero (i.e. the distance between a symbol and itself). Since a direct transition is impossible, the conceptual distance between '–' and '+' is equal to two (one for '–' to '0' and one for '0' to '+'). The overall conceptual distance between two QTC relations can then be calculated by summing the conceptual distance over all relation symbols. For instance, for two QTC relations consisting of four symbols, the conceptual distance ranges from zero to eight.

## Types of QTC

Due to the consideration of different spaces and frames of reference, the following types of QTC have been elaborated:

- Basic type: $QTC_B$ (Van de Weghe, Cohn, De Tré, & De Maeyer, 2006), Figure 2a
- Double Cross type: $QTC_C$ (Van de Weghe, Cohn, De Maeyer, & Witlox, 2005), Figure 2b
- Network type: $QTC_N$ (Bogaert, Van de Weghe, Cohn, Witlox, & De Maeyer, 2006), Figure 2c
- Shape type: $QTC_S$ (Van de Weghe, De Tré, Kuijpers, & De Maeyer, 2005)

The Basic ($QTC_B$) and the Double Cross ($QTC_C$) types both deal with MPOs that have a free trajectory in an *n* dimensional space. $QTC_B$ relations are determined by referring to the Euclidian distance between two MPOs (Figure 2a). $QTC_C$ relations on the other hand rely on the double cross, a concept introduced by Zimmerman and Freksa (1996), as a spatial reference frame (Figure 2b). $QTC_B$ and $QTC_C$ will be discussed in detail in the next two sections.

$QTC_N$ (Network) focuses on the special case of MPOs which trajectories are constrained by a network, such as cars in a city. Since both the Euclidean distance and the double cross concepts ignore the spatial configuration of a potential underlying network, they are not well suited for $QTC_N$. Therefore, $QTC_N$ relations rely on the shortest paths in the network between the considered MPOs (Figure 2c). In essence, $QTC_N$ employs the philosophy of $QTC_B$ in the context of a space constrained by a network. $QTC_N$ will not be considered further in this chapter.

Finally, $QTC_S$ (Shape) employs the double cross concept in order to describe trajectory shapes or even arbitrary undirected polylines in a qualitative way. Thus, $QTC_S$ deals with the relative configuration of a trajectory, rather than with the relation between MPOs. Due to this different focus, it is out of the scope of this chapter.

## QTC: BASIC ($QTC_B$)

An MPO is always characterised by an origin and a destination, whether explicit or implicit. Hence, a basic dichotomy concerning MPOs, perhaps the most fundamental one, is the distinction between *towards* and *away from* relations. This very generic idea underlies $QTC_B$ where this binary relation is evaluated on the basis of Euclidean distance in an unconstrained $n$-dimensional space. In addition, also the relative speed between both objects can be taken into account. As mentioned earlier, QTC relations consist of qualitative symbols that share the threefold domain $U = \{-, 0, +\}$. $QTC_B$ relations are constructed from the relationships in Box 1.

Two levels of $QTC_B$ relations have been proposed: a first level $QTC_{B1}$ that only considers the distance constraints (relationships A and B), and a second level $QTC_{B2}$ taking account of the speed constraint (relationship C) as well. The resulting relation syntaxes are respectively the tuples $(A\ B)_{B1}$ and $(A\ B\ C)_{B2}$. Note that relationship C dually represents the relative speed of $l$ with respect to $k$, and hence trivialises a fourth relationship.

Relation icons for $QTC_B$ are shown in Figure 3, where $k$ is always on the left side, and $l$ on the right side. The line segments and crescents represent potential motion areas. Note that their boundaries are open, and, for the crescents, the straight boundaries correspond to elements of another relation. A filled dot indicates that an MPO might be stationary, whereas an open dot means that it must be moving. Dashed lines represent uncertain boundaries that follow from the ignorance of relative speed. The Roman numerals below the icons specify the minimum number of spatial dimensions required for a relation to be feasible.

There are 9 ($3^2$) base relations in $QTC_{B1}$ (Figure 3a). All these relations are possible in a one- or higher-dimensional space. $QTC_{B2}$ on the other hand has 27 ($3^3$) base relations (Figure 3b), which are all possible in two- or higher-dimensional spaces. However, in a one-dimensional space, only 17 (63.0%) $QTC_{B2}$ relations can occur. This reduction follows from a dependency between the distance constraints and the speed constraint in the case of a 1D space. In a 1D space, the direction of movement is always collinear with the direction of Euclidean distance, and hence a '0' in the distance constraints always corresponds to a stationary MPO. As a consequence, it is impossible for an MPO to be stationary and to have a higher speed than another MPO. In a two- or higher-dimensional space on the other hand, a '0' distance constraint does not necessarily indicate a stationary object, e.g. in the case of 'tangential motion' such as when one MPO is circling around the other MPO.

## QTC: DOUBLE CROSS ($QTC_C$)

In addition to the *towards / away from* dichotomy of $QTC_B$, $QTC_C$ employs another fundamental distinction in navigation, i.e. the *left / right* dichotomy. Hence, an intrinsic ‡-shaped frame of reference is obtained, called the Double Cross, after a concept introduced by Freksa (1992b) (Figure 4). The reference line associated with the *left / right* distinction is the straight connection line between both MPOs. Besides the *left / right* dichotomy, $QTC_C$ also takes into account the relative difference in relative motion angle with respect to this reference line (see Box 2).

As for $QTC_B$, two levels of $QTC_C$ have been defined: a first level $QTC_{C1}$ that simply considers the *towards / away from* and *left / right* distinctions and a second level $QTC_{C2}$ considering the speeds and angle constraints as well. The rela-

*Box 1.*

Assume: MPOs $k$ and $l$ and time point $t$

$k \mid t$ denotes the position of an MPO $k$ at $t$

$d(u,v)$ denotes the Euclidean distance between two positions $u$ and $v$

$\overrightarrow{v_k^t}$ denotes the velocity vector of $k$ at $t$

$t_1 \prec t_2$ denotes that $t_1$ is temporally before $t_2$

A. Movement of $k$ with respect to $l$ at $t$ (distance constraint):

-: $k$ is moving towards $l$:

$$\exists t_1 \left(t_1 \prec t \wedge \forall t^- \left(t_1 \prec t^- \prec t \rightarrow d\left(k|t^-, l|t\right) > d\left(k|t, l|t\right)\right)\right) \wedge$$
$$\exists t_2 \left(t \prec t_2 \wedge \forall t^+ \left(t \prec t^+ \prec t_2 \rightarrow d\left(k \mid t, l \mid t\right) > d\left(k \mid t^+, l \mid t\right)\right)\right) \quad (1)$$

+: $k$ is moving away from $l$:

$$\exists t_1 \left(t_1 \prec t \wedge \forall t^- \left(t_1 \prec t^- \prec t \rightarrow d\left(k|t^-, l|t\right) < d\left(k|t, l|t\right)\right)\right) \wedge$$
$$\exists t_2 \left(t \prec t_2 \wedge \forall t^+ \left(t \prec t^+ \prec t_2 \rightarrow d\left(k \mid t, l \mid t\right) < d\left(k \mid t^+, l \mid t\right)\right)\right) \quad (2)$$

0: $k$ is stable with respect to $l$ (all other cases)

B. Movement of $l$ with respect to $k$ at $t$ (distance constraint), can be described as in A with $k$ and $l$ interchanged, and hence:

-: $l$ is moving towards $k$ (3)

+: $l$ is moving away from $k$ (4)

0: $l$ is stable with respect to $k$ (all other cases)

C. Relative speed of $k$ with respect to $l$ at $t$ (speed constraint):

-: $k$ is moving slower than $l$

$$\left|\overrightarrow{v_k^t}\right| < \left|\overrightarrow{v_l^t}\right| \quad (5)$$

+: $k$ is moving faster than $l$

$$\left|\overrightarrow{v_k^t}\right| > \left|\overrightarrow{v_l^t}\right| \quad (6)$$

0: $k$ and $l$ are moving equally fast

$$\left|\overrightarrow{v_k^t}\right| = \left|\overrightarrow{v_l^t}\right| \quad (7)$$

*Figure 3. $QTC_{B1}$ (a), and $QTC_{B2}$ (b) relation icons*

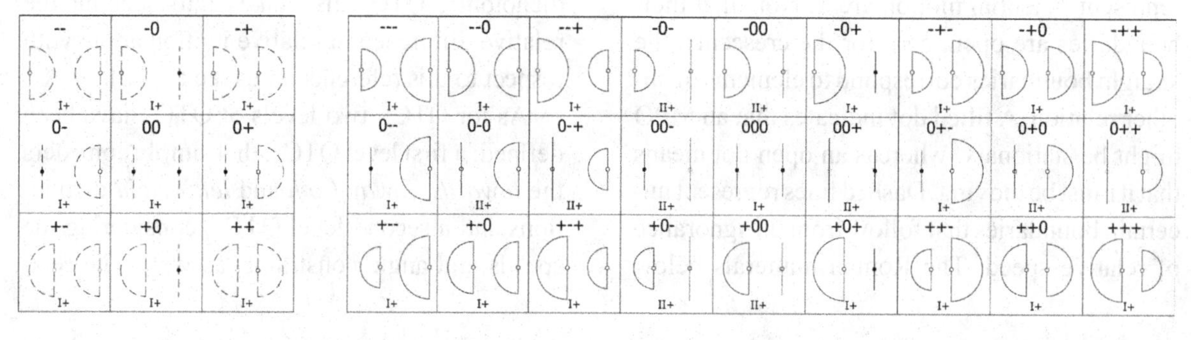

*Figure 4. Different use of the double cross in the double cross calculus (Zimmermann & Freksa, 1996) (a), and the $QTC_C$ calculus (b)*

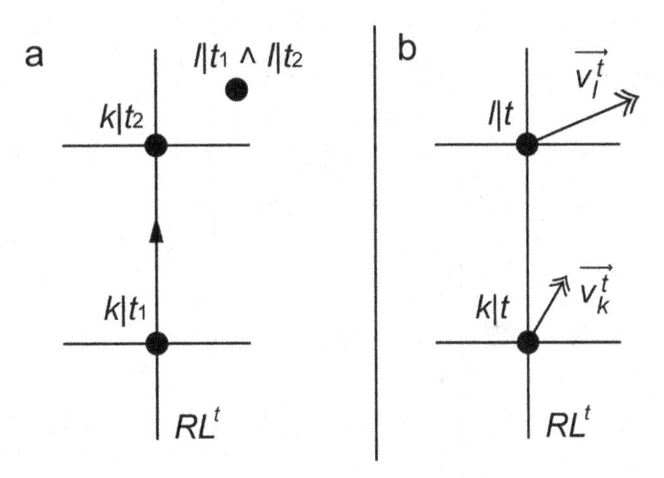


*Box 2.*

Assume: MPOs $k$ and $l$ and time point $t$

$RL^t$ denotes the reference line through $k|t$ and $l|t$

$MAA\left(\vec{v}_k^t, RL^t\right)$ denotes the minimum absolute angle between $v_k^t$ and $RL^t$

Movement of $k$ with respect to $RL^t$ at $t$ (side constraint):

-: $k$ is moving to the left side of $RL^t$

$$\exists t_1 \left(t_1 \prec t \wedge \forall t^- \left(t_1 \prec t^- \prec t \rightarrow k \text{is on the right side of } RL^t \text{at } t\right)\right) \wedge \exists t_2 \left(t \prec t_2 \wedge \forall t^+ \left(t \prec t^+ \prec t_2 \rightarrow k \text{ is on the left side of } RL^t \text{ at } t\right)\right) \quad (8)$$

+: $k$ is moving to the right side of $RL^t$

$$\exists t_1 \left(t_1 \prec t \wedge \forall t^- \left(t_1 \prec t^- \prec t \rightarrow k \text{is on the left side of } RL^t \text{at } t\right)\right) \wedge \exists t_2 \left(t \prec t_2 \wedge \forall t^+ \left(t \prec t^+ \prec t_2 \rightarrow k \text{ is on the right side of } RL^t \text{ at } t\right)\right) \quad (9)$$

0: $k$ is moving along $RL^t$ (all other cases)

Movement of $l$ with respect to $RL^t$ at $t$ (side constraint), can be described as in D with $k$ and $l$ interchanged, and hence:

-: $l$ is moving to the left side of $RL^t$ (10)

+: $l$ is moving to the right side of $RL^t$ (11)

0: $l$ is moving along $RL^t$ (all other cases)

D. Angle constraint:

$$-: \; MAA\left(\vec{v}_k^t, RL^t\right) < MAA\left(\vec{v}_l^t, RL^t\right) \quad (12)$$

$$+: \; MAA\left(\vec{v}_k^t, RL^t\right) > MAA\left(\vec{v}_l^t, RL^t\right) \quad (13)$$

0: all other cases

*Figure 5.* $\dot{Q}TC_{C1}$ *relation icons*

| ---- II+ | ---0 II+ | ---+ II+ | --0- II+ | --00 I+ | --0+ II+ | --+- II+ | --+0 II+ | --++ II+ |
|---|---|---|---|---|---|---|---|---|
| -0-- II+ | -0-0 II+ | -0-+ II+ | -00- II+ | -000 I+ | -00+ II+ | -0+- II+ | -0+0 II+ | -0++ II+ |
| -+-- II+ | -+-0 II+ | -+-+ II+ | -+0- II+ | -+00 I+ | -+0+ II+ | -++- II+ | -++0 II+ | -+++ II+ |
| 0--- II+ | 0--0 II+ | 0--+ II+ | 0-0- II+ | 0-00 I+ | 0-0+ II+ | 0-+- II+ | 0-+0 II+ | 0-++ II+ |
| 00-- II+ | 00-0 II+ | 00-+ II+ | 000- II+ | 0000 I+ | 000+ II+ | 00+- II+ | 00+0 II+ | 00++ II+ |
| 0+-- II+ | 0+-0 II+ | 0+-+ II+ | 0+0- II+ | 0+00 I+ | 0+0+ II+ | 0++- II+ | 0++0 II+ | 0+++ II+ |
| +--- II+ | +--0 II+ | +--+ II+ | +-0- II+ | +-00 I+ | +-0+ II+ | +-+- II+ | +-+0 II+ | +-++ II+ |
| +0-- II+ | +0-0 II+ | +0-+ II+ | +00- II+ | +000 I+ | +00+ II+ | +0+- II+ | +0+0 II+ | +0++ II+ |
| ++-- II+ | ++-0 II+ | ++-+ II+ | ++0- II+ | ++00 I+ | ++0+ II+ | +++- II+ | +++0 II+ | ++++ II+ |

tional syntaxes are respectively $(A\ B\ D\ E)_{C1}$ and $(A\ B\ D\ E\ C\ F)_{C2}$. Let us consider relationship F if one of the objects is not moving at $t$. The object can move in every direction at $t^-$ and at $t^+$. Assume that F is '–' at $t^-$ and '+' at $t^+$. Since we assume continuous motion, F has to be '0' at $t$. Thus, if at least one MPO is stationary, F will be '0.'

$QTC_{C1}$ and $QTC_{C2}$ respectively have 81 ($3^4$) and 729 ($3^6$) theoretical JEPD base relations (Figure 5, Figure 6). In a one-dimensional space, left and right of the reference line through $k$ and $l$ cannot be distinguished, and hence the side and angle constraints will always be '0.' Thus, in essence, $QTC_{C1}$ reduces to $QTC_{B1}$ and $QTC_{C2}$ reduces to $QTC_{B2}$ for the one-dimensional case, with, respectively, 9 (11.1% of the theoretical number) and 17 (2.3%) base relations.

In two dimensions, all $QTC_{C1}$ base relations exist (as for all higher dimensions), whereas only 305 (42.4%) $QTC_{C2}$ relations are possible, due to the interdependence of relational symbols. Since in 2D space, objects must be stationary whenever their distance and side constraints are '0,' the speed constraint is restricted and the angle constraint must be '0' in that case. Also, an object with a '0' distance constraint and non-'0' side constraint must be moving with a bigger or equal angle with respect to $RL^t$, and hence the restriction on the angle constraint. Analogously, objects with a non-'0' distance constraint and '0' side constraint move with smaller or equal angles with respect to $RL^t$. Moreover, when the latter two rules are combined, the inequality turns into either a strict equality, or a strict inequality, and thereby restricts the angle constraint to a singleton.

In three-dimensional space, the distance and side constraints are insufficient to deduce the stationarity of the objects. However, as in 2D, they

*Figure 6. $QTC_{C2}$ relations and the minimal number of spatial dimensions supporting them: respectively the dotted, dashed, and straight boundaries for one, two, and three dimensions*

| | | | | | | | | | | | | | | | | | | | | | | | | | | |
|---|---|---|---|---|---|---|---|---|---|---|---|---|---|---|---|---|---|---|---|---|---|---|---|---|---|---|
| ---<br>--- | ---<br>--0 | ---<br>--+ | ---<br>-0- | ---<br>-00 | ---<br>-0+ | ---<br>-+- | ---<br>-+0 | ---<br>-++ | ---<br>0-- | ---<br>0-0 | ---<br>0-+ | ---<br>00- | ---<br>000 | ---<br>00+ | ---<br>0+- | ---<br>0+0 | ---<br>0++ | ---<br>+-- | ---<br>+-0 | ---<br>+-+ | ---<br>+0- | ---<br>+00 | ---<br>+0+ | ---<br>++- | ---<br>++0 | ---<br>+++ |
| --0<br>--- | --0<br>--0 | --0<br>--+ | --0<br>-0- | --0<br>-00 | --0<br>-0+ | --0<br>-+- | --0<br>-+0 | --0<br>-++ | --0<br>0-- | --0<br>0-0 | --0<br>0-+ | --0<br>00- | --0<br>000 | --0<br>00+ | --0<br>0+- | --0<br>0+0 | --0<br>0++ | --0<br>+-- | --0<br>+-0 | --0<br>+-+ | --0<br>+0- | --0<br>+00 | --0<br>+0+ | --0<br>++- | --0<br>++0 | --0<br>+++ |
| --+<br>--- | --+<br>--0 | --+<br>--+ | --+<br>-0- | --+<br>-00 | --+<br>-0+ | --+<br>-+- | --+<br>-+0 | --+<br>-++ | --+<br>0-- | --+<br>0-0 | --+<br>0-+ | --+<br>00- | --+<br>000 | --+<br>00+ | --+<br>0+- | --+<br>0+0 | --+<br>0++ | --+<br>+-- | --+<br>+-0 | --+<br>+-+ | --+<br>+0- | --+<br>+00 | --+<br>+0+ | --+<br>++- | --+<br>++0 | --+<br>+++ |
| -0-<br>--- | -0-<br>--0 | -0-<br>--+ | -0-<br>-0- | -0-<br>-00 | -0-<br>-0+ | -0-<br>-+- | -0-<br>-+0 | -0-<br>-++ | -0-<br>0-- | -0-<br>0-0 | -0-<br>0-+ | -0-<br>00- | -0-<br>000 | -0-<br>00+ | -0-<br>0+- | -0-<br>0+0 | -0-<br>0++ | -0-<br>+-- | -0-<br>+-0 | -0-<br>+-+ | -0-<br>+0- | -0-<br>+00 | -0-<br>+0+ | -0-<br>++- | -0-<br>++0 | -0-<br>+++ |
| -00<br>--- | -00<br>--0 | -00<br>--+ | -00<br>-0- | -00<br>-00 | -00<br>-0+ | -00<br>-+- | -00<br>-+0 | -00<br>-++ | -00<br>0-- | -00<br>0-0 | -00<br>0-+ | -00<br>00- | -00<br>000 | -00<br>00+ | -00<br>0+- | -00<br>0+0 | -00<br>0++ | -00<br>+-- | -00<br>+-0 | -00<br>+-+ | -00<br>+0- | -00<br>+00 | -00<br>+0+ | -00<br>++- | -00<br>++0 | -00<br>+++ |
| -0+<br>--- | -0+<br>--0 | -0+<br>--+ | -0+<br>-0- | -0+<br>-00 | -0+<br>-0+ | -0+<br>-+- | -0+<br>-+0 | -0+<br>-++ | -0+<br>0-- | -0+<br>0-0 | -0+<br>0-+ | -0+<br>00- | -0+<br>000 | -0+<br>00+ | -0+<br>0+- | -0+<br>0+0 | -0+<br>0++ | -0+<br>+-- | -0+<br>+-0 | -0+<br>+-+ | -0+<br>+0- | -0+<br>+00 | -0+<br>+0+ | -0+<br>++- | -0+<br>++0 | -0+<br>+++ |
| -+-<br>--- | -+-<br>--0 | -+-<br>--+ | -+-<br>-0- | -+-<br>-00 | -+-<br>-0+ | -+-<br>-+- | -+-<br>-+0 | -+-<br>-++ | -+-<br>0-- | -+-<br>0-0 | -+-<br>0-+ | -+-<br>00- | -+-<br>000 | -+-<br>00+ | -+-<br>0+- | -+-<br>0+0 | -+-<br>0++ | -+-<br>+-- | -+-<br>+-0 | -+-<br>+-+ | -+-<br>+0- | -+-<br>+00 | -+-<br>+0+ | -+-<br>++- | -+-<br>++0 | -+-<br>+++ |
| -+0<br>--- | -+0<br>--0 | -+0<br>--+ | -+0<br>-0- | -+0<br>-00 | -+0<br>-0+ | -+0<br>-+- | -+0<br>-+0 | -+0<br>-++ | -+0<br>0-- | -+0<br>0-0 | -+0<br>0-+ | -+0<br>00- | -+0<br>000 | -+0<br>00+ | -+0<br>0+- | -+0<br>0+0 | -+0<br>0++ | -+0<br>+-- | -+0<br>+-0 | -+0<br>+-+ | -+0<br>+0- | -+0<br>+00 | -+0<br>+0+ | -+0<br>++- | -+0<br>++0 | -+0<br>+++ |
| -++<br>--- | -++<br>--0 | -++<br>--+ | -++<br>-0- | -++<br>-00 | -++<br>-0+ | -++<br>-+- | -++<br>-+0 | -++<br>-++ | -++<br>0-- | -++<br>0-0 | -++<br>0-+ | -++<br>00- | -++<br>000 | -++<br>00+ | -++<br>0+- | -++<br>0+0 | -++<br>0++ | -++<br>+-- | -++<br>+-0 | -++<br>+-+ | -++<br>+0- | -++<br>+00 | -++<br>+0+ | -++<br>++- | -++<br>++0 | -++<br>+++ |
| 0--<br>--- | 0--<br>--0 | 0--<br>--+ | 0--<br>-0- | 0--<br>-00 | 0--<br>-0+ | 0--<br>-+- | 0--<br>-+0 | 0--<br>-++ | 0--<br>0-- | 0--<br>0-0 | 0--<br>0-+ | 0--<br>00- | 0--<br>000 | 0--<br>00+ | 0--<br>0+- | 0--<br>0+0 | 0--<br>0++ | 0--<br>+-- | 0--<br>+-0 | 0--<br>+-+ | 0--<br>+0- | 0--<br>+00 | 0--<br>+0+ | 0--<br>++- | 0--<br>++0 | 0--<br>+++ |
| 0-0<br>--- | 0-0<br>--0 | 0-0<br>--+ | 0-0<br>-0- | 0-0<br>-00 | 0-0<br>-0+ | 0-0<br>-+- | 0-0<br>-+0 | 0-0<br>-++ | 0-0<br>0-- | 0-0<br>0-0 | 0-0<br>0-+ | 0-0<br>00- | 0-0<br>000 | 0-0<br>00+ | 0-0<br>0+- | 0-0<br>0+0 | 0-0<br>0++ | 0-0<br>+-- | 0-0<br>+-0 | 0-0<br>+-+ | 0-0<br>+0- | 0-0<br>+00 | 0-0<br>+0+ | 0-0<br>++- | 0-0<br>++0 | 0-0<br>+++ |
| 0-+<br>--- | 0-+<br>--0 | 0-+<br>--+ | 0-+<br>-0- | 0-+<br>-00 | 0-+<br>-0+ | 0-+<br>-+- | 0-+<br>-+0 | 0-+<br>-++ | 0-+<br>0-- | 0-+<br>0-0 | 0-+<br>0-+ | 0-+<br>00- | 0-+<br>000 | 0-+<br>00+ | 0-+<br>0+- | 0-+<br>0+0 | 0-+<br>0++ | 0-+<br>+-- | 0-+<br>+-0 | 0-+<br>+-+ | 0-+<br>+0- | 0-+<br>+00 | 0-+<br>+0+ | 0-+<br>++- | 0-+<br>++0 | 0-+<br>+++ |
| 00-<br>--- | 00-<br>--0 | 00-<br>--+ | 00-<br>-0- | 00-<br>-00 | 00-<br>-0+ | 00-<br>-+- | 00-<br>-+0 | 00-<br>-++ | 00-<br>0-- | 00-<br>0-0 | 00-<br>0-+ | 00-<br>00- | 00-<br>000 | 00-<br>00+ | 00-<br>0+- | 00-<br>0+0 | 00-<br>0++ | 00-<br>+-- | 00-<br>+-0 | 00-<br>+-+ | 00-<br>+0- | 00-<br>+00 | 00-<br>+0+ | 00-<br>++- | 00-<br>++0 | 00-<br>+++ |
| 000<br>--- | 000<br>--0 | 000<br>--+ | 000<br>-0- | 000<br>-00 | 000<br>-0+ | 000<br>-+- | 000<br>-+0 | 000<br>-++ | 000<br>0-- | 000<br>0-0 | 000<br>0-+ | 000<br>00- | 000<br>000 | 000<br>00+ | 000<br>0+- | 000<br>0+0 | 000<br>0++ | 000<br>+-- | 000<br>+-0 | 000<br>+-+ | 000<br>+0- | 000<br>+00 | 000<br>+0+ | 000<br>++- | 000<br>++0 | 000<br>+++ |
| 00+<br>--- | 00+<br>--0 | 00+<br>--+ | 00+<br>-0- | 00+<br>-00 | 00+<br>-0+ | 00+<br>-+- | 00+<br>-+0 | 00+<br>-++ | 00+<br>0-- | 00+<br>0-0 | 00+<br>0-+ | 00+<br>00- | 00+<br>000 | 00+<br>00+ | 00+<br>0+- | 00+<br>0+0 | 00+<br>0++ | 00+<br>+-- | 00+<br>+-0 | 00+<br>+-+ | 00+<br>+0- | 00+<br>+00 | 00+<br>+0+ | 00+<br>++- | 00+<br>++0 | 00+<br>+++ |
| 0+-<br>--- | 0+-<br>--0 | 0+-<br>--+ | 0+-<br>-0- | 0+-<br>-00 | 0+-<br>-0+ | 0+-<br>-+- | 0+-<br>-+0 | 0+-<br>-++ | 0+-<br>0-- | 0+-<br>0-0 | 0+-<br>0-+ | 0+-<br>00- | 0+-<br>000 | 0+-<br>00+ | 0+-<br>0+- | 0+-<br>0+0 | 0+-<br>0++ | 0+-<br>+-- | 0+-<br>+-0 | 0+-<br>+-+ | 0+-<br>+0- | 0+-<br>+00 | 0+-<br>+0+ | 0+-<br>++- | 0+-<br>++0 | 0+-<br>+++ |
| 0+0<br>--- | 0+0<br>--0 | 0+0<br>--+ | 0+0<br>-0- | 0+0<br>-00 | 0+0<br>-0+ | 0+0<br>-+- | 0+0<br>-+0 | 0+0<br>-++ | 0+0<br>0-- | 0+0<br>0-0 | 0+0<br>0-+ | 0+0<br>00- | 0+0<br>000 | 0+0<br>00+ | 0+0<br>0+- | 0+0<br>0+0 | 0+0<br>0++ | 0+0<br>+-- | 0+0<br>+-0 | 0+0<br>+-+ | 0+0<br>+0- | 0+0<br>+00 | 0+0<br>+0+ | 0+0<br>++- | 0+0<br>++0 | 0+0<br>+++ |
| 0++<br>--- | 0++<br>--0 | 0++<br>--+ | 0++<br>-0- | 0++<br>-00 | 0++<br>-0+ | 0++<br>-+- | 0++<br>-+0 | 0++<br>-++ | 0++<br>0-- | 0++<br>0-0 | 0++<br>0-+ | 0++<br>00- | 0++<br>000 | 0++<br>00+ | 0++<br>0+- | 0++<br>0+0 | 0++<br>0++ | 0++<br>+-- | 0++<br>+-0 | 0++<br>+-+ | 0++<br>+0- | 0++<br>+00 | 0++<br>+0+ | 0++<br>++- | 0++<br>++0 | 0++<br>+++ |
| +--<br>--- | +--<br>--0 | +--<br>--+ | +--<br>-0- | +--<br>-00 | +--<br>-0+ | +--<br>-+- | +--<br>-+0 | +--<br>-++ | +--<br>0-- | +--<br>0-0 | +--<br>0-+ | +--<br>00- | +--<br>000 | +--<br>00+ | +--<br>0+- | +--<br>0+0 | +--<br>0++ | +--<br>+-- | +--<br>+-0 | +--<br>+-+ | +--<br>+0- | +--<br>+00 | +--<br>+0+ | +--<br>++- | +--<br>++0 | +--<br>+++ |
| +-0<br>--- | +-0<br>--0 | +-0<br>--+ | +-0<br>-0- | +-0<br>-00 | +-0<br>-0+ | +-0<br>-+- | +-0<br>-+0 | +-0<br>-++ | +-0<br>0-- | +-0<br>0-0 | +-0<br>0-+ | +-0<br>00- | +-0<br>000 | +-0<br>00+ | +-0<br>0+- | +-0<br>0+0 | +-0<br>0++ | +-0<br>+-- | +-0<br>+-0 | +-0<br>+-+ | +-0<br>+0- | +-0<br>+00 | +-0<br>+0+ | +-0<br>++- | +-0<br>++0 | +-0<br>+++ |
| +-+<br>--- | +-+<br>--0 | +-+<br>--+ | +-+<br>-0- | +-+<br>-00 | +-+<br>-0+ | +-+<br>-+- | +-+<br>-+0 | +-+<br>-++ | +-+<br>0-- | +-+<br>0-0 | +-+<br>0-+ | +-+<br>00- | +-+<br>000 | +-+<br>00+ | +-+<br>0+- | +-+<br>0+0 | +-+<br>0++ | +-+<br>+-- | +-+<br>+-0 | +-+<br>+-+ | +-+<br>+0- | +-+<br>+00 | +-+<br>+0+ | +-+<br>++- | +-+<br>++0 | +-+<br>+++ |
| +0-<br>--- | +0-<br>--0 | +0-<br>--+ | +0-<br>-0- | +0-<br>-00 | +0-<br>-0+ | +0-<br>-+- | +0-<br>-+0 | +0-<br>-++ | +0-<br>0-- | +0-<br>0-0 | +0-<br>0-+ | +0-<br>00- | +0-<br>000 | +0-<br>00+ | +0-<br>0+- | +0-<br>0+0 | +0-<br>0++ | +0-<br>+-- | +0-<br>+-0 | +0-<br>+-+ | +0-<br>+0- | +0-<br>+00 | +0-<br>+0+ | +0-<br>++- | +0-<br>++0 | +0-<br>+++ |
| +00<br>--- | +00<br>--0 | +00<br>--+ | +00<br>-0- | +00<br>-00 | +00<br>-0+ | +00<br>-+- | +00<br>-+0 | +00<br>-++ | +00<br>0-- | +00<br>0-0 | +00<br>0-+ | +00<br>00- | +00<br>000 | +00<br>00+ | +00<br>0+- | +00<br>0+0 | +00<br>0++ | +00<br>+-- | +00<br>+-0 | +00<br>+-+ | +00<br>+0- | +00<br>+00 | +00<br>+0+ | +00<br>++- | +00<br>++0 | +00<br>+++ |
| +0+<br>--- | +0+<br>--0 | +0+<br>--+ | +0+<br>-0- | +0+<br>-00 | +0+<br>-0+ | +0+<br>-+- | +0+<br>-+0 | +0+<br>-++ | +0+<br>0-- | +0+<br>0-0 | +0+<br>0-+ | +0+<br>00- | +0+<br>000 | +0+<br>00+ | +0+<br>0+- | +0+<br>0+0 | +0+<br>0++ | +0+<br>+-- | +0+<br>+-0 | +0+<br>+-+ | +0+<br>+0- | +0+<br>+00 | +0+<br>+0+ | +0+<br>++- | +0+<br>++0 | +0+<br>+++ |
| ++-<br>--- | ++-<br>--0 | ++-<br>--+ | ++-<br>-0- | ++-<br>-00 | ++-<br>-0+ | ++-<br>-+- | ++-<br>-+0 | ++-<br>-++ | ++-<br>0-- | ++-<br>0-0 | ++-<br>0-+ | ++-<br>00- | ++-<br>000 | ++-<br>00+ | ++-<br>0+- | ++-<br>0+0 | ++-<br>0++ | ++-<br>+-- | ++-<br>+-0 | ++-<br>+-+ | ++-<br>+0- | ++-<br>+00 | ++-<br>+0+ | ++-<br>++- | ++-<br>++0 | ++-<br>+++ |
| ++0<br>--- | ++0<br>--0 | ++0<br>--+ | ++0<br>-0- | ++0<br>-00 | ++0<br>-0+ | ++0<br>-+- | ++0<br>-+0 | ++0<br>-++ | ++0<br>0-- | ++0<br>0-0 | ++0<br>0-+ | ++0<br>00- | ++0<br>000 | ++0<br>00+ | ++0<br>0+- | ++0<br>0+0 | ++0<br>0++ | ++0<br>+-- | ++0<br>+-0 | ++0<br>+-+ | ++0<br>+0- | ++0<br>+00 | ++0<br>+0+ | ++0<br>++- | ++0<br>++0 | ++0<br>+++ |
| +++<br>--- | +++<br>--0 | +++<br>--+ | +++<br>-0- | +++<br>-00 | +++<br>-0+ | +++<br>-+- | +++<br>-+0 | +++<br>-++ | +++<br>0-- | +++<br>0-0 | +++<br>0-+ | +++<br>00- | +++<br>000 | +++<br>00+ | +++<br>0+- | +++<br>0+0 | +++<br>0++ | +++<br>+-- | +++<br>+-0 | +++<br>+-+ | +++<br>+0- | +++<br>+00 | +++<br>+0+ | +++<br>++- | +++<br>++0 | +++<br>+++ |

determine whether the direction of movement must be along or perpendicular to $RL^t$. From this observation restrictions follow on the angle constraint. The special case where both the distance and side constraints are '0' may indicate either a stationary object, or an object moving perpendicular to $RL^t$ and perpendicular to both the *left* / *right* and *towards* / *away from* directions. We obtain 591 (81.1%) feasible $QTC_{C2}$ relations in 3D.

*Figure 7. CNDs for $QTC_{B1}$ in n-dimensional space (a), for $QTC_{B2}$ in a one-dimensional space (b), and for $QTC_{B2}$ in a two- or higher-dimensional space (c). The straight, dashed and dotted lines respectively represent the conceptual distances one, two, and three.*

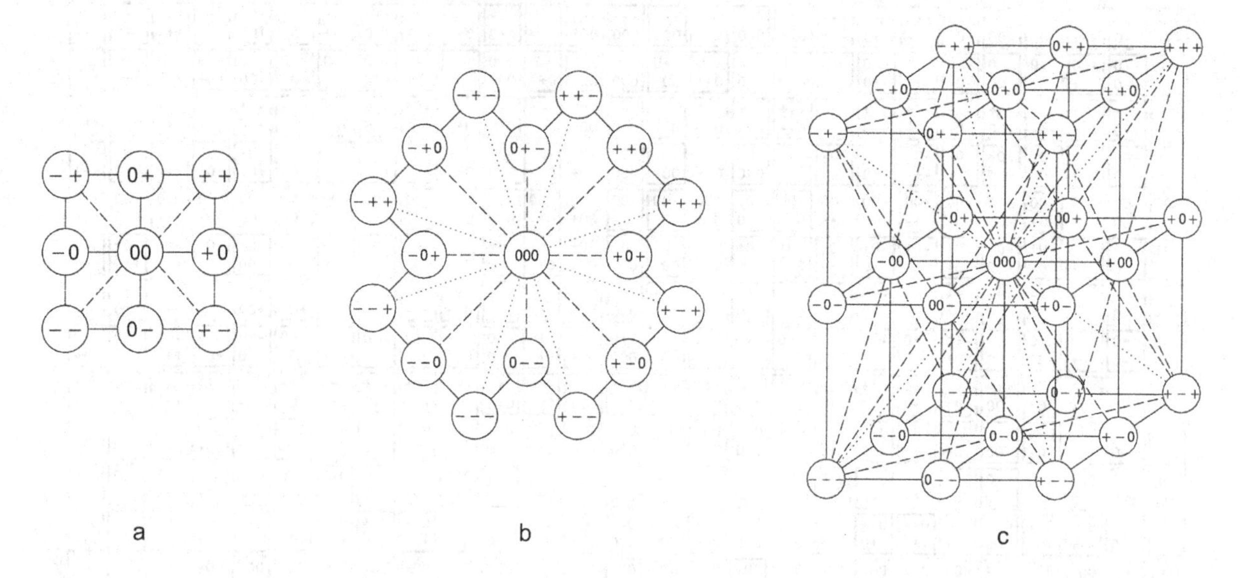


## REPRESENTING AND REASONING WITH QTC

QTC has been confronted with key concepts in qualitative reasoning. In this section, we will discuss three of these issues, respectively Conceptual Neighbourhood Diagrams (CNDs), Composition Tables (CTs), and incomplete knowledge.

### Conceptual Neighbourhood Diagrams

As mentioned earlier, the construction of CNDs for QTC is based on the concepts of dominance (Galton, 2001) and conceptual distance. For an in depth description, we refer to Van de Weghe and De Maeyer (2005). CNDs for the Basic and Double Cross QTC calculi in 2D space are respectively shown in Figure 7 and Figure 8. For each link between conceptual neighbours the conceptual distance between the adjacent relations has been indicated. The CND for $QTC_{C1}$ in 1D has been omitted, since it would be the same as the CND for $QTC_{B1}$ except for two additional '0' values in each relation. The CND for $QTC_{C2}$ is also not shown, as it is too complex to visualise on a two-dimensional medium.

From the CNDs, we learn that, due to the laws of continuity, the conceptual neighbours of each particular relation constitute only a subset of base relations. This set comprises the candidate relations that may directly precede or follow the relation at hand in time, i.e. the set of possible transitions from/to this relation. This set of candidates is thereby highly limited when compared to the set of theoretical possibilities, as can be seen from Table 1. Note that each pair of conceptual neighbours $R_1$ and $R_2$ is associated with two transitions, i.e. a transition from $R_1$ to $R_2$, and its converse from $R_2$ to $R_1$. Similarly, to a CND, a transition graph can be constructed with directed links to represent existing transitions. However, for $QTC_B$ and $QTC_C$, all converse transitions do exist and thus one conceptual neighbour relation can be counted for two transitions (Table 1). Note that this may not be the case for other types of QTC, e.g. for $QTC_{N'}$ (Delafontaine, Van de Weghe, Bogaert, & De Maeyer, 2008).

*Figure 8. CND for $QTC_{C1}$ in a two-or higher-dimensional space. Links have been gray-shaded according to the conceptual distance between the adjacent relations.*

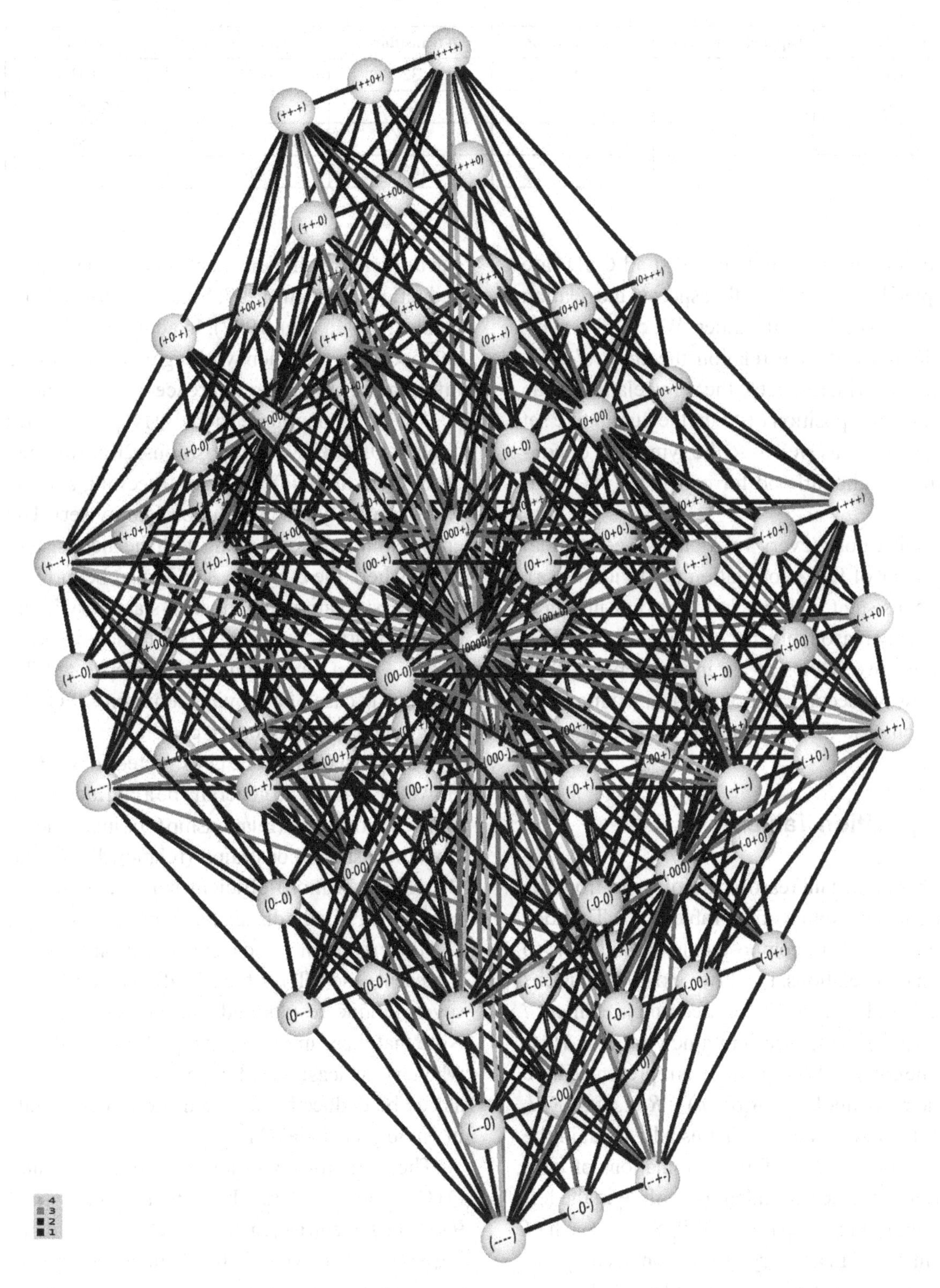

*Table 1. The number of base relations, transitions, theoretical combinations of base relations, and the ratio transitions / theoretical combinations for QTC basic and double cross calculi*

| QTC calculus | #spatial dimensions | # base relations | # transitions | # combinations | ratio |
|---|---|---|---|---|---|
| B1 | 1+ | 9 | 32 | 72 | 44,4% |
| B2 | 1 | 17 | 64 | 272 | 23,5% |
|  | 2+ | 27 | 196 | 702 | 27,9% |
| C1 | 2+ | 81 | 1088 | 6480 | 16,8% |

Another notable finding is that all CNDs are completely symmetric with respect to the relation consisting solely of '0' values. We call this symmetric and reflexive relation the *zero-relation*. Symmetry with respect to the zero-relation is due to the central position of '0' in the qualitative set $U = \{-, 0, +\}$, as well as to the symmetry of conceptual neighbourhood for converse QTC relations.

Furthermore, every relation is a conceptual neighbour of the zero-relation (and vice versa), as is consistent with our intuition. For instance, it is highly reasonable that, whatever the relation between two MPOs at a certain moment, they may always become stationary the next moment, in which case their relation turns into the zero-relation.

## Composition Tables

Another important reasoning tool, apart from the CND, is the Composition Table (CT). The idea behind a CT is to compose existing relations to obtain new relations, i.e. if two existing relations $R_1(k, l)$ and $R_2(l, m)$ share a common element $l$ they can be composed into a new relation $R_3(k, m)$. The composition operation is represented here by the $\otimes$ symbol, e.g. $R_3(k, m) = R_1(k, l) \otimes R_2(l, m)$. CTs are cross tables that usually contain the composition results of all combinations of base relations for a certain calculus, with $R_1$ in the left column, $R_2$ in the top row, and $R_1 \otimes R_2$ in each of the entries. CTs are very useful from a computational point of view, since a simple table look-up can be far more efficient than complex theoretical deduction (Bennett, 1997; Skiadopoulos & Koubarakis, 2004; Vieu, 1997). In addition, CTs play an important role when working with incomplete information and larger inference mechanisms.

The CT for one-dimensional $QTC_{B1}$ is shown in Table 2. Of its 81 ($9^2$) compositions, 20 are unique, 20 of them are twofold, 4 are threefold, and the remaining 36 yield no solution (empty set). The empty solutions come along with the inconsistent cases where the common MPO must be moving in the first relation and must be stationary in the second relation, and vice versa. Hence, in order to avoid them, one might use two separate CTs: one for the case of a moving common MPO, the other one for the stationary case.

Complete CTs can be constructed for $QTC_{B2}$. However, this would generally be a bad idea, since the speed constraint (relationship C) is independent from the distance constraints (relationships A and B). Hence, a more efficient solution is to use separate CTs for the distance and speed constraints, and then recombine the results afterwards. Table 3 presents the CT for the speed constraint, with seven unique results and two universe results. Note that these universe sets are further reduced whenever at least one of the objects is stationary, as can be deduced from the distance constraints in one-dimensional $QTC_B$.

The CTs for two-dimensional $QTC_{C1}$ and $QTC_{C2}$ would respectively contain 6561 ($81^2$) and 93025 ($305^2$) entries, each of these entries containing a set of up to 81 and 305 elements. Since CTs soon become very large, a so-called *Composition-*

*Table 2. CT for $QTC_{B1}$ in a one-dimensional space*

| ⊗ | (--) | (0-) | (+-) | (-0) | (00) | (+0) | (-+) | (0+) | (++) |
|---|---|---|---|---|---|---|---|---|---|
| (--) | (-+)∨(+-) | ∅ | (--) | (0+)∨(0-) | ∅ | (0-) | (--)∨(++) | ∅ | (+-) |
| (0-) | (-0)∨(+0) | ∅ | (-0) | (00) | ∅ | (00) | (-0)∨(+0) | ∅ | (+0) |
| (+-) | (--)∨(++) | ∅ | (-+) | (0+)∨(0-) | ∅ | (0+) | (-+)∨(+-) | ∅ | (++) |
| (-0) | ∅ | (-+)∨(--) ∨(+-) | ∅ | ∅ | (0+)∨(0-) | ∅ | ∅ | (--)∨(+-) ∨(++) | ∅ |
| (00) | ∅ | (0+)∨(0-) | ∅ | ∅ | (00) | ∅ | ∅ | (0+)∨(0-) | ∅ |
| (+0) | ∅ | (--)∨(-+) ∨(++) | ∅ | ∅ | (0+)∨(0-) | ∅ | ∅ | (-+)∨(++) ∨(+-) | ∅ |
| (-+) | (--) | ∅ | (-+)∨(+-) | (0-) | ∅ | (0+)∨(0-) | (+-) | ∅ | (--)∨(++) |
| (0+) | (-0) | ∅ | (-0)∨(+0) | (00) | ∅ | (00) | (+0) | ∅ | (-0)∨(+0) |
| (++) | (-+) | ∅ | (--)∨(++) | (++) | ∅ | (0+)∨(0-) | (++) | ∅ | (-+)∨(+-) |

*Table 3. CT for the speed constraint*

| ⊗ | − | 0 | + |
|---|---|---|---|
| − | − | − | *U* |
| 0 | − | 0 | + |
| + | *U* | + | + |

*Rule Table* (CRT) was introduced by Van de Weghe, Kuijpers, Bogaert, and De Maeyer (2005). A CRT differs from a traditional CT as it does not contain all individual composition results. Nevertheless, a CRT does provide all the information offered by a traditional CT. Instead of the full CT, a CRT uses a set of composition rules to generate the composition results for the relations at hand. These rules can be implemented in information systems in order to automatically generate compositions, which might be preferable to CTs due to their extent.

CRTs for QTC can be obtained by using diagrammatic reasoning on the basis of relation icons (e.g. Figure 3: $QTC_{B1}$ [a], and $QTC_{B2}$ [b] relation iconsFigure 3 and Figure 5). As $R_1$ and $R_2$ are given, their corresponding relation icons can be translated so that the position of $l$ in the icon of $R_2$ matches the position of $l$ in the icon of $R_1$. Then, in order to find the composition result, two central issues have to be considered. First, which rotation do we need, such that the velocity vector of $l$ in $R_2$ matches the one of $l$ in $R_1$? Second, how is $k$ moving with respect to $l$ in $R_1$, and how is $m$ moving with respect to $l$ in $R_2$?

Let us consider the case of two-dimensional $QTC_{C1}$. For the first issue, nine rotational possibilities have to be taken into account[1]: the crisp rotations 0°, 90°, 180°, 270°, the range rotations [0°, 90°], [90°, 180°], [180°, 270°], [270°, 360°], and the option of no possible match by rotation. The latter case occurs due to the impossibility of inference between a moving and a stationary MPO. For the second issue, only the first and the third relational symbols of $R_1$ (relationships A and C) and the second and fourth symbols of $R_2$ (relationships B and D) have to be considered to determine the composition result.

Table 4 presents the CRT for $QTC_{C1}$ in 2D. It has 324 entries, which is a compression to less than 5% compared to the original CT with 6561 entries. The CRT consists of two halves: the upper half to look up the first and third symbol (relationships A and C) of $R_3$, and the lower half to determine the second and fourth symbol (relationships B and D).

We briefly explain the CRT with an example. The velocity vector of $l$ in the icon of $R_2(l, m) = (+ + 0\ 0)_{C1}$ needs to be rotated over 270° in order

*Table 4. CRT for $QTC_{C1}$ in a two-dimensional space*

| | | 0° | | 90° | | 180° | | | | 270° | | 0°-90° | | 90°-180° | | | | | | | | | | 180°-270° | | | | | | | | | | 270°-360° | | X |
|---|---|---|---|---|---|---|---|---|---|---|---|---|---|---|---|---|---|---|---|---|---|---|---|---|---|---|---|---|---|---|---|---|---|---|---|---|
| A | C | A | C | A | C | A | C | A | C | A | C | A | C | A | C | A | C | A | C | A | C | A | C | A | C | A | C | A | C | A | C | A | C | A | C | |
| 0 | 0 | 0 | 0 | 0 | 0 | 0 | 0 | 0 | 0 | 0 | 0 | 0 | 0 | 0 | 0 | 0 | 0 | 0 | 0 | 0 | 0 | 0 | 0 | 0 | 0 | 0 | 0 | 0 | 0 | 0 | 0 | 0 | 0 | 0 | 0 | |
| – | 0 | – | 0 | – | + | – | 0 | + | 0 | – | – | – | + | – | + | – | + | – | + | 0 | + | + | + | + | – | 0 | – | – | – | – | – | – | – | – | – | |
| – | – | – | – | – | U | – | – | + | + | U | – | – | U | – | U | – | U | – | + | U | + | + | U | + | – | U | - | U | – | U | – | U | – | U | – | |
| 0 | – | 0 | – | – | – | 0 | – | 0 | + | + | – | – | – | – | – | – | – | – | – | – | 0 | – | + | + | + | + | 0 | + | - | + | – | + | – | + | – | |
| + | – | + | – | U | – | + | – | – | + | + | U | U | – | U | – | U | – | U | – | – | – | – | U | U | + | + | + | + | U | + | U | + | U | + | U | |
| + | 0 | + | 0 | + | – | + | 0 | – | 0 | + | + | + | – | + | – | + | – | + | – | 0 | – | – | – | – | + | 0 | + | + | + | + | + | + | + | + | + | |
| + | + | + | + | + | U | + | + | – | – | U | + | + | U | + | U | + | U | + | U | + | – | U | – | – | U | - | + | U | + | U | + | U | + | U | + | |
| 0 | + | 0 | + | + | + | 0 | + | 0 | – | – | + | + | + | + | + | + | + | + | + | + | 0 | + | – | – | – | – | 0 | – | + | – | + | – | + | – | + | |
| – | + | – | + | U | + | – | + | + | – | – | U | U | + | U | + | U | + | U | + | + | + | + | U | U | – | – | – | – | U | – | U | – | U | – | U | |
| B | D | B | D | B | D | B | D | B | D | B | D | B | D | B | D | B | D | B | D | B | D | B | D | B | D | B | D | B | D | B | D | B | D | B | D | |
| 0 | 0 | 0 | 0 | 0 | 0 | 0 | 0 | 0 | 0 | 0 | 0 | 0 | 0 | 0 | 0 | 0 | 0 | 0 | 0 | 0 | 0 | 0 | 0 | 0 | 0 | 0 | 0 | 0 | 0 | 0 | 0 | 0 | 0 | 0 | 0 | |
| + | 0 | + | 0 | + | + | – | 0 | + | 0 | + | – | + | + | – | + | 0 | + | + | + | + | + | + | + | + | – | + | – | + | – | 0 | – | – | – | + | – | |
| + | + | + | + | U | + | – | – | + | + | + | U | U | + | – | U | – | + | U | + | U | + | U | + | + | U | + | U | + | U | + | – | U | – | + | U | |
| 0 | + | 0 | + | – | + | 0 | – | 0 | + | + | + | – | + | – | – | – | 0 | – | + | – | + | – | + | + | + | + | + | + | + | + | 0 | + | – | + | + | |
| – | + | – | + | – | U | + | – | – | + | U | + | – | U | U | – | – | – | – | U | – | U | – | U | U | + | U | + | U | + | + | + | + | U | U | + | |
| – | 0 | – | 0 | – | – | + | 0 | – | 0 | – | + | – | – | + | – | 0 | – | – | – | – | – | – | – | – | + | – | + | – | + | 0 | + | + | + | – | + | |
| – | – | – | – | U | – | + | + | – | – | – | U | U | – | + | U | + | – | U | – | U | – | U | – | – | U | – | U | – | U | – | + | U | + | – | U | |
| 0 | – | 0 | – | + | – | 0 | + | 0 | – | – | – | + | – | + | + | + | 0 | + | – | + | – | + | – | – | – | – | – | – | – | – | 0 | – | + | – | – | |
| + | – | + | – | + | U | – | + | + | – | U | – | + | U | U | + | + | + | + | U | + | U | + | U | U | – | U | – | U | – | – | – | – | U | U | – | |

to match the vector of $l$ in $R_1(k, l) = (-\ 0 -\square-)_{C1}$. Hence, to find $R_3(k, m)$, we use the column of 270° of Table 4. Then, the relationships A & C of $R_3(k, m)$ are in the row corresponding to A & C of $R_1$, i.e. the row of '–,"–,' and the column of 270°: we obtain $U$ for A and '–' for C. Analogously, B and D of $R_3(k, m)$ depend on B and D of $R_2$: we get '+' for B, '–' for D. Thus, we find $R_3(k, m) \in \{(-\ +\ -\square-)_{C1}, (0\ +\ -\square-)_{C1}, (+\ +\ -\square-)_{C1}\}$. Note that results for A & C in one column always have to be combined with results for B & C in the same column, even when multiple columns correspond to the same rotation angle, e.g. for 180°. Thus, we should not take the cross product.

## Incomplete Knowledge

Not everything has to be known about a situation to make inferences which are important for the issue at hand (Frank, 1996). Obviously, in these situations information may lack for offering complete answers to queries. However, '*a partial answer may be better than no answer at all,*' as Freksa (1992a, p. 203) argues. By abstracting away from the mass of metrical details, qualitative representations are much more appropriate for handling such incomplete knowledge, rather than quantitative approaches (Cristani, Cohn, & Bennett, 2000).

As mentioned before, the development of the QTC has been inspired by some major QR calculi, especially the temporal Semi-Interval Calculus (Freksa, 1992a) and the spatial Double-Cross Calculus (Freksa, 1992b; Zimmermann & Freksa, 1996). Central in these theories is the specific attention to incomplete knowledge, and hence, one might expect QTC to be able to handle incomplete knowledge as well.

One kind of incomplete knowledge results from natural language expressions. Consider the expression "$k$ is moving towards $l$, which is not slower than $k$." This expression can be represented in QTC, for instance by $(-\square U\ U_+)_{B2}$ with $U_+ = U \setminus \{+\}$. Hence, we obtain a union of six solutions. Interestingly, these solutions constitute a conceptual neighbourhood, i.e. they are mutually path-connected through conceptual neighbour relations when isolated from the complete CND of base relations (see Figure 7). According to Freksa (1992a), we achieve *coarse knowledge*, i.e. a kind of incomplete knowledge that allows to be represented by a conceptual neighbourhood of relations at a certain level of granularity. When relations between MPOs are perceived or described incompletely through natural language, the resulting knowledge will typically be coarse.

Whenever one expression may lead us to incomplete knowledge, multiple expressions can be combined in order to deduce finer knowledge. Table 5 gives an example of four expressions, each of which has a coarse result, for which the intersection results in complete knowledge. In addition, composition offers an appropriate inference mechanism to integrate expressions about three or more objects.

*Table 5. Intersection of coarse solutions to obtain fine knowledge, with $U_0 = U \setminus \{0\}$*

| natural language expression | $QTC_{B2}$ solution | integrated solution |
|---|---|---|
| " $k$ is moving towards $l$ " | $(-\square U\ U)_{B2}$ | $(-\square U\ U)_{B2} \cap (U_0\ U_0\ U)_{B2} \cap (U +\ U)_{B2} \cap (U\ U\ 0)_{B2} = (-\ +\ 0)_{B2}$ |
| " $k$ and $l$ are moving along the same straight line " | $(U_0\ U_0\ U)_{B2}$ | |
| " $l$ is moving away from $k$ " | $(U +\ U)_{B2}$ | |
| " $l$ is moving equally fast as $k$ " | $(U\ U\ 0)_{B2}$ | |

## EXTENDING QTC

Complex real-life motions go far beyond the earlier described simplifications applied in QTC. Can we relax these constraints? Obviously, not all simplifications can be ignored. Therefore, we now focus on how QTC can be extended, whilst still accepting the object simplification, i.e. the abstraction of moving objects to MPOs. In the remainder of this section, we will discuss the respective and cumulative releases of the relational, temporal, and topological simplifications.

### Multiple MPOs

The relations between multiple MPOs can be represented by means of a QTC cross table or matrix (Table 6). An element (*i,j*) in this matrix represents the QTC relation between MPOs *i* and *j*. A QTC matrix can be computed at each time point. The following compression rules and techniques can be used in order to reduce its size:

- The diagonal of the matrix can be excluded, as it is empty due to the topological constraint.
- Only the upper right (or lower left half) of the matrix has to be considered, as is gray shaded in bold in Table 6. The lower part of the matrix holds the converse relations of the upper part and vice versa and is therefore redundant.

Hence, for *n* objects, the number of elements can be reduced from $n^2$ to $(n^2-n)/2$. Note that research has been done in order to further simplify topological relations (Rodríguez, Egenhofer, & Blaser, 2003) and simplifying temporal relations (Rodríguez, Van de Weghe, & De Maeyer, 2004) over multiple elements. It could be interesting to combine both in order to simplify spatiotemporal relations, such as QTC relations. Thus, the number of elements in a QTC matrix could be further reduced so that it only contains relevant information, i.e. no redundancies.

*Table 6. $QTC_{B1}$ matrix for four MPOs k, l, m, and n at time t*

| *t* | *k* | *l* | *m* | *n* |
|---|---|---|---|---|
| *k* | X | -- | -+ | -0 |
| *l* | -- | X | ++ | +0 |
| *m* | +- | ++ | X | -0 |
| *n* | 0- | 0+ | 0- | X |

### Multiple Time Points and Intervals

What if we consider QTC matrices at different time moments? According to the philosophy of qualitative reasoning, new relations only need to be calculated whenever transitions occur. As a consequence, it will be the most efficient to compute one initial matrix and to store only relations which have transitioned in all subsequent matrices.

### Multiple Topological Relations

QTC does not distinguish topological relations, and might hence be complemented by topological calculi. As mentioned earlier, point objects only have two topological relations: *disjoint* and *equal*. Though QTC is developed to reason about *disjoint* objects, this constraint might be relaxed. Note that in case of *equal* MPOs, we will always obtain zero-relations.

## EXAMPLE CASE

This section discusses an example application of QTC in one of the major domains of applied science that in essence deals with objects moving in a geographical space, namely transportation research. Ever since their invention, cars have been a focus of research for numerous traffic engineers

*Table 7. Trajectory sample points of two cars k and l during an overtake event*

| sample point | car *k* | | | car *l* | | |
|---|---|---|---|---|---|---|
| | *x* (m) | *y* (m) | *t* (s) | *x* (m) | *y* (m) | *t* (s) |
| **1** | 15 | 0 | 0 | 15 | 10 | 0 |
| **2** | 15 | 5 | 1 | 15 | 13 | 1 |
| **3** | 10 | 13 | 2 | 15 | 17 | 2 |
| **4** | 10 | 23 | 3 | 15 | 23 | 3 |
| **5** | 10 | 33 | 4 | 15 | 28 | 4 |
| **6** | 15 | 41 | 5 | 15 | 33 | 5 |
| **7** | 15 | 46 | 6 | 15 | 38 | 6 |

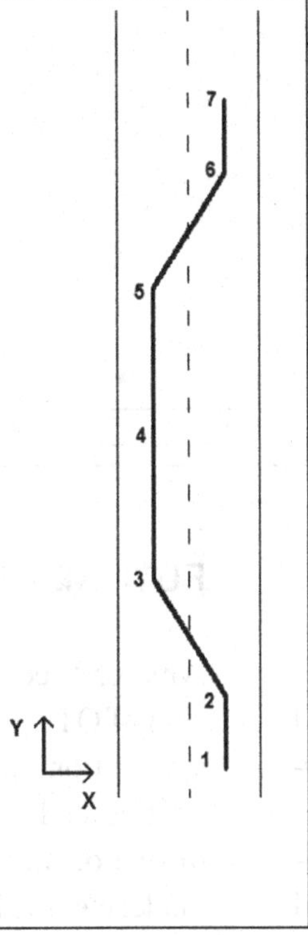

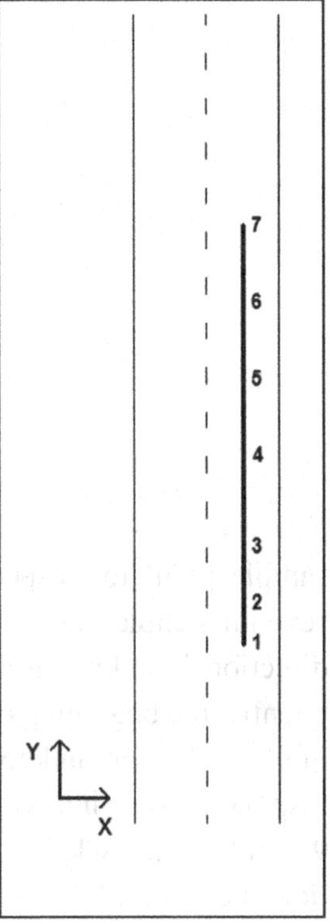

that have tried to represent and understand their complex physics. A typical example is the case of an overtake event (André, Herzog, & Rist, 1989; Fernyhough, Cohn, & Hogg, 2000). In this section, we will analyse this case in QTC starting from raw trajectory sample points as received from position aware devices. As the *left / right* distinction is crucial in overtake events, we will utilise $QTC_C$.

Let us consider two cars *k* and *l*. Table 7 gives their two-dimensional sample coordinates during an overtake event at regular time steps of one second. As QTC assumes continuity, such a discrete set of sample points has to be interpolated in order to obtain continuous trajectories. Although several approaches are possible, we will, for this example case, rely on simple linear interpolation in space and time. This is also shown in Table 7.

Figure 9 gives an overview of the spatial configuration of the objects and their instantaneous velocity vector for all sample times during the overtake event. Also, the $QTC_{C1}$ relations are given at and in between these sample instants. We find the following relation pattern: $(- + 0\ 0)_{C1} \rightarrow (- + - +)_{C1} \rightarrow (0\ 0 - +)_{C1} \rightarrow (+ -□- +)_{C1} \rightarrow (+ - 0\ 0)_{C1}$. Since this is a pattern of subsequent conceptual neighbours, we call it a *conceptual animation* (Van de Weghe, et al., 2005). It consists of five relations, four of which hold over a time interval, whereas $(0\ 0 - +)_{C1}$ occurs instantaneously at 3 s. Although all others last over intervals, continuity theory induces some subtle differences between them. As pointed out earlier, a '0' value must always last over a closed time interval (of which a time instant is a special case), whereas '–' and '+' must always hold over an open time interval. Therefore, it follows that $(- + - +)_{C1}$ and $(+ -□- +)_{C1}$ persist over open time intervals, whereas $(0\ 0 - +)_{C1}$ occurs at an instantaneous closed time interval. Note that, as Table 7 does not provide a preceding and following

*Figure 9. Configuration of two cars k and l at sample time stamps during an overtake event*

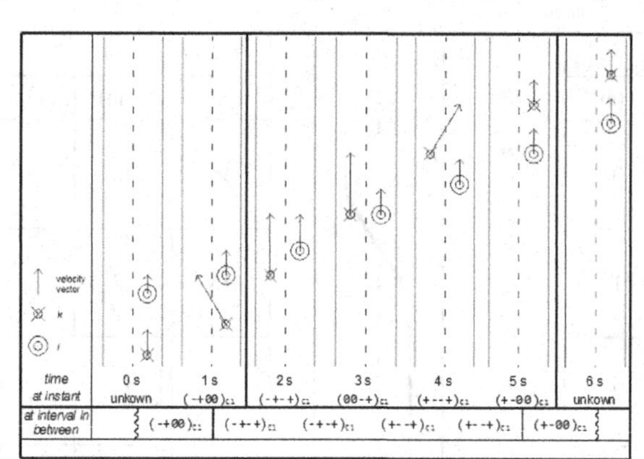


sample point for respectively the first and the seventh sample point, the change in movement direction is unknown at these instants. Consequently, the beginning of $(- + 0\ 0)_{C1}$ and the end of $(+ - 0\ 0)_{C1}$ are unknown, and hence their corresponding time intervals are half-closed (Figure 9). With this knowledge, a more complete description of the complete conceptual animation would be:

$]0, 1]:(- + 0\ 0)_{C1} \rightarrow ]1, 3[:(- + - +)_{C1} \rightarrow [3]:(0\ 0 - +)_{C1} \rightarrow ]3, 5[:(+ -\square- +)_{C1} \rightarrow [5, 6[:(+ - 0\ 0)_{C1}$.

The overtake event illustrated here would be a legal manoeuvre if we consider right-hand driving in Continental Europe. What about the case of left-hand driving? In that case, the trajectories of *k* and *l* are mirrored along the main road axis, and hence *left* interchanges with *right*. As can be expected for $QTC_{C1}$, we obtain a symmetrical animation with the last two characters inverted, while the first two remain: $(- + 0\ 0)_{C1} \rightarrow (- + + -)_{C1} \rightarrow (0\ 0 + -)_{C1} \rightarrow (+ - + -)_{C1} \rightarrow (+ - 0\ 0)_{C1}$.

Similarly to the overtake event, numerous other traffic situations can be modelled by means of conceptual animations. A qualitative framework can then be composed of such QTC patterns in order to reason about, recognise, or simulate traffic events.

## FUTURE RESEARCH DIRECTIONS

A major direction for further research is the extension of QTC theory. New types of QTC, perhaps application-specific types, can be elaborated. To this end, opportunities lie in the relaxation of one or more of the simplifications that were made, e.g. to allow moving line, region and body objects, next to the conventional MPOs. Also, more realistic scenarios, spatial and temporal constraints, or frames of reference can be taken into account. Delafontaine et al. (2008) already made an attempt in that direction by studying the implications for $QTC_N$ when considering dynamic instead of static networks.

Other directions lie in the implementation, application, and evaluation of QTC. Efforts in that direction have already been undertaken by Delafontaine (2008) and Delafontaine and Van de Weghe (2008). We plan to evaluate the usefulness of QTC-based information systems through extensive case studies.

Finally, future research may consider how QTC relates to other domains, such as psychological, cognitive and behavioural sciences, linguistics, information visualisation, and human-computer interaction. It is our aim to study how QTC relates to cognition and natural language, e.g. in simple prepositions such as 'towards' and 'away from' (Bogaert, Van der Zee, Maddens, Van de Weghe, & De Maeyer, 2008).

## CONCLUSION

This chapter has presented the Qualitative Trajectory Calculus as a qualitative spatiotemporal calculus to handle the relations between moving objects adequately. The development of QTC and which spatial and temporal calculi inspired QTC has been discussed. The chapter has focused on the two most general and fundamental QTC calculi, i.e. the Basic and Double Cross types, as they constitute the basis of all other types. The principal reasoning mechanisms such as conceptual neighbourhoodness and composition have been considered in some detail, as well as the ability for QTC to deal with incomplete knowledge. The usefulness and applicability of QTC has been illustrated in a simple case where, starting from raw trajectory data, a conceptual QTC animation is obtained. Finally, although QTC is not yet fully theoretically well-documented, we presented three useful directions for future research.

## REFERENCES

Allen, J. F. (1983). Maintaining knowledge about temporal intervals. *Communications of the ACM*, *26*(11), 832–843. doi:10.1145/182.358434

André, E., Herzog, G., & Rist, T. (1989). *Natural language access to visual data: Dealing with space and movement*. Saarbrücken, Germany: German Research Center for Artificial Intelligence (DFKI).

Bennett, B. (1997). *Logical representations for automated reasoning about spatial relationships*. Leeds, UK: University of Leeds.

Bitterlich, W., Sack, J. R., Sester, M., & Weibel, R. (2008). *08451 abstracts collection - Representation, analysis and visualization of moving objects*. Paper presented at the Representation, Analysis and Visualization of Moving Objects. Dagstuhl, Germany.

Bogaert, P., Van de Weghe, N., Cohn, A. G., Witlox, F., & De Maeyer, P. (2006). *The qualitative trajectory calculus on networks*. Paper presented at the Spatial Cognition V Reasoning, Action, Interaction. Bremen, Germany.

Bogaert, P., Van der Zee, E., Maddens, R., Van de Weghe, N., & De Maeyer, P. (2008). *Cognitive and linguistic adequacy of the qualitative trajectory calculus*. Paper presented at the International Workshop on Moving Objects: From Natural to Formal Language. Park City, UT.

Cohn, A. G., & Renz, J. (2007). Qualitative spatial reasoning. In Van Hermelen, F., Lifschitz, V., & Porter, B. (Eds.), *Handbook of Knowledge Representation*. Elsevier Science.

Cristani, M., Cohn, A. G., & Bennett, B. (2000). *Spatial locations via morpho-mereology*. Paper presented at the Conference on Principles of Knowledge Representation and Reasoning (KR 2000). Breckenridge, CO.

Delafontaine, M. (2008). *The qualitative trajectory calculus - From theory to practice*. Paper presented at the Representation, Analysis and Visualization of Moving Objects (Dagstuhl Seminar 08451). Zurich, Switzerland.

Delafontaine, M., & Van de Weghe, N. (2008). Towards an implementation of the qualitative trajectory calculus to analyze moving objects. In *Proceedings of the International Conference Spatial Cognition 2008, Poster Presentations*. Spatial Recognition.

Delafontaine, M., Van de Weghe, N., Bogaert, P., & De Maeyer, P. (2008). Qualitative relations between moving objects in a network changing its topological relations. *Information Sciences*, *178*(8), 1997–2006. doi:10.1016/j.ins.2007.11.027

Egenhofer, M. J., & Al-Taha, K. K. (1992). *Reasoning about gradual changes of topological relationships*. Paper presented at the Theory and Methods of Spatio-Temporal Reasoning in Geographic Space. Pisa, Italy.

Egenhofer, M. J., & Franzosa, R. D. (1991). Point-set topological spatial relations. *International Journal of Geographical Information Systems*, *5*(2), 161–174. doi:10.1080/02693799108927841

Fernyhough, J., Cohn, A. G., & Hogg, D. C. (2000). Constructing qualitative event models automatically from video input. *Image and Vision Computing*, *18*(2), 81–103. doi:10.1016/S0262-8856(99)00023-2

Frank, A. U. (1996). Qualitative spatial reasoning: Cardinal directions as an example. *International Journal of Geographical Information Systems*, *10*(3), 269–290. doi:10.1080/02693799608902079

Freksa, C. (1992a). Temporal reasoning based on semi-intervals. *Artificial Intelligence*, *54*, 199–127. doi:10.1016/0004-3702(92)90090-K

Freksa, C. (1992b). *Using orientation information for qualitative spatial reasoning*. Paper presented at the Theories and Methods of Spatio-Temporal Reasoning in Geographic Space. Pisa, Italy.

Galton, A. (2001). Dominance diagrams: A tool for qualitative reasoning about continuous systems. *Fundamenta Informaticae*, *46*(1-2), 55–70.

Gudmundsson, J., van Kreveld, M., & Speckmann, B. (2004). Efficient detection of motion patterns in spatio-temporal data sets. In *Proceedings of the 12th Annual ACM International Workshop on Geographic Information Systems*. ACM Press.

Guting, R. H., Bohlen, M. H., Erwig, M., Jensen, C. S., Lorentzos, N. A., & Schneider, M. (2000). A foundation for representing and querying moving objects. *ACM Transactions on Database Systems*, *25*(1), 1–42. doi:10.1145/352958.352963

Hallot, P., & Billen, R. (2008). *Generalized life and motion configurations reasoning model*. Paper presented at the International Worshop on Moving Objects: From Natural to Formal Language. Park City, UT.

Ibrahim, Z., & Tawfik, A. (2007). An abstract theory and ontology of motion based on the regions connection calculus. In *Proceedings of the Abstraction, Reformulation, and Approximation*, (pp. 230-242). Abstraction Reformation and Approximation.

Kurata, Y., & Egenhofer, M. J. (2009). Interpretation of behaviours from a viewpoint of topology. In Gottfried, B., & Aghajan, H. (Eds.), *Behaviour Monitoring and Interpretation-Ambient Intelligence and Smart Environments* (*Vol. 3*). Amsterdam, The Netherlands: IOS Press.

Laube, P. (2005). *Analysing point motion-spatio-temporal data mining of geospatial lifelines*. Zürich, Switzerland: Universität Zürich.

Muller, P. (2002). Topological spatio-temporal reasoning and representation. *Computational Intelligence*, *18*(3), 420–450. doi:10.1111/1467-8640.00196

Noyon, V., Claramunt, C., & Devogele, T. (2007). A relative representation of trajectories in geographical spaces. *GeoInformatica*, *11*(4), 479–496. doi:10.1007/s10707-007-0023-2

Peuquet, D. J. (2001). Making space for time: Issues in space-time data representation. *GeoInformatica*, *5*(1), 11–32. doi:10.1023/A:1011455820644

Randell, D. A., Cui, Z., & Cohn, A. G. (1992). A spatial logic based on regions and connection. In B. Nebel, C. Rich, & W. Swartout (Eds.), *Principles of Knowledge Representation and Reasoning: Proceedings of the Third International Conference* (pp. 165-176). Springer.

Skiadopoulos, S., & Koubarakis, M. (2004). Composing cardinal direction relations. *Artificial Intelligence*, *152*(2), 143–171. doi:10.1016/S0004-3702(03)00137-1

Van de Weghe, N. (2004). *Representing and reasoning about moving objects: A qualitative approach*. Ghent, Belgium: Ghent University.

Van de Weghe, N., Cohn, A. G., De Maeyer, P., & Witlox, F. (2005). Representing moving objects in computer-based expert systems: The overtake event example. *Expert Systems with Applications*, *29*(4), 977–983. doi:10.1016/j.eswa.2005.06.022

Van de Weghe, N., Cohn, A. G., De Tré, G., & De Maeyer, P. (2006). A qualitative trajectory calculus as a basis for representing moving objects in Geographical Information Systems. *Control and Cybernetics*, *35*(1), 97–119.

Van de Weghe, N., & De Maeyer, P. (2005). Conceptual neighbourhood diagrams for representing moving objects. In *Proceedings of the Perspectives in Conceptual Modeling,* (pp. 228-238). Perspectives in Conceptual Modeling.

Van de Weghe, N., De Tré, G., Kuijpers, B., & De Maeyer, P. (2005). *The double-cross and the generalization concept as a basis for representing and comparing shapes of polylines.* Paper presented at the First International Workshop on Semantic-Based Geographical Information Systems (SeBGIS'05). Agia Napa, Cyprus.

Van de Weghe, N., Kuijpers, B., Bogaert, P., & De Maeyer, P. (2005, 2005). *A qualitative trajectory calculus and the composition of its relations.* In *Proceedings of the 1st International Conference on Geospatial Semantics (GeoS)*. GeoS.

Vieu, L. (1997). Spatial representation and reasoning in artificial intelligence. In Stock, O. (Ed.), *Spatial and Temporal Reasoning* (pp. 5–41). Dordrecht, The Netherlands: Kluwer. doi:10.1007/978-0-585-28322-7_1

Wolter, F., & Zakharyaschev, M. (2000, 2000). *Spatio-temporal representation and reasoning based on RCC-8.* In *Proceedings of the seventh Conference on Principles of Knowledge Representation and Reasoning, KR2000*. Morgan Kaufmann.

Zimmermann, K., & Freksa, C. (1996). Qualitative spatial reasoning using orientation, distance, and path knowledge. *Applied Intelligence*, *6*(1), 49–58. doi:10.1007/BF00117601

## ENDNOTE

1 According to trigonometry, we take anticlockwise angles as being positive.

# Chapter 5
# Methodologies for Qualitative Spatial and Temporal Reasoning Application Design

**Carl Schultz**
*The University of Auckland, New Zealand*

**Robert Amor**
*The University of Auckland, New Zealand*

**Hans W. Guesgen**
*Massey University, New Zealand*

## ABSTRACT

*Although a wide range of sophisticated Qualitative Spatial and Temporal Reasoning (QSTR) formalisms have now been developed, there are relatively few applications that apply these commonsense methods. To address this problem, the authors of this chapter developed methodologies that support QSTR application design. They established a theoretical foundation for QSTR applications that includes the roles of application designers and users. The authors adapted formal software requirements that allow a designer to specify the customer's operational requirements and the functional requirements of a QSTR application. The chapter presents design patterns for organising the components of QSTR applications, and a methodology for defining high-level neighbourhoods that are derived from the system structure. Finally, the authors develop a methodology for QSTR application validation by defining a complexity metric called H-complexity that is used in test coverage analysis for assessing the quality of unit and integration test sets.*

DOI: 10.4018/978-1-61692-868-1.ch005

# 1. INTRODUCTION

Over the last two and a half decades researchers have made significant progress in the theoretical foundations and analysis of Qualitative Spatial and Temporal Reasoning (QSTR) calculi, and a range of commonsense formalisms have now been developed for representing and reasoning about different aspects of space and time (Cohn & Renz, 2008). Moreover, while many QSTR formalisms have been shown to be NP hard, maximal tractable subsets of well known calculi have been identified (Nebel & Bürckert, 1995; Renz, 1999) and automatic methods for finding tractable subsets have been developed (Renz, 2007), thus informing a user about the classes of problems that are practical to solve. Techniques have also been developed that greatly improve reasoning performance (Westphal & Wölfl, 2009; Li, et al., 2009).

Despite this theoretically advanced state of the field, there is a distinct absence of applications that make significant use of QSTR formalisms. There are five critical barriers to QSTR application design that have not yet been addressed.

1. QSTR researchers have not clearly identified the characteristics of the problems that can be uniquely addressed by QSTR applications.
2. In many cases, no pre-existing QSTR formalism will perfectly and completely satisfy the requirements of an application. In most cases, the designer will need to formalise domain knowledge, and design complex, heterogeneous models that build on top of a mix of different existing QSTR formalisms.
3. There is no methodology for developing QSTR applications, and even researchers in the field currently develop QSTR applications in a very ad hoc manner.
4. There are no methodologies for analysing QSTR applications, and therefore no way to make informed design decisions. This contributes to the problem of ad hoc QSTR application development.
5. Making QSTR accessible means having designers from outside the field applying QSTR, that is, the designers will not be experts in QSTR. Design methodologies derived from concepts in software engineering are required to bridge the gap between expert QSTR logicians and application designers from other disciplines.

We address these issues in this chapter with specialised methodologies for QSTR application design, motivated by research in software engineering, knowledge representation, artificial intelligence, and finite model theory. Section 2 reviews unifying frameworks and development tools in related areas and establishes a theoretical foundation for QSTR applications. Section 3 identifies the salient characteristics of QSTR applications that are the focus of our design methodologies. Section 4 characterises the problems that QSTR applications address and enumerates the tasks that they can perform, by adapting formal software requirements from software engineering. Section 5 presents design patterns for organising the components of QSTR applications, and Section 6 presents a methodology for defining high level neighbourhoods that are derived from the system structure. Section 7 presents a methodology that supports designers in QSTR application validation by identifying important classes for unit testing and integration testing based on a novel measure of complexity. Sections 8 and 9 present the future work and conclusions of this chapter.

# 2. BACKGROUND

A number of unifying QSTR frameworks are now being developed in order to make the field more cohesive and accessible. Three prominent projects are SparQ (Dylla, 2006), GQR (Gantner, 2008), and an investigation into formal algebraic properties (Ligozat, 2004). Although developing a library of efficient and robust implementations of QSTR calculi is a necessary step in making these formalisms more accessible, this does not directly address the five key problems given in the introduction.

Researchers in the related field of Qualitative Reasoning (QR) have developed a workbench software application called Garp3 (Bredeweg, 2007) to support the process of designing and reasoning with qualitative models. Note that QR is distinct from QSTR as it is primarily concerned with treating scalar quantities in a qualitative discrete way, rather than directly modelling commonsense spatial and temporal relationships. Garp3 is an integrated development environment for designing and reasoning about qualitative models of physical systems. The motivation for Garp3 is identical to the problems that the QSTR field currently encounters, namely that wider audiences can be reluctant to employ the advanced methods for modelling qualitative physics that have been developed (although this problem does not appear to be as significant as with QSTR, for example [Iwasaki, 1997]). The central aim of Garp3 is to overcome this inertia by supporting modellers in specifying and reasoning about qualitative models in a graphically based, user-friendly, homogeneous workbench. A QSTR equivalent to Garp3 would be highly desirable.

In the field of software engineering, the well known Unified Modelling Language (UML) is used to specify and visualise object oriented software systems (Pooley, 2004). UML is particularly relevant because it is well known within the software engineering community, and thus by adapting UML concepts (such as use cases and object classes) we can help to bridge the gap between software engineers and QSTR logicians.

According to standard software engineering practices, formal software requirements are necessary for software development and validation (Burnstein, 2003). Defining equivalent formal requirements for QSTR applications may also be necessary for the development of powerful QSTR based applications. Five standard requirements categories are operational requirements, functional requirements, performance requirements, design requirements, and allocated requirements (SETC, 1984). In Section 4, we adapt two of these requirements, namely customer's operational requirements and functional requirements, to the QSTR application domain. We also provide methodologies adapted from UML to support the designer in specifying QSTR application requirements.

## 2.1. Definition of QSTR Applications

Informally, QSTR applications model, infer, and check the consistency of object relations in a scenario. We will define QSTR applications in terms of model theory (Marker, 2002; Hodges, 1997) and then define the roles of QSTR application designers and users.

We use the notation $\uparrow$ to represent the exponent operator, $x{\uparrow}y{=}x^y$. In model theoretic terms, a language $L$ (or *vocabulary*, or *signature*) is a finite set of relation symbols $\mathbf{R}$ and arities $a_R$ for each $R{\in}\mathbf{R}$. A model $\mathbf{M}$ of language $L$ (or *L-structure*, or *interpretation*) consists of a *universe* $U$ (or *domain*, or *underlying set*) and for each relation symbol $R{\in}\mathbf{R}$ there is a set $R_{\mathbf{M}} \subseteq U{\uparrow}a_R$. That is, $\mathbf{M}$ provides a concrete interpretation of the symbols in $L$ based on the underlying set $U$. Finally, a *scenario* (or *configuration*, or *substructure*) is a model $\mathbf{V}$ that can be *embedded* into $\mathbf{M}$, that is, an injective homomorphism $\mathrm{f}{:}V{\to}U$ exists such that, for each $R{\in}\mathbf{R}$ with arity $a$,

$$\forall v_1, \ldots, v_a \in V^a \cdot (v_1, \ldots, v_a) \in R_{\mathbf{V}} \leftrightarrow (\mathrm{f}(v_1), \ldots, \mathrm{f}(v_a)) \in R_{\mathbf{M}}.$$

A QSTR application has a language $L$ that specifies the set of relation symbols that the designer has deemed relevant to the task at hand. The model $\mathbf{M}$ of a QSTR application is the interpreta-

*Table 1. Comparing the domains of model theory, QSTR applications, and the roles of QSTR application designers and users*

| *Model Theory* | *QSTR Application Domain* | *Actor* |
|---|---|---|
| language $L$ | specification of useful qualitative relations | QSTR application *designer* |
| model **M** based on $L$ | constraints that determine the interaction between the relations | |
| model **V** based on $L$ embedded in **M** | Using a QSTR application to represent and reason about objects. | QSTR application *user* |

tion of the relations, implemented using first order *constraints* between the relations (what objects must, or must not, exist in different combinations of relations). For each relation type $R \in \mathbf{R}$ with arity $a_R$, and for each tuple of arity $a_R$, the relation either *holds*, *does not hold*, or is *not applicable* for that tuple. Thus, for each relation symbol $R \in \mathbf{R}$ in the language, a QSTR application model **M** requires three sets, $R_{\mathbf{M}}^{+}$ (holds), $R_{\mathbf{M}}^{-}$ (does not hold) and $R_{\mathbf{M}}^{\sim}$ (not applicable), with the axiom:

*Axiom 1.* $\forall\, R \in \mathbf{R} \cdot U \uparrow a_R = R_{\mathbf{M}}^{+} \,\Delta\, R_{\mathbf{M}}^{-} \,\Delta\, R_{\mathbf{M}}^{\sim}$,

where $\Delta$ is symmetric difference (the set theoretic equivalent of mutual exclusion). For brevity we will omit the $_{\mathbf{M}}$ and simply write $R^{+}$.

A QSTR application *designer* is responsible for determining the application language and model, given formal software requirements. This involves selecting an appropriate set of relation symbols and encoding an appropriate set of constraints. Appropriateness means satisfying specific test criteria and conditions on metrics that imply that the software requirements have been met. A QSTR application *user* constructs scenarios in a QSTR application by specifying a model **V** and employing reasoning to accomplish tasks such as determining scenario consistency with respect to the model **M**, envisioning potential future scenarios, and so on (a complete set of basic QSTR application task types with respect to this model of QSTR applications is presented in Section 4). Table 1 summarises the relationship between model theory, QSTR applications, and actor roles.

Often parts of the user's scenario are indefinite or unknown, and reasoning with the application constraints is used to help resolve this ambiguity. For each relation $R \in \mathbf{R}$, the user can place tuples (of objects from $V$) with arity $a_R$ in a fourth *indefinite* set, $R_{\mathbf{M}}^{?}$ that is mutually exclusive with the three corresponding *definite* sets. This *partial scenario* is a shorthand for specifying a set of models $\mathbf{V}_1, \ldots, \mathbf{V}_n$ each representing a possible scenario.

An example of a scenario is:

- $V$={*kitchen*, *lounge*, *study*},
- *adjacent*$^{+}$ ={(*lounge*, *study*), (*lounge*, *kitchen*)},
- *adjacent*$^{?}$ ={(*lounge*, *lounge*), (*study*, *lounge*), …},
- *adjacent*$^{-}$ ={},
- *adjacent*$^{\sim}$ ={}.

The *adjacent* relation can be defined as symmetric using the constraint $\{(x,y) \mid (y,x) \in adjacent^{+}\} \subset adjacent^{+}$. The *LHS* of the constraint as evaluated in the scenario is {(*study*,*lounge*), (*kitchen*,*lounge*)}. The *RHS* as evaluated in the

*Table 2. Defines permitted fundamental operations on QSTR scenarios based on the combination of components that are variable. The left hand column assigns actor roles to variables available. Variables are represented by v, constants by c, non-applicable components by n/a, available operations by ✓, and unavailable operations by ×. Partial scenario models distinguish between definite relations where $\alpha=\{+,-,\sim\}$, and indefinite relations.*

| | *L* | **M** | | **V'** | | | *permitted operations* | | |
|---|---|---|---|---|---|---|---|---|---|
| | | *M* | $\mathbf{R}^{\mathbf{M}}$ | *V* | $\mathbf{R}_{\alpha}^{\mathbf{V}}$ | $\mathbf{R}_{?}^{\mathbf{V}}$ | *select tuples* | *refine scenario* | *edit objects* |
| *application design* | v | v | v | n/a | n/a | n/a | n/a | | |
| *scenario design* | c | c | c | v | v | v | n/a | | |
| *scenario reasoning* | c | c | c | c | c | v | ✓ | ✓ | × |
| | c | c | c | v | c | v | ✓ | ✓ | ✓ |

scenario does not contain these tuples as required by the proper subset relation, and so reasoning moves the offending tuples out of $adjacent^{?}$ and into $adjacent^{+}$ thus satisfying symmetry.

## 2.2. Fundamental Operations on QSTR Scenarios

In this section, we use our model theoretic definitions to derive the complete set of fundamental operations that can be performed on a QSTR application model. In Section 4 we combine these operations to enumerate a set of basic purely qualitative tasks, and show how the application designer can use this information to determine their software requirements, and to develop their QSTR application.

Given a partial scenario, what operations can be performed on the model theoretic structure? The features involved are language symbols, constraints, the scenario universe, and the collection of sets that interpret the relation symbols. The relation symbols and constraints are determined at QSTR application design time and so are fixed when reasoning about scenarios. Once a partial scenario has been specified, either the user has declared all the relevant objects, and thus the set is also fixed, or objects may appear and disappear from the set (e.g. in dynamic scenarios). Thus, the only component that is variable in all scenarios is the set of interpreting models, that is, which models are included and which models are excluded from the partial scenario (although the models themselves are immutable). Furthermore, in some applications the set of objects may also be variable. This leaves only three fundamental operations that can be performed on a qualitative (partial) scenario:

- selecting subsets of tuples in the partial scenario,
- refining the partial scenario by eliminating particular complete scenarios, and
- editing the set of objects in the scenario.

Therefore, all QSTR application tasks can be defined as a series of tuple selections, partial scenario refinements and scenario universe edits. Table 2 illustrates a comparison between actor roles, variable components, and permitted operations on QSTR scenarios.

## 3. CHARACTERISTICS OF QSTR APPLICATIONS

This section presents four central properties of QSTR applications. We argue that methodologies for the development of QSTR applications must focus on supporting the designer in these four areas.

### 3.1. Reasoning across a Broad Range of Abstraction Levels

QSTR applications often employ a broad range of abstraction levels in the same model. For example, a QSTR application can model very abstract high-level emotional responses and very low-level concrete spatial configurations of light fixtures, compared to a numerical GIS database that simply stores numerical descriptions of features (points and lines describing a polygon for a region). QSTR application designers require special techniques for rapidly designing and validating models that have a very layered and hierarchical structure. Section 5 presents the concept of fragments and two design patterns for organising QSTR application relations.

### 3.2. Continuity Assumption and Neighbourhoods for Changing Scenarios

QSTR relies heavily on the concept of continuity, stating that temporal and spatial objects cannot morph and translate discontinuously, but must change in a continuous fashion. A fundamental relationship exists between continuity and compositional reasoning (the prominent reasoning mechanism for standard QSTR calculi), and is used directly in critical QSTR tasks such as envisioning. Continuity is formally defined using conceptual neighbours and neighbourhood graphs (Freksa, 1992).

The standard definition of conceptual neighbours is (Cohn, 2008) $R_1$ and $R_2$ are conceptual neighbours if it is possible for $R_1$ to hold over a tuple of objects at one point in time, and for $R_2$ to hold over the tuple at a later time, with no other mutually exclusive relation holding over the tuple in between. A neighbourhood graph has one node for each relation $R \in \mathbf{R}$ and an edge between two nodes if the corresponding relations are neighbours. Section 6 generalises the definition of conceptual neighbours to apply to QSTR applications, and presents a methodology for designers to customise their conceptual neighbour definitions.

### 3.3. Modelling Infinite Domains

QSTR application models typically have infinite domains, in contrast to, for example, relational database models and Constraint Satisfaction Programming (CSP) models which typically have finite domains (Cohn & Renz, 2008). This significantly complicates the process of validating a specific QSTR calculi's reasoning mechanism so that even expert logicians find this to be a non-trivial task (Wölfl, et al., 2007).

When considering the perspective of QSTR applications, two further problems are that QSTR applications are significantly more complicated than a given calculi, and the application designers are not necessarily expert logicians. Thus, more practical software engineering based approaches to validating constraints over infinite domains are required for QSTR applications. Section 7 presents novel test coverage metrics for QSTR application validation by adapting complexity measures and techniques from finite model theory.

### 3.4. Reasoning about Objects in Multi-Dimensional Models

QSTR applications very often model multi-dimensional structures. Prominent tasks that use qualitative reasoning, particularly composition, apply transitivity to determine whether a scenario is consistent, and thus rely on relations having an ordering. In QR relations map to scalar one

*Figure 1. QSTR problem characteristics, ordered according to the dependencies between characteristics*

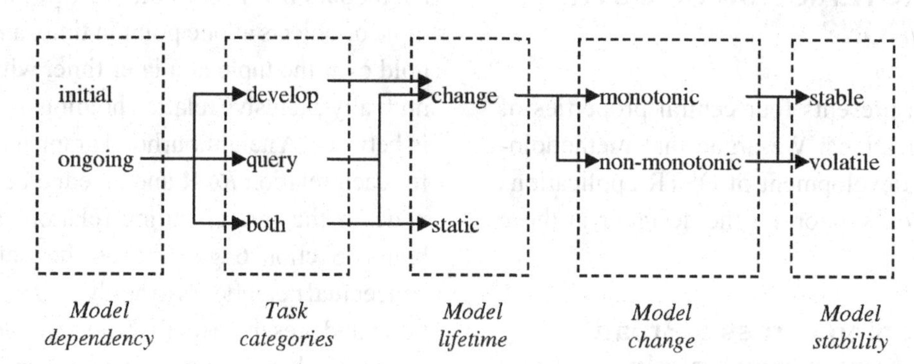


dimensional quantities, and thus have an obvious total order. On the other hand, spatial scenarios often apply at least two dimensions, thus admitting only partial orderings. Temporal scenarios can also apply multiple dimensions in the form of branching and parallel time streams, resulting in a partial ordering of events.

Multi-dimensional models significantly complicate the design of qualitative reasoning methods, as the designer needs to determine the structure of the partial ordering to employ transitivity. This issue is the focus of future research.

## 4. FORMAL SOFTWARE REQUIREMENTS FOR QSTR APPLICATIONS

In this section, we adapt two standard formal requirements from software engineering, namely customer's operational requirements and functional requirements, to the QSTR application domain.

### 4.1. Customer's Operational Requirements

Customer's operational requirements define the essential needs of the customer (SETC, 1984). In particular, operational requirements specify:

- the context of deployment,
- the typical environment in which the application must function correctly,
- how the application will address the current problem (mission profile),
- the critical aspects of the application,
- how the application will be used,
- the application's minimum allowable efficiency required to solve the problem, and
- the operational life cycle.

We now define critical characteristics of QSTR problems, and show how these characteristics determine the customer's operational profile. By considering how each of these characteristics relate to the problem at hand, the designer can formalise the requirements of the application. Figure 1 illustrates an appropriate sequence for considering some of the application characteristics based on their dependencies. The collection of characteristics presented below has been developed from an analysis of the formal definitions of QSTR applications, for example to determine what aspects of a model can vary between applications, such as initial or ongoing dependency, and a review of QSTR literature, for example to determine the different environments for which researchers have developed calculi.

*Model dependency*: the duration of dependency on the working model during the problem solving process. A problem may only have initial dependency, where all the information required for processing is initially available, for example, checking the qualitative consistency of an existing spatial database. Alternatively, other problems require information that is not initially available and thus the dependency on the working model is ongoing, for example, checking the consistency of a spatial database whenever modifications are made.

*Task categories*: QSTR tasks fall into two basic categories, either querying the model or developing the model. Further task details are specified in the functional requirements.

*Model lifetime*: the state of the application's working model over its lifetime. Once initialised the working model may never change, for example, bootstrapping a robot with a qualitative description of an environment on which the robot runs qualitative queries for accomplishing navigation tasks. Alternatively, the working model may change, for example, if a robot performs simultaneous qualitative location and mapping.

*Model change*: models either change monotonically or non-monotonically.

*Model stability*: the frequency of changes that occur to a model. Models are either stable and changes occur rarely, or volatile and changes occur frequently.

*Element relationships*: elements in a model can have simple relationships, with only superficial or limited interaction, for example, a GIS application that describes the qualitative spatial relationships between arbitrary features in terms of orientation and proximity. Alternatively, model elements can have complex relationships, with a lot of significant interaction and strong dependencies, for example, a town planning GIS application that incorporates a high degree of semantic content about the types of buildings being modelled, and constraints between buildings such as ensuring all residences are suitably accessible from some fire station.

*Spatial Granularity*: the spatial context of the application model primarily defined by the scale. Basic categories of environments for which existing QSTR calculi have been designed to reason about, ranging from smallest to largest, are: hand (e.g. inside a pencil case), desktop, indoor, outdoor (e.g. a sports field), neighbourhood, geographical, and astronomical.

*Spatial Dimensionality*: the number of dimensions used to model spatial relationships, typically a combination of one, two, or three dimensions, and may also model arbitrary dimensions.

*Spatial and Temporal Entities*: the context of the application model in terms the entities being modelled. This includes time points, time intervals, spatial points, spatial intervals (directed or undirected), and spatial regions.

While this set of characteristics is likely to be incomplete, it establishes a methodology for specifying the customer requirements of a QSTR application. Future research will focus on expanding the list of characteristics, and determining which characteristics are the most significant.

## 4.2. Functional Requirements

Functional requirements define what tasks the system needs to be capable of performing, and how the system will behave during execution (SETC, 1984). These requirements are specified as the inputs, behaviours, and outputs of system components. In this section, we enumerate the basic set of purely qualitative tasks that includes tasks commonly found in the QSTR literature. The set of basic QSTR tasks are derived by considering all possible sequences of operations that can be performed on the application parameters, namely the set of relations, constraints, and the universe. Therefore, this derivation defines the exact extent to which QSTR can be applied, and thus provides a standard with which a software developer can determine, firstly, whether or not QSTR is applicable to their problem, and secondly,

*Table 3. Tasks that can be performed on a scenario with respect to the underlying parameters. In the state diagram, states are black circles, tasks (composed of states) are ovals with a task label, terminating states are double-lined circles, arrows are state transitions annotated with QSTR operations, and the arrow with no source state is the task entry point.*

| Task | Parameters involved | Formal description | State diagram |
|---|---|---|---|
| *Query.* Isolates relevant subsets of a model. | *Select:* **R**, C, *V* | Select from **R**, C, *V* such that conditions are satisfied (specified using **R**, C, *V*). | select |
| *Query relaxation.* Accept relations that are within a threshold neighbourhood distance of the given target relation. | *Select:* **R**, C, G, *V* | Select from **R**, C, *V* such that conditions are satisfied (specified using **R**, C, *V*), and relations are within threshold distance through specified graph in G. | |
| *Modify.* Changes a partial scenario. | *Modify:* *V* | Refine *R* by eliminating possible scenarios or edit the universe *U* by adding or removing objects. | edit U; refine |
| *Check consistency.* Ensures that the model does not break any application constraints. | *Query:* **R**, C, *V* | Execute a query (using **R**, C, *V*) and then test conditions on the result (specified using **R**, C, *V*). | pass; query; fail |
| *Infer.* Manipulates the model based on premise information. | *Check:* **R**, C, *V* | Execute a consistency check. Terminate if check passes, or fails and cannot be corrected. Otherwise, modify the model to correct the fail and repeat from start. | modify; pass; chk cons.; fail uncorrectable |

what specific qualitative tasks may be suitable for their problem.

### 4.2.1. Deriving Standard QSTR Tasks Using Fundamental Operations

We define a task as a sequence of operations on a mathematical structure. The set of basic QSTR tasks is established by considering sequences of operations that can be performed on the parameters of a scenario in a QSTR application.

As presented in Section 2.1, an application has a set of relations **R** and constraints C. A scenario consists of a universe *V* and a set of relation state sets *R*. As presented in Section 2.2, the fundamental operations that can be applied to scenarios are selection, refinement and editing the scenario universe (adding or removing objects). The select operator can only be performed on application parameters, i.e. **R**, C, and *V*. During application runtime the only variables are *V* and the relation state sets. This limits the number of task categories that can be performed, which will now be enumerated. Table 3 presents a summary of the basic tasks and their associated model parameters.

The most basic task is to simply execute a selection operation. *Querying* is used to isolate relevant subsets of a model. For example, in Qayyum and Cohn (2007), the authors use a qualitative description of images (adapted from Allen's interval calculus) to provide a method for searching through an image database based on semantic content. TreeSap (Schultz, et al., 2007) is a geographic information system that accepts qualitative queries such as "find all bus stops near Downtown" and displays objects that meet the given criteria.

In many cases, a QSTR application user may not have complete information about the criteria of the query that they want to execute, for example, a robot reasoning with noisy sensor readings (Dylla & Wallgrün, 2007). It may be the case that certain conditions are more flexible than others, and moreover, if a user executes a query that returns no results, then it would be highly desirable for the user to be able to relax the conditions of their query in an intuitive way (Schultz, et al., 2006; Guesgen, 2002). *Query relaxation* accepts relations that are within a threshold neighbourhood distance of the given target relation through graph G. Because selection is a fundamental operation, all QSTR tasks can be relaxed using this approach, such as relaxed consistency checking and relaxed inference. Conceptual neighbourhoods provide an ideal mechanism for query relaxation because they encode the structure of relations based on continuous change. Thus, relations that are physically similar will have a smaller distance through the neighbourhood graph.

The next basic task is applying refinement and universe edits. *Modify* changes a partial scenario by either eliminating possible scenarios (refinement) or by adding or removing objects from the universe (universe edit).

The next task builds on the previous querying task by testing conditions on the returned subsets, for example to check the consistency of a scenario with respect to the application constraints. *Consistency checking* ensures that the model does not break any application constraints. The model is contradictory if an inconsistent subset (with respect to some application constraint) contains definite tuples, or if an indefinite subset still violates the constraint regardless of how the indefiniteness is resolved.

The next basic task is to execute a check consistency task and then refine the model based on the condition results. *Inference* accepts a partial qualitative description of a model as premise information and infers as much about the indefinite components of the model as possible (typically by composing relations to approximate path-consistency), i.e. deductive closure. Inference typically applies the check consistency and modify tasks to identify and eliminate inconsistent possible scenarios from a partial scenario description, that is, moving tuples out of indefinite relations $R^?$ and into definite relations.

These basic tasks are very general and can be employed in any QSTR application. The following sections build on these basic tasks by formally characterising more specialised QSTR tasks for models that contain two or more scenarios. In these cases, reasoning is applied to the relationship between partial scenarios in a group, and the type of ordering between scenarios is critical for determining the tasks that can be performed.

### 4.2.2. Deriving QSTR Tasks for Multiple Scenarios

Given two or more scenarios, we can formally characterise a number of QSTR tasks. Sequences of scenarios representing change can refer to a change in space (e.g. zooming into a map and increasing the resolution) or a change in time (e.g. modelling a car travelling down a road). Tasks that specifically apply to sequences of scenarios are envisioning, diagnosis, and checking consistency.

Two general multi-scenario tasks are merging scenarios and splitting scenarios.

*Checking the consistency* of a sequence of scenarios is determining whether the sequence is valid with respect to neighbourhood graphs. That is, for each tuple that has a relation state change in $R_1$ from does not hold to holds, there is a relation $R_2$ that holds in the previous scenario state, and an edge from $R_2$ to $R_1$ in a neighbourhood graph.

*Envisioning* is the generation of potential successor scenarios based on the conceptual neighbourhood graph. Envisioning is with respect to either (a) time, by forecasting into the future, or (b) space, by increasing the resolution of the model. Given a scenario, envisioning to depth $n$ is the set of consistent sequences of length $n$.

*Refined envisioning* selects a subset of the set of consistent sequences. For example, contextual information can be used to determine the most likely sequence of scenarios. Refined envisioning makes it possible to generate scenarios that are a greater number of steps away from the initial scenario. Contextual information includes conditional probabilities with respect to the current scenario state (e.g. a cup is very likely to fall if it is not on top of some other object like a table), conditional probabilities with respect to previous scenario states (e.g. trajectories), and domain knowledge about the movement patterns and behaviour of specific objects (e.g. in a predator-prey scenario it is more likely that a predator will follow prey, rather than simply follow a trajectory [Van de Weghe, 2006]).

*Diagnosis* is the inverse of envisioning by generating potential predecessor scenarios based on the conceptual neighbourhood graph. Similarly, refined diagnosis is the inverse of refined envisioning (Bhatt, 2007).

*Completing sequences* accepts an incomplete sequence of scenarios (i.e. a sequence that has gaps where some scenarios are missing) and applies a combination of envisioning and diagnosis to determine potential scenarios that can complete the sequence consistently.

*Merging* is the union of two scenarios and is applied when the mapping of objects between two scenarios is not known. The key challenge is to identify and pair off objects that appear in both scenarios by applying matching criteria with respect to qualitative relation states and the relative perspectives of the agents involved. This task can be useful for combining multiple perspectives of the same scenario, for example, from a number of different autonomous agents. Changing space and time can also be parameters as follows:

1. *Merging snapshots of a dynamic scene*. For example, a robot attempting to label dynamic objects across a sequence of sensor readings by referring to conceptual neighbourhoods to decide what sequence of qualitative relations is more likely to belong to a single object, such as correctly labeling which object is the 'coffee cup' and which object is the 'spoon' in each scenario snapshot.
2. *Merging snapshots of a scene taken at different granularities*. For example, combining satellite images taken at different heights, such as correctly labelling which object is the 'mountain' and which object is the 'house' in each scenario snapshot.

*Splitting* is the inverse of merging, where a scenario is divided into two possibly overlapping scenarios. Splitting can be used, for example, where agents do not need to maintain global information about a scenario and instead can efficiently specialise in certain parts of a scenario.

### 4.2.3. Characterising QSTR Application Execution Behaviour

In this section, we establish a template for the behaviour of QSTR applications based on the purely qualitative tasks from Section 4.2.1. Software developers can use this to characterise their application by explicitly incorporating task requirements into its behaviour.

*Figure 2. QSTR application behaviour during the execution of a software application. (left) Statechart diagram of an executing QSTR application where circles represent states, arrows represent possible state transitions, and the arrow annotations describe the effect of the transition on the QSTR system. (right) Substitution of low-level state diagrams from Table 3 specifying fundamental model operations (arrows without annotation indicate that a sub-task has been completed).*

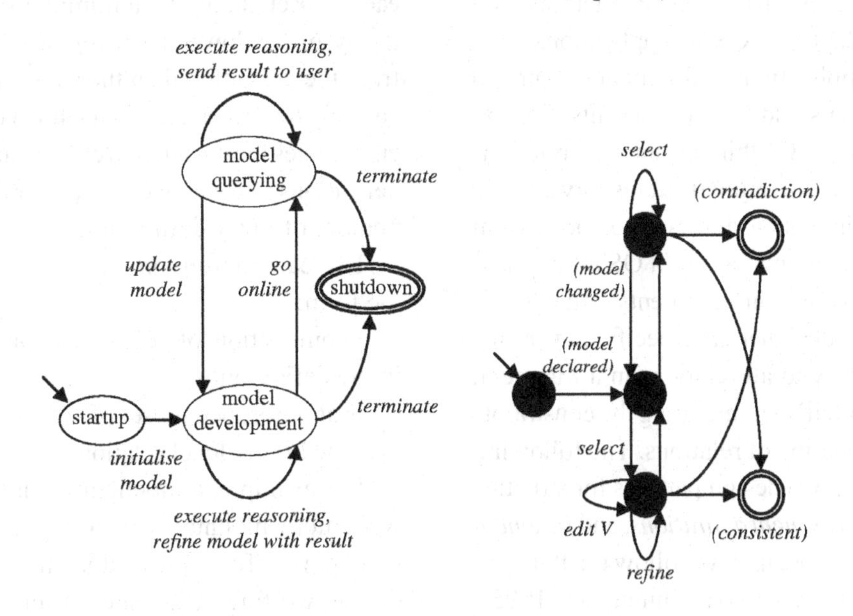


Figure 2 (left) illustrates the statechart diagram describing the generic behaviour of QSTR applications during execution, derived from the tasks in Table 3. States represent how the application is manipulating the model. During the model development state, inference tasks refine the model and edit scenario universes. During the model querying state, querying and check consistency tasks isolate and compare relevant parts of the model. Model changed occurs when an agent external to the reasoning process modifies the model, such as a user updating geographical data, or a sensor delivering new information. Figure 2 (right) shows the underlying low-level model operations that are performed in each state.

This template represents all possible QSTR application behaviour patterns, and all possible QSTR tasks are definable as a sequence of fundamental operations. The significance is that, if the designer requires a task that is not a sequence of the fundamental QSTR operations then no QSTR application will be able to satisfy the designer's software requirements.

## 5. STRUCTURING QSTR APPLICATIONS

Certain relations in QSTR application models can often be grouped together, because they refer to a similar aspect of a domain at the same abstraction level. Moreover, relations within a group often share a constraint such as mutual exclusivity, symmetry, having inverse pairs, and so on. To help manage the various abstraction levels being modelled and to speed up the design process, the application designer requires a methodology, analogous to design patterns, for grouping and organising the relations and expressing constraints over these groups.

In the area of Qualitative Reasoning (QR) about physical systems the term *model fragment* refers to modular, partial models composed of different components, and can be reused and extended in other models (Iwasaki, 1997). The concept of a qualitative reasoning fragment is very appropriate for representing groups of QSTR relations, and will now be adapted to QSTR applications.

In QSTR applications, a fragment is simply a group of relations and their constraints. For example, Allen's (1983) thirteen interval relations and their constraints (mutual exclusivity and the operators for inversion and composition) form a fragment that can be reused in QSTR applications. Relations within fragments often share properties. The designer can specify constraints so that they apply to all relations in a fragment, rather than explicitly enumerating the constraints for each combination of relations. The following sections present two design patterns for structuring fragments, *fragment definitions,* and *fragment specialisations*. Note that we follow the Portland Form design pattern format (Cunningham, 1995): <problem description (paragraph text)> *Therefore*: <solution description (paragraph text)> <solution examples>.

## 5.1. Design Pattern: Fragment Definitions

Relations in one fragment can be tightly associated to relations in a collection of other fragments because they refer to the same concept in the domain, but at different levels of abstraction. The designer might notice that each higher level concept is composed of collections of lower level concepts. That is, the lower level relations represent properties or attributes, and specific combinations of these properties realise some particular higher level concepts.

Therefore:

Designate the higher-level fragment as the abstraction domain, and the lower level fragment as the reference domain. For each abstraction domain relation, select a subset of reference domain relations that together describe or define the higher level relation; this subset is a definition of the higher level relation.

Firstly, note that there can be more than one definition for each higher-level concept. Secondly, each subset should be a minimal subset, that is, if any of the lower level relations are removed from the definition then the subset no longer accurately describes the higher-level concept. This encourages the designer to create multiple precise definitions that can overlap, rather than a smaller number of fuzzy definitions.

For each definition, specify a constraint of the form:

<conjunction of reference domain relations in the definition>

is an improper subset of

<the higher level relation>.

For example, a mountain image is an image with more mountains than sky, and more sky than grass. To express this, the designer can define two fragments, one for qualitative image categories, including the relation mountain, and another for qualitative differences in features of an image, including "mountain > sky" and "sky > grass". The conjunction between fragments is then implemented with the constraint

$\{x|x\in\text{"mountain>sky"}^{+} \wedge x\in\text{"sky>grass"}^{+}\} \subseteq \{y|y\in\text{mountain}^{+}\}$.

## 5.2. Design Pattern: Fragment Specialisation

Relations in one fragment can be tightly associated to relations in exactly one other fragment because, again, they refer to the same aspect of the domain, but at different levels of abstraction. The designer may notice that the difference between two fragments is an issue of granularity, so that relations in one fragment are a coarse, incomplete, ambiguous, or generalised representation of relations in another, more fine grained fragment.

Therefore:

Designate the higher-level fragment as the abstraction domain, and the lower-level fragment as the reference domain. For each abstraction domain relation, select a subset of reference domain relations that individually represent the same concept as the abstraction domain relation, but to a more precise degree; this subset is a specialisation.

Firstly, there is always exactly one specialisation subset for each higher-level relation. Secondly, two specialisations for two different high-level relations can overlap. Thirdly, each subset should be a maximal subset, that is, if any lower-level relations are not included in the subset then in no way do they refine the higher-level relation. This ensures that a specialisation represents all possible refinements of a high-level concept, and tends to prevent the designer ruling out potential, albeit improbable, refinements, which would compromise reasoning soundness. Following this strategy, a designer can clearly identify when a high-level relation is too coarse or general (i.e. the specialisation subset is too large), and may decide to either partition the overly general relation into different relations within the abstraction domain, or introduce an entirely new intermediate abstraction layer fragment.

For each specialisation, specify a constraint of the form:

<disjunction of reference domain relations in the specialisation>

is an improper subset of

<the higher level relation>.

For example, consider the incomplete temporal information that "Mozart is older than Beethoven." In Freka's semi-interval calculus (Freksa, 1992), a time interval $t_1$ is older than time interval $t_2$ if $t_1$ started before $t_2$. This semi-interval knowledge says nothing about the relationship between the endings of the two time intervals. Thus, the high-level semi-interval relation *older than* can potentially be refined to one of the following interval relations: *before*, *meets*, *overlaps*, *finished by*, or *contains*. The disjunction of relations is implemented with the constraint

$\{(t_1,t_2)|(t_1,t_2)\in before^{+}\vee\ldots\vee(t_1,t_2)\in contains^{+}\}$
$\subseteq\{(u_1,u_2)|(u_1,u_2)\in older\ than^{+}\}$.

## 6. DESIGNING NEIGHBOURHOODS OVER FRAGMENTS

In Section 3, we discussed how continuity about spatial and temporal change is a standard assumption in QSTR, leading to conceptual neighbours. Cohn's definition of conceptual neighbours is that "...[a] pair of relations R1 and R2 are conceptual neighbors if it is possible for R1 to hold at a certain time, and R2 to hold later, with no third relation holding in between" (Cohn, 2008).

Ideally, the designer would want their expected neighbourhood for relations in a higher-level abstraction domain fragment to be consistent with the neighbourhood of relations in the associated reference domain fragment. Alternatively, the designer should be able to derive neighbourhoods for a group of relations if no other neighbour information is available. However, a number of issues arise when considering neighbourhoods that are derived from the relationship between fragments. For example, in many cases standard neighbour definitions permit all high-level concepts to be neighbours, producing an ineffective neighbourhood graph.

This section presents a methodology for defining high-level neighbourhoods that are consistent with the structure of fragments in a QSTR application. We define conceptual neighbours in terms of fragment constraints, and focus neighbour tests by applying two novel aspects of conceptual neighbours: path restrictions and equivalence classes. Once the designer has decided on an appropriate definition of a neighbour, then a neighbourhood graph can be generated.

### 6.1. An Illustrative Running Example

The following running example will be used to explain the problems with the standard neighbourhood definition when applied to fragments, and the novel neighbourhood definitions that overcome these limitations. Figure 3 illustrates a reference domain fragment $f_2$ that includes eight mutually

*Figure 3. Reference domain fragment $f_2$ containing relations $R_1, ..., R_8$ and $R'_1, ..., R'_6$ with simple ordered neighbourhoods (left). The fragment definition space (right) consists of fragment definitions that specify one relation from $R_1, ..., R_8$ and one relation from $R'_1, ..., R'_6$. The abstraction domain fragment $f_1$ contains three relations $R_x$ (black), $R_y$ (striped), $R_z$ (grey), that have fragment definitions in $f_2$ illustrated in the fragment definition space (right).*

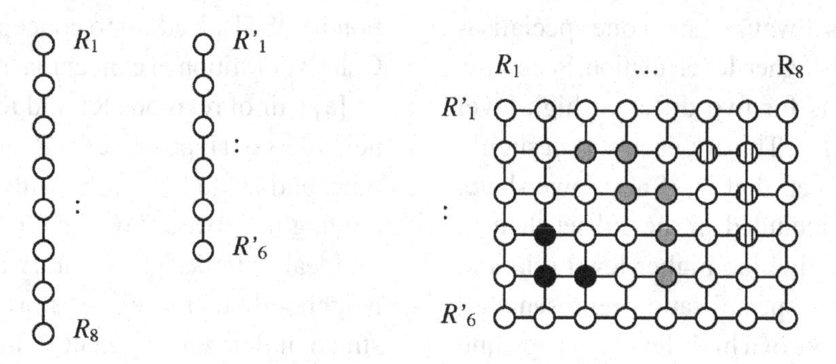


exclusive relations $R_1,...R_8$ and six mutually exclusive relations $R'_1,...,R'_6$ each having a simple totally ordered conceptual neighbourhood. Each vertex in the grid illustrated in Figure 3 (right) represents a valid conjunction of relations in $f_2$, called the *fragment definition space*. An abstraction domain fragment $f_1$ includes three relations $R_x$, $R_y$, $R_z$ (black, striped, grey, respectively, in Figure 3), and each of these relations has a set of fragment definitions in $f_2$, shown by the filled vertices in the grid.

## 6.2. Defining Conceptual Neighbours as Transitions between Low-Level Relations

Conceptual neighbours are derived from fragment definitions by defining transitions. First, *transition via the neighbourhood graph* is defined. Given two relations $R_i$, $R_j$ from a fragment, a transition via the neighbourhood graph $g$, written $\Delta_g(R_i, R_j)$, is a sequence of relations that is a path in $g$, from $R_i$ to $R_j$. Note that there may be more than one path, and that paths can contain cycles.

Next, *transitions via fragment definitions* is defined. Let a fragment definition of relation $R$, written $\sigma_c(R)$ where $c$ is the constraint that implements the definition as described in Section 5.1, be a subset of relations from the reference domain that appear in the constraint. Transitioning between two high-level relations (from the abstraction domain fragment) is a sequence of fragment definitions, where adjacent fragment definitions differ by an incremental change, i.e. they differ by exactly one pair of adjacent lower level relations according to the low level neighbourhood graph $g$.

For example, consider the fragment definitions space in Figure 3. One transition from the fragment definition $\{R_2, R'_1\}$ to $\{R_5, R'_3\}$ is $(\{R_2, R'_1\}, \{R_3, R'_1\}, \{R_4, R'_1\}, \{R_5, R'_1\}, \{R_5, R'_2\}, \{R_5, R'_3\})$, and another transition is $(\{R_2, R'_1\}, \{R_2, R'_2\}, \{R_3, R'_2\}, \{R_4, R'_2\}, \{R_5, R'_2\}, \{R_5, R'_3\})$.

Next, *transition classes via fragment definitions* is defined. Consider the set of all possible *transitions via fragment definitions* between two high level relations. The ordering of some particular low-level changes is essential. In particular, transitions can not violate the continuity assumption by skipping relations in the low-level neighbourhood graph $g$, for example, a transition $(..., \{R_2, R'_1\}, \{R_4, R'_1\}...)$ is invalid. Other changes can occur in any order, for example, the transition from $R_3$ to $R_4$ is completely independent of the transition from $R'_1$ to $R'_2$ and these transitions can occur in any order.

Thus, a class of transitions can be succinctly expressed by representing a high-level transition as a partial ordering of low-level transitions. A *transition class via fragment definitions* between two high level relations, written $\Delta_{c,c'}(R, R')$ is a set of transitions from $\Delta_g(R, R')$ such that:

- for each relation $R_i$ in $\sigma_c(R)$ there is a transition $\Delta_g(R_i, R_j)$ that starts from $R_i$ and ends at some relation $R_j$ in $\sigma_{c'}(R')$, and
- (vice versa) for each relation $R_j$ in $\sigma_{c'}(R')$ there is a transition $\Delta_g(R_i, R_j)$ that starts from some relation $R_i$ in $\sigma_c(R)$ and ends $R_j$.

For example, one class of transitions from $\{R_2, R'_1\}$ to $\{R_5, R'_3\}$ is $\{(R_2, R_3, R_4, R_5), (R'_1, R'_2, R'_3)\}$. Another class is $\{(R_2, R_1, R_2, R_3, R_4, R_5), (R'_1, R'_2, R'_3)\}$.

Therefore, a transition class $\Delta_{c,c'}(R, R')$ specifies a partial ordering of incremental changes at the lower fragment definition level (i.e. from $\Delta_g$) required to move from the fragment definition of $R$ to the fragment definition of $R'$. Note that if there are multiple paths between two low-level relations in the low-level neighbourhood graph $g$, as shown in the example (i.e. different options for $\Delta_g$) then there are multiple transition classes and $\Delta_{c,c'}(R, R')$ returns one class out of a set of possible classes.

Finally, *conceptual neighbours* is defined. $R$ and $R'$ are neighbours in the standard sense, written $N(R, R')$, if it is possible to start from a low level fragment definition of $R$, make incremental changes, and eventually transition into $R'$ without passing through another relation's fragment definition. That is, $N(R, R')$ is true if and only if there is some sequence of fragment definitions that is in some class $\Delta_{c,c'}(R, R')$ such that none of the fragment definitions in the sequence correspond to some other high level relation.

For example, the relations $R_x$ and $R_y$ are conceptual neighbours according to this definition because there exists a transition class $\Delta_{c,c'}(R,R')=\{(R_2,R_3,R_4,R_5,R_6),(R'_4,R'_3,R'_2,R'_1,R'_2)\}$ that contains a fragment definition sequence $(\{R_2,R'_4\},\ldots,\{R_2,R'_1\},\ldots,\{R_6,R'_1\},\{R_6,R'_2\})$ that does not include any of $R_z$'s fragment definitions.

A later subsection highlights the problems with this conceptual neighbour definition, and the remainder of the section presents a methodology that allows the designer to appropriately refine the neighbour test. The next section summarises the steps that a designer must go through in order to derive a high-level neighbourhood graph.

## 6.3. Deriving a High-Level Neighbourhood Graph

The designer can construct a high-level conceptual neighbourhood graph $g_{f1}$ by applying the following procedure.

1. Define an abstraction domain fragment $f_1$ and a reference domain fragment $f_2$.
2. Define a low-level neighbourhood graph $g$ for $f_2$.
3. For each high level relation $R$ in $f_1$, define the fragment definitions $\sigma_{ci}(R)$ into the reference domain $f_2$ by implementing constraints $c_i$.
4. Decide on the appropriate definition of conceptual neighbours $N_{f1}$.
5. Construct the neighbourhood graph $g_{f1}$ such that
   a. there is exactly one vertex for each high level relation, and
   b. for each pair of high level relations $R,R'$ there is an edge between the corresponding vertices iff $N_{f1}(R, R')$ is true.

In practice, steps 1 and 2 will require the designer to select a pair of appropriate fragments that have already been defined in the application. A methodology for configuring the neighbour test is described in the following subsections, and summarised in Section 6.9 below. The designer can automate step 5 with a simple nested for-loop algorithm that executes the neighbour test on each pair of high-level relations.

## 6.4. Limitations of the Standard Neighbour Definition

The problem with the standard conceptual neighbour definition is that two relations *possibly* being neighbours results in relations almost always being neighbours, thus the definition is too weak to be useful. Moreover, this may lead to counter-intuitive neighbours. For example, as illustrated in Figure 3, if any path from $R_x$ to $R_y$ is unobstructed then the relations are considered neighbours. It may be more intuitive in the context of a particular application to assume that a transition between two relations will take the most convenient, shortest transition path. In this case, a user will expect $R_x$ and $R_y$ to not be neighbours.

In order to develop more appropriate neighbour definitions, the neighbour test is summarised as follows: given a set of paths, if any of the paths are unobstructed then the two relations are neighbours. Hence, there are two ways to focus the conceptual neighbour definition, by restricting the set of paths considered for determining neighbour status, and by grouping paths together into equivalence classes.

## 6.5. Path Restrictions to Focus the Neighbour Test

The designer can avoid impractical and counter-intuitive neighbourhoods by restricting the set of paths used to determine whether two relations are neighbours. Two types of paths are *direct* paths and *critical* paths.

The *direct* path restriction requires that low level neighbourhood transition sequences take a shortest path in $\Delta_g(R_i,R_j)$ (note that there can be multiple shortest paths). This ensures that all transitions monotonically approach the target fragment definition. Figure 4a illustrates the admissible paths with this restriction, and that $R_x$ and $R_y$ are no longer neighbours.

The *critical* path restriction requires that paths only include relations that are guaranteed to conflict between the high-level fragment definitions of two relations. Intuitively, certain relations in the reference domain will be very important cues for interpreting higher-level concepts, while some (probably most) combinations will lie in the vast fragment definition space between these critical points. The necessarily conflicting relations are the important, prototypical relations that separate two high-level relations and therefore critical transition paths can be a useful measure of conceptual neighbour status. More formally, when transitioning from high-level relation $R$ to $R'$, fragment definition relations with neighbourhood graph $g_i$ fall into one of the following three categories.

- Transition *always* required: *no* pair of fragment definitions from $R$ and $R'$ share a relation from $g_i$.
- Transition *never* required: *all* pairs of fragment definitions from $R$ and $R'$ share a relation from $g_i$.
- Transition *possibly* required: *some, but not all*, pairs of fragment definitions from $R$ and $R'$ share a relation from $g_i$.

The designer can use these distinctions to refine their neighbour definition. For example, as illustrated in Figure 3, one fragment definition of $R_x$ is $\{R'_4,R_2\}$ and one fragment definition of $R_y$ is $\{R'_4,R_7\}$, thus when transitioning from $R_x$ to $R_y$ it is possible that $R'_4$ is already satisfied and no transition through the neighbourhood of relations $R'_1,\ldots,R'_6$ is required. On the other hand, regardless of the $R_x$ fragment definition, a transition through the relations in $R_1,\ldots,R_8$ will always be required.

Figure 4b illustrates the admissible transition paths through the critical paths where transitions

*Figure 4. Refined fragment definition spaces: (a) direct path restrictions, (b) critical path restrictions, (c) equivalence class of direct paths, (d) equivalence class of critical paths in conjunction with a direct path restriction*

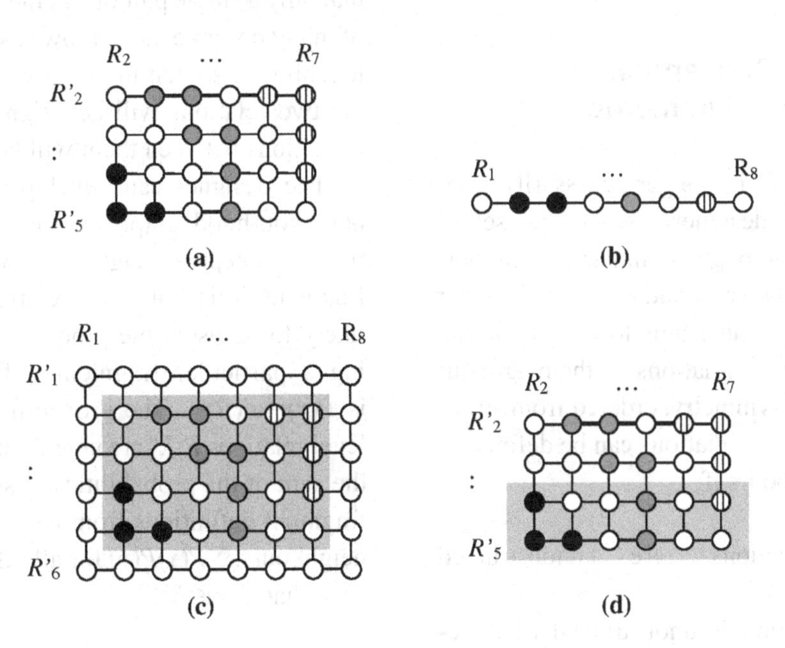


are always required, and shows that $R_x$ and $R_y$ are no longer neighbours.

## 6.6. Transition Path Equivalence Classes to Focus the Neighbour Test

Consider the following counter-intuitive scenario with the standard neighbour definition illustrated in Figure 3. The transitions required to get from a fragment definition of $R_x$ to a fragment definition of $R_y$ always include $\{(R_3,R_4),(R_4,R_5),(R_5,R_6)\}$. The transitions to get from a fragment definition of $R_z$ to a fragment definition of $R_y$ always include $\{(R_4,R_5),(R_5,R_6)\}$, which is a subset of $R_x$'s required transitions. Moreover, for any fragment definition of $R_x$ there is some fragment definition of $R_z$ where the required transitions to arrive at any given fragment definition of $R_y$ are a proper subset of those required by the fragment definition of $R_x$.

Because $R_z$'s required transitions are a proper subset, in some applications it might be intuitive to view $R_z$ as an intermediate relation between $R_x$ and $R_y$. However, the standard definition does not distinguish this special case of intermediate relations.

A designer can control any such special cases by grouping a set of paths into an equivalence class. This has the effect of removing the ordering of transitions taken in the set of paths in the equivalence class. An alternative perspective is that, previously the neighbour test checked whether it was possible to avoid intermediate relations, but now it is checking the stronger condition whether it is guaranteed to avoid intermediate relations within the equivalence class of paths.

Equivalence classes must be applied to a restricted set of paths (otherwise, the neighbour test will fail whenever there are three or more relations). Figure 4c illustrates defining the direct paths as an equivalence class. Figure 4d illustrates defining the critical paths as an equivalence class so that the conflicting paths must be guaranteed to be unobstructed, and at least one path through the non-conflicting paths must be unobstructed.

Thus, transition path equivalence classes afford the designer considerable flexibility in defining neighbourhoods.

## 6.7. Ensuring Conceptual Neighbours are Symmetric

Neighbour status is no longer necessarily symmetric when the designer restricts the set of transition paths. Although asymmetric neighbourhood graphs can be valid and useful, a designer may require neighbour status to be symmetric. The following three variations on the neighbour definition ensure symmetry, ordered from strongest to weakest. Two relations can be defined as symmetric neighbours if:

- both directions are unobstructed (conjunction),
- either direction is unobstructed (disjunction), and
- no single intermediate relation obstructs both directions (restricted disjunction).

The first variant is the strongest stating that both directions must be clear before the relations are considered neighbours. The second variant weakens this by only requiring one of the directions to be unobstructed. The third variant states that no single obstruction occurs in both directions, so that two high level relations are not neighbours if the fragment definition of a third relation obstructs both relevant transition paths (this is useful in cases where the designer wants the third relation to represent a guaranteed intermediate concept in between two relations).

## 6.8. Dealing with Multiple Fragment Definitions

If a high level relation $R$ has multiple fragment definitions then some of its fragment definitions may permit it to be a neighbour to some other high level relation $R'$, while some of its other fragment definitions do not. It may be the case that only a single pair of fragment definitions out of many possible pairs allows two relations to be neighbours, so that in practice it is unlikely that the two relations will be neighbours, and most transitions between them will be obstructed.

The designer can develop a more accurate neighbourhood graph by annotating probabilities to conceptual neighbours. Assuming that all fragment definitions of a relation $R$ are equally likely to be used, the probability $P$ of employing a particular fragment definition $x \in \sigma_c(R)$ is $P(x)=|\sigma_c(R)|^{-1}$. The probability that two high level relations $R,R'$ are neighbours $P(N(R,R'))$ is the sum of the probabilities of selecting pairs of fragment definitions from each relation that are neighbours, $\sum P(x)P(y)$ for all $x \in \sigma_c(R)$, $y \in \sigma_c(R')$ such that $(x,y) \in N$.

## 6.9. Summary and Engineering Implications

Table 4 presents guidelines to help the designer select the appropriate neighbour definition. The guidelines relate a problem that the designer can experience when deriving neighbourhood graphs, the appropriate actions defined in the previous subsections, and associated effects of the action. Note that a complete graph is not useful for any typical task that requires a neighbourhood such as envisioning, because it does not distinguish between relations within the fragment. Equivalently, edgeless graphs provide no information that is useful for performing neighbourhood-based tasks.

# 7. VALIDATING QSTR APPLICATION USING H-COMPLEXITY

The aim of program validation in software engineering is to determine if the system is fit for purpose (Burnstein, 2003), explicitly evaluating

*Table 4. QSTR application designer guidelines for deriving effective neighbourhood graphs. Columns list the problems with deriving neighbourhood graphs, actions that will help to address the problem, and related effects. Rows that contain main categories of problems and actions have a white background, and rows that immediately follow contain specific problems and actions within a category with a grey background.*

| *Problem with current derived neighbourhood* | *Designer Action* | *Effect on neighbourhood* |
|---|---|---|
| Relations are almost always neighbours (i.e. neighbour test is too weak). | *Path restrictions.* | Rules out irrelevant outlier paths which bias the neighbour tests in an unhelpful way. Outlier paths contain impractical or counter-intuitive low level relation transitions. |
| Relations that clearly lie between two relations have no effect on their neighbour status. | *Path restriction*: only accept shortest paths through reference domain. | Transitions will now monotonically approach the target definition. This avoids paths that 'side step' obstructions by taking impractical and counter-intuitive transitions. |
| Interesting and important cores of relations are obstructed by other relations, but this has no effect on their neighbour status. | *Path restriction*: only accept paths that change core low level relations. Core relations are those that conflict between every definition of two high level relations. | Transitions now only change the prototypical core of a high level relation when determining neighbour status. This avoids irrelevant and uninformative paths that lie in the vast and sparse 'transition space' between these critical points. |
| Relations that clearly lie between two relations have no effect on their neighbour status, even after applying path restrictions. | *Equivalence classes*: pick a restricted set of paths that strongly determines neighbour status and define the set as an equivalence class of paths. | Ordering of transitions is ignored when determining whether the path between two relations is obstructed. The neighbour test is strengthened to guarantee that no matter what order the transitions are made, no obstruction will occur. |
| Relations have multiple definitions, and the neighbour test is too coarse grained. The user needs more information about boundary cases where relations are *sometimes* or *partially* neighbours. | *Neighbour probability*: include probability scores with neighbour status. | Probabilities are a measure of the strength of neighbour status where high probability indicates that relations are closer neighbours than a low probability; the user can get an indication of the likelihood that a transition to some other relation will be interrupted. |
| Sometimes $R_1$ is a neighbour of $R_2$ when $R_2$ is not a neighbour of $R_1$, i.e. the neighbour test must be symmetric. | *Symmetric neighbours*: consider both transition directions between relations before determining their shared neighbour status. | Neighbour test now involves both transition directions. Care must be taken in understanding and communicating to users what the neighbour test now entails, as one transition direction can completely hide the neighbour status of the other direction. |
| If two relations are neighbours, then transitioning between them must never be obstructed. | *Symmetric neighbours*: neighbour test requires both directions to be unobstructed (conjunction). | This is the strongest symmetric neighbour test. If $R_1$ **is not** a neighbour of $R_2$, it does not necessarily mean that the transition from $R_1$ to $R_2$ can be obstructed. |
| If two relations are neighbours, then it is possible to transition between them without being obstructed. | *Symmetric neighbours*: neighbour test requires either direction to be unobstructed (disjunction). | If $R_1$ **is** a neighbour of $R_2$, it does not necessarily mean that it is possible to directly transition from $R_1$ to $R_2$. |
| When a transition between relations is obstructed the intermediate relation is often different, which is too inconsistent. | *Symmetric neighbours*: neighbour test requires that no single intermediate relation obstructs both directions (restricted disjunction). | This is the weakest symmetric neighbour test. If $R_1$ **is** a neighbour of $R_2$, it does not necessarily mean that it is possible to directly transition **in either direction**. |

the program in terms of its application context. Researchers in QSTR typically apply general first-order theorem provers (and higher) for system validation (Wölfl, et al., 2007). However, the use of theorem provers for application level validation is not practical in general. Firstly, applying theorem provers can be very manually intensive, and even expert logicians in the QSTR research field find the task non-trivial (e.g. refer to page 292 and Section 6.2 in Cohn, et al., 1997). Secondly, they require axioms for the logic, which in many cases will not be available, making theorem provers impossible to use. For example, particularly during the early stages of application design, software developers may need to rapidly encode informal qualitative domain knowledge with the intention of refining the logic later if necessary. Thus, a thorough axiomatisation would not be necessary or appropriate.

We present a significantly different methodology for QSTR application validation, inspired by research in software engineering and finite model theory. We focus on adapting two white-box testing approaches, namely unit testing and integration testing, so that our validation methodology can be used iteratively during application development (rather than as a black-box post development validation tool).

## 7.1. Unit Testing and Integration Testing for QSTR Applications

Unit testing aims to validate small components of a program by exercising isolated aspects of functionality in an independent way (Burnstein, 2003). We define the units of QSTR applications to be the two set expressions on the left hand side and right hand side of constraints. Once the units have been exercised, the next step is to test that the constraint's set comparator is correct. A unit test is simply a set of inputs and a set of expected outputs, and the domain is the collection of relations in the unit set expression being tested.

Integration testing is used to validate the interaction between different program components (Burnstein, 2003). An integration test for a QSTR application exercises some subset of constraints. An integration test is a set of inputs and a set of expected outputs, where the domain is the collection of relations that appear in the set expressions of the constraints being tested.

The primary issue is determining which tests the designer must execute to achieve an adequate degree of confidence that the application is fit for purpose. In standard software engineering, the set of tests that can be executed on a typical software program (called the test space) is determined by the system inputs and outputs, and the system structure such as statements, decisions and control paths. Executing all possible tests is clearly impractical and thus software engineers employ methods that isolate critical subsets such as boundary checking, equivalence class partitioning, and cause-effect graphs (Burnstein, 2003).

One standard technique for identifying significant test classes is to measure the test coverage of some type of program component (Zhu, et al., 1997). For example, the set of tests that execute every statement in a program at least once is typically considered to be a minimum coverage requirement for validation. We adapt this software engineering methodology by defining a concept called homogeneous sets (called H sets). H sets are used to measure the test coverage of QSTR application components.

## 7.2. Homogeneous Sets

In model theory (Hodges, 1997; Marker, 2002), a set $X$ is *definable* (in model **M**) if there is some query in first order logic that can distinguish precisely this set of objects (that is, a formula $\phi$ exists such that $X=\{(v_1,\ldots,v_n)\in U^n \mid \mathbf{M} \vDash \phi(v_1,\ldots,v_n)\}$, where entails $\vDash$ means that the formula is true in **M**).

Homogeneous sets (or H sets) are a special class of definable sets. H sets are atomic definable sets, that is, no query exists that can separate two objects within the same H set, thus objects within an H set are equivalent and indistinguishable. Let $H=\{h_1,\ldots,h_n\}$ be a set of homogeneous sets, where each $h_i \subseteq U$. By definition, $h_1, \ldots, h_n$ partition $U$. We define H-complexity of a language to be $|H|$.

## 7.3. Using H Sets to Measure Complexity

Complexity of a QSTR application language can be considered as either the number of distinct queries that can be expressed, or (equivalently) the number of distinct scenarios that can be encoded.

A query is used to access a subset of objects in a scenario, and query complexity of a language is defined as the maximum number of unique non-empty subsets that can be accessed by some query. H sets are indivisible and mutually exclusive (by definition), so the query that defines an H set must also be the query that returns the smallest non-empty subset of those objects. The smallest subset containing objects from two different H sets $h_1$, $h_2$ must be the union of the queries that define those two H sets, $h_1 \cup h_2$. It follows that any accessible subset of objects must be the union of some combination of H sets, and thus query complexity is equal to the number of different combinations of H sets, $2^{|H|}$.

We now consider scenario complexity. Intuitively, qualitative models do not distinguish between numerical quantities, unlike metric systems. If two objects in a scenario can not be separated by a query, then the objects are considered equivalent and indistinguishable, that is, the objects must be in the same H set. Accordingly, if the only difference between two scenarios is the number of indistinguishable objects in each non-empty H set then the scenarios are considered equivalent. Thus, a scenario equivalence class is defined by the combination of H sets from which objects are selected, and the number of such scenario classes, or the scenario complexity of the language, is $2^{|H|}$.

## 7.4. Using H-Complexity to Quantify Test Coverage

H sets are a natural option for analysing test classes because, on one hand, they specify the absolute limit for distinguishing between objects, and on the other hand, they can be used to describe any possible distinct set of objects. This section presents our methodology for applying H-complexity to measure test coverage.

When quantifying test coverage, the designer initially has a set of QSTR application components that are currently being tested, and the set of tests (called the test suite). Five activities that the designer must undertake are to:

1. identify the domain of the components being tested,
2. refine the test space by specifying conditions that are not appropriate for exhaustive testing,
3. calculate the complexity of the original test space and the refined test space,
4. determine the class of each test in the test suite, and
5. calculate test coverage results.

The following sections present the details of each activity.

## 7.5. Activity 1: Identify Component Domains

Firstly, the designer must identify the domain (a set of relations) of the components being tested. For a unit test, the domain contains the relations in the set expression, e.g. the domain of the set expression $\{x_1 | (x_1,x_2) \in R_1^+ \wedge (x_3,x_2) \in R_2^-\}$ is $\{R_1, R_2\}$. For an integration test, the domain contains the relations that appear in the subset of constraints being tested, e.g. the domain of the constraints:

$\{x_1 \mid (x_1, x_2) \in R_1^+ \wedge (x_3, x_2) \in R_2^\sim\}$
$= \{x_1 \mid (x_2, x_1) \in R_3^+\}$
$\{x_1 \mid (x_1, x_2) \in R_3^+ \wedge (x_3, x_2) \in R_2^\sim\}$
$\subseteq \{x_1 \mid x_1 \in R_4^+\}$

is $\{R_1, R_2, R_3, R_4\}$.

## 7.6. Activity 2: Specifying Conditions to Refine the Test Space

H-complexity is calculated as all possible combinations of H sets. When considered as a test space, each H set is being exercised in conjunction with every other combination of H sets. However, many H sets represent conditions that may not require this exhaustive testing. By isolating such conditions and testing them independently, the designer can achieve a smaller, more focused and hence more practical and effective test space.

For example, the relation *in* is not (usually) symmetric, that is, if *x* is *in y*, then *y* cannot also be *in x*. If this condition is violated then the scenario is clearly inconsistent with the QSTR application, regardless of the other remaining components of the scenario. Rather than exhaustively testing *in* for every unit that it is used, the designer can isolate the erroneous symmetric condition and test it once. They can then assume that every time *in* is used the application will respond correctly regarding symmetry. Table 5 presents our suggestions for common conditions that can be used to refine test spaces.

## 7.7. Activity 3: Calculating H-Complexity

This section derives the formula for calculating H-complexity of a language (i.e. a domain) by counting the number of H sets, $|H|$. Firstly we calculate the number of H sets permitted by a single unary relation, and then a single relation of arbitrary arity. We then observe that binary relations (and higher) admit an infinite number of H sets, making H-complexity unusable. To overcome this we employ restrictions on the query language to calculate the number of basic queries that can be expressed for a set of relations. We then show that basic queries are not Jointly Exhaustive and Pairwise Disjoint (JEPD) and so do not correspond to H sets. Thus, we finally calculate H complexity as the smallest number of unique JEPD queries that can be expressed using combinations of basic queries.

Initially, assume that all relations have an arity of 1 (i.e. they represent qualitative properties such as *round* or *large*). Tuples can take one of $|A_R|$ states for a relation $R$ (such as *holds*), hence the complexity of a unary relation is $|H_R|=|A_R|$. However, once relations have an arity greater than 1 there are an infinite number of potential $H$ sets, because a binary relation constitutes a total order. We proceed in our analysis by using a graph to represent a scenario that consists of a single binary relation $R_i$, where objects represent vertices and directed edges represent tuples as illustrated in Figure 5.

A set theoretic query describes the structure of a graph and specifies the vertex to be selected with $v$ bound variables (universally or existentially quantified), e.g.

$$\forall x_1 ... \exists x_v \cdot x_1 \neq x_2 \wedge ... \wedge x_1 \neq x_v \wedge ... \wedge x_{v\text{-}1} \neq x_v.$$

For brevity, we will omit explicitly stating these quantifications and conditions for all further queries, and for simplicity, the variables in our examples are only existentially quantified. For example, the query $\{x_2 \mid (x_1, x_2) \in R_1 \wedge (x_3, x_2) \in R_1\}$ will access $b$ from the graph of $R_1$ in Figure 5.

While there are an infinite number of potential graphs and unique accessible subsets, homogeneous sets still exist that contain indistinguishable objects. Indeed, homogeneous sets correspond to graph symmetries. For example, regarding the graph of $R_1$, no query exists that can separate objects *a* and *c* (without directly referring to those objects),

*Table 5. Common conditions for refining test spaces*

| Condition | Mathematical Property | Example (application specific) | Formal description |
|---|---|---|---|
| *Using Object Types (special unary relations)* | | | |
| During testing, assume certain objects are certain types. | n/a | Object $x$ is always a *room*, and object $y$ is always a *light*. | given $x,\ldots,z$ in $U$, $R_1^+(x)$ and … and $R_n^+(z)$ *used in conjunction with other constraints* |
| Semantically, certain types of objects can never have certain relations. | n/a | No objects are ever *inside* a *light bulb* object. | for all $x,\ldots,z$ in $U$, $R_1^+(x) \rightarrow R_2^-(x,\ldots,z)$ |
| *One Binary Relation* | | | |
| An object is necessarily related to itself with respect to this relation. | Reflexive | Objects are always *near* themselves. | for all $x$ in $U$, $R^+(x,x)$ |
| An object can never be related to itself with respect to this relation. | Irreflexive | No object is *inside* itself. | for all $x$ in $U$, $R^-(x,x)$ |
| If the relation holds from one object to another object, then it must also hold in the other direction (i.e. from the latter object to the former object). | Symmetric | If an object $x$ is *near* another object $y$, then object $y$ must also be *near* object $x$. | for all $x,y$ in $U$, $R^+(x,y) \rightarrow R^+(y,x)$ |
| If the relation holds from one object to another object, then it can never hold in the other direction. | Asymmetric | If an object $x$ is *inside* object $y$, then object $y$ can never be *inside* object $x$. | for all $x,y$ in $U$, $R^+(x,y) \rightarrow R^-(y,x)$ |
| *Two Binary Relations* | | | |
| If relation $R_1$ holds from one object to another object, then relation $R_2$ must also hold in the other direction (i.e. from the latter object to the former object). | Inverse (or converse) | If time interval $x$ is *before* time interval $y$, then interval $y$ must be *after* interval $x$. | for all $x,y$ in $U$, $R_1^+(x,y) \rightarrow R_2^+(y,x)$ |
| If relation $R_1$ holds from one object to another object, then relation $R_2$ can never hold in the other direction. | n/a | If object $x$ *contains* object $y$, then $y$ can never be *larger than* $x$. | for all $x,y$ in $U$, $R_1^+(x,y) \rightarrow R_2^-(y,x)$ |
| *Pairs of Relations, Arbitrary Arity* | | | |
| One relation trivially implies another relation. | Implication | If an object $x$ is *accelerating* then it must also be *moving*. | for all $x,\ldots,z$ in $U$, $R_1^+(x,\ldots,z) \rightarrow R_2^+(x,\ldots,z)$ |
| If one relation does not hold, then it trivially implies that another particular relation must hold. | Complement | If an object $x$ is not *stationary*, then it must be *moving*. | for all $x,\ldots,z$ in $U$, $R_1^-(x,\ldots,z) \rightarrow R_2^+(x,\ldots,z)$ |
| *Groups of Relations, Arbitrary Arity* | | | |
| No two relations (out of a set of relations **R**) can both hold for a given set of objects at the same time. | Pairwise mutually exclusive | No pair of the relations *near*, *moderately near*, and *far* can ever hold at the same time. | for all $x,\ldots,z$ in $U$, and for all relations $R_1,R_2$ in **R**, *not* $(R_1^+(x,\ldots,z)$ and $R_2^+(x,\ldots,z))$ |
| At least one relation (out of a set of relation **R**) must hold for a given set of objects at any time. | Jointly exhaustive | All objects are either *moving* or *stationary* at any time. | for all $x,\ldots,z$ in $U$, there exists relation $R$ in **R**, $R^+(x,\ldots,z)$ |

*Figure 5. Three graphs representing binary relations $R_1$, $R_2$ and $R_3$. In $R_3$, subgraphs {a,b} and {c,d} correspond to basic queries, where {e,f,g} contains more than one basic query as induced subgraphs*

| | |
|---|---|
| $R_1$={ (a,b), (c,b)} | a → b, c → b |
| $R_2$={(a,a), (a,b), (b,c), (d,d), (d,e), (e,c)} | a ↺, a → b → c; d ↺, d → e → c |
| $R_3$={(a,b), (c,d), (d,d), (e,f), (e,g), (g,g)} | a → b; c → d ↺; e → f, e → g ↺ |

$$\{a,c\} = \{x_1 \mid (x_1,x_2) \in R_1 \wedge (x_3,x_2) \in R_1\}$$
$$= \{x_3 \mid (x_1,x_2) \in R_1 \wedge (x_3,x_2) \in R_1\},$$

and the graph of $R_2$ has three $H$ sets, accessed by the query

$$\{x_i \mid (x_1,x_1) \in R_2 \wedge (x_1,x_2) \in R_2 \wedge (x_2,x_3) \in R_2 \wedge (x_4,x_4) \in R_2 \wedge (x_4,x_5) \in R_2 \wedge (x_5,x_3) \in R_2\},$$

namely $\{a, d\}$ when $i = 1$ or 4, $\{b, e\}$ when $i = 2$ or 5 and $\{c\}$ when $i = 3$.

Given a graph of a scenario, the number of $H$ sets is the number of vertices minus the number of symmetries. However, to make $|H_R|$ a function of the entire QSTR application language, rather than just isolated scenarios (i.e. rather than particular graphs), we apply the concept of restricted query languages from finite model theory (normally used for studying descriptive complexity [Marker, 2002]). If the restricted query language only recognises a finite number of graphs, it will admit a finite number of $H$ sets. It is then possible to quantify the complexity of a relation independent of a particular scenario, and measure the relative difference in expressiveness between two languages.

One common query restriction is to limit the number of variables (vertices). Previously, queries have referred to variables $x_i$ where $i$ can be any positive integer. For example, if $i \leq 2$ then the allowable tuples are $(x_1, x_1)$, $(x_1, x_2)$, $(x_2, x_1)$, and $(x_2, x_2)$. If $v$ is the number of variables allowed in a query, and $a_R$ is the arity of relation $R$ (i.e. the size of the tuples) then for each query, the number of tuples is $v \uparrow a_R$. We refer to these queries as *basic queries*. For example, if $v = 2$ then one basic query on a binary relation is $\{x_1 \mid (x_1, x_1) \in R^- \wedge (x_1, x_2) \in R^+ \wedge (x_2, x_1) \in R^- \wedge (x_2, x_2) \in R^-\}$. Each tuple can be assigned to one of $|A_R|$ relation states, thus, the number of *unique* basic queries for relation $R$ is $|A_R|^{number\ of\ tuples}$, where *number of tuples* $= v \uparrow a_R$.

Previously we only referred to one relation within a query. Given $v$ bound variables, queries will now take the form, $\{x_1 \mid query\ R_1, query\ R_2, \ldots, query\ R_n\}$, where $query\ R_i$ is one of the unique basic queries for relation $R_i$. Hence, the total number of queries permitted over $n$ relations is $|basic\ R_1\ queries| \times \ldots \times |basic\ R_n\ queries|$. Moreover, each query variable can be either existentially or universally quantified, i.e. the query can use any one of the combinations from $\exists x_1 \exists x_2 \ldots \exists x_v$ to $\forall x_1 \forall x_2 \ldots \forall x_v$. In general, the number of allowable variable quantifications $q$ is $2^v$ if all combinations are acceptable. Thus the number of unique basic relations including the acceptable variable quantifications is $q \times |basic\ R_1\ queries| \times \ldots \times |basic\ R_n\ queries|$.

For H sets to truly represent the maximum refinement possible, they must be JEPD so that every object in a scenario will appear in exactly one H set. This property is critical; if it did not hold then further refinements could be achieved by taking H set intersections and differences. Basic queries are not necessarily JEPD (specifically, when their corresponding graphs are overlapping induced subgraphs of the full scenario graph) and so they do not specify H sets. For example, consider the scenario graph $R_3$ in Figure 5. If $v = 2$ then two basic queries are:

$\{x_1 \mid (x_1, x_1) \in R^- \wedge (x_1, x_2) \in R^+ \wedge (x_2, x_1) \in R^- \wedge (x_2, x_2) \in R^-\} = \{a, e\}$,

$\{x_1 \mid (x_1, x_1) \in R^- \wedge (x_1, x_2) \in R^+ \wedge (x_2, x_1) \in R^- \wedge (x_2, x_2) \in R^+\} = \{c, e\}$.

Vertex $e$ appears in both results, and therefore the basic queries are not JEPD.

To calculate $|H|$ we must determine the smallest JEPD queries that contain the basic queries. This is achieved by taking all combinations of basic queries by intersection and difference, hence $|H|=2^{\text{number of unique basic queries}} - 1$ (we can ignore the trailing'$-1$').

To summarise,

- the language being measured has a set of relations $\mathbf{R}$,
- $A_R$ is the number of relation states allowed for relation $R$ (such as *holds* and *does not hold*),
- $a_R$ is the arity of relation $R$ (e.g. binary relations have arity 2),
- $v$ is the number of variables allowed in a query $(1 \leq v)$,
- $q$ is the number of variable quantifications $(1 \leq q \leq 2^v)$, and
- $H$ is the set of H sets, and $|H|$ is the H-complexity of the language.

The formula for calculating H-complexity is:

$$
\begin{aligned}
|H| &= 2 \uparrow (q \times |\, basic\ R_1\ queries\,| \\
&\quad \times \ldots \\
&\quad \times |\, basic\ R_n\ queries\,|) \\
&= 2 \uparrow (q(|A_{R1}| \uparrow v \uparrow a_{R1}) \times \ldots \times (|A_{Rn}| \uparrow v \uparrow a_{Rn})) \\
&= 2 \uparrow (q \textstyle\prod_{R \in \mathbf{R}} (|A_R| \uparrow v \uparrow a_R)
\end{aligned} \tag{1}
$$

## 7.8. Activity 3: Calculating H-Complexity for Refined Test Spaces

The complexity of a language can be calculated simply by applying the formula in the previous section. However, once the designer has specified conditions for refining the test space, the formula can no longer be used. In this section we present a method for calculating the refined test space complexity by encoding it as a Constraint Satisfaction Problem (CSP). The designer can then use any standard CSP solver, such as JaCoP (Kuchcinski, 2003), to calculate the complexity.

A CSP is a finite number of variables (where each variable has a finite domain), and a set of constraints between variables. In our case, given a domain of relations $\mathbf{R}$ and the number of allowable query variables $v$, the CSP solver will return the number of basic queries permitted, $\prod_{R \in \mathbf{R}} |$basic $R$ queries$|$. Equation 1 from the previous section can then be used to calculate the refined test space complexity.

We now present our CSP encoding. Each variable represents a tuple from a basic query. From the previous section, the number of tuples for relation $R$ is $v \uparrow a_R$. Let integers 1,2,3,4 represent *holds*, *does not hold*, *not applicable*, and *indefinite*, respectively. For each relation $R$, declare $v \uparrow a_R$ variables with domain $A_R$, encoded as the appropriate subset of $\{1,2,3,4\}$. Next, specify the refinement conditions from Section 7.6. Finally, execute the solver and have it return the number of solutions (there is no need to record the solutions).

If computation is not too time consuming, the solver can be executed multiple times to determine the impact of each constraint. Do this by executing the solver with only one constraint at a time, and record the different complexities. Alternatively, execute the solver with all but one constraint (for each constraint) to quickly determine whether any constraints are redundant.

For example, given the domain **R**={*light*, *room*, *warm*, *in*}, $v$=2 allowable query variables, and for every relation $A_R$={+,−,~,?}, $q$=1 variable quantification (both variables existentially quantified), the number of basic queries is:

$$
\begin{aligned}
& q\prod_{R\in\mathbf{R}}(|A_R| \uparrow v \uparrow a_R) \\
&= (4\uparrow 2\uparrow 1)\cdot(4\uparrow 2\uparrow 1)\cdot(4\uparrow 2\uparrow 1)\cdot(4\uparrow 2\uparrow 2) \\
&= 16\cdot 16\cdot 16\cdot 256 \\
&= 1048576,
\end{aligned}
$$

yielding a completely intractable test space, with complexity $|H|$ = 2↑1048576. A designer then refines this test space by specifying the following conditions:

- only test when $x$ is a *light* and $y$ is a *room*
- because both object types are assumed, ignore the *not applicable* relation state (all relations apply for *lights* and *rooms*)
- the types *light* and *room* are mutually exclusive
- *in* is not reflexive
- *in* is not symmetric
- nothing is ever *in* a *light*

The designer then encodes the CSP problem[1] using JaCoP (Kuchcinski, 2003). Firstly the variables are declared, using a restricted domain that excludes *not applicable*. Next, the designer encodes the constraints. (see Box 1.)

Next, the designer runs the solver which returns 27 solutions. The test space of size $2^{27}$ is now practical for certain important coverage metrics, although further refinements can be made, for example, choosing to only test one *room* at a time (Schultz, et al., 2009).

The designer executes the solver multiple times, each run using only one of the constraints, and determines that constraints 1 and 4 have the most impact. Once again, the designer executes the solver multiple times, each run using all but one constraint (for each constraint) and determines that some constraints are redundant and can be removed such as shown in Box 2.

Note that, after removing one constraint, the process should be repeated rather than removing multiple constraints at once.

## 7.9. Activity 4: Calculate the Class of a Given Test Instance

To determine the test coverage of a given set of tests, the designer must compare the tests to the test space in terms of H-complexity. That is, the designer needs to determine which combination of H sets are exercised in a given test.

A test is a set of input premises and expected outputs. The input premise information is a set of relations that contain object tuples, such as $within^{+}$={(a,b), (b,c)}, $school^{+}$={a}, $Downtown^{+}$={b}, $Auckland^{+}$={c}, $near^{-}$={(c,d)}, $within^{?}$={(a,c)}. By convention, for each relation, any unspecified tuples can be assumed to be in the *indefinite* relation state (e.g. $Auckland^{?}$={a,b,d}). The expected output is again a set of relations that contain object tuples, such as $within^{+}$={(a,b), (b,c), (a,c)}. A test is satisfied by a QSTR application if, given the premises, reasoning produces a scenario that satisfies the expected outputs.

Given a domain being tested and a test instance, the designer needs to determine which test class the given test is in with respect to the domain's test space. Using H sets we define a test class as the premise scenario specified in the test (that is, we ignore the expected output). To calculate the class of a given test we use a CSP encoding.

To summarise, query variables and scenario objects are encoded. CSP is then used to select every possible combination of scenario objects for the query variables, and for each combination

*Box 1.*

```
Store network = new Store();
Variable light_x        = new Variable(network, "light_x", domain(1,2,4));
Variable light_y        = new Variable(network, "light_y", domain(1,2,4));
Variable room_x         = new Variable(network, "room_x", domain(1,2,4));
Variable room_y         = new Variable(network, "room_y", domain(1,2,4));
Variable warm_x         = new Variable(network, "warm_x", domain(1,2,4));
Variable warm_y         = new Variable(network, "warm_y", domain(1,2,4));
Variable in_x_x         = new Variable(network, "in_x_x", domain(1,2,4));
Variable in_y_y         = new Variable(network, "in_y_y", domain(1,2,4));
Variable in_x_y         = new Variable(network, "in_x_y", domain(1,2,4));
Variable in_y_x         = new Variable(network, "in_y_x", domain(1,2,4));

//- only test when x is a light and y is a room
network.impose(new XeqC(light_x, 1));
network.impose(new XeqC(room_y, 1));

//- types "light" and "room" are mutually exclusive
network.impose(new IfThen( new XeqC(light_x, 1),
                           new XeqC(room_x, 2)));
network.impose(new IfThen( new XeqC(light_y, 1),
                           new XeqC(room_y, 2)));
network.impose(new IfThen( new XeqC(room_x, 1),
                           new XeqC(light_x, 2)));
network.impose(new IfThen( new XeqC(room_y, 1),
                           new XeqC(light_y, 2)));

//- "in" is not reflexive
network.impose(new XeqC(in_x_x, 2));
network.impose(new XeqC(in_y_y, 2));

//- "in" is not symmetric
network.impose(new IfThen( new XeqC(in_x_y, 1),
                           new XeqC(in_y_x, 2)));
network.impose(new IfThen( new XeqC(in_y_x, 1),
                           new XeqC(in_x_y, 2)));

//- nothing is ever "in" a "light"
network.impose(new IfThen( new XeqC(light_x, 1),
                           new XeqC(in_y_x, 2)));
network.impose(new IfThen( new XeqC(light_y, 1),
                           new XeqC(in_x_y, 2)));
```

*Box 2.*

```
network.impose(new IfThen(  new XeqC(light_y, 1),
                            new XeqC(room_y, 2)));
```

*Box 3.*

```
Variable x = new Variable(store, "x", 0, n-1)
Variable y = new Variable(store, "y", 0, n-1)
Variable x_x = new Variable(store, "x_x", n, n*n+n-1)
Variable x_y = new Variable(store, "x_y", n, n*n+n-1)
Variable y_x = new Variable(store, "y_x", n, n*n+n-1)
Variable y_y = new Variable(store, "y_y", n, n*n+n-1)
```

*Box 4.*

```
store.impose(new Alldifferent(new Variable[]{x,y}));
store.impose(new Alldifferent(new Variable[]{x_x,x_y,y_x,y_y}));
```

it constructs the H set from the relation states for the particular chosen objects.

Firstly, we use an integer coding system for representing each unary object tuple, binary object tuple, and so on, up to each $n$-ary tuple. The following integer coding is one example of how this can be accomplished. The greatest tuple arity (i.e. the $n$-ary tuples) required to express the scenario is equal to the greatest relation arity; in the above example the greatest relation arity is 2. Thus, given a scenario with $n$ objects, let integers 0 to $n - 1$ represent each object. Next, let integers $n$ to $2n - 1$ represent tuples (0, 0), (0, 1), …, (0, $n - 1$), integers $2n + 1$ to $3n - 1$ represent tuples (1, 0), (1, 1), …, (1, $n$−1), and so on; hence, $n^2$ binary tuples are represented by integers $n$ to $n + n^2 - 1$. The relationship between the object identifiers and the tuple identifier is $(x+1)n + y$ (that is, the last tuple is represented by the integer $(n - 1 + 1)n + n - 1 = n + n^2 - 1$).

Secondly, for each allowable tuple of query variables, create one CSP variable, with domains of values representing every object tuple of the appropriate arity. For example, if $v$=2 then six variable tuples are required (see Box 3).

Impose the constraint that the variables are not equal to ensure that they represent different objects in each solution (see Box 4.)

Thirdly, encode the basic queries in terms of H sets using the method from the previous section. That is, for each tuple from a basic query of relation $R$, create a variable with a domain that represents the allowable tuple states $A_R$, i.e. some subset of {1,2,3,4} where integers 1,2,3,4 represent *holds*, *does not hold*, *not applicable*, and *indefinite*, respectively. Do not encode the test space refinement constraints.

Finally, link the scenario encoding to the basic query encoding. For each relation, create an implication constraint that associates the object tuple selected by the query variables to the relation state

*Box 5.*

```
store.impose(new IfThenElse(
  new Or(XeqC(x_y,5), XeqC(x_y,10)),     //- if variable matches a tuple
  new XeqC(within_x_y,1),                //- then H set relation state holds
  new XeqC(within_x_y,2)));              //- else relation state does not hold
```

in the H set. For example, encoding $within^{+}$={(a,b), (b,c)}, where a=0, b=1, c=2, d=3, (a,b)=5 and (b,c)=10 requires the constraint shown in Box 5.

Note that further nested IfThenElse constraints are required to also explicitly specify the *not holds*, *not applicable* and *indefinite* states.

Execute the solver to get all solutions. The class of a test is determined by the set of solutions for the basic query encoding variables, and the value of the object variables that satisfy those basic queries. Once the designer knows the class that each test is in (that is, the combination of H sets from which objects are specified), they can run the test coverage metrics presented in the following section.

## 7.10. Activity 5: Test Coverage Metrics

This section presents four test coverage metrics based on H-complexity. To illustrate the test coverage metrics we will use the following running example. Let the domain being tested contain one binary relation $R$ that can take two states $A_R=\{+,-\}$. Two query variables are allowed, $v=2$ and one variable quantification, $q=1$. The number of query tuples is $v\uparrow a_R=2^2=4$, which are:

$(x_1,x_1)\in R$, $(x_1,x_2)\in R$, $(x_2,x_1)\in R$, and $(x_2,x_2)\in R$.

The number of basic queries is $q \prod_{R\in\mathbf{R}} (|A_R|\uparrow v\uparrow a_R)=1\cdot 2^4=16$, which are:

$b_1=\{x_1 \mid (x_1,x_1)\in R^+ \wedge (x_1,x_2)\in R^+ \wedge (x_2,x_1)\in R^+ \wedge (x_2,x_2)\in R^+\}$,

$b_2=\{x_1 \mid (x_1,x_1)\in R^+ \wedge (x_1,x_2)\in R^+ \wedge (x_2,x_1)\in R^+ \wedge (x_2,x_2)\in R^-\}$,

$b_3=\{x_1 \mid (x_1,x_1)\in R^+ \wedge (x_1,x_2)\in R^+ \wedge (x_2,x_1)\in R^- \wedge (x_2,x_2)\in R^+\}$,

...

$b_{16}=\{x_1 \mid (x_1,x_1)\in R^- \wedge (x_1,x_2)\in R^- \wedge (x_2,x_1)\in R^- \wedge (x_2,x_2)\in R^-\}$.

The number of H sets is $|H| = 2\uparrow(q \prod_{R\in\mathbf{R}} (|A_R|\uparrow v\uparrow a_R))=2^{16}$. The number of scenario classes is $2^{|H|}=2\uparrow(2^{16})$. Let the example test set consist of two tests with the following H sets:

- test t1: $(b_1, b_2)$
- test t2: $(b_1)$, $(b_2,b_3)$.

Our four test coverage metrics, strictly ordered in terms of coverage strength (from weakest to strongest) are:

- tuple state coverage (TS),
- basic query coverage (BQ),
- H set coverage (H), and
- scenario coverage (S).

Tuple State (TS) coverage measures the number of query tuples that have taken a particular state in at least one test. Full TS coverage means that every query tuple has been assigned to every allowable relation state in at least one test. This should be viewed as an absolute minimum coverage requirement that all QSTR application test sets must satisfy. The total number of tuples with states that a language admits is $\sum_{R\in\mathbf{R}} |A_R|\cdot(v\uparrow a_R)$. In the running example there are 4 query tuples, and each tuple can take 2 states, giving 2·4=8 possible tuples with states, namely

$(x_1,x_1)\in R^+$, $(x_1,x_2)\in R^+$, $(x_2,x_1)\in R^+$, $(x_2,x_2)\in R^+$,

$(x_1,x_1)\in R^-$, $(x_1,x_2)\in R^-$, $(x_2,x_1)\in R^-$, $(x_2,x_2)\in R^-$.

The example test set contains the following tuples $(x_1,x_1)\in R^+$, $(x_1,x_2)\in R^+$, $(x_2,x_1)\in R^+$, $(x_2,x_2)\in R^+$, $(x_2,x_1)\in R^-$, $(x_2,x_2)\in R^-$. Hence percent TS coverage is 5/8=62.5%.

Basic Query (BQ) coverage measures the number of basic queries that have appeared in at least one test. Full BQ coverage means that every basic query has been used to describe some test scenario. While stronger than full TS coverage, full BQ coverage should also be viewed as a minimum coverage requirement for application validation. In the running example, the test set contains 3 basic queries ($b_1$, $b_2$, $b_3$), giving a percent BQ coverage of 3/16=18.75%.

H set (H) coverage measures the number of H sets that have been used to specify scenarios in at least one test. In practice, full H coverage is often very difficult to achieve, as it constitutes a vast class of tests. Instead the designer should focus on satisfying important subclasses within full H coverage, discussed below. The running example test set has 3 H sets, giving a percent H coverage of $3/(2^{16})\approx 0\%$.

Scenario (S) coverage measures the number of scenario classes exercised in at least one test, where a scenario class is some unique combination of H sets from which objects in the class of scenarios are drawn. In practice, full S coverage is impossible to achieve, except for trivially small domains. However, after test space refinement S coverage can be a useful measure. In the running example two scenario classes are exercised, namely $\{(b_1, b_2)\}$ and $\{(b_1), (b_2,b_3)\}$. This gives a percent S coverage of $2/(2\uparrow 2^{16})\approx 0\%$.

Full BQ coverage is trivially easy to achieve, for example full BQ coverage is satisfied by one test where the scenario returns objects from all 16 basic queries. On the other hand, achieving full H coverage is often difficult in practice, and achieving full S coverage is, in almost all cases, impossible. Our current research is focused on identifying valuable classes within this test space in terms of H and S coverage. For example, two potentially significant H coverage criteria are

- all H sets that consist of exactly one basic query, and
- all H sets that consist of exactly two basic queries

The first class of tests will ensure that all basic queries have been exercised in isolation (giving full TS and BQ coverage). The second class ensures that the interactions between all pairs of basic queries have been exercised. Both of these test classes are relatively small and often practical to achieve. If the number of basic queries is $b$ then the test class sizes are $b$ and $b(b-1)$ respectively, where the maximum size of $b$ is $(q \prod_{R\in\mathbf{R}} (|A_R|\uparrow v\uparrow a_R))$.

## 8. FUTURE RESEARCH

Our long-term aim is to develop a QSTR application development environment inspired by Garp3 and other UML software tools. This will be used for designing, validating and automatically implementing the reasoning component of a QSTR application, and will integrate software tools that support the methodologies discussed in this chapter. The workbench will allow the designer to easily employ existing QSTR libraries such as SparQ and GQR, structure their application by declaring fragments and design patterns such as fragment definitions derive high-level neighbourhoods, automatically generate tests from critical test classes, and execute validation metrics such as test coverage. Additionally, a suite of metrics will be available that analyse an application based on external test data, e.g. using classification techniques on test data to analyse the quality of a designer's fragment definitions. Once a QSTR application design has been finalised, our workbench will generate a standalone implementation, such as a jar file, that will accept a scenario description and perform the required task, such as envisioning.

We are also planning to compile a library of application contexts, such as a qualitative GIS suite, an office environment suite, a sports field suite, architectural lighting suite, and so on. Each library component would consist of the relevant existing QSTR calculi, along with other standard high-level commonsense relations and rules.

## 9. CONCLUSION

A number of critical barriers to QSTR application development must be addressed, namely that the important characteristics of QSTR problems need to be defined, QSTR application designers need to develop task specific qualitative relations and constraints, there are no methodologies for developing or analysing QSTR applications, and that application designers will typically be software engineers rather than logicians. In this chapter, we address these problems with a collection of methodologies that support the design and validation of QSTR applications.

We established a theoretical foundation for QSTR applications, and used this to define the roles of application designers and users, and to identify three fundamental QSTR application operations, selection, insertion, and scenario universe modification.

We presented four central properties of QSTR applications, specifically, reasoning across a broad range of abstraction levels, continuity assumption, modelling infinite domains, and reasoning about objects in multi-dimensional models. Our methodologies for QSTR application development focused on supporting the designer in three of these key areas.

We adapted two standard formal requirements from software engineering for QSTR applications, which were the customer's operational requirements and functional requirements. We presented critical characteristics of QSTR problems based on our theoretical foundations of QSTR applications and a review of existing QSTR literature, and showed how these characteristics determine the customer's operational profile. We enumerated a set of significant purely qualitative tasks that defines the exact extent to which QSTR can be applied, and we established a template that covers all general QSTR application behaviour sequences in a UML state diagram.

QSTR applications are organised into groups of relations, called fragments. We presented two design patterns, fragment definitions, and fragment generalisations, for structuring fragments.

We presented a methodology for defining high-level neighbourhoods that are consistent with the structure of fragments in a QSTR application. For this, we defined two novel components of conceptual neighbours, path restrictions and transition equivalence classes, and showed how the designer can use these to customise a derived high-level neighbourhood graph.

Finally, we presented a novel methodology for QSTR application validation, inspired by research in software engineering and finite model theory. We defined a complexity metric called H-complexity, and developed test coverage metrics for assessing the quality of unit and integration test sets.

## REFERENCES

Allen, J. F. (1983). Maintaining knowledge about temporal intervals. *Communications of the ACM*, *26*(11), 832–843. doi:10.1145/182.358434

Bhatt, M. (2007). A causal approach for modelling spatial dynamics: A preliminary report. In *Proceedings of the Workshop on Spatial and Temporal Reasoning, 20th International Joint Conference on Artificial Intelligence (IJCAI-07)*. IJCAI.

Bredeweg, B., Bouwer, A., Jellema, J., Bertels, D., Linnebank, F., & Liem, J. (2007). Garp3: A new workbench for qualitative reasoning and modelling. In *Proceedings of the 4th International Conference on Knowledge Capture (K-CAP'07)*, (pp. 183-184). K-CAP.

Burnstein, I. (2003). *Practical software testing: A process oriented approach*. New York, NY: Springer.

Cohn, A. (2008). Conceptual neighborhood. In Shekhar, S., & Xiong, H. (Eds.), *Encyclopedia of GIS* (p. 123). New York, NY: Springer Science. doi:10.1007/978-0-387-35973-1_173

Cohn, A. G., & Renz, J. (2008). Qualitative spatial representation and reasoning. In van Hermelen, F., Lifschitz, V., & Porter, B. (Eds.), *Handbook of Knowledge Representation* (pp. 551–596). London, UK: Elsevier. doi:10.1016/S1574-6526(07)03013-1

Cunningham, W. (1995). *About the Portland form*. Retrieved on August 8, 2009, from http://c2.com/ppr/about/portland.html.

Dylla, F., Frommberger, L., Wallgrün, J. O., & Wolter, D. (2006). SparQ: A toolbox for qualitative spatial representation and reasoning. In *Proceedings of the Workshop on Qualitative Constraint Calculi: Application and Integration*. Qualitative Constraint Calculi.

Dylla, F., & Wallgrün, J. O. (2007). Qualitative spatial reasoning with conceptual neighborhoods for agent control. *Journal of Intelligent & Robotic Systems, 48*(1), 55–78. doi:10.1007/s10846-006-9099-4

Freksa, C. (1992). Temporal reasoning based on semi-intervals. *Artificial Intelligence, 54*, 199–227. doi:10.1016/0004-3702(92)90090-K

Gantner, Z., Westphal, M., & Wölfl, S. (2008). GQR-a fast reasoner for binary qualitative constraint calculi. In *Proceedings of the AAAI'08 Workshop on Spatial and Temporal Reasoning* (pp. 24-29). Chicago, IL: AAAI.

Guesgen, H. W. (2002). Fuzzifying spatial relations. In Matsakis, P., & Sztandera, L. (Eds.), *Applying Soft Computing in Defining Spatial Relations* (pp. 1–16). Heidelberg, Germany: Physica-Verlag.

Hodges, W. (1997). *A shorter model theory*. Cambridge, UK: Cambridge University Press.

Iwasaki, Y. (1997). Real-world applications of qualitative reasoning. *IEEE Expert, 12*(3), 16–21. doi:10.1109/64.590068

Kuchcinski, K. (2003). Constraints-driven scheduling and resource assignment. *ACM Transactions on Design Automation of Electronic Systems, 8*(3), 355–383. doi:10.1145/785411.785416

Li, J. J., Huang, J., & Renz, J. (2009). A divide-and-conquer approach for solving interval algebra networks. In *Proceedings of the 21st International Joint Conference on Artificial Intelligence (IJCAI 2009)*, (pp. 572-577). Pasadena, CA: IJCAI.

Ligozat, G., Mitra, D., & Condotta, J. (2004). Spatial and temporal reasoning: Beyond Allen's calculus. *AI Communications, 17*(4), 223–233.

Marker, D. (2002). *Model theory: An introduction*. New York, NY: Springer Verlag.

Nebel, B., & Bürckert, H. J. (1995). Reasoning about temporal relations: A maximal tractable subclass of Allen's interval algebra. *Journal of the ACM, 42*(1), 43–66. doi:10.1145/200836.200848

Pooley, R. J. (2004). *Applying UML advanced application*. Oxford, UK: Elsevier.

Qayyum, Z. U., & Cohn, A. G. (2007). Image retrieval through qualitative representations over semantic features. In *Proceedings of the 18th British Machine Vision Conference (BMVC2007)*, (pp. 610-619). BMVC.

Renz, J. (1999). Maximal tractable fragments of the region connection calculus: A complete analysis. In *Proceedings of the 16th International Joint Conference on Artificial Intelligence (IJCAI'99)*, (pp. 448-455). Stockholm, Sweden: IJCAI.

Renz, J. (2007). Qualitative spatial and temporal reasoning: Efficient algorithms for everyone. In *Proceedings of the 20th International Joint Conference on Artificial Intelligence (IJCAI-07)*, (pp. 526-531). Hyderabad, India: IJCAI.

Schultz, C., Amor, R., & Guesgen, H. W. (2009). Unit testing for qualitative spatial and temporal reasoning. In *Proceedings of the 22nd Florida Artificial Intelligence Research Society Conference (FLAIRS-22)*. Sanibel Island, FL: FLAIRS.

Schultz, C., Clephane, T. R., Guesgen, H. W., & Amor, R. (2006). Utilisation of qualitative spatial reasoning in geographic information systems. In *Proceedings of the International Symposium on Spatial Data Handling (SDH-06)*, (pp. 27-42). Vienna, Austria: SDH.

Schultz, C., Guesgen, H. W., & Amor, R. (2007). A system for querying with qualitative distances in networks. In *Proceedings of the IEEE International Conference on Fuzzy Systems (FUZZ-IEEE'07)*, (pp. 640-645). London, UK: IEEE Press.

SETC. (1984). *IEEE guide to software requirements specifications*. New York, NY: IEEE Computer Society.

Van de Weghe, N., Cohn, A. G., De Tré, G., & De Maeyer, P. (2006). A qualitative trajectory calculus as a basis for representing moving objects in geographical information systems. *Control and Cybernetics*, *35*(1), 97–119.

Westphal, M., & Wölfl, S. (2009). Qualitative CSP, finite CSP, and SAT: Comparing methods for qualitative constraint-based reasoning. In *Proceedings of the 21st International Joint Conference on Artificial Intelligence (IJCAI 2009)*, (pp. 628-633). Pasadena, CA: IJCAI.

Wölfl, S., Mossakowski, T., & Schröder, L. (2007). Qualitative constraint calculi: Heterogeneous verification of composition tables. In *Proceedings of the 20th International Florida Artificial Intelligence Research Society Conference (FLAIRS 2007)*, (pp. 665-670). AAAI Press.

Zhu, H., Hall, P. A. V., & May, J. H. R. (1997). Software unit test coverage and adequacy. *ACM Computing Surveys*, *29*(4), 366–427. doi:10.1145/267580.267590

## KEY TERMS AND DEFINITIONS

**Application Designer:** Determines the QSTR application language and model, given formal software requirements.

**Validation:** Process conducted to ensure that a software system is fit for purpose.

**Complexity:** A measure of the expressiveness of a relational language; specifically, the number of distinct scenarios that can be represented.

**Requirements:** The necessary properties of the intended application for that application to have value, such as characteristics of the domain being modelled, the tasks that the intended system needs to be capable of performing, and the system's behaviour during runtime.

**Neighbourhood:** A graph where vertices represent relations are edges represent conceptual neighbours; two relations are conceptual neighbours if it is possible for a tuple of objects to transition between those relations without requiring a third, intermediate relation.

**Test Coverage:** The proportion of a selected class of software components exercised by a test suite.

**QSTR Applications:** A class of relational systems, typically characterised by modelling a broad range of abstraction levels, modelling continuity in dynamic scenarios, and modelling infinite, partially ordered domains.

## ENDNOTE

[1] Here we have explicitly enumerated variables and constraints for clarity. In practice, generator methods should be used that accept a set of relation names, domains $A_R$, and the number of query variables $v$, and return the set of variables. Convenience methods should also be created that accept relation names, parameter patterns, and a constraint type, and impose the appropriate set of constraints (rather than explicit enumeration).

# Chapter 6
# Enriching the Qualitative Spatial Reasoning System RCC8

**Ahed Alboody**
*Université Paul Sabatier (UPS), France*

**Florence Sedes**
*Université Paul Sabatier (UPS), France*

**Jordi Inglada**
*Centre National d'Etudes Spatiales (CNES), France*

## ABSTRACT

*The field of qualitative spatial reasoning is now an active research area in Geographical Information Systems (GIS) and also in Artificial Intelligence (AI). Different kinds of spatial relations play an important role in spatial reasoning, spatial analysis, and query languages for geospatial databases. GIS and image databases are often based on the description of relations between spatial regions. One kind of these relations is the topological relations, where the general description of region-region topological relations in detail is still an unsolved issue, although much effort has been done.*

*The eight basic topological relations between two spatial regions are written without any details in the classical form of the spatial reasoning system RCC8:* ***DC, EC, PO, TPP, NTPP, TPPi, NTPPi,*** *and* ***EQ*** *with the names of:* ***DisConnected, Externally Connected, Partial Overlap, Tangential Proper Part, Non-Tangential Proper Part, Tangential Proper Part Inverse, Non-Tangential Proper Part Inverse,*** *and* ***Equally****. In some applications, such as GIS and satellite imagery, need to be described in detail to get new spatial information by enriching these topological relations of the RCC8 system. In order to extract all the necessary details at all possible levels and to differentiate between relations of the same kind, multi-level topological relations are introduced by using two concepts: the Separation Number and the Types of Spatial Elements (Points and Lines) of the Boundary-Boundary Intersection Spatial Set (BBISS).*

*In this chapter, the major contribution is the definition of multi-level topological relations to enrich the RCC8 system. The authors focus their research on the four relations* ***EC, PO, TPP,*** *and* ***TPPi,*** *which*

DOI: 10.4018/978-1-61692-868-1.ch006

*can be detailed and enriched at two levels. First, at the first detailed level (**Level-1**), these four relations are written in general detailed forms by using the concept of Separation Number of Spatial Elements (Points and Lines) of BBISS as: **EC** given as: $EC_{mL}$, $EC_{nP}$, $EC_{mL, nP}$; **PO** given as: $PO_{mL}$, $PO_{nP}$, $PO_{mL, nP}$; **TPP** given as: $TPP_{mLT}$, $TPP_{nPT}$, $TPP_{mLT, nPT}$; and **TPPi** given as: $TPPi_{mLT}$, $TPPi_{nPT}$, $TPPi_{mLT, nPT}$; where the notations (mL, mLT, nP and nPT) are the separation number of the spatial elements of BBISS. Secondly, at the second detailed level (**Level-2**), the same relations are expressed in other general forms more detailed by using the concept of Types of Spatial Elements (Points and Lines) of BBISS as following: **EC** given as: $EC_{m(TOL)}$, $EC_{n(TOP)}$, $EC_{m(TOL), n(TOP)}$; **PO** given as: $PO_{m(TOL)}$, $PO_{n(TOP)}$, $PO_{m(TOL), n(TOP)}$; **TPP** given as: $TPP_{m(TOL)}$, $TPP_{n(TOP)}$, $TPP_{m(TOL), n(TOP)}$; and **TPPi** given as: $TPPi_{m(TOL)}$, $TPPi_{n(TOP)}$, $TPPi_{m(TOL), n(TOP)}$; where the notations m(TOL) and n(TOP) are the separation number of the types of spatial elements of BBISS.*

*In this context, the authors develop definitions for the generalization of these detailed topological relations at these two levels (**Level-1** and **Level-2**). The chapter presents two tables of these four detailed relations. Finally, examples for GIS applications are provided to illustrate the determination of the detailed topological relations studied in this chapter.*

## INTRODUCTION

We start this chapter by giving an overview of the field of qualitative spatial representation and reasoning. The Region Connection Calculus (RCC) proposed by Randell et al. (1992a) and in particular RCC8 is the best known approach to qualitative spatial reasoning. The RCC8 system consists of eight basic topological relations between two spatial regions written as following: ***DC, EC, PO, TPP, NTPP, TPPi, NTPPi and EQ,*** or with the topological names of: ***DisConnected (Disjoint), Externally Connected (Meet), Partial Overlap (Overlaps), Tangential Proper Part (CoveredBy), Non-Tangential Proper Part (ContainedBy or Inside), Tangential Proper Part inverse (Covers), Non-Tangential Proper Part inverse (Contains) and Equally (Equal).***

Then, we summarize the state of the art about the topological models (such as *4- and 9- intersections, Intersection and Difference*...) used to get the eight basic topological relations between spatial regions of the RCC8 system as a basis for qualitative spatial representation and reasoning (Egenhofer, 1991; Cohn, et al.,1997; Cohn & Renz, 2008). Then, we present the topological models at the detailed level which are studied in Egenhofer (1993), Egenhofer and Franzosa (1995), and Deng et al. (2007).

We present the problem that arises at the detailed level on the topological relations of the same kind (***EC, PO, TPP,*** and ***TPPi***) of the RCC8 system represented by many graphical representations (circular, rectangular, polygon...). This problem is expressed by the question: *At the detailed level, which are the differences between the topological relations of the same kind between its several graphical representations?* We present our motivation and the most important application such GIS which is becoming increasingly popular methods of representing and reasoning with geographical data.

Our objective in this chapter is to answer the precedent question by enriching and detailing the topological relations of the RCC8 system using the term of the *Boundary-Boundary Intersection Spatial Set* (*BBISS*) and the Separation Number and the Types of Spatial Elements (Points and Lines) of BBISS. Among the eight topological relations of the RCC8 system, we see that only four relations ***EC, PO, TPP,*** and ***TPPi*** can be characterized in details by the terms BBISS. Consequently, these four relations is detailed and enriched at two additional levels (***Level-1*** and ***Level-2***) using the

*Figure 1. Spatial region (A) with its three parts: interior (A°), boundary (∂A), and exterior or closure (A⁻)*

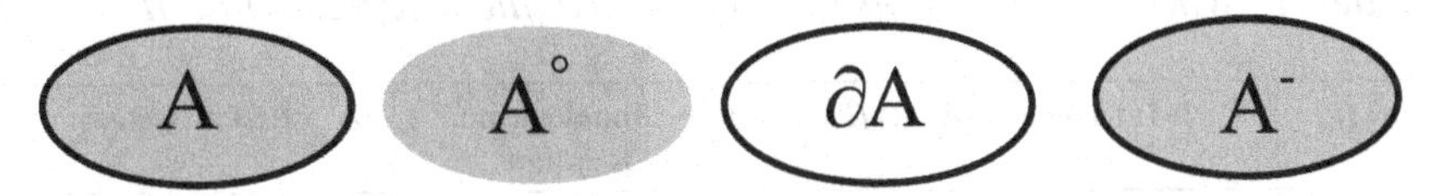


concepts of Separation Number and the Types of Spatial Elements (Points and Lines) of BBISS.

Before concluding, examples in some applications (GIS and satellite image processing) are provided. Then, we present our perspectives to be included in our future work. Finally, we conclude this chapter.

## TOPOLOGICAL MODELS AS BASIS OF THE RCC8 SYSTEM

In this section, we will give an overview about the topological models as basis of the RCC8 system. The topological relations can describe a type of qualitative spatial information between spatial regions. In a two-dimensional space ($IR^2$), most topological existing models can distinguish the eight basic topological relations of the RCC8 system (Region Connection Calculus) (Randell, et al., 1992a).

For region-region topological relations, the most representative models are *4-intersection model* developed by Egenhofer (Egenhofer, 1989; Egenhofer & Franzosa, 1991), *9-intersection model* proposed in Egenhofer and Herring (1991) and Egenhofer and Sharma (1993), and the *Intersection and Difference (**ID**) model* introduced by Deng et al. (2007). Where a spatial region is defined by its interior and boundary; and based on this definition, sets of intersections and differences are included according to the topological models (only sets of intersections for *4- and 9-intersection models*; or with two difference and two intersection sets for the *Intersection and Difference [**ID**] model*).

In the *4-intersection model* (Egenhofer, 1989; Egenhofer & Franzosa, 1991), a spatial region is defined by its interior and boundary, and four intersection sets are included. This model can differentiate the eight topological relations between two spatial regions A and B. The *4-intersection model* ($I_4$) is given by:

$$I_4(A,B) = \begin{bmatrix} A^\circ \cap B^\circ & A^\circ \cap \partial B \\ \partial A \cap B^\circ & \partial A \cap \partial B \end{bmatrix} = \left[A^\circ \cap B^\circ,\ A^\circ \cap \partial B,\ \partial A \cap B^\circ,\ \partial A \cap \partial B\right]$$

Where the interior of A is $A°$ and the boundary of A is $\partial A$; and the interior of B is $B°$ and the boundary of B is $\partial B$ (as shown as in Figure 1). Due to the fact that the *4-intersection model* possibly leads to some confusion in the description of relations between two spatial lines, and between a spatial line and a spatial region, the *4-intersection model* is extended to the *9-intersection model* by introducing the exterior of a spatial region. The three parts (*Interior*, *Boundary,* and *Exterior* or *Closure*) of a spatial region is represented in Figure 1.

The *9-intersection model* (Egenhofer & Herring, 1991; Egenhofer & Sharma, 1993) is an extension of the *4-intersection model* by taking into account the exterior of a spatial region (also called its *Complement* or *Closure*) denoted by $A^-$ for the exterior of A and $B^-$ for the exterior of B. The *9-intersection model* ($I_9$) is written as in Egenhofer and Herring (1991) and Egenhofer and Sharma (1993) by the matrix:

$$I_9(A,B) = \begin{bmatrix} A^\circ \cap B^\circ & A^\circ \cap \partial B & A^\circ \cap B^- \\ \partial A \cap B^\circ & \partial A \cap \partial B & \partial A \cap B^- \\ A^- \cap B^\circ & A^- \cap \partial B & A^- \cap B^- \end{bmatrix}$$

*Table 1. Matrix of the topological relations of the RCC8 system using the 4-intersection model ($I_4$) and 9-intersection model ($I_9$) with spatial regions of circular graphical representation*

| 4-Intersection Model ($I_4$) | 9-Intersection Model ($I_9$) | Topological Relations | RCC8 System | Icons |
|---|---|---|---|---|
| $I_4(A,B)=\begin{bmatrix}\emptyset & \emptyset\\ \emptyset & \emptyset\end{bmatrix}$ | $I_9(A,B)=\begin{bmatrix}\emptyset & \emptyset & \neg\emptyset\\ \emptyset & \emptyset & \neg\emptyset\\ \neg\emptyset & \neg\emptyset & \neg\emptyset\end{bmatrix}$ | *Disjoint* | *DisConnected (DC)* | B A |
| $I_4(A,B)=\begin{bmatrix}\emptyset & \emptyset\\ \emptyset & \neg\emptyset\end{bmatrix}$ | $I_9(A,B)=\begin{bmatrix}\emptyset & \emptyset & \neg\emptyset\\ \emptyset & \neg\emptyset & \neg\emptyset\\ \neg\emptyset & \neg\emptyset & \neg\emptyset\end{bmatrix}$ | *Meet* | *Externally Connected (EC)* | B A |
| $I_4(A,B)=\begin{bmatrix}\neg\emptyset & \neg\emptyset\\ \neg\emptyset & \neg\emptyset\end{bmatrix}$ | $I_9(A,B)=\begin{bmatrix}\neg\emptyset & \neg\emptyset & \neg\emptyset\\ \neg\emptyset & \neg\emptyset & \neg\emptyset\\ \neg\emptyset & \neg\emptyset & \neg\emptyset\end{bmatrix}$ | *Overlaps* | *Partial Overlap (PO)* | B A |
| $I_4(A,B)=\begin{bmatrix}\neg\emptyset & \emptyset\\ \neg\emptyset & \neg\emptyset\end{bmatrix}$ | $I_9(A,B)=\begin{bmatrix}\neg\emptyset & \emptyset & \emptyset\\ \neg\emptyset & \neg\emptyset & \emptyset\\ \neg\emptyset & \neg\emptyset & \neg\emptyset\end{bmatrix}$ | *CoveredBy* | *Tangential Proper Part (TPP)* | B A |
| $I_4(A,B)=\begin{bmatrix}\neg\emptyset & \emptyset\\ \neg\emptyset & \emptyset\end{bmatrix}$ | $I_9(A,B)=\begin{bmatrix}\neg\emptyset & \emptyset & \emptyset\\ \neg\emptyset & \emptyset & \emptyset\\ \neg\emptyset & \neg\emptyset & \neg\emptyset\end{bmatrix}$ | *ContainedBy or Inside* | *Non-Tangential Proper Part (NTPP)* | B A |
| $I_4(A,B)=\begin{bmatrix}\neg\emptyset & \emptyset\\ \neg\emptyset & \neg\emptyset\end{bmatrix}$ | $I_9(A,B)=\begin{bmatrix}\neg\emptyset & \neg\emptyset & \neg\emptyset\\ \emptyset & \neg\emptyset & \neg\emptyset\\ \emptyset & \emptyset & \neg\emptyset\end{bmatrix}$ | *Covers* | *Tangential Proper Part inverse (TPPi)* | A B |
| $I_4(A,B)=\begin{bmatrix}\neg\emptyset & \neg\emptyset\\ \emptyset & \emptyset\end{bmatrix}$ | $I_9(A,B)=\begin{bmatrix}\neg\emptyset & \neg\emptyset & \neg\emptyset\\ \emptyset & \emptyset & \neg\emptyset\\ \emptyset & \emptyset & \neg\emptyset\end{bmatrix}$ | *Contains* | *Non-Tangential Proper Part inverse (NTPPi)* | A B |
| $I_4(A,B)=\begin{bmatrix}\neg\emptyset & \emptyset\\ \emptyset & \neg\emptyset\end{bmatrix}$ | $I_9(A,B)=\begin{bmatrix}\neg\emptyset & \emptyset & \emptyset\\ \emptyset & \neg\emptyset & \emptyset\\ \emptyset & \emptyset & \neg\emptyset\end{bmatrix}$ | *Equal* | *Equally (EQ)* | A B |

In the literature, for these two models of *4- and 9-intersections*, the topological relations of the RCC8 system are written without any details in the form: ***DC, EC, PO, TPP, NTPP, TPPi, NTPPi, and EQ***, or with the names of: ***DisConnected (Disjoint), Externally Connected (Meet), Partial Overlap (Overlaps), Tangential Proper Part (CoveredBy), Non-Tangential Proper Part (ContainedBy or Inside), Tangential Proper***

***Part inverse (Covers), Non-Tangential Proper Part inverse (Contains), and Equally (Equal).***

The martice of the topological relations of the RCC8 system using the *4-intersection model* ($I_4$) and *9-intersection model* ($I_9$) with spatial regions of circular graphical representation is given in Table 1. Where the symbol $\emptyset$ and $\neg\emptyset$ denotes an empty and a non-empty set.

In the ***Intersection and Difference (ID) model*** introduced by Deng et al. (2007), a spatial region is also defined by its interior and boundary, but with the ***ID*** *model* (Deng, et al., 2007), we see that there are two intersection sets which are the interior-interior intersection ($A^\circ \cap B^\circ$) and the boundary-boundary intersection ($\partial A \cap \partial B$). And there are also two difference sets which are the difference between A and B (*A-B*); and the difference between B and A (*B-A*). The ***ID*** *model* can also distinguish the eight topological relations and it is represented by the matrix:

$$ID(A,B) = \begin{bmatrix} A^\circ \cap B^\circ & A - B \\ B - A & \partial A \cap \partial B \end{bmatrix} = \begin{bmatrix} A^\circ \cap B^\circ, & A - B, & B - A, & \partial A \cap \partial B \end{bmatrix}$$

The main difference between the *4-intersection* ($I_4$) and ***ID*** *models* is that both intersection sets ($A^\circ \cap \partial B$) and ($\partial A \cap B^\circ$) of *4-intersection model* are replaced by two differences (*A-B*) and (*B-A*), respectively. This change has two advantages (Deng, et al., 2007): first, it reduces the computational complexity by avoiding topological spatial operations between topological components with different dimensions, for example, ($A^\circ \cap \partial B$) and ($\partial A \cap B^\circ$) with $A^\circ$, $B^\circ$ as ***2-D*** and with $\partial A$, $\partial B$ as ***1-D***; and the second advantage, it reduces the computational cost due to only two intersections in the ***ID*** *model*.

The topological relations of the ***ID*** *model* are equivalent to the topological relations of the spatial reasoning system RCC8 (Deng, et al., 2007). Indeed, the eight topological relations differentiated by the ***ID*** *model* are completely the same as the topological relations by the *4- and 9-intersection models*. In Table 2, the matrix of ***ID*** *model* for all topological relations compared with the RCC8 system is presented. Where the symbol $\emptyset$ and $\neg\emptyset$ denotes an empty and a non-empty set.

Three graphical representations of spatial regions to representing the topological relations of the qualitative spatial reasoning system RCC8 are shown using ***MATLAB*** in Figure 2 (*Circular [Icons (1)] as in Table 2.*), Figure 3 (*Rectangular [Icons (2)] as in Table 2.*), and Figure 4 (*General Polygons [General Icons (3)] as in Table 2.*) as following:

Finally, from the above investigation about the topological models at the coarse level, these three models of *4-intersections* ($I_4$), *9-intersections* ($I_9$) and the ***ID*** *model* can distinguish the eight topological relations of the RCC8 system.

In the GIS spatial analysis, detecting topological changes in satellite images and topological inconsistency, it often needs detailed topological relations (Egenhofer, 1993; Egenhofer & Franzosa, 1995; Deng, et al., 2007). It is also demonstrated that additional details of relations can provide crucial information to specify the semantics of spatial relations in query languages for GIS and image databases. In this objective, our contribution in this chapter focuses exclusively on enriching and detailing the topological relations of the qualitative spatial reasoning system RCC8 at two additional levels.

## ENRICHING THE QUALITATIVE SPATIAL REASONING SYSTEM RCC8 AT THE DETAILED LEVEL WITH TWO ADDITIONAL LEVELS (LEVEL-1 AND LEVEL-2)

In this section, we present our contributions, which consist of enriched topological relations of the RCC8 system at two additional levels using

*Table 2. Matrix of the topological relations by using the ID model compared with the RCC8 system for three graphical representations of spatial regions as: circular (icons [1]), rectangular (icons [2]), and general polygons (general icons [3])*

| ID Model | Topological Relations | RCC8 System | Icons (1) | Icons (2) | General Icons (3) |
|---|---|---|---|---|---|
| $ID(A,B)=\begin{bmatrix}\varnothing & \neg\varnothing\\ \neg\varnothing & \varnothing\end{bmatrix}$ | *Disjoint* | *Disconnected (DC)* | | | |
| $ID(A,B)=\begin{bmatrix}\varnothing & \neg\varnothing\\ \neg\varnothing & \neg\varnothing\end{bmatrix}$ | *Meet* | *Externally Connected (EC)* | | | |
| $ID(A,B)=\begin{bmatrix}\neg\varnothing & \neg\varnothing\\ \neg\varnothing & \neg\varnothing\end{bmatrix}$ | *Overlaps* | *Partially Overlapping (PO)* | | | |
| $ID(A,B)=\begin{bmatrix}\neg\varnothing & \varnothing\\ \neg\varnothing & \neg\varnothing\end{bmatrix}$ | *CoveredBy* | *Tangential Proper Part (TPP)* | | | |
| $ID(A,B)=\begin{bmatrix}\neg\varnothing & \varnothing\\ \neg\varnothing & \varnothing\end{bmatrix}$ | *ContainBy or Inside* | *Non-Tangential Proper Part (NTPP)* | | | |
| $ID(A,B)=\begin{bmatrix}\neg\varnothing & \neg\varnothing\\ \varnothing & \neg\varnothing\end{bmatrix}$ | *Covers* | *Tangential Proper Part inverse (TPPi)* | | | |
| $ID(A,B)=\begin{bmatrix}\neg\varnothing & \neg\varnothing\\ \varnothing & \varnothing\end{bmatrix}$ | *Contains* | *Non-Tangential Proper Part inverse (NTPPi)* | | | |
| $ID(A,B)=\begin{bmatrix}\neg\varnothing & \varnothing\\ \varnothing & \neg\varnothing\end{bmatrix}$ | *Equal* | *Equal (EQ)* | | | |

two principal concepts. As similar as in the works (Egenhofer, 1993; Egenhofer & Franzosa, 1995; Deng, et al., 2007), only the four relations (***EC, PO, TPP, and TPPi***) of the RCC8 system are written and described in general detailed forms at the first detailed level (***Level-1***) by using the concept of Separation Number of Spatial Elements (Points and Lines) of the Boundary-Boundary Intersection Spatial Set (BBISS) as: ***EC*** given as: $EC_{mL}$, $EC_{nP}$, $EC_{mL, nP}$; ***PO*** given as: $PO_{mL}$, $PO_{nP}$, $PO_{mL, nP}$; ***TPP*** given as: $TPP_{mLT}$, $TPP_{nPT}$, $TPP_{mLT, nPT}$; and ***TPPi*** given as: $TPPi_{mLT}$, $TPPi_{nPT}$, $TPPi_{mLT, nPT}$; where the notations (*mL*, *mLT*, *nP* and *nPT*) are the separation number of the spatial elements (for Lines: *mL*, Tangential Lines: *mLT*, for Points: *nP*, and Tangential Points: *nPT*) of the terms BBISS. Secondly, the same relations are expressed in other general forms more detailed at the second detailed level (***Level-2***) by using the concept of Types of Spatial Elements (Points and Lines) of BBISS as follwing: ***EC*** can be written as: $EC_{m(TOL)}$, $EC_{n(TOP)}$, $EC_{m(TOL), n(TOP)}$; ***PO*** can be written as:

*Figure 2. Graphical representation of spatial regions as circular (icons [1])*

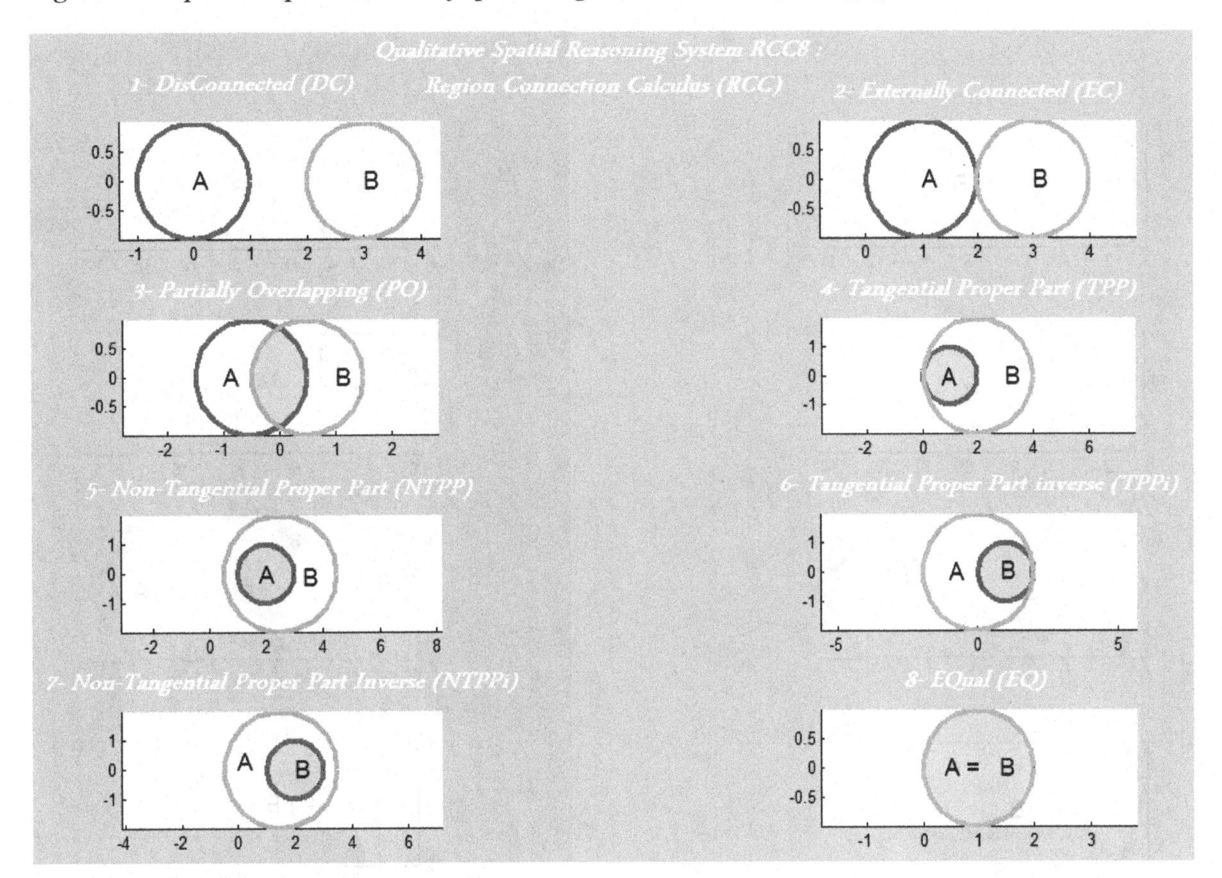


$\boldsymbol{PO}_{m(TOL)}$, $\boldsymbol{PO}_{n(TOP)}$, $\boldsymbol{PO}_{m(TOL),\, n(TOP)}$; ***TPP*** can be written as: $\boldsymbol{TPP}_{m(TOL)}$, $\boldsymbol{TPP}_{n(TOP)}$, $\boldsymbol{TPP}_{m(TOL),\, n(TOP)}$; and ***TPPi*** can be written as: $\boldsymbol{TPPi}_{m(TOL)}$, $\boldsymbol{TPPi}_{n(TOP)}$, $\boldsymbol{TPPi}_{m(TOL),\, n(TOP)}$; where the notations *m(TOL)* and *n(TOP)* are the separation number of the types of spatial elements (for Lines and Tangential Lines: *m[TOL],* for Points and Tangential Points: *n[TOP])* of the terms BBISS.

## Topological Models at the Detailed Level

Qualitative spatial representation and reasoning is necessary in spatial data mining, spatial reasoning, the GIS spatial analysis (Schultz, et al., 2006), satellite image inetrpretation (Inglada & Michel, 2009), Geospatial Semantic Web (Wang, et al., 2006), detection of topological changes (Alboody, et al., 2008) and topological inconsistency. It often needs detailed topological relations and to describe the topological equivalence of two spatial configurations as studied in the works (Egenhofer, 1993; Egenhofer & Franzosa, 1995; Deng, et al., 2007).

In the objective to distuingish further details about topological relations, the concept of the *dimension* and the *separation number* are used in the works of Egenhofer (1993) and Egenhofer and Franzosa (1995) to refine the invariants of *4-intersection model*, so that the spatial configurations with different dimensions and numbers of connected components in the intersection set between boundaries of two spatial regions can be discriminated. The distinction between empty and non-empty intersection is called ***content invariant***, as a property topological of *4-intersection model.*

*Figure 3. Graphical representation of spatial regions as rectangular (icons [2])*

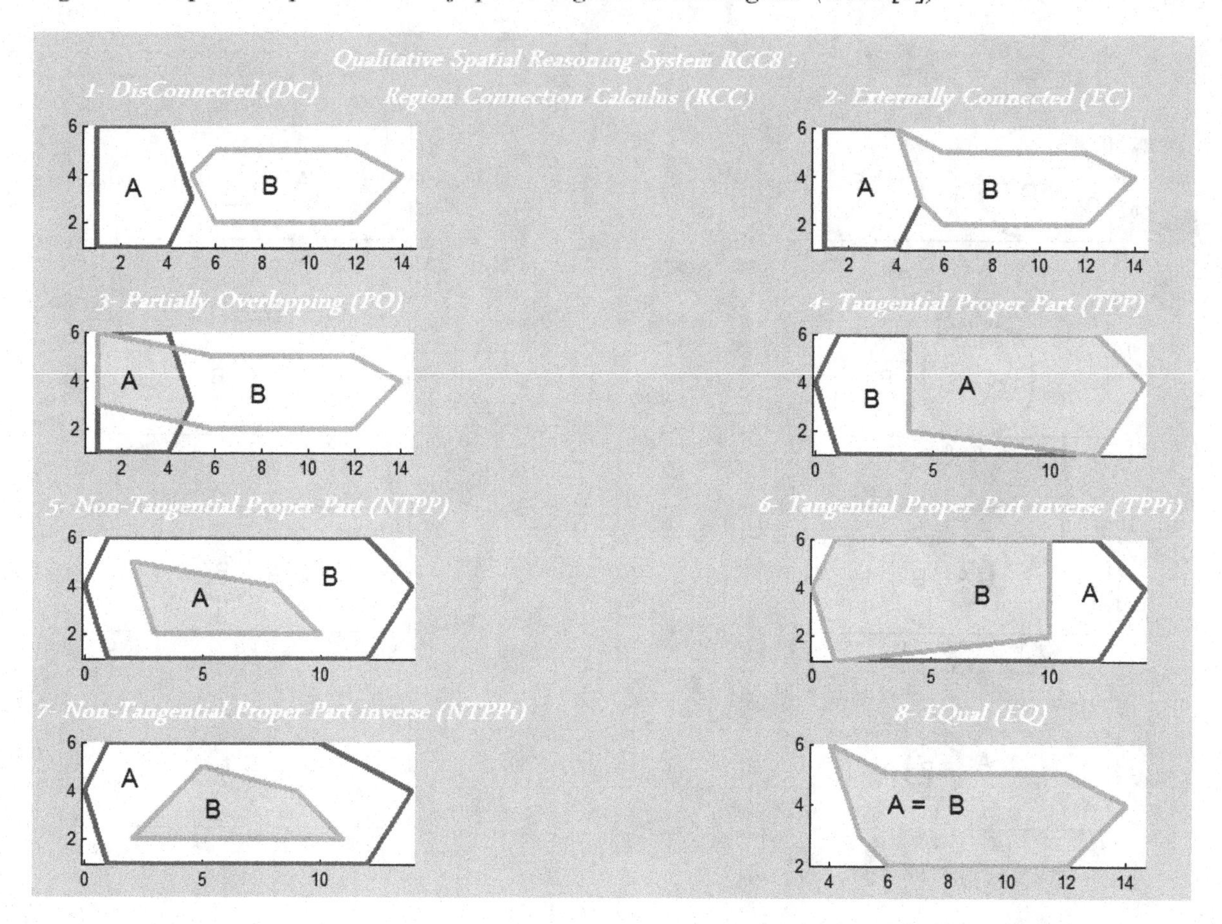


To better describe the topological equivalence of two spatial configurations, Egenhofer (1993), Egenhofer and Franzosa (1995) have developed a set of topological invariants (*dimension, sequence, type, complement relationship, boundedness,* and *crossing direction*) for more detailed description of the topological relations between spatial regions. At the detailed level, among the detailed relations taking into account various dimensions of the non-empty boundary-boundary intersection are given as following: ***EC*** (***Meet***) relation into ***0D-Meet*** and ***1D-Meet*** as in (a) and (b) of Figure 5., ***PO*** (***Overlaps***) relation into ***0D-Overlaps*** and ***1D-Overlaps*** as in (c) and (d) of Figure 5., ***TPP*** (***CoveredBy***) relation into ***0D-CoveredBy*** and ***1D-CoveredBy*** as in (e) and (f) of Figure 5., ***TPPi*** (***Covers***) relation into ***0D-Covers*** and ***1D-Covers*** as in (g) and (h) of Figure 5., where ***0D*** and ***1D*** refers to ***"0"*** and ***"1"*** dimensions of intersection set between boundaries, respectively as in (Egenhofer, 1989 & 1993). Only, the four relations: ***EC*** (***Meet***), ***PO*** (***Overlaps***), ***TPP*** (***CoveredBy***), and ***TPPi*** (***Covers***) are detailed.

However, there are two aspects of problems on those invariants (Egenhofer & Franzosa, 1995). On the one hand, parts of invariants (such as ***inner/outer crossing*** and ***into/out of crossing***) is heavily incompatible to fundamental property of topological invariant that excludes any consideration of region geometry, such as size, shape, distance and direction; on the other hand, it is very difficult to define those invariants formally. Unfortunately, parts of the defined topological invariants are closely related to the assumed ori-

*Figure 4. Graphical representation of spatial regions as general polygons (general icons [3])*

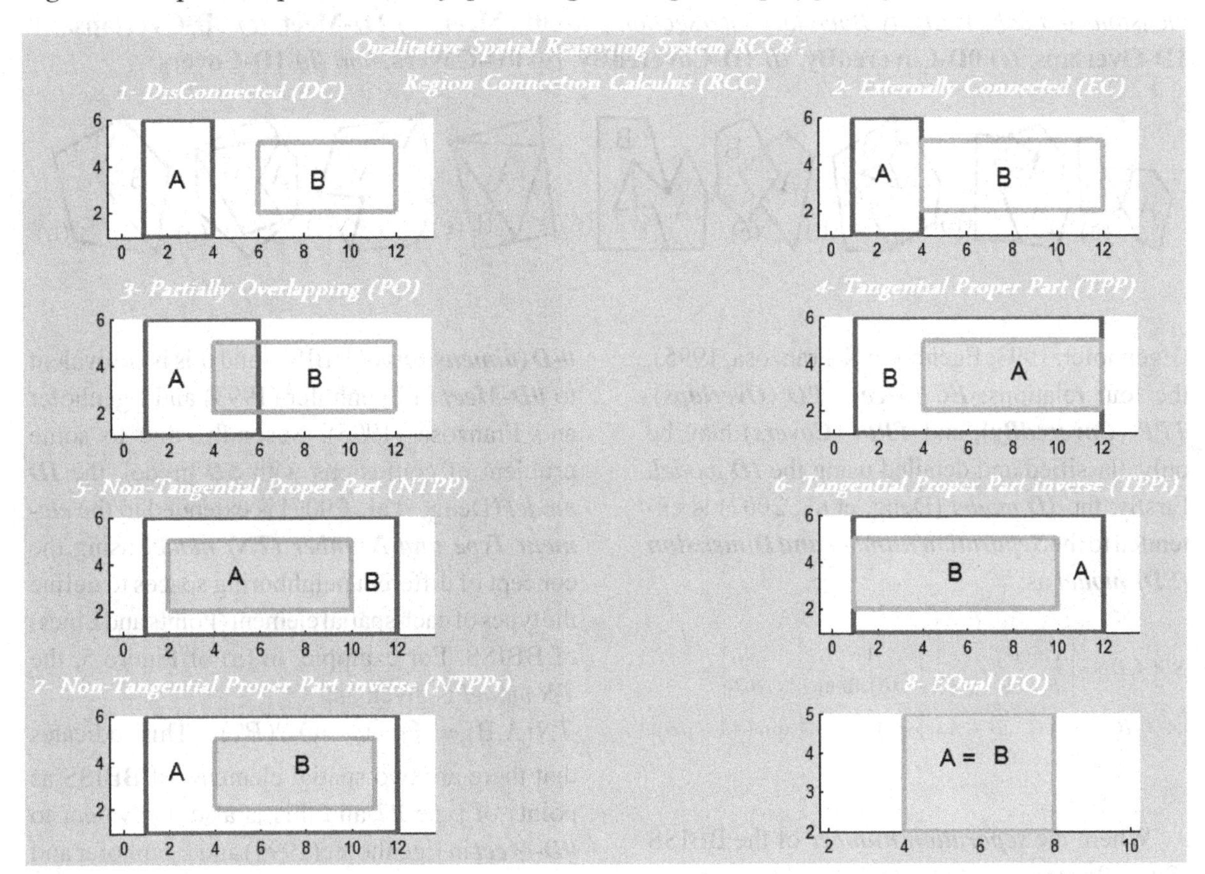


entations of regions themselves and their configurations (Egenhofer & Franzosa, 1995).

As shown in (a) of Figure 6, both intersection components ***C0*** and ***C1*** are distinguished as ***into crossing*** and ***out of crossing***, while the description results would be contrary if different orientations are assigned to a spatial configuration presented in (b) of Figure 6 (Egenhofer & Franzosa, 1995). In fact, types of these two components are of same topology, that is, they are same type of components. In addition, the priority and hierarchy of the defined topological invariants are not given, so that it is difficult to decide when and how to apply what invariants for need of topological relations in a given application.

Recently, in the paper of Deng et al. (2007), they have proposed the ***Intersection and Diffrence (ID) model*** at two levels. The ***Intersection and Difference model*** at the *coarse level* is a new version of *4-intersection model*. It has more topological information to be associated with the models at the detailed level. Therefore, in this work, a multi-level modeling approach is proposed to describe all the details necessary for region-region relations based upon topological invariants. In this approach, a set of invariants topological relations is defined based upon the boundary-boundary intersection. Five types of topological invariants are defined in Deng et al. (2007) from a ***spatial set***, including the ***separation number*** and the ***dimension*** of a spatial set and the ***dimension*** of each spatial element, the ***neighborhoods*** for each spatial element with its types and the ***holistic sequence*** (Deng, et al., 2007). At the detailed level, the ***ID*** *model* is extended to three levels using these five types. Also as in the works

*Figure 5. Examples of the Detailed Relations Between Two Spatial Regions Considering Different Dimensions in the Non-Empty Boundary intersections: (a)* **0D-Meet***, (b)* **1D-Meet***, (c)* **0D-Overlaps***, (d)* **1D-Overlaps***, (e)* **0D-CoveredBy***, (f)* **1D-CoveredBy***, (g)* **0D-Covers***, and (h)* **1D-Covers**

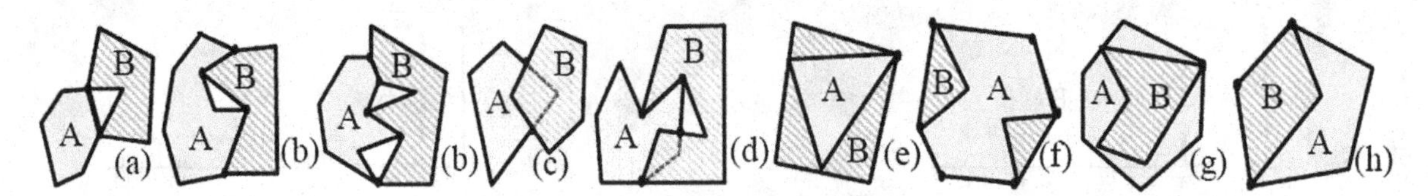


(Egenhofer, 1993; Egenhofer & Franzosa, 1995), the four relations: ***EC*** ***(Meet)***, ***PO*** ***(Overlaps)***, ***TPP*** ***(CoveredBy)***, and ***TPPi*** ***(Covers)*** may be only classified and detailed using the ***ID*** *model*. Firstly, the ***ID*** *model* (Deng, et al., 2007) is extended to the ***Separation number and Dimension (SD) model*** as:

$$SD(A,B) = \begin{bmatrix} A^{\circ} \cap B^{\circ} & A - B \\ B - A & \chi(\partial A \cap \partial B), \dim(\partial A \cap \partial B) \end{bmatrix} =$$
$$\left[A^{\circ} \cap B^{\circ},\ A - B,\ B - A,\ \chi(\partial A \cap \partial B),\ \dim(\partial A \cap \partial B)\right]$$

Where the ***separation number*** of the BBISS *(∂A∩∂B)* is $\chi(\partial A \cap \partial B)$, and the ***dimension*** of the BBISS is ***dim(∂A∩∂B)*** as similar as in (Egenhofer & Franzosa, 1995). For example, in (a) of Figure 5, the ***SD*** *model* is given as: $SD(A,B) = [\varnothing,\ \neg\varnothing,\ \neg\varnothing, 2, 0]$. This indicates that there are two spatial elements of BBISS with ***0-D*** ***(dimensions*** of BBISS) and this is equivalent to ***0D-Meet*** in Egenhofer (1993) and Egenhofer and Franzosa (1995). Secondly, due to some problem of confusions with ***SD*** model, the ***ID*** *model* (Deng, et al., 2007) is extended to the ***element Type and Number (TN) model*** using the concept of different neighboring spaces to define the types of each spatial element (Points and Lines) of BBISS. For example, in (a) of Figure 5, the ***TN*** *model* is given as: $TN(A,B) = [\varnothing, \neg\varnothing, \neg\varnothing, 2(P7)]$. This indicates that there are two spatial elements of BBISS as points of type P7 and this is also equivalent to ***0D-Meet*** in Egenhofer (1993) and Egenhofer and Franzosa (1995). Thirdly, in order to take into consideration the order of each spatial element (Points and Lines), the ***ID*** *model* (Deng, et al., 2007) is extended to the ***SequenCe (SC) model*** at the integrated level. For example, in (a) of Figure 5, the ***SC*** *model* is given as:

*Figure 6. Identification of* **into crossing** *and* **out of crossing** *associated with the setting of the plane* **orientation***, where* **C0** *is identified as* **into crossing***,* **C1** *as* **out of crossing** *in (a), while the results are inverse in (b)*

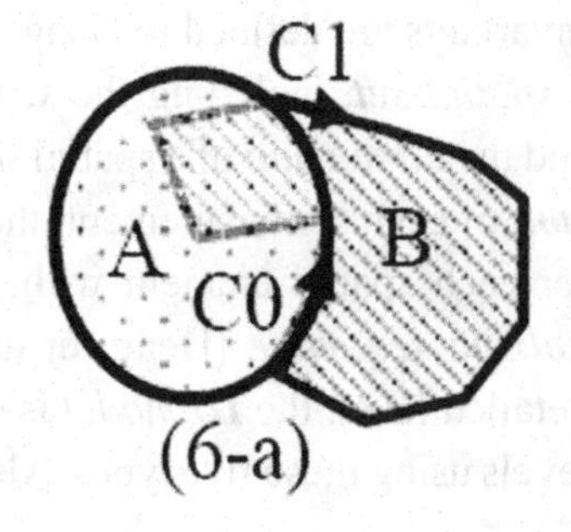


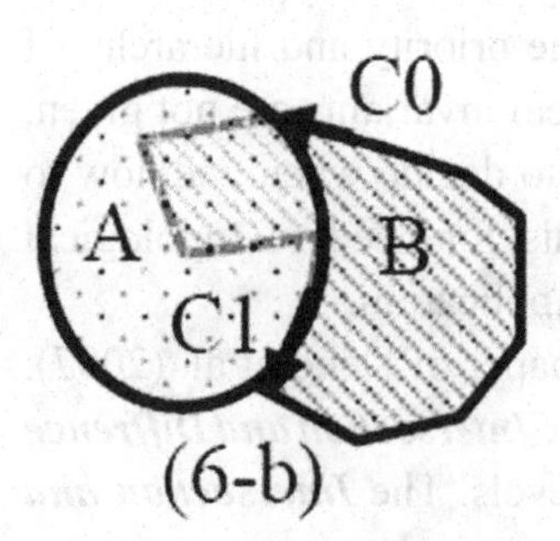

*Figure 7. Example: how to detect the topological changes at the detailed level*

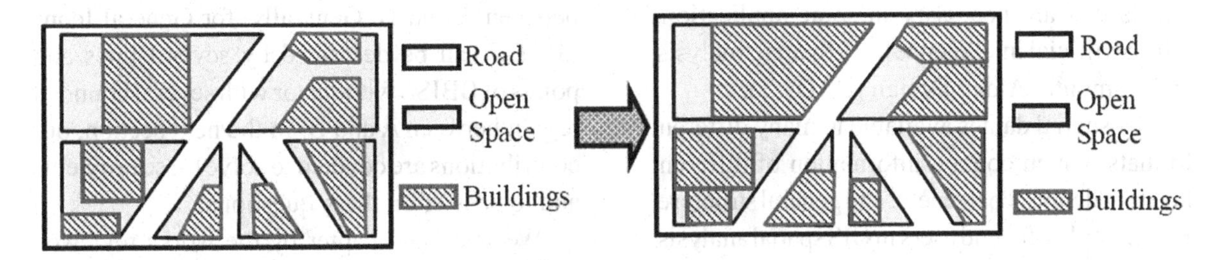


$SC(\mathrm{A,B}) = [\varnothing, \neg\varnothing, \neg\varnothing, 1(P7), 2(P7)]$. This indicates that there are two spatial elements of BBISS as points of type P7 with the following order: (1) the first point is a point of type P7 and (2) the second point is also a point of type P7 (refers to Deng, et al., 2007), and this is also equivalent to ***0D-Meet*** in Egenhofer (1993) and Egenhofer and Franzosa (1995).

Finally, from the above investigation about the topological models at the detailed level and as in Egenhofer (1993), Egenhofer and Franzosa (1995), and Deng et al. (2007), these four relations ***EC (Meet)***, ***PO (Overlaps)***, ***TPP (CoveredBy)***, and ***TPPi (Covers)*** are not generalized and easily detailed in simple forms to understand with their topological names (***EC, PO, TPP, and TPPi***). For example, in Egenhofer (1993) and Egenhofer and Franzosa (1995) the detailed relation ***EC (Meet)*** is written in the form ***0D-Meet, 1D-Meet***. While in Deng et al. (2007), the spatial elements of boundary-boundary intersection are defined to detail these four relations with three levels under very complicated forms to understand. For example, the relation ***EC (Meet)*** is written, firstly, for the ***dimension*** and the ***separation number*** at the set level as $SD(A,B) = [\varnothing,\ \neg\varnothing,\ \neg\varnothing,1,1]$ equivalent to ***1D-Meet*** and $SD(A,B) = [\varnothing,\ \neg\varnothing,\ \neg\varnothing,2,0]$ equivalent to ***0D-Meet***; and secondly, for the ***element type*** at the element level as $TN(\mathrm{A,B}) = [\varnothing, \neg\varnothing, \neg\varnothing, 2(L11)]$ equivalent to ***1D-Meet***, and $TN(\mathrm{A,B}) = [\varnothing, \neg\varnothing, \neg\varnothing, 2(P7)]$ equivalent to ***0D-Meet***; and thirdly the ***sequence*** at the integrated level as $SC(\mathrm{A,B}) = [\varnothing,\neg\varnothing,\neg\varnothing,1(P7),2(L12)]$ equivalent to ***1D-Meet***, and $SC(\mathrm{A,B}) = [\varnothing,\neg\varnothing,\neg\varnothing,1(P7),2(P7)]$ equivalent to ***0D-Meet***.

Unfortunately, the concept of separation number of each spatial element (points and lines) of BBISS, certain types of spatial elements (points and lines) of BBISS with the separation number of intersection regions ($RI = A^{\circ} \cap B^{\circ}$) and bounded regions between two spatial regions are neither defined nor taken into account in these works. Even the expressions of these relations are poorly detailed and difficult to understand. Finally, at the detailed level, the ***ID*** *model* is better than the *4-intersection model* (Deng, et al., 2007). For that, we will take the ***ID*** *model* in our work in this chapter. Also, we will search to find solutions for these desadvantages and problems of these reviewed works (Egenhofer, 1993; Egenhofer & Franzosa, 1995; Deng, et al., 2007) in order to find easily forms to describe in details the topological relations of the RCC8 system.

## Motivation and Applications

GIS is becoming increasingly popular methods of representing and reasoning with geographical data. In order to do this, we require approaches that will allow spatial reasoning such as RCC8 to be used at the detailed level. More importantly, there are needs to use topological models which are able to differentiate not only the eight basic topological relations, but also more topological details that are necessary in some applications (GIS, Artificial Intelligence [AI], Spatial Analysis, and Computer Aided Design [CAD]...).

Geospatial data is available in many different formats, which contain information of different levels of details, coarseness, and general structure. For examples, for end users in GIS spatial analysis, questions such as: "*how many times two regions touch*?" and, "*are the two regions points touch or lines touch or together*?" These questions will be easily answered by means of the separation number and the type of spatial elements of the boundary-boundary intersection for four relations of the RCC8 system.

Firstly, we take this example given in Figure 7. One can find the changes in geometry of "*Buildings*" and "*Open space*," which may be caused by data uncertainty due to measurement error, acquisition means, and/or cartographic scale, or caused by a real change of the location and shape of "*Buildings*" and "*Open space*" in reality with time. Such geometric change further leads to the topological changes in details. The end users need to know how topological details change.

Secondly, The RCC8 system consists of eight relations. In the literature, we find that the spatial regions under several representations (see Table 2. and Figures 2, 3, and 4) are also poorly studied under general polygonal representations (Figure 4, and General Icons 3) at the detailed level.

The main problem that arises on relations represented by these graphical representations in Table 2 (Icons [1], Icons [2], and General Icons [3]) and Figures (2, 3, and 4 is: what are the differences between the relations of the same kind between its representations? For example, how to differentiate and define in details the ***EC*** relation for all its graphical representations in Table 2?; From the topological point of view, we find that for the ***EC*** relation: for Icons (1), ***EC*** is described only by one point of BBISS; and for Icons (2), ***EC*** is described only by one line of BBISS; and for General Icons (3), ***EC*** is described by two lines and one point of BBISS with one bounded region between A and B. Generally, for General Icons (3), ***EC*** can be described by several lines and points of BBISS without /or with several bounded region between A and B. In the next section, our contributions are devoted to solve these problems and to answer on these questions.

We start our chapter by the works reviewed herein which serves as a basis for the extension of the ***ID*** *model* studied in the topological models as a basis of the RCC8 system at the coarse level and at the detailed level. In order to explain the extension of the ***ID*** *model*, topological invariants such as the concept of *seperation number* and the *types of spatial elements* (points and lines) of BBISS are firstly studied.

Thereafter, at the first detailed level using the concept of *Separation Number of Spatial Elements* (Points and Lines) of BBISS, the extension of ***ID*** *model* is used to generalize the four relations ***EC, PO, TPP, and TPPi*** under general detailed forms. We will develop definitions for the generalization of these detailed relations with some examples. The major contribution is the generalization of new detailed topological relations written under detailed forms at the first level (***Level-1***): ***EC*** given as: $EC_{mL}$, $EC_{nP}$, $EC_{mL,\,nP}$; ***PO*** given as: $PO_{mL}$, $PO_{nP}$, $PO_{mL,\,nP}$; ***TPP*** given as: $TPP_{mLT}$, $TPP_{nPT}$, $TPP_{mLT,\,nPT}$; and ***TPPi*** given as: $TPPi_{mLT}$, $TPPi_{nPT}$, $TPPi_{mLT,\,nPT}$; where the notations (*mL*, *mLT*, *nP* and *nPT*) are the separation number of the spatial elements (for Lines: *mL*, Tangential Lines: *mLT*, for Points: *nP*, and Tangential Points: *nPT*) of the terms BBISS as in our contributions (Alboody, et al., 2009a, 2009b). Some problems of confusions between relations of the same kind (***EC, PO, TPP, and TPPi***) will lead us to define the types of points and lines of BBISS, for more details about these topological relations in general at the second detailed level.

At the second detailed level (***Level-2***) using the types of points and lines of BBISS, the new detailed topological relations will be detailed with the types of spatial elements of BBISS and they will be written under these three general detailed forms: $(Topological\_Relation)_{m(Type\_Of\_Lines)}$, $(Topological\_Relation)_{n(Type\_Of\_Points)}$, and $(Topological\_Relation)_{m(Type\_Of\_Lines),\ n(Type\_Of\_Points)}$; where the notation $Topological\_Relation$ is one of the four topological relations of the RCC8 system: ***EC, PO, TPP and TPPi*** as in our paper (Alboody, et al., 2009b).

In other expressions, the same four relations are expressed in other general forms more detailed at the second detailed level (***Level-2***) by using the concept of Types of Spatial Elements (Points and Lines) of BBISS as following: ***EC*** given as: $EC_{m(TOL)}$, $EC_{n(TOP)}$, $EC_{m(TOL),\ n(TOP)}$; ***PO*** given as: $PO_{m(TOL)}$, $PO_{n(TOP)}$, $PO_{m(TOL),\ n(TOP)}$; ***TPP*** given as: $TPP_{m(TOL)}$, $TPP_{n(TOP)}$, $TPP_{m(TOL),\ n(TOP)}$; and ***TPPi*** given as: $TPPi_{m(TOL)}$, $TPPi_{n(TOP)}$, $TPPi_{m(TOL),\ n(TOP)}$; where the notations *m(TOL)* and *n(TOP)* are the separation number of the types of spatial elements (for Lines and Tangential Lines: *m(TOL),* and for Points and Tangential Points: *n(TOP))* of the terms BBISS as in our work (Alboody, et al., 2009b).

## Properties of Topological Relations and Topological Invariants for the Extension of ID Model

In the ***ID*** *model* proposed by Deng et al. (2007) which consists of two intersection sets ($A^\circ \cap B^\circ$) and ($\partial A \cap \partial B$); and two difference sets (*A-B*) and (*B-A*). This ***ID*** *model* can distinguish the eight relations of the RCC8 system and can be represented by the matrix:

$$ID(A,B) = \begin{bmatrix} A^\circ \cap B^\circ & A - B \\ B - A & \partial A \cap \partial B \end{bmatrix} = \left[A^\circ \cap B^\circ,\ A - B,\ B - A,\ \partial A \cap \partial B\right]$$

Next, we study the properties of topological relations extracted by using the ***ID*** *model* to show that the ***ID*** *model* is sound and effective for describing these eight relations of the RCC8 system.

## Properties of Topological Relations

We study the properties of topological relations extracted by using the ***ID*** *model.* Based upon the ***ID*** *model*, the properties of topological relations can be formally analyzed like in the 9-intersection model (Egenhofer, 1991, 1994).

For this study about the properties of topological relations, we suppose that: ($I\,[^\circ, {}^\circ] = A^\circ \cap B^\circ$) refers to the ***Interior-Interior Intersection*** between A and B; and ($D^1[-, -] = A-B$) refers to the ***First Difference*** between A and B; and ($D^2[-, -] = B-A$) refers to the ***Second Difference*** between B and A; and ($I\,[\partial, \partial] = \partial A \cap \partial B$) refers to the ***Boundary-Boundary Intersection*** between A and B. Where ***I*** indicates the ***Intersection*** of interiors or boundaries between A and B; meanwhile ***D*** indicates the ***Difference*** between A and B or B and A.

Then, the ***ID*** *model* can be written by the matrix:

$$ID(A,B) = \begin{bmatrix} A^\circ \cap B^\circ & A - B \\ B - A & \partial A \cap \partial B \end{bmatrix} = \left[A^\circ \cap B^\circ,\ A - B,\ B - A,\ \partial A \cap \partial B\right] = \left[I\,[^\circ, {}^\circ],\ D^1[-,-],\ D^2[-,-],\ I\,[\partial, \partial]\right]$$

A ***topological relation R*** between two spatial regions A and B is ***symmetric if and only if:*** *(A-B = B-A) or ($D^1[-, -] = D^2[-, -]$)* in terms of empty or non-empty values. For example, the $\boldsymbol{R_{Overlaps}}$ ***(PO)*** relation is ***symmetric*** because: *(($D^1[-, -] = \neg\emptyset$) = ($D^2[-, -] = \neg\emptyset$))*. From Table 2., the ***symmetric*** relations are $\boldsymbol{R_{Disjoint}}$, $\boldsymbol{R_{Meet}}$, $\boldsymbol{R_{Overlaps}}$ and $\boldsymbol{R_{Equal}}$. In other words, the topological relations ***DC, EC, PO,*** and ***EQ*** are ***symmetric.***

A ***topological relation R*** is ***non- symmetric if and only if***: *(A-B ≠ B-A) or ($D^1[-, -] \neq D^2[-, -]$)* in terms of empty or non-empty values. For example, the $\boldsymbol{R_{Inside}}$ or $\boldsymbol{R_{ConatainedBy}}$ ***(NTPP)*** topological relation is ***non-symmetric*** because: *(($D^1[-, -] = \emptyset$) ≠ ($D^2[-, -] = \neg\emptyset$))*. From Table 2., the ***non-symmetric*** relations are $\boldsymbol{R_{CoveredBy}}$, $\boldsymbol{R_{Inside}}$, $\boldsymbol{R_{Covers}}$ and $\boldsymbol{R_{Contains}}$.

The topological relations ***TPP, NTPP, TPPi,*** and ***NTPPi*** are ***non-symmetric*** (from Table 2).

***Likewise, two topological relations $R_n$,*** and ***$R_m$*** (with ($1 \leq n \leq 8$, and $1 \leq m \leq 8$) and here refers to one of the eight topological relations of the RCC8 system) are ***converse if and only if:*** $(I_n\,[\partial, \partial] = I_m\,[\partial, \partial])$ ^ $(I_n\,[°, °] = I_m\,[°, °])$ ^ $(D^1_n\,[-, -] \neq D^1_m\,[-, -])$ ^ $(D^2_n\,[-, -] \neq D^2_m\,[-, -])$; where "^" refers to the logical operator ***"and"***. For example, from Table 2., ***$R_{Inside}$*** ***(NTPP)*** and ***$R_{Contains}$*** ***(NTPPi)*** (with ***n = 5*** and ***m = 7***) are ***converse*** because: $(I_5\,[\partial, \partial] = \emptyset = I_7\,[\partial, \partial])$ ^ $(I_5\,[°, °] = \neg\emptyset = I_7\,[°, °])$ ^ $((D^1_5\,[-, -] = \emptyset) \neq (D^1_7\,[-, -] = \neg\emptyset))$ ^ $((D^2_5\,[-, -] = \neg\emptyset) \neq (D^2_7\,[-, -] = \emptyset))$.

The other pair of ***converse*** relations is ***$R_{Covers}$*** ***(TPPi)*** and ***$R_{CoveredBy}$*** ***(TPP)*** because: $(I_4\,[\partial, \partial] = \neg\emptyset = I_6\,[\partial, \partial])$ ^ $(I_4\,[°, °] = \neg\emptyset = I_6\,[°, °])$ ^ $((D^1_4\,[-, -] = \emptyset) \neq (D^1_6\,[-, -] = \neg\emptyset))$ ^ $((D^2_4\,[-, -] = \neg\emptyset) \neq (D^2_6\,[-, -] = \emptyset))$. The ***converse*** pairs of topological relations are ***$R_{Covers}$ (TPPi) and $R_{CoveredBy}$ (TPP), $R_{Inside}$ (NTPP), and $R_{Contains}$ (NTPPi).***

The four ***empty/non-empty*** intersections and differences of the ***ID** model* describe a set of relations that provides a complete coverage of the RCC8 system. Furthermore, these eight relations are also ***Jointly Exhaustive and Pairwise Disjoint*** (***JEPD***). Where a ***JEPD*** relation means that for any two definite spatial regions, only one relation can be satisfied in the relation set of RCC8 system. From this study about the properties of topological relations, we can classify the topological relations of the RCC8 system defined by the ***ID** model* as given as in the next.

The ***principal and sufficient conditions*** to discriminate the eight topological relations of the RCC8 system, which are determined using the ***ID** model* (see Table 2.), are summarized as follows:

1. The topological relation is ***DC***: ***if and only if*** $(I\,[°, °] = A° \cap B° = \emptyset)$ ^ $(I\,[\partial, \partial] = \partial A \cap \partial B = \emptyset)$
2. The topological relation is ***EC***: ***if and only if*** $(I\,[°, °] = A° \cap B° = \emptyset)$ ^ $(I\,[\partial, \partial] = \partial A \cap \partial B = \neg\emptyset)$
3. The topological relation is ***PO***: ***if and only if*** $(I\,[°, °] = A° \cap B° = \neg\emptyset)$ ^ $(D^1[-, -] = A\text{-}B = \neg\emptyset)$ ^ $(D^2[-, -] = B\text{-}A = \neg\emptyset)$
4. The topological relation is ***TPP***: ***if and only if*** $(I\,[\partial, \partial] = \partial A \cap \partial B = \neg\emptyset)$ ^ $(D^1[-, -] = A\text{-}B = \emptyset)$ ^ $(D^2[-, -] = B\text{-}A = \neg\emptyset)$
5. The topological relation is ***NTPP***: ***if and only if*** $(I\,[\partial, \partial] = \partial A \cap \partial B = \emptyset)$ ^ $(D^1[-, -] = A\text{-}B = \emptyset)$
6. The topological relation is ***TPPi***: ***if and only if*** $(I\,[\partial, \partial] = \partial A \cap \partial B = \neg\emptyset)$ ^ $(D^1[-, -] = A\text{-}B = \neg\emptyset)$ ^ $(D^2[-, -] = B\text{-}A = \emptyset)$
7. The topological relation is ***NTPPi***: ***if and only if*** $(I\,[\partial, \partial] = \partial A \cap \partial B = \emptyset)$ ^ $(D^2[-, -] = B\text{-}A = \emptyset)$
8. The topological relation is ***EQ***: ***if and only if*** $(D^1[-, -] = A\text{-}B = \emptyset)$ ^ $(D^2[-, -] = B\text{-}A = \emptyset)$

It was shown that the ***ID** model* is sound and effective for describing these eight relations of RCC8. In spatial analysis and query languages, there may be a need for more topological details. For that, a concept of spatial set and topological invariants is developed in Deng et al. (2007). Therefore, this section is devoted to develop the topological invariants to be included in the extension of the ***ID** model* to provide more information about the detailed topological relations.

## The Concept of Spatial Set

For spatial object as building, it is treated as a set in the GIS spatial analysis. The concept of spatial set for representation of spatial regions is developed in Deng et al. (2007). A spatial set is considered a special set of certain properties related to the spatial location. Let S be a spatial set with its elements $s_1, s_2 ..., s_i ... s_N$, , then, we can express this spatial set defined as $S = \{s_1, s_2 ..., s_i ... s_N\}$ where $s_i (1 \leq i \leq N)$ is called a *spatialelement*, and these elements must satisfy the two following conditions: (1) $s_i \cap \overline{s_j} = \emptyset$ for $1 \leq i, j \leq N$ and

*Table 3. Example about the concept of separation number and subspaces neighbors of spatial elements (points: P1 and P2) of BBISS for Figure 8*

| Figure 8 | Separation Number of BBISS | Neighboring Subspaces of Spatial Elements |
|---|---|---|
| (a) | $r = 5, n = 3, m = 1, k = 1, j = 1$ | For Point *P1*: *(A-B)*, *(A°∩B°)* and $(A \cup B)^-_{ub}$ |
| (b) | $r = 6, n = 2, m = 2, k = 2, j = 1$ | For Point *P2*: *(A-B)*, *(B-A)*, $(A \cup B)^-_b$ and $(A \cup B)^-_{ub}$ |

i ≠ j, $\overline{s_j}$ is the closure of $s_j$; (2) $s_i (1 \le i \le N)$ is a spatial element of S.

## Topological Invariants

**The Concept of Separation Number:** By definition, all the elements in a spatial set are separated each other in spatial distribution. From the view of topology, number of spatial elements in a spatial set can be regarded as a measure of separability of the spatial set, called as the ***Separation Number*** of a spatial set. Then, the spatial set ($S = \partial A \cap \partial B$) of boundary-boundary intersection between two spatial regions is called the *Boundary-Boundary Intersection Spatial Set (BBISS) of separation* and *the separation number of BBISS* is denoted by $r = \chi(\partial A \cap \partial B)$ (Egenhofer, 1993; Deng, et al., 2007).

In our work, we will search the separation number of the spatial elements (points and lines) of BBISS by using the separation number defined by $r = \chi(\partial A \cap \partial B)$ as in Deng et al. (2007). The BBISS consists of points and lines. In order to separate between these points and lines from the separation number $r = \chi(\partial A \cap \partial B)$, we determine the ***separation number of points*** of BBISS as $n = \chi(\partial A \cap \partial B)_P$ and ***lines*** of BBISS as $m = \chi(\partial A \cap \partial B)_L$ (see Table 3). We introduce the separation number $k = \chi((A \cup B)^-_b)$ of ***Bounded Regions*** (***R***) defined as the number of bounded regions; and the separation number $j = \chi(A^\circ \cap B^\circ)$ of ***Intersection Regions*** (***RI***) defined as the number of intersection regions. These separation numbers will be used to detail and enrich the topological relations.

The ***Intersection Regions (RI)*** represents the intersection regions obtained by ($A^\circ \cap B^\circ$). The ***Bounded Regions (R)*** $(A \cup B)^-_b$ represent an exterior space with a bounded region between A and B. While the ***UnBounded Region*** $(A \cup B)^-_{ub}$ represents an exterior space with an unbounded region as shown as in Figure 8. The ***ID*** *model*, unbounded region, bounded regions (***R***) and intersection regions (***RI***) are shown in Figure 8. In Table 3, the separation numbers "*r, n, m, k, j*" for both cases (8-a) and (8-b) in Figure 8 are given.

In this part, the separation number is defined to enrich the topological relations. We will detail and generalize the four relations ***EC, PO, TPP, and TPPi*** based upon the separation number. Definitions will be developed for the generalization of the detailed relations of ***EC, PO, TPP, and TPPi***.

**The Concept of Neighborhoods of a Spatial Element:** In the point set topology, the definition of topology is built upon the concept of neighborhood. Therefore, the topology of a spatial element can be distinguished based on its neighboring subspaces. In order to make a general identification of all neighbors of spatial elements, all possible neighbors are defined in five *neighborhoods subspaces* (or *Neighboring Subspaces*) as *(A-B)*, *(B-A)*, *(A°∩B°)*, $(A \cup B)^-_{ub}$ and $(A \cup B)^-_b$ shown in (a) and (b) in Figure 8 and also taken in Deng et al. (2007). This notion of neighborhood will be used to define the type of spatial elements (points and lines) of BBISS. The notion of neighborhoods

*Figure 8. Graphical representation of the ID model, bounded regions (R), and intersection regions (RI) with the neighborhoods of spatial elements (points: P1 and P2) of BBISS*

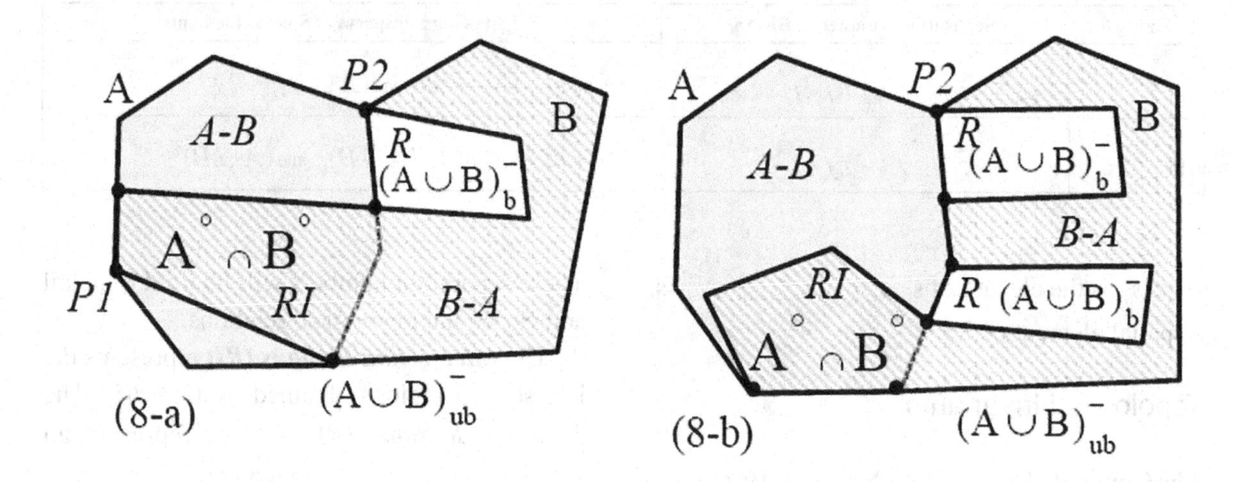


with the ***ID model*** is shown in Figure 8. Based upon this concept of neighborhood (neighboring subspaces), we will find the ***Types of Spatial Elements*** (Points and Lines) of BBISS as applied in Deng et al. (2007).

The topological invariant called the separation number has been defined. This invariant is needed to enrich the topological relations at the first level (***Level-1***). Meanwhile, the concept of neighborhoods of spatial elements of BBISS will be used to define their types. Then, the topological relations will be detailed at the second level (***Level-2***) by using the concept of type spatial element. In the next section, we will detail and generalize the four relations ***EC, PO, TPP, and TPPi*** of the RCC8 system under two additional levels (***Level-1*** and ***Level-2***) based upon the separation number and the type element. Definitions will be developed for the generalization of theses detailed relations as in our papers (Alboody, et al., 2009a, 2009b).

## Contributions: Multi-Level Topological Relations of the RCC8 System

In our contributions (Alboody, et al., 2009a, 2009b), the topological relations of the RCC8 system are written under three levels by using the concept of the *Separation Number* and the *Types of Spatial Elements* of the Boundary-Boundary Intersection Spatial Set (BBISS) as following:

### At the Level-0: Topological Relations at the Coarse Level without Any Details

At the coarse level by using the ***ID model*** (Deng, et al., 2007; Alboody, et al., 2009a, 2009b), the topological relations of the RCC8 system are written without any details in the form: ***DC, EC, PO, TPP, NTPP, TPPi, NTPPi, and EQ,*** or with the names of: ***DisConnected (Disjoint), Externally Connected (Meet), Partial Overlap (Overlaps), Tangential Proper Part (CoveredBy), Non-Tangential Proper Part (Covers), Tangential Proper Part inverse (ContainedBy or Inside), Non-Tangential Proper Part inverse (Contains), and Equally (Equal).*** We call the coarse level by the ***Level-0*** (Alboody, et al., 2009a, 2009b). In the next part, at the detailed level, the fundamental approach is to utilize topological invariants for detailed description of topological relations where four relations ***EC, PO, TPP, and TPPi*** will be detailed by the extension of ***ID model*** based upon the concept of separation number and the types of spatial elements (Points and Lines) of BBISS.

## At the Level-1: Topological Relations at the Detailed Level-1 Based Upon the Separation Number

In this part, we will combine the topological invariant of the ***Separation Number*** with the ***ID model*** to describe all the necessary details of topological relations at the first level. We say that the ***ID** model* is extended by the concept of separation number. In our works (Alboody, et al., 2009a, 2009b), we have been developed a part of the ***Level-1***. Here in this work as in Alboody et al. (2009a, 2009b), we identify the separation number $r = \chi(\partial A \cap \partial B)$ of BBISS. Then, we enrich the four topological relations ***EC, PO, TPP and TPPi*** of the RCC8 system at the first level (***Level-1***) based upon the seperation number of spatial elements (Points [*nP/nPT*] and Lines [*mL/mLT*]) of BBISS, and the seperation number of bounded regions (*kR*) and the seperation number of intersection regions (*RI*). These seperation numbers of Points, Lines, bounded Regions and Intersection Regions depend on the detailed topological relations of ***EC***, ***PO***, ***TPP,*** and ***TPPi,*** as we will see.

In other words, The BBISS consists of points and lines. In order to separate between these points and lines from the separation number of BBISS $r = \chi(\partial A \cap \partial B)$, we determine the separation number of points of BBISS as $n = \chi(\partial A \cap \partial B)_P$ and lines of BBISS as $m = \chi(\partial A \cap \partial B)_L$ (Refers to Alboody, et al., 2009a, 2009b).

The ***separation number*** $r = \chi(\partial A \cap \partial B)$ of BBISS is presented in general as follows:

$$r = \chi(S) = \chi(\partial A \cap \partial B) = \left\{s_1, \ldots, s_i, \ldots s_N\right\} = \left\{\begin{matrix} m : for \;\; m(Lines) \geq 1, and \;\; n(Po\inf s) = 0 \\ n : for \;\; m(Lines) = 0, and \;\; n(Po\inf s) \geq 1 \\ m + n : for \;\; m(Lines) \geq 1, and \;\; n(Po\inf s) \geq 1 \end{matrix}\right\}$$

For detailing these two relations ***EC and PO***, the BBISS is presented using the separation number of points (***nP***) and lines (***mL***) as:

$$r = \chi(S) = \chi(\partial A \cap \partial B) = \left\{s_1, \ldots, s_i, \ldots s_N\right\} = \left\{\begin{matrix} mL : for \;\; m \geq 1 \;\; and \;\; n = 0 \\ nP : for \;\; n \geq 1 \;\; and \;\; m = 0 \\ mL + nP : for \;\; m \geq 1 \;\; and \;\; n \geq 1 \end{matrix}\right\}$$

For detailing these two relations ***TPP*** and ***TPPi***, the BBISS is presented using the separation number of tangential points (***nPT***) and tangential lines (***mLT***) as:

$$r = \chi(S) = \chi(\partial A \cap \partial B) = \left\{s_1, \ldots, s_i, \ldots s_N\right\} = \left\{\begin{matrix} mLT : for \;\; m \geq 1 \;\; and \;\; n = 0 \\ nPT : for \;\; n \geq 1 \;\; and \;\; m = 0 \\ mLT + nPT : for \;\; m \geq 1 \;\; and \;\; n \geq 1 \end{matrix}\right\}$$

The relations ***EC*** and ***PO*** will be described by the separation number of Lines (***mL***) and Points (***nP***) of BBISS. The relations ***TPP*** and ***TPPi*** will be described by the separation number of Tangential Lines (***mLT***) and Tangential Points (***nPT***) of BBISS.

## Generalization of the Detailed EC Topological Relation at the Level-1

In this part, we study the enriching and detailing of the ***EC*** relation at the first level (***Level-1***) as in our papers (Alboody, et al., 2009a, 2009b). In order to study the generalization of the ***EC*** relation, we take the ***EC*** relation represented in Figure 9 with several representations. For ***EC*** relation, the bounded region (*R*) is defined as $(A \cup B)_b^-$ (see Figure 8 and Figure 9a). These regions (*R*) between A and B do not belong neither to A nor to B. In general, cases of ***EC***, there are

*Figure 9. EC topological relation in several graphical representations*

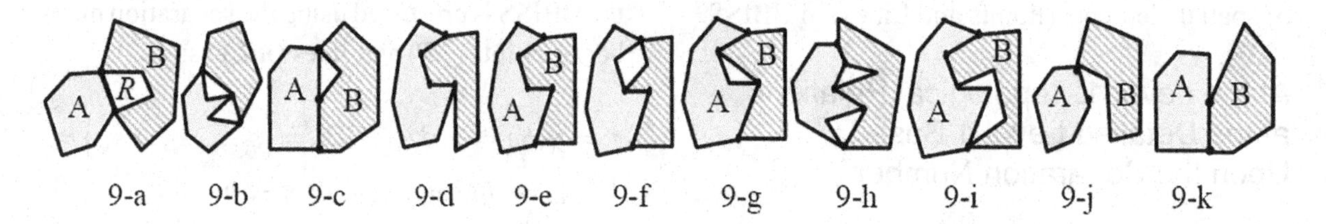


several bounded regions. To distinguish between these relations of the same kind ***EC***, which describe these different configurations, we will develop a definition to enrich and generalize these relations in details which may be externally connected in *n-different ways*.

**Definition:** *For the* **ID** *model,* **if** *the boundary-boundary intersection ($\partial A \cap \partial B$) of two spatial regions A and B is non-empty ($\neg\emptyset$), and the interior-interior intersection ($A^\circ \cap B^\circ$) of A and B is empty ($\emptyset$),* **therefore***, the topological relation between A and B is* **EC** *(***Meet***):*

$$EC(Meet) \Leftrightarrow ID(A,B) = \begin{bmatrix} A^\circ \cap B^\circ & A - B \\ B - A & \partial A \cap \partial B \end{bmatrix} = \begin{bmatrix} \emptyset & \neg\emptyset \\ \neg\emptyset & \neg\emptyset \end{bmatrix}$$

Or, based upon the properties of topological relations using the ***ID*** *model*: The topological relation is ***EC***: ***if and only if*** *($I[^\circ, ^\circ] = A^\circ \cap B^\circ = \emptyset$) ^ ($I[\partial, \partial] = \partial A \cap \partial B = \neg\emptyset$).*

Therefore, these two spatial regions of *2-dimensions* may be externally connected in *n-different ways*. In order to detail and generalize these *n-different ways* of the ***EC*** relation, it's sufficient to identify the separation number $r = \chi(\partial A \cap \partial B)$ of the spatial set BBISS ($S = \partial A \cap \partial B$), the separation number of points (***nP***) of BBISS as $n = \chi(\partial A \cap \partial B)_P$ and lines (***mL***) of BBISS as $m = \chi(\partial A \cap \partial B)_L$, and the separation number of bounded regions (***kR***) defined by $k = \chi((A \cup B)^-_b)$. Hence, for the generalization of detailed ***EC*** relation, we have three possible general cases as follows:

a. **If** we have only lines "mL" (see Figure 9d, e, g, and k) where "m" is the separation number of lines (L), **therefore**, the detailed **EC** relation is written in the general form $\mathbf{EC_{mL}}$. For more of details and information and to limit some possible confusions, the detailed relation $\mathbf{EC_{mL}}$ takes also two detailed possible cases:
   - ***Either***, *we have only lines "mL" without any bounded region (0R) (see Figure 9d, e, and k);* ***therefore***, *the detailed relation* $\mathbf{EC_{mL}}$ *is written in the general form* $\mathbf{EC_{mL, 0R}}$*, where "0R" indicates that there is no bounded region between A and B. A very simple case is the case (k) in Figure 9 where the detailed* **EC** *relation is described by one line (1L) of external connection without any bounded region (0R) and the detailed* **EC** *relation is given by the expression* $\mathbf{EC_{1L, 0R}}$.
   - ***Or***, *we have only lines "mL" with bounded regions (kR) (see Figure 9g) where "k" is the separation number of bounded regions (R) between A and B,* ***therefore***, *the detailed relation* $\mathbf{EC_{mL}}$ *is written in the general form* $\mathbf{EC_{mL, kR}}$. *For example, the case (g) in Figure 9, the detailed* **EC** *relation is described by two lines (2L) of externally connection with one bounded region (1R) and the detailed*

*Table 4. Generalization of the detailed EC topological relation at the level-1*

<table>
<tr><th rowspan="2">EC<br>Topological Relation of the RCC8 System at the Level-0</th><th colspan="2">Generalization of the Detailed EC Topological Relation at the Level-1</th></tr>
<tr><th>With Points (nP) and Lines (mL)</th><th>With Bounded Regions (kR)</th></tr>
<tr><td rowspan="7"></td><td rowspan="2">Only Lines (mL):<br>$EC_{mL}$</td><td>Without any bounded Region (0R): $EC_{mL, 0R}$</td></tr>
<tr><td>With "k" bounded Regions (kR): $EC_{mL, kR}$</td></tr>
<tr><td rowspan="2">Only Points (nP):<br>$EC_{nP}$<br>This case is always with at least one bounded Region (1R) between A and B for: $n > 1$</td><td>With only one Point "1" and without any bounded Region (0R): $EC_{1P, 0R}$</td></tr>
<tr><td>With "k" bounded Regions (kR): $EC_{nP, kR}$</td></tr>
<tr><td>Both Lines (mL) and Points (nP):<br>$EC_{mL, nP}$<br>This case is always with at least one bounded Region (1R) between A and B</td><td>With "k" bounded Regions (kR): $EC_{mL, nP, kR}$</td></tr>
</table>

*EC topological relation is given by the expression* $EC_{2L, 1R}$.

b. **If** we have only points "nP" (see Figure 9a, b, and j) where "n" is the separation number of points (P), **therefore**, the detailed **EC** relation is written under the general form $EC_{nP}$. In this case, we have two interesting cases, the first one is a very simple, and the other is a very general. In order to details this relation and eliminate some possible confusions, the detailed relation $EC_{nP}$ is generalized in these two next cases:
   - ***Either***, *we have only a single point "1P" without any bounded region (0R) (see Figure 9j), where the separation number of points is equal to "1";* ***therefore***, *the detailed relation* $EC_{nP}$ *is written always in the general form* $EC_{1P, 0R}$. *This form of relation* $EC_{nP}$ *is very simple* ***EC*** *relation of the RCC8 system.*
   - ***Or***, *we have only points "nP" with bounded regions (kR) (see Figure 9a and b). In this case, there is always at least one bounded region between A and B.* ***So***, *the detailed* $EC_{nP}$ *relation is written in the general form* $EC_{nP, kR}$ *where "k" is the separation number of bounded regions (kR). A very simple case of this relation* $EC_{nP, kR}$ *is the case (a) in Figure 9 with the separation number of points is equal to "n=2," and with one bounded region (1R) between A and B,* ***therefore***, *the detailed topological relation* $EC_{nP, kR}$ *is given by the expression* $EC_{2P, 1R}$.

c. **If** we have both lines "mL" and points "nP" (see Figure 9c, f, h, and i) where "m" is the separation number of lines (L) and "n" is the separation number of points (P), **therefore**, the detailed **EC** relation is written in the general form $EC_{mL, nP}$. In this case, there is always at least one bounded region (1R) between A and B. So, the detailed **EC** relation is written in the general form $EC_{mL, nP, kR}$ where "k" is the separation number of bounded regions (kR) between A and B. For example, the case (h) in Figure 9, the detailed **EC** relation is described by two lines (2L) and one point of externally connection with two bounded region (2R) and the detailed **EC** topological relation is given by the expression $EC_{2L, 1P, 2R}$.

In general, in very simple cases, we can see that the detailed ***EC*** topological relation is always described with at least one point (*1P*) of externally connection (as in Figure 9j) or with one line (*1L*) of externally connection (as in Figure 9k) and without any bounded region (*0R*) (see Figure 9j

Figure 10. PO topological relation in several graphical representations

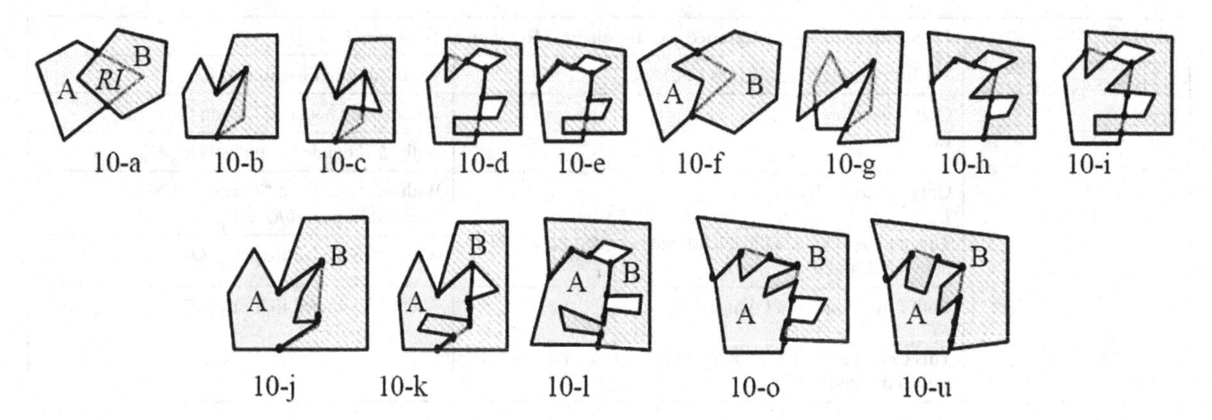


and k). The three general cases of the detailed ***EC*** topological relation at the ***Level-1*** are given in Table 4.

## Generalization of the Detailed PO Topological Relation at the Level-1

In this part, we study the enriching and detailing of the ***PO*** relation at the first level (***Level-1***) as in our papers (Alboody, et al., 2009a, 2009b). To compare relations of kind ***PO*** in various configurations, we take the ***PO*** relation represented in Figure 10 in several graphical representations. These several graphical representations, in Figure 10, may be in relation of ***partially overlapping*** in *n-different ways*.

In this case of ***PO*** relation, the Intersection Regions (***RI***) belong to A and B at the same time and they represent the interior-interior intersection ($RI = A°\cap B°$) which is non-empty set ($A°\cap B° = \neg\emptyset$) (see Figure 8 and Figure 10a). The characterization of these regions is very interesting to detail the ***PO*** relation because they provide important information to determine how the interior-interior intersection of A and B can be changed.

**Definition: If** *the four operators of the* **ID** *model are non-empty ($\neg\emptyset$),* **therefore**, *the topological relation between A and B is* **PO (Overlaps).**

$$PO, Overlaps \Leftrightarrow ID(A,B) = \begin{bmatrix} A^{\circ} \cap B^{\circ} & A - B \\ B - A & \partial A \cap \partial B \end{bmatrix} = \begin{bmatrix} \neg\emptyset & \neg\emptyset \\ \neg\emptyset & \neg\emptyset \end{bmatrix} = [\neg\emptyset]$$

Or, based upon the properties of topological relations using the ***ID*** *model*: The topological relation is ***PO***: ***if and only if*** *($I[°, °] = A°\cap B° = \neg\emptyset$) ^ ($D^1[-, -] = A\text{-}B = \neg\emptyset$) ^ ($D^2[-, -] = B\text{-}A = \neg\emptyset$).*

So, these two spatial regions of *2-dimensions* may be in relation of ***partially overlapping*** in *n-different ways*. In order to detail and generalize these *n-different ways* of the ***PO*** relation, it is sufficient to identify the points (*P*), lines (*L*) of the boundary-boundary intersection spatial set ($S = \partial A\cap\partial B$), the Intersection Regions (*RI*) defined by ($A°\cap B°$) and the bounded regions (*R*) defined by $(A \cup B)_b^-$ between A and B, with the separation number $r = \chi(\partial A \cap \partial B)$ of the spatial set BBISS ($S = \partial A\cap\partial B$), the separation number of points (***nP***) of BBISS as $n = \chi(\partial A \cap \partial B)_P$ and lines (***mL***) of BBISS as $m = \chi(\partial A \cap \partial B)_L$, the separation number of intersection regions (***jRI***) defined by $j = \chi(A^{\circ} \cap B^{\circ})$ and the separation number of bounded regions (***kR***) defined by $k = \chi((A \cup B)_b^-)$. Hence, for the generalization of the detailed ***PO*** relation, we have three possible general cases as follows:

a. **If** we have only lines "mL" (see Figure 10j, k, l, o, and u) where "m" is the separation number of lines (L), **therefore**, the detailed **PO** relation is written in the general form $\mathbf{PO}_{\mathbf{mL}}$. For more information and to limit some possible confusions, the detailed $\mathbf{PO}_{\mathbf{mL}}$ topological relation takes also two possible cases:
   - ***Either***, *we have only lines "mL" with intersection regions (jRI) and without any bounded region (0R) (see Figure 10j and u) where "j" is the separation number of intersection regions (RI),* ***therefore***, *the detailed* $\boldsymbol{PO}_{mL}$ *relation is written in the general form* $\boldsymbol{PO}_{mL,\, jRI,\, 0R}$. *For example, the case (j) in Figure 10, the detailed* ***PO*** *relation is described by two lines (2L) of partially overlapping with one intersection region (1RI) and without any bounded region (0R) and* ***then***, *the detailed* ***PO*** *relation is given by the expression* $\boldsymbol{PO}_{2L,\, 1RI,\, 0R}$.
   - ***Or***, *we have only lines "mL" with intersection regions (jRI) and with bounded regions (kR) (see Figure 10k, l, and o) where "j" is the separation number of Intersection Regions (RI),* ***therefore***, *the detailed* $\boldsymbol{PO}_{mL}$ *relation is written in the general form* $\boldsymbol{PO}_{mL,\, jRI,\, kR}$ *where "k" is the separation number of bounded regions (kR). For example, the case (k) in Figure 10, the detailed* ***PO*** *relation is described by three lines (3L) of partially overlapping with one intersection region (1RI) and with one bounded region (1R) and* ***then***, *the detailed* ***PO*** *relation is given by the expression* $\boldsymbol{PO}_{3L,\, 1RI,\, 1R}$.

b. **If** we have only points "nP" (see Figure 10a, f, and i) where "n" is the separation number of points (P), **therefore**, the detailed relation is written in the general form $\mathbf{PO}_{\mathbf{nP}}$. For more information and to limit some possible confusions, the detailed $\mathbf{PO}_{\mathbf{nP}}$ relation takes also two possible cases:
   - ***Either***, *we have only points "nP" with intersection regions (jRI) and without any bounded region (0R) (see Figure 10a and f) where "j" is the separation number of intersection regions (RI),* ***therefore***, *the detailed* $\boldsymbol{PO}_{nP}$ *relation is written in the general form* $\boldsymbol{PO}_{nP,\, jRI,\, 0R}$. *For example, the case (10-a) in Figure 10, the detailed* ***PO*** *relation is described by two points (2P) of partially overlapping with one intersection region (1RI) and without any bounded region (0R) and* ***then***, *the detailed* ***PO*** *relation is given by the expression* $\boldsymbol{PO}_{2P,\, 1RI,\, 0R}$.
   - ***Or***, *we have only points "nP" with intersection regions (jRI) and with bounded regions (kR) (see Figure 10-i) where "j" is the separation number of Intersection Regions (RI),* ***therefore***, *the detailed relation* $\boldsymbol{PO}_{nP}$ *is written in the general form* $\boldsymbol{PO}_{nP,\, jRI,\, kR}$ *where "k" is the separation number of bounded regions (kR). For example, the case (i) in Figure 10, the detailed* ***PO*** *relation is described by six points (6P) of partially overlapping with three intersection regions (3RI) and with two bounded regions (2R) and* ***then***, *the detailed* ***PO*** *relation is given by the expression* $\boldsymbol{PO}_{6P,\, 3RI,\, 2R}$.

c. ***If*** *we have both lines "mL" and points "nP" (see Figure 10b, c, d, e, g, and h) where "m" is the separation number of lines (L) and "n" is the separation number of points (P),* ***therefore***, *the detailed* ***PO*** *relation is written in the general form* $\boldsymbol{PO}_{mL,\, nP}$. *For more* *information and to limit some problems of confusions, the detailed* ***PO***$_{mL, nP}$ *topological relation takes also two possible cases:*

- ***Either***, *we have both lines "mL" and points "nP" with intersection regions (jRI) and without any bounded region (0R) (see Figure 10b and g) where "j" is the separation number of intersection regions (RI),* ***therefore***, *the detailed relation* ***PO***$_{mL, nP}$ *is written in the general form* ***PO***$_{mL, nP, jRI, 0R}$. *For example, the case (b) in Figure 10, the detailed* ***PO*** *relation is described by one line (1L) and one point (1P) of partially overlapping with one intersection region (1RI) and without any bounded region (0R) and* ***then***, *the detailed* ***PO*** *relation is given by the expression* ***PO***$_{1L, 1P, 1RI, 0R}$.
- ***Or***, *we have both lines "mL" and points "nP" with intersection regions (jRI) and with bounded regions (kR) (see Figure 10-c, 10-d, 10-e, and 10-h) where "j" is the separation number of intersection regions (RI),* ***therefore***, *the detailed relation* ***PO***$_{mL, nP}$ *is written in the general form* ***PO***$_{mL, nP, jRI, kR}$ *where "k" is the separation number of bounded regions (kR). For example, the case (d) in Figure 10, the detailed* ***PO*** *relation is described by one line (1L) and four points (4P) of partially overlapping with two intersection regions (2RI) and with two bounded regions (2R) and* ***then***, *the detailed* ***PO*** *relation is given by the expression* ***PO***$_{1L, 4P, 2RI, 2R}$.

In general, we observe that the detailed ***PO*** topological relation at the ***Level-1*** is always described with at least two points (*2P*) of partially overlapping (see Figure a and f) or one line (*1L*) of partially overlapping and one point (*1P*) of partially overlapping (see Figure 10-b) and with one intersection region (*1RI*) defined by ($A°\cap B°$) and without any bounded region (*0R*) (see Figure a, b, and f).

To conclude about this definition of ***PO*** relation, the generalization of the detailed ***PO*** topological relation at the ***Level-1*** is given in Table 5.

## Generalization of the Detailed TPP Topological Relation at the Level-1

In this part, we study the enriching and detailing of the ***TPP*** relation at the first level (***Level-1***) as in our papers (Alboody, et al., 2009a, 2009b). In order to study the ***TPP*** relation in details, it is represented in Figure 11 in several graphical representations which a spatial region A is a tangential proper part of B in *n-different ways*. The spatial elements of ($S = \partial A\cap\partial B$) are tangential lines and points. In this study to detail the ***TPP*** relation, we take a bounded region (*R*) belonging to B and it represent the difference (*B-A*) between B and A which is non-empty set ($B\text{-}A = \neg\emptyset$) (see Figure 11). In the general case, there are several bounded regions that are parts of B. In our study, the ***TPP*** relation is described by the separation number of Tangential Lines (***LT***), Tangential Points (***PT***), and the bounded regions (*R*).

**Definition:** *For the* **ID** *model,* **if** *the boundary-boundary intersection ($\partial A\cap\partial B$) of two regions A and B, the interior-interior intersection ($A°\cap B°$) of A and B and the difference (B-A) are non-empty ($\neg\emptyset$), and the difference (A-B) is empty ($\emptyset$).* **Hence**, *the topological relation between A and B is* **TPP** *(***A CoveredBy B, or B Covers A***).*

$$TPP, CoveredBy \Leftrightarrow ID(A,B) = \begin{bmatrix} \overset{\circ}{A} \cap \overset{\circ}{B} & A - B \\ B - A & \partial A \cap \partial B \end{bmatrix} = \begin{bmatrix} \neg\emptyset & \emptyset \\ \neg\emptyset & \neg\emptyset \end{bmatrix}$$

*Table 5. Generalization of the detailed PO topological relation at the level-1*

| PO Topological Relation of the RCC8 System at the *Level-0* | Generalization of the Detailed PO Topological Relation at the *Level-1* | |
|---|---|---|
| | **With Points *(nP)* and Lines *(mL)*** | **With Bounded Regions *(kR)* and Intersection Regions *(jRI)*** |
| | Only Lines *(mL)*: $PO_{mL}$ | With "*j*" Intersection Regions *(jRI)* and without any bounded Region *(0R)*: $PO_{mL, jRI, 0R}$ |
| | | With "*j*" Intersection Regions *(jRI)* and with "*k*" bounded Regions *(kR)*: $PO_{mL, jRI, kR}$ |
| | Only Points *(nP)*: $PO_{nP}$ | With "*j*" Intersection Regions *(jRI)* and without any bounded Region *(0R)*: $PO_{nP, jRI, 0R}$ |
| | | With "*j*" Intersection Regions *(jRI)* and with "*k*" bounded Regions *(kR)*: $PO_{nP, jRI, kR}$ |
| | Both Lines *(mL)* and Points *(nP)*: $PO_{mL, nP}$ | With "*j*" Intersection Regions *(jRI)* and without any bounded Region *(0R)*: $PO_{mL, nP, jRI, 0R}$ |
| | | With "*j*" Intersection Regions *(jRI)* and with "*k*" bounded Regions *(kR)*: $PO_{mL, nP, jRI, kR}$ |

*Figure 11. TPP topological relation in several graphical representations*

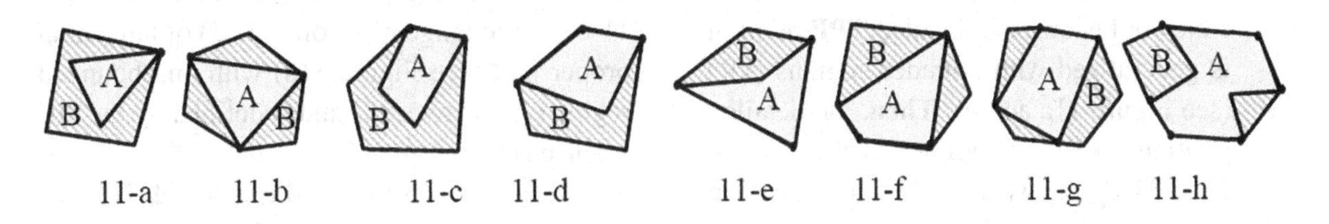


Or, based upon the properties of topological relations using the ***ID** model*: The topological relation is ***TPP***: ***if and only if*** *(I [∂, ∂] = ∂A∩∂B = ¬Ø) ^ (D¹[-, -] = A-B = Ø) ^ (D²[-, -] = A-B = ¬Ø).*

So, in a *two-dimensional* space, a spatial region A is a tangential proper part of B in *n-different ways*. In order to detail and generalize these *n-different ways* of the ***TPP*** relation, it is sufficient to the separation number $r = \chi(\partial A \cap \partial B)$, the separation number of tangential points (***nPT***) of BBISS as $n = \chi(\partial A \cap \partial B)_{PT}$ and tangential lines (***mLT***) of BBISS as $m = \chi(\partial A \cap \partial B)_{LT}$, and the separation number of bounded regions (***kR***) defined by $k = \chi(B - A)$. In this case, there is always at least one bounded region (*1R*) between A and B, where the value of "*k*" is greater than or equal to "1" ($k \geq 1$). Hence, we have three possible general cases as follows:

a. **If** we have only tangential lines "mLT" (see Figure 11c, d, e, and h) where "m" is the separation number of tangential lines (LT), **therefore**, the detailed **TPP** relation is written in the general form $\mathbf{TPP_{mLT}}$. In order to have more information and limit some possible confusions, the detailed $\mathbf{TPP_{mLT}}$ relation is written in the general form $\mathbf{TPP_{mLT, kR}}$ with bounded regions (kR) (see Figure 11e and h) where "k " is the separation number of bounded regions (kR) between A and B. A very simple case of this detailed **TPP** relation is the case (c) in Figure 11 with one tangential line (1LT) and one bounded region (1R), **therefore**, the detailed **TPP**

*Table 6. Generalization of the detailed TPP topological relation at the level-1*

| TPP Topological Relation of the RCC8 System at the *Level-0* | **Generalization of the Detailed TPP Topological Relation at the *Level-1*** | |
|---|---|---|
| | **With Tangential Points *(nPT)* and Tangential Lines *(mLT)*** | **With Bounded Regions *(kR)*** |
| | Only Tangential Lines *(mLT)*: $TPP_{mLT}$ | With "*k*" bounded Regions *(kR)*: $TPP_{mLT, kR}$ |
| | Only Tangential Points *(nPT)*: $TPP_{nPT}$ | With "*k*" bounded Regions *(kR)*: $TPP_{nPT, kR}$ |
| | Both Tangential Lines *(mLT)* and Tangential Points *(nPT)*: $TPP_{mLT, nPT}$ | With "*k*" bounded Regions *(kR)*: $TPP_{mLT, nPT, kR}$ |

topological relation is given by the expression $\mathbf{TPP}_{\mathbf{1LT, 1R}}$.

b. **If** we have only tangential points "nPT" (see Figure 11a and b) where "n" is the separation number of Tangential Points (PT), **therefore**, the detailed **TPP** relation is written in the general form $\mathbf{TPP}_{\mathbf{nPT}}$. For more of details about this relation and eliminate some possible confusions, the detailed **TPP** relation is generalized with bounded regions (kR) (see Figure 11a and b). **Then**, the detailed relation $\mathbf{TPP}_{\mathbf{nPT}}$ is written in the general form $\mathbf{TPP}_{\mathbf{nPT, kR}}$ where "k" is the separation number of bounded regions (kR). A very simple case of this relation is the case (a) in Figure 11 with one tangential point (1PT) and one bounded region (1R), **therefore**, the detailed **TPP** topological relation is given by the expression $\mathbf{TPP}_{\mathbf{1PT, 1R}}$.

c. **If** we have tangential lines "mLT" and tangential points "nPT" (see Figure 11f and g) where "m" is the separation number of lines (LT) and "n" is the separation number of points (PT), **therefore**, the relation is written in the general form $\mathbf{TPP}_{\mathbf{mLT, nPT}}$. For more of details about this detailed **TPP** relation with bounded regions (kR) where "k" is the separation number of bounded regions (kR), we can write the detailed relation $\mathbf{TPP}_{\mathbf{mLT, nPT}}$ in the general form $\mathbf{TPP}_{\mathbf{mLT, nPT, kR}}$. For example, the case (g) in Figure 11, the detailed **TPP** relation is described by one tangential line (1LT) and two tangential points (2PT) of tangential proper part with three bounded regions (3R), and **therefore**, the detailed **TPP** topological relation is given by the expression $\mathbf{TPP}_{\mathbf{1LT, 2PT, 3R}}$.

In general as in very simple cases, we see that the detailed ***TPP*** topological relation at the ***Level-1*** is always described with at least one tangential line (*1LT*) of tangential proper part (see Figure 11-c) or one tangential point (*1PT*) of tangential proper part (see Figure 11a) with one bounded region (*1R*) between B and A defined by the difference ($B\text{-}A = \neg\varnothing$).

The generalization of the detailed ***TPP*** topological relation at the ***Level-1*** is given by the Table 6.

## Generalization of the Detailed TPPi Topological Relation at the Level-1

In this part, we study the enriching and detailing of the ***TPPi*** relation at the first level (***Level-1***) as in our papers (Alboody, et al., 2009a, 2009b). The ***TPPi*** relation is represented in Figure 12 in several graphical representations which a spatial region A is a tangential proper part inverse of a spatial region B in *n-different ways*.

As seen as for the ***TPP*** relation, the spatial elements of BBISS ($S = \partial A \cap \partial B$) for the ***TPPi*** relation are also tangential lines and tangential points. In this case of ***TPPi*** relation, the bounded regions (*R*) between A and B belong to A and represent difference (*A-B*) between A and B which is non-empty set ($A\text{-}B = \neg\varnothing$) (see Figure 12). This

*Figure 12. TPPi topological relation in several graphical representations*

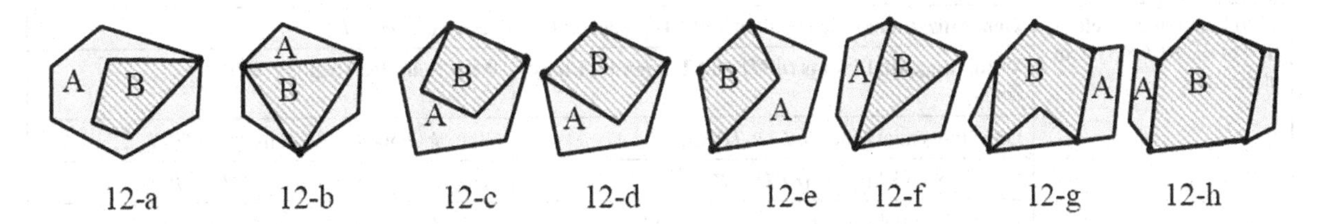


is the only difference between the detailed ***TPPi*** relation and ***TPP*** relation.

In general cases, there are several bounded regions (*kR*) that are parts of A. For the detailed ***TPPi*** relation (inverse of ***TPP***), it is necessary to develop this part although the ***TPP*** relation is already detailed for two reasons: Firstly, for the ***TPP*** relation, the *bounded region* called (*R*) is ($B\text{-}A = \neg\emptyset$), while for the ***TPPi*** relation, the *bounded region* called also (*R*) is ($A\text{-}B = \neg\emptyset$). Then, this is the only important difference between the detailed ***TPPi*** relation and ***TPP*** relation. Secondly, it is indispensable to take in our study these two detailed ***TPP*** and ***TPPi*** relations in order to detailing these relations at the ***Level-2*** using the concept of types of spatial elements (points and lines) of BBISS in the next part and in order to confront some problems of confusion between two detailed ***TPP*** and ***TPPi*** relations of the same kind.

The generalization of the ***TPPi*** relation is very similar to the generalization of ***TPP*** relation.

**Definition: If** *the boundary-boundary intersection ($\partial A \cap \partial B$) of two regions A and B, the interior-interior intersection ($A° \cap B°$) of A and B and the difference (A-B) are non-empty ($\neg\emptyset$), and the difference (B-A) is empty ($\emptyset$).* **Hence,** *the topological relation between A and B is* **TPPi** ***(Covers).***

$$TPPi, Covers \Leftrightarrow I\!D(\text{A,B}) = \begin{bmatrix} A^{\circ} \cap B^{\circ} & A - B \\ B - A & \partial A \cap \partial B \end{bmatrix} = \begin{bmatrix} \neg\emptyset & \neg\emptyset \\ \emptyset & \neg\emptyset \end{bmatrix}$$

Or, based upon the properties of topological relations using the ***ID*** *model*: The topological relation is ***TPPi***: ***if and only if*** *($I\,[\partial, \partial] = \partial A \cap \partial B = \neg\emptyset$) ^ ($D^1[-, -] = B\text{-}A = \neg\emptyset$) ^ ($D^2[-, -] = B\text{-}A = \emptyset$).*

So, in a *two-dimensional space*, a spatial region A is a tangential proper part inverse of a spatial region B in *n-different ways*. In order to detail and generalize these *n-different ways* of the ***TPPi*** relation, it is sufficient to identify the tangential points (*PT*), and the tangential lines (*LT*) of the boundary-boundary intersection *($\partial A \cap \partial B$)* and the bounded regions (*R*) defined by the difference *(A-B)* between A and B, with the number separation of BBISS $r = \chi(\partial A \cap \partial B)$, the separation number of tangential points (***nPT***) of BBISS as $n = \chi(\partial A \cap \partial B)_{PT}$ and tangential lines (***mLT***) of BBISS as $m = \chi(\partial A \cap \partial B)_{LT}$, and the separation number of bounded regions (***kR***) defined by $k = \chi(A - B)$. In this case, there is always at least a bounded region (*1R*) between A and B, where the value of "*k*" is greater than or equal to "1" ($k \geq 1$). Hence, we have three possible general cases as follows:

a. **If** we have only tangential lines "mLT" (see Figure 12c, d, e, and h) where "m" is the separation number of Tangential Lines (LT), **therefore**, the detailed relation is written in the general form $\mathbf{TPPi_{mLT}}$. In order to have more information and to limit some possible confusions, the detailed relation $\mathbf{TPPi_{mLT}}$ is written in the general form $\mathbf{TPPi_{mLT,kR}}$ with bounded regions (kR) (see Figure 12e and h) where "k " is the separation number of bounded regions (R) between A and B. A very simple case of this detailed relation is

*Table 7. Generalization of the detailed TPPi topological relation at the level-1*

| TPPi Topological Relation of the RCC8 System at the *Level-0* | **Generalization of the Detailed TPPi Topological Relation at the *Level-1*** | |
|---|---|---|
| | **With Tangential Points *(nPT)* and Tangential Lines *(mLT)*** | **With Bounded Regions *(kR)*** |
| | Only Tangential Lines *(mLT)*: $TPPi_{mLT}$ | With "*k*" bounded Regions *(kR)*: $TPPi_{mLT, kR}$ |
| | Only Tangential Points *(nPT)*: $TPPi_{nPT}$ | With "*k*" bounded Regions *(kR)*: $TPPi_{nPT, kR}$ |
| | Both Tangential Lines *(mLT)* and Tangential Points *(nPT)*: $TPPi_{mLT, nPT}$ | With "*k*" bounded Regions *(kR)*: $TPPi_{mLT, nPT, kR}$ |

the case (c) in Figure 12 with one tangential line (1LT) and one bounded region (1R), therefore, the detailed **TPPi** relation is given by the expression $\mathbf{TPPi_{1LT, 1R}}$.

b. **If** we have only tangential points "nPT" (see Figure 12a and b) where "n" is the separation number of Tangential Points (PT), **therefore**, the detailed relation is written in the general form $\mathbf{TPPi_{nPT}}$. For more of details about this relation and to eliminate some possible confusions, the detailed **TPPi** relation is generalized with bounded regions (kR) (see Figure 12a and b). **Then**, the detailed relation $\mathbf{TPPi_{nPT}}$ is written in the general form $\mathbf{TPPi_{nPT, kR}}$ where "k" is the separation number of bounded regions (kR). A very simple case of this relation is the case (a) in Figure12 with one tangential point (1PT) and one bounded region (1R), therefore, the detailed **TPPi** topological relation is given by the expression $\mathbf{TPPi_{1PT, 1R}}$.

c. **If** we have both tangential lines "mLT" and tangential points "nPT" (see Figure 12f and g) where "m" is the separation number of lines (LT) and "n" is the separation number of points (PT), **therefore**, the detailed relation is written in the general form $\mathbf{TPPi_{mLT, nPT}}$. For more of details about this detailed relation with bounded regions (kR) where "k" is the separation number of bounded regions (kR), we can write the detailed relation $\mathbf{TPPi_{mLT, nPT}}$ in the general form $\mathbf{TPPi_{mLT, nPT, kR}}$. For example, the case (g) in Figure 12, the detailed **TPP** relation is described by two tangential lines (2LT) and two tangential points (2PT) of tangential proper part inverse with three bounded regions (3R), and **therefore**, the detailed **TPP** relation is given by the expression $\mathbf{TPPi_{2LT, 2PT, 3R}}$.

In general, we can see that the detailed ***TPPi*** relation at the ***Level-1*** is always described with at least one tangential line (*1LT*) of tangential proper part inverse (see Figure 12c) or one tangential point (*1PT*) of tangential proper part inverse (see Figure 12-c) with one bounded region (*1R*) between B and A defined by the difference ($A\text{-}B = \neg\emptyset$).

Finally, the generalization of the detailed ***TPPi*** topological relation at the ***Level-1*** given by the Table 7 is similar to the generalization of the detailed ***TPP*** topological relation given by the Table 6.

## Summary about the Detailed Topological Relations of the RCC8 System at the Level-1

The main contribution in this section is new detailed relations of the RCC8 system at the ***Level-1***. To conclude, new topological relations at the first detailed level (***Level-1***) to discriminate between relations of the same kind (see Table 2) are introduced. These new detailed relations are very necessary to detect the topological changes and for query in spatial databases such as GIS and image databases. The four detailed topological relations (***EC***, ***PO***, ***TPP***, ***and TPPi***) of RCC8 at the ***Level-1*** are given by Table 8.

*Table 8. Generalization of the four detailed topological relations EC, PO, TPP, and TPPi of the RCC8 system at the level-1*

| Topological Relations of the RCC8 System at the *Level-0* Without Any Details | Detailed Topological Relations of the RCC8 System: *EC, PO, TPP,* and *TPPi* at the *Level-1* | |
|---|---|---|
| | With Points *(nP/nPT)* and Lines *(mL/mLT)* | With Bounded Regions *(kR)* and Intersection Regions *(jRI)* |
| EC | $EC_{mL}$ | $EC_{mL, 0R}$ |
| | | $EC_{mL, kR}$ |
| | $EC_{nP}$ | $EC_{1P, 0R}$ |
| | | $EC_{nP, kR}$ |
| | $EC_{mL, nP}$ | $EC_{mL, nP, kR}$ |
| PO | $PO_{mL}$ | $PO_{mL, jRI, 0R}$ |
| | | $PO_{mL, jRI, kR}$ |
| | $PO_{nP}$ | $PO_{nP, jRI, 0R}$ |
| | | $PO_{nP, jRI, kR}$ |
| | $PO_{mL, nP}$ | $PO_{mL, nP, jRI, 0R}$ |
| | | $PO_{mL, nP, jRI, kR}$ |
| TPP | $TPP_{mLT}$ | $TPP_{mLT, kR}$ |
| | $TPP_{nPT}$ | $TPP_{nPT, kR}$ |
| | $TPP_{mLT, nPT}$ | $TPP_{mLT, nPT, kR}$ |
| TPPi | $TPPi_{mLT}$ | $TPPi_{mLT, kR}$ |
| | $TPPi_{nPT}$ | $TPPi_{nPT, kR}$ |
| | $TPPi_{mLT, nPT}$ | $TPPi_{mLT, nPT, kR}$ |

By using the ***ID model*** and the concept of separation number, the four detailed topological relations at the ***Level-1*** are given as seen in this work and in Alboody et al. (2009a, 2009b): ***EC*** becomes as: $EC_{mL}$, $EC_{nP}$, $EC_{mL, nP}$; ***PO*** becomes as: $PO_{mL}$, $PO_{nP}$, $PO_{mL, nP}$; ***TPP*** becomes as: $TPP_{mLT}$, $TPP_{nPT}$, $TPP_{mLT, nPT}$; and ***TPPi*** becomes as: $TPPi_{mLT}$, $TPPi_{nPT}$, $TPPi_{mLT, nPT}$.

Based upon these four detailed topological relations at the ***Level-1***, the enriched version of the RCC8 system consists of sixteen (16) relations and can be written as: ***DC***, $EC_{mL}$, $EC_{nP}$, $EC_{mL, nP}$, $PO_{mL}$, $PO_{nP}$, $PO_{mL, nP}$, $TPP_{mLT}$, $TPP_{nPT}$, $TPP_{mLT, nPT}$, ***NTPP***, $TPPi_{mLT}$, $TPPi_{nPT}$, $TPPi_{mLT, nPT}$, ***NTPPi***, and ***EQ***.

We call this new set of (16) detailed topological relations of the RCC8 system by *the extended version of the RCC8 system at the **Level-1*** or we can call this *extended version of the RCC8 system* by ***the RCC-16 system at the Level-1.***

To conclude on this study, we find that there are some problems of confusion between detailed relations of the same kind ***EC, PO, TPP,*** and ***TPPi*** at the first detailed level (at the ***Level-1***). Therefore, we give some examples to demonstrate the confusion problems. Such problems are encountered at the detailed level (herein the ***Level-1***) in the paper of Deng et al. (2007).

For example, for the detailed ***EC*** relation at the ***Level-1***, we find that there is a confusion between two cases 13a ($EC_{2L, 1P, 1R}$) and 13b ($EC_{2L, 1P, 1R}$) in Figure 13, it can be shown that these two detailed relations of the same kind (***EC***) are equal to each other, but visually, it's not correct because the two lines are in first place and then after a point in the second place for the case 13b; while the point is in first place and the two lines are in second place in the case 13a. The same problem of confusion appears also in the case of relations ***PO, TPP,***

*Figure 13. Examples about the confusion problems using several graphical representations*

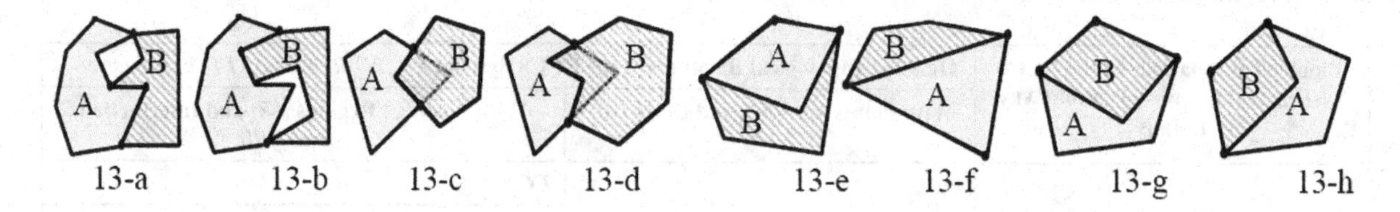


*Table 9. Examples and summary about the confusion problems between the four detailed topological relations EC, PO, TPP, and TPPi of the same kind at the level-1*

| RCC8 Topological Relations Without Any Details at the *Level-0* | | Detailed Topological Relations of the RCC8 System at the *Level-1* | | Summary about the Confusion Problems at the *Level-1* |
|---|---|---|---|---|
| *EC* | *Figures 13-a, 13-b* | $EC_{2L, 1P}$ | $EC_{2L, 1P, 1R}$ | *Importance more and more for detailing these relations.* There are also differences between these relations of the same kind ***EC, PO, TPP and TPPi*** at different levels (***Level-2***, ***Level-3*** and ***Level-4***): ***1. Level-2:*** By defining ***the Types of Spatial Elments*** (Points and Lines) of BBISS ***2. Level-3***: By defining ***the Order of occurrence of Spatial Elments*** (Points and Lines) of BBISS 3. Level-4: By defining the Orientation and the Position of Spatial Elments (Points and Lines) of BBISS |
| *PO* | *Figures 13-c, 13-d* | $PO_{2P}$ | $PO_{2P, 1RI}$ | |
| *TPP* | *Figures 13-e, 13-f* | $TPP_{2LT}$ | $TPP_{2LT, 1R}$ | |
| *TPPi* | *Figures 13-g, 13-h* | $TPPi_{2LT}$ | $TPPi_{2LT, 1R}$ | |

and ***TPPi*** as shown in Table 9 and Figure 13. To confront this problem of confusion, we will take into account the concept of types of spatial elments (Points and Lines) of BBISS. At the second level (***Level-2***), we will define the types of each spatial elment (Points and Lines) of BBISS and then we will integrate these types with the concept of separation number at the ***Level-1*** into the ***ID*** model. We can also take the concepts of order of occurrence at the third level (at the ***Level-3***); and the orientation and the poisition of spatial elments (Points and Lines) of BBISS at the fourth level (at the ***Level-4***) to solve these problems.

In our study, we will only find the detailed topological relations at the second level (***Level-2***).

## At the Level-2: Topological Relations at the Detailed Level-2 Based Upon the Definition of the Types of Spatial Elements (Points and Lines) of BBISS

In this part, we will combine the topological invariant of the *Types and Neighborhoods* of a Spatial Element of BBISS with the ***ID model*** to describe all the necessary details of topological relations, which cannot be exactly extracted at the ***Level-1***. In this part, we will develop and define the types of points and lines that will serve us to overcome some confusion problems that we encountered in the previous study of detailed relations at the ***Level-1***. First, we will expand the definition of the types of points based upon the concept of neighborhoods studied in the topological invariants. Then, from such points, we will define the types of lines. Certain types of points and lines are studied based upon the ***ID model*** in Deng et al. (2007). We will add the types of points and lines

*Figure 14. Graphical representations for the types of points (TOP)*

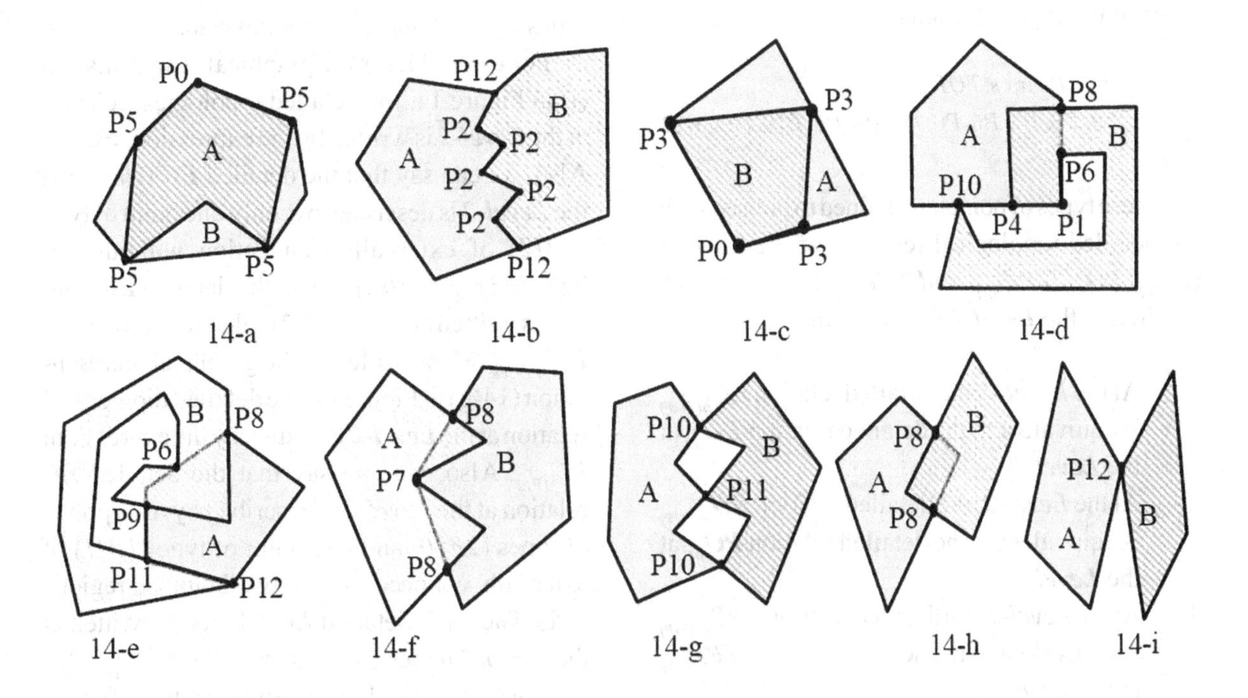


that are not already defined in the paper of Deng et al. (2007). Finally, we will introduce the types of points and lines in the generalization of the four detailed topological relations ***EC, PO, TPP,*** and ***TPPi*** at the second detailed level (***Level-2***). We will present a summary of our contribution at the ***Level-2*** as in our work (Alboody, et al., 2009b).

## Definition of the Types of Points

The concept of neighborhoods is used to define the type of points of BBISS. Neighbors of each spatial element (point) are defined by the following five operators: (*A-B*), (*B-A*), ($A^{\circ} \cap B^{\circ}$), $(A \cup B)^{-}_{ub}$ and $(A \cup B)^{-}_{b}$ as shown in Figure 8. We determine ***thirteen (13) points*** with their types (Alboody, et al., 2009b). The types of some of these points are defined in Deng et al. (2007). We will use these types of points to generalize the detailed topological relations ***EC, PO, TPP and TPPi*** at the ***Level-1*** to be written in the general form at the ***Level-2***:

$$(Topological\_Relation)_{n(Type\_Of\_Points)}$$

Where *"n"* is the separation number of each type of points. And all the types of points are represented in Figure 14, and denoted by (*TOP*):

$$Type\_Of\_Points(TOP) = P0, P1, P2, P3, P4, P5, P6, P7, P8, P9, P10, P11, P12$$

Then, we give the general form of the four detailed topological relation at the second level (***Level-2***) for *"n"* points (*nP/nPT*) by the expression as in (Alboody et al., 2009b):

$$(Topological\_Relation)_{n(Type\_Of\_Points)} = (EC, PO, TPP, TPPi)_{n(P0,\ P1,\ P2,\ P3, P4,\ P5,\ P6,\ P7,\ P8,\ P9,\ P10,\ P11,\ P12)}$$

Where the notation ($Topological\_Relation$) is one of the four topological relations of the RCC8 system: ***EC, PO, TPP and TPPi***; and the notation ($Type\_Of\_Po\text{int}\,s(TOP)$) is one or more of the types of points:

$Type\_Of\_Po\text{int}\,s(TOP) =$
$P0, P1, P2, P3, P4, P5, P6, P7, P8, P9, P10, P11, P12$

These types of points are defined to be used with the detailed topological relations at the ***Level-1*** (***EC***$_{nP}$, ***PO***$_{nP}$, ***TPP***$_{nPT}$, ***and TPPi***$_{nPT}$) which can be detaited at the ***Level-2*** as following:

1. At the ***Level-2***, the detailed relation ***EC***$_{n(TOP)}$ is equivalent to the detailed relation ***EC***$_{nP}$ at the ***Level-1***.
2. At the ***Level-2***, the detailed relation ***PO***$_{n(TOP)}$ is equivalent to the detailed relation ***PO***$_{nP}$ at the ***Level-1***.
3. At the ***Level-2***, the detailed relation ***TPP***$_{n(TOP)}$ is equivalent to the detailed relation ***TPP***$_{nPT}$ at the ***Level-1***.
4. At the ***Level-2***, the detailed relation ***TPPi***$_{n(TOP)}$ is equivalent to the detailed relation ***TPPi***$_{nPT}$ at the ***Level-1***.

For example, the four detailed topological relation at the ***Level-2*** (with their equivalent at the ***Level-1***) can be written under the general forms such as:

- ***EC***$_{2P10}$ (***EC***$_{n(TOP)}$) at the ***Level-2*** is equivalent to ***EC***$_{2P}$ (***EC***$_{nP}$) at the ***Level-1***;
- ***PO***$_{2P8}$ (***PO***$_{n(TOP)}$) at the ***Level-2*** is equivalent to ***PO***$_{4P}$ (***PO***$_{nP}$) at the ***Level-1***;
- ***TPP***$_{1P5}$ (***TPP***$_{n(TOP)}$) at the ***Level-2*** is equivalent to ***TPP***$_{1PT}$ (***TPP***$_{nPT}$) at the ***Level-1***;
- And ***TPPi***$_{1P3}$ (***TPPi***$_{n(TOP)}$) at the ***Level-2*** is equivalent to ***TPPi***$_{1PT}$ (***TPPi***$_{nPT}$) at the ***Level-1***.

In Table 10, the types of points are given as shown as in Figure 14. Where *"1"* indicates that the region (***Neighboring Subspaces***) defined by the operators (*A-B*), (*B-A*), ($A°\cap B°$), $(A\cup B)^-_{ub}$ and $(A\cup B)^-_{b}$ is in the neighborhoods of such types and *"0"* indicates the inverse.

For example, for the graphical representation (i) in Figure 14, the detailed topological relation at the ***Level-2*** is written by the expression: ***EC***$_{1P12}$. Also, we can say that the detailed ***EC*** relation at the ***Level-2*** is described by: only one point of type (*1P12*) of externally connection without any bounded region (*0R*). Then, the detailed ***EC*** relation is written at the ***Level-2*** under the expression: ***EC***$_{1P12,\,0R}$. Meanwhile, for the graphical representation (14-g) in Figure 14, the detailed topological relation at the ***Level-2*** is written by the expression: ***EC***$_{1P12}$. Also, we can say that the detailed ***EC*** relation at the ***Level-2*** is described by: two points of types (*2P10*) and one point of type (*1P11*) of externally connection with two bounded regions (*2R*). Then, the detailed ***EC*** relation is written at the ***Level-2*** under the expression: ***EC***$_{2P10,\,1P11,\,2R}$.

Another example is given about the ***PO*** relation. For the graphical representation (f) in Figure 14, the detailed topological relation at the ***Level-2*** is written by the expression: ***PO***$_{2P8,\,1P7}$. Also, we can say that the detailed ***PO*** relation at the ***Level-2*** is described by: two points of type (*2P8*), one point of type (*1P7*) of partially overlaping with two intersection regions (*2RI*) and without any bounded region (*0R*). Then, the detailed ***PO*** relation is written at the ***Level-2*** in the form: ***PO***$_{2P8,\,1P7,\,2RI,\,0R}$. Meanwhile, for the graphical representation (h) in Figure 14, the detailed topological relation at the ***Level-2*** is written by the expression: ***PO***$_{2P8}$. Also, we can say that the detailed ***PO*** relation at the ***Level-2*** is described by: only two points of type (*2P8*) of partially overlaping with one intersection region (*1RI*) and without any bounded region (*0R*). Then, the detailed ***PO*** relation is written at the ***Level-2*** in the form: ***PO***$_{2P8,\,2RI,\,0R}$.

To conclude on these types of points, we find that we can determine the detailed topological relation at the ***Level-2*** based upon determining and defining the types of points. Finally, these

*Table 10. Definitions of the types of points (TOP) using the neighboring subspaces*

| Types Of Points (TOP) | | Neighboring Subspaces of Points | | | | |
|---|---|---|---|---|---|---|
| N | Type | A-B | B-A | $A^{\circ} \cap B^{\circ}$ | $\overline{(A \cup B)}_{ub}$ | $\overline{(A \cup B)}_{b}$ |
| 1 | P0 | 0 | 0 | 1 | 1 | 0 |
| 2 | P1 | 0 | 0 | 1 | 0 | 1 |
| 3 | P2 | 1 | 1 | 0 | 0 | 0 |
| 4 | P3 | 1 | 0 | 1 | 1 | 0 |
| 5 | P4 | 1 | 0 | 1 | 0 | 1 |
| 6 | P5 | 0 | 1 | 1 | 1 | 0 |
| 7 | P6 | 0 | 1 | 1 | 0 | 1 |
| 8 | P7 | 1 | 1 | 1 | 0 | 0 |
| 9 | P8 | 1 | 1 | 1 | 1 | 0 |
| 10 | P9 | 1 | 1 | 1 | 0 | 1 |
| 11 | P10 | 1 | 1 | 0 | 1 | 1 |
| 12 | P11 | 1 | 1 | 0 | 0 | 1 |
| 13 | P12 | 1 | 1 | 0 | 1 | 0 |

*Table 11. Types of points (TOP) at the level-2 are always and without doubt with these detailed topological relations of the RCC8 system at the level-1*

| Detailed Topological Relations of the RCC8 System at the Level-1 | EC (Meet) $EC_{nP}$ $EC_{mL, nP}$ | PO (Overlaps) $PO_{nP}$ $PO_{mL, nP}$ | TPP (CoveredBy) $TPP_{nPT}$ $TPP_{mLT, nPT}$ | TPPi (Covers) $TPPi_{nPT}$ $TPPi_{mLT, nPT}$ |
|---|---|---|---|---|
| Types Of Points (TOP) for using at the Level-2 | P12 | P8, P9 | P0 | P0 |

types of points will serve us to determine and define the types of lines.

## Conclusion about the Definiton of the Types of Points (TOP)

We find that the types of points can participate to identify and characterize only one of the four detailed topological relations. For example, the type of points (*P8*) and (*P9*) can characterize the detailed relations ***PO*** ***(***$PO_{nP}$ ***and*** $PO_{mL, nP}$***)***. In Table 11, we present the types of points which are always true and undoubtedly with the detailed topological relations at the ***Level-1*** corresponding to such types. The same thing is true for the type of point (*P12*) which can describe only the detailed topological relation $EC_{1P12, 0R}$ (see Figure 14i).

We find that the types of points can participate to identify and characterize several topological relations at the same time. For example, the type of point (*P4*) can characterize both detailed relations $TPPi_{nPT}$ and $PO_{nP}$. This may be also help to

*Table 12. Types of points (TOP) at the level-2 are without doubt with these detailed topological relations of the RCC8 system at the level-1*

| *Detailed Topological Relations of the RCC8 System at the Level-1* | *EC (Meet)* $EC_{nP}$ $EC_{mL,nP}$ | *PO (Overlaps)* $PO_{nP}$ $PO_{mL,nP}$ | *TPP (CoveredBy)* $TPP_{nPT}$ $TPP_{mLT,nPT}$ | *TPPi (Covers)* $TPPi_{nPT}$ $TPPi_{mLT,nPT}$ |
|---|---|---|---|---|
| *Types Of Points (TOP) for using at the Level-2* | *P1, P2, P4, P6, P10, P11* | *P1, P2, P3, P4, P5, P6, P7, P10, P11* | *P5, P7* | *P1, P3, P4* |

characterize the relation $EC_{nP}$. In Table 12, we present the types of points which are undoubtedly true but not always with the detailed topological relations at the ***Level-1*** corresponding to such types.

## Definition of the Types of Lines

In the previous part of the definition of the types of points, we have defined the types of points. Then, we will use these types of points to define the types of lines in this part. The types of lines of BBISS are defined by the same five operators (***Neighboring Subspaces***) for the types of points: (*A-B*), (*B-A*), ($A^{\circ} \cap B^{\circ}$), $(A \cup B)^{-}_{ub}$ and $(A \cup B)^{-}_{b}$ presented in Figure 8. Each type of lines is defined by ***its start-point (1)*** and ***end-point (2)*** with the type of these two points. The types of points are used to define the types of lines. We search the types of ***start-point*** and ***end-point*** of each line in the ***clockwise direction*** as in Deng et al. (2007) and Alboody et al. (2009b). Some types of these types of lines are defined in Deng et al. (2007). We use the orientation of ***clockwise direction*** to avoid the orientation problem (***into crossing*** and ***out of crossing***) studied and presented in Figure 6 (Egenhofer & Franzosa, 1995).

Then, we will use these types of lines to determine the detailed topological relation ***EC, PO, TPP, and TPPi*** to be written in the general form at the ***Level-2***:

$$(Topological\_Relation)_{m(Type\_Of\_Lines)}$$

Where *"m"* is the separation number of each type of lines. The type of each line is denoted by (*TOL*):

$$Type\_Of\_Lines(TOL) = L0, L1, L2, L3, L4, L5, L6, L7, L8, L9, L10, L11, L12, L13, L14, L15, L16, L17, L18, L19, L20, L21, L22, L23, L24, L25, L26, L27, L28, L29, L30$$

Where the notation $(Topological\_Relation)$ is one of the four topological relations of the RCC8 system: ***EC, PO, TPP, and TPPi***; and the notation $(Type\_Of\_Lines(TOL))$ is one or more of the types of lines.

For example, we give the detailed topological relation at the ***Level-2*** with these types of lines denoted by:

$$(Topological\_Relation)_{m(Type\_Of\_Lines)} = (EC, PO, TPP, TPPi)_{m(L0,\ L1,\ L2,\ L3,\ L4,\ L5,\ L6,\ L7,\ L8,\ L9,\ L10,\ L11,\ L12,\ L13,\ L14,\ L15,\ L16,\ L17,\ L18,\ L19,\ L20,\ L21,\ L22,\ L23,\ L24,\ L25,\ L26,\ L27,\ L28,\ L29,\ L30)}$$

We determine thirty (30) possible lines with their types presented in Figure 5 and Figure 6 (Alboody, et al., 2009b). In Table 13, the types of lines (*TOL*) are also given with ***Types of Start-Point (1)*** and ***End-Point (2)***.

All these types of lines (*TOL*) are represented with the *clockwise direction* in Figure 15 and Figure 16. These types of lines are defined to be used with the detailed topological relations at the ***Level-1*** ($EC_{mL}$, $PO_{mL}$, $TPP_{mLT}$, ***and*** $TPPi_{mLT}$) which can be detaited at the ***Level-2*** as following:

*Table 13. Definitions of the types of lines (TOL) using the definitions of the types of points (TOP)*

| Types of Start-Point (1) *(TOP)* | Types of End-Point (2) *(TOP)* | Type Of Lines *(TOL)* |
|---|---|---|
| P0 | ***P0*** | ***L24*** |
| | ***P3*** | ***L26*** |
| | ***P5*** | ***L28*** |
| ***P1*** | ***P4*** | ***L23*** |
| P2 | ***P2*** | ***L12*** |
| | ***P7*** | ***L29*** |
| | ***P11*** | ***L21*** |
| | ***P12*** | ***L15*** |
| P3 | ***P0*** | ***L25*** |
| | ***P3*** | ***L6*** |
| | ***P5*** | ***L8*** |
| P4 | ***P4*** | ***L7*** |
| | ***P6*** | ***L9*** |
| P5 | ***P0*** | ***L27*** |
| | ***P3*** | ***L18*** |
| | ***P5*** | ***L10*** |
| P6 | ***P1*** | ***L22*** |
| | ***P4*** | ***L19*** |
| | ***P6*** | ***L11*** |
| P7 | ***P2*** | ***L30*** |
| | ***P7*** | ***L5*** |
| | ***P11*** | ***L4*** |
| | ***P12*** | ***L3*** |
| ***P8*** | - | - |
| ***P9*** | - | - |
| ***P10*** | - | - |
| P11 | ***P2*** | ***L20*** |
| | ***P7*** | ***L17*** |
| | ***P11*** | ***L2*** |
| | ***P12*** | ***L13*** |
| P12 | ***P2*** | ***L14*** |
| | ***P11*** | ***L1*** |
| | ***P12*** | ***L0*** |
| | ***P7*** | ***L16*** |

1. At the ***Level-2***, the detailed relation $\boldsymbol{EC}_{m(TOL)}$ is equivalent to the detailed relation $\boldsymbol{EC}_{mL}$ at the ***Level-1***.
2. At the ***Level-2***, the detailed relation $\boldsymbol{PO}_{m(TOL)}$ is equivalent to the detailed relation $\boldsymbol{PO}_{mL}$ at the ***Level-1***.
3. At the ***Level-2***, the detailed relation $\boldsymbol{TPP}_{m(TOL)}$ is equivalent to the detailed relation $\boldsymbol{TPP}_{mLT}$ at the ***Level-1***.
4. At the ***Level-2***, the detailed relation $\boldsymbol{TPPi}_{m(TOL)}$ is equivalent to the detailed relation $\boldsymbol{TPPi}_{mLT}$ at the ***Level-1***.

For example, the four detailed topological relation at the ***Level-2*** (with their equivalent at the ***Level-1***) can be written under the forms such as:

- $\boldsymbol{EC}_{1L0}$ ($\boldsymbol{EC}_{m(TOL)}$) at the ***Level-2*** is equivalent to $\boldsymbol{EC}_{1L}$ ($\boldsymbol{EC}_{mL}$) at the ***Level-1***;
- $\boldsymbol{PO}_{1L14, 1L15, 1L29, 1L30}$ ($\boldsymbol{PO}_{m(TOL)}$) at the ***Level-2*** is equivalent to $\boldsymbol{PO}_{4L}$ ($\boldsymbol{PO}_{mL}$) at the ***Level-1***;
- $\boldsymbol{TPP}_{1L27, 1L28}$ ($\boldsymbol{TPP}_{m(TOL)}$) at the ***Level-2*** is equivalent to $\boldsymbol{TPP}_{2LT}$ ($\boldsymbol{TPP}_{mLT}$) at the ***Level-1***;
- And $\boldsymbol{TPPi}_{2L6}$ ($\boldsymbol{TPPi}_{m(TOL)}$) at the ***Level-2*** is equivalent to $\boldsymbol{TPPi}_{2LT}$ ($\boldsymbol{TPPi}_{mLT}$) at the ***Level-1***.

For example, for the graphical representation (a) in Figure 15, the detailed topological relation at the ***Level-2*** is written by the expression: $\boldsymbol{EC}_{1L1, 1L13}$. Also, we can say that the detailed ***EC*** relation at the ***Level-2*** is described by: one line of type (*1L1*) and one line of type (*1L13*) of externally connection with one bounded region (*1R*). Then, the detailed ***EC*** relation is written at the ***Level-2*** under the expression ($\boldsymbol{EC}_{1L1, 1L13, 1R}$).

Meanwhile, for the graphical representation (b) in Figure 15, the detailed topological relation at the ***Level-2*** is written by the expression: $\boldsymbol{EC}_{1L1, 1L2, 1L13}$. Also, we can say that the detailed ***EC*** relation at the ***Level-2*** is described by: one line of type (1L1), one line of type (*1L2*) and one line of type (*1L13*) of externally connection with two bounded regions (*2R*). Then, the detailed ***EC*** relation is written at the ***Level-2*** under the expression: $\boldsymbol{EC}_{1L1, 1L2, 1L13, 2R}$.

Another example is given here. For the graphical representation (a) in Figure 16, the detailed topological relation at the ***Level-2*** is written by the expression: $\boldsymbol{TPP}_{1L27, 1L28}$. Also, we can say that the detailed ***TPP*** relation at the ***Level-2*** is described by: one line of type (*1L27*) and one line of type (*1L28*) of externally connection with one bounded region (*1R*). Then, the detailed ***TPP*** relation is written at the ***Level-2*** under the expression ($\boldsymbol{TPP}_{1L27, 1L28, 1R}$).

Meanwhile, for the graphical representation (b) in Figure 16, the detailed topological relation at the ***Level-2*** is written by the expression: $\boldsymbol{TPP}_{1L10, 1L24, 1L27, 1L28}$. Also, we can say that the detailed ***TPP*** relation at the ***Level-2*** is described by: one line of type (*1L10*), one line of type (*1L24*), one line of type (*1L27*) and one line of type (*1L28*) of tangential proper part with two bounded regions (*2R*). Then, the detailed ***TPP*** relation is written at the ***Level-2*** under the expression: $\boldsymbol{TPP}_{1L10, 1L24, 1L27, 1L28, 2R}$.

Finally, for the cases of the detailed topological relation at the ***Level-1*** ($\boldsymbol{EC}_{mL, nP}$, $\boldsymbol{PO}_{mL, nP}$, $\boldsymbol{TPP}_{mLT, nPT}$, ***and*** $\boldsymbol{TPPi}_{mLT, nPT}$), we integrate the types of points (*TOP*) and lines (*TOL*) for detailing and enriching these detailed topological relations at the ***Level-2*** as following:

1. At the ***Level-2***, the detailed relation $\boldsymbol{EC}_{m(TOL), n(TOP)}$ is equivalent to the detailed relation $\boldsymbol{EC}_{mL, nP}$ at the ***Level-1***.
2. At the ***Level-2***, the detailed relation $\boldsymbol{PO}_{m(TOL), n(TOP)}$ is equivalent to the detailed relation $\boldsymbol{PO}_{mL, nP}$ at the ***Level-1***.
3. At the ***Level-2***, the detailed relation $\boldsymbol{TPP}_{m(TOL), n(TOP)}$ is equivalent to the detailed relation $\boldsymbol{TPP}_{mLT, nPT}$ at the ***Level-1***.
4. At the ***Level-2***, the detailed relation $\boldsymbol{TPPi}_{m(TOL), n(TOP)}$ is equivalent to the detailed relation $\boldsymbol{TPPi}_{mLT, nPT}$ at the ***Level-1***.

*Figure 15. Part (1): graphical representations for the types of lines (TOL)*

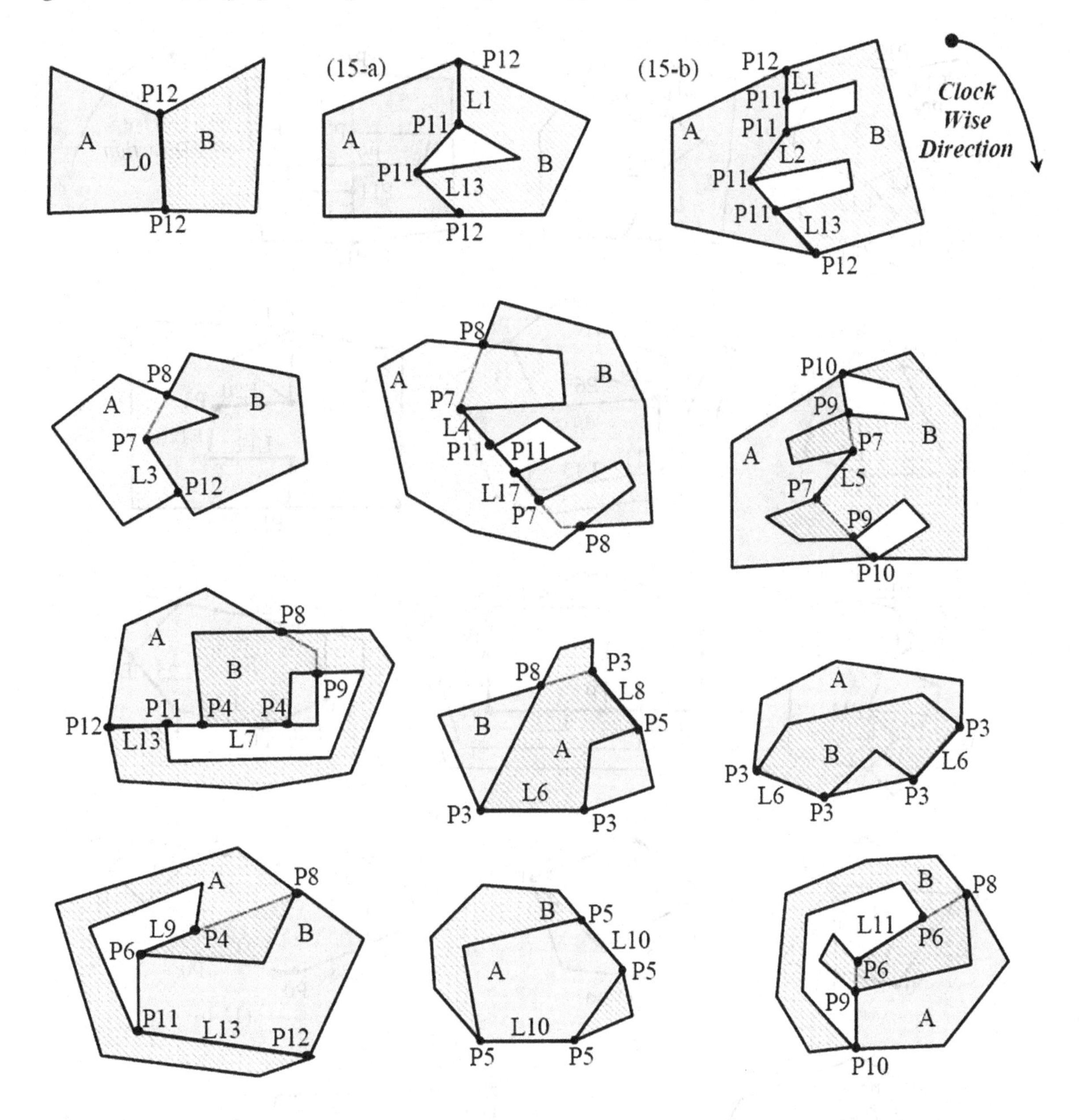


For example, the four detailed topological relation at the ***Level-2*** (with their equivalent at the ***Level-1***) can be written under the forms such as:

- $EC_{1L1,\ 1P10}$ ($EC_{m(TOL),\ n(TOP)}$) at the ***Level-2*** (see Figure 17a) is equivalent to $EC_{1L,\ 1P}$ ($EC_{mL,\ nP}$) at the ***Level-1***;
- $PO_{1L3,\ 1P8}$ ($PO_{m(TOL)}$) at the ***Level-2*** (see Figure 17b) is equivalent to $PO_{1L,\ 1P}$ ($PO_{mL}$) at the ***Level-1***;
- $TPP_{1L27,\ 1L28,\ 2P5}$ ($TPP_{m(TOL),\ n(TOP)}$) at the ***Level-2*** (see Figure 17c) is equivalent to $TPP_{2LT,\ 2PT}$ ($TPP_{mLT,\ nPT}$) at the ***Level-1***;

*Figure 16. Part (2): graphical representations for the types of lines (TOL)*

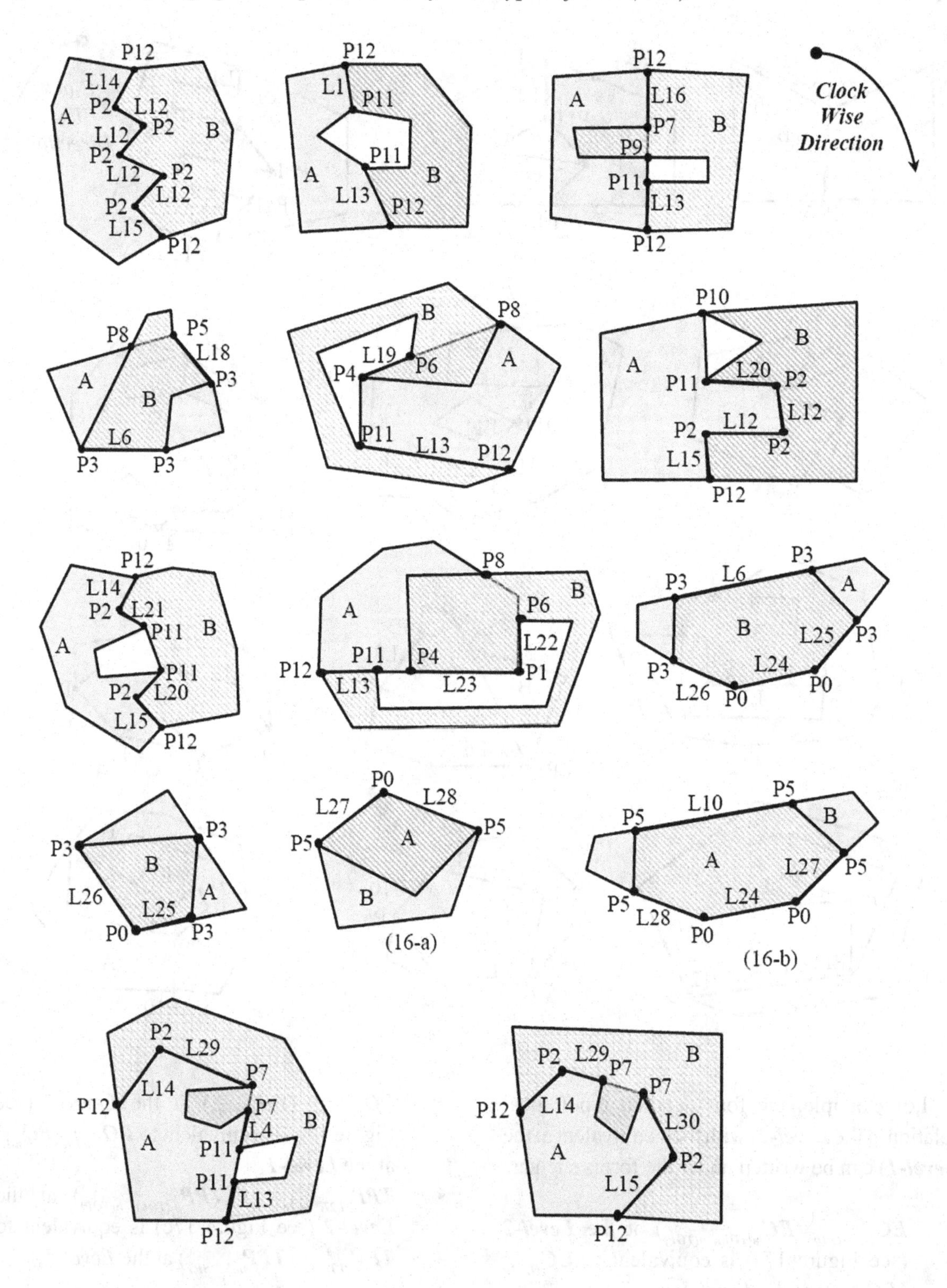

*Figure 17. Graphical representations for the types of lines (TOL) and points (TOP)*

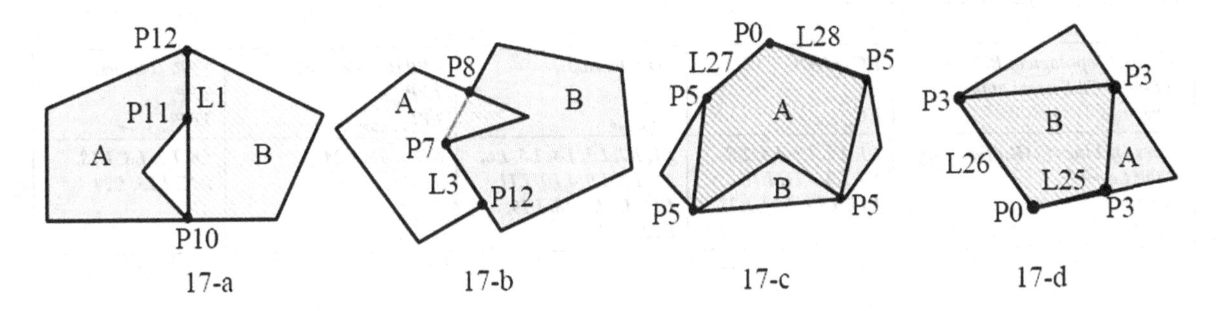


*Table 14. Types of lines (TOL) at the level-2 are always and without doubt with these detailed topological relations of the RCC8 system at the level-1*

| *Detailed Topological Relations of the RCC8 System at the Level-1* | *EC (Meet)* $EC_{mL}$ $EC_{mL,nP}$ | *PO (Overlaps)* $PO_{mL}$ $PO_{mL,nP}$ | *TPP (CoveredBy)* $TPP_{mLT}$ $TPP_{mLT,nPT}$ | *TPPi (Covers)* $TPPi_{mLT}$ $TPPi_{mLT,nPT}$ |
|---|---|---|---|---|
| *Types Of Lines (TOL) for using at the Level-2* | *L0, L12, L13, L14, L15, L20, L21* | *L29, L30* | *L27, L28* | *L25, L26* |

- And $\boldsymbol{TPPi}_{1L25,\ 1L26,\ 1P3}$ ($\boldsymbol{TPPi}_{m(TOL),\ n(TOP)}$) at the ***Level-2*** (see Figure 17d) is equivalent to $\boldsymbol{TPPi}_{2LT,\ 1PT}$ ($\boldsymbol{TPPi}_{mLT,\ nPT}$) at the ***Level-1***.

## Conclusion about the Definiton of the Types of Lines (TOL)

To conclude on the definition of the types of lines, we find that we can determine the detailed topological relation at the ***Level-2*** based upon the determination of the types of lines (*TOL*) of BBISS.

In the two following tables, we give the detailed topological relation corresponding to each type of lines. In Table 14, detailed topological relations at the ***Level-2*** are always and undoubtedly with these types of lines and vice-versa. For example, the types of lines (*L25*) and (*L26*) are always and without doubt correspond to the detailed ***TPPi*** topological relation ($\boldsymbol{TPPi}_{mLT}$ ***and*** $\boldsymbol{TPPi}_{mLT,\ nPT}$).

In Table 15, the types of lines can participate to identify several detailed topological relations at the ***Level-2***. The detailed relations at the ***Level-2*** corresponding to the types of lines are without doubt, but not always true with these types. That is to say that each of these types of lines can characterize and describe two or more of these detailed topological relations (***EC, PO, TPP, and TPPi***). For example, the type of line (*L1*) can characterize both detailed relations ***EC*** ($\boldsymbol{EC}_{mL}$ ***and*** $\boldsymbol{EC}_{mL,\ nP}$) and ***PO*** ($\boldsymbol{PO}_{mL}$ ***and*** $\boldsymbol{PO}_{mL,\ nP}$). For example, the type of line (*L24*) is always corresponding to the two detailed topological relations ***TPPi*** ($\boldsymbol{TPPi}_{mLT}$ ***and*** $\boldsymbol{TPPi}_{mLT,nPT}$) ***and TPP*** ($\boldsymbol{TPPi}_{mLT}$ ***and*** $\boldsymbol{TPPi}_{mLT,\ nPT}$).

## Summary about the Detailed Topological Relations of the RCC8 System at the Level-2

In the two principal parts (defintions of types of points [*TOP*] and lines [*TOL*]), we have defined the types of points and lines. The main contribution in this section is new detailed topological relations of the RCC8 system at the ***Level-2***.

To conclude, new topological relations at the second detailed level (***Level-2***) to discriminate between relations of the same kind are introduced.

*Table 15. Types of lines (TOL) at the level-2 are without doubt with these detailed topological relations of the RCC8 system at the level-1*

| *Detailed Topological Relations of the RCC8 System at the Level-1* | *EC (Meet)* $EC_{mL}$ $EC_{mL, nP}$ | *PO (Overlaps)* $PO_{mL}$ $PO_{mL, nP}$ | *TPP (CoveredBy)* $TPP_{mLT}$ $TPP_{mLT, nPT}$ | *TPPi (Covers)* $TPPi_{mLT}$ $TPPi_{mLT, nPT}$ |
|---|---|---|---|---|
| *Types Of Lines (TOL) for using at the Level-2* | *L1, L2, L3, L4, L5, L7, L9, L11, L16, L17, L19, L22, L23* | *L1, L2, L3, L4, L5, L6, L7, L8, L9, L10, L11, L16, L17, L18, L19, L22, L23* | *L10, L18, L24* | *L6, L7, L8, L18, L22, L23, L24* |

The four detailed topological relations of the RCC8 system at the ***Level-2*** are given by Table 16. The four detailed topological relations at the ***Level-2*** are written under these general forms:

$$(Topological\_Relation)_{n(Type\_Of\_Points)},$$

$$(Topological\_Relation)_{m(Type\_Of\_Lines)}$$

and

$$(Topological\_Relation)_{m(Type\_Of\_Lines),\ n(Type\_Of\_Points)}.$$

Where the notation

$$Topological\_Relation = EC, PO, TPP, TPPi$$

is one of the four relations: ***EC, PO, TPP, and TPPi.***

In other words, four relations ***EC, PO, TPP, and TPPi*** of the RCC8 system are determined in details at the ***Level-2*** in Table 16 under these general forms:

$$(EC, PO, TPP, TPPi)_{n(TOP)},$$

$$(EC, PO, TPP, TPPi)_{m(TOL)}$$

and

$$(EC, PO, TPP, TPPi)_{m(TOL), n(TOP)}.$$

Where the notation (*TOP*) denotes (*Type_Of_Points*) and the notation (*TOL*) denotes (*Type_Of_Lines*).

By using the ***ID model*** and the concept of types of spatial elements (Points and Lines) with the separation number, the four detailed topological relations at the ***Level-2*** are given as seen in this work and in Alboody et al. (2009b):

- ***EC*** becomes as: $EC_{m(TOL)}$, $EC_{n(TOP)}$, $EC_{m(TOL), n(TOP)}$;
- ***PO*** becomes as: $PO_{m(TOL)}$, $PO_{n(TOP)}$, $PO_{m(TOL), n(TOP)}$;
- ***TPP*** becomes as: $TPP_{m(TOL)}$, $TPP_{n(TOP)}$, $TPP_{m(TOL), n(TOP)}$;
- And ***TPPi*** becomes as: $TPPi_{m(TOL)}$, $TPPi_{n(TOP)}$, $TPPi_{m(TOL), n(TOP)}$.

Based upon these four detailed topological relations at the ***Level-2***, the enriched version of the RCC8 system consists of sixteen (16) relations and can be written as: ***DC***, $EC_{m(TOL)}$, $EC_{n(TOP)}$, $EC_{m(TOL), n(TOP)}$, $PO_{m(TOL)}$, $PO_{n(TOP)}$, $PO_{m(TOL), n(TOP)}$, $TPP_{m(TOL)}$, $TPP_{n(TOP)}$, $TPP_{m(TOL), n(TOP)}$, ***NTPP***, $TPPi_{m(TOL)}$, $TPPi_{n(TOP)}$, $TPPi_{m(TOL), n(TOP)}$, ***NTPPi***, and ***EQ***.

We call this new set of (16) detailed topological relations of the RCC8 system by *the extended version of the RCC8 system at the **Level-2*** or we can call this *extended version of the RCC8 system* by ***the RCC-16 system at the Level-2.***

*Table 16. Generalization of the four detailed topological relations EC, PO, TPP, and TPPi of the RCC8 system at the level-2*

| Topological Relations of the RCC8 System: at the *Level-0* Without Any Details | Detailed Topological Relations of the RCC8 System: *EC, PO, TPP and TPPi* at the *Level-2* | |
|---|---|---|
| | With Type Of Points *(TOP)* and Type Of Lines *(TOL)* | With Bounded Regions (*kR*) and Intersection Regions (*jRI*) |
| EC | $EC_{m(TOL)}$ | $EC_{m(TOL), 0R}$ |
| | | $EC_{m(TOL), kR}$ |
| | $EC_{n(TOP)}$ | $EC_{n(TOP), 0R}$ |
| | | $EC_{n(TOP), kR}$ |
| | $EC_{m(TOL), n(TOP)}$ | $EC_{m(TOL), n(TOP), kR}$ |
| PO | $PO_{m(TOL)}$ | $PO_{m(TOL), jRI, 0R}$ |
| | | $PO_{m(TOL), jRI, kR}$ |
| | $PO_{n(TOP)}$ | $PO_{n(TOP), jRI, 0R}$ |
| | | $PO_{n(TOP), jRI, kR}$ |
| | $PO_{m(TOL), n(TOP)}$ | $PO_{m(TOL), n(TOP), jRI, 0R}$ |
| | | $PO_{m(TOL), n(TOP), jRI, kR}$ |
| TPP | $TPP_{m(TOL)}$ | $TPP_{m(TOL), kR}$ |
| | $TPP_{n(TOP)}$ | $TPP_{n(TOP), kR}$ |
| | $TPP_{m(TOL), n(TOP)}$ | $TPP_{m(TOL), n(TOP), kR}$ |
| TPPi | $TPPi_{m(TOL)}$ | $TPPi_{m(TOL), kR}$ |
| | $TPPi_{n(TOP)}$ | $TPPi_{n(TOP), kR}$ |
| | $TPPi_{m(TOL), n(TOP)}$ | $TPPi_{m(TOL), n(TOP), kR}$ |

## Summary of Contributions

In this chapter, the main contribution is different levels (***Level-1*** and ***Level-2)*** of detailed topological relations of the qualitative spatial reasoning system RCC8 to differentiate different kinds of topological details. We say that the qualitative spatial reasoning system RCC8 is enriched at two levels (***Level-1*** and ***Level-2)*** using two principal concepts: the *Seperation Number* and the *Types of Spatial Elements* of BBISS. In Table 17, a multi-level (***Level -0, Level-1,*** and ***Level-2***) topological relation of the RCC8 system is presented. We have developed and implemented algorithms on ***MATLAB*** (not included here in this chapter) to find all these detailed topological relations at two levels (***Level-1*** and ***Level-2)*** with the separation number and the types of spatial elements.

## Examples of Multi-Level Detailed Topological Relations of the RCC8 System

In this part, we will show how to describe the four detailed relations ***EC, PO, TPP,*** and ***TPPi*** by using the types of points and lines with its separation number and the separation number of intersection regions (*jRI*) and bounded regions (*kR*). Further, questions such as: (*1) how many times two regions touch, and (2) they are only points, lines or both points and lines touch, and (3) how many times two regions overlap can be answered.* For examples, in Table 18, multi-level detailed topological relations are determined based upon the concept of separation number and the types of spatial elements (points and lines) for spatial configurations presented in Figure 18. We

*Table 17. Contributions: generalization of the four detailed topological relations **EC, PO, TPP,** and **TPPi** of the RCC8 system at two levels: **level-1** with the concept of separation number and **level-2** with the concept of types of spatial elements (points and lines) of BBISS*

| Topological Relations of the RCC8 System: at the *Level-0* Without Any Details | Detailed Topological Relations of the RCC8 System: *EC, PO, TPP and TPPi* at the *Level-1* | | Detailed Topological Relations of the RCC8 System: *EC, PO, TPP and TPPi* at the *Level-2* | |
|---|---|---|---|---|
| | With Points *(nP/nPT)* and Lines *(mL/mLT)* | With Bounded Regions *(kR)* and Intersection Regions *(jRI)* | With Type Of Points *(TOP)* and Type Of Lines *(TOL)* | With Bounded Regions *(kR)* and Intersection Regions *(jRI)* |
| EC | $EC_{mL}$ | $EC_{mL, 0R}$ | $EC_{m(TOL)}$ | $EC_{m(TOL), 0R}$ |
| | | $EC_{mL, kR}$ | | $EC_{m(TOL), kR}$ |
| | $EC_{nP}$ | $EC_{1P, 0R}$ | $EC_{n(TOP)}$ | $EC_{n(TOP), 0R}$ |
| | | $EC_{nP, kR}$ | | $EC_{n(TOP), kR}$ |
| | $EC_{mL, nP}$ | $EC_{mL, nP, kR}$ | $EC_{m(TOL), n(TOP)}$ | $EC_{m(TOL), n(TOP), kR}$ |
| PO | $PO_{mL}$ | $PO_{mL, jRI, 0R}$ | $PO_{m(TOL)}$ | $PO_{m(TOL), jRI, 0R}$ |
| | | $PO_{mL, jRI, kR}$ | | $PO_{m(TOL), jRI, kR}$ |
| | $PO_{nP}$ | $PO_{nP, jRI, 0R}$ | $PO_{n(TOP)}$ | $PO_{n(TOP), jRI, 0R}$ |
| | | $PO_{nP, jRI, kR}$ | | $PO_{n(TOP), jRI, kR}$ |
| | $PO_{mL, nP}$ | $PO_{mL, nP, jRI, 0R}$ | $PO_{m(TOL), n(TOP)}$ | $PO_{m(TOL), n(TOP), jRI, 0R}$ |
| | | $PO_{mL, nP, jRI, kR}$ | | $PO_{m(TOL), n(TOP), jRI, kR}$ |
| TPP | $TPP_{mLT}$ | $TPP_{mLT, kR}$ | $TPP_{m(TOL)}$ | $TPP_{m(TOL), kR}$ |
| | $TPP_{nPT}$ | $TPP_{nPT, kR}$ | $TPP_{n(TOP)}$ | $TPP_{n(TOP), kR}$ |
| | $TPP_{mLT, nPT}$ | $TPP_{mLT, nPT, kR}$ | $TPP_{m(TOL), n(TOP)}$ | $TPP_{m(TOL), n(TOP), kR}$ |
| TPPi | $TPPi_{mLT}$ | $TPPi_{mLT, kR}$ | $TPPi_{m(TOL)}$ | $TPPi_{m(TOL), kR}$ |
| | $TPPi_{nPT}$ | $TPPi_{nPT, kR}$ | $TPPi_{n(TOP)}$ | $TPPi_{n(TOP), kR}$ |
| | $TPPi_{mLT, nPT}$ | $TPPi_{mLT, nPT, kR}$ | $TPPi_{m(TOL), n(TOP)}$ | $TPPi_{m(TOL), n(TOP), kR}$ |

find that we can distinguish between relations of the same kind ***EC***, ***PO***, ***TPP,*** and ***TPPi***.

For example, the detailed ***EC*** topological relation for the case (a) in Figure 18 is described by: ***at the Level-1:*** three points (*3P*) of externally connection with two bounded regions (*2R*), and ***then*** detailed ***EC*** relation is written at the ***Level-1*** under the expression: $EC_{3P, 2R}$. While, ***at the Level-2:*** two points of type (*2P10*), one point of type (*1P11*) of externally connection with two bounded regions (*2R*), and ***then*** detailed ***EC*** relation is written at the ***Level-2*** in the form: $EC_{2P10, 1P11, 2R}$.

## APPLICATIONS

In some applications such as GIS spatial analysis, detecting topological changes, spatial reasoning, and satellite image inetrpretation where qualitative spatial representation and reasoning is necessary and it often needs detailed topological relations. It is also demonstrated that additional details of relations can provide crucial information to specify the semantics of spatial relations in query languages for GIS and images databases. As GIS spatial analysis application, we take CORINE Land Cover (CLC) database (CORINE Land Cover, 2000) as geospatial data, which is available in many different formats (vector…) and contains spatial information of different levels of details, coarseness, and general structure. CORINE Land

*Table 18. Examples of multi-level detailed topological relations of the RCC8 system*

| Figure | Topological Relations of the RCC8 System at the *Level-0* Without Any Details | Detailed Topological Relations of the RCC8 System with the Concept of Separation Number at the *Level-1* | | Detailed Topological Relations of the RCC8 System with the Concept of Types of Points *(TOP)* and Lines *(TOL)* at the *Level-2* | |
|---|---|---|---|---|---|
| | | With Points *(nP/nPT)* and Lines *(mL/mLT)* | With Bounded Regions *(kR)* and Intersection Regions *(jRI)* | With Type Of Points *(TOP)* and Type Of Lines *(TOL)* | With Bounded Regions *(kR)* and Intersection Regions *(jRI)* |
| *18-a* | *EC* | $EC_{3P}$ | $EC_{3P, 2R}$ | $EC_{2P10, 1P11}$ | $EC_{2P10, 1P11, 2R}$ |
| *18-b* | *EC* | $EC_{4L}$ | $EC_{4L, 0R}$ | $EC_{1L14, 2L12, 1L15}$ | $EC_{1L14, 2L12, 1L15, 0R}$ |
| *18-c* | *EC* | $EC_{2L, 1P}$ | $EC_{2L, 1P, 2R}$ | $EC_{1L1, 1L2, 1P10}$ | $EC_{1L1, 1L2, 1P10, 2R}$ |
| *18-d* | *PO* | $PO_{2P}$ | $PO_{2P, 1RI, 0R}$ | $PO_{2P8}$ | $PO_{2P8, 1RI, 0R}$ |
| *18-e* | *PO* | $PO_{3L}$ | $PO_{3L, 1RI, 1R}$ | $PO_{1L1, 1L3, 1L17}$ | $PO_{1L1, 1L3, 1L17, 1RI, 1R}$ |
| *18-f* | *PO* | $PO_{1L, 4P}$ | $PO_{1L, 4P, 2RI, 2R}$ | $PO_{1L2, 2P8, 2P9}$ | $PO_{1L2, 2P8, 2P9, 2RI, 2R}$ |
| *18-g* | *TPP* | $TPP_{3PT}$ | $TPP_{3PT, 3R}$ | $TPP_{3P5}$ | $TPP_{3P5, 3R}$ |
| *18-h* | *TPP* | $TPP_{2LT}$ | $TPP_{2LT, 1R}$ | $TPP_{1L27, 1L28}$ | $TPP_{1L27, 1L28, 1R}$ |
| *18-i* | *TPP* | $TPP_{2LT, 1PT}$ | $TPP_{2LT, 1PT, 2R}$ | $TPP_{1L27, 1L28, 1P5}$ | $TPP_{1L27, 1L28, 1P5, 2R}$ |
| *18-j* | *TPPi* | $TPPi_{3PT}$ | $TPPi_{3PT, 3R}$ | $TPPi_{3P3}$ | $TPPi_{3P3, 3R}$ |
| *18-k* | *TPPi* | $TPPi_{2LT}$ | $TPPi_{2LT, 1R}$ | $TPPi_{1L25, 1L26}$ | $TPPi_{1L25, 1L26, 1R}$ |
| *18-o* | *TPPi* | $TPPi_{2LT, 2PT}$ | $TPPi_{2LT, 2PT, 3R}$ | $TPPi_{1L25, 1L26, 2P3}$ | $TPPi_{1L25, 1L26, 2P3, 3R}$ |

Cover (CLC) uses a unique combination of satellite images and other data (such as aerial photographs, maps…) to reveal all kinds of information on land resources which has a broad range of applications: from nature conservation to urban planning. The standard CLC nomenclature includes 44 land cover classes. These are grouped in a three level hierarchy. The five level-one categories are: 1) artificial surfaces, 2) agricultural areas, 3) forests and semi-natural areas, 4) wetlands, 5) water bodies.

We use CORINE Land Cover (CLC2000) vector database (CORINE Land Cover, 2000) for the department (45) of ***Loiret*** in ***France*** as a geospatial database where a part of the map CLC2000D45 of the database CLC2000 is presented in Figure 19. We have developed and implemented algorithms on ***MATLAB*** in order to search and to find the detailed topological relations at the first level (***Level-1***) from the map CLC2000D45. We give in Figure 20 (a and b) some results of the detailed topological relations at the ***Level-1*** of the kind $EC_{mL, 0R}$ extracted from the map CLC2000D45. For Figure 20a, the detailed topological relation at the ***Level-1*** is given as $EC_{3L, 0R}$ with three lines (*3L*) of externally connection and without any bounded region (*0R*). At the ***Level-2***, the detailed topological relation for Figure 20a can be written as $EC_{1L12, 1L14, 1L15, 0R}$ with one line of type (*1L12*), one line of type (*1L14*) and one line of type (*1L15*) of externally connection and without any bounded region (*0R*)

Meanwhile for Figure 20b, the detailed topological relation at the ***Level-1*** is given as $EC_{18L, 0R}$ with eigtheen lines (*18L*) of externally connection and without any bounded region (*0R*). At the ***Level-2***, the detailed topological relation for Figure 20b can be written as $EC_{1L14, 16L12, 1L15, 0R}$ with one line of type (*1L14*), sixteen lines of type (*16L12*) and one line of type (*1L15*) of externally connection and without any bounded region (*0R*).

Another example is given in Figure 21 (a and b) about the detailed topological relations at the ***Level-1*** of the kind $EC_{mL, kR}$. For Figure 21a, the detailed topological relation at the ***Level-1*** is given as $EC_{6L, 1R}$ with six lines (*6L*) of externally connection and one bounded region (*1R*). At the ***Level-2***, the detailed topological relation for Figure 21a can

*Figure 18. Graphical representations for examples about multi-level detailed topological relations of the RCC8 system*

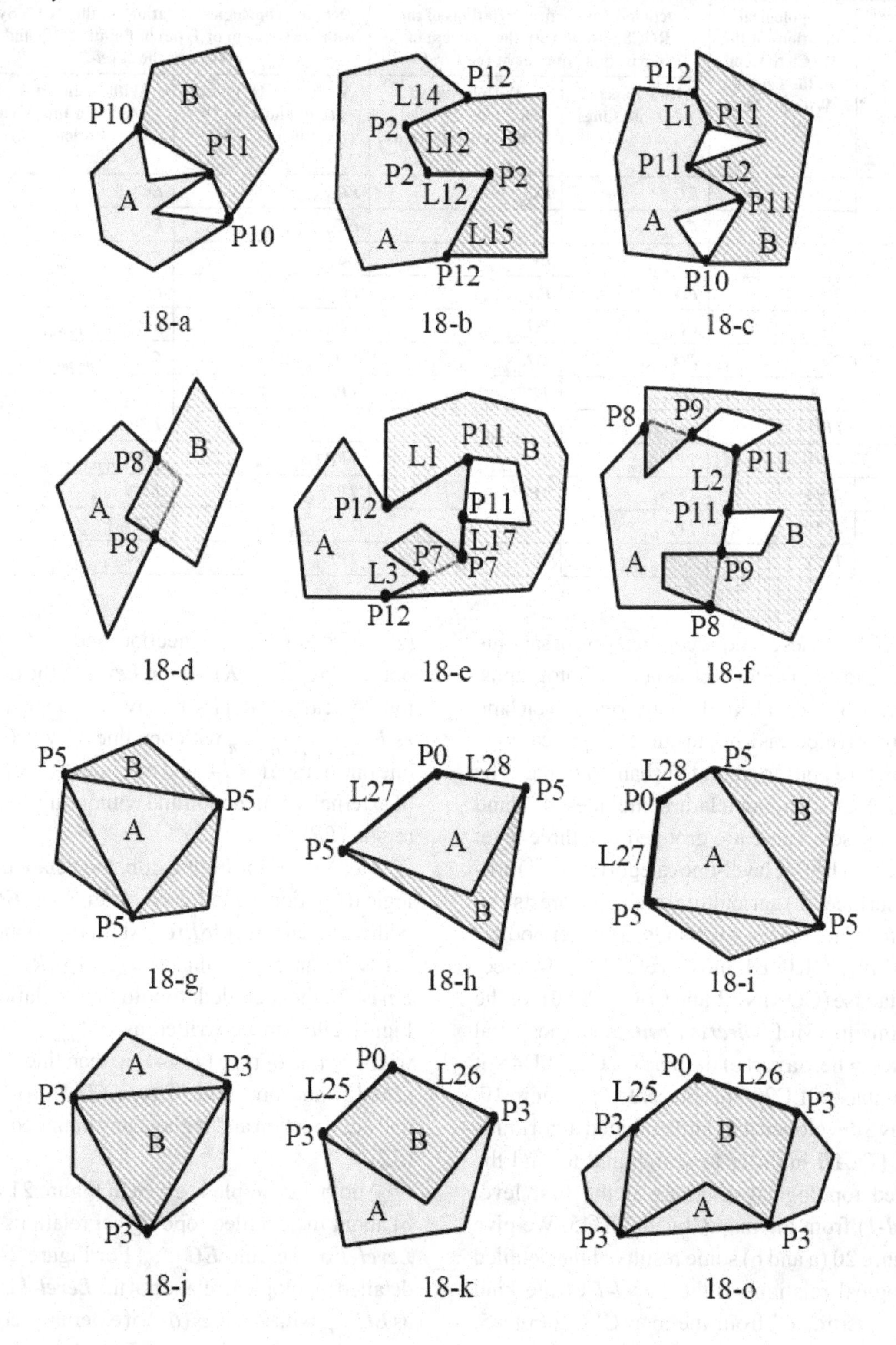

*Figure 19. Part of the map CLC2000D45 of the CLC2000 vector database*

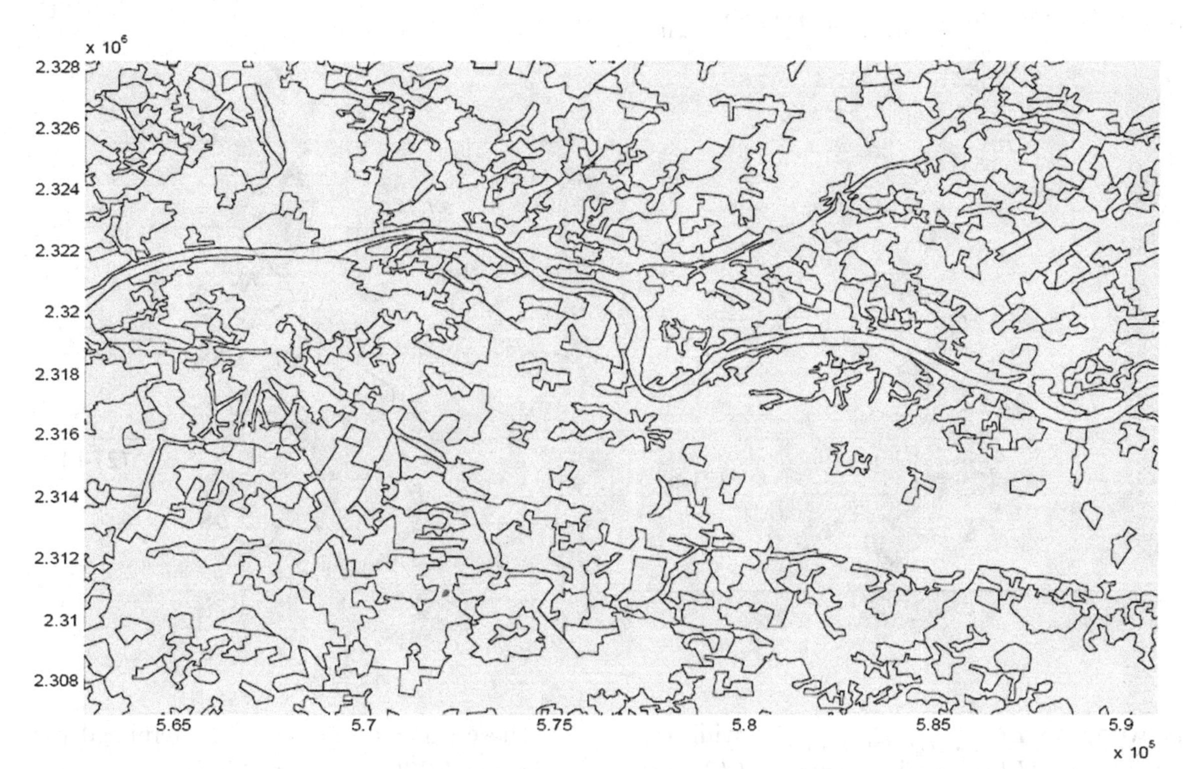


*Figure 20. Some results of the detailed topological relations at the* **level-1** *for* $\mathbf{EC}_{\mathbf{mL,\,0R}}$ *with CLC2000 vector database: (a)* $\mathbf{EC}_{\mathbf{3L,\,0R}}$ *; and (b)* $\mathbf{EC}_{\mathbf{18L,\,0R}}$

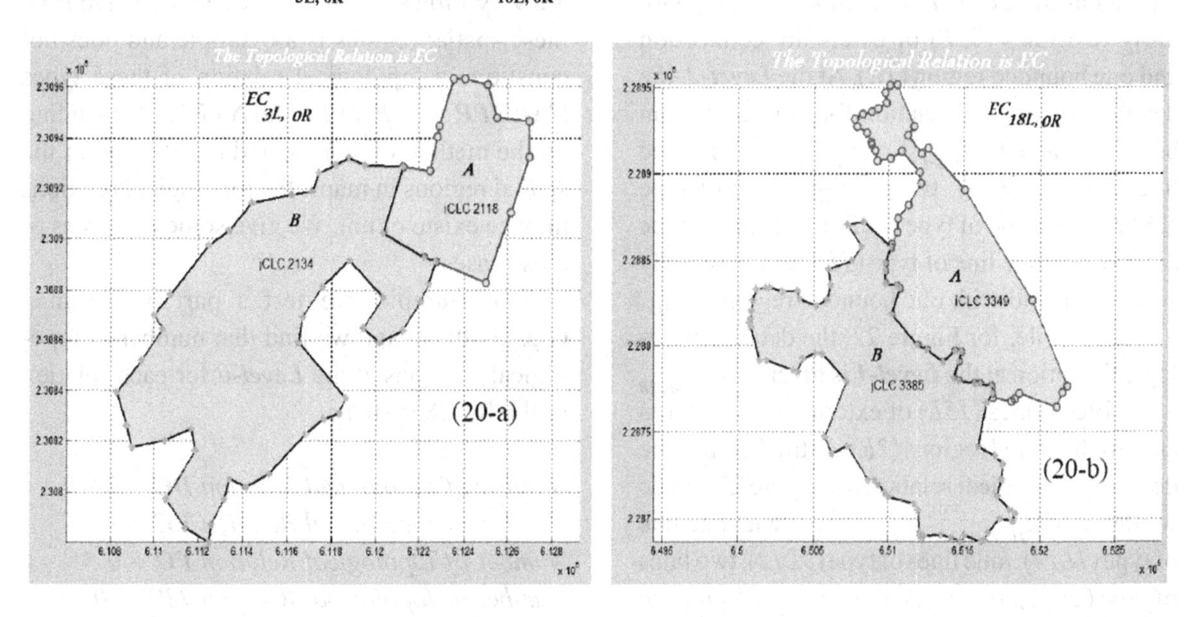

*Figure 21. Some results of the detailed topological relations at the* **level-1** *for* $\mathbf{EC}_{\mathbf{mL,\,kR}}$ *with CLC2000 vector database: (a)* $\mathbf{EC}_{\mathbf{6L,\,1R}}$ *; and (b)* $\mathbf{EC}_{\mathbf{32L,\,1R}}$

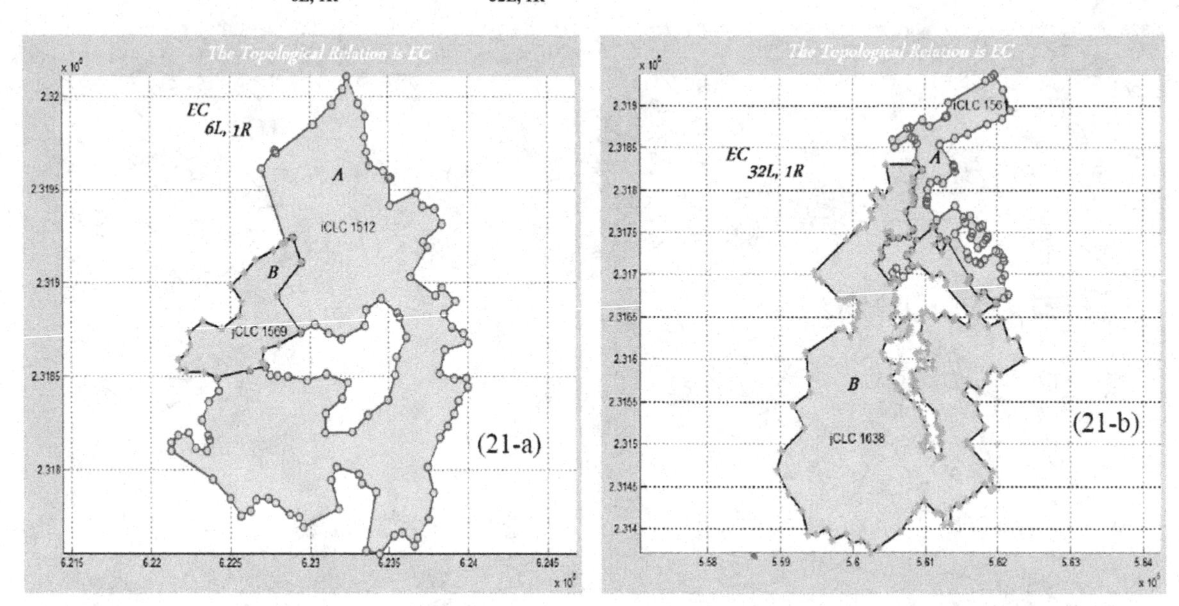


be written as $EC_{1L14,\ 2L12,\ 1L21,\ 1L20,\ 1L15,\ 1R}$ with one line of type (*1L14*), two lines of type (*2L12*), one line of type (*1L21*), one line of type (*1L20*), and one line of type (*1L15*) of externally connection and with one bounded region (*1R*).

And for Figure 21b, the detailed topological relation at the ***Level-1*** is given as $EC_{32L,\ 1R}$ with thirty two lines (*32L*) of externally connection and one bounded region (*1R*). At the ***Level-2***, the detailed topological relation for Figure 21b can be written as $EC_{1L14,\ 28L12,\ 1L21,\ 1L20,\ 1L15,\ 1R}$ with one line of type (*1L14*), twenty eight lines of type (*28L12*), one line of type (*1L21*), one line of type (*1L20*), and one line of type (*1L15*) of externally connection and with one bounded region (*1R*).

Meanwhile, for Figure 22, the detailed topological relation at the ***Level-1*** is given as $EC_{15L,\ 2R}$ with fifteen lines (*15L*) of externally connection and two bounded regions (*2R*). At the ***Level-2***, the detailed topological relation for Figure 22 can be written as $EC_{1L14,\ 28L12,\ 1L21,\ 1L20,\ 1L15,\ 1R}$ with one line of type (*1L14*), nine lines of type (*9L12*), two lines of type (*2L21*), two lines of type (*2L20*), and one line of type (*1L15*) of externally connection and with two bounded regions (*2R*).

These examples are taken and determined from the map CLC2000D45 (see Figure 19).

Most of the topological relations between two spatial regions of the spatial database CLC2000 are ***DC***, ***EC,*** and ***EQ***. The other topological relations (***PO, TPP, NTPP, TPPi,*** and ***NTPPi***) are very little because the way to store and save these spatial regions is too simple and does not constitute a topological relation of these types (***PO, TPP, NTPP, TPPi,*** and ***NTPPi***). Depending on the method of storage and registration of the spatial regions in maps, the topological relations may be existe or not. We give some examples of these cases.

For example, we test a part of the map CLC2000D45 and we find that number of topological relations at the ***Level-0*** for each relation of the RCC8 system:

*Number of Topological Relation* ***DC*** *= 7449*
*Number of Topological Relation* ***EC*** *= 76*
*Number of Topological Relation* ***PO*** *= 0*
*Number of Topological Relation* ***TPP*** *= 0*
*Number of Topological Relation* ***NTPP*** *= 0*
*Number of Topological Relation* ***TPPi*** *= 0*

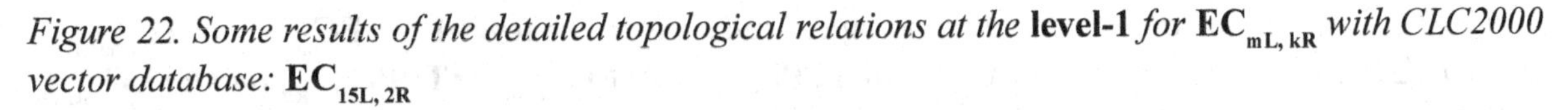

*Figure 22. Some results of the detailed topological relations at the* **level-1** *for* $\mathbf{EC}_{\mathbf{mL,\,kR}}$ *with CLC2000 vector database:* $\mathbf{EC}_{\mathbf{15L,\,2R}}$

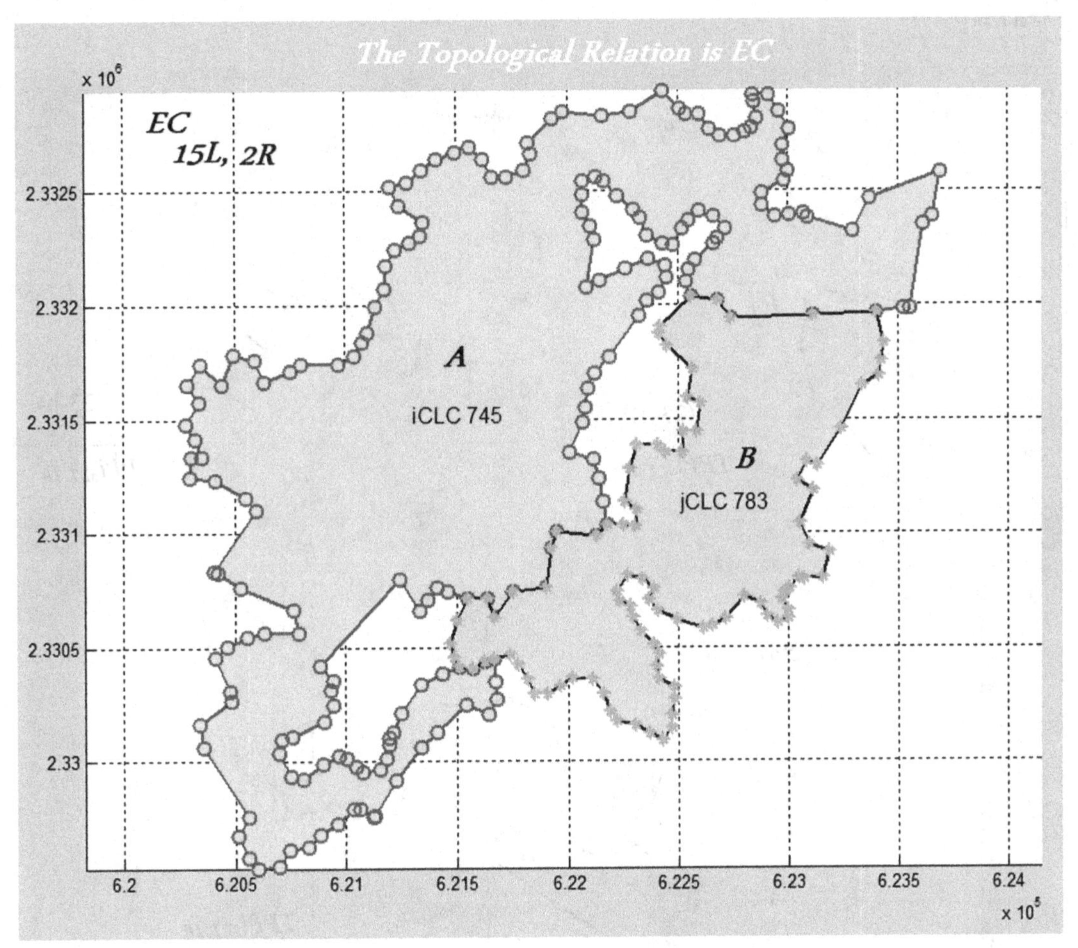


*Number of Topological Relation* ***NTPPi*** *= 0*
*Number of Topological Relation* ***EQ*** *= 50*
*Total Number of Topological Relations = 7575*

We give also some results of queries to find all detailed topological relations of kind $\boldsymbol{TPP}_{mLT,\,kR}$ at the ***Level-1***. For example, the detailed relation of Figure 23a is given in the form $\boldsymbol{EC}_{12L,\,0R}$. While the detailed relation of Figure 23a may be written in the form $\boldsymbol{TPPi}_{4LT,\,1R}$ ($\boldsymbol{TPP}_{mLT,\,kR}$) with four tangential lines (*4LT*) of tangential proper part inverse and one bounded region (*1R*). At the ***Level-2***, the detailed topological relation for Figure 23a can be written as $\boldsymbol{TPPi}_{1L25,\,2L24,\,1L26,\,1R}$ with one line of type (*1L25*), two lines of type (*2L24*), and one line of type (*1L26*) of tangential proper part inverse and with one bounded region (*1R*).

Another example is also given in Figure 23b where the detailed topological relation is written under the form $\boldsymbol{EC}_{14L,\,0R}$. Meanwhile the detailed topological relation of Figure 23b may be written in the form $\boldsymbol{TPPi}_{5LT,\,1R}$ ($\boldsymbol{TPP}_{mLT,\,kR}$) with five tangential lines (*5LT*) of tangential proper part inverse and one bounded region (*1R*). At the ***Level-2***, the detailed topological relation for Figure 23b can be written as $\boldsymbol{TPPi}_{1L25,\,3L24,\,1L26,\,1R}$ with one line of type (*1L25*), three lines of type (*3L24*), and one line of type (*1L26*) of tangential proper part inverse and with one bounded region (*1R*).

*Figure 23. Some results of the detailed topological relations at the* **level-1** *for* $\mathbf{EC_{mL,0R}}$ **or** $\mathbf{TPP_{mLT,kR}}$ *with CLC2000 vector database: (a)* $\mathbf{EC_{12L,0R}}$ **or** $\mathbf{TPPi_{4LT,1R}}$*; (b)* $\mathbf{EC_{14L,0R}}$ **or** $\mathbf{TPPi_{5LT,1R}}$*; and (c)* $\mathbf{EC_{35L,0R}}$ **or** $\mathbf{TPPi_{2LT,1R}}$

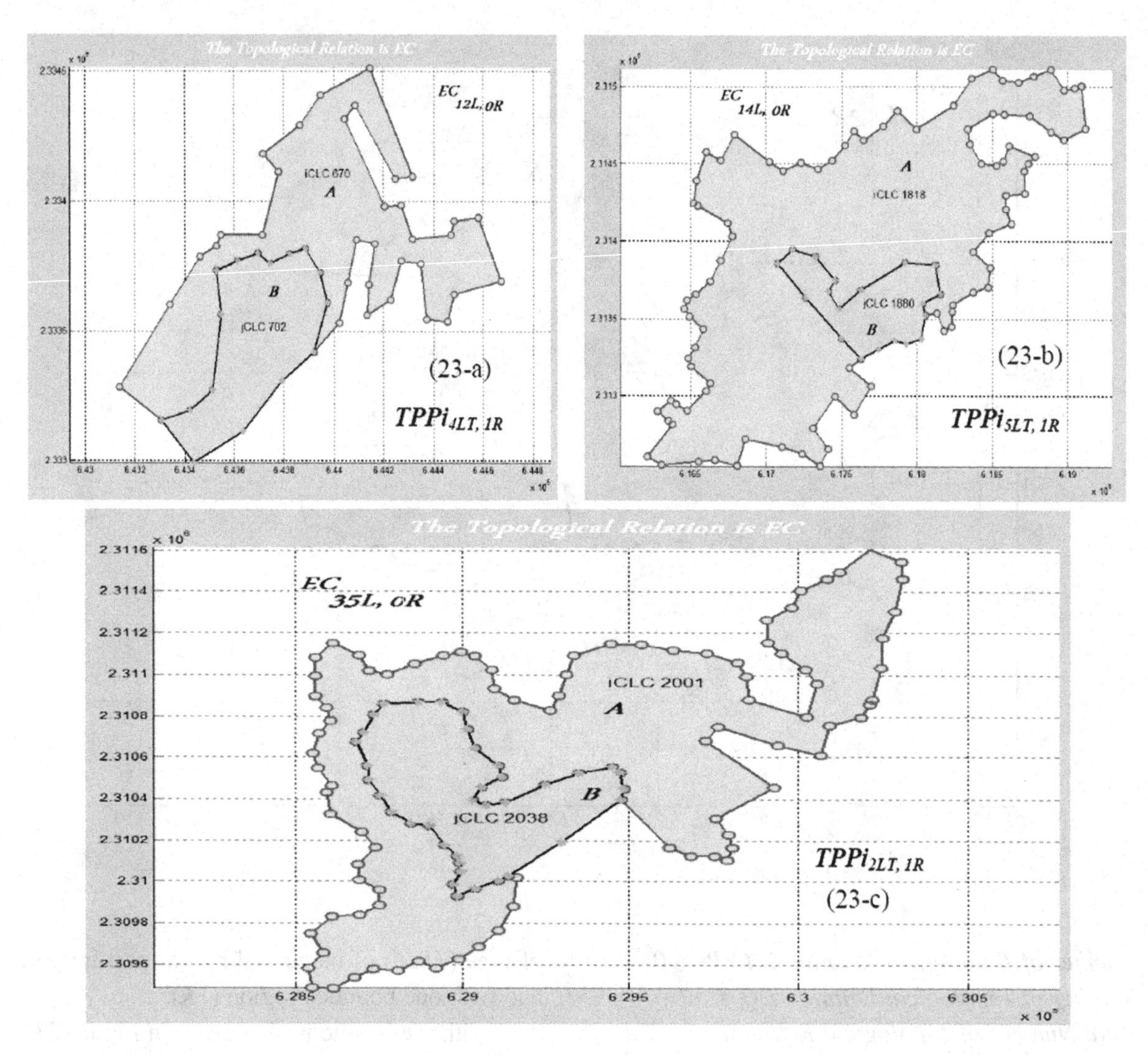


The same thing is applied for the case in Figure 23c where the detailed topological relation may be written in two forms: $EC_{35L,\,0R}$ *or* $TPPi_{2LT,\,1R}$ ($TPP_{mLT,\,kR}$) at the ***Level-1***. At the ***Level-2***, the detailed topological relation for Figure 23b can be written as $TPPi_{1L25,\,1L26,\,1R}$ with one line of type (*1L25*) and one line of type (*1L26*) of tangential proper part inverse and with one bounded region (*1R*).

Another example about the relationship between the detailed topological relation and the used storage method of spatial regions is given in Figure 24. The spatial region *A* consists of three regions (*A1*, *A2*, and *A3*). Two regions (*A1* and *A2*) are in the interior of the spatial region *A3*. The detailed topological relation between *A* and *B* can be written as $EC_{28L,\,0R}$ ($EC_{mL,\,0R}$) at the ***Level-1***. And the topological relation between *A3* and *A1* or between *A3* and *A2* should be holded as

*Figure 24. Some results of the detailed topological relations at the* **level-1:** $\mathbf{EC_{mL,kR}}$ *and* **NTPP** *or* **NTPPi** *with CLC2000 vector database*

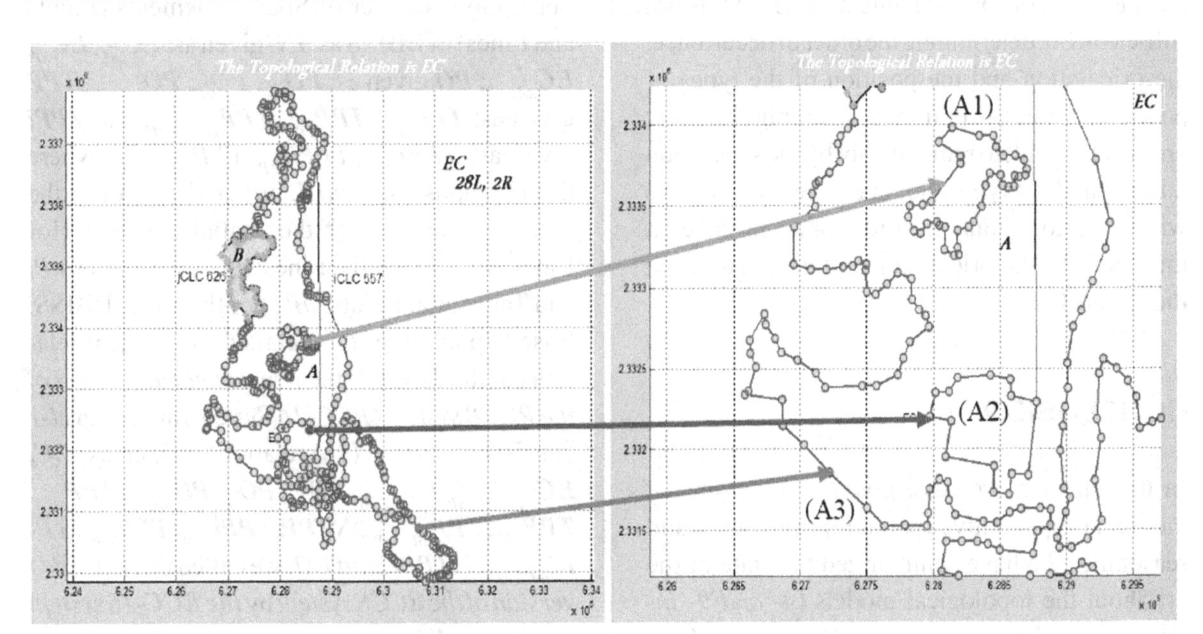


***NTPP*** or ***NTPPi*** and this isn't the case because the storage method considere the three regions (*A1*, *A2*, and *A3*) as one spatial region *A*.

The solution for these problems is to redefine the data storage method with small number of points for each spatial region in the CLC2000 Database. This solution can optimize the memory of storage, the search time and to find more and more of the detailed topological relations of the RCC8 system. For example, in Figure 23a, the spatial region *A* is presented by (47) points of spatial elements. This number of points can be reduced to (39) points (see Figure 23a) instead of (47) points. And the detailed topological relation can be written in the form $\boldsymbol{TPPi_{4LT,1R}}$ ($\boldsymbol{TPP_{mLT,kR}}$) at the ***Level-1***.

In the next section, we will give our perspectives and our future work to be completed and continued.

## FUTURE RESEARCH: NEW COMPOSITION TABLE OF THE RCC8 SYSTEM

Based on the topological relations of the RCC8 system at the ***Level-0***, the composition table of RCC8 is deriving in Randell et al. (1992b) and Egenhofer (1991, 1994) and also presented in Wikipedia (2009).

In our future work, we will try to establish the new composition table of the RCC8 system based upon these new detailed relations at the ***Level-1*** by simulation on ***MATLAB***, mathematically using the ***ID*** model and the old composition table of RCC8. Where the *extended version of the RCC8 system (RCC-16 System)* at the ***Level-1*** consists of sixteen (16) relations written as: $\boldsymbol{DC, EC_{mL}, EC_{nP}, EC_{mL,nP}, PO_{mL}, PO_{nP}, PO_{mL,nP}, TPP_{mLT}, TPP_{nPT}, TPP_{mLT,nPT}, NTPP, TPPi_{mLT}, TPPi_{nPT}, TPPi_{mLT,nPT}}$, ***NTPPi, and EQ***.

Finally, we note that the description of these four detailed topological relations (***EC, PO, TPP, and TPPi***) of the RCC8 system at these two levels

(***Level-1*** and ***Level-2***) by the seperation number and the types of spatial elements of BBISS is not sufficient. So, determining the order of occurrence, the orientation and the position of the types of points and lines can eliminate all ambiguities that are very difficult to remove only by the seperation number and the types. So, in our perspective, we will take into account the order of occurrence (at the ***Level-3***), the orientation and the position (at the ***Level-4***).

## CONCLUSION

In this chapter, we have given an overview of the field of qualitative spatial representation and reasoning. We have summarized the state of the art about the topological models (*4- and 9- intersections, Intersection and Difference **ID**...*) used to get the eight basic topological relations of the RCC8 system at the coarse level and the detailed level. We have studied the properties of the topological relations defined using the ***ID** model*. The concepts of separation number, the neighborhoods, and the types of spatial elements (points and lines) of the Boundary-Boundary Intersection Spatial Set (BBISS) are presented. Then, we detailed the four topological relations ***EC, PO, TPP, and TPPi*** of the RCC8 system at two additional levels (***Level-1*** and ***Level-2***). These topological relations are written under classical forms at the ***Level-0***.

The novel major contribution is the generalization of new detailed topological relations written under general detailed forms at two levels (***Level-1*** and ***Level-2***). Every spatial element (points and lines) of BBISS is important to determine the detailed topological relation. Such details are very useful for qualitative spatial reasoning, spatial analysis in GIS, and automated detection of the spatial inconsistency for updating GIS maps using satellite images.

At the first detailed level (***Level-1***), these four topological relations are written and described in general detailed forms by using the concept of Separation Number of Spatial Elements (Points and Lines) of BBISS as: ***EC*** given as: $EC_{mL}$, $EC_{nP}$, $EC_{mL,\,nP}$; ***PO*** given as: $PO_{mL}$, $PO_{nP}$, $PO_{mL,\,nP}$; ***TPP*** given as: $TPP_{mLT}$, $TPP_{nPT}$, $TPP_{mLT,\,nPT}$; and ***TPPi*** given as: $TPPi_{mLT}$, $TPPi_{nPT}$, $TPPi_{mLT,\,nPT}$; where the notations (*mL*, *mLT*, *nP*, and *nPT*) are the separation number of the spatial elements (for Lines: *mL*, Tangential Lines: *mLT*, for Points: *nP*, and Tangential Points: *nPT*) of the terms BBISS. Based upon these four detailed topological relations at the ***Level-1***, the *new extended version of the RCC8 system* (*RCC-16 System*) at the ***Level-1*** consists of sixteen (16) relations written as: ***DC***, $EC_{mL}$, $EC_{nP}$, $EC_{mL,\,nP}$, $PO_{mL}$, $PO_{nP}$, $PO_{mL,\,nP}$, $TPP_{mLT}$, $TPP_{nPT}$, $TPP_{mLT,\,nPT}$, ***NTPP***, $TPPi_{mLT}$, $TPPi_{nPT}$, $TPPi_{mLT,\,nPT}$, ***NTPPi, and EQ***. we called this *extended version of the RCC8 system* by ***the RCC-16 system at the Level-1.***

Secondly, in order to enrich these topological relations and to confront some problems of ambiguities and confusions, we have developed the definition of the Types of Spatial Elements (Points and Lines) of BBISS. Based upon the concept of type of spatial elements, the topological relations at the ***Level-1*** are written under other general detailed forms at the ***Level-2***.

In other words, the same topological relations at the first detailed level (***Level-1***) are expressed in other general forms more detailed at the second detailed level (***Level-2***) by using the concept of Types of Spatial Elements (Points and Lines) of BBISS as following: ***EC*** given as: $EC_{m(TOL)}$, $EC_{n(TOP)}$, $EC_{m(TOL),\,n(TOP)}$; ***PO*** given as: $PO_{m(TOL)}$, $PO_{n(TOP)}$, $PO_{m(TOL),\,n(TOP)}$; ***TPP*** given as: $TPP_{m(TOL)}$, $TPP_{n(TOP)}$, $TPP_{m(TOL),\,n(TOP)}$; and ***TPPi*** given as: $TPPi_{m(TOL)}$, $TPPi_{n(TOP)}$, $TPPi_{m(TOL),\,n(TOP)}$; where the notations *m(TOL)* and *n(TOP)* are the separation number of the types of spatial elements (for Lines and Tangential Lines: *m(TOL)*; and for Points and Tangential Points: *n(TOP)*) of the terms BBISS. In this context, we have developed definitions for the generalization of these detailed relations at these two levels (***Level-1*** and ***Level-2***).

Based upon these four detailed topological relations at the ***Level-2***, the *new extended version of the RCC8 system* (*RCC-16 System*) consists of sixteen (16) relations and can be written as: ***DC***, $EC_{m(TOL)}$, $EC_{n(TOP)}$, $EC_{m(TOL),\ n(TOP)}$, $PO_{m(TOL)}$, $PO_{n(TOP)}$, $PO_{m(TOL),\ n(TOP)}$, $TPP_{m(TOL)}$, $TPP_{n(TOP)}$, $TPP_{m(TOL),\ n(TOP)}$, ***NTPP***, $TPPi_{m(TOL)}$, $TPPi_{n(TOP)}$, $TPPi_{m(TOL),\ n(TOP)}$, ***NTPPi, and EQ***. we called this *extended version of the RCC8 system* by ***the RCC-16 system at the Level-2.***

Thirdly, we presented one table of these four detailed topological relations (***EC, PO, TPP, and TPPi***) of the RCC8 system at three levels (***Level-0***, ***Level-1***, and ***Level-2***).

Finally, some examples and applications about these four detailed topological relations at different levels (***Level-0***, ***Level-1***, and ***Level-2***) are given.

## REFERENCES


Alboody, A., Inglada, J., & Sèdes, F. (2009a). Enriching the spatial reasoning system RCC8. *The SIGSPATIAL Special*, *1*(1), 14–20. doi:10.1145/1517463.1517464

Alboody, A., Sèdes, F., & Inglada, J. (2008). Post-classification and spatial reasoning: New approach to change detection for updating GIS database. In *Proceedings of the IEEE International Conference on Information and Communication Technologies: From Theory to Applications (ICTTA2008)*, (pp. 1-7). Damascus, Syria. IEEE Press. Retrieved from http://ieeexplore.ieee.org/xpls/abs_all.jsp?arnumber=4530039.

Alboody, A., Sèdes, F., & Inglada, J. (2009b). Multi-level topological relations of the spatial reasoning system RCC-8. In *Proceedings of The First International Conference on Advances in Databases, Knowledge, and Data Applications (DBKDA 2009), IARIA Conferences – GlobeNet2009*, (pp. 13-21). IEEE Press.

Cohn, A. G., Bennett, B., Gooday, J., & Gotts, M. M. (1997). Qualitative spatial representation and reasoning with the region connection calculus. *International Journal of GeoInformatica*, *1*, 275–316. doi:10.1023/A:1009712514511

Cohn, A. G., & Renz, J. (2008). Qualitative spatial representation and reasoning. In *Handbook of Knowledge Representation: Foundations of Artificial Intelligence* (*Vol. 3*, pp. 551–596). London, UK: Elsevier.

Deng, M., Cheng, T., Chen, X., & Li, Z. (2007). Multi-level topological relations between spatial regions based upon topological invariants. *International Journal of GeoInformatica*, *11*(2), 239–267. doi:10.1007/s10707-006-0004-x

Egenhofer, M. J. (1989). A formal definition of binary topological relationships. In *Foundations of Data Organization and Algorithms: Interfaces and Formal Models* (pp. 457–472). Berlin, Germany: Springer-Verlag. doi:10.1007/3-540-51295-0_148

Egenhofer, M. J. (1991). Reasoning about binary topological relations. In *Proceedings of the Second Symposium on Large Spatial Databases*, (pp. 143–160). Springer-Verlag.

Egenhofer, M. J. (1993). A model for detailed binary topological relationships. *International Journal of Geomatica*, *47*(3-4), 261–273.

Egenhofer, M. J. (1994). Deriving the composition of binary topological relations. *Journal of Visual Languages and Computing*, *5*(2), 133–149. doi:10.1006/jvlc.1994.1007

Egenhofer, M. J., & Franzosa, R. (1991). Point-set topological spatial relations. *International Journal of Geographical Information Systems*, *5*(2), 161–174. doi:10.1080/02693799108927841

Egenhofer, M. J., & Franzosa, R. (1995). On the equivalence of topological relations. *International Journal of Geographical Information Systems*, *9*(2), 133–152. doi:10.1080/02693799508902030

Egenhofer, M. J., & Herring, J. (1991). Categorizing binary topological relationships between regions, lines and points in geographic databases. In Egenhofer, M., & Herring, J. (Eds.), *A Framework for the Definition of Topological Relationships and an Approach to Spatial Reasoning within this Framework* (pp. 1–28). Santa Barbara, CA: Morgan Kaufmann.

Egenhofer, M. J., & Sharma, J. (1993). Topological relations between regions in R2 and Z2. In *Third International Symposium on Large Spatial Databases and Advances in Spatial Databases,* (pp. 316-336). Springer-Verlag.

Inglada, J., & Michel, J. (2009). Qualitative spatial reasoning for high-resolution remote sensing image analysis. *IEEE Transactions on Geoscience and Remote Sensing, 47*(2), 599–612. doi:10.1109/TGRS.2008.2003435

Land Cover, C. O. R. I. N. E. (2000). *CLC2000.* Retrieved from http://terrestrial.eionet.europa.eu/CLC2000.

Randell, D. A., Cohn, A. G., & Cui, Z. (1992b). Computing transivity tables: A challenge for automated theorem provers. In *Proceedings of the 11th International Conference on Automated Deduction: Automated Deduction,* (pp. 786-790). Automated Deduction.

Randell, D. A., Cui, Z., & Cohn, A. G. (1992a). A spatial logic based on regions and connection. In *Proceedings of the 3rd International Conference on Knowledge Representation and Reasoning,* (pp. 165-176). San Mateo, CA: Morgan Kaufmann.

Schultz, C. P. L., Clephane, T. R., Guesgen, H. W., & Amor, R. (2006). Utilization of qualitative spatial reasoning in geographic information systems. In Riedl, A., Kainz, W., & Elmes, G. A. (Eds.), *Progress in Spatial Data Handling, Part 2* (pp. 27–42). Berlin, Germany: Springer. doi:10.1007/3-540-35589-8_3

Wang, S. S., & Liu, D. Y. (2006). Qualitative spatial relation database for semantic web. In Mizoguchi, R., Shi, Z., & Giunchiglia, F. (Eds.), *The Semantic Web* (pp. 387–399). Berlin, Germany: Springer-Verlag. doi:10.1007/11836025_39

Wikipedia. (2009). *Region connection calculus.* Retrieved from http://en.wikipedia.org/wiki/Region_Connection_Calculus.

## ADDITIONAL READING

Alboody, A., Sèdes, F., & Inglada, J. (2009). Fuzzy intersection and difference model for topological relations. In *Proceedings of the International Fuzzy Systems Association World Congress and Conference of the European Society for Fuzzy Logic and Technology (13th IFSA - 6th EUSFLAT 2009).* Lisbon, Portugal: EUSFLAT. Retrieved from http://ifsa2009.ist.utl.pt/Docs/ProgramGlance_IFSA_EUSFLAT_2009Final.pdf.

Brennan, J., & Sowmya, A. (1998). Satellite image interpretation using spatial reasoning. In *Proceedings of the Australasian Remote Sensing Photogrammet Conference,* (Vol. 1). Sydney, Australia: Australasian Conference. Retrieved from http://citeseerx.ist.psu.edu/viewdoc/summary?doi=10.1.1.39.6506.

Chen, J., Li, C., Li, Z., & Gold, C. (2001). A Voronoi-based 9-intersection model for spatial relations. *International Journal of Geographical Information Science, 15*(3), 201–220. doi:10.1080/13658810151072831

Chen, J., Li, Z., Li, C., & Gold, C. M. (1998). Describing topological relations with voronoi-based 9-intersection model. *IAPRS, 32*(4), 99–104.

Clementini, E., Sharma, J., & Egenhofer, M. (1994). Modeling topological spatial relations: Strategies forquery processing. *Computers & Graphics, 18*(6), 815–822. doi:10.1016/0097-8493(94)90007-8

El-Geresy, B. A., & Abdelmotyb, A. I. (2004). SPARQS: A qualitative spatial reasoning engine. *Journal of Knowledge-Based Systems*, *17*(2-4), 89–102. doi:10.1016/j.knosys.2004.03.004

Guo, P., Tao, H.-F., & Luo, Y. (2003). Research on the relationship between 4-intersection and classifying invariant based on the simple regions. In *Proceedings of the Second International Conference on Machine Learning and Cybernetics*, (Vol. 3), (pp. 1642-1647). IEEE Press.

Li, S., & Ying, M. (2002). Extensionality of the RCC8 composition table. *Fundamenta Informaticae*, *55*(3-4), 363–385.

Li, S., & Ying, M. (2003). Region connection calculus: Its models and composition table. *Artificial Intelligence*, *145*(1-2), 121–146. doi:10.1016/S0004-3702(02)00372-7

Liu, K., & Shi, W. (2007). Extended model of topological relations between spatial objects in geographic infromation systems. *International Journal of Applied Earth Observation and Geoinformation*, *9*(3), 264–275. doi:10.1016/j.jag.2006.09.004

Renz, J., & Nebel, B. (1999). On the complexity of qualitative spatial reasoning: A maximal tractable fragment of the region connection calculus. *Artificial Intelligence*, *108*(1-2), 69–123. doi:10.1016/S0004-3702(99)00002-8

Seixas, J., & Aparicio, J. (1994). A framework for spatial reasoning the task of image interpretation. In *Proceedings of the EGIS Foundation, Fifth European Conference and Exhibition on Geographical Information Systems,* (Vol. 1). Retrieved from http://libraries.maine.edu/Spatial/gisweb/spatdb/egis/eg94015.html.

Vafaeinezhad, A., Alesheikh, A. A., & Parvinnezhad, D. (2006). Advanced topological structure in GIS. *Map Middle East 2006.* Retrieved from http://www.gisdevelopment.net/proceedings/mapmiddleeast/2006/poster/mm06pos_149.htm.

## KEY TERMS AND DENITIONS

**Geographic Information System (GIS):** Captures, stores, analyzes, manages, and presents data that is linked to spatial object, location etc. Technically, *GIS* is geographic information systems which includes mapping software and its application with *remote sensing images*, *land surveying*, *aerial photography*, *mathematics*, *photogrammetry*, *geography*, and *tools* that can be implemented with *GIS software*. Still, many refer to "*geographic information system*" as *GIS* even though it doesn't cover all tools connected to topology. *GIS* refers to spatial databases which are interacted with through geographically accurate models (or representations) of the real world information they represent.

**Qualitative Spatial Reasoning:** Is an approach to represent spatial knowledge using a limited vocabulary such as qualitative relations (Topological, Directional…) between spatial entities.

**Region Connection Calculus (RCC):** The RCC is intended to provide a logical framework for incorporating qualitative spatial representation and reasoning into *GIS* and Artificial Intelligence systems.

**Satellite Imagery:** A picture of the earth taken from an *earth orbital satellite*. *Satellite images* may be produced photographically or by on-board scanner and it's always in *raster format*, where each pixel has its own *signature* that have been interpreted by an expert or a computer to produce a *land use map* can be "*read into*" the *GIS* in *raster format*. *Satellite imagery* such as *Landsat TM* and *SPOT* provide multispectral images of the earth, some containing seven or more bands.

**Spatial Analysis:** Includes any of the formal techniques which study entities using their *topological*, *geometric*, or *geographic* properties. Spatial analysis confronts also many fundamental issues in the definition of its *objects* of study, in the construction of the analytic operations to be used, in the use of computers for analysis, in the limitations and particularities of the analyses which are known, and in the presentation of analytic results. In other words, ***spatial analysis*** is the process of modeling, examining, interpreting model results, and extracting or creating new information about a set of geographic objects or features.

**Spatial Database:** A database that is optimized to store and query spatial data related to objects in space, including points, lines and polygons. In other words, ***Spatial Database*** is a database containing information indexed by *location*. For example, CORINE Land Cover (CLC) database and GIS databases are a spatial database.

**Spatial Reasoning System RCC8:** RCC8 consists of eight basic topological relations that are possible between two spatial regions given as: ***DC, EC, PO, TPP, NTPP, TPPi, NTPPi, and EQ.***

**Topological Models:** Topological approaches (*4- and 9- intersection models, ID model...*) are usually used to extract and find the topological relations between spatial regions.

**Topological Relations:** Is used to describe the relations between spatial entities (regions, lines and points) by considering a particular spatial aspect called *topology*.

# Chapter 7
# A Region-Based Ontology of the Brain Ventricular System and Its Relation to Schizophrenia

**Paulo E. Santos**
*Centro Universitário da FEI, Brazil*

**Carlos E. Thomaz**
*Centro Universitário da FEI, Brazil*

**Rodolpho Freire**
*Centro Universitário da FEI, Brazil*

**Paulo C. Sallet**
*Universidade de São Paulo, Brazil*

**Danilo N. dos Santos**
*Centro Universitário da FEI, Brazil*

**Mario Louzã**
*Universidade de São Paulo, Brazil*

**Anthony G. Cohn**
*University of Leeds, UK*

## ABSTRACT

*This chapter describes an initial region-based formalisation of some concepts about neuroanatomy into ontological and epistemic terms, as part of a major effort into the formalisation of the knowledge contained in neuroimages of patients with schizophrenia. The long-term goal is to build an ontology that is a formal basis for the expectations generated from statistical data analysis. To this end, the chapter presents an example of applying this ontology to interpret the results of image-based analysis of neuroimages from schizophrenic patients.*

## 1. INTRODUCTION

Schizophrenia is a mental disorder that affects approximately 1% of the population worldwide and whose causes are still unknown[1]. Both genetic (Harrison & Owen, 2003) and environmental factors (including biological—e.g., prenatal infection and obstetric complications—and psychosocial factors) appear to play a role in its etiology. These factors, however, are not sufficient for the emergence of schizophrenia (Nuechterlein & Dawson, 1984). Previous studies (Gattaz, et al., 1988; Thomaz, et al., 2007b) investigated the possibility that the neuroanatomical changes of this disease are diffuse, therefore suggesting that

DOI: 10.4018/978-1-61692-868-1.ch007

multidimensional techniques may be the right tools for providing information of the possible influence of structural brain anomalies related to the disease. In another work (Santos, et al., 2009), we have proposed an integrated framework for extracting and describing patterns of changes from neuroimages of schizophrenic patients using a combination of linear discriminant analysis and active contour models. As a result, we obtained clusters of the most statistically significant differences of neuroimages between healthy controls and patients (an example of such clusters is shown in Figure 1).

The voxels within these clusters were mapped using the Talairach atlas (Lancaster, et al., 2000) to the corresponding labels of neuroanatomic structures. However, that work falls short on placing the obtained descriptions into the context of neuroanatomy, as the relationships between the labels and the structures they describe were not represented explicitly. Besides, the knowledge about the known facts of how anatomical changes are related to schizophrenia was also absent.

The goal of the present work is to describe a spatial ontology for the brain structure more frequently reported as altered in schizophrenia: the Ventricular Brain System (VBS). This ontology provides both the neuroanatomical context for parts of the VBS, and also the findings relating brain structures to schizophrenia as published in the literature. For this purpose, in this chapter, we assume the Basic Inclusion Theory (BIT) (Donnelly, et al., 2006), a spatial theory for formalising biomedical ontologies. The main reason for assuming BIT is the distinction that it makes between mereological and location relations. Mereological relations are properties defined in terms of parts and their respective wholes (Casati & Varzi, 1999). For instance, in BIT we could express formally that the fourth ventricle is part of the ventricular system, but it would be a mistake to say that it is also part of the hindbrain, although it is located within it. This distinction is explicit in BIT. BIT is one of many existing frameworks

*Figure 1. Results of the active contour model segmentation from statistical*

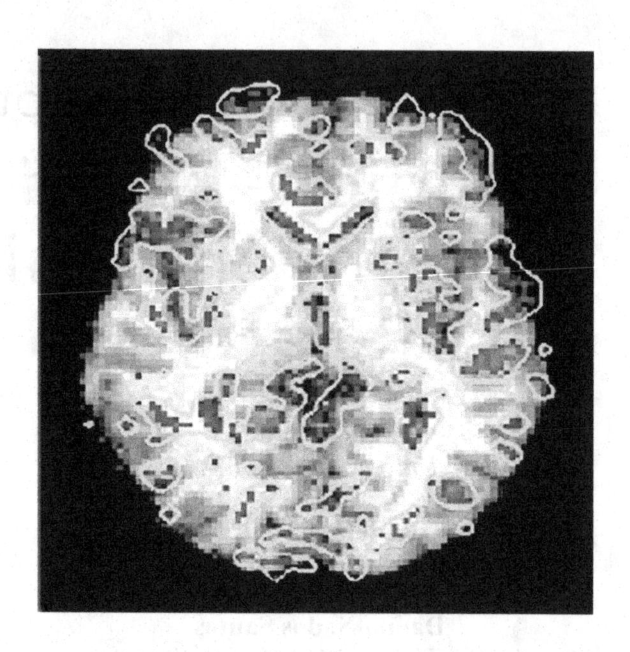

for building bio-ontologies. Perhaps central to this area are the Foundational Model of Anatomy Ontology (FMA) (Rosse & Mejino, 2003) and the Open Biomedical Ontologies (Smith, et al., 2005), among others (Chen, et al., 2006). FMA is a knowledge source of classes and relations about observable characteristics of the human body structure; thus, FMA is mainly concerned with representing anatomical information. The OBO Foundry project is a collaborative development, which includes a large amount of biological information, such as amphibian gross anatomy, chemical entities of biological interest, as well as human disease information and so on. There are a few attempts to build ontologies of neuroanatomical structures. The work proposed in Martin et al. (2001) integrates into FMA a terminology whose purpose is to model the structure of knowledge of neuroanatomy. An ontology specifically about the nervous system is proposed in Bota and Swanson (2008). However, to the best of our knowledge, the present chapter is the first attempt to encode neuroanatomical terms into BIT, providing thus a clear account of the mereological and location relations underlying this field. The main reason for choosing the Basic Inclusion Theory in this work, instead of FMA or OBO (for instance), is that BIT provides a clear formalisation for the structure underlying the elements of bio-ontologies in terms of spatial regions. We believe that the region-based relations of BIT provide a proper basis for describing the main differences between neuroimages of controls and patients, such as those shown in Figure 1.

There are a number of decision support systems for schizophrenia reported in the literature (Spitzer & Endicott, 1968; Bronzino, et al., 1989; First, et al., 1993), all of them were based on formalising the symptomatology of the disease (Razzouk, 2001). The challenge of the present work is to develop a knowledge representation and reasoning system that incorporates (as elementary entities) spatial regions in neuroimages that represent structures that are known to be affected in mental disorders. This chapter is part of a major effort to formalise the basic concepts for an automated process of image interpretation that would facilitate the medical assessment of the information contained in neuroimages. The pursuit of an ontological basis for this investigation resides in the largely believed fact that the pathogenesis of schizophrenia may rely on a myriad of factors, ranging from neuroanatomical and neurochemical abnormalities to genetic predisposition (Kandel, et al., 2000). Defining a common ontology underlying the search of the possible causes of this disease is essential in order to develop computer systems that process findings from distinct analysis of the same data sets. The present paper reports initial steps towards these goals.

In order to provide a region-based formalisation for the ventricular brain system we define consensual (fiat) boundaries using BIT relations. We also present axioms constraining the idea of spatial continuity. In this work, variables are universally quantified, unless explicitly stated otherwise.

This chapter is organised as follows: the next subsection describes informally the ventricular brain system; Section 2 summarises Basic Inclusion Theory; Section 3 presents our definitions of fiat boundaries and continuity used to represent the VBS; Section 4 presents the bio-ontology for the VBS; Section 5 presents an example of how the proposed ontology can be used along with neuroimage analysis. Finally, Section 6 concludes this paper.

### 1.1. Ventricular Brain System (VBS)

The ventricular brain system (Figure 2) is a cavity disposed within the brain, which is composed of the third, fourth, and lateral ventricles. The lateral ventricles are subdivided as body, frontal horn, occipital horn, and temporal horn. The communication between the lateral ventricles and the third ventricle is done via the Monro foramina (Parent & Carpenter, 1996).

The third ventricle is sub-divided into optical recess, supra-parietal recess, and infundibulum. The third ventricle also communicates with the fourth ventricle by the cerebral aqueduct and in the centre of the third ventricle is located the interthalamic connection.

The fourth ventricle is composed of the lateral recess and the Luschka foramina linking up with the third ventricle through the brain aqueduct.

As we shall discuss further in this paper, enlarged lateral and third ventricles are the most commonly found anatomical abnormalities in schizophrenic patients.

## 2. THE BASIC INCLUSION THEORY

In this section we describe the Basic Inclusion Theory (BIT) (Donnelly, et al., 2006), a region-based formalism for building biomedical ontologies, which makes a clear distinction between mereological and location relations.

*Figure 2. Ventricular brain system: a lithography plate from Gray's Anatomy (Gray, 1918)*

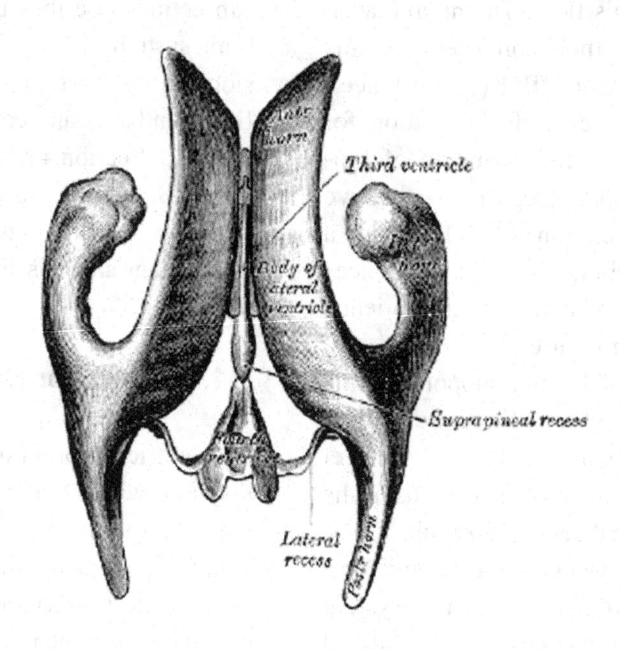


In the mereological part of BIT, variables range over domain individuals, in the present case, over distinct neuroanatomical structures.

Axioms (1), (2), and (3) constrain the meaning of the primitive BIT relation part of (P/2).

$$P(x, x). \quad (1)$$

$$P(x, y) \land P(y, x) \rightarrow x = y. \quad (2)$$

$$P(x, y) \land P(y, z) \rightarrow P(x, z). \quad (3)$$

Axiom (1) states that every individual x is a part of itself; Axiom (2) states that if x is part of y (and y is a part of x) then x and y are the same individual. Finally, Axiom (3) represents the fact that if x is part of y and y is part of z, then x is part of z. With P/2, two important relations can be defined: the proper part relation PP (Formula [4]) and the overlap relation O (Formula [5]).

$$PP(x, y) \equiv P(x, y) \land \neg x = y \quad (4)$$

$$O(x, y) \equiv \exists z (P(z, x) \land P(z, y)) \quad (5)$$

In other words, x is proper part of y if and only if x is part of y and x and y are distinct individuals (cf. Formula [5]); similarly, x overlaps with y if there is at least one z that is part of both x and y.

The distinction between mereological and location relations is accomplished by defining location relations with spatial regions as arguments. In this chapter, spatial regions are unique mappings from neuroanatomical structures to the distinct spatial regions they occupy. Thus, location relations can be defined using relations from the mereological part of BIT using a region function r(x) that maps each individual x to its occupancy region.

There are two basic location relations in BIT: the LocIn, standing for "object x is located in object y" which holds if and only if the occupancy region of x, r(x), is part of the occupancy region of y" (cf. Formula [6]) and PCoin, read as "objects x and y partially coincide," which holds if and only if their occupancy regions overlap (cf. Formula [7]).

$$LocIn(x, y) \equiv P(r(x), r(y)). \quad (6)$$

$$PCoin(x, y) \equiv O(r(x), r(y)). \quad (7)$$

*Figure 3. Basic inclusion theory relations*

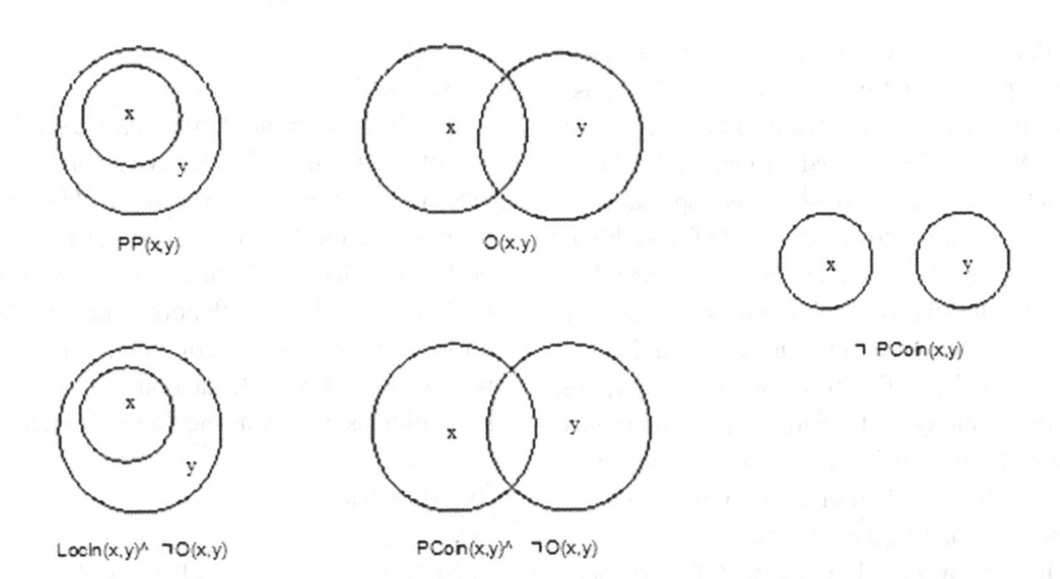


The qualitative distinctions within the basic part of BIT (Axioms [1]–[7]) are shown in Figure 3 (Donnelly, et al., 2006).

The BIT axioms imply a number of theorems that in turn can be used to infer many facts about biomedical ontologies (Donnelly, et al., 2006). Assertions about classes of individuals, rather than about particular instances, are also feasible in an extension of BIT that includes an instantiation relation, linking a class to its individual instances. Therefore, in this extended version of BIT, it is possible to express (for instance) the spatial relation between the classes Ventricular System and Cerebrospinal Fluid, as well as the spatial relation between the individuals' right and left lateral ventricles. The instantiation relation is represented as Inst(x, A) read as "x is an instance of the class A."

This class instantiation relation is defined in Donnelly et al. (2006) as the relation Is_a(A, B) (Formula 8) which represents that the class A is a subclass of B and that if x is an instance of A, it is also an instance of B.

$$\text{Is\_a}(A, B) \equiv \forall x(\text{Inst}(x, A) \rightarrow \text{Inst}(x, B)) \quad (8)$$

Also relevant to this work is the relation PP12(A, B) which represents that "every instance of A has an instance of B as proper part, and every instance of B has an instance of A as proper part" (Donnelly, et al., 2006). With this relation, it is possible to state, for instance, that every lateral ventricle is a proper part of the ventricular brain system and every ventricular brain system has a lateral ventricle as proper part.

## 3. CONTINUITY AND FIAT BOUNDARIES

In order to represent the ventricular brain system, we have to characterise regions that do not have physical boundaries, i.e., they are consensually defined by the experts (such as the body, the anterior or posterior horns of the lateral ventricles, Figure 2). Besides, we also want to be able to represent continuous portions of the ventricular system (the foramina for instance). In order to accomplish these tasks we define the notion of fiat boundaries and maximal continuous part, as introduced below.

## 3.1 Continuity

In order to define the notion of maximum continuous part, we introduce a relation about discontinuity (Disc/2), following some ideas in the "hole ontology" presented in (Varzi, 1996). A discontinuity can be thought of as a special case of a hole: a hole is normally thought of something, which is part of the convex hull of an object but not part of the object itself, normally manifesting itself as an interior void or a surface concavity. We can think of discontinuities as a third case where the discontinuity is formed by two (or more) separated parts, and the discontinuity again is part of the convex hull of the sum of these parts but not overlapping any of them.

This notion is used to represent, for instance, the material discontinuity in the third ventricle called the interthalamic connection.

We represent a discontinuity using the relation Disc(x, y) ("x is a discontinuity in y") which is constrained by the following axioms:

$$\exists y \, Disc(x, y) \quad (9)$$

"Every discontinuity x has a host y";

$$Disc(x, y) \rightarrow LocIn(x, y) \quad (10)$$

"Every discontinuity x is located in its host y";

$$Disc(x, y) \rightarrow \neg \exists z Disc(z, x) \quad (11)$$

"no discontinuity hosts a discontinuity itself."

Using Disc/2 we can define a relation for continuous part: PCont(x, y), meaning that "x is a continuous part of y," (Formula [12]). This relation was first introduced in Santos and Cabalar (2008).

$$PCont(x, y) \equiv P(x, y) \wedge \forall z \neg Disc(z, x). \quad (12)$$

Then, we define a segment x of an object y (Segm(x, y)) as the maximal continuous part of y, according to Formula (13).

$$Segm(x, y) \equiv PCont(x, y) \wedge \neg \exists z (PP(y, z) \wedge PP(x, z) \wedge PCont(z, y)). \quad (13)$$

3.2 Fiat Boundaries

Fiat boundaries are limits that are commonly accepted but which do not have a concrete existence (Varzi, 1997; Smith & Varzi, 2000). In this paper we define the relation Fiat(x, y), read as "x is a fiat boundary in y," constrained by axioms (14) to (17), below. It is worth noting that, in order to provide a region-based definition for boundaries, we assume in this work that boundaries are of the same dimensionality as the domain objects.

$$\exists y \, Fiat(x, y), \quad (14)$$

"Every fiat boundary x has a host y."

$$Fiat(x, y) \rightarrow PCoin(x, y), \quad (15)$$

"Every fiat boundary x partially coincides with its host y."

$$Fiat(x, y) \rightarrow \neg \exists z \, Fiat(z, x), \quad (16)$$

"a fiat boundary cannot host a fiat boundary itself."

$$Fiat(x, y) \rightarrow \neg \exists z \, Disc(x, z). \quad (17)$$

"no fiat boundary is a discontinuity."

Axiom 17 guarantees that a fiat boundary is not a physical discontinuity. The next section presents how these notions are used to formalise the ventricular brain system.

## 4. A SPATIAL BIO-ONTOLOGY FOR THE VENTRICULAR BRAIN SYSTEM

In the top level of the ontology for the ventricular brain system resides statements about its constituent parts. We assume three classes: VBS (Ventricular Brain System), Ventricle, and Foramina.

The statements are expressed in Formulae 18 to 27, where the following abbreviations are used: LV, lateral ventricle; LLV, left lateral ventricle; RLV, right lateral ventricle; TV, third ventricle; FV, fourth ventricle; LIF, RIF: left and right interventricular foramina (Monro foramina); and CA, Cerebral aqueduct. For the sake of brevity, we omit in the description below more specific parts of the ventricular brain system, such as the anterior or the posterior horns of the lateral ventricles. In the formulae below we use the relation PP12 (A, B) (every instance of A has an instance of B as proper part, and every instance of B has an instance of A as proper part" (Donnelly, et al., 2006) as described in Section 2.

PP12(VENTRICLE, VBS) (18)

Is_a(LV, VENTRICLE) (19)

PP12(LLV, LV) (20)

PP12 (RLV, LV) (21)

Is_a(TV, VENTRICLE) (22)

Is_a(V, VENTRICLE) (23)

PP12(FORAMINA, VBS) (24)

Is_a(LIF, FORAMINA) (25)

Is_a(RIF, FORAMINA) (26)

Is_a(CA, FORAMINA) (27)

We enumerated 21 fiat boundaries limiting all ventricular anatomical elements. We define each fiat boundary according to the structure that hosts it.

Formula 28 states this fact for each fiat boundary Zi .

Fiat(Zi, Ai) (28)

"Zi is a fiat boundary on a structure Ai."

In order to distinguish individual ventricles (or any neuroanatomical region) within images, the representation and autonomous recognition of shapes are key issues. However, the efficient processing of shapes is still a difficult problem (Costa & Cesar, 2006; Cohn & Hazarika, 2001; Cohn & Renz, 2008).

In the present paper, we single out the ventricles using their relative volumes. In order to do that, we use a function Vol: VENTRICLE $\rightarrow$ R, mapping an instance of VENTRICLE to a real value. Formulae (29)–(31) formalise this idea.

Formula 29 states that x is an instance of the Lateral Ventricle (LV) if its volume is greater than both the volume of the Third Ventricle (TV) and the volume of the Fourth Ventricle (F V). The fourth conjunct on the right hand side of Formula 29 states that x is a maximal continuous part of the ventricular brain system (cf. Section 3). Formulae 30 and 31 are analogous.

$$Inst(x, LV) \leftarrow LV(x) \wedge TV(y) \wedge FV(z) \wedge (Vol(x) > Vol(y)) \wedge (Vol(x) > Vol(z)) \wedge Segment(x, VBS) \quad (29)$$

$$Inst(x, T V) \leftarrow LV(x) \wedge TV(y) \wedge FV(z) \wedge (Vol(x) > Vol(y)) \wedge (Vol(y) > Vol(z)) \wedge \wedge Segment(x, VBS) \quad (30)$$

$$Inst(x, F V) \leftarrow LV(x) \wedge TV(y) \wedge FV(z) \wedge (Vol(x) > Vol(z)) \wedge (Vol(y) > Vol(z)) \wedge \wedge Segment(x, VBS) \quad (31)$$

We can write analogous formulae for the remainder structures of the ventricular brain system, omitted here for brevity.

The statements presented in this section can be summarised in Figures 4 and 5.

In order to define common characteristics among distinct groups, the medical specialist relies on the relative literature (using information from meta-analysis), image, or statistical analysis. The information available in these sources is not

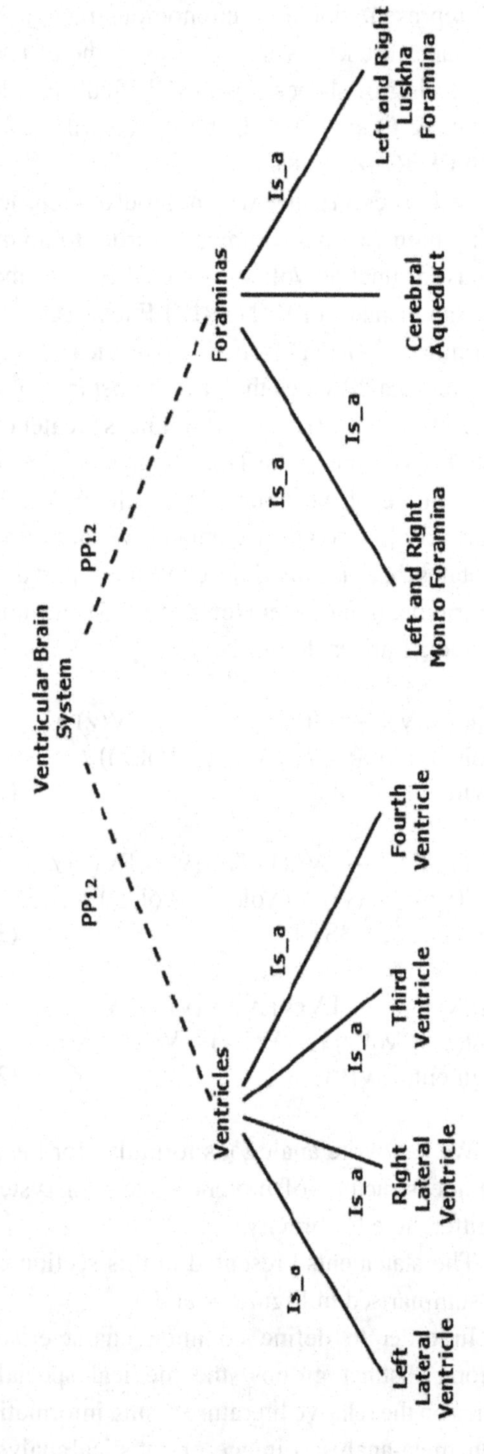

*Figure 4. Classes of the VBS formalisation*

part of the domain *per se* (so it cannot be captured by an ontology) but it is knowledge about it. The next section defines epistemic classes that are used to include knowledge about the domain in the ontology discussed above.

## 4.1. Epistemic Classes

The knowledge about things are not the things themselves, therefore, including it in the ontology would lead to a Kantian confusion (Smith & Ceusters, 2007). In this work, we avoid this confusion by assuming epistemic classes, which are related to the ontological classes by a modified Is_a relation ($Is\_a_{EPIST}$). Given an epistemic class E, an ontological class O and a binary primitive relation $\kappa(x, y)$ (representing that x is the knowledge about a domain y), we define $Is\_a_{EPIST}$ in BIT in the following way:

$$Is\_a_{EPIST}(E, O) \equiv \forall x\, Inst(x, E) \rightarrow \neg Inst(x, O) \wedge \kappa(x, O). \qquad (32)$$

Informally, E is an epistemic class within the ontology O if and only if every instance of E is not an instance of O but is knowledge about it. Therefore, we can include both ontological and epistemic individuals in the same formalism. In this work, an epistemic individual is a piece of knowledge about anatomical changes in the VBS (related to schizophrenia) that comes from the medical literature (meta-analysis for instance) or from image data analysis procedures.

In order to be absolutely precise, it would be desirable to provide a complete axiomatisation of $\kappa(x, y)$ according to epistemic logics (Rescher, 2005; Baader, et al., 2003). However, for brevity, we introduce it here as a primitive relation, leaving its formal treatment for a future work.

The epistemic classes are described by Formulae 33 to 40, whereby the basic epistemic classes are CONTROL and PATIENT.

*Figure 5. Partonomy of the VBS*

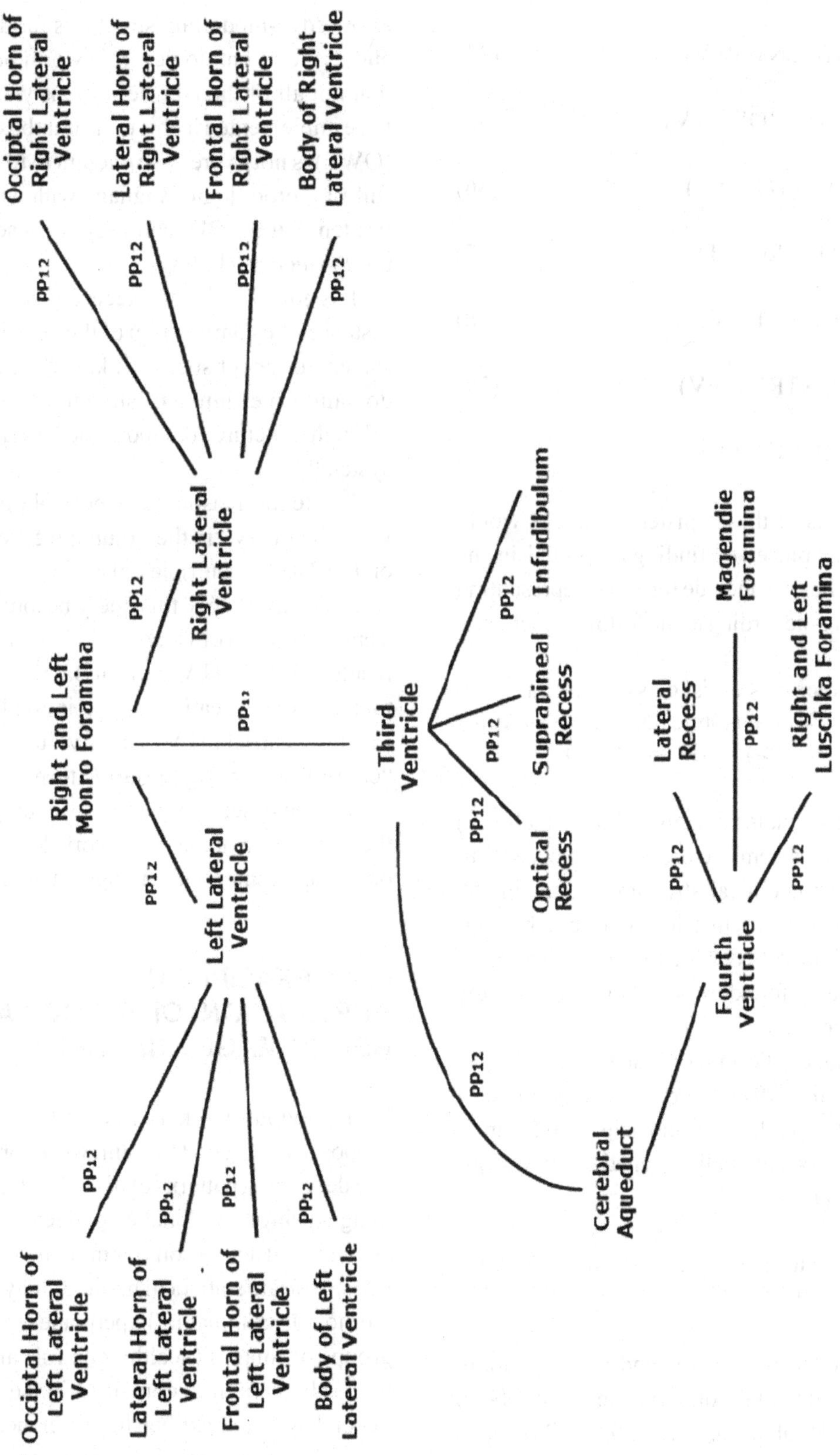

Occipital Horn of Left Lateral Ventricle
Lateral Horn of Left Lateral Ventricle
Frontal Horn of Left Lateral Ventricle
Body of Left Lateral Ventricle
Left Lateral Ventricle
Right and Left Monro Foramina
Right Lateral Ventricle
Occipital Horn of Right Lateral Ventricle
Lateral Horn of Right Lateral Ventricle
Frontal Horn of Right Lateral Ventricle
Body of Right Lateral Ventricle
Third Ventricle
Optical Recess
Suprapineal Recess
Infudibulum
Cerebral Aqueduct
Fourth Ventricle
Lateral Recess
Magendie Foramina
Right and Left Luschka Foramina
PP12

$$Is\_a_{EPIST}\ (\text{CONTROL, RLV}) \qquad (33)$$

$$Is\_a_{EPIST}\ (\text{PATIENT, RLV}) \qquad (34)$$

$$Is\_a_{EPIST}\ (\text{CONTROL, LLV}) \qquad (35)$$

$$Is\_a_{EPIST}\ (\text{PATIENT, LLV}) \qquad (36)$$

$$Is\_a_{EPIST}\ (\text{CONTROL, TV}) \qquad (37)$$

$$Is\_a_{EPIST}\ (\text{PATIENT, TV}) \qquad (38)$$

$$Is\_a_{EPIST}\ (\text{CONTROL, FV}) \qquad (39)$$

$$Is\_a_{EPIST}\ (\text{PATIENT, FV}) \qquad (40)$$

Subclasses of these epistemic classes would be particular pieces of findings reported in the literature. Thus, we include formulae representing these findings according to the following scheme:

$$Is\_a(<\text{author}>, <\text{espist.class}>) \wedge Is\_a_{EPIST}(<\text{espist.class}>, <\text{anatomical.struct.}>) \leftrightarrow Vol(<\text{anatomical.struct}>) \in (\Theta + \sigma, \Theta - \sigma) \qquad (41)$$

Formula 41 states that an author (< author >) assigned an epistemic class < espist.class > to a particular anatomical structure < anatomical. struct. > iff this structure has a volume belonging to the interval $(\Theta + \sigma, \Theta - \sigma)$ (where $\Theta$ is the mean value found by < author > and $\sigma$ is the standard variation).

For instance, Formula 42 states that Barr et al. (Barr et al., 1997) reports a mean volume of the control right lateral ventricle as 6.52 mm. Table 1 shows the findings cited from various reference sources.

$$Is\_a(\text{Barr, Control}) \wedge Is\_a_{EPIST}\ (\text{Control, RLV}) \leftrightarrow Vol(RLV) = 6.52\ (\pm 2.69) \qquad (42)$$

We encoded the classes and the partonomy (Figures 4 and 5) of the ontology described above in *Protégé* (Knublauch, et al., 2004). *Protégé* is an open source tool that combines a number of knowledge-modelling structures for the creation and usage of ontologies. It is worth pointing out that not all of the BIT definitions were possible to be implemented in this tool, as its base language (OWL) is not expressive enough to to encode the full first-order logic language with which BIT is written, but the BIT ontology was used to guide the *Protégé* modelling.

It is now possible to execute queries about, for instance, the composition of the ventricular brain system, or about specialist knowledge about the domain. An example of an ontological query is: "Which structures compose the ventricular brain system?"

Epistemic reasoning is possible in a similar way: the query "is the volume 6.52 of the right or left lateral ventricles classified as patient or control?" In Protégé this query becomes "Lateral Ventricles and Vol value 6.52," and produces the result: "Vol Right LV Control Barr," which means that the classification of an individual whose Lateral Ventricle (LV) has a volume of 6.52 is "control" according to Barr (Steen, et al., 2006).

The next section presents ongoing work on the application of the framework described above on the assessment of findings on neuroimages.

## 5. AN EXAMPLE OF APPLICATION: ONTOLOGY AND NEUROIMAGE ANALYSIS

In a previous work (Santos, et al., 2009) we proposed an integrated framework for extracting and describing patterns of disorders from medical images using a combination of linear discriminant analysis and active contour models. We first used a multivariate statistical methodology to identify the most discriminating hyperplane separating two groups of images (healthy controls and patients with schizophrenia) contained in the input data. Second, we made explicit the differences found by the multivariate statistical method by subtracting

*Table 1. Epistemic classes as stated in formula 41*

| Epistemic classes as cited in Steen et al. (Steen et al., 2006) | | | | |
|---|---|---|---|---|
| **Epistemic subclass** | **Epist. class** | **Onto. class** | **Θ (mm)** | **σ (mm)** |
| Barr et al. (1997) | Control | RLV | 6.52 | 2.69 |
| Chua et al. (2003) | Control | RLV | 4.40 | 1.70 |
| Degreef et al. (1992) | Control | RLV | 6.75 | 6.75 |
| Fannon et al. (2000b) | Control | RLV | 4.70 | 1.90 |
| Fannon et al. (2000a) | Control | RLV | 4.70 | 1.90 |
| James et al. (1999) | Control | RLV | 5.89 | 2.28 |
| Lawrie et al. (1999) | Control | RLV | 3.50 | 2.00 |
| Barr et al. (1997) | Patient | RLV | 8.22 | 4.22 |
| Chua et al. (2003) | Patient | RLV | 5.10 | 1.70 |
| Degreef et al. (1992) | Patient | RLV | 8.15 | 3.05 |
| Fannon et al. (2000b) | Patient | RLV | 4.60 | 2.10 |
| Fannon et al. (2000a) | Patient | RLV | 5.80 | 2.90 |
| James et al. (1999) | Patient | RLV | 8.12 | 3.32 |
| Lawrie et al. (1999) | Patient | RLV | 3.70 | 2.60 |
| Barr et al. (1997) | Control | LLV | 6.98 | 2.90 |
| Chua et al. (2003) | Control | LLV | 5.00 | 2.00 |
| Degreef et al. (1992) | Control | LLV | 6.70 | 2.14 |
| Fannon et al. (2000b) | Control | LLV | 4.50 | 1.90 |
| Fannon et al. (2000a) | Control | LLV | 4.50 | 1.90 |
| James et al. (1999) | Control | LLV | 6.16 | 2.30 |
| Lawrie et al. (1999) | Control | LLV | 3.80 | 2.80 |
| Barr et al. (1997) | Patient | LLV | 9.16 | 4.22 |
| Chua et al. (2003) | Patient | LLV | 6.00 | 1.50 |
| Degreef et al. (1992) | Patient | LLV | 8.91 | 3.96 |
| Fannon et al. (2000b) | Patient | LLV | 5.10 | 3.00 |
| Fannon et al. (2000a | Patient | LLV | 6.20 | 3.20 |
| James et al. (1999) | Patient | LLV | 9.66 | 4.00 |
| Lawrie et al. (1999) | Patient | LLV | 3.90 | 2.50 |
| Degreef et al. (1992) | Control | TV | 1.62 | 0.32 |
| Fannon et al. (2000b) | Control | TV | 0.68 | 0.21 |
| Fannon et al. (2000a) | Control | TV | 0.70 | 0.35 |
| James et al. (1999) | Control | TV | 1.60 | 0.35 |
| Lawrie et al. (1999) | Control | TV | 0.40 | 0.20 |
| Degreef et al. (1992) | Patient | TV | 1.33 | 0.38 |
| Fannon et al. (2000b) | Patient | TV | 0.77 | 0.20 |
| Fannon et al. (2000a) | Patient | TV | 0.90 | 0.40 |
| James et al. (1999) | Patient | TV | 2.08 | 0.66 |
| Lawrie et al. (1999) | Patient | TV | 0.60 | 0.40 |

the discriminant models of controls and patients, weighted by the pooled variance between the two groups. The proposed method was evaluated contrasting its results with well-known anatomical changes related to schizophrenia as described in the literature.

To illustrate the performance of this approach, we present below (in Figures 6, 7, and 8) some results on a Magnetic Resonance Imaging (MRI) dataset that contains 44 patients with schizophrenia and 26 healthy controls. All these images were acquired using a 1.5T Philips Gyroscan S15-ACS MRI scanner (Philips Medical Systems, Eindhoven, The Netherlands), including a series of contiguous 1.2mm thick coronal images across the entire brain, using a T1-weighted fast field echo sequence (TE = 9ms, TR = 30ms, ⟩ip angle 30°, field of view = 240mm, 256 x 256 matrix).

All images were reviewed by a MR neuro-radiologist. Ethical permission for this study was granted by the Ethics Committee of the Hospital das Clínicas, University of São Paulo Medical School.

The statistical differences between the control and schizophrenia MRI samples captured by the discriminant analysis are illustrated in Figure 7. It shows the differences between the patient (on the top left) and control (on the right bottom) images captured by the multivariate statistical classifier using MR intensity features as inputs and all the spatially normalised samples for training.

These 14 images (from top left to bottom right) correspond to the 14 asterisks (on the horizontal axis, from left to right) shown on Figure 6 projected back into the image domain. We can interpret this mapping procedure as a way of defining intensity changes that come from "definitely schizophrenia" and "definitely control" samples captured by the knowledge extraction approach (Thomaz, et al., 2007a).

The discriminant analysis is able to distinguish regions that have changed between images, however it is unable to measure the variation with respect to each voxel. In order to analyse the variation in a single point we use a voxel-to-voxel statistical test to obtain the effect size of the changes. Formula 43 represents the statistical test used, where $x_c$ is the extreme control image model (bottom right image in Figure 7), $x_p$ is the extreme patient image model (top left image in Figure 7), $\sigma$ is the pooled variance between both groups, $N_c$ is the number of control samples, and $N_p$ is the number of patient samples.

$$\text{Changes} = (x_c - x_p) / (\sigma^2/N_c + \sigma^2/N_p)^{1/2} \qquad (43)$$

A sample result of this procedure is shown in Figure 8 (and Figure 1), where one slice of the 3D MRI multivariate discriminant differences extracted is presented, superimposed on a control brain image randomly selected. In the picture, the gray-scale shows relative intensity change as a range of this thresholding. The dots in the images (Figures 1 and 8) show voxels whose difference of intensity between control and patient exceeded three pooled variances (i.e., differences that we consider as statistically significant). By normalising these resulting images with the Talairach atlas (Lancaster, et al., 2000), it is possible to point out specific neuroanatomic structures where the changes occur. However, the findings on Figure 8 only show that there are differences between the two groups in the dataset, leaving aside any information about how the structures are affected (whether an enlargement or a shrinkage occurred).

The ontology delineated in Section 4 above is a step towards finding a solution to this issue, whereby the structures found by the image analysis could be compared to the body of knowledge relating schizophrenia (for instance) to neuroanatomical changes. This method provides, in an autonomous way, interpretations to the resulting images that are grounded on the literature available.

We currently can accomplish this for the ventricular brain system. More specifically, given a set of voxels representing statistically significant changes localised in the lateral ventricles (for instance), the ontology can provide a description of

*Figure 6. The most discriminant hyperplane found by the multivariate statistical approach. In the scatter plot, schizophrenia patients are coded with a cross whereas healthy controls are coded with a circle*

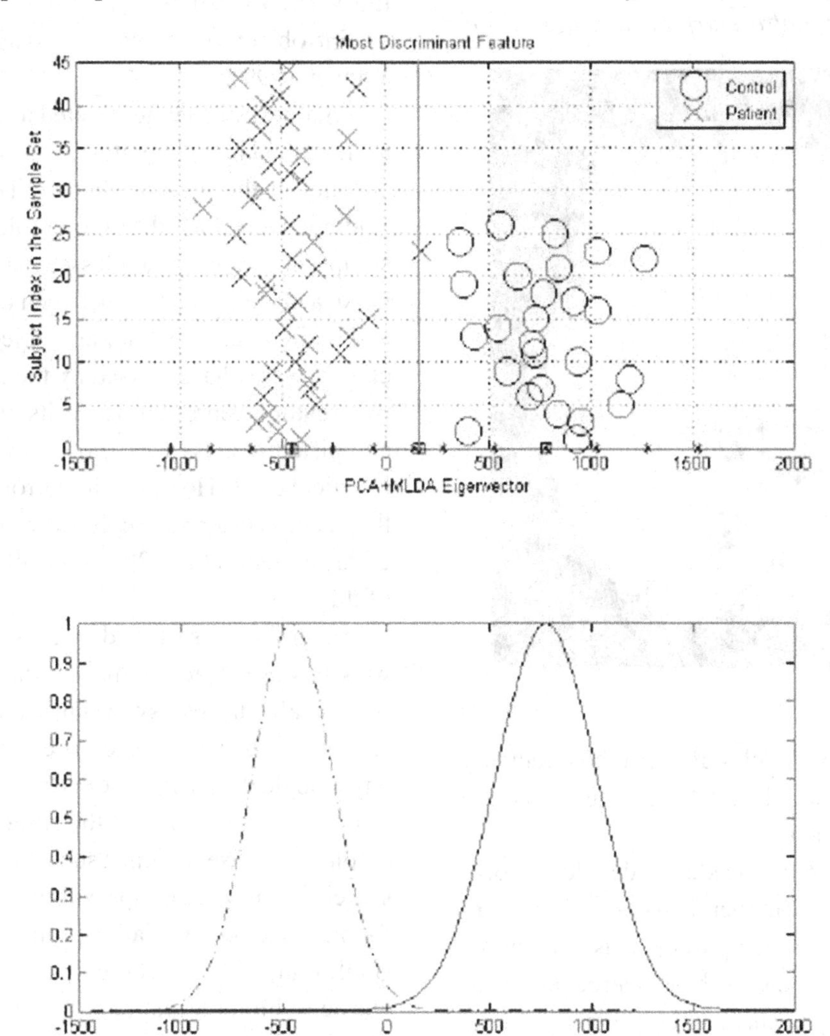


*Figure 7. Statistical differences between the schizophrenia (on top left) and healthy controls (on bottom right) images captured by the discriminant analysis approach*

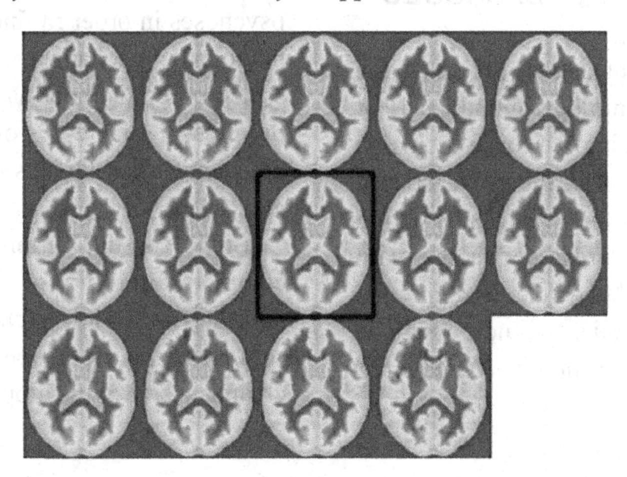

*Figure 8. Effect size of the multivariate statistical differences comparing the intensity values described by the control and patient image models*

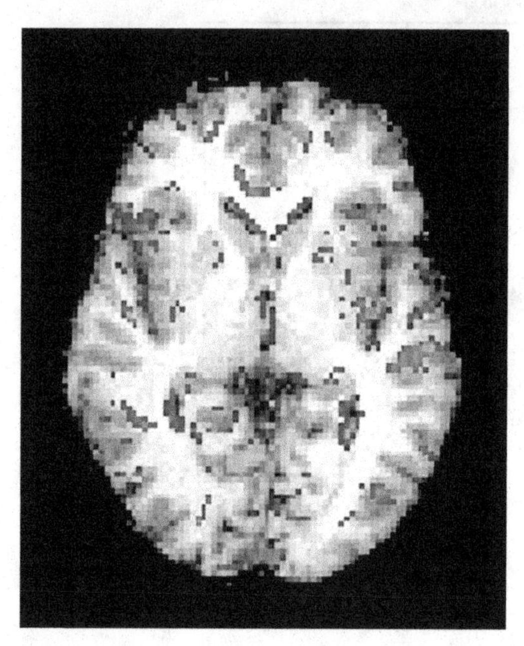

the parts of the ventricles affected, how they are affected and a list of literature findings related to this portion of the brain.

Further research is needed to develop a complete ontology about the neuroanatomical structure changes related to schizophrenia. It is also important to note that some of these neuroanatomical changes may be present in other mental disorders, such as bipolar disorders.

## 6. DISCUSSION AND OPEN ISSUES

The present work delineated some aspects in the development of a bio-ontology about a part of human neuroanatomy using the Basic Inclusion Theory (BIT) (Donnelly, et al., 2006). We focused on the formalisation of the Ventricular Brain System (VBS), since it is regarded as the main anatomical structure related to schizophrenia. In order to accomplish this, two new relations had to be defined to represent, respectively, fiat boundaries and maximally continuous parts of the VBS. We left for future work the definition of fiat objects from fiat boundaries (Bittner & Winter, 1999).

Anatomical changes related to schizophrenia, as described in the literature, were also taken into account in the present chapter. These literature findings were linked to the ontology by the assumption of epistemic classes, so that we could make a clear distinction between domain objects and knowledge about domain objects. Epistemic classes were characterised by the use of a primitive relation representing, in its arguments, that an epistemic class was knowledge about an ontological class. However, a rigorous treatment of this relation in terms of epistemic logics (Rescher, 2005; Baader, et al., 2003) is still an open issue of this work.

Several pieces of evidence suggest that what we know as schizophrenia is in fact an ensemble of clinically discrete syndromes in which biological and environmental factors exert partial pathophysiological effecs (Joyce & Roiser, 2007; Fatemi & Folson, 2009). One of the strategies currently employed in disentangling such mechanisms is the search for endophenotipe, subtypes of psychoses found based on association with quantitative and stable clinical (e.g. neurocognitive performance) and neurobiologic markers (e.g. genetic polymorphisms, neurochemical biomarkers, and discrete patterns of neuroanatomic abnormalities obtained by neuroimaging) (Tan, et al., 2008). The aim is to identify more homogeneous subgroups of psychoses in order to find their underlying etiopathogenic mechanisms. Searching for different structural brain abnormalities (as investigated in the present chapter) is of utmost importance in advancing such models of research (Lawrie, et al., 2008).

Subject to our current investigations are the complete description of neuroanatomy using BIT and the further interpretation of findings about schizophrenia from neuroimages, such as the change in size of the hippocampus, amongst others (Harrison, 1999). The interpretation of results obtained from neuroimaging statistical analysis, using the ideas discussed in this paper, was shown as an example in this chapter (Section 5).

Key to the future development of this investigation is the development of theories capable of representing the shapes of brain regions and what changes they may suffer under psychiatric diseases.

## REFERENCES


Baader, F., Küsters, R., & Wolter, F. (2003). Extensions to description logics. In *The Description Logic Handbook: Theory, Implementation, and Applications* (pp. 219–261). New York, NY: Cambridge University Press.

Barr, W., Ashtari, M., Bilder, R., Degreef, G., & Lieberman, J. (1997). Brain morphometric comparison of first-episode schizophrenia and temporal lobe epilepsy. *The British Journal of Psychiatry, 170*, 515–519. doi:10.1192/bjp.170.6.515

Bittner, T., & Winter, S. (1999). On ontology in image analysis. In *Selected Papers from the International Workshop on Integrated Spatial Databases, Digital Images and GIS*, (pp. 168–191). London, UK: Springer-Verlag.

Bota, M., & Swanson, L. (2008). Bams neuroanatomical ontology: Design and implementation. *Frontiers in Neuroinformatics, 2*(2).

Bronzino, J., Morelli, R. A., & Goethe, J. (1989). Overseer: A prototype expert system for monitoring drug treatment in the psychiatric clinic. *IEEE Transactions on Bio-Medical Engineering, 36*(5), 533–540. doi:10.1109/10.24255

Casati, R., & Varzi, A. C. (1999). *Parts and places: The structures of spatial representation*. Cambridge, MA: MIT Press.

Chen, H., Fuller, S. S., Friedman, C., & Hersh, W. (Eds.). (2006). *Medical informatics, volume 8 of Integrated Series in Information Systems: Biomedical ontologies*, (pp. 211–236). Springer.

Chua, S., Lam, I., Tai, K., Cheung, C., Tang, W. N., & Chen, E. (2003). Brain morphological abnormality in schizophrenia is independent of country of origin. *Acta Psychiatrica Scandinavica, 108*, 269–275. doi:10.1034/j.1600-0447.2003.00134.x

Cohn, A. G., & Hazarika, S. M. (2001). Qualitative spatial representation and reasoning: An overview. *Fundamenta Informaticae, 46*(1-2), 1–29.

Cohn, A. G., & Renz, J. (2008). Qualitative spatial representation and reasoning. In van Hermelen, F., & Lifschitz, V. (Eds.), *Handbook of Knowledge Representation* (pp. 551–596). Amsterdam, The Netherlands: Elsevier. doi:10.1016/S1574-6526(07)03013-1

Costa, L., & Cesar, R. M. Jr. (2006). *Shape analysis and classification: Theory and practice*. Boca Raton, FL: CRC Press.

Degreef, G., Ashtari, M., Bogerts, B., Bilder, R. M., Jody, D. N., Alvir, J. M. J., & Lieberman, J. A. (1992). Volumes of ventricular system subdivisions measured from magnetic resonance images in first-episode schizophrenic patients. *Archives of General Psychiatry, 49*(7), 531–537. doi:10.1001/archpsyc.1992.01820070025004

Donnelly, M., Bittner, T., & Rosse, C. (2006). A formal theory for spatial representation and reasoning in biomedical ontologies. *Artificial Intelligence in Medicine, 36*(1), 1–27. doi:10.1016/j.artmed.2005.07.004

Fannon, D., Chitnis, X., Doku, V., Tennakoon, L., O'Ceallaigh, S., & Soni, W. (2000a). Features of structural brain abnormality detected in first-episode psychosis. *The American Journal of Psychiatry, 157*, 1829–1834. doi:10.1176/appi.ajp.157.11.1829

Fannon, D., Tennakoon, L., O'Ceallaigh, S., Doku, V., Soni, W., & Chitnis, X. (2000b). Third ventricle enlargement and developmental delay in first-episode psychosis: Preliminary findings. *The British Journal of Psychiatry*, *177*, 354–359. doi:10.1192/bjp.177.4.354

Fatemi, S. H., & Folsom, T. D. (2009). The neurodevelopmental hypothesis of schizophrenia revisited. *Schizophrenia Bulletin*, *35*(3), 528–548. doi:10.1093/schbul/sbn187

First, M., Opler, L., Hamilton, R., Linder, J., Linfield, L., & Silver, J. (1993). Evaluation in a inpatient setting of DTREE, a computer-assisted diagnostic assessment procedure. *Comprehensive Psychiatry*, *34*(3), 171–175. doi:10.1016/0010-440X(93)90043-4

Gattaz, W. F., Rost, W., Kohlmeyer, K., Bauer, K., Hubner, C., & Gasser, T. (1988). CT scans and neuroleptic response in schizophrenia: A multidimensional approach. *Psychiatry Research*, *26*(3), 293–303. doi:10.1016/0165-1781(88)90124-2

Gray, H. (1918). *Anatomy of the human body*. Philadelphia, PA: Lea & Febiger.

Harrison, P. J. (1999). The neuropathology of schizophrenia: A critical review of the data and their interpretation. *Brain*, *122*(4), 593–624. doi:10.1093/brain/122.4.593

Harrison, P. J., & Owen, M. J. (2003). Genes for schizophrenia: Recent findings and their pathophysiological implications. *Lancet*, *361*, 417–419. doi:10.1016/S0140-6736(03)12379-3

James, A., Crow, T., Renowden, S., Wardell, A., Smith, D., & Anslow, P. (1999). Is the course of brain development in schizophrenia delayed? Evidence from onsets in adolescence. *Schizophrenia Research*, *40*, 1–10. doi:10.1016/S0920-9964(99)00042-0

Joyce, E. M., & Roiser, J. P. (2007). Cognitive heterogeneity in schizophrenia. *Current Opinion in Psychiatry*, *20*(3), 268–272.

Kandel, E. R., Schwartz, J. H., & Jessell, T. M. (2000). *Principles of neural science*. New York, NY: McGraw-Hill.

Knublauch, H., Fergerson, R. W., Noy, N. F., & Musen, M. A. (2004). The protégé owl plugin: An open development environment for Semantic Web applications. In *Proceedings of the 3rd International Semantic Web Conference (ISWC 2004)*, (pp. 229–243). Springer.

Lancaster, J., Woldorff, M., Parsons, L., Liotti, M., Freitas, C., & Rainey, L. (2000). Automated Talairach atlas labels for functional brain mapping. *Human Brain Mapping*, *10*(3), 120–131. doi:10.1002/1097-0193(200007)10:3<120::AID-HBM30>3.0.CO;2-8

Lawrie, S. M., Hall, J., McIntosh, A. M., Cunningham-Owens, D. G., & Johnstone, E. C. (2008). Neuroimaging and molecular genetics of schizophrenia: Pathophysiological advances and therapeutic potential. *British Journal of Pharmacology*, *153*, 120–124. doi:10.1038/sj.bjp.0707655

Lawrie, S. M., Whalley, H., Kestelman, J. N., Abukmeil, S. S., Byrne, M., & Hodges, A. (1999). Magnetic resonance imaging of brain in people at high risk of developing schizophrenia. *Lancet*, *353*, 30–33. doi:10.1016/S0140-6736(98)06244-8

Martin, R. F., Mejino, J. L. V., Bowden, D. M., Brinkley, J., & Rosse, C. (2001). Foundational model of neuroanatomy: Implications for the human brain project. In *Proceedings of the American Medical Informatics Association Fall Symposium*, (pp. 438–442). Philadelphia, PA: Hanley & Belfus.

National Institute of Health. (2009). *National institute of mental health*. Retrieved from http://www.nimh.nih.gov.

Nuechterlein, K. H., & Dawson, M. E. (1984). A heuristic vulnerability/stress model of schizophrenic episodes. *Schizophrenia Bulletin*, *10*, 300–312.

Parent, A., & Carpenter, M. (1996). *Carpenter's human neuroanatomy*. Baltimore, MD: Williams & Wilkins.

Razzouk, D. (2001). *Construção de uma base de conhecimento de um sistema de apoio a decisao*. PhD Thesis. São Paulo, Brazil: UNIFESP.

Rescher, N. (2005). *Epistemic logic: A survey of the logic of knowledge*. Pittsburgh, PA: University of Pittsburgh Press.

Rosse, C., & Mejino, J. (2003). A reference ontology for biomedical informatics: The foundational model of anatomy. *Journal of Biomedical Informatics*, *36*(6), 478–500. doi:10.1016/j.jbi.2003.11.007

Santos, P., & Cabalar, P. (2008). The space within fisherman's folly: Playing with a puzzle in mereotopology. *Spatial Cognition and Computation*, *8*(1-2), 47–64. doi:10.1080/13875860801944804

Santos PE, Thomaz CE, dos Santos D, Freire R, Sato JR, Louzã M, Sallet P, Busatto G, Gattaz WF. (2010). Exploring the knowledge contained in neuroimages: Statistical discriminant analysis and automatic segmentation of the most significant changes, *Artificial Intelligence in Medicine*, *49*(2), 105-115, Doi:10.1016/j.artmed.2010.03.003.

Smith, B., & Ceusters, W. (2007). Ontology as the core discipline of biomedical informatics: Legacies of the past and recommendations for the future direction of research. In Crnkovic, G., & Stuart, S. (Eds.), *Computing, Philosophy, and Cognitive Science* (pp. 104–122). Newcastle, UK: Cambridge Scholars Press.

Smith, B., Ceusters, W., Klagges, B., Köhler, J., Kumar, A., & Lomax, J. (2005). Relations in biomedical ontologies. *Genome Biology*, *5*(6).

Smith, B., & Varzi, A. (2000). Fiat and bona fide boundaries. *Philosophy and Phenomenological Research*, *60*(2), 401–420. doi:10.2307/2653492

Spitzer, R. L., & Endicott, J. (1968). Diagno: Computerized program for psychiatric diagnosis utilizing the differential diagnostic procedure. *Archives of General Psychiatry*, *18*, 747–756. doi:10.1001/archpsyc.1968.01740060106013

Steen, R. G., Mull, C., McClure, R., Hamer, R. M., & Lieberman, J. A. (2006). Brain volume in first-episode schizophrenia. *The British Journal of Psychiatry*, *188*, 510–518. doi:10.1192/bjp.188.6.510

Tan, H.-Y., Callicott, J. H., & Weinberger, D. R. (2008). Intermediate phenotypes in schizophrenia genetics redux: Is it a no brainer? *Molecular Psychiatry*, *13*, 233–238. doi:10.1038/sj.mp.4002145

Thomaz, C. E., Boardman, J. P., Counsell, S., Hill, D. L. G., Hajnal, J. V., & Edwards, A. D. (2007a). A multivariate statistical analysis of the developing human brain in preterm infants. *Image and Vision Computing*, *25*(6), 981–994. doi:10.1016/j.imavis.2006.07.011

Thomaz, C. E., Duran, F. L. S., Busatto, G. F., Gillies, D. F., & Rueckert, D. (2007b). Multivariate statistical differences of MRI samples of the human brain. *Journal of Mathematical Imaging and Vision*, *29*(2-3), 95–106. doi:10.1007/s10851-007-0033-6

Varzi, A. (1997). Boundaries, continuity, and contact. *Nous (Detroit, Mich.)*, *31*(1), 26–58. doi:10.1111/0029-4624.00034

Varzi, A. C. (1996). Reasoning about space: The hole story. *Logic and Logical Philosophy*, *4*, 3–39.

## KEY TERMS AND DEFINITIONS

**Active Contour Models:** Also known as snakes are methods for segmenting an object outline from a possibly noisy image by means of minimizing an energy function associated to the current contour.

**Basic Inclusion Theory:** A region-based formalism for building biomedical ontologies, which makes a clear distinction between mereological and location relations.

**Epistemic Logics:** Logical formalisms that represent (and reason about) knowledge and how knowledge is acquired.

**Fiat boundaries:** limits that are commonly accepted but which do not have a concrete existence.

**Kantian Confusion:** Usually referred to the confusion between objects and concepts.

**Linear Discriminant Analyses:** Set of statistical methods used to find the linear combination of features which best separate two groups of data points.

**Meta Analysis:** A statistical procedure for combining the results of independent studies (usually from the published research material).

**Spatial Ontology:** Logical formalisms that make clear the spatial foundations of domains.

## ENDNOTE

1 (National Institute of Health, 2009).

# Chapter 8
# Explanation Generation over Temporal Interval Algebra

**Debasis Mitra**
*Florida Institute of Technology, USA*

**Florent Launay**
*Florida Institute of Technology, USA*

## ABSTRACT

*Temporal interval algebra has generated strong interest for both theoretical and practical reasons. All its Maximal Tractable Subalgebras (MTS) have been identified. Now is the time to make the transition toward their practical applications. In this chapter, the authors have proposed a formalism on how to classify an input temporal network in one of these MTSs or decide its intractability. They have also proposed a linear algorithm for checking consistency when the input belongs to one of the seventeen MTSs, and for finding the constraints responsible for inconsistency in case the network is unsatisfiable.*

## INTRODUCTION

Interval Algebra (IA) is possibly the most studied algebra related to automated reasoning, for its theoretical elegance and feasible practical applications in scheduling, natural language engineering, etc. Some of the hallmark works in the area are: Vilain and Kautz's (1986) proof of NP-hardness of IA; Nebel and Bürckert's (1995) detecting the first maximal tractable algebra, namely, the ORD-Horn algebra (OH); Ligozat's (1996) reinterpretation of that algebra in a canonical and geometrical representation space; and Krokhin et al.'s (2003) discovery of the exhaustive set of eighteen non-trivial Maximal Tractable Subalgebras (MTS). Sometimes we will use the word "algebra" or "subalgebra" synonymously with MTS.

A motivation behind studying the maximal tractable algebras is that an application domain may fall into one of these classes, or may be restricted to one of these classes making temporal reasoning more practical for that application. Given such an expectation it is only reasonable to ask, how can we identify an input system of interval constraints

DOI: 10.4018/978-1-61692-868-1.ch008

whether it belongs to any of the MTSs? In this paper we develop a classification structure of the MTSs and we propose an algorithm for identifying an input network if it belongs to any particular MTS. We use a novel geometrical interpretation of the MTSs for this purpose. Although, polynomial-time Path Consistency algorithm (PC) is complete for any MTS, we show that each MTS, other than the OH, has a similar behavior as the point-based reasoning problem (van Beek, 1992; Drakengren, et al., 1997), thus, enabling one to apply a more efficient cycle-checking algorithm than the PC. This new algorithm also has an extension for detecting *culprit* constraints when the input is inconsistent. *Culprit* detection is equivalent to the diagnosis as a task.

In the following section, we provide some background information on IA for uninitiated readers. Subsequently we will show the geometrical interpretation of the MTSs in Ligozat's canonical space. We will then introduce the classification algorithm for an arbitrary interval constraint network. Lastly we provide the scheme for checking consistency of some Qualitative Temporal Constraint Networks (QTCNs) belonging to any of the MTSs, other than the OH.

## BACKGROUND ON TEMPORAL REASONING

Qualitative reasoning with intervals involves thirteen atomic relations, $B$: {*before(p), after(*$p^{-1}$*), meets(m), met-by(*$m^{-1}$*), overlaps(o), overlapped-by(*$o^{-1}$*), starts(s), started-by(*$s^{-1}$*), during(d), contains(*$d^{-1}$*), finishes(f), finished-by (*$f^{-1}$*), equal(eq)*}, between any pair of intervals (Allen, 1983). The corresponding relational algebra is comprised of the power set $P(B)$, the power set of $B$, which is closed under the traditional reasoning operators like composition, converse, set union, and set intersection.

*Definition 1*: A *Qualitative Temporal Constraint Network* (QTCN) is a graph $G=(V, E)$, where each node denotes an interval, and each directed labeled edge $(v_1, v_2, R) \in E$ represents disjunctive constraint $R$ between $v_1$ and $v_2$, where $R \in P(B)$. Two special relations are *tautology* (disjunction of all thirteen atomic relations or no constraint), and Ø (empty relation leading to inconsistency). Reasoning may be restricted to a subset $\Theta$, where $R \in \Theta \subseteq P(B)$, in case $\Theta$ is closed under composition, converse and intersection, thus, forming a $\Theta$-subalgebra.

*Definition 2: Qualitative Temporal Reasoning Problem* (QTR($\Theta$)) is to answer, given a QTCN $Q$ in which only relations form $\Theta$ occur, if a satisfiable assignment for each of the nodes exists, such that all the constraints $R$ in $Q$ are satisfied. For $\Theta = P(B)$, the full algebra is called the *Interval Algebra* or *IA*. The reasoning problem over full *IA* is known to be NP-hard (Vilain & Kautz, 1986). For $\Theta \subset P(B)$, restricted reasoning is interesting if such a $\Theta$-subalgebra is tractable.

*Definition 3 (Maximal Tractable Subalgebra, or MTS)*: A tractable subalgebra $\Theta$ is maximal if it has no super-algebra $\Theta$' that is tractable, other than the full algebra $P(B)$.

Eighteen MTSs for the *IA* have been found such that the list is exhaustive—no other MTS of *IA* exists (Theorem 2.3 of Krokhin, et al., 2003). This is true at least from linguistic perspective, i.e., we do not know if the graph structure of temporal network may provide more MTS. The list includes ORD-Horn MTS, which is the only MTS that includes all thirteen atomic relations in $B$. We call the set of MTSs other than OH as the *Krokhin-MTS.*

Ligozat (1996) developed a canonical way of representing time interval relations geometrically, which appears as a useful tool for understanding the MTSs (Figure 1): An intervals is placed as a point in a 2D-Cartesian space, where the starting point of the interval is $X$-coordinate, the ending point is $Y$-coordinate, and the valid space is $Y>X$, forbidding the interval ending point to occur before the starting point. For instance, if interval $A$ '*precedes*' interval $B$, then $A$ will be located as a point

*Figure 1. Canonical representation of interval relations*

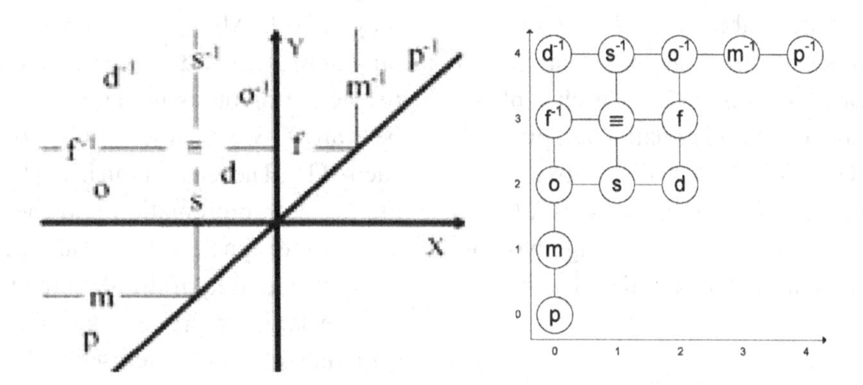


anywhere in the angular open space '*p*' while *B* is at the position designated as '≡.' The topological relationships between the regions corresponding to the atomic relations in this space constitute a lattice (Figure 1b, "*p*" as inferior [0,0] and "$p^{-1}$" as superior [4,4]).

We need the following definitions from Ligozat (1996).

*Definition 4* (Convex relation): A *convex* relation is a closed lattice-interval on the lattice in Figure 1b.

*Example 1*: An interval between (0,2) and (2,4) in the lattice, which is a disjunctive set $\{o, s, d, f^{-1}, \equiv, f, d^{-1}, s^{-1}, o^{-1}\}$ is a convex relation.

*Example 2*: An interval from (0,3) to (2,3): $\{f^{1}, \equiv, f\}$.

*Definition 5* (Convex closure *Cl*(*r*)): Convex closure of a relation *p* is the disjunction of all atomic relations within the minimum lattice-interval over the lattice enclosing *r*.

*Example 3*: $Cl(\{o, d^{1}, \equiv\}) = \{o, f^{1}, d^{-1}, s, \equiv, s^{-1}\}$, or the range (0,2) through (1,4).

*Definition 6* (Dimension *dim*(*l*)): For an atomic relation *b*, *dim*(*b*) is the dimension of *b* in the Canonical representation in Figure 1a. For any relation *r*, $dim(r) = \max\{dim(b) \mid b \in r\}$.

*Example 4*: "*p*" is adjacent to "*m*," dim(*p*)=2 and dim(*m*)=1.

*Definition 7* (Preconvex relation): A preconvex relation *l* is such that $dim(cl(l) \setminus l) < dim(l)$. In other words, missing atomic relations from *cl*(*l*) are of relatively lower dimensions.

*Example 5*: $\{o, s, d, d^{1}, o^{-1}\}$ is a preconvex relation, where the missing relations are $(f, \equiv, f^{1}, s^{-1})$ in order to form the respective convex closure. The convex closure being $\{o, s, d, f, \equiv, f^{1}, d^{1}, s^{-1}, o^{-1}\}$ with the range from (0,2) to (2, 4) on the lattice.

*Example 6*: $\{f^{1}, f\}$ is another preconvex relation. Missing lower dimensional relation is (≡) from the convex closure. The $Cl(\{f^{1}, f\})$ is $\{f^{1}, \equiv, f\}$ with the range from (0, 3) to (2, 3).

*ORD-Horn relations* are the same as the *preconvex* relations (Ligozat, 1996). Set of ORD-Horn relations form a MTS (OH) of *IA*.

## GEOMETRICAL REPRESENTATION OF MTSs

The following Figures 2-5 visualize the seventeen MTSs.

As described in the last section Ligozat (1996) provided the geometrical representation of the OH MTS. In this work, we provide similar representation of the other seventeen non-trivial MTSs on the same canonical lattice over the atomic relations. Each MTS (except Alj(17)) *M* splits the lattice into up to four partitions (for the lack of any better term we will call them as "sublattices," although mathematically that is not necessarily accurate): sublattices *L1*, possibly *L2* and *L3*, and a set of "free" atomic relations *F* (explained shortly, see Figure 2). In each sublattice we call a specific atomic relation as "pivot," $pv_i$ ($i$=1, 2, and possibly 3). Any disjunctive relation $R \in M$ has the following property: if $R \cap L_i \neq \emptyset$, then $pv_i \in R$, i.e., the corresponding pivot to the lattice must be in $R$. Any atomic relation belonging to the "free" set $F$ (not in any sublattice) may be in $R$. Alj(17) has the whole lattice as the only sublattice and ≡ as the pivot. Presence of respective pivots is imperative for a relation to be in an MTS. Sublattices and pivots characterize each MTS. The left column in the figures contains the lattice representation and the right column shows the original Krokhin et al.'s definition along with the counting of the algebra elements.

The lattice representation shows the corresponding sublattices enclosed by dashed lines, and the pivots as dark circles. Each algebra in Figure 2 (Alj 1 through 8) has (see Figure 4) one dimen-

*Figure 2. Lattice representation of MTSs Alj 1-8*

| | |
|---|---|
| 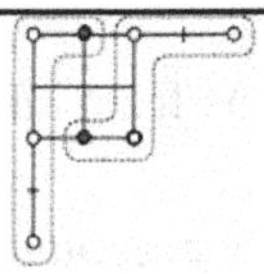 | Alj(1) or *A1* (Krohkin et al., 2003)<br>$\{r \mid r \cap (pmod^{-1}f^{1})^{\pm 1} \neq \emptyset \Rightarrow (s^{-1})^{\pm 1} \subseteq r\}$<br>$2^{11}+2^6+2^6+2 = 2178$ |
| 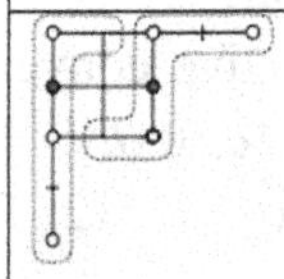 | Alj(2) or *B3*<br>$\{r \mid r \cap (pmod^{-1}s^{-1})^{\pm 1} \neq \emptyset \Rightarrow (f^{1})^{\pm 1} \subseteq r\}$<br>$2^{11}+2^6+2^6+2 = 2178$ |
| 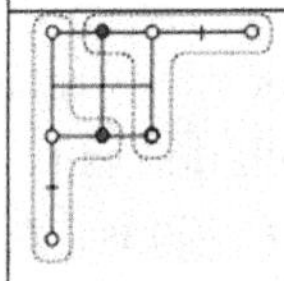 | Alj(3) or *A2*<br>$\{r \mid r \cap (pmod^{-1}f^{1})^{\pm 1} \neq \emptyset \Rightarrow (s)^{\pm 1} \subseteq r\}$<br>$2^{11}+2^6+2^6+2 = 2178$ |
| 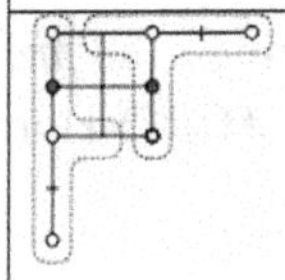 | Alj(4) or *B4*<br>$\{r \mid r \cap (pmod^{-1}s^{-1})^{\pm 1} \neq \emptyset \Rightarrow (f^{1})^{\pm 1} \subseteq r\}$<br>$2^{11}+2^6+2^6+2 = 2178$ |
| 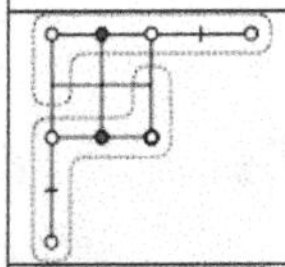 | Alj(5) or *A3*<br>$\{r \mid r \cap (pmodf)^{\pm 1} \neq \emptyset \Rightarrow (s)^{\pm 1} \subseteq r\}$<br>$2^{11}+2^6+2^6+2 = 2178$ |
| 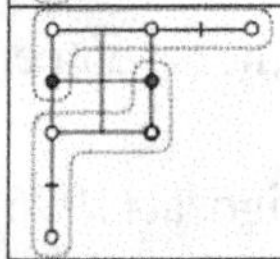 | Alj(6) or *B2*<br>$\{r \mid r \cap (pmods)^{\pm 1} \neq \emptyset \Rightarrow (f)^{\pm 1} \subseteq r\}$<br>$2^{11}+2^6+2^6+2 = 2178$ |
| 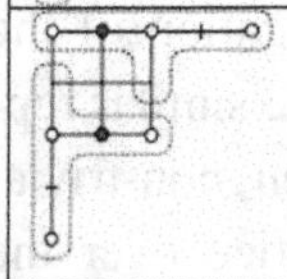 | Alj(7) or *A4*<br>$\{r \mid r \cap (pmodf^{1})^{\pm 1} \neq \emptyset \Rightarrow (s)^{\pm 1} \subseteq r\}$<br>$2^{11}+2^6+2^6+2 = 2178$ |
| 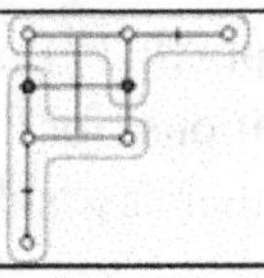 | Alj(8) or *B1*<br>$\{r \mid r \cap (pmods)^{\pm 1} \neq \emptyset \Rightarrow (f^{1})^{\pm 1} \subseteq r\}$<br>$2^{11}+2^6+2^6+2 = 2178$ |

*Figure 3. Lattice representation of MTSs Alj 9-14*

| | |
|---|---|
| 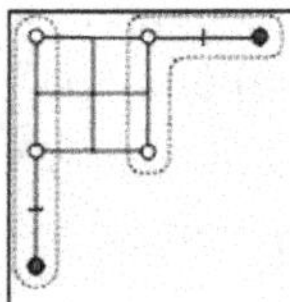 | Alj(9) or *Sp*<br>$\{r \mid r \cap (pmod^{-1}f^{1})^{\pm 1} \neq \emptyset \Rightarrow (p)^{\pm 1} \subseteq r\}$<br>$2^{11}+2^7+2^7+2^3 = 2312$ |
| 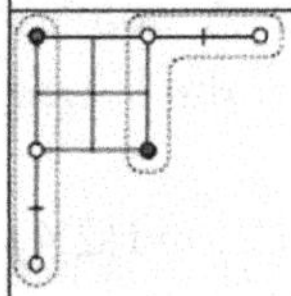 | Alj(10) or *Sd*<br>$\{r \mid r \cap (pmod^{-1}f^{1})^{\pm 1} \neq \emptyset \Rightarrow (d^{-1})^{\pm 1} \subseteq r\}$<br>$2^{11}+2^7+2^7+2^3 = 2312$ |
| 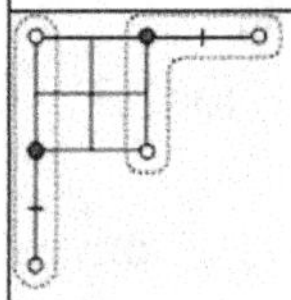 | Alj(11) or *So*<br>$\{r \mid r \cap (pmod^{-1}f^{1})^{\pm 1} \neq \emptyset \Rightarrow (o)^{\pm 1} \subseteq r\}$<br>$2^{11}+2^7+2^7+2^3 = 2312$ |
| 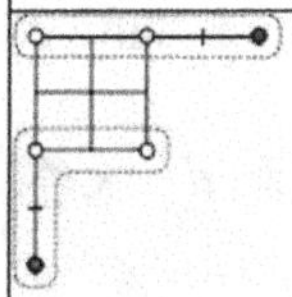 | Alj(12) or *Ep*<br>$\{r \mid r \cap (pmods)^{\pm 1} \neq \emptyset \Rightarrow (p)^{\pm 1} \subseteq r\}$<br>$2^{11}+2^7+2^7+2^3 = 2312$ |
| 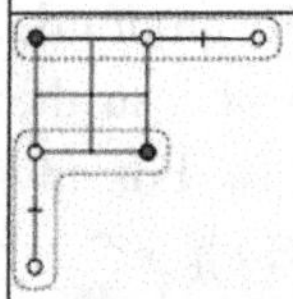 | Alj(13) or *Ed*<br>$\{r \mid r \cap (pmods)^{\pm 1} \neq \emptyset \Rightarrow (d)^{\pm 1} \subseteq r\}$<br>$2^{11}+2^7+2^7+2^3 = 2312$ |
| 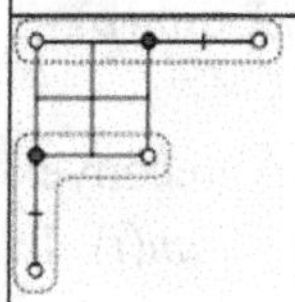 | Alj(14) or *Eo*<br>$\{r \mid r \cap (pmods)^{\pm 1} \neq \emptyset \Rightarrow (o)^{\pm 1} \subseteq r\}$<br>$2^{11}+2^7+2^7+2^3 = 2312$ |

sional pivots ($s^{\pm 1}$ and $f^{\pm 1}$), and ≡ as the only free atom, in Figure 3 (Alj 9–14) has two-dimensional pivots and three free atoms each, in Figure 4 (Alj 15-16) has three lattices, lower dimensional pivots ($s^{\pm 1}$, $f^{\pm 1}$ and ≡) and no free atom, and in Figure 5 the trivial "equality" Alj(17) has no free atom, the whole lattice is the only sublattice and the pivot is the ≡. Note that OH cannot be visualized with a static depiction over the lattice as these seventeen MTSs could be (Figure 5).

We will call OH algebra as Alj(18), which has no static geometrical representation as those of the Krokhin algebras.

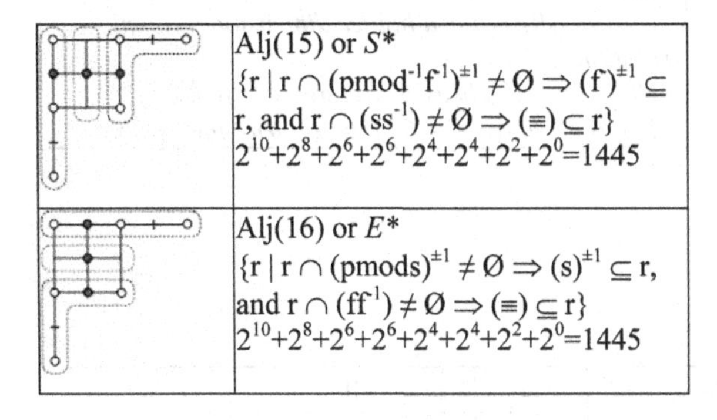

| | |
|---|---|
| | Alj(15) or $S^*$<br>$\{r \mid r \cap (pmod^{-1}f^{-1})^{\pm 1} \neq \emptyset \Rightarrow (f)^{\pm 1} \subseteq$ r, and $r \cap (ss^{-1}) \neq \emptyset \Rightarrow (\equiv) \subseteq r\}$<br>$2^{10}+2^8+2^6+2^6+2^4+2^4+2^2+2^0=1445$ |
| | Alj(16) or $E^*$<br>$\{r \mid r \cap (pmods)^{\pm 1} \neq \emptyset \Rightarrow (s)^{\pm 1} \subseteq r,$ and $r \cap (ff^{-1}) \neq \emptyset \Rightarrow (\equiv) \subseteq r\}$<br>$2^{10}+2^8+2^6+2^6+2^4+2^4+2^2+2^0=1445$ |

*Figure 4. Lattice representation of MTSs Alj 15-16*

## MTS CLASSIFICATION

As one can clearly see from the above discussion—there are only a few lattices and pivots that together comprise the seventeen MTSs. In Table 1, we tabulate the algebras according to these criteria. The table clearly visualizes the clustering of the algebras. Algebras appearing in a cluster have many similar properties, e.g., the number of elements.

A given QTCN $C$ belongs to an algebra $A$ if each constraint $R$ ($R \in C$) belongs to $A$. A QTCN $C$ may belong to multiple MTSs, or none—in case the input is intractable. For this reason we initially presume that $C$ belongs to all the algebras (step 1 of the algorithm in Figure 6). For any atomic relation $r$ to belong to a relation $R$ in an algebra, the algebra demands a strict inclusion of

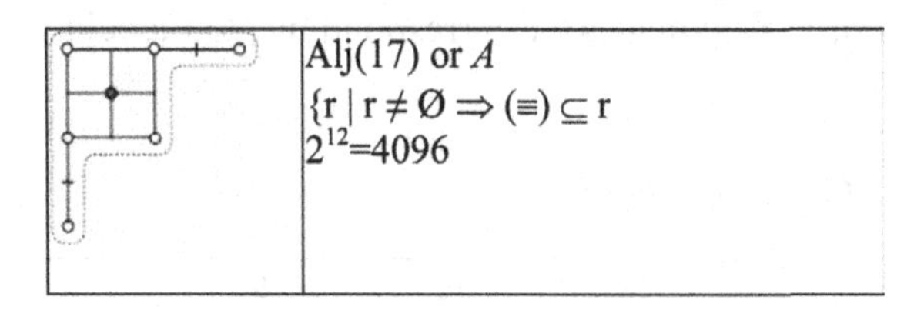

| | |
|---|---|
| | Alj(17) or $A$<br>$\{r \mid r \neq \emptyset \Rightarrow (\equiv) \subseteq r$<br>$2^{12}=4096$ |

*Figure 5. Lattice representation of the MTS Alj 17*

*Table 1. Algebra clusters*

| **Sub-lattice struct → Pivots ↓** | 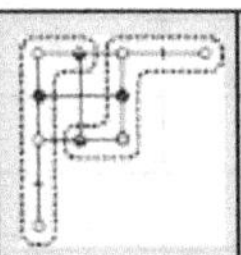 | 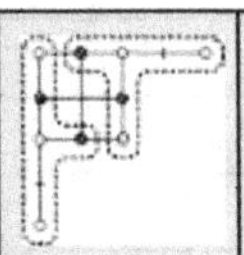 | 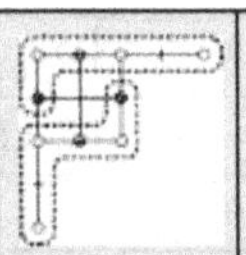 | 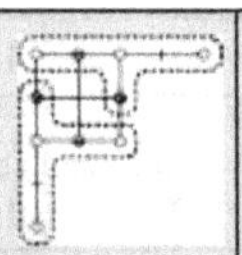 | 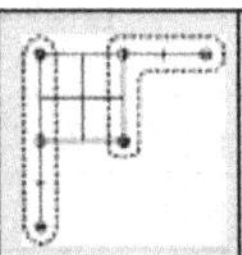 | 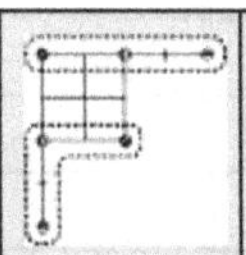 | 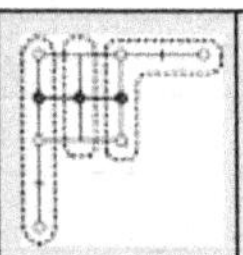 | 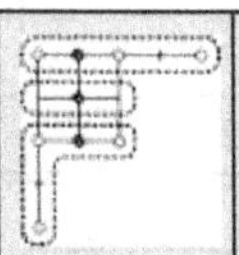 | 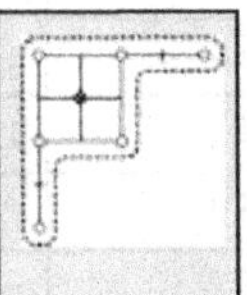 |
|---|---|---|---|---|---|---|---|---|---|
| (s)($s^{-1}$) | **Alj(1)** | **Alj(3)** | **Alj(5)** | **Alj(7)** | | | | | |
| (f)($f^{-1}$) | **Alj(2)** | **Alj(4)** | **Alj(6)** | **Alj(8)** | | | | | |
| (p) ($p^{-1}$) | | | | | **Alj(9)** | **Alj(12)** | | | |
| (d) ($d^{-1}$) | | | | | **Alj(10)** | **Alj(13)** | | | |
| (o) ($o^{-1}$) | | | | | **Alj(11)** | **Alj(14)** | | | |
| (f)(≡) ($f^{-1}$) | | | | | | | **Alj(15)** | | |
| (s)(≡) ($s^{-1}$) | | | | | | | | **Alj(16)** | |
| (≡) | | | | | | | | | **Alj(17)** |

the corresponding pivot *pv* in the relation *R* unless *r* is a free atom (in *F*). This information led us to develop a 13x13 table (*AljTable* as Table 2) over the set of atomic relations (*B*). The rows indicate the atomic relations (*r*), columns indicate the absence of the pivot (*!pv*), and an entry in the *AljTable* indicates the algebras that the relation *R* may not belong to if $r \in R$ and $pv \notin R$. (See example 7 in section 5). Only first seven of the thirteen columns are shown in the Table 2, the rest of the entries can be derived from the symmetry. For example, Alj(*o*)(*!f* $^{-1}$) = Alj(*o* $^{-1}$)(*!f*).

Lines 2-5 of the algorithm *FindMTSs* excludes all the seventeen Krokhin-MTSs that the input QTCN *C* cannot belong to. A relation *R* belonging to OH algebra may not have any dimension 2 atomic relation in *cl(R)\R,* where *cl(R)* is the convex closure of *R.* Lines 6-10 checks for that. The *X* and *Y* coordinates on the lattice (Figure 1) of an atomic relation *r*, namely the *r(X)* and *r(Y)* are used for this purpose. The inverse function *rel(X, Y)* indicates the corresponding atomic rela-

*Figure 6. Algorithm FindMTSs*

```
Algorithm FindMTSs
  Input: A QTCN C
  Returns: Find the set of algebras C belongs to, or
  "intractable"
(1) Initialize Algebras = {all eighteen MTSs};
(2) ∀relations R ∈ C do {
      // check for the seventeen Krokhin-MTSs
(3)       ∀atomic relation r, p ∈ B do
(4)           if r ∈ R && p ∉ R then
(5)               Algebras := Algebras\
AljTable(r)(!p);
      // check for the OH MTS
(6)     (lowX, lowY) := Min {r(X), r(Y) | r ∈ R };
(7)     (highX, highY) := Max {r(X), r(Y) | r ∈ R };
      // computed cl(R), the convex closure of R
(8)     for (X:=lowX, Y:=lowY;
                    X ≤ highX, Y ≤ highY; X++, Y++) do
(9)         if rel(X, Y) ∉ R && dim(rel(X, Y)) = = 2
then
          // cl(R)\R has a higher dimensional atomic
relation
(10)            Algebras := Algebras\ Alj(18); };
(11) if Algebras == ∅ then return "intractable";
```

*Table 2. AljTable()()*

| | !b | !m | !o | !s | !d | !f | !≡ |
|---|---|---|---|---|---|---|---|
| b | | | 11,14 | 3,5,7,16 | 13 | 6 | 17 |
| m | 9,12 | | 11,14 | 3,5,7,16 | 13 | 6 | 17 |
| o | 9,12 | | | 3,5,7,16 | 13 | 6 | 17 |
| s | 12 | | 14 | | 13 | 2,6 | 15,17 |
| d | 12 | | 14 | 1,5,7,16 | | 2,4,6,15 | 17 |
| f | | | | 1,5 | 10 | | 16,17 |
| ≡ | | | | | | | |
| $f^{-1}$ | 9 | | 11 | 3,7 | | | 16,17 |
| $d^{-1}$ | 9 | | 11 | 3 | | 8 | 17 |
| $s^{-1}$ | | | | | | 4,8 | 15,17 |
| $o^{-1}$ | | | | 1 | 10 | 2,4,8,15 | 17 |
| $m^{-1}$ | | | | 1 | 10 | 2,4,8,15 | 17 |
| $b^{-1}$ | | | | 1 | 10 | 2,4,8,15 | 17 |

tion on the lattice. If dimension 2 atomic relation is found in *cl(R)\R, C* does not belong to the ORD-Horn MTS, and is removed from the *Algebras* set (line 10). Finally, if *C* does not belong to any MTS, then *C* is an intractable problem (line 11). For a proof of the intractability, see Krokhin et al.(2003).

**Proposition 1:** An entry in Table 2, *AljTable(x) (!y)*, correctly shows the respective MTS to be excluded if any relation *R* in a TCN has an atomic relation *x*, but not the corresponding pivot *y*.

This is easy to verify from Table 1. For example, any relation R in Alj(11) may not have 'p' (from left vertical sublattice), while the corresponding pivot 'o' is absent from R (see Table 1).

**Theorem 1:** *Algorithm FindMTSs identifies a TCN C with the respective MTSs, or declares C to be intractable, in O(|C|) time, where |C| = the number of non-trivial relations in C (not tautology, or not Ø).*

*Proof*: Algorithm utilizes the defining characteristics (proposition 1) of the MTSs. The two *for-loops* on lines 3 and 8 are bounded by constant integers. Hence, the complexity from the loop on line 2 is O(|*C*|).

## CONSISTENCY CHECKING AND CULPRIT DETECTION FOR SEVENTEEN KROKHIN-MTSs

Drakengren et al. (1997) suggested an algorithm to solve 21 large tractable subclasses of Allen's Interval algebra. The algorithm practically converts the input QTCN to a directed graph and looks for cycles to detect inconsistency. In that work, only nine of the algebras were identified as maximal. Those are the algebras we named Alj(i) for $1 \leq i \leq 8$ (Figure 2) and the OH algebra (ORD-Horn [Nebel & Bürckert, 1995]). The remaining 12 algebras were actually subalgebras of Alj(j) for $9 \leq j \leq 14$ mentioned in Figure 3. For those algebras, excluding the ORD-Horn Algebra, Drakengren et al. (1997) suggested a polynomial time algorithm, which runs in linear time in the number of intervals input.

In this section, we first modify the existing algorithm to fit our terminologies, and enhance the former in two ways, (1) make sure that it is applied over all the Krokhin-MTSs, (2) suggest how the algorithm may be extended with new development toward OH MTS, so that one can com up with a complete algorithm for all MTS, and (3) store the constraints responsible for inconsistency (*culprits*) when the system is not satisfiable (Algorithm *SAT-TR* in Figure 7). To repeat, this algorithm can be applied to the remaining algebras (than the ones for which Drakengren et al. (1997) developed their algorithm for) presented in Figures 4 and 5, and for OH algebra. Identifying culprits is also a new direction in this line of work.

For the purpose of OH algebra, the *Proposition 4.8* of Drakengren et al. (1995) may be used:

**Proposition 2.** The only *maximal acyclic relations* (MAR) in *IA* are *(b d o m s f), (b d o m s $f^1$), (b $d^1$ o m s $f^1$), and (b $d^1$ o m $s^{-1}$ $f^1$)*, and their respective converses.

An acyclic relation is such that *iff* all the arcs in a QTCN are labeled with a particular acyclic relation or its subsets, then the presence of a cycle in the QTCN indicates inconsistency. Maximal acyclic relation is maximal for all such acyclic relations in the usual sense of maximality. Let us call *(b d o m s f), (b d o m s $f^1$), (b $d^1$ o m s $f^1$), or (b $d^1$ o m $s^{-1}$ $f^1$)* as a Forward MAR or *FMAR*, and an inverse of an FMAR as Backward MAR or *BMAR*.

**Theorem 2:** *Algorithm SAT-TR correctly solves satisfiability for Alj(i) for $1 \leq i \leq 17$.*

*Proof*: Drakengren & Jonsson's (1997) proof is trivially extendable for all the first 14 MTS. *Alj(15)* and *Alj(16)* has three sublattices each (Figure 4), and the proof relies on the correctness of the theorem for some of those algebras. First, we must assume that no edge is labeled with Ø, otherwise, the problem is not satisfiable. For *Alj(15)*, it is easy to see that if no relation from the middle sublattice including *(≡)* is present,

*Figure 7. Algorithm SAT-TR*

```
Algorithm SAT-TR
Input: a temporal constraint network C over θ-subalgebra, where θ∈(Alj(i), 1≤i≤ 18)
Output: accept, or a set of culprit constraints
(1)  let C' := C, Culprit := ∅;
(1)  if i<18 in the input Alj(i)   // a Krohin-MTS
(1)      let pv be the forward non-zero dimensional pivot of Alj(i)
(3)      ∀constraints (n1R n2)  ∈ C do
(4)          if pv ∉ R and pv^-1 ∈ R do
(5)              redirect (n1R n2)  to (n2 R^-1 n1);
(6)          if pv ∈ R and pv^-1 ∈ R do
(7)              C' := C' – R;

(8)      SC := the set of all nodes of all strong components in C';
(9)      ∀constraints (n1R n2) ∈ C  do {
(10)         if R ∩{≡} == ∅ do
(11)             if n1 and  n2 ∈ SC do
(12)                 Culprit := Culprit ∪(n1R n2);
(13)         if R  == ∅
(14)             Culprit := Culprit ∪(n1R n2)};
(15) if Culprit == ∅   return 'accept';
(16) else return Culprit
```

Note that a *culprit* edge may exist in two different strong components or may belong to the same strong component (line 12). This is why we collect all nodes belonging to the strong components in *SC* in line 8, which are the only important information for our purpose.

then the problem can be solved using *Alj(1)* or *Alj(3)*. If on the contrary, the middle sublattice is present, then so is the *(≡)* relation on every concerned labeled edge that is the pivot for middle lattices. Therefore, the output set '*Culprit*' will not be populated on this iteration, since the conditional statement in line 13 is not true, as long as the relation contains the *(≡)* relation. Similarly for *Alj(16)*, the two algebras that can be used are *Alj(5)* or *Alj(7)*. For *Alj(17)* every relation must include the *(≡)* and the problem is satisfiable for any input (as long as $\varnothing \notin C$).

Proof for *Alj(18)* (OH) is somewhat tricky for absence of any fixed pivots. Thus, the arcs here may not be directed as in line 5. Also, even if in some cases MAR's are used for directing the arcs the existence of the strong connected components are not sufficient condition for unstaisfiability of a network. This is because '*equality*' and '*inequality*' of the end points may for an inconsistent cycle. For example, *Interval1* $\{f, f^{-1}\}$ *Interval2* $\{s, s^{-1}\}$ *Interval3* {≡} *Interval1*, no directed cycle exists in this case, but '*equality*' relations over the end points of the respective intervals conflict.

**Theorem 3:** *Algorithm SAT-TR runs in linear time in the size of C.*

*Proof*: See Drakengren et al. (1997) for the constraint checking parts of the algorithm. The culprit detection part (line 18) does not increase the asymptotic complexity of the algorithm.

Note that the consistency checking may terminate after detecting the first *culprit*, whereas

*Figure 8. The constraint network C*

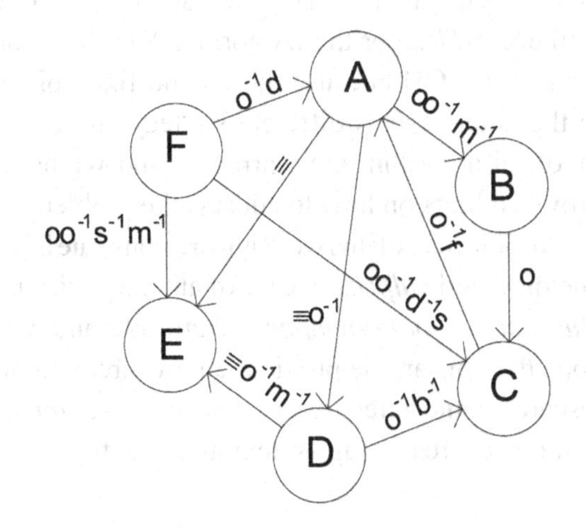


*Figure 9. C revised*

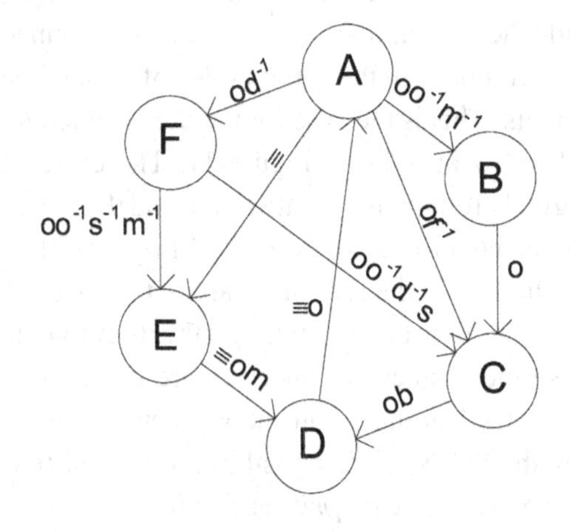


*Figure 10. C'*

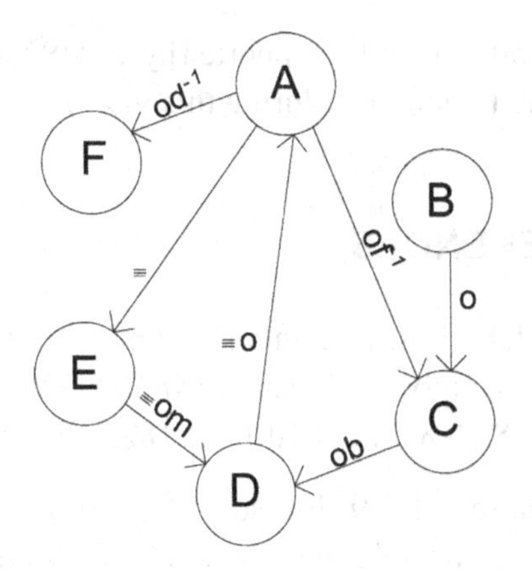


*Figure 11. Strong component*

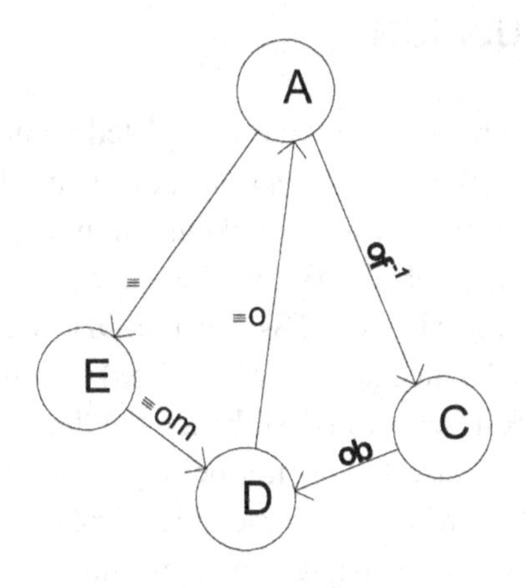


*SAT-TR* runs through all edges in $C$ to find *all* the culprits.

*Example 7:* Consider the following set of constraint over intervals *{A, B, C, D, E, F}*: $A\ (oo^{-1}m^{-1})\ B$, $B\ (o)\ C$, $C\ (o^{-1}f)\ A$, $A\ (\equiv o^{-1})\ D$, $D\ (o^{-1}b^{-1})\ C$, $D\ (\equiv o^{-1}m^{-1})\ E$, $A\ (\equiv)\ E$, $F\ (o\ o^{-1}s^{-1}m^{-1})\ E$, $F\ (oo^{-1}d^{-1}s)\ C$, and $F\ (o^{-1}d)\ A$.

The corresponding interval constraint network $C$ is shown in Figure 8.

Algorithm *FindMTSs* will find out which algebras this problem does not belong to. For example, constraint $C_1$ excludes the following algebras, Table($o$)($!b$) ⇒ 9, 12; Table($o$)($!s$) ⇒ 3, 5, 7, 16; Table($o$)($!b$) ⇒ 9, 12; Table($o$)($!d$) ⇒ 13; Table($o$)($!f$) ⇒ 6; Table($o$)($!eq$) ⇒ 17; Table($o$)($!f$) ⇒ 2, 4, 8, 15; Table($o$)($!d^{-1}$) ⇒ 10; and Table($o$)($!\,s^{-1}$) ⇒ 1.

Algorithm *FindMTSs* will finally return a set for which only the value for Alj(11) remains true. The problem is tractable, and some possible pivots $(oo^{-1})$ have been identified. We can now use Algorithm *SAT-TR* to decide satisfiability of the problem. First, we must redirect every edge so that C does not have any arc labeled only with $o^{-1}$ pivot (lines 4-5). The new constraint network C is shown in Figure 9. *C'* is the graph *C* where every arc labeled with both the pivots are removed (lines 6-7). *C'* is shown in Figure 10. The next step consists in finding every strong component in C'. These components are shown in Figure 11.

Finally, for every arc *A* in C that does not include the (≡) relation, return 'reject' if *A* connects any two nodes in the set of nodes of strong components. This is the case for the arcs labeled *(ob)* and *(of*$^{-1}$*)* in bold on Figure 11. Therefore, the original problem is not satisfiable and the *culprits* are detected to be {*(C (od) D)*, *(A (of*$^{-1}$*) C)*}.

The arcs in the *culprit* set are not individually responsible for inconsistency, rather they together cause inconsistency. Since we are detecting all the SCCs leading to an inconsistent TCN, and only the SCCs are responsible for inconsistency (Theorem 3), the *culprit* set is unique.

## DISCUSSION

In this chapter, we have completed some gaps left in Drakengren, Krokhin, Jeavon, and Johnsson's series of works (Drakengren, et al., 1997; Krokhin, et al., 2003) on the Interval Algebra identifying all its MTSs but the OH. We have proposed a mechanism (*FindMTSs*) to classify a network in some or possibly none of the eighteen MTSs. In case it does not belong to any one of them, the problem is intractable (Krokhin, et al., 2003). We have adapted an algorithm from those works to check for consistency when a network does belong to any of those MTSs (except the OH). Even though OH is expected to be the most "useful" algebra because it contains all the atomic relations as its elements, other MTS's may also be useful in practical situations where all the basic relations are not needed (e.g., 1D-atomic relations like '*meet*' are often impractical). Our algorithm not only checks for consistency but in case of inconsistency it returns the arcs (*culprits*) that are responsible for inconsistency. Although Allen's path consistency algorithm (less efficient than Drakengen et al.'s and our algorithms) can check for consistency over tractable problems, it is not easy to modify Allen's algorithm (1983) for identification of culprits or detect intractable problems. In a future work, we will develop an algorithm toward the OH MTS that is not covered by the *SAT-TR* algorithm. Algorithm *SAT-TR* is not suitable for OH because there is no fixed pivot in the latter case. A different strategy and more involved algorithm are warranted and we have provided hints on how to address the problem.

An objective of this work is to demonstrate how one may find *culprits* in case of any inconsistent *Qualitative Spatio-temporal Network*, and we hope that this article provides a new direction of research in the latter area, as detection of *culprits* will make a reasoning system more useful.

## ACKNOWLEDGMENT

This work was partly supported by the US National Science Foundation during this work.

## REFERENCES

Allen, J. F. (1983). Maintaining knowledge about temporal intervals. *Communications of the ACM, 26*(11), 832–843. doi:10.1145/182.358434

Drakengren, T., & Jonsson, P. (1997). Twenty one large tractable subclasses of Allen's algebra. *Artificial Intelligence Journal, 93*, 297–319. doi:10.1016/S0004-3702(97)00021-0

Krokhin, A., Jeavons, P., & Jonsson, P. (2003). Reasoning about temporal relations: The tractable subalgebras of Allen's interval algebra. *Journal of the ACM, 50*(5), 591–640. doi:10.1145/876638.876639

Ligozat, G. (1996). A new proof of tractability for ORD-Horn relations. In *Proceedings of the Thirteenth National Conference on Artificial Intelligence (AAAI-96)*, (pp. 395-401). Menlo Park, CA: AAAI Press.

Nebel, B., & Bürckert, H. J. (1995). Reasoning about temporal relations: A maximal tractable subclass of Allen's algebra. *Journal of the ACM*, *42*(1), 43–66. doi:10.1145/200836.200848

Van Beek, P. (1992). Reasoning about qualitative temporal information. *Artificial Intelligence*, *58*, 297–326. doi:10.1016/0004-3702(92)90011-L

Vilain, M., & Kautz, H. (1986). Constraint propagation algorithms for temporal reasoning. In *Proceedings of the Fifth National Conference on Artificial Intelligence (AAAI)*, (pp. 377-382). AAAI.

# Chapter 9
# Reasoning about Space, Actions, and Change:
## A Paradigm for Applications of Spatial Reasoning

**Mehul Bhatt**
*University of Bremen, Germany*

## ABSTRACT

*Qualitative spatial conceptualizations provide a relational abstraction and interface to the metrical realities of the physical world. Humans, robots, and systems that act and interact, are embedded in space. The space itself undergoes change all the time, typically as a result of volitional actions performed by an agent, and events, both deterministic and otherwise, which occur in the environment. Both categories of occurrences are a critical link to the external world, in a predictive as well as an explanatory sense: anticipations of spatial reality conform to commonsense knowledge of the effects of actions and events on material entities. Similarly, explanations of the perceived reality too are established on the basis of such apriori established commonsense notions. The author reasons about space, actions, and change in an integrated manner, either without being able to clearly demarcate the boundaries of each type of reasoning, or because such boundaries do not exist per se. This chapter is an attempt to position such integrated reasoning as a useful paradigm for the utilization of qualitative spatial representation and reasoning techniques in relevant application domains. From a logical perspective, the author notes that formalisms already exist and that effort need only be directed at specific integration tasks at a commonsense conceptual, formal representational, and computational level.*

DOI: 10.4018/978-1-61692-868-1.ch009

## 1. INTRODUCTION

The field of Qualitative Spatial Reasoning (QSR) investigates abstraction mechanisms and the technical computational apparatus for representing and reasoning about space within a formal, non-metrical framework (Freksa, 1991b; Cohn & Renz, 2007). Logical formalizations of space and tools for efficiently reasoning with them are now well-established (Renz & Nebel, 2007). Similarly, temporal calculi, in a minimalist sense of the interval-interval relations of Allen (1983), and other more elaborate formal methods in reasoning about change provide the general mechanisms required to handle various aspects such as continuity, concurrency, causality and the fundamental problems resulting therefrom (Shanahan, 1997; Davis & Morgenstern, 2004; Mueller, 2006). Developments in this latter field, generally referred to as Reasoning about Actions and Change (RAC) (Van Harmelen, et al., 2007), have primarily been motivated by some of the fundamental epistemological problems that arise in reasoning about actions and their effects, e.g., the *frame* (McCarthy & Hayes, 1969), *ramification* (Finger, 1987), and *qualification* (McCarthy, 1977) problems. Within RAC, efforts have resulted in formal calculi such as the Situation Calculus (McCarthy & Hayes, 1969), Event Calculus (Kowalski & Sergot, 1986), and Fluent Calculus (Thielscher, 1998), and other more specialized formalisms also similarly grounded in mathematical logic (Davis & Morgenstern, 2004). In contrast to the field of RAC, QSR has acquired its present status as a sub-division within Artificial Intelligence (AI) only relatively recently (Stock, 1997), and has its most direct origins in the work on Qualitative Reasoning in the late 80s and early 90s (Weld & de Kleer, 1989).

With the aim of realizing practical applications of '*logic-based*' reasoning about space and spatial change, this article poses the question of the integration of formal methods in qualitative spatial representation and reasoning on the one hand, and general commonsensical approaches to represent and reason about action and change on the other. The question is posed within the context of a certain class of application scenarios, and ensuing computational requirements therefrom, which inherently require the ability to model and reason about changing spatial datasets. In a rather specific sense, this posits the question of the integration of qualitative spatial theories encompassing one or more aspects of space with calculi of action and change such as the Situation Calculus, Event Calculus and Fluent Calculus; the range of available specialized formalism for modelling commonsense reasoning, and reasoning about action and change being rather extensive (Davis & Morgenstern, 2004; Van Harmelen, et al., 2007).

### 1.1. Why is Integration Necessary?

The integration of qualitative spatial representation and reasoning techniques within general commonsense reasoning frameworks in AI is an essential next-step for their applicability in realistic (relevant) domains, e.g., in the form of spatial control and spatial planning in cognitive robotics, for spatial decision-support in intelligent systems and as explanatory models in a wide-range of systems requiring the formulation of hypothesis, e.g., diagnosis, event-based geographic information systems, robotic control scenarios. It is also imperative that the intended integration be achieved at uniform ontological, representational and computational levels, or aptly, a paradigm such as '*Reasoning about Space, Actions, and Change*' (RSAC) is needed. Indeed, if 'spatial reasoning,' both qualitative and otherwise, and commonsense notions of space and spatial change are to be embedded or utilized within practical or larger application scenarios in AI, for instance to model the qualitative spatial reasoning abilities of a robot, their integration with formal calculi and tools to model change in general needs to be adequately investigated in a fundamental manner.

Furthermore, it is necessary that the integration and the supported computational mechanisms therefrom be generic / applicable in a wide-range of application domains, such as the ones highlighted in this chapter.

## 1.2. Integration and Sub-Division in AI

The proposed integration is also closely related to the general problem pertaining to the sub-division of endeavours (McCarthy, 1977), such as spatial reasoning, in artificial intelligence in general. Within the context of the formalisation of common-sense knowledge, McCarthy (1977) singled out spatial reasoning as an important task, mostly concentrating on the aspects necessary to resolve some specific problems. Such separation of tasks is necessary and important from an AI research viewpoint; however, within the context of the integration of such sub-divided endeavours, an important question is what is more fundamental: spatial reasoning or general logic-based reasoning (Freksa, 1992). To quote Freksa (1992) on the issue:

*'From a formal position, these two viewpoints may appear equivalent; however, from a cognitive and computational position they are not; the logic-based view assumes that spatial reasoning involves special assumptions regarding the properties of space which must be taken into account while the space-based view assumes that abstract (non-spatial) reasoning involves abstraction from spatial constraints which must be treated explicitly.'*

Our viewpoint here is that the issue of *integration* in the aforementioned context, which is at least as important as the issue of *sub-division,* has been accorded a secondary status by researchers in the qualitative spatial reasoning domain in favour of the development of fundamental modes of spatial information representation and reasoning. Indeed, specialised problems need to be approached individually, but it is also necessary that the resulting solutions can be integrated seamlessly and/or be embedded within a larger unified theory, with the intended integration happening at conceptual, representational and computational levels. The development of such a unifying semantics is necessary to, for instance, realize the intrinsic representation and reasoning capabilities of an intelligent entity such as the 'well-designed child' of McCarthy (2008), or its more specialized form by way of the 'well-designed (young) mathematician' of Sloman (2008). Among other things, it is this application-centered '*integration*' aspect and its logical '*well-designed'ness*' that are discussed in this chapter.

## 1.3. Organisation of Chapter

The chapter is written in the form of an opinion piece that advocates a particular line of research. The chapter does not strive to provide an in-depth literature review. I highlight the importance of the proposed integration by way of the RSAC paradigm, the problems that may be solved in this context, point out related research that addresses these questions explicitly, and present immediate agenda for furthering the proposed paradigm. The chapter is organized as follows:

- Section 2 provides diverse motivating application domains where integrated reasoning about space, actions and change is useful. Each application domain is independent in itself and does not affect the continuity of the chapter.
- Section 3 discusses the key challenges connected to the RSAC paradigm vis-à-vis the logical well-designed'ness. The section also includes a more or less chronological discussion of perspectives related to the proposed integration.
- Section 4 builds-up on Section 3 and discusses the ontological, representational,

commonsensical and computational challenges involved in integrated logical reasoning about space, actions and change.
- Section 5 concludes with a brief summary of the chapter. In addition to references, key reading material is also cited at the end.

## 2. SPACE, ACTIONS, AND CHANGE: APPLICATION PERSPECTIVES

Actions and events are a crucial connecting-link between space and spatial change, i.e., spatial configurations typically change as a result of interaction within the environment, whatever be the ontological status of the interaction or the nature of the environment. Actions and events, both in a predictive as well as an explanatory sense, also constitute the mechanisms by which we establish and nurture commonsense knowledge about the world that we live in: our anticipations of spatial reality conform to our commonsense knowledge of the effects of actions and events in the real world. Similarly, our explanations of the perceived reality too are established on the basis of such apriori established commonsense notions. In the following subsections, I present some application domains where this interpretation of integrated reasoning about space, actions and change is applicable.

### 2.1. Spatial Control and Decision-Making in Cognitive Robotics

High-level spatial planning/re-configuration, or more generally spatial control and decision-making (Bhatt, 2009b) in *Cognitive Robotics* (Levesque & Lakemeyer, 2007) is a domain where integrated reasoning about space, actions and change is most directly applicable. High-level agent / robot control languages such as INDIGOLOG (Giacomo & Levesque, 1999) and FLUX (Thielscher, 2005), which pursue a vision of cognitive robotics from a logical viewpoint, share many important common features, chiefly among them being the availability of imperative programming style constructs for robot/agent-control tasks, i.e., statements in the program correspond to actions, events and properties of the world in which an agent is operating. What these languages lack, and rightly so, is a generic domain-independent spatial theory that could be used as a basis of a high-level spatial planning in arbitrary tasks. For instance, consider a robot such as in Figure 1 with grasping, locomotion, and vision capabilities. On the table lie a few solid/rigid boxes and balls, containers that are either empty or filled with some liquid and possibly other specialized bodies. Further, presuppose that the robot is equipped with basic vision and scene grounding[1] (by qualification) capabilities at least in this limited context. From the viewpoint of the RSAC paradigm, it is *desired* that the robot's built-in spatial reasoning capabilities be general (i.e., be applicable in new situations and completely different domains) and elaboration tolerant[2] from the viewpoint of the representational and computational requirements.

For this robot, spatial changes could be denoted by relational variations (e.g., topological and orientation changes), which accrue as a result of actions, in the grounded spatial configurations of objects, or possibly incremental updates to the layout and structuring of the environment as perceived (and grounded) by less than perfect sensory devices in real-time as the robot performs *move* and *turn* actions. The range of application possibilities for integrated reasoning about space, actions and change in the domain of cognitive robotics are rather extensive, and also perhaps most natural (Bhatt, 2009b).

### 2.2. Dynamic Object and Event-Based GIS

Modelling and analysis of dynamic geospatial phenomena within *Geographic Information Systems* (GIS) and the integration of time in GIS (Temporal GIS or T-GIS) has emerged as a

*Figure 1. Spatial planning in cognitive robotics*

(a) Spatial reconfiguration

(b) Control and decision-making

major research topic within the GIS community. Although present representational and analytical apparatus to examine the dynamics of such phenomena is nascent at best, the issue is increasingly being considered as a major research priority in GIS (Yuan, et al., 2004). Integrating time with GIS is clearly necessary toward the development of GIS capable of monitoring and analysing successive states of spatial entities (Claramunt & Thériault, 1995). Such capability, necessitating the representation of instances of geographic entities and their change over time rather than change to layers or scenes is the future of GIS and has been emphasized in the National Imagery and Mapping Agency's (NIMA) vision for Integrated Information Libraries (NIMA, 2000). A (temporal) GIS should, in addition to accounting for spatial changes, also consider the events behind changes and the facts which enable observation of these changes (Beller, 1991). In the words of Claramunt and Thériault (1995):

*'To respond adequately to scientific needs, a TGIS should explicitly preserve known links between events and their consequences. Observed relationships should be noted (e.g., entities A and B generate entity C) to help scientists develop models that reproduce the dynamics of spatio-temporal processes. Researchers will thus be able to study complex relationships, draw conclusions and verify causal links that associate entities through influence and transformation processes.'*

Clearly, such a facility necessitates a formal approach encompassing events, actions and their effects toward representing and reasoning about dynamic spatial changes. Such an approach will be advantageous in GIS applications concerned with retrospective analysis or diagnosis of observed spatial changes involving either fine-scale object level analysis or macro-level (aggregate) analysis of dynamic geospatial phenomena. For instance, within GIS, spatial changes could denote (environmental) changes in the geographic sphere at a certain temporal granularity and could bear a significant relationship to natural events and human actions, e.g., changes in land-usage, vegetation, cluster variations among aggregates of demographic features, and wild-life migration patterns. Here, event-based and object-level reasoning at the spatial level could serve as a basis of explanatory analyses, for instance by abduction, within a GIS (Galton & Hood, 2004; Worboys, 2005; Couclelis, 2009). For instance,

*Figure 2. Abduction in GIS*

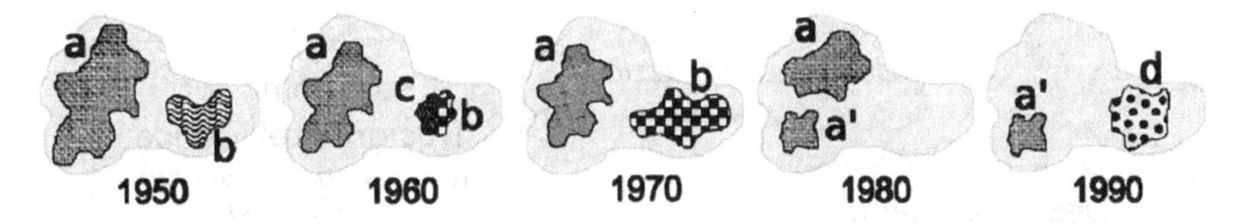


a useful reasoning mechanism that applications may benefit from could be the task of causal explanation (Bhatt, 2009a), which is the process of retrospective analysis by the extraction of an event-based explanatory model from available spatial data (e.g., temporally-ordered snap-shots such as in Figure 2)[3]. Indeed, the explanation would essentially be an event-based history of the observed spatial phenomena defined in terms of both domain-independent and domain-dependent occurrences. At the domain-independent level, the explanation may encompass behaviour such as *emergence*, *growth* and *shrinkage*, *disappearance*, *spread*, *stability*, etc, in addition to the sequential/parallel composition of the behavioural primitives aforementioned, e.g., *emergence* followed by *growth*, *spread / movement*, *stability* and *disappearance* during a time-interval. At a domain-dependent level, such patterns may characterize high-level processes, environmental / natural and human activities such as deforestation, urbanisation, transformations in land-use types etc. Such explanatory analysis is especially important (e.g., in the context of a query-based GIS system) where the available data needs to be analysed for various purposes such as managerial decision making, policy formation and so forth. This aspect is further discussed in Section 4.3.3.

## 2.3. Spatial Computing for Design

Spatial computing for design refers to the use of formal methods in qualitative spatial representation and reasoning for solving requirement modelling and consistency problems in the domain of spatial design (Bhatt & Freksa, 2010). Here, the main goal is to develop the formal representational and computational framework that may be used as a basis of providing assistive design intelligence within a conventional spatial design workflow.

The availability of assistive intelligence capability for *spatial design* tasks, e.g., within a Computer Assisted Architecture Design (CAAD) tool, is essential to reduce design errors and failures, and also to ensure that functional requirements of a design are met when the design is actually deployed/constructed in reality (Bhatt & Freksa, 2010; Bhatt, et al., 2010). An operational overview of the iterative design refinement cycle is illustrated in Figure 3. Here, a design is modelled in an architectural design tool such as ArchiCAD (Graphisoft Inc., 2010). Subsequently, the geometrical / quantitative data-model of a concrete design (e.g., a CAD model) is transformed to an alternate symbolic representation within the intelligent system, wherein reasoning is performed with a potentially symbolic / qualitative spatial model, and the work-in-progress design is evaluated along different dimensions. The results of the reasoning process, e.g., detected inconsistencies, are then provided as feedback to the designer in a cognitively adequate manner, and the design (re) adjustments are incorporated within the iterative refinement phase. The process is ideally repeated until certain design objectives and/or functional requirements are satisfied, e.g., until no requirement inconsistencies occur.

The crux of such a iteratively-refined, intelligence assisted design approach is that it becomes possible to automatically validate a designer's

Figure 3. Iterative refinement by intelligent design assistance

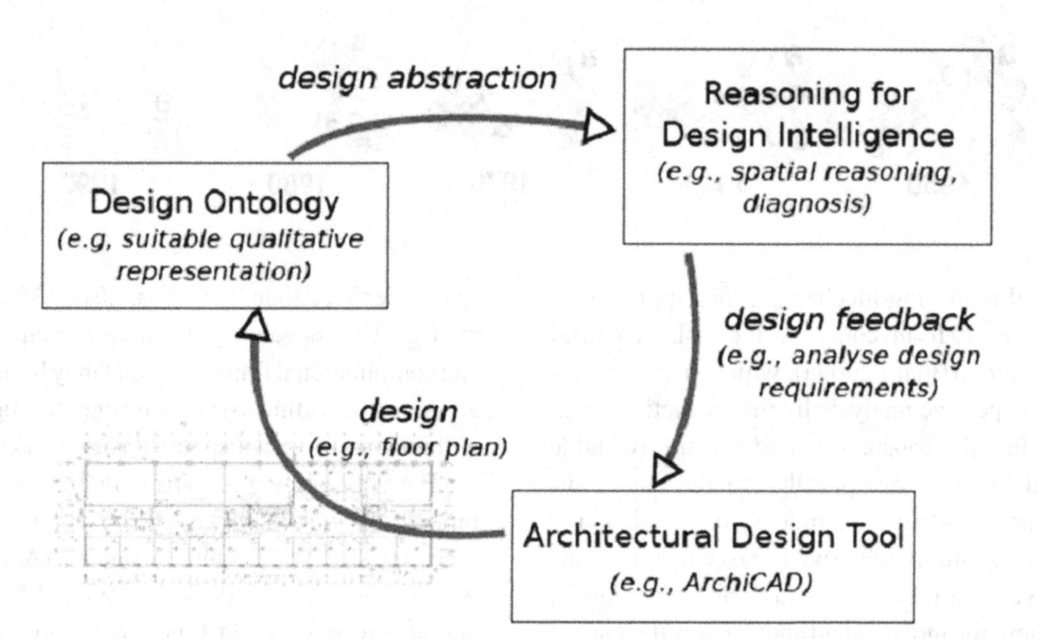


*conceptual space* against the precisely modeled *quantity space*, as constituted by a work-in-progress design. As an example, Bhatt et al. (2009) illustrate the approach for the specific case where the new generation of smart environments and building-automation systems are being designed. Consider the example in Figure 4 illustrates two alternatives of a selected part of a sample floor plan. Here, a requirement constraint that stipulates the non-existence of security blind-spots (e.g., wrt. $Sensor_1$ and $Sensor_2$) whilst people utilise the door ($Door_1$) can be easily checked for (topological) (in)consistency at the design stage itself. For a reasoner that aims at not only detecting the inconsistencies, but also at coming up with alternate recommendations that are consistent, spatial re-configurations and transformations (e.g., translation and deformation actions) at the qualitative level that solve inconsistencies may represent a useful solution approach in this domain. In general, within an decision-support or design assistance tool, metrical changes in the structural layout or changes in the relative spatial relationships of the design elements—i.e., qualitative changes along the conceptual space of the designer—will directly or indirectly entail differing end-product realizations in terms of spatial design requirements, building construction costs, human-factors (e.g., traversability, way-finding complexity), aesthetics aspects, and energy efficiency and long-term maintenance expenses thereof.

## 2.4. Activity Recognition in Smart Environments

The field of *Ambient Intelligence* (AmI) is beginning to manifest itself in everyday application scenarios in public and private spheres. Key domains include security and surveillance applications and other utilitarian purposes in smart homes and office environments, ambient assisted living, and so forth (Streitz, et al., 2007; Augusto & Shapiro, 2007). Notwithstanding the primarily commercial motivations in the field, there has also been active academic (co)engagement and, more importantly, an effort to utilize mainstream artificial intelligence tools and techniques as a foundational basis within the field (Ramos, et al.,

*Figure 4. A two room scenario with the requirement that the door must be supervised by sensors, i.e., the functional space of the door must be completely covered by some sensor range (not necessarily only from a single sensor). Source: Bhatt et al. (2009)*

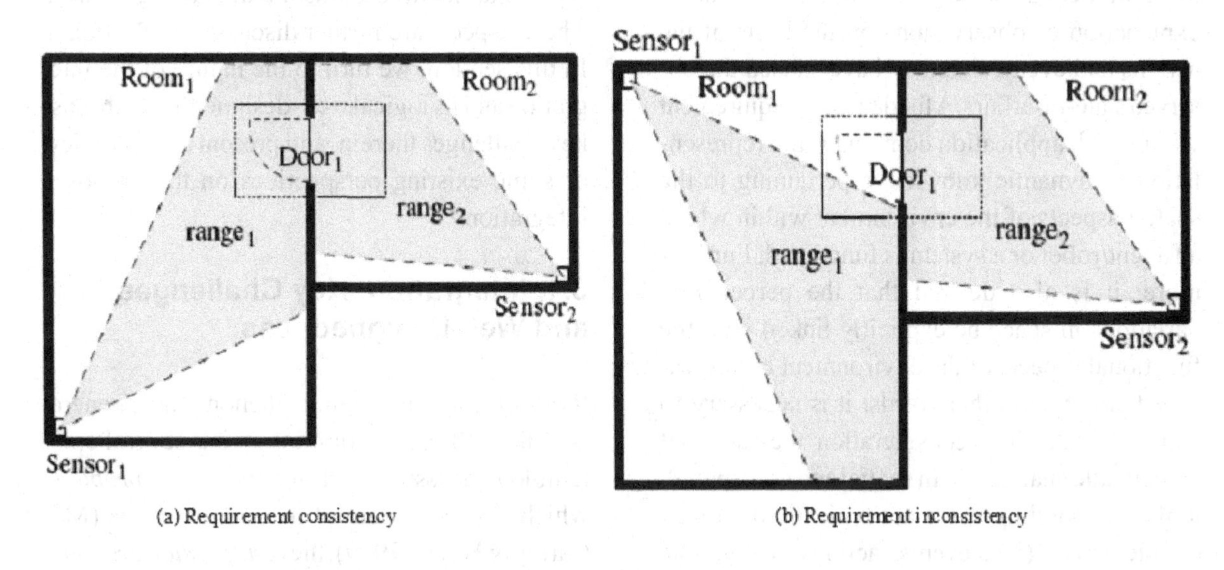


*Figure 5. Activity recognition in smart environments (source: Bhatt & Dylla, 2009)*

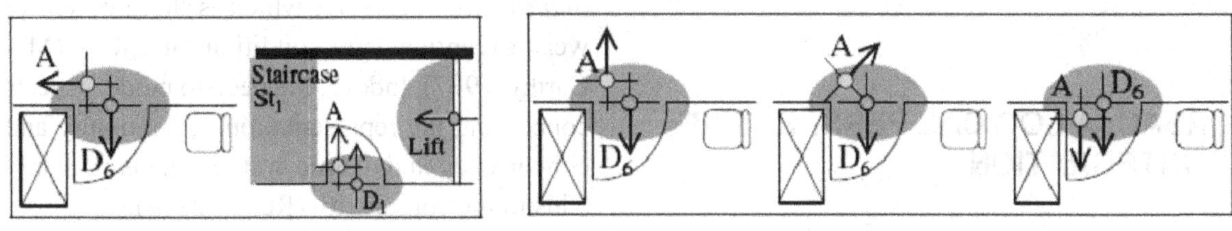


2008; Augusto & Nugent, 2006). For instance, the use of quantitative techniques for sensor data analysis and mining, e.g., to look for patterns in motion-data, and for activity and behavior recognition has found wide acceptability (Youngblood & Cook, 2007; Philipose, et al., 2004) (see Figure 5).

AmI systems that monitor and interact with an environment populated by humans and other artefacts require a formal means for representing and reasoning with spatio-temporal and event-based phenomena that are grounded to real aspects of the environment (Bhatt & Guesgen, 2009). Here, the location of a mobile entity may be required to be projected or abduced (i.e., be explainable) within a (dynamic) spatial environment being modelled (e.g., smart homes, airports, shopping-malls, traffic junctions, smart factories) for purposes of dynamic scene analysis and interpretation, event-recognition, alert generation, surveillance and so forth (Bhatt & Dylla, 2009). For instance, within a *behavior monitoring* and/or security system for a smart environment (e.g., home, office), *recognition of dynamic scenes* from changes in pre-designated configurations of qualified spatial configurations could be used as a basis of activity recognition and alert generation (Bhatt & Dylla, 2009; Galton, 2006). Similarly, the unfolding of sequences of spatial configurations that correspond to certain activities within the application domain of interest may be required to be modelled too, e.g., in the form of causal explanation of observations on the basis of the actions and events that may have caused the observed state-of-affairs. A fundamental requirement within such application domains is the representation of dynamic knowledge pertaining to the spatial aspects of the environment within which an agent/robot or a system is functional. Furthermore, it is also desired that the perceivable variations in space be explicitly linked with the functional aspects of the environment being reasoned about—in other words, it is necessary to explicitly take into consideration the fact that perceivable changes, both spatial and non-spatial, in the surrounding space are typically the result of interaction (i.e., events, actions) within the environment. Therefore, a unified view of space, change and occurrences—events and actions—is necessitated.

## 3. RSAC: A LOGICAL PERSPECTIVE TO INTEGRATION

To realise the predictive and explanatory reasoning capabilities for the class of application domains identified in Sections 2.3–2.1, a foundational approach and a formal (logical) basis for representing and reasoning about space, actions and change at uniform ontological and computational levels is needed; indeed, the integration is approachable from a cognitive perspective too, however, this is beyond the scope of the logical perspective of the present discussion. The key aspects to bear in mind before embarking on a particular logical approach to integration are the reasoning patterns that the respective approach / formalism lends itself to. To re-iterate, for the class of applications being considered herein, predictive (e.g., projection, planning and simulation) and explanatory (e.g., causal explanation) capabilities may be deemed essential. From a computational viewpoint, it is intended that these reasoning tasks follow directly from the semantics of the foundational approach or representational formalism that is being utilised. These aspects are further discussed in Section 4. In this section, we turn to the nature of the integration and its logical well-designed'ness, discuss key challenges therein, and present a brief review of some existing perspectives on the proposed integration.

### 3.1. Integration: Key Challenges and Well-Designedness

Reasoning about dynamic phenomena in general is a difficult proposition involving several epistemological issues such as: the *frame problem*, which is the problem of modelling inertia (McCarthy & Hayes, 1969), the *ramification problem*, which pertains to accounting for the indirect effects of actions and events (Finger, 1987) and the *qualification problem*, which is the problem of weak/exceptional pre-conditions of actions (McCarthy, 1977). Indeed, the need to model aspects concerning the representation of continuity and concurrency in dynamic systems in general only adds to the complexity (Reiter, 2001).

Along the (strictly) spatial dimension alone, the complexity first of all stems from the fact that space is characterized via various aspects—topology, orientation, size, shape, and some other attributes that are not purely geometrical (Galton, 2000). Furthermore, the complexity is compounded for the specific case of dynamic spatial systems where it is known that sets of qualitative spatial relationships pertaining to more than one aspect of space (e.g., orientation, topology, direction, distance) undergo changes as a result of actions and events occurring within the system (Bhatt & Loke, 2008). Since the respective sets of qualitative spatial relationships correspond to a *qualitative calculus*[4], it is imperative to ensure that all high-level axiomatic aspects[5] of the concerned calculi being modelled are preserved within the dynamic context. Indeed, the need to reason about space, spatial change, events and actions in a unified manner takes the complexity to a completely new level. For instance, such reasoning involves functional specifications of entities and their interaction with the environment, typically encompassing explicit accounts of the causal and goal-directed aspects of the (spatial) changes that are being modeled and reasoned upon. Key problematic aspects herein that have to be accounted for in the context of qualitative spatial calculi pertaining to any arbitrary aspect of space can be classified in following fundamental categories:

### F1. Epistemological

Problems that are *epistemological* in nature (Bhatt, 2010), namely problems of global spatial (compositional) consistency of spatial information and the modeling of spatial persistence and ramification/indirect effects within the context of dynamic spatial system.

### F2. Phenomenal

Problems pertaining to *phenomenal* aspects (Bhatt, 2009a) that are intrinsic to dynamic spatial systems, and involve behaviours such as *appearance*, *disappearance*, *re-appearance*, and other transformations of properties, spatial or non-spatial, which characterize an object, and the closely connected issue of object identity (Bennett, 2002; Hornsby & Egenhofer, 2000).

### F3. Reasoning Requirements

Specific *reasoning requirements* (e.g., abduction for causal explanation) (Bhatt, 2009a) that are required in the class of application domains, such as those discussed in Sections 2.3–2.1. This can have a significant bearing on the choice of the representational formalism, since it is the semantics of the formalism that will dictate the essential nature (e.g., monotonic vs. non-monotonic) of the reasoning patterns that are possible per se.

These aspects in (F1–F3) are further discussed in the rest of the chapter in Section 4. At this stage, the significance of (F1–F3) is further discussed in light of the need to have an integration that is logically well-designed with respect to a specific notion of logical well-designedness (McCarthy, 2008). Basically, McCarthy exemplifies the notion using the idea of a '*well-designed child*,' and more specifically, that of a well-designed logical robot child that is innately equipped with abilities to interact with the world that it lives in. To quote McCarthy (2008, section 7)[6]:

*Consider designing a logical robot child, although using logic is not the only approach that might work. In a logical child, the innate information takes the form of axioms in some language of mathematical logic.*

For McCarthy, the scale and complexity of the abilities of the robot or of the realities / phenomena of the world being represented are secondary. What is important is that the child's '*innate structures*,' or from a logical viewpoint, the child's innate logical structures, be well-designed. McCarthy's *well-designedness* in this logical context explicitly corresponds to the inclusion of following categories of innate structures in (I1–I4):[7]:

- I1 persistence of objects in terms of their composition and absolute position in space
- I2 spatial and temporal continuity of perceptions
- I3 relations of appearance and reality—"*how do we describe the appearance of an object to a blind person who has not felt it with his hands?* "
- I4 commonsense conservation laws pertaining to spatial quantities (Piaget & Inhelder, 1967)

Primarily, and in a broader sense, the issue of integration discussed in this article in fact echoes the same principle for the specific case where the *innate structures and reasoning abilities* correspond to the commonsense and qualitative conceptions pertaining to space, spatial change, and interaction within a dynamic spatial system. The *well-designedness* here corresponds to the use of formal conceptualizations—both for space as well as change—within a logical framework for modelling aspects concerning the different categories of innate structures that are identified by McCarthy. In a rather focussed or narrow sense, the issue of the integration proposed herein, and specifically of this notion of logical well-designedness, has been exemplified by Bhatt and Loke (2008), where the innate logical structures for representing domain-independent truths pertaining to space, spatial change and dynamic spatial phenomena are represented in the situation calculus. Some categories that have been accounted for include (C1–C5):[8]:

- C1 *global consistency* of relational (spatial) information, an aspect that is closely related to the ramification problem or the problem of modelling indirect-effect yielding state constraints (Section 4.2.3)
- C2 spatial property *persistence*, which is connected to the frame problem (e.g., the inference-pattern involved in making the default assumption that the spatial relationship between two objects *typically* stays the same, or that the absolute position of an object in space stays the same)
- C3 *continuity* of spatial change, involving the modelling of the conceptual neighbourhood of qualitative relationships
- C4 *phenomenal* aspects such as the *appearance* and *disappearance* of entities and the inference mechanisms required to account for an incompletely known domain of discourse
- C5 *explanatory* capability, for instance modelled as an abductive inference pattern, that provides a logical basis to formulate hypotheses about observed spatial phenomena

Needless to say, the range of innate categories pertaining to commonsense notions of space, spatial change and dynamic spatial phenomena covered by Bhatt and Loke (2008), or those enumerated in a much broader context by McCarthy (2008) for the "logical well-designedness" of a robot are by no means all-encompassing. Whereas the potentialities to further refine and extend the categories of innate structures are enormous[9], we further discuss the ones that have been presented here in Section 4.

## 3.2. (Some) Related Perspectives on Integration

There exist several works that either explicitly addresses the issue of integration or bear a close relationship to it. For the purposes of this chapter, we broadly classify these works in two categories[10]: foundational techniques that use some form of logic of action and change, possibly involving commonsense and non-monotonic researching frameworks, and other early work grounded in the area of qualitative simulation of physical/spatial system. The term 'foundational approach' corresponds to the use of mathematical logic based formalisms, in the spirit of the logical well-designedness discussed in Section 3.1; it does not imply that other works are non-foundational or ad hoc.

### 3.2.1. Integration within Qualitative Simulation Systems

One of the earliest explicitly stated accounts of an attempt toward a unifying semantics of space, time and actions, done within the context of the Qualitative Process Theory (QPT), can be found in the work of Forbus (1989). Forbus proposed *action-augmented envisionments*, which incorporate both the effects of an agent's actions and what will happen in the physical world whether or not the agent does something. Most research in this area, which gathered momentum during the mid-80s and early-90s, focussed on techniques for modelling and predicting the behaviour of physical systems in general (Bobrow, 1984; Weld & de Kleer, 1989). In addition to the qualitative process theory (Forbus, 1984), another notable outcome during this time was Kuipers's qualitative simulation system QSIM (Kuipers, 1986, 1994). The basic functionality supported in all of these systems is usually the same—the capability to generate some form of a behaviour model (usually a tree-based structure) in the form of a temporal partial ordering of the qualitative states that a modelled physical system can evolve into given some indexed state. Such a behaviour model, also referred to as an *envisionment* (Weld & de Kleer, 1989), is meant to trace the evolution of the system being modelled with respect to time. Depending on which aspects of change, encompassing space, time and causality, have been accounted for in the theory, envisionment-based qualitative simulation can be used as the basis of a planning and/or prediction function. The theory per se can be regarded to be general or rich enough to model the set of rules of behavioural dynamics involving several spatial attributes (e.g., changing location, orientation or the manipulation of objects) of the objects, both autonomous or human-controlled, in the domain being modelled to an extent to which it accounts for these differing aspects that are relevant to the domain. For example, the qualitative simulation system QSSIM in Cui et al. (1992) and Cohn et al. (1997c) is based on a topological view of space—qualitative states in their system are sets of distinct dyadic topological relations holding between the primitive objects of the theory's spatial ontology. In this sense, QSSIM can be only regarded as a topological theory of simulation. Albeit novel and different from QSIM or qualitative process theory in its use of a spatial ontology of regions and states based on sets of simultaneously satisfiable formulae, QSSIM still left a few open questions by considering merely one aspect of space, viz topology. To quote Cui et al. (1992, Sec. 5):

*Further envisaged extensions to the theory would include motion as a sub-theory...other useful extensions would include explicit information about causality and processes, the latter including teleological accounts of a physical systems behaviour*

An extended theory that includes causal and teleological accounts of a physical systems behaviour (i.e., is based on an integration of various aspects of space, time and causality) provides a far richer basis for planning and procedure generation, with varied applications in intelligent analysis and control, robot planning etc. A similar viewpoint, which is presently a general consensus within the GIS community, is also promoted in the context of event-based models of dynamic geographic phenomena in the GIS area where the use of dynamic aspects of geographic phenomena has been considered essential toward serving a useful explanatory and prediction function within GIS (Worboys, 1998, 2005; Beller, 1991; Allen, et al., 1995; NIMA, 2000)[11].

### 3.2.2. (Strictly) Logical Perspectives to Integration

A foundational approach toward the broader integration of spatial and logic-based common-sense reasoning frameworks is adopted in the works of Allen and Ferguson (1994), Bennett and Galton (2004), Bhatt and Loke (2008); Bhatt (2008b), Shanahan (1995), and Davis (2008, 2009).

#### 3.2.2.1. Foundational Approaches

Allen (1984) and Allen and Ferguson (1994) addressed the much broader (and still open-ended) problem of developing a general representation of actions and events that uniformly supports a wide range of reasoning tasks, including planning, explanation, prediction, natural language understanding, and commonsense reasoning in general. According to Allen and Ferguson (1994, p. 51), the novelty of their work is the combination of techniques (relevant to temporal reasoning and reasoning about action and change) into a unified framework that supports explicit reasoning about temporal relationships, actions, events and their effects. Here, the temporal part of Allen's theory is based on his seminal interval temporal logic (Allen, 1983; Allen & Hayes, 1985). Bennett and Galton (2004) propose Versatile Event Logic (VEL), which consists of a general temporal ontology and semantics encompassing many other representations such as the situation calculus and event calculus. In essence, VEL includes a temporal ontology and an expressive mechanism for representing temporal relationships and events. The main motivation for the development of VEL is its use as a foundational representational framework for comparing and interfacing different AI languages. Bennett and Galton illustrate this in the context of the situation and event calculus. Although spatial reasoning is not addressed in this context by Bennett and Galton, the general utility of an interfacing language such as VEL is promising from the viewpoint of the proposed RSAC paradigm.

Shanahan (1995) describes a default reasoning problem, analogous to the frame problem, which arises when an attempt is made to construct a logic-based calculus for reasoning about the movement of objects in a real-valued co-ordinate system. As Shanahan (1995) elaborates:

*If we are to develop a formal theory of commonsense, we need a precisely defined language for talking about shape, spatial location and change. The theory will include axioms, expressed in that language, that capture domain-independent truths about shape, location and change, and will also incorporate a formal account of any non-deductive forms of commonsense inference that arise in reasoning about the spatial properties of objects and how they vary over time.*

Indeed, what Shanahan's all-encompassing theory refers to is a unification of spatial, temporal and causal aspects at representational and computational levels. Bhatt (2009a, 2008b) extends the aforementioned default reasoning about spatial occupancy of Shanahan (1995), also within the situation calculus, by presenting scenarios where default and/or non-monotonic reasoning patterns are useful and (sometimes) necessary for the modelling of dynamic spatial domains. Here, the identified instances bear a direct relationship to the fundamental epistemological issues relevant to the frame and ramification problems and are utilized to realize essential computational tasks such as (abductive) causal explanation and spatial property projection[12] The use of commonsense reasoning about the physical properties of objects within a first-order logical framework has been investigated by Davis (2008, 2009). The key highlight of this work is that it combines commonsense qualitative reasoning about 'continuous time, Euclidean space, commonsense dynamics of solid objects, and semantics of partially specified plans' (Davis, 2009).

Gooday and Cohn (1996) propose an event-based qualitative spatial simulation system by employing the transition calculus (Gooday & Galton, 1997), which is a high-level formalism for reasoning about action and change, as the basic representation tool. Using this event-based approach, the behaviour model of the system corresponds to the set of landmark *events* that occur in it. With the spatial-temporal ontology and the envisionment axioms that are used as the basis of temporal projections still being the same, the system is basically a reformulation of QSSIM (Cui, et al., 1992) using the transition calculus. Although most of the important features of transition calculus involving concurrency and non-monotonic reasoning remained unutilized, the general utility of the proposed approach is in

*Figure 7. Topological and orientation calculi*

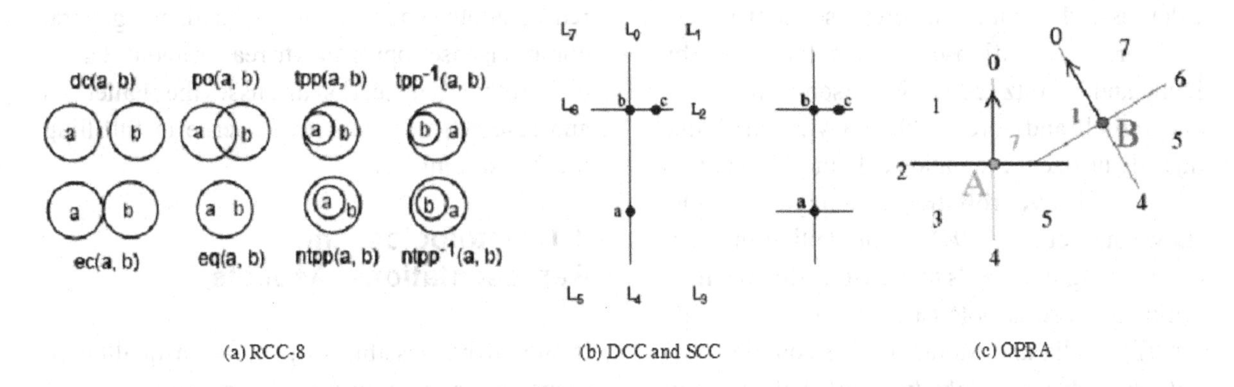


line with overall objective of a unifying semantics for space, time and events.

Bhatt and Loke (2008) and Bhatt (2008a) explicitly formalize a *Dynamic Spatial Systems* ( $\mathcal{DSS}$ ) approach for the modelling of changing spatial domains. A dynamic spatial system here is regarded as an instantiation of the generic *dynamic systems* approach (Sandewall, 1994; Reiter, 2001) for the specific case where sets of qualitative spatial relationships (grounded in formal spatial calculi) pertaining to one or more aspect of space undergo change as a result of actions and events in the system. The $\mathcal{DSS}$ formalization adheres to the semantics of the situation calculus and includes a systematic account of key aspects that are necessary to embed a domain-independent qualitative spatial theory within the situation calculus. The spatial theory itself is primarily derivable from the all-pervasive generic notion of 'qualitative spatial calculi' that are representative of differing aspects of space. The key advantage of the $\mathcal{DSS}$ approach is that based on the structure and semantics of the underlying situation calculus framework, fundamental reasoning tasks such as projection and explanation directly follow. As elaborated on in Section 4, these translate to spatial planning/re-configuration and causal explanation. The work of Bhatt and Loke may be regarded as a rather specific instantiation of the general RSAC proposal, which is paradigmatic and a much broader call than what any individual piece of research may encompass.

#### 3.2.2.2. Application-Oriented Approaches

Ferguson et al. (2003) describe an architecture consisting of JEPD spatial relation sets as nodes in a dependency network for dynamically handling spatial information in an incremental, non-monotonic diagrammatic reasoning system. These spatial relation sets include interval relations, relative orientation relations, and connectivity relations, but in theory could include any Jointly Exhaustive and Pair-Wise Disjoint (JEPD) sets of spatial relations, e.g., such as those illustrated in Figure 7 (Section 4). The system is designed with the aim to support higher-level reasoning, including support for creating default assumptions. Albeit indirectly related to the theme of integration, also important is the work of Cardelli and Gordon (2000, 2006) on ambient modal logics, where the truth of a modal formula is defined to be relative to its spatial and temporal location. In their work on defining mobile interactions, mobility is understood as a change of spatial configurations over time. Although the work does not explicitly refer to spatial properties in the strictly spatial sense (e.g., orientation or topological relationships), the approach is nevertheless useful toward formalising concurrent interactions within a spatio-temporal framework, given its foundations in the process calculus and its model-theoretic semantics.

More application-centric is the work by Dylla and Moratz (2004), Ferguson et al. (2003) and Cardelli and Gordon (2006). Dylla and Moratz directly utilize the situation calculus based high-level cognitive robotics language GOLOG (Levesque, et al., 1997) for modelling the conceptual neighborhoods that arise within the line-segment-based Dipole calculus (Moratz, et al., 2000)[13]. Dylla and Moratz define complex *turn actions* such as *go-right, turn-left* on the basis of primitive (intrinsic) orientation relations of the Dipole calculus (Moratz, et al., 2000). Their work adopts a high-level approach by directly utilising the cognitive robotics language GOLOG (Levesque, et al., 1997), but leaves out finer representational problems (e.g., concerning issues such as the ramification problem) that arise whilst modelling a qualitative theory of space within a formalism to model change in general. Regardless, together with the cognitive robotics centered application perspective in Section 2.1 and the discussion of spatial property projection and planning in Sections 4.3.1 and 4.3.2 respectively, this work further reinforces the indicated robotic application scenarios that may be tackled with a foundational integrative approach as envisaged by the proposed RSAC paradigm.

## 4. RSAC: KEY CHALLENGES AND QUESTIONS

From the perspective of the computational requirements of the application domains discussed in Section 2, it is expected that a 'Reasoning about space, actions and change' approach should essentially provide predictive and explanatory reasoning capabilities. From the viewpoint of the logical well-designedness of the overall framework discussed in Section 2, it is desired that these reasoning capabilities be available within a (preferably) first-order logical framework, in the context of existing formal methods to model and reason about space on the one hand, and general commonsense approaches to reason about change on the other. This section discusses the challenges and research questions that accrue in fulfilling these requirements.

### 4.1. Ontological and Representational Aspects

It should be possible to generate a qualitative scene description backed by a formal spatial ontology that is grounded in adequate spatial calculi. Depending on the richness of the spatial calculi being utilized, this will primarily consist of qualitative spatial relationships relevant to one or more spatial dimensions, e.g., with topological, orientation, directional and size information. At a basic level, the scene description ontology should provide for the following:

#### 4.1.1. Multi-Perspective Characterizations

When one considers the potential areas where computational tasks such as spatial planning/reconfiguration and explanation are applicable, it becomes clear that conventional approaches that are based on a uniform ontological handling of primitive spatial entities are not sufficient. For instance, one need only conceptualize the qualitative descriptions that would be required to represent the configuration of objects for the *table-and-blocks* world or for a *room* with everyday objects in it—some objects are best conceptualized or modeled as two-dimensional entities (the *table-top*), some as three-dimensional semi-rigid (a *container*) or rigid entities (e.g., a *ball*), some as fully deformable entities (e.g., *liquids*), some as directed line-segments with an intrinsic orientation (the *agent* itself), and some simply as points (e.g., *landmarks* and possibly some *locations* such as the corner of a *table* or of a *room*). Therefore,

*Figure 6. Dynamic properties: fluids*

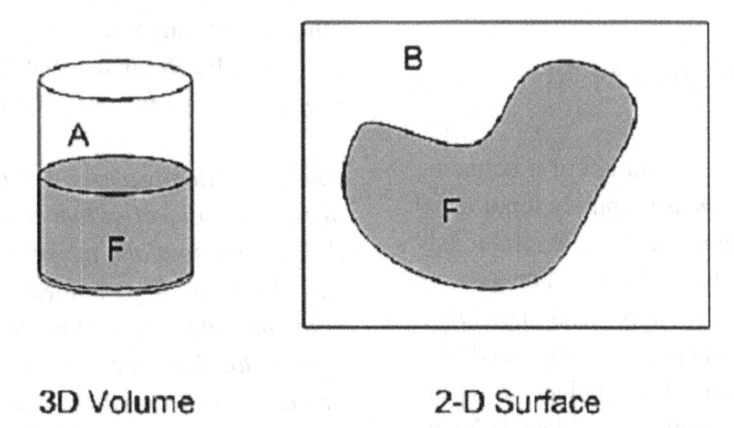


a mixed ontology with regions, points and line-segments is required.

### 4.1.2. Mixed-Dimensions

Regularity or uniform dimensionality of the object space within one spatial theory is sometimes restrictive. Take the case of fully-flexible *fluids* that acquire the dimensionality of the containing object, i.e., they may be regarded as two-dimensional surfaces and three-dimensional volumes in different situations (Figure 6). For instance, *water*, when contained in something, is volumetric, whereas when spilt on the *table-top*, acquires a planar form at least from a commonsense viewpoint. Therefore, there should be an inherent way to account for the multi-faceted nature of such a transformation of dimensionality within one theory. For the case where an ontology of mixed-dimensional entities is not feasible or does not exist, the suggestion by Hazarika (2005) is interesting: "One way of reasoning about regions of different dimensionality would be to impose a sort structure (one sort for each dimension) and essentially taking a copy of the theory for each dimension-sort." Whereas the respective merits and demerits of such an approach need closer examination, intrinsic (ontological) support within a spatial theory for allowing entities of mixed dimensions seems to be a more preferred approach in comparison to dimension-sorted approach (Gotts, 1996; Galton, 1996; Cohn, et al., 1997a).

### 4.1.3. Dynamic Physical / Object Properties and Constraints

Objects in the domain may have varying properties relevant to their physical aspects at different times. To aid the discussion, let's appeal to a commonsense notion of rigidity where objects tend to maintain their shape; this is essentially similar to the physics-based notion where a rigid body is an idealization of a solid body of finite size in which deformation is completely neglected. In other words, the distance between any two given points of a rigid body remains constant, regardless of external forces exerted on it. Given this interpretation, an important issue that concerns the characterisation of dynamic object properties is that of classification of objects into 'strictly rigid' and 'non-rigid' types. Consider the following scenarios:

A 'delivery object' ( $o$ ) is *disconnected* (*dc*)[14] '*next to*' a 'delivery vehicle' ( $v$ ) in one situation ( $s_1$ ) and in a later situation ( $s_2$ ), is *inside* (*tpp*) the delivery vehicle. Topologically, this is equivalent to the following:

situation $s_1: Holds(\phi_{top}(o,v), dc, s_1)$

situation $s_2: Holds(\phi_{top}(o,v), tpp, s_2)$

2. Consider the representation of a bouncing *ball* inside a *room* using purely topological primitives. Here, the state continuously oscillates for a finite duration between *tpp* and *ntpp* until eventually steadying at *tpp*.
3. A *container* object is completely filled with *water*. In this state, the container (or water) can still contain some other object, let's say, by way of *dropping* a small metal *ball* in the *container*. Now let's say that in a later situation, the *water* is frozen and stays that way for eternity.

When dealing with material (rigid) objects, such as the metal ball in scenario 3, the observed topological changes can be understood to be the result of motion, rather than other possibilities such as continuous deformation that are possible with non-rigid objects, such as fluids. However, a coarse distinction into strictly rigid and non-rigid objects is not sufficient. For example, consider the delivery vehicle (or the room) in the examples aforementioned. Although the object identifying the vehicle cannot *grow* or *shrink*, it can certainly contain other objects[15]. Therefore, the vehicle can neither be classified as being strictly rigid (being in a similar class as that of a metal ball), thereby not allowing interpenetration, nor is it a fully flexible non-rigid object like a water body that can *grow*, *shrink* or change *shape*. To take the case further, the solidification of the water-body in scenario 3 reveals that upon it being frozen, there is a fundamental change in the physical property of water. This change, namely water being solidified into ice, is important and must be reflected as a change of spatial (physical) property from a fully flexible to a strictly rigid object so that the container, which was previously filled with water and could still contain other objects cannot contain other objects anymore.

It may be stipulated that a *dynamic physical property* (Bhatt & Loke, 2008) is one that:

*characteristically pertains to the physical nature of a material object and which necessarily restricts the range of spatial relationships that the respective object, or class of objects, can participate in with other objects, or class of objects. Using this notion, for instance, certain configurations of objects may be completely disregarded from the state space in view of the implausibility of their physical realisation.*

Like physical properties, dynamic physical constraints are definable only within a specific spatial framework. For instance, containment constraints can be identified within the context of a mereotopological framework. Likewise, constraints on the potential rotation and direction of motion of objects (e.g., by *turn* and *move* actions) can be defined within a spatial framework consisting of orientation and direction information.

Commonsense Ontologies: An interesting exercise in this direction would be the identification of taxonomies of generic spatial actions and single and multi-object motion patterns that may be definable, given specific ontological assumptions and spatial calculi under consideration. It may be added that an integration of constraints relevant to more than one aspect of space is necessary in realistic applications, e.g., if distinctions such as an object approaching another from the right and from the left are to be made. It is essential that dynamic physical properties be modelled at the level of a domain-independent spatial theory. This way, domain-independent constraints on the potential spatial transformations, and spatial action taxonomies may be used by modellers in arbitrary spatial scenarios.

In general, the utility of elaborate commonsense characterizations for spatial entities cannot be overemphasized—these are useful in wide-ranging applications, e.g., for the qualitative abstraction of low-level motion control tasks in robotics or high-level spatial planning, for the modelling of taxonomies of spatial changes in event-based GIS and so forth. Commonsense characterizations corresponding to aspects concerning (dynamic) physical properties such as *containment, deformity, semi-rigidity, full-rigidity non-rigidity, surface information, stability, graspability* and their impact vis-à-vis the actions / affordances that may be possible / performed given the backdrop of such knowledge.

## 4.2. Commonsense Spatial Dynamics

Commonsense notions of spatial change—naive physics—to reason about the (ontologically) grounded material world should also be part of a domain-independent spatial theory, e.g., for the cognitive robotics domain, these should be a part of the innate abilities of McCarthy's *child robot* (Section 3.1). This section presents some spatial calculi specific as well as foundational epistemological and phenomenal aspects that need to be given consideration whilst handling spatial change within a commonsensical framework.

### 4.2.1. Consistency with Axiomatic Aspects of Spatial Calculi

We presume that spatial information representation corresponds to the use of spatial calculi such as the Region Connection Calculus (RCC) (Randell, et al., 1992; Cohn, et al., 1997b), Single-Cross and Double-Cross Calculi (SCC, DCC) (Freksa, 1992), Oriented Point Relation Algebra (OPRA) (Moratz, 2006) (Figure 7).

When spatial configurations change as a result of spatial actions and events, it is necessary that the spatial scene descriptions corresponding to the changing state of the system at each situation/time-point/interval be globally consistent with respect to the constraints and properties of the underlying (qualitative) relationship space, as encompassed by the respective spatial calculi that are being modelled.

To aid the discussion, let $\mathcal{R} = \{\mathcal{R}_1, \mathcal{R}_2, \ldots, \mathcal{R}_n\}$ be a finite set of n-ary base relationships of a qualitative spatial calculus over a domain $\mathcal{U}$ with some spatial/spatio-temporal interpretation. From a high-level axiomatic viewpoint, a spatial calculus defined on $\mathcal{R}$ has the following properties that must be preserved within a dynamic context:

#### P1. JEPD Property

$\mathcal{R}$ has the Jointly Exhaustive and Pair-Wise Disjoint (JEPD) property, meaning that for any two entities in $\mathcal{U}$, one and only one spatial relationship from $\mathcal{R}$ holds in a given situation. Any integration of a spatial theory within a theory of action and change will need to preserve this basic property.

#### P2. Basic Relational Structure

Just like the JEPD'ness of $\mathcal{R}$, the basic transitivity, symmetry and asymmetry properties of the relationship space should be explicitly modelled or preserved in the context of the changing logic of action and change.

#### P3. Continuity Structure

The primitive relationships in $\mathcal{R}$ have a continuity structure, referred to its Conceptual Neighborhood (CND) (Freksa, 1991a), which determines the direct, continuous changes in the quality space (e.g., by deformation, and/or translational/rotational motion). This continuity structure for $\mathcal{R}$ also needs to be explicitly modelled so that spatial projection and abduction tasks that are performed in the context of a given logic of action and change conform to the conceptual neighbourhood of the spatial calculus that is being modelled within.

Figure 8. Incorporating spatial / qualitative inertia

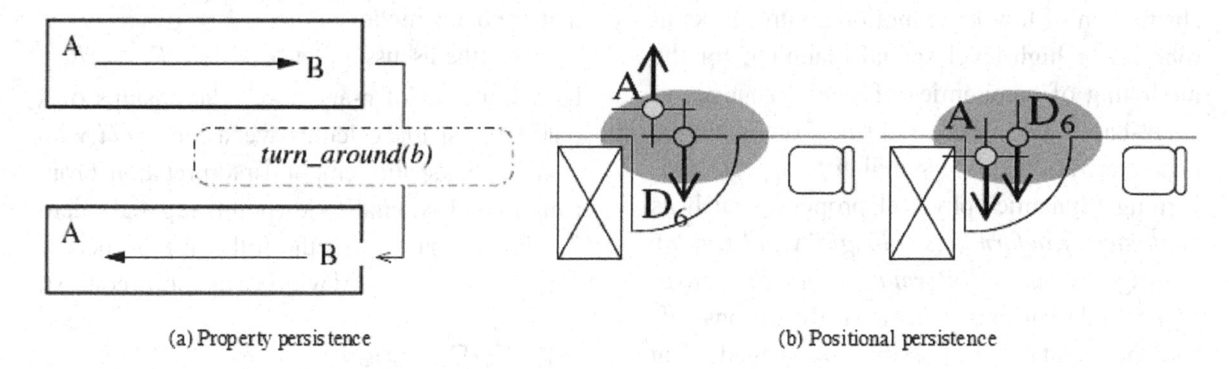


(a) Property persistence

(b) Positional persistence

## P4. Composition Theorems

For a spatial calculus with $n = |\mathcal{R}|$ JEPD relationships, $[n \times n]$ composition theorems are known apriori. These composition theorems need to be modelled comprehensively in order to achieve global compositional consistency within the dynamic context of the logic of action and change that is being utlized. Composition theorems, and the resulting notion of global compositional consistency, is a key (contributing) notion in operationalizing the principle of 'physically realizable/ plausible' situations for spatial planning and (abductive) explanation tasks. For instance, in finding potential models abductively, the composition theorems are usable in eliminating models that may not be physically possible in reality (Bhatt, 2010).

## P5. Axioms of Interaction

Axioms of interaction that explicitly model interactions between interdependent spatial calculi, when more than one calculi are being applied in a non-integrated manner (i.e., with independent composition theorems).

From the viewpoint of integration with a logic of action and change, one may assume that for any spatial calculus, (P1–P5) are known apriori. In order to realize a domain-independent spatial theory that is re-usable across arbitrary dynamic domains, it is necessary to preserve all the high-level axiomatic semantics in (P1–P5), and implicitly the underlying algebraic properties, that collectively constitutes a 'qualitative spatial calculus' (Ligozat & Renz, 2004).

### 4.2.2. Spatial Inertia

Inertial aspects of a dynamic spatial system determining what remains unchanged need to be accounted. The following forms of persistence may be identified (see Figure 8):

#### *4.2.2.1. Spatial Property Persistence*

The intuition that the spatial relationship between two (or more) objects typically remains the same, is one default reasoning pattern rooted in the *frame problem* that is identifiable within the spatial context. The frame problem, first identified by McCarthy and Hayes (1969) in the context of mathematical logic, is one of the most fundamental problems that occurs whilst reasoning about the effects of actions (Shanahan, 1997). In so far as the limited context of logic-based AI is concerned, the general problem is this: '*How do we reason about those aspects of the state that remain unchanged as a result of performing an action*? ' Imagine if there were a set of spatial actions / events involving the translation and rotation of

*Figure 9. Default reasoning about 'emptiness' in discrete space*

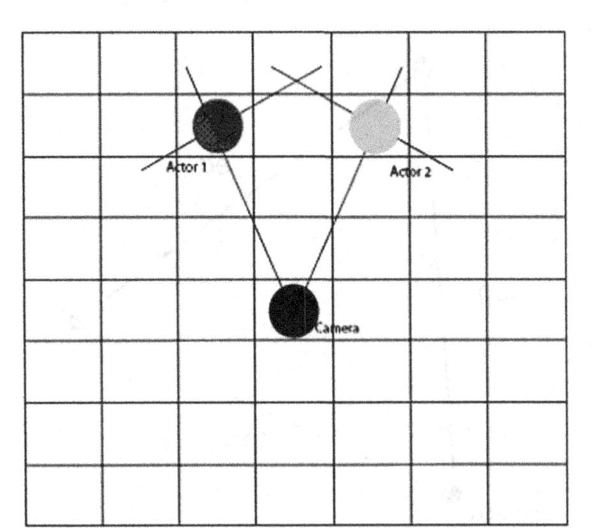


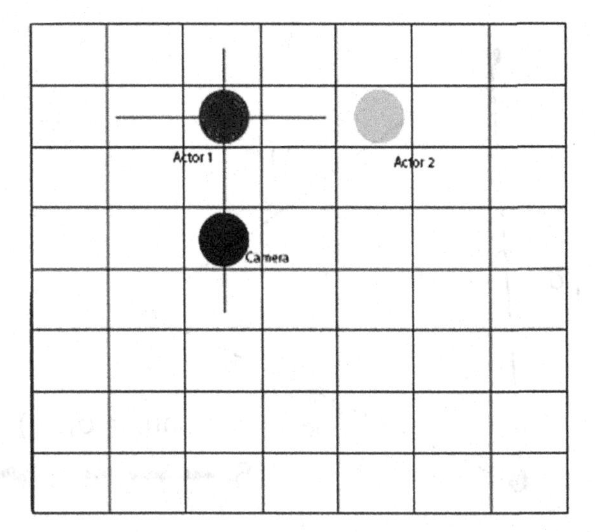


objects, we would have quite a number of conditions to write down that certain spatial actions do not change the state in some way. Precisely, with $m$ actions and $n$ values (representing the state), we would have to write down $m \times n$ such conditions.

For the spatial case, the frame problem translates to spatial property / relational persistence: assuming that dynamic topological and orientation information constitutes the state descriptions, the problem is that of formalizing the intuition that the topological / directional relationship between two objects or the orientation of an object relative to another '*typically*' remains the same.

#### 4.2.2.2. Absolute Positional Persistence

In addition to persistence at the qualitative or relational level, absolute positional persistence at the metric level is also required to formalize the intuition that the absolute spatial extension of an object, whatever that may be from a geometric viewpoint, remains the same

#### Emptiness

Default reasoning about empty space is another useful inference pattern that is useful within a dynamic context. Here, the intuition that needs to be formalised is that an empty region of space *typically* remains empty (Shanahan, 1995). This is a default assumption that a robot must make before moving objects from one location to another, or before moving itself to a new location. As an example, consider the discrete grid world of Figure 9: the illustration consists of three point-abstracted entities, and their relative orientation relationships modelled as per the partitioning scheme of the Single-Cross Calculus (see Section 4.2.1, Figure 7). Here, one (or more) of the three entities / agents that may want to move to a new location in the grid should be able to perform a *move* action by implicitly making a default assumption of the emptiness of the target location. Indeed, such an assumption is possible only if default reasoning about emptiness has been incorporated within the underlying commonsense reasoning approach.

### 4.2.3. Ramifications: Indirect Effects

The *ramification problem* (Finger, 1987) is concerned with the capability to model actions whose execution causes indirect effects. These effects, not formally accounted for in the respective action specification, are consequences of general laws

*Figure 10. Compositional constraints and ramifications*

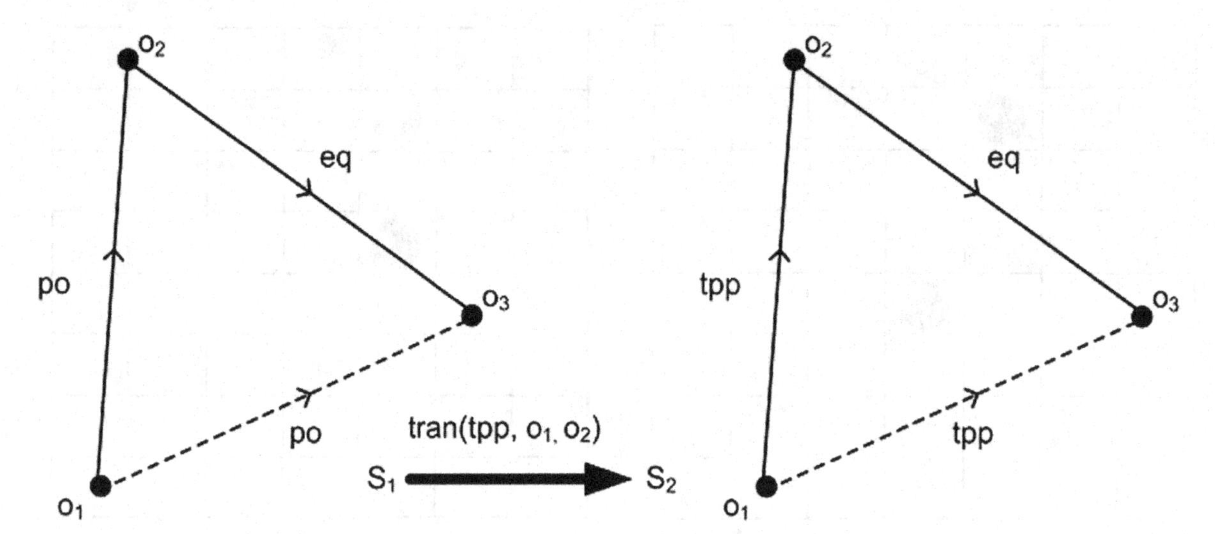


describing dependencies between components of the world description (Thielscher, 1997). The concept of ramification is closely related to the notion of domain constraints, causality and transitive dependencies that exist between various properties of a particular dynamic system that is being modelled (Thielscher, 1997; Lin, 1995; Papadakis & Plexousakis, 2003; Hall, 2000).

Basically, ramification yielding state constraints contain implicit side-effects in them that need to be accounted for whilst reasoning about the effects of events and actions. Since indirect effects are a recurring problem whilst modelling several aspects of qualitative spatial calculi, the ramification problem is of special significance from the viewpoint of commonsense reasoning about spatial change (Bhatt, 2010)[16]. As an example of how this is relevant to spatial change, consider the basic case of compositional inference with three objects $o_1$, $o_2$ and $o_3$ in Figure 10: when $o_1$ and $o_2$ undergo a transition to a different qualitative state (either by translational motion and/or deformation), this also has an indirect effect, although not necessarily, on the spatial relationship between $o_1$ and $o_3$ since the relationship between the latter two is constrained by at least one of the $[n \times n]$ compositional constraints (Section 4.2.1; P4) of the relational space.

For a more action and event oriented example, consider the illustration in Figure 11: the scenario depicted herein consists of the topological relationships between three objects '*a*,' '*b*,' and '*c*.' In the initial situation '$S_0$,' the spatial extension of '*a*' is a *non-tangential part* of that of '*b*.' Further, assume that there is a change in the relationship between '*a*' and '*b*,' as depicted in Figure 11, as a result of a direct effect of an event such as *growth* or an action involving the *motion* of '*a*.' Indeed, as is clear from Figure 11, for the spatial situation description in the resulting situation (either '$S_1$' or '$S_2$'), the compositional dependencies between '*a*,' '*b*,' and '*c*' must be adhered to, i.e., the change of relationship between '*a*' and '*c*' must be derivable as an indirect effect from the underlying compositional constraints. The new relationship between *a* and *c* in situation $S_2$ can either result in: increased ambiguity, decreased ambiguity and in some cases no change at all[17]. For instance, in the case of the RCC-8 topological calculus, there exist a total of 64 composition theorems, 27 of which provide unambiguous information as to the potential relation-

*Figure 11. Ramifications / indirect effects*

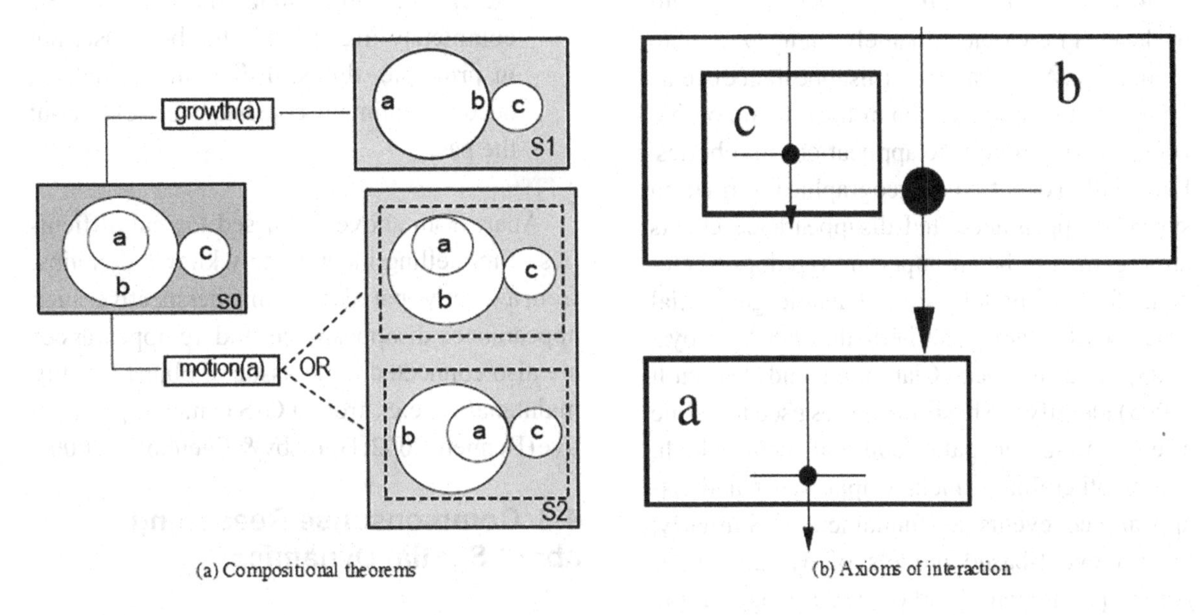


(a) Compositional theorems

(b) Axioms of interaction

ship. All other compositions provide disjunctive information that may further be refined by the inclusion of complementary spatial calculi, e.g., in a manner such as in (Randell & Witkowski, 2004). Modelling of complementary aspects of space requires the so called "*axioms of interaction*" (Bhatt, 2010), which produce ramification similar in nature to the compositional constraints. This is illustrated Figure 11 for the case of three extended and (also) point-abstracted entities *a*, *b*, and *c* —the interpretation of the ramification is left to the reader.

## 4.2.4. Dynamic Spatial Phenomena

The range of *phenomenal* aspects that may be accounted for from a commonsensical viewpoint is, in principle, open-ended. The identification of default spatial reasoning patterns, the general utility of non-monotonic reasoning about change from a specific spatial reasoning viewpoint is broadly an interesting and open research area. In the following, some instances are summarised:

### *4.2.4.1. Appearance and Disappearance of Objects*

Appearance of new objects and disappearance of existing ones, either abruptly or explicitly formulated in the domain theory, is characteristic of non-trivial dynamic spatial systems. In robotic applications, it is necessary to introduce new objects into the model, since it is unlikely that a complete description of the robot's environment is either specifiable or even available. Similarly, it is also typical for a mobile robot operating in a dynamic environment, with limited perceptual or sensory capability, to lose track of certain objects because of issues such as noisy sensors or a limited field-of-vision.

As an example, consider a '*delivery scenario*' (Figure 12) in which a vehicle/robot is assigned the task of delivering '*object*(*s*)' from one '*way-station*' to another. In the initial situation description, the domain consists of a finite number of '*way-stations*' and deliverable '*objects*.' However, the scheduling of new objects for delivery in future situations will involve introducing new 'objects' into the domain theory. For example, an external event[18] such as

'$schedule\_delivery(new\_load, loc_1, loc_5)$' introduces a new object, namely '*new_load,*' into the domain. Appearance and disappearance events involving the modification of the domain of discourse are not unique to applications in robotics. Even within event-based geographic information systems, appearance and disappearance events are regarded to be an important typological element for the modelling of dynamic geospatial processes (Claramunt & Thériault, 1995; Worboys, 2005). For instance, Claramunt and Thériault (1995) identify the basic processes used to define a set of low-order spatio-temporal events which, among other things, include appearance and disappearance events as fundamental. Similarly, toward event-based models of dynamic geographic phenomena, Worboys (2005) suggests the use of the appearance and disappearance events at least in so far as single object behaviours are concerned (see Figure 12).

Within a logical framework, appearance and disappearance has ramifications from the (model-theoretic) viewpoint of modelling an incompletely known domain of discourse. The case of disappearance is not too problematic, however, for the case of appearance and re-appearance, some questions that need to be addressed include:

- What is the spatial relationship (e.g., topological, directional) of the newly appearing object with other existing objects? Clearly, within a relational spatial framework, the whole notion of the existence of an object/entity is based on its spatial relationship with at least one other existing entity
- Given the fact that a newly appearing object is, from a model-theoretic viewpoint, *unknown* in the past, how to make it 'known' and 'not exist' in the past? Clearly, here it is important that the approach to handle this problem be domain-independent
- How to make past and present situation descriptions 'compositionally consistent'?[19] Here, knowledge about the past may be completely irrelevant in the best case, but in principle, this still does not dispel the need to maintain consistent beliefs about the past

Apart from above-discussed logical difficulties of modelling incompletely known domains, from a strictly spatial reasoning perspective, such appearance, disappearance and re-appearances are also connected to the issue of object identity maintenance, e.g., from a GIS centered perspective (Bennett, 2002; Hornsby & Egenhofer, 2000).

## 4.3. Commonsense Reasoning about Spatial Dynamics

Given some 'Action Description Logic' ( $\mathcal{ADL}$ ) and the 'Domain theory' ( $\mathcal{D}$ ) for the application under consideration, basic reasoning capabilities encompassing *projection*, *simulation*, *planning* and *explanation* should be available in the context of $\mathcal{ADL} \cup \mathcal{D}$. It must be emphasized that all desirable reasoning patterns or computational tasks should directly follow from the semantics of the underlying $\mathcal{ADL}$ and the domain-specific instance as presented by way of $\mathcal{D}$. For instance, standard computational techniques such as *regression* and *abductive explanation* should remain applicable within the context of the $\mathcal{ADL}$ being utilized. Depending on the richness required with respect to *time*, *continuity*, *concurrency*, and the *action ontology*, there are many possibilities for the choice of the $\mathcal{ADL}$. Whereas Bhatt and Loke (2008) illustrate this for the case where the $\mathcal{ADL}$ corresponds to a basic situation calculus based causal theory, this may be substituted with the event calculus, fluent calculus and possibly even other specialised formalisms (Davis & Morgenstern, 2004). In principle, any *basic action theory* in a sorted first-order logic with action and event types, preconditions and effect axioms, and a general mechanism to handle the frame problem and ramification problems should be sufficient.

*Figure 12. Phenomenal aspects*

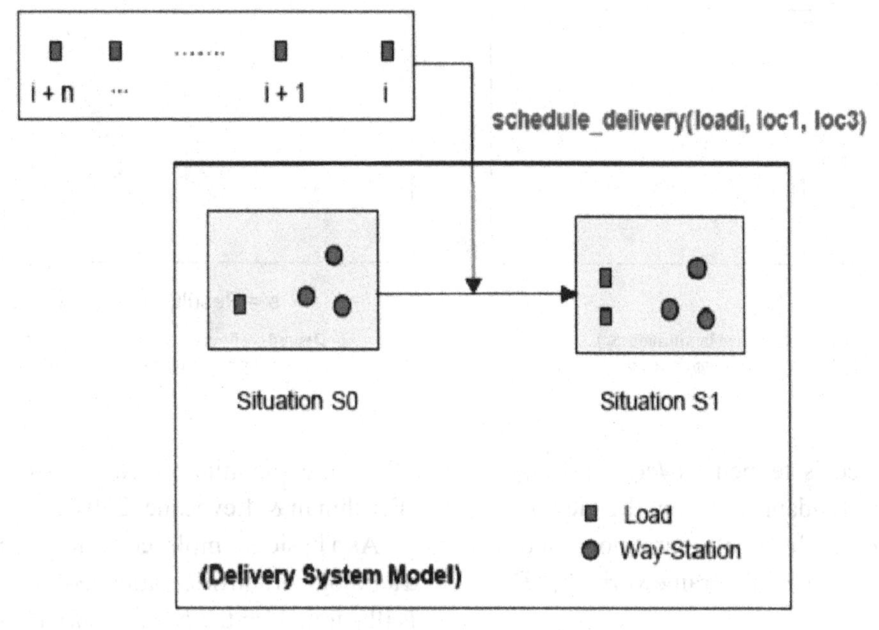


(a) Appearance and disappearance - Delivery example

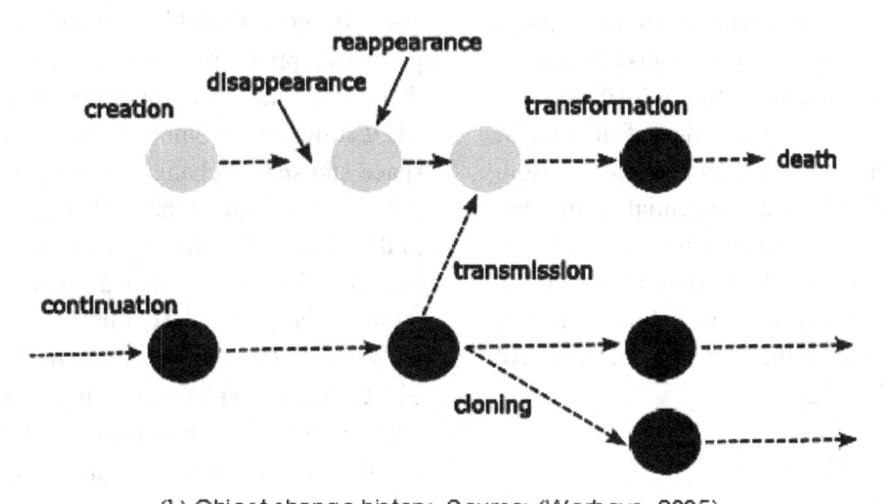


(b) Object change history, Source: (Worboys, 2005)

### 4.3.1. Spatial Property Projection and Simulation

Given a sequence consisting of events and/or actions, *projection* corresponds to the task of determining what would be true if those actions were performed or if the events occurred starting in the initial situation. It is of course a separate matter to determine whether or not the events and actions present in the sequence could in fact occur or be possible/performed sequentially in compliance with the action/event preconditions and the relational constraints of the spatial theory that is being modelled. The related task of determining

*Figure 13. Spatial re-configuration with $[\mathcal{ADL}]$ for the blocks world*

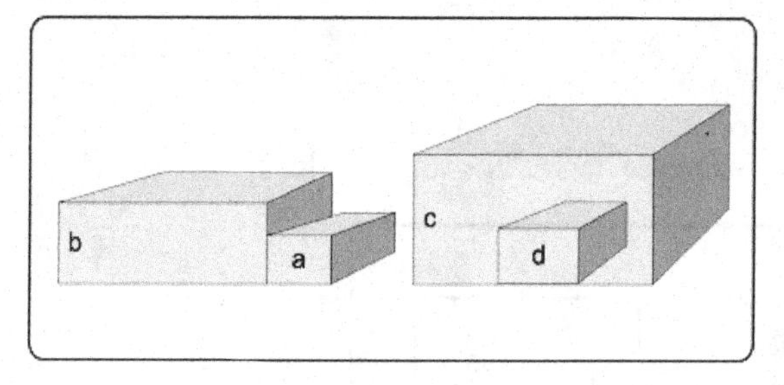


$S_0$

(a) Initial configuration (denoted by situation $S_0$) representing the initial configuration of objects.

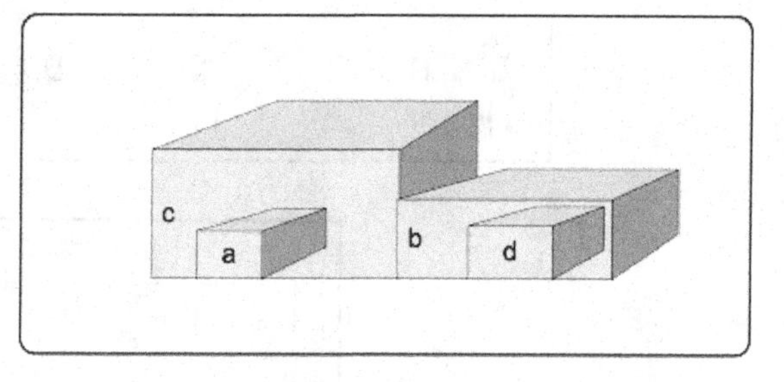


$s = Result(<\theta_1, \theta_2, \ldots, \theta_n>, S_0)$

(b) Desired configuration $s$ is the *Result* of sequentially performing $[\theta_1, \theta_2, \theta_n]$ in $S_0$.

such compliance is termed as *legality testing*. These tasks are fundamental from the viewpoint of planning (e.g., by goal regression) and/or theorem-proving within the framework of $\mathcal{ADL}$ .

Projection and simulation are necessary to apply *'what if...'* scenarios on one or more spatial and non-spatial properties (or fluents) that reflect the state (e.g., spatial configurations) of the system. Differences in the axiomatisation of the precise $\mathcal{ADL}$ notwithstanding, the fundamental reasoning task of *projection* and its essential counterpart of *legality testing* are definable within the context of the underlying action theory (e.g., Reiter, 2001). To reiterate, these tasks should directly follow from the semantics of the foundational axioms of the concerned $\mathcal{ADL}$ .

### 4.3.2. Spatial Planning / Re-Configuration

The objective in *spatial planning* is to derive a sequence of spatial actions that will achieve a goal, e.g., *transfer* of *liquid* from one *container* to another, and other forms of spatial re-configuration, e.g., topological and orientational *re-arrangement*, involving physical manipulation and movement of objects by translation and rotation. Given a basic mechanism for projection and legality testing with an $\mathcal{ADL}$ , the formulation of offline planning is rather straight-forward (Brachman & Levesque, 2004).

As a basic example, consider Figure 13 where a topological and orientation re-configuration task is illustrated for the *block world*. Here, instead of a naive representation of relationships such as $on(a,b)$ and $on(b,table)$, which is common approach adopted in planning tasks, it is desired that there be an inherent way within the underlying $\mathcal{ADL}$ to maintain commonsense knowledge about space and spatial changes by way of a generic / domain-independent spatial theory. The objective in doing so is that the spatial semantics, e.g., as constituted by the formal properties of one or more spatial calculi, be explicitly integrated with the semantics of the $\mathcal{ADL}$ . With this setup, the $\mathcal{ADL}$ together with the domain-specific instance $\mathcal{D}_{blocks}$ may be directly applied for planning tasks. For the re-configuration example of Figure 13, given an *initial* and *desired* situation description, a plan by way of a sequence of movement actions $[\theta_1, \theta_2, \theta_n]$ is directly obtainable in a conventional planner[20] from the spatial theory encoded within the $\mathcal{ADL}$ , or precisely, from $\mathcal{ADL} \cup \mathcal{D}_{blocks}$ .

### 4.3.3. Causal Explanation (by Abduction)

Diametrically opposite to projection and planning is the task of post-dictum or explanation (Pierce,

*Figure 14. Domain independent and specific abduction*

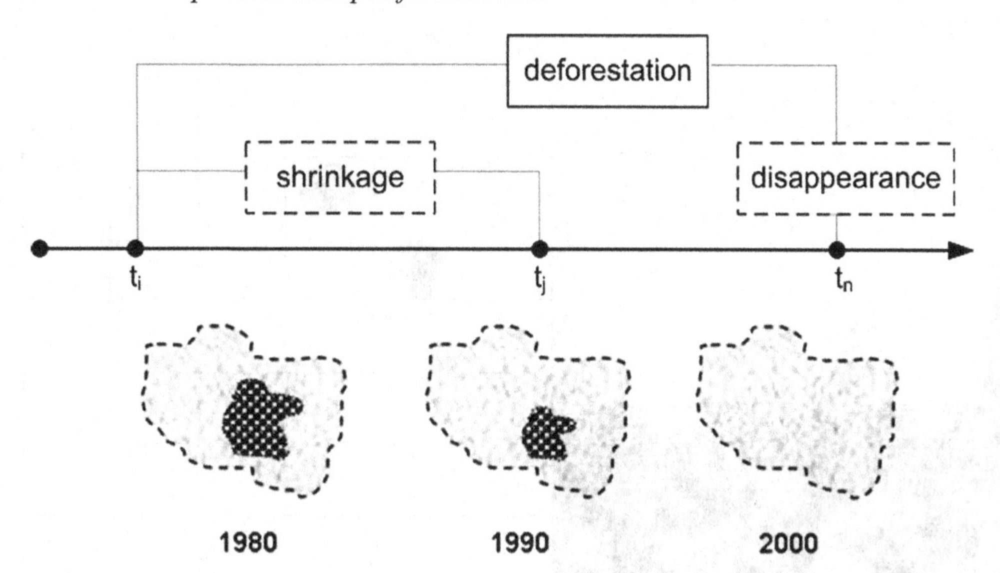


1935; Poole, et al., 1987), where given a set of time-stamped observations or snap-shots (e.g., observation of a mobile-robot or time-stamped GIS data), the objective is to explain which events and/or actions may have caused the resulting state-of-affairs. Explanation, in general, is regarded as a converse operation to temporal projection essentially involving reasoning from effects to causes, i.e., reasoning about the past (Shanahan, 1989).

For the spatial case, causal explanation refers to the explanation of observations (e.g., observations of a robot, sensor readings in a smart home, datasets in a GIS) from temporally-ordered spatial snapshots. Here, explanation involves the interpolation of missing spatial scenes (i.e., consistent constraint networks) in adherence to the continuity and relational constraints of the relationship space (Section 4.2.1), and the derivation of high-level spatial and non-spatial actions and events that may have occurred and caused the observed state-of-affairs. Based on the (circumscriptive) abductive approach of Shanahan (1993) for explanation in the context of the situation calculus, Bhatt (2009a) formalizes and demonstrates the manner in which causal explanation may be performed within the spatial domain. The approach, as illustrated later in this section, has been further been applied in the context of the event calculus (Bhatt & Flanagan, 2010). For the purposes of this chapter, we further illustrate and exemplify the practical concepts involved in explanation within the spatial domain. Consider the examples in (E1–E2) from two very different domains. Whereas example E1 illustrates the concept of the *adequacy* of an explanation, E2 demonstrates the nature of *scenario and narrative completion*:

## E1. Abduction in GIS

Consider a geographic information system domain / scenario as depicted in Figure 14. At a domain-independent level (i.e., at the level of a general spatial theory), the scene may be described using topological and qualitative size relationships. Consequently, the only changes that are identifiable at the level of the spatial theory are *shrinkage* and eventual *disappearance*—this is because a domain-independent spatial theory may only include a generic typology (*appearance, disappearance, growth, shrinkage, deformation, splitting, merging,* etc.) of spatial change. However, at a domain-specific level, these changes could

*Figure 15. Automatic cinematography domain: 2 avatars and 1 virtual camera (black circle) (source: Bhatt & Flanagan, 2010)*

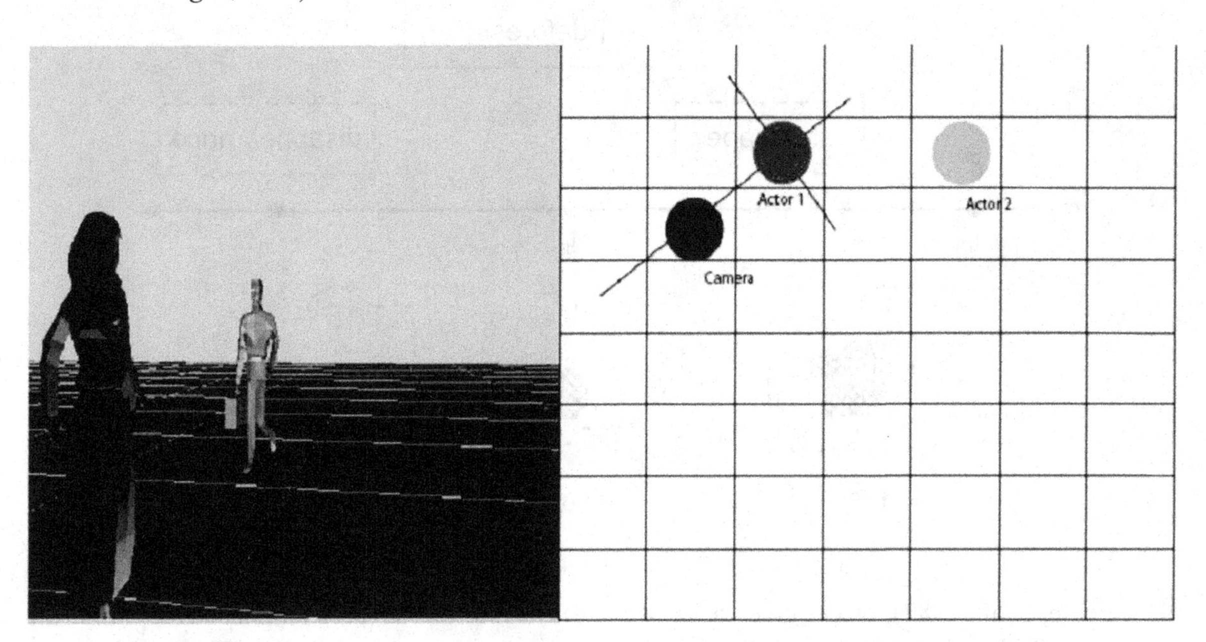


characterize a specific event (or process) such as, for instance, *deforestation*. The hypotheses or explanations that are generated during a explanation process should necessarily consist of the domain-level occurrences in addition to the underlying (associated) spatial changes (as per the generic typology) that are identifiable. That is to say, that the explanations more or less take a form such as: '*Between time-points $t_i$ and $t_j$, the process of deforestation is abducible as one potential hypothesis*.' Derived hypothesis / explanations that involve both domain-dependent and as well their corresponding domain-independent typological elements are referred to as being '*adequate*' from the viewpoint of causal explanation.

## E2. Scenario and Narrative Completion by Abduction

Consider the illustration in Figure 15 for the domain of automatic cinematography: the world consists of three point-abstracted entities—2 *avatars* and 1 virtual *camera*[21]. For minimality, suppose that container space is modelled a discrete grid world together with relative orientation relationships among the entities as per the partitioning scheme of the Single-Cross Calculus (see Section 4.2.1, Figure 7). For this discussion, further suppose that the *camera* is the only entity that is able to move, i.e., change location from one grid-cell to another.

For a scenario such as this, causal explanation could be the basis of *scenario and narrative completion*, and for this particular example, the derivation of ideal *camera placements* as a side-effect of the abduction process. Figure 16 consists of a *narrative* (completion) from time-points $t_1$ to $t_{12}$, denoting an *abduced* evolution of the system, as represented the sequence of qualitative state descriptions for 2 stationery and 1 moving entity. For clarity, images from a 3D simulation are included together with the relational / graph-based illustrations for each of the time-points. From an initial narrative description consisting of information about only some of the time-points[22], the narrative completion has been abduced on the

*Figure 16. Scenario and narrative completion by abduction (source: Bhatt & Flanagan, 2010)*

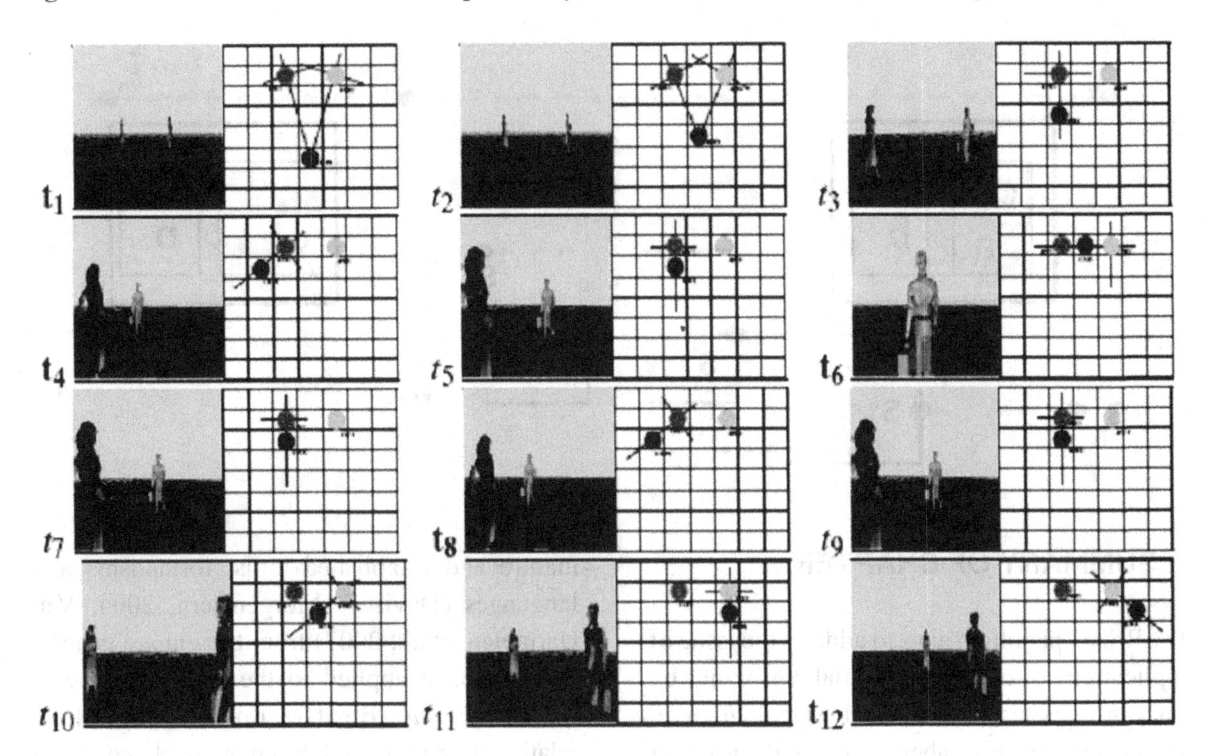


basis of available *camera actions—pan, zoom, move*—and pre-specified knowledge or heuristics, referred to as *film idioms*, about desired camera placements, e.g., *establishing shot, external shot, mid-shot, close-up* and so forth. In this example, the resulting narrative is usable by a virtual reality and/or an automatic cinematography system to generate automatic visualizations for a script.

**Structure of Causal Explanation**: Given the examples in (E1–E2), it is easy to intuitively infer the general structure of causal explanation (by abduction) within spatial information. Consider the illustration in Figure 17 for a branching / hypothetical situation space that characterizes the complete evolution of a system. In Figure 17—the situation-based history $< s_0, s_1, \ldots, s_n >$ represents one path, corresponding to a actual time-line $< t_0, t_1, \ldots, t_n >$, within the overall branching-tree structured situation space. Given incomplete narrative descriptions, e.g., corresponding to only some ordered time-points (such as in Figure 16) in terms of high-level *spatial (e.g.,* topological, orientation) and occurrence information, the objective of causal explanation is to derive one or more paths from the branching situation space, that could best fit the available narrative information. Of course, the completions that bridge the narrative by interpolating the missing spatial and action/event information have to be consistent with domain-specific and domain-independent rules/dynamics.

Many different formalizations of causal explanation with spatial knowledge, such as within a belief revision framework (Alchourrón, et al., 1985), nonmonotonic causal formalizations in the manner of (Giunchiglia, et al., 2004) are possible and the subject of ongoing study. Additionally, the suitability of event calculus (Kowalski & Sergot, 1986; Mueller, 2009) vis-à-vis the situation calculus is also a topic that especially merits detailed treatment.

*Figure 17. Branching / hypothetical situation space*

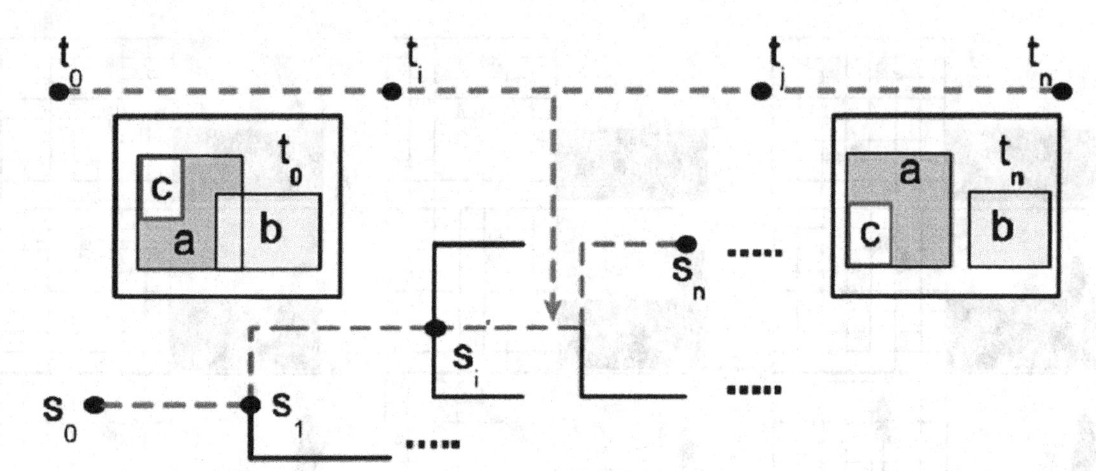


## 5. SUMMARY OF CHAPTER

The RSAC paradigm aims to address the issue of applications of qualitative spatial reasoning: by what bridges may we connect formal '*logical*' methods in reasoning about space, and reasoning about change, with applications / their computational requirements, such as those mentioned in Section 2, that are considered befitting of such methods. A secondary focus, closely related to the main issue of integration, has been on the conventional emphasis of research in the QSR domain—*qualitative spatial reasoning* (Freksa, 1991b) methods have primarily remained focused on the development of new calculi for spatial information representation and on the construction of efficient algorithms for solving spatial reasoning problems (Cohn & Renz, 2007; Renz & Nebel, 2007). The emphasis in QSR has primarily been on reasoning with static spatial configurations. However, for the range of applicationdomains such as those identified in Section 2, spatial reasoning methods require a dynamic interpretation, and more importantly, support for high-level forms of inference such as prediction, planning and explanation.

In general, the areas of *commonsense reasoning*, and *reasoning about action and change* are mature and established tools, formalisms and languages (Davis & Morgenstern, 2004; Van Harmelen, et al., 2007) from therein are general enough to be applied to the case of *dynamic spatial systems* (Bhatt & Loke, 2008), where relational spatial models undergo change as a result of interaction (i.e., actions and events) occurring within the system or environment being modeled. Consequently, the formal embedding of arbitrary spatial calculi—whilst preserving their high-level axiomatic semantics and low-level algebraic properties—has to be investigated from the viewpoint of formalisms such as the situation calculus, event calculus, fluent calculus and possibly other specialized formalisms. Broadly, this will result in the incorporation of *commonsense notions of space and spatial change*, and *dynamic spatial phenomena* of a general sort within general logic-based frameworks in artificial intelligence, and their use in application domains requiring predictive and explanatory reasoning capabilities within a dynamic context. As research in QSR moves toward practical application considerations, it is expected that the conventional focus of QSR will extend itself from reasoning about space in isolation to *logical* reasoning about space, actions and change in an integrated manner.

## LITERATURE AND COMMUNITY

In line with the aims of this chapter, and the book, some key reading material has been pointed-out here explicitly. Hopefully, this will be of utility to new research students and practitioners from other fields of computer science.

The textbook on *Qualitative Spatial Change* (Galton, 2000) is an excellent introduction and in-depth study of the advancements in the spatial reasoning area; taken together with Stock (1997), the demystification of qualitative spatial representation and reasoning for a beginner should be easily possible. The *Handbook of Spatial Logics* (Aiello, et al., 2007) is a more advanced text that presents a rather formal analysis.

The *Knowledge Representation Handbook* (Van Harmelen, et al., 2007) is the definitive text for the KR community; there are several chapters within that serve as an excellent starting point for many of the topics discussed in this chapter (e.g., chapters on cognitive robotics, qualitative spatial representation and reasoning, commonsense reasoning).

The text *Knowledge in action: Logical foundations for describing and implementing Dynamical systems* by Reiter (2001) is the most comprehensive and intense study of modelling dynamic domains within the framework of the situation calculus. A good companion text for beginners would be the text *Knowledge Representation and Reasoning* by Brachman and Levesque (2004). The textbook on *Commonsense Reasoning* (Mueller, 2006) is a comprehensive study of modelling commonsense reasoning within the framework of the Event Calculus (Mueller, 2006).

Workshops and special sessions on Qualitative Spatial Representation and Reasoning (and derivatives) are regularly organised at all major AI conferences such as AAAI, ECAI, IJCAI. Furthermore, the Conference Series on Spatial Information Theory (COSIT) is a specialized forum devoted to theoretical and application-oriented issues surrounding QSR and related topics. These events should be a rich source of the latest advancements in the community.

## ACKNOWLEDGMENT

I acknowledge the funding and support by the Alexander von Humboldt, Stiftung, Germany, and the overall scientific and infrastructural support available at the SFB/TR 8 center via funding by the German Research Foundation (DFG). Comments by reviewers of some of the previous works cited herein have been helpful in refining the discussed ideas. The referees for this article have played a very constructive role with their comments and suggestions for improvements. Many application specific ideas have been influenced by my discussions with colleagues in Project R3-[Q-Shape] (2003), and by my close collaborations with John Bateman, Frank Dylla, Gregory Flanagan, Shyamanta Hazarika, Joana Hois, Oliver Kutz, and Jan-Oliver Wallgruen. All shortcomings are indeed of my own making.

## REFERENCES

R3-[Q-Shape]. (2003). *SFB/TR 8 spatial cognition*. Berlin, Germany: Project R3-[Q-Shape]: Reasoning about Paths, Shapes, and Configurations.

(2007). Advances in ambient intelligence. In Augusto, J. C., & Shapiro, D. (Eds.), *Frontiers in Artificial Intelligence and Applications* (*Vol. 164*). IOS.

Aiello, M., Pratt-Hartmann, I. E., & Benthem, J. F. V. (2007). *Handbook of spatial logics*. Secaucus, NJ: Springer-Verlag New York, Inc. doi:10.1007/978-1-4020-5587-4

Alchourrón, C. E., Gärdenfors, P., & Makinson, D. (1985). On the logic of theory change: Partial meet contraction and revision functions. *Journal of Symbolic Logic*, *50*(2), 510–530. doi:10.2307/2274239

Allen, E., Edwards, G., & Bédard, Y. (1995). Qualitative causal modeling in temporal GIS. In *Proceedings of COSIT*, (pp 397–412). COSIT.

Allen, J. F. (1983). Maintaining knowledge about temporal intervals. *Communications of the ACM*, *26*(11), 832–843. doi:10.1145/182.358434

Allen, J. F. (1984). Towards a general theory of action and time. *Artificial Intelligence*, *23*(2), 123–154. doi:10.1016/0004-3702(84)90008-0

Allen, J. F., & Ferguson, G. (1994). Actions and events in interval temporal logic. *Journal of Logic and Computation*, *4*(5), 531–579. doi:10.1093/logcom/4.5.531

Allen, J. F., & Hayes, P. J. (1985). A common sense theory of time. In *Proceedings of IJCAI*. Los Altos, CA: Morgan Kaufmann.

Augusto, J. C., & Nugent, C. D. (Eds.). (2006). *Designing smart homes, the role of artificial intelligence. (LNCS 4008)*. Springer.

Beller, A. (1991). Spatio/temporal events in a GIS. In *Proceedings of GIS/LIS*, (pp. 766–775). ASPRS/ACSM.

Bennett, B. (2002). Physical objects, identity and vagueness. In D. Fensel, D. McGuinness, & M.-A. Williams (Eds.), *Principles of Knowledge Representation and Reasoning: Proceedings of the Eighth International Conference (KR2002)*. San Francisco, CA: Morgan Kaufmann.

Bennett, B., & Galton, A. P. (2004). A unifying semantics for time and events. *Artificial Intelligence*, *153*(1-2), 13–48. doi:10.1016/j.artint.2003.02.001

Bhatt, M. (2008a). Dynamical spatial systems-A potential approach for the application of qualitative spatial calculi. In D. Wilson & H. C. Lane (Eds.), *FLAIRS Conference*, (pp. 580–585). AAAI Press.

Bhatt, M. (2008b). (Some) default and non-monotonic aspects of qualitative spatial reasoning. In *Proceedings of AAAI-08 Technical Reports, Workshop on Spatial and Temporal Reasoning*, (pp. 1–6). AAAI.

Bhatt, M. (2009a). Commonsense inference in dynamic spatial systems: Phenomenal and reasoning requirements. In *Proceedings of the 23rd International Workshop on Qualitative Reasoning (QR 09)*, (pp. 1-6). Ljubljana, Slovenia: QR.

Bhatt, M. (2009b). Toward an experimental cognitive robotics framework: A position statement. In *Proceedings of the International Workshop on Hybrid Control of Autonomous Systems: Integrating Learning, Deliberation and Reactive Control (HYCAS 2009)*, (pp. 7-12). Pasadena, CA: HYCAS.

Bhatt, M. (2010). Commonsense inference in dynamic spatial systems: Epistemological requirements. In *Proceedings of FLAIRS Conference: Special Track on Spatial and Temporal Reasoning*. AAAI Press.

Bhatt, M., & Dylla, F. (2009). A qualitative model of dynamic scene analysis and interpretation in ambient intelligence systems. *International Journal of Robotics and Automation*, *24*(3). doi:10.2316/Journal.206.2009.3.206-3274

Bhatt, M., Dylla, F., & Hois, J. (2009). Spatio-terminological inference for the design of ambient environments. In *Proceedings of the 9th International Conference on Spatial Information Theory (COSIT)*, (p. 505). Springer-Verlag.

Bhatt, M., & Flanagan, G. (2010). *Spatio-temporal abduction in the event calculus*. Unpublished.

Bhatt, M., & Freksa, C. (2010). Spatial computing for design: An artificial intelligence perspective. In *Proceedings of NSF International Workshop on Studying Visual and Spatial Reasoning for Design Creativity (SDC'10)*. SDC.

Bhatt, M., & Guesgen, H. (Eds.). (2009). *Spatial and temporal reasoning for ambient intelligence systems (STAMI 09)*. (SFB/TR 8 Spatial Cognition Report Series, No. 020-08/2009). STAMI.

Bhatt, M., Ichim, A., & Flanagan, G. (2010). DSIM: A tool for assisted spatial design. In *Proceedings of the 4th International Conference on Design Computing and Cognition (DCC'10)*. DCC.

Bhatt, M., & Loke, S. (2008). Modelling dynamic spatial systems in the situation calculus. *Spatial Cognition and Computation*, *8*(1), 86–130. doi:10.1080/13875860801926884

Bobrow, D. G. (1984). Special volume on qualitative reasoning about physical systems. *Artificial Intelligence*, *24*(1-3). doi:10.1016/0004-3702(84)90036-5

Brachman, R., & Levesque, H. (2004). *Knowledge representation and reasoning*. San Francisco, CA: Morgan Kaufmann Publishers Inc.

Cardelli, L., & Gordon, A. D. (2000). Anytime, anywhere: Modal logics for mobile ambients. In *Proceedings of POPL*, (pp. 365–377). ACM.

Cardelli, L., & Gordon, A. D. (2006). Ambient logic. *Mathematical Structures in Computer Science*.

Claramunt, C., & Thériault, M. (1995). Managing time in GIS: An event-oriented approach. In *Proceedings of Temporal Databases* (pp. 23–42). Temporal Databases. doi:10.1007/978-1-4471-3033-8_2

Cohn, A., Bennett, B., Gooday, J., & Gotts, N. (1997a). Representing and reasoning with qualitative spatial relations about regions. In Stock, O. (Ed.), *Spatial and Temporal Reasoning* (pp. 97–134). Dordrecht, The Netherlands: Kluwer Academic Publishers. doi:10.1007/978-0-585-28322-7_4

Cohn, A. G., Bennett, B., Gooday, J., & Gotts, N. M. (1997b). Qualitative spatial representation and reasoning with the region connection calculus. *GeoInformatica*, *1*(3), 275–316. doi:10.1023/A:1009712514511

Cohn, A. G., Gotts, N. M., Randell, D. A., Cui, Z., Bennett, B., & Gooday, J. M. (1997c). Exploiting temporal continuity in qualitative spatial calculi. In Golledge, R. G., & Egenhofer, M. J. (Eds.), *Spatial and Temporal Reasoning in Geographical Information Systems*. London, UK: Elsevier.

Cohn, A. G., & Renz, J. (2007). Qualitative spatial reasoning. In van Harmelen, F., Lifschitz, V., & Porter, B. (Eds.), *Handbook of Knowledge Representation*. London, UK: Elsevier.

Couclelis, H. (2009). The abduction of geographic information science: Transporting spatial reasoning to the realm of purpose and design. In Hornsby, K. S., Claramunt, C., Denis, M., & Ligozat, G. (Eds.), *COSIT* (pp. 342–356). Springer. doi:10.1007/978-3-642-03832-7_21

Cui, Z., Cohn, A. G., & Randell, D. A. (1992). Qualitative simulation based on a logical formalism of space and time. In *Proceedings of, AAAI-92*, 679–684.

Davis, E. (2008). Pouring liquids: A study in commonsense physical reasoning. *Artificial Intelligence*, *172*(12-13), 1540–1578. doi:10.1016/j.artint.2008.04.003

Davis, E. (2009). How does a box work? A study in the qualitative dynamics of solid objects. *Artificial Intelligence*, *175*(1), 299–345. doi:10.1016/j.artint.2010.04.006

Davis, E., & Morgenstern, L. (2004). Introduction: Progress in formal commonsense reasoning. *Artificial Intelligence*, *153*(1-2), 1–12. doi:10.1016/j.artint.2003.09.001

Dylla, F., & Moratz, R. (2004). Exploiting qualitative spatial neighborhoods in the situation calculus. In *Proceedings of Spatial Cognition* (pp. 304–322). Spatial Cognition. doi:10.1007/978-3-540-32255-9_18

Ferguson, R. W., Bokor, J. L., Mappus, R. L., IV, & Feldman, A. (2003). Maintaining spatial relations in an incremental diagrammatic reasoner. In *Proceedings of COSIT*, (pp. 136–150). COSIT.

Finger, J. (1987). *Exploiting constraints in design synthesis*. Unpublished Doctoral Dissertation. Palo Alto, CA: Stanford University.

Forbus, K. D. (1984). Qualitative process theory. *Artificial Intelligence*, *24*(1-3), 85–168. doi:10.1016/0004-3702(84)90038-9

Forbus, K. D. (1989). Introducing actions into qualitative simulation. In N. S. Sridharan (Ed.), *Proceedings of the Eleventh International Joint Conference on Artificial Intelligence*, (pp. 1273–1278). San Mateo, CA: Morgan Kaufmann.

Freksa, C. (1991a). Conceptual neighborhood and its role in temporal and spatial reasoning. In Singh, M., & Travé-Massuyès, L. (Eds.), *Decision Support Systems and Qualitative Reasoning* (pp. 181–187). Amsterdam, The Netherlands: North-Holland Publishers.

Freksa, C. (1991b). Qualitative spatial reasoning. In Mark, D., & Frank, A. (Eds.), *Cognitive and Linguistic Aspects of Geographic Space* (pp. 361–372). Dordrecht, The Netherlands: Kluwer.

Freksa, C. (1992). Using orientation information for qualitative spatial reasoning. In *Proceedings of the International Conference on GIS, From Space to Territory: Theories and Methods of Spatio-Temporal Reasoning in Geographic Space*, (pp. 162–178). Berlin, Germany: Springer-Verlag.

Galton, A. (1996). Taking dimension seriously in qualitative spatial reasoning. In *Proceedings of ECAI*, (pp. 501–505). ECAI.

Galton, A. (2000). *Qualitative spatial change*. Oxford, UK: Oxford University Press.

Galton, A. (2006). Causal reasoning for alert generation in smart homes. In *Proceedings of Designing Smart Homes* (pp. 57–70). Designing Smart Homes. doi:10.1007/11788485_4

Galton, A., & Hood, J. (2004). Qualitative interpolation for environmental knowledge representation. In de Mántaras, R. L., & Saitta, L. (Eds.), *ECAI* (pp. 1017–1018). IOS Press.

Giacomo, G. D., & Levesque, H. J. (1999). An incremental interpreter for high-level programs with sensing. In Levesque, H. J., & Pirri, F. (Eds.), *Logical Foundation for Cognitive Agents: Contributions in Honor of Ray Reiter* (pp. 86–102). Berlin, Germany: Springer. doi:10.1007/978-3-642-60211-5_8

Giunchiglia, E., Lee, J., Lifschitz, V., McCain, N., & Turner, H. (2004). Nonmonotonic causal theories. *Artificial Intelligence*, *153*(1-2), 49–104. doi:10.1016/j.artint.2002.12.001

Gooday, J., & Cohn, A. (1996). Transition-based qualitative simulation. In *Proceeding of the 10th International Workshop on Qualitative Reasoning*, (pp. 74–82). AAAI Press.

Gooday, J., & Galton, A. (1997). The transition calculus: A high-level formalism for reasoning about action and change. *Journal of Experimental & Theoretical Artificial Intelligence*, *9*(1), 51–66. doi:10.1080/095281397147239

Gotts, N. M. (1996). Formalizing commonsense topology: The inch calculus. In *Proceedings of Fourth International Symposium on Artificial Intelligence and Mathematics*. Artificial Intelligence in Mathematics.

Graphisoft Inc. (2010). *ArchiCAD 13*. Retrieved from http://www.graphisoft.com/.

Hall, N. (2000). Causation and the price of transitivity. *The Journal of Philosophy*, *97*(4), 198–222. doi:10.2307/2678390

Hazarika, S. M. (2005). *Qualitative spatial change: Space-time histories and continuity*. Unpublished Doctoral Dissertation. Leeds, UK: The University of Leeds.

Hornsby, K., & Egenhofer, M. (2000). Identity-based change: A foundation for spatio-temporal knowledge representation. *International Journal of Geographical Information Science*, *14*(3), 207–224. doi:10.1080/136588100240813

Kowalski, R., & Sergot, M. (1986). A logic-based calculus of events. *New Generation Computing*, *4*(1), 67–95. doi:10.1007/BF03037383

Kuipers, B. (1994). *Qualitative reasoning: Modeling and simulation with incomplete knowledge*. Cambridge, MA: MIT Press.

Kuipers, B. J. (1986). Qualitative simulation. *Artificial Intelligence*, *29*(3), 289–338. doi:10.1016/0004-3702(86)90073-1

Levesque, H., & Lakemeyer, G. (2007). Cognitive robotics. In Lifschitz, V., van Harmelen, F., & Porter, F. (Eds.), *Handbook of Knowledge Representation*. London, UK: Elsevier.

Levesque, H. J., Reiter, R., Lespérance, Y., Lin, F., & Scherl, R. B. (1997). Golog: A logic programming language for dynamic domains. *The Journal of Logic Programming*, *31*(1-3), 59–83. doi:10.1016/S0743-1066(96)00121-5

Ligozat, G., & Renz, J. (2004). What is a qualitative calculus? A general framework. In *Proceedings of PRICAI*, (pp. 53–64). PRICAI.

Lin, F. (1995). Embracing causality in specifying the indirect effects of actions. In *Proceedings of IJCAI*, (pp. 1985–1993). IJCAI.

McCarthy, J. (1977). Epistemological problems of artificial intelligence. In *Proceedings of IJCAI*, (pp. 1038–1044). IJCAI.

McCarthy, J. (1998). *Elaboration tolerance*. New York, NY: CommonSense.

McCarthy, J. (2008). The well-designed child. *Artificial Intelligence*, *172*(18), 2003–2014. doi:10.1016/j.artint.2008.10.001

McCarthy, J., & Hayes, P. J. (1969). Some philosophical problems from the standpoint of artificial intelligence. In Meltzer, B., & Michie, D. (Eds.), *Machine Intelligence 4* (pp. 463–502). Edinburgh, UK: Edinburgh University Press.

Moratz, R. (2006). Representing relative direction as a binary relation of oriented points. In *Proceedings of ECAI*, (pp. 407–411). ECAI.

Moratz, R., Renz, J., & Wolter, D. (2000). Qualitative spatial reasoning about line segments. In *Proceedings of ECAI*, (pp. 234–238). ECAI.

Mueller, E. T. (2006). *Commonsense reasoning*. San Francisco, CA: Morgan Kaufmann Publishers Inc.

Mueller, E. T. (2009). Automating commonsense reasoning using the event calculus. *Communications of the ACM*, *52*(1), 113–117. doi:10.1145/1435417.1435443

NIMA. (2000). *The big idea framework*. Washington, DC: National Imagery and Mapping Agency.

Papadakis, N., & Plexousakis, D. (2003). Actions with duration and constraints: The ramification problem in temporal databases. *International Journal of Artificial Intelligence Tools*, *12*(3), 315–353. doi:10.1142/S0218213003001265

Philipose, M., Fishkin, K. P., Perkowitz, M., Patterson, D. J., Fox, D., Kautz, H., & Hahnel, D. (2004). Inferring activities from interactions with objects. *IEEE Pervasive Computing / IEEE Computer Society and IEEE Communications Society*, *3*(4), 50–57. doi:10.1109/MPRV.2004.7

Piaget, J., & Inhelder, B. (1967). *The child's conception of space*. New York, NY: Basic Books.

Pierce, C. S. (1935). *The collected papers of Charles Sanders Peirce*. Cambridge, MA: Harvard University Press.

Poole, D., Goebel, R., & Aleliunas, R. (1987). Theorist: A logical reasoning system for defaults and diagnosis. In Cercone, N., & McCalla, G. (Eds.), *The Knowledge Frontier* (pp. 331–352). New York, NY: Springer. doi:10.1007/978-1-4612-4792-0_13

Ramos, C., Augusto, J. C., & Shapiro, D. (2008). Ambient intelligence: The next step for artificial intelligence. *IEEE Intelligent Systems*, *23*(2), 15–18. doi:10.1109/MIS.2008.19

Randell, D., & Witkowski, M. (2004). Tracking regions using conceptual neighbourhoods. In *Proceedings of the Workshop on Spatial and Temporal Reasoning*, (pp. 63–71). ECAI.

Randell, D. A., Cui, Z., & Cohn, A. (1992). A spatial logic based on regions and connection. In *Proceedings of KR'92: Principles of Knowledge Representation and Reasoning*, (pp. 165–176). San Mateo, CA: Morgan Kaufmann.

Reiter, R. (2001). *Knowledge in action: Logical foundations for describing and implementing dynamical systems*. Cambridge, MA: MIT Press.

Renz, J., & Nebel, B. (2007). *Qualitative spatial reasoning using constraint calculi*. Retrieved from http://users.cecs.anu.edu.au/~jrenz/papers/renz-nebel-los.pdf.

Sandewall, E. (1994). *Features and fluents: The representation of knowledge about dynamical systems*. New York, NY: Oxford University Press, Inc.

Shanahan, M. (1989). Prediction is deduction but explanation is abduction. In *Proceedings of IJCAI*, (pp. 1055–1060). IJCAI.

Shanahan, M. (1993). Explanation in the situation calculus. In *Proceedings of IJCAI*, (pp. 160–165). IJCAI.

Shanahan, M. (1995). Default reasoning about spatial occupancy. *Artificial Intelligence*, *74*(1), 147–163. doi:10.1016/0004-3702(94)00071-8

Shanahan, M. (1997). *Solving the frame problem: A mathematical investigation of the common sense law of inertia*. Cambridge, MA: MIT Press.

Sloman, A. (2008). The well-designed young mathematician. *Artificial Intelligence*, *172*(18), 2015–2034. doi:10.1016/j.artint.2008.09.004

Stock, O. (1997). *Spatial and temporal reasoning*. Dordrecht, The Netherlands: Kluwer Academic Publishers. doi:10.1007/978-0-585-28322-7

Streitz, N. A., Kameas, A., & Mavrommati, I. (Eds.). (2007). *The disappearing computer, interaction design, system infrastructures and applications for smart environments. (LNCS 4500)*. Springer.

Thielscher, M. (1997). Ramification and causality. *Artificial Intelligence*, *89*(1-2), 317–364. doi:10.1016/S0004-3702(96)00033-1

Thielscher, M. (1998). Introduction to the fluent calculus. *Electronic Transactions in Artificial Intelligence*, *2*, 179–192.

Thielscher, M. (2005). Flux: A logic programming method for reasoning agents. *Theory and Practice of Logic Programming, 5*(4-5), 533–565. doi:10.1017/S1471068405002358

Van Harmelen, F., Lifschitz, V., & Porter, B. (Eds.). (2007). *Handbook of knowledge representation (foundations of artificial intelligence)*. Elsevier Science.

Weld, D. S., & de Kleer, J. (1989). *Readings in qualitative reasoning about physical systems*. San Mateo, CA: Morgan Kaufmann Publishers.

Worboys, M. (1998). Modelling changes and events in dynamic spatial systems with reference to socio-economic units. In *Proceedings of ESF GISDATA Conference on Modelling Change in Socio-Economic Units*. Taylor and Francis.

Worboys, M. F. (2005). Event-oriented approaches to geographic phenomena. *International Journal of Geographical Information Science, 19*(1), 1–28. doi:10.1080/13658810412331280167

Youngblood, G. M., & Cook, D. J. (2007). Data mining for hierarchical model creation. *IEEE Transactions on Systems, Man, and Cybernetics. Part C, 37*(4), 561–572.

Yuan, M., Mark, D. M., Egenhofer, M. J., & Peuquet, D. J. (2004). *Extensions to geographic representations in a research agenda for geographic information science*. Boca Raton, FL: CRC Press.

## ENDNOTES

1. Here, *grounding* should be interpreted in a limited sense to correspond to the derivation of qualified relational scene information from (noisy) quantitative or metrical data.
2. Broadly, elaboration tolerant theories are those where addition of new domain-independent truths or axioms may be easily achieved to account for "*new phenomena or changed circumstances*" (McCarthy, 1998).
3. This example is further discussed in the context of causal explanation in Section 4.3.3.
4. See "*What is a qualitative calculus*? (Ligozat & Renz, 2004).
5. These, for instance, correspond to the following properties of the underlying relationship space: Jointly Exhaustive and Pair-Wise Disjoint Property (JEPD), the composition theorems, basic symmetric and asymmetric properties, continuity constraints. See Section 4.
6. The robotics centered discussion suffices here since the same principles extend to arbitrary spatial domains / systems of a dynamic nature (Bhatt & Loke, 2008).
7. Only categories closely related to the topic of the present discussion are included.
8. Note the correspondences between I1-C2, I2-C3, I3-C4, and I4-C5.
9. For instance, an important next step in this direction is to further identify phenomenal aspects that may be considered inherent in a wide-range of dynamic spatial systems.
10. A comprehensive literature review has not been attempted in this chapter. Instead, I have only reviewed closely related works that are directly connected to the RSAC paradigm being pursued herein.
11. Application and resulting computational aspects are discussed in Sections 2.2 and 4.3.3, respectively.
12. These works are discussed in detail in Section 4.
13. Continuity constraints resulting from the conceptual neighbourhood of a spatial calculus constitute one aspect of modelling a spatial theory within a logic of action and change. Additional properties that constitute a "*qualitative calculus*" (Ligozat & Renz, 2004) also need to be accounted for.

[14] See Figure 7 for 2D interpretations of the topological relationships *{dc; ec; po; eq, tpp, ntpp,* $tpp^{1}$; $ntpp^{1}$*}* in the context of the Region Connection Calculus (Randell, et al., 1992).

[15] The vehicle and room can be conceived as one hollow object bounded by the sides with an opening at one end so as to allow containment relationships with other objects.

[16] The computational tasks where such commonsense reasoning is relevant are discussed in Section 4.3.

[17] The former two cases involve ramifications whereas the last case pertains to *spatial inertia* (Section 4.2.2).

[18] An external event is an event that may occur non-deterministically at some time-point.

[19] Recall that compositional consistency refers to the satisfaction of the global constraints formulated by composition theorems relevant to every spatial calculus that is modelled.

[20] For instance, "*plans can be synthesized as a side-effect of theorem proving*" (Reiter, 2001).

[21] The third entity in the simulation is a virtual camera that records the other two entities in the scene, and hence is not visible within the 3D illustration of Figure 15.

[22] These are, for instance, (implicitly) available from linguistic descriptions about *acts* and *scenes* within a drama or film script. The progression of the script can be thought of as an imaginary evolution of the system.

# Chapter 10
# Integrated Ontologies for Spatial Scene Descriptions

**Sotirios Batsakis**
*Technical University of Crete, Greece*

**Euripides G.M. Petrakis**
*Technical University of Crete, Greece*

## ABSTRACT

*Scene descriptions are typically expressed in natural language texts and are integrated within Web pages, books, newspapers, and other means of content dissemination. The capabilities of such means can be enhanced to support automated content processing and communication between people or machines by allowing the scene contents to be extracted and expressed in ontologies, a formal syntax rich in semantics interpretable by both people and machines. Ontologies enable more effective querying, reasoning, and general use of content and allow for standardizing the quality and delivery of information across communicating information sources. Ontologies are defined using the well-established standards of the Semantic Web for expressing scene descriptions in application fields such as Geographic Information Systems, medicine, and the World Wide Web (WWW). Ontologies are not only suitable for describing static scenes with static objects (e.g., in photographs) but also enable representation of dynamic events with objects and properties changing in time (e.g., moving objects in a video). Representation of both static and dynamic scenes by ontologies, as well as querying and reasoning over static and dynamic ontologies are important issues for further research. These are exactly the problems this chapter is dealing with.*

DOI: 10.4018/978-1-61692-868-1.ch010

## BACKGROUND

Formal spatial, temporal and spatio-temporal representations have been studied extensively in the Database (Gutting, 1994) and recently, in the Semantic Web literature (Arpinal, Sheth, Ramakrishnan, Usery, Azami, & Kwan, 2006). The related work is surveyed in the following sections focusing on work inspired by ontologies and the Semantic Web.

Spatial entities (e.g., objects, regions) in classic database systems are typically represented based upon a reference coordinate system using points, lines (polygonal lines) or Minimum Bounding Rectangles (MBRs) enclosing objects or regions and their relationships (Petrakis, 2002). Relations among spatial entities can be topological, orientation or distance relations. In turn, spatial relations can be qualitative (i.e. described using lexical terms) or quantitative (i.e. described using numerical values).

Many spatial ontologies for the semantic Web are known to exist, the majority of them being defined based upon a reference coordinate system and qualitative topological and direction relations (e.g., RCC-8 relations). Reasoning rules for various relation sets have been proposed as well (Cohn & Hazarika, 2001; Renz & Nebel, 2007). Recent approaches use specialized representation languages such as GML or general-purpose Semantic Web languages such as OWL (Abdelmoty, Smart, Jones, Fu, & Finch, 2005). The SPIRIT spatial search system (Jones, Abdelmoty, Finch, Fu, & Vaid, 2004) combines an ontology with indexing mechanisms. In Katz and Grau (2005) RCC-8 topological relations are represented using OWL-DL. In the work by Hazarika (Hazarika & Roy, 2008), information retrieval is enhanced using RCC-5 topological relations among objects. Along the same lines, Grutter (Grutter & Bauer-Messmer, 2007) suggest extracting RCC-8 relations using a separate coordinate system which is not part of the ontology. SWETO-GS (Arpinal, Sheth, Ramakrishnan, Usery, Azami, & Kwan, 2006) is a geospatial ontology enhanced with Spatiotemporal Thematic Proximity (STTP) reasoning and interactive visualization capabilities. Liu and Hao (2005), combine topological and direction relations. A combination of RCC-5 with cardinal direction relations is proposed by Chen, Liu, Zhang, and Xie (2009). An almost orthogonal (to representation) issue is speed of search. Petrakis (2002a) and Dellis and Paliouras (2007) emphasize on the indexing of spatial information using R-trees for improving the speed of search of nearest-neighbor and range queries.

The representation of spatio-temporal knowledge has also motivated research within the Semantic Web community. Related work includes Chen, Perich, Finin, and Joshi (2004) where the temporal ontology is enhanced by Allen's temporal relations. In this work, the RCC-8 relations form the core of the spatial representation. Worboys and Hornby (2004) suggest a model for representing objects and events combining spatial and temporal information. Wang et al. (2004) introduce a spatiotemporal representation in OWL supporting logic-based reasoning by limiting spatial relations to inclusion relations. In the work by Sheth et al. (Sheth, Arpinar, Perry, & Hakimpour, 2009), the SPIRIT spatial query engine (Jones, Abdelmoty, Finch, Fu, & Vaid, 2004) is combined with temporal RDF (Gutierrez, Hurtado, & Vaisman, 2007) in an integrated spatiotemporal representation mechanism. Finally, the MOQL query language (Li, Ozsu, Szafron, & Oria, 1997) has been proposed for querying spatio-temporal information in databases.

## INTEGRATED SCENE DESCRIPTION ONTOLOGIES

Issues relating to spatial and temporal aspects of scene descriptions are discussed next. Particular emphasis in given to ontology models integrating both kinds of knowledge.

## Temporal Representation

Dealing with information that changes over time is a critical problem in Knowledge Representation (KR). Representation languages such as OWL (description logics), frame-based and object-oriented languages (F-logic) are all based on binary relations (e.g., being the employee of a company) without any temporal information. Adding the time dimension to this information would lead to ternary relations which are not supported by OWL (Hayes & Welty, 2006). However, representation of temporal information using OWL is still feasible, although complicated.

The OWL-Time (formerly DAML-Time) temporal ontology describes the temporal content of Web pages and the temporal properties of Web services. Apart from language constructs for the representation of time in ontologies, there is a need for mechanisms for the representation of the evolution of concepts (events) in time. Existing solutions for dealing with this problem include: Versioning, Reification, the 4-D perdurantist (fluent) approach (Welty & Fikes, 2006) and Temporal Description Logics (Artale & Franconi, 2000; Lutz, Wolter, & Zakharyaschev, 2008). This is related to the problem of the representation of time in temporal (relational and object oriented) databases (Ozsoyoglu & Snodgrass, 1995). Existing methods are relying mostly on temporal Entity Relation (ER) models (Gregersen & Jensen, 1999) taking into account valid time (i.e., the time interval during which a relation holds), transaction time (i.e., the time at which a database entry is updated) or both. Also, time is represented by time points, intervals or finite sets of intervals. Representation of time in the semantic web standards differs from representation in databases (Gutierrez, Hurtado, & Vaisman, 2007) as (a) OWL semantics are not equivalent to ER model semantics (e.g., OWL adopts the Open World Assumption) while ER model adopts the Closed World Assumption and (b) relations in OWL are restricted to binary ones.

### Ontology Versioning

Ontology Versioning (Klein & Fensel, 2001) suggests that the ontology has different versions (one per instance of time). When a change takes place, a new version is created. Versioning suffers from several disadvantages: (a) changes even on single attributes require that a new version of the ontology be created leading to information redundancy, (b) searching for events occurred at time instances or during time intervals requires exhaustive searches in multiple versions of the ontology, and (c) it is not clear how the relation between evolving classes is represented within the ontology.

### Temporal Description Logics

Temporal description logics (Artale & Franconi, 2000; Lutz, Wolter, & Zakharyaschev, 2008) form the basis of Semantic Web standards such as OWL-DL and are based on Description Logics (DL). In addition to the features of standard DLs, Temporal DLs allow additional operators such as "until," "sometime in the past," and "always in the future." They extend the expressive power of standard description logics and they do not suffer from the data redundancy problem of other approaches (versioning, 4-D fluent, and reification). They also require extending standard Semantic Web languages such as OWL, which is not desirable when compatibility with existing standards and tools is required.

### Reification

Reification (Andronikos, Stefanidakis, & Papadakis, 2009) is a general-purpose technique applied when relations involving more than two objects-attributes (such as temporal relations) have to be represented using languages restricting relations to binary ones. For example, when the relation *Rel* holds between objects $Obj_1$ and $Obj_2$ at time $time_1$ then a new object is created which has three properties: Objects $Obj_1$ and $Obj_2$ and the time value $time_1$. Data redundancy is a problem of this method, since a new object is created whenever a temporal relation must be represented. In addition, since relations are represented as objects and not as OWL relations, the semantics offered by the OWL specification regarding object relations cannot be applied when reification is used.

### The 4-Dimensional (Perdurantist) Approach

The 4D-fluent (perdurantist) approach (Welty & Fikes, 2006) shows how temporal information can be represented effectively in OWL. However, similarly to versioning and reification, it still suffers from data redundancy. Concepts in time are represented as 4-dimensional objects with the 4th dimension being the time. Time instances and time intervals are represented as instances of a *time interval* class, which in turn, is related with time concepts varying in time.

The ontology comprises of a static and a dynamic part. Changes occur on the properties of the temporal part of the ontology keeping the entities of the static part unchanged. To add the time dimension to an ontology, classes *TimeSlice* and *TimeInterval* with properties *tsTimeSliceOf* and *tsTimeInterval* respectively are introduced into the ontology representation. Class *TimeSlice* is the domain class for entities representing temporal parts (i.e., "time slices") and class *TimeInterval* is the domain class of time intervals. A time interval holds the temporal information of a time slice. Property *tsTimeSliceOf* connects an instance of class *TimeSlice* with an entity, and property *tsTimeInterval* connects an instance of class *TimeSlice* with an instance of class *TimeInterval*. Properties having a time dimension are called *fluent* properties and connect instances of class *TimeSlice*.

Figure 1 illustrates an example temporal ontology with classes *Company* with data type property *companyName* and *Product* with datatype properties *price* and *productName*. In this example, *CompanyName* is a static property (its value does not change in time), while properties *produces*, *productName* and *price* are dynamic (fluent) properties whose values may change in time. Because they are fluent properties, their domain (and range) is of class *TimeSlice*. *CompanyTimeSlice* and *ProductTimeSlice* are instances of class *TimeSlice* and are provided to denote that the domain of properties *produces*, *productName*, and *price* are time slices restricted to be slices of a specific class. For example, the domain of property *productName* is not class *TimeSlice* but it is restricted to instances that are time slices of class *Product*.

## Spatio-Temporal Representations

Representing spatial knowledge has been studied extensively within the context of spatial database research (Gutting, 1994). Existing representations refer mostly to quantitative data (i.e., points, lines and minimum bounding rectangles). Quantitative representation mechanisms are best suited to Geographical Information Systems (GIS). Spatial relations holding between objects can be topological, directional and distance relations. Qualitative relations although less accurate than quantitative relations have been proposed as well. The vast majority of scene descriptions expressed in natural language involve mostly qualitative expressions, which are more common than quantitative ones. For instance, the relative position between two regions is commonly expressed by qualitative expressions such as "North of" rather than by quantitative ones, such as by providing longitude and latitude values. Quantitative descriptions are

*Figure 1. Ontology for representation of dynamic objects using 4D fluents*

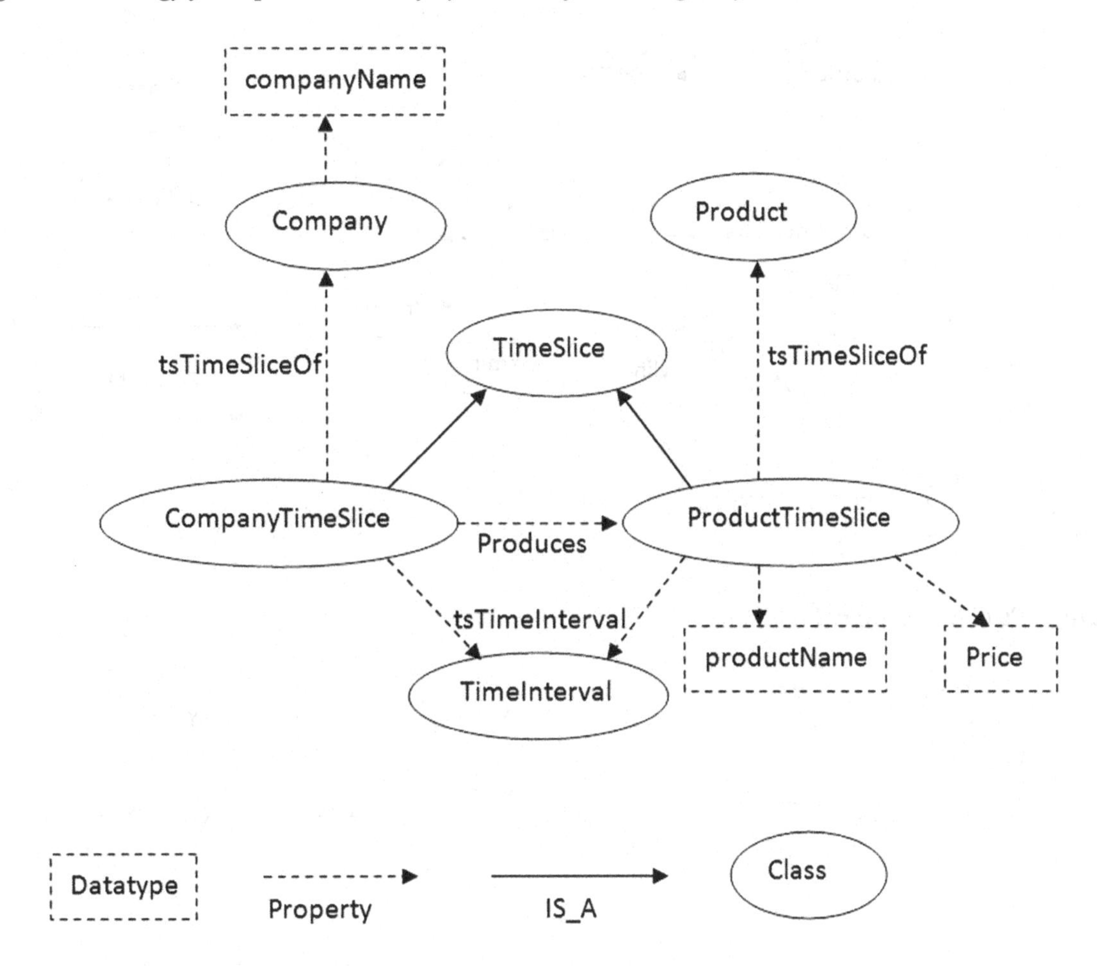


restricted to specialized domains (such as navigation in GIS) while, in everyday use qualitative relations are more common.

Similarly to spatial relations, temporal relations (e.g., "before," "after") often appear without numerical values denoting time instants or intervals. Integrating temporal and spatial representations in a unified model has been studied in Abraham and Roddick (1999) and Sheth, Arpinar, Perry, and Hakimpour (2009) in the context of database and semantic Web research respectively. Integrating spatial with temporal representations in a unified ontology representation model is discussed next.

## Spatial Ontology Representation

The 4-D fluent mechanism will form the basis of the proposed spatio-temporal ontology representation. The spatial representation mechanism below supports several types of qualitative spatial relations (topological, directional, distance). Although many applications require only one category of relations, a general-purpose ontology model should offer support for all types of spatial relations.

Figure 2 illustrates a general ontology representation model for spatial information. Class *Location* has attribute *name* (of type string). In addition, a *Location* object can be optionally con-

*Figure 2. Ontology representation of spatial objects*

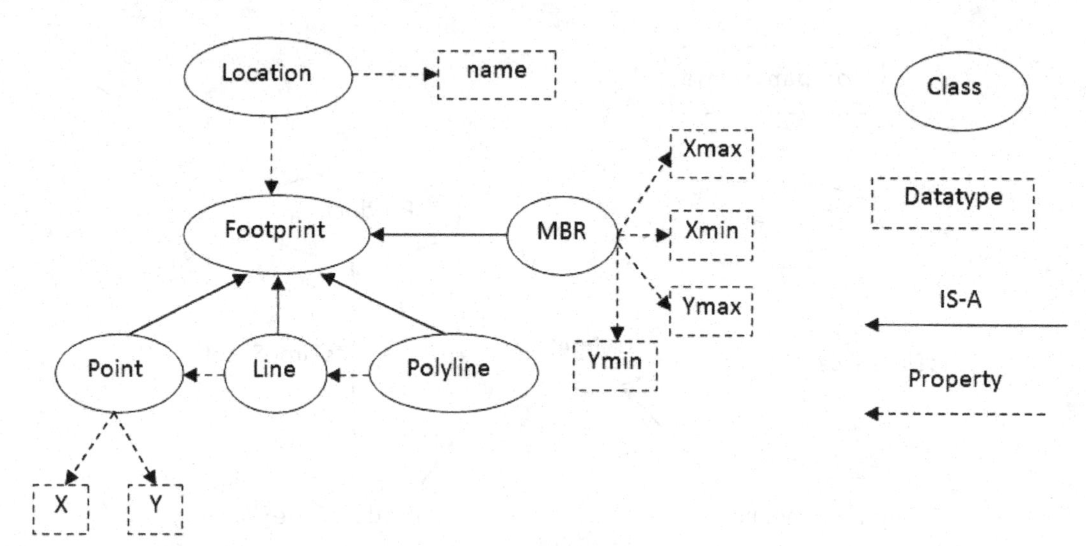


*Figure 3. RCC-8 topological relations*

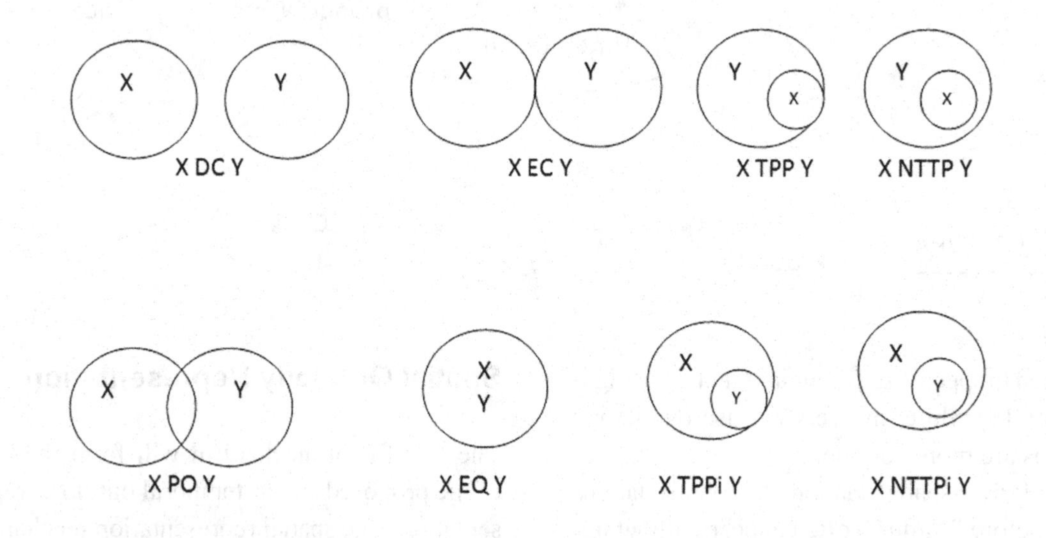


nected with a *footprint* class object with subclasses: *Point, Line, Polyline,* and *MBR*. Class *Point* has two (or three in a three-dimensional representation) numerical attributes, namely *X, Y* (also *Z* in a three-dimensional representation). For example, *Point* will be the footprint of entities such as cities in a large-scale map. Class *Line* has *point*$_1$ and *point*$_2$ as attributes representing the ending points of a line segment. Class *PolyLine* may represent region boundaries by a set of consecutive line segments (e.g. roads, rivers). Finally, a region can be represented by the polygonal line surrounding its contour (*Polyline*) or by its Minimum Bounding Rectangle (MBR). In the later case, the MBR of a region is denoted by four numerical attributes *Xmax, YmaxY, Xmin* and *Ymin*. As Figure 2 demonstrates, both *Polyline* and *MBR* attributes can be taking part in the same representation.

*Figure 4. Projection based direction relations*

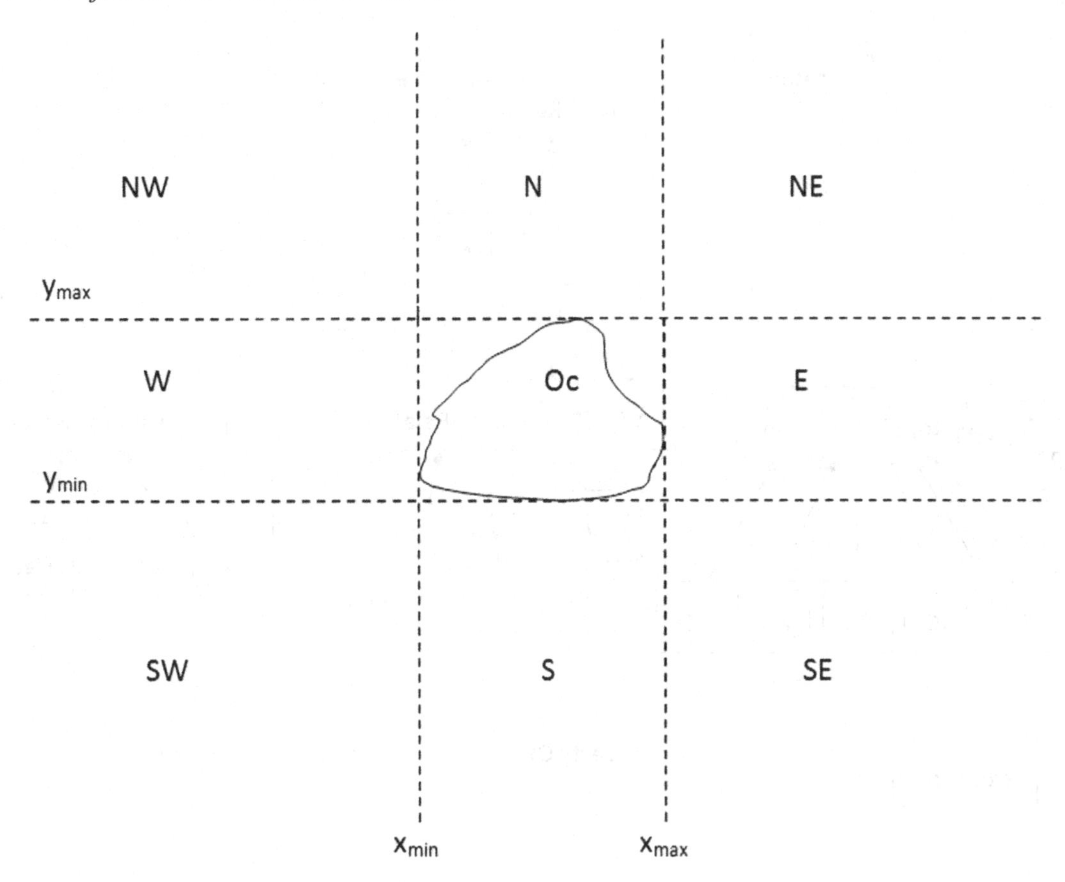


Figure 3 summarizes all types of spatial relations within a common ontology schema. Omitting one or more types of spatial relations is a design decision, which is taken given application domain and user requirements.

The spatial relations between regions can be easily extracted from their surrounding MBRs (or surrounding polygonal lines) by comparing their coordinates. In an ontology, each *spatialRelation* connects two locations and has three subproperties namely: *topologicRelation*, *directionalRelation* and *distanceRelation*. These types of relations may co-exist within the same representation although in most cases, depending on the application, an ontology schema calls for either direction or topologic relations. The following topological relations (DC, EC, EQ, NTTP, NTTPi, TTP, TPPi, PO), shown in Figure 4, referred to as RCC-8 relations (Randell, Cui, & Cohn, 1992) are also defined and can be used as well.

Direction relations are defined based on 2D or cone shaped projections (Renz & Nebel, 2007). As shown in Figure 5, nine direction relations can be identified namely North (N), North East (NE), East (E), South East (SE), South (S), South West (SW), West (W), North West (NW), and the neutral direction (Oc) based on 2D-projections (Frank, 1996). In addition, the relations *Front*, *Left*, *Behind,* and *Right* can also be used.

Finally, the distance relations *far* and *near* can be defined. However, distance relations may be ambiguous especially in application where a common scale for measuring distances is not provided. Also, distance relations can be expressed

*Figure 5. Ontology schema with all spatial relations*

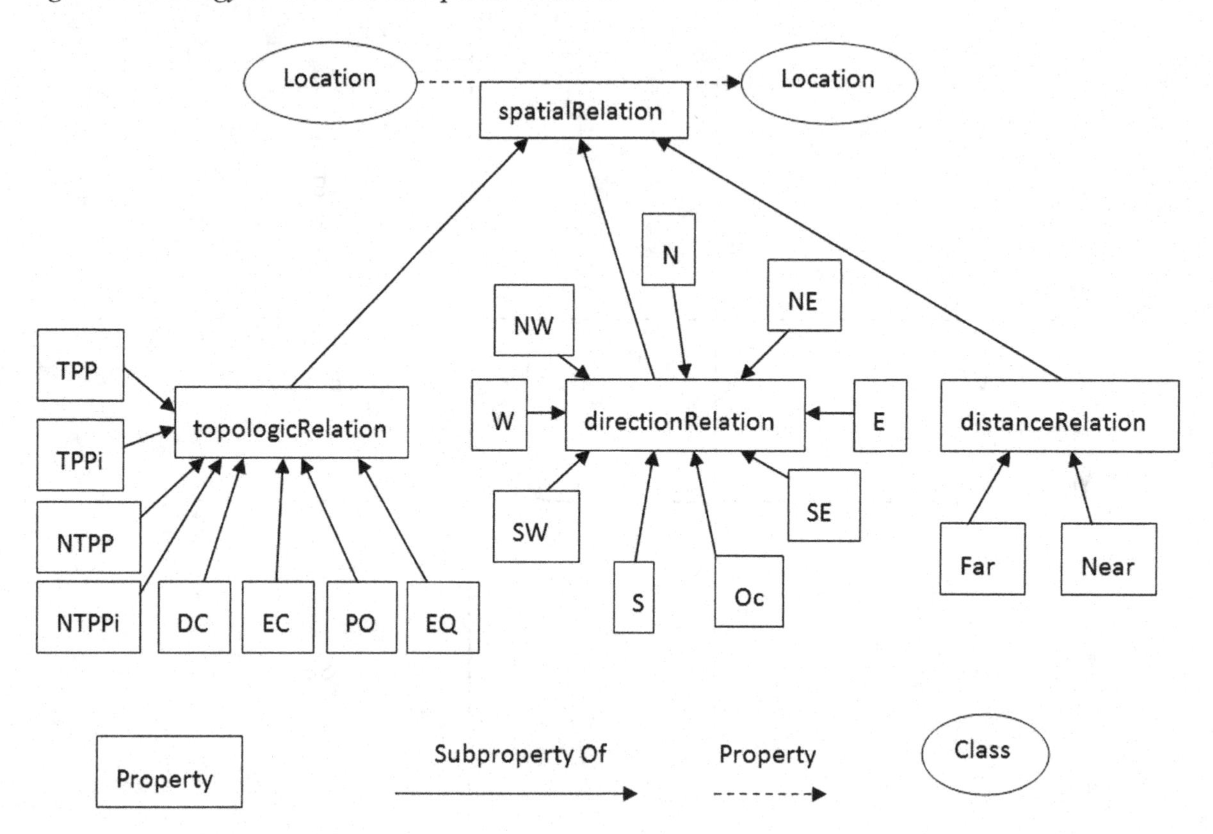


quantitatively (e.g., 3Km far from city A) and stored in the ontology using reification (i.e., by defining a distance object with attributes the two related locations and a numerical attribute representing distance).

Summarizing, it is likely that only topological and direction relations will be used in practice since they can be easily extracted from natural scenes. Distance relations, although common in natural scene descriptions, are less likely to be used since they cannot be extracted from natural scenes (unless a reference coordinate system or scale for measuring distances is provided). For instance, given the MBRs of two regions, the *EQ* relation holds when all four coordinates are equal, *DC* relation holds when either *x-axis* or *y-axis* coordinates—or both—do not overlap (i.e., the min value of a region is greater than the corresponding maximum value of the other) etc. Additional relations can be inferred by the defined ones using composition tables which are defined for both topological and direction relations.

A composition table defines the possible spatial relations holding between two objects, given their spatial relations with a third one. Table 1 and Table 2 illustrate example composition tables using RCC-8 topological and 2D projection based direction relations respectively. Spatial reasoning is then achieved by applying rules implementing the inferred relations of a composition table.

A limited set of table entries leads to an unambiguously defined result. For example, the composition of the S and SE direction relations (i.e., object A is south of B and object B south-east of C) yields (as defined by the table entry at the intersection of the *S*-row and the *SE*-column of Table 2) the *SE* relation as a result meaning that A is south east of C. However, the composition

*Table 1. Composition of RCC-8 topological relations*

| | DC | EC | PO | TPP | NTPP | TPPi | NTPPi | EQ |
|---|---|---|---|---|---|---|---|---|
| DC | DC,EC,PO, TPP,NTPP, TPPi,NTPPi, EQ | DC,EC,PO, TPP,NTPP | DC,EC,PO, TPP,NTPP | DC,EC,PO, TPP,NTPP | DC,EC,PO, TPP,NTPP | DC | DC | DC |
| EC | DC,EC,PO, TPPi,NTPPi | DC,EC,PO,TPP TPPi,EQ | DC,EC,PO, TPP,NTPP | EC,PO, TPP,NTPP | PO,TPP,NTPP | DC,EC | DC | EC |
| PO | DC,EC,PO, TPPi,NTPPi | DC,EC,PO, TPPi,NTPPi | DC,EC,PO,TPP, NTPP,TPPi, NTPPi,EQ | PO,TPP,NTPP | PO,TPP,NTPP | DC,EC,PO, TPPi,NTPPi | DC,EC,PO, TPPi,NTPPi | PO |
| TPP | DC | DC,EC | DC,EC,PO, TPP,NTPP | TPP,NTPP | NTPP | DC,EC,PO, TPP,NTPP | DC,EC,PO, TPPi,NTPPi | TPP |
| NTPP | DC | DC | DC,EC,PO, TPP,NTPP | NTPP | NTPP | DC,EC,PO, TPP,NTPP | DC,EC,PO TPP,NTPP, TPPi,NTPPi EQ | NTPP |
| TPPi | DC,EC,PO, TPPi,NTPPi | EC,PO, TPPi,NTPPi | PO,TPPi, NTPPi | EQ,PO,TPPi, NTPPi | PO,TPP,NTPP | TPPi,NTPPi | NTPPi | TPPi |
| NTPPi | DC,EC,PO, TPPi,NTPPi | PO,TPPi, NTPPi | PO,TPPi, NTPPi | PO,TPPi, NTPPi | PO,TPP,NTPP EQ,TPPi,NTPPi | NTPPi | NTPPi | NTPPi |
| EQ | DC | EC | PO | TPP | NTPP | TPPi | NTPPi | EQ |

*Table 2. Composition of 2D projection based direction relations*

| | N | NE | E | SE | S | SW | W | NW | Oc |
|---|---|---|---|---|---|---|---|---|---|
| N | N | N,NE | N,NE,E | N,NE,E,SE | N,NE,E,SE S, SW,W NW,Oc | W,NW, SW,N | NW,N,W | NW,N | N |
| NE | NE,N | NE | NE,E | E,NE,SE | E,NE, SE,S | N,NE,E,SES, SW, W,NW,Oc | N,NE, NW,W | N,NE,NW | NE |
| E | NE,E,N | NE,E | E | SE,E | SE,E,S | S,SW,SE E, | N,NE,E, SE,S, SW W,NW,Oc | N,NW, NE,E | E |
| SE | E,SE, NE,N | E,SE,NE | SE,E | SE | SE,S | S,SE,SW | S,SE,SW | N,NE,E,SE,S, SW,W,NW,Oc | SE |
| S | N,NE,E,SE,S SW,W NW,Oc | E,S,NE,SE | SE,E,S | SE,S | S | S,SW | S,W,SW | W,S,NW, SW | S |
| SW | W,SW N,NW | N,NE,E,SE,S SW,W NW,Oc | S,SW SE,E | S,SW,SE | SW,S | SW | SW,W | W,NW,SW | SW |
| W | N,W,NW | N,NW,NE W | N,NE,E,SE,S ,SW,W NW,Oc | S,SE,SW W | W,S,SW | W,SW | W | W,NW | W |
| NW | N,NW | N,NW,NE | N,NW,NE,E | N,NE,E,SES,SW,W, NW,Oc | W,NW,SW,S | W,NW, SW | NW,W | NW | NW |
| Oc | N | NE | E | SE | S | SW | W | NW | Oc |

of *E* and *NW* relations does not yield a unique relation as a result. Therefore, only a subset of the above table entries (27 in the case of RCC-8 relations and 49 in the case of projection based direction relations) can be used to infer other relations. If the directional relations "*front*," "*left*," "*right*," and "*behind*" are used then, the corresponding reasoning mechanism has to be used (Freksa, 1992). In this case determining the relation between two objects A and B does not determine the inverse relation holding between object B and A.

Figure 6. Static objects

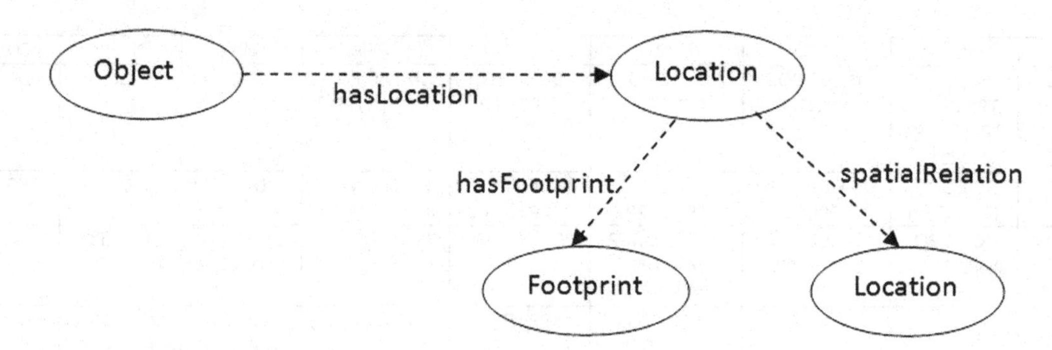


## Spatio-Temporal Ontology Representation

In the following, we show how spatial representations are combined with the prevailing temporal representation presented in the previous sections (the 4D fluent approach) into an integrated spatio-temporal ontology model. For the ease of presentation, we distinguish between application cases involving static or moving objects.

### Static Objects

Figure 6 illustrates a static object (i.e. objects without fluent properties) which is related with the *hasLocation* property with a *Location* object, which in turn is related with a footprint (Figure 2) or with other locations using user defined or footprint extracted relations (Figure 3).

### Dynamic Objects

In the case of dynamic objects whose location is static (i.e., although the objects do not change location, other properties of the object, e.g., the color of a house, may change) the location property must be defined at the static part of the ontology, as illustrated in Figure 7. Note that, the location of an object is represented using a single entry although multiple time slices of this object may exist.

In the case of moving objects, the *hasLocation* property applies to the *TimeSlice* class and not to the static object. It is also related to a corresponding time interval. This is illustrated in Figure 8. This is the most complicated case and refers to moving objects (i.e., objects whose position change) or events that evolve in space and time (i.e., taking place in different locations as time evolves).

Figure 9 illustrates the dynamic ontology schema representing the scenario "… from the city of Chania, John went to the city of Athens located further north."

In the above representation, the following temporal semantics hold:

- A spatial relation between two static objects holds at all times (e.g. the direction relation between two cities)
- A spatial relation between the location of a static object and a location of a *timeslice* object, holds for the time interval the timeslice holds true (e.g., if a ship is at a port for a given time interval then the inclusion topological relation between the ship and the port holds for that time interval only).
- A spatial relation between the locations of two timeslices holds as long as both timeslices hold true (i.e., for the time defined by the intersection of their corresponding time intervals, e.g., being passenger in a ship).

*Figure 7. Dynamic objects with static position*

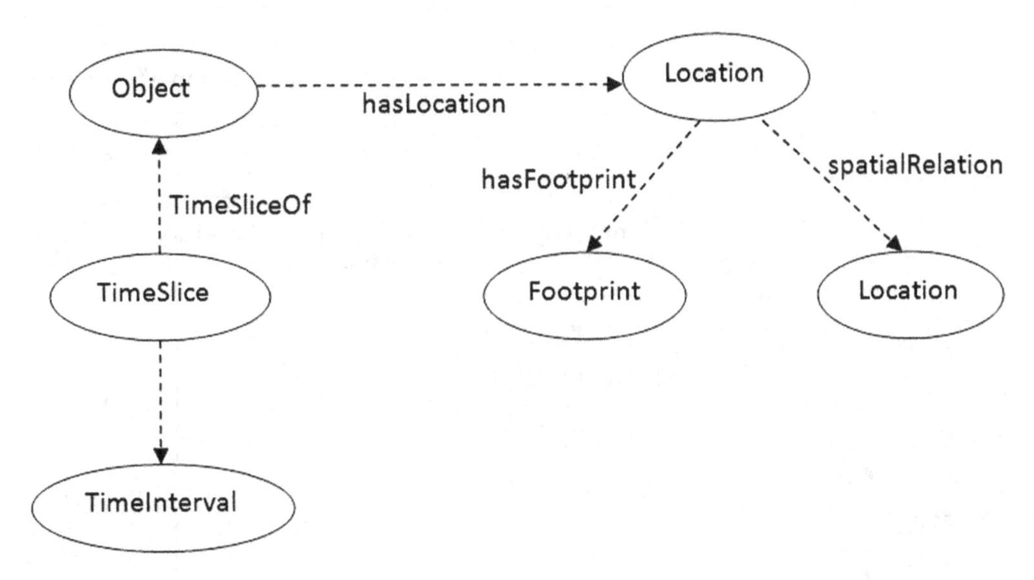


*Figure 8. Dynamic moving objects*

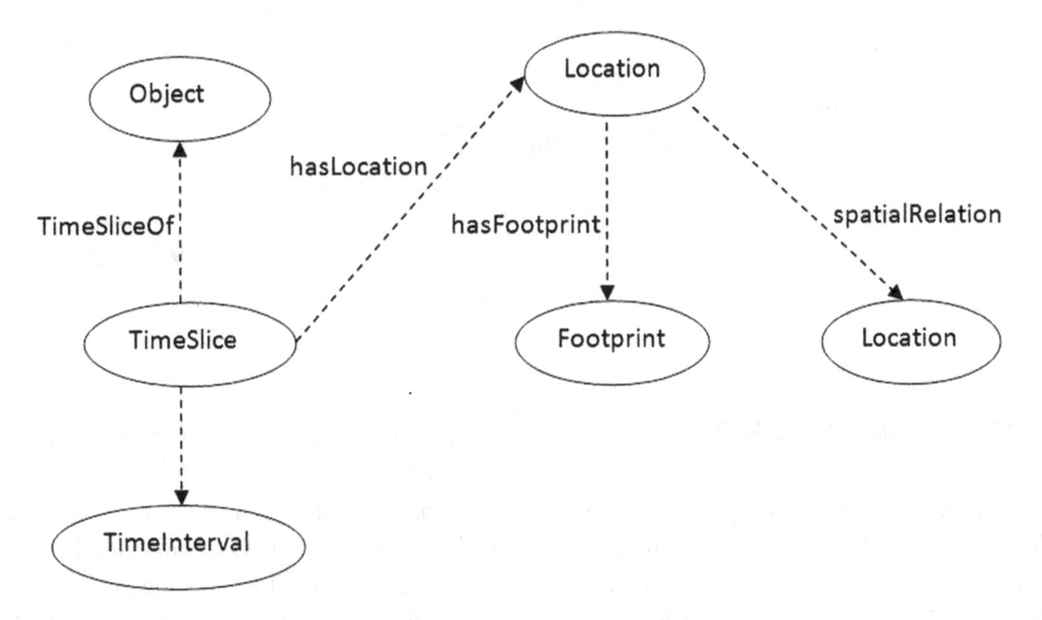


The *far* and *near* relations can be included in the representation model as user defined properties (i.e., the user can manually assert that the near or far relation holds between two objects). However, because they are application and scale dependent, automatic extraction is not suitable for a general-purpose representation. The point and MBR based representation can be used in the ontology as well, although specific applications might require more accurate location representations based on polygonal approximations of objects or regions (which however are more complicated than MBRs as the algorithms for extracting and handling such representations are computationally more involved).

*Figure 9. Instantiation example*

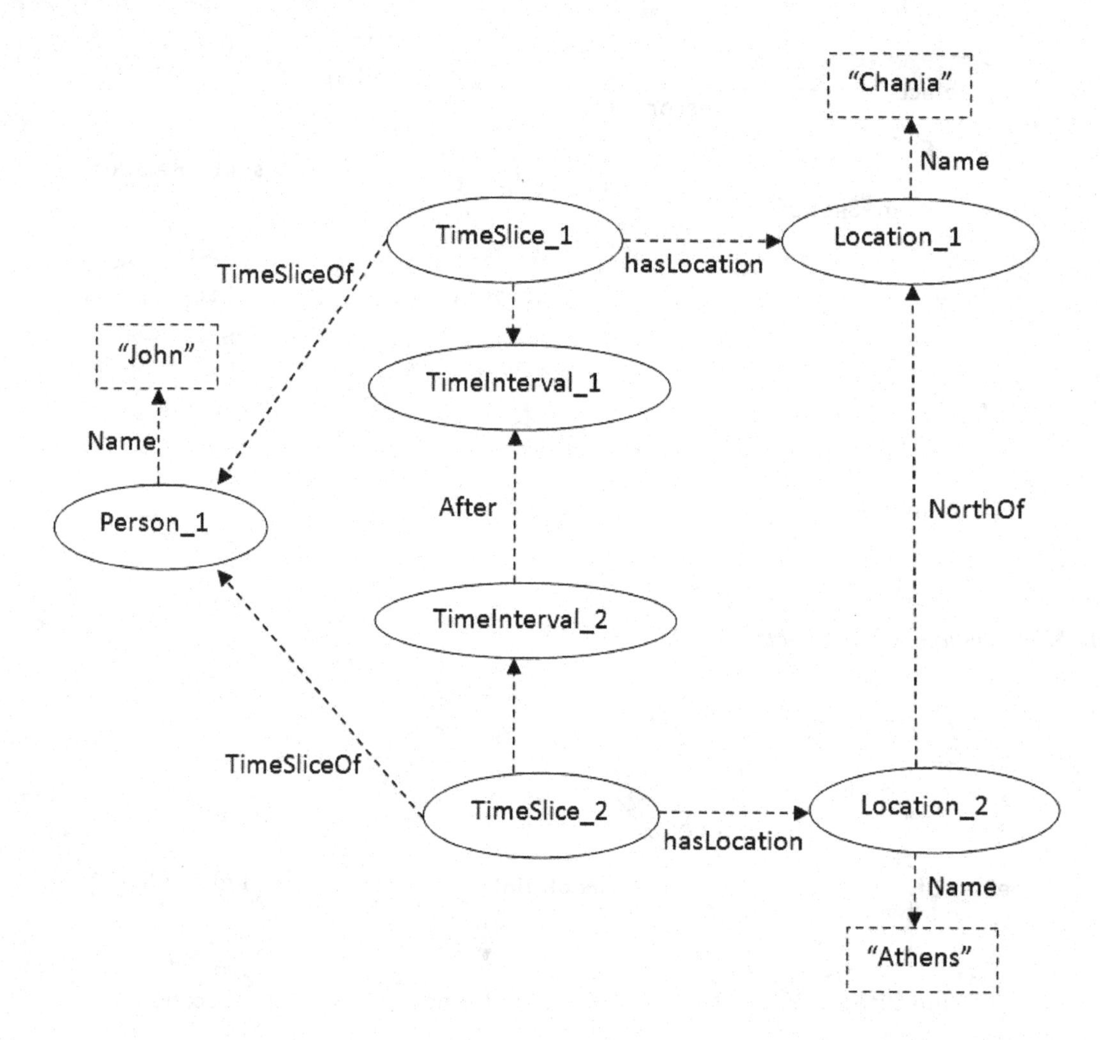


## FUTURE RESEARCH DIRECTIONS

Ontology representations of dynamic scene descriptions can be realized using a combination of existing temporal and spatial representations mechanisms. Crafting and instantiating such dynamic ontologies manually can be tedious and time consuming tasks that can be carried out only by domain experts. Instantiating information to a spatio-temporal ontology usually calls for application of information extraction (ACE, 2007) or text mining approaches (Camiano, 2006) for the extraction or recognition of concepts, events and locations (as the majority of information residing in information sources such as the Web is in textual form). Querying spatio-temporal information in ontologies using general-purpose Semantic Web query languages such as SPARQL and SeRQL leads to formation of complicated queries. Developing ontology query languages (or extending existing languages) for handling spatio-temporal information in ontologies is a direction of promising research (Baratis, Petrakis, Batsakis, Maris, & Papadakis, 2009).

## CONCLUSION

In this chapter, ontology approaches for representing static and dynamic scene contents are discussed. Example representations based on the 4-D fluent temporal representation mechanism combined with topological RCC-8 and projection based 2D directional relations are presented. The resulting ontology can be instantiated using both qualitative and quantitative information. Different types of temporal and spatial representations are all integrated into a unique spatio-temporal ontology representation capable of representing static, temporal, and both or combined spatio-temporal information. The proposed representation is a general purpose one, and is capable of representing temporal and spatial aspects of the events and of the objects involved in a scene.

## REFERENCES


Abdelmoty, A., Smart, P., Jones, C., Fu, G., & Finch, D. (2005). A critical evaluation of ontology languages for geographic information retrieval on the Internet. *Journal of Visual Languages and Computing, 16*(4), 331–358. doi:10.1016/j.jvlc.2004.11.001

Abraham, T., & Roddick, J. (1999). Survey of spatio-temporal databases. *GeoInformatica, 3*(1), 61–99. doi:10.1023/A:1009800916313

ACE. (2007). *The ACE evaluation plan: Evaluation of the detection and recognition of ACE entities, values, temporal expressions, relations and events, ver. 1.9*. Retrieved from http://www.nist.gov/speech/tests/ace/2007/index.html.

Andronikos, T., Stefanidakis, M., & Papadakis, I. (2009). Adding temporal dimension to ontologies via OWL reification. In *Proceedings of Panhellenic Conference on Informatics*, (pp. 19-22). Panhellenic Conference.

Arpinal, B., Sheth, A., Ramakrishnan, C., Usery, L., Azami, M., & Kwan, M.-P. (2006). Geospatial ontology development and semantic analytics. *Transactions in GIS, 10*(14), 551–575.

Artale, A., & Franconi, E. (2000). A survey of temporal extensions of description logics. *Annals of Mathematics and Artificial Intelligence, 30*(1-4), 171–210. doi:10.1023/A:1016636131405

Baratis, E., Petrakis, E. G., Batsakis, S., Maris, N., & Papadakis, N. (2009). TOQL: Temporal ontology querying language. In *Proceedings of the 11th International Symposium on Spatial and Temporal Databases (SSTD 2009)*, (pp. 338-354). SSTD.

Camiano, P. (2006). *Ontology learning and population from text: Algorithms, evaluation and applications*. London, UK: Springer.

Chen, H., Perich, F., Finin, T., & Joshi, A. (2004). Soupa: Standard ontology for ubiquitous and pervasive applications. In *Proceedings of International Conference on Mobile and Ubiquitous Multimedia (MOBIQUITOUS)*, (pp. 258-267). Baltimore, MD: MOBIQUITOUS.

Chen, J., Liu, D., Zhang, C., & Xie, Q. (2009). *Combinative reasoning with RCC5 and cardinal direction relations*. Berlin, Germany: Springer.

Cohn, A., & Hazarika, S. (2001). *Qualitative spatial representation and reasoning: An overview* (pp. 179–182). Berlin, Germany: Springer.

Dellis, E., & Paliouras, G. (2007). *Management of large spatial ontology bases*. Berlin, Germany: Springer.

Frank, A. (1996). Qualitative spatial reasoning: Cardinal directions as an example. *International Journal of Geographic Information Systems, 10*(3), 269–290.

Freksa, C. (1992). Using orientation information for qualitative spatial reasoning. In *Theories and Methods of Spatio-Temporal Reasoning in Geographic Space* (pp. 162–178). Springer. doi:10.1007/3-540-55966-3_10

Gregersen, H., & Jensen, C. (1999). Temporal entity-relationship models-a survey. *IEEE Transactions on Knowledge and Data Engineering, 11*(3), 464–497. doi:10.1109/69.774104

Grutter, R., & Bauer-Messmer, B. (2007). *Towards spatial reasoning in the semantic web: A hybrid knowledge representation system architecture* (pp. 349–364). Berlin, Germany: Springer.

Gutierrez, C., Hurtado, C., & Vaisman, A. (2007). Introducing time into RDF. *IEEE Transactions on Knowledge and Data Engineering, 19*(2), 207–218. doi:10.1109/TKDE.2007.34

Gutting, R. (1994). An introduction to spatial database systems. *The VLDB Journal, 3*, 357–399. doi:10.1007/BF01231602

Hayes, P., & Welty, C. (2006). Defining n-ary relations on the semantic web. *W3C Working Group*. Retrieved from http://www.w3.org/TR/swbp--n-aryRelations/.

Hazarika, J., & Roy, B. (2008). Semantic search of unstructured knowledge using qualitative analysis. *International Journal of Knowledge Management, 4*(2), 35–45. doi:10.4018/jkm.2008040103

Jones, C., Abdelmoty, A., Finch, D., Fu, G., & Vaid, S. (2004). *The SPIRIT search engine: Architecture, ontologies and spatial indexing*. Berlin, Germany: Springer.

Katz, Y., & Grau, B. (2005). Representing qualitative spatial information in OWL-DL. In *Proceedings of International Workshop: OWL Experiences and Directions*. Galway, Ireland: OWL.

Klein, M., & Fensel, D. (2001). Ontology versioning for the semantic web. In *Proceedings of International Semantic Web Working Symposioum (SWWS 2001)*, (pp. 75-92). SWWS.

Li, J., Ozsu, M., Szafron, D., & Oria, V. (1997). MOQL: A multimedia object query language. In *Proceedings of the 3rd International Workshop on Multimedia Information Systems*, (pp. 19-28). Multimedia Information Systems.

Liu, Y., & Hao, Z. (2005). The cardinal direction relations and the rectangle algebra. In *Proceedings of International Workshop on Machine Learning and Cybernetics*, (pp. 3115-3118). Machine Learning and Cybernetics.

Lutz, C., Wolter, F., & Zakharyaschev, M. (2008). Temporal description logics: A survey. In *Proceedings of International Conference on Temporal Representation and Reasoning (TIME 2008)*, (pp. 3-14). TIME.

Ozsoyoglu, G., & Snodgrass, R. (1995). Temporal and real-time databases: A survey. *IEEE Transactions on Knowledge and Data Engineering, 7*(4), 513–532. doi:10.1109/69.404027

Petrakis, E. G. (2002). Fast retrieval by spatial structure in image databases. *Journal of Visual Languages and Computing, 13*(5), 545–569. doi:10.1006/jvlc.2002.0233

Petrakis, E. G. (2002a). Design and evaluation of spatial similarity approaches for image retrieval. *Image and Vision Computing, 20*(1), 59–76. doi:10.1016/S0262-8856(01)00077-4

Randell, D., Cui, Z., & Cohn, A. (1992). A spatial logic based on regions and connection. In *Proceedings of the 3rd International Conference on Knowledge Representation and Reasoning*, (pp. 165-176). San Mateo, CA: Morgan Kaufmann.

Renz, J., & Nebel, B. (2007). Qualitative spatial reasoning using constraint calculi. In *Handbook of Spatial Logics* (pp. 161–215). Springer. doi:10.1007/978-1-4020-5587-4_4

Sheth, A., Arpinar, I., Perry, M., & Hakimpour, F. (2009). Geospatial and temporal semantic analytics. In Karimi, H. A. (Ed.), *Handbook of Research in Geoinformatics*. Hershey, PA: IGI Global.

Wang, X., Zhang, D., Gu, T., & Pung, H. (2004). Ontology based context modeling and reasoning using OWL. In *Proceedings of the Second IEEE Conference on Pervasive Computing and Communications Workshops.* Orlando, FL: IEEE Press.

Welty, C., & Fikes, R. (2006). A reusable ontology for fluents in OWL. In *Proceedings of International Conference on Formal Ontology in Information Systems (FOIS-2006),* (pp. 226-236). FOIS.

Worboys, M., & Hornby, K. (2004). From objects to events: GEM, the geospatial event model. In *Proceedings of International Conference on GIScience 2004,* (pp. 327-344). Springer Verlag.

# Chapter 11
# Qualitative Spatial Reasoning for Applications:
## New Challenges and the SparQ Toolbox

**Diedrich Wolter**
*Universität Bremen, Germany*

**Jan Oliver Wallgrün**
*Universität Bremen, Germany*

## ABSTRACT

*About two decades ago, the field of Qualitative Spatial and Temporal Reasoning (QSTR) emerged as a new area of AI research that set out to grasp human-level understanding and reasoning about spatial and temporal entities, linking formal approaches to cognitive theories. Empowering artificial agents with QSTR capabilities is claimed to facilitate manifold applications, including robot navigation, Geographic Information Systems (GIS), natural language understanding, and computer-aided design. QSTR is an active field of research that has developed many representation and reasoning approaches so far, but only comparatively few applications exist that actually build on these QSTR techniques.*

*This chapter approaches QSTR from an application perspective. Considering the exemplary application domains of robot navigation, GIS, and computer-aided design, the authors conclude that reasoning must be interpreted in a broader sense than the often-considered constraint-based reasoning and that supporting tools must become available. The authors then discuss the newly identified reasoning tasks and how they can be supported by QSTR toolboxes to foster the dissemination of QSTR in applications. Furthermore, the authors explain how they aim to overcome the lack-of-tools dilemma through the development of the QSTR toolbox SparQ.*

DOI: 10.4018/978-1-61692-868-1.ch011

## 1. INTRODUCTION

Qualitative Spatial and Temporal Reasoning (QSTR) (Cohn & Hazarika, 2001; Cohn & Renz, 2007; Renz & Nebel, 2007) is the subfield of knowledge representation and symbolic reasoning that deals with knowledge about an infinite spatio-temporal domain using a finite set of *qualitative relations*. One particular aim is to model human common-sense understanding of space. Qualitative approaches have therefore been promoted as a basis for connecting human cognition and intelligent agents. Moreover, qualitative approaches offer compact representations that are supposed to enable complex decision tasks. However, despite these rationales, we still observe a lack of success stories of QSTR in the sense of successful applications that make use of QSTR, or, ultimately, applications that are successful *because* they make use of QSTR.

In this chapter, we explore qualitative reasoning from an application oriented point of view. One possible reason for the comparatively small number of QSTR applications could be seen in a lack of adequate software toolboxes which provide the results of QSTR research in a form which enables application developers to incorporate QSTR techniques easily into their own software. Throughout the last years, first QSTR toolboxes have started to emerge (e.g., GQR [Gantner, Westphal, & Wölfl, 2008], QAT [Condotta, Ligozat, & Saade, 2006], and our own toolbox SparQ [Wallgrün, Frommberger, Wolter, Dylla, & Freksa, 2007]). However, so far these efforts have been very much concentrated on the problem of deciding satisfiability of sets of qualitative constraints. This emphasis on what we will term *constraint-based reasoning* is easily understandable because, technically speaking, qualitative relations constrain the valuation of variables and, hence, deciding satisfiability has been in the center of theoretical research in QSTR during the last two decades. Contrary to classical constraint-based techniques, QSTR has pursued a purely relation algebraic approach: qualitative relations and operations on them constitute a qualitative calculus (Ligozat & Renz, 2004) and the operations provide a symbolic approach to deciding consistency (Renz & Nebel, 2007)[1].

One thesis underlying this work is that qualitative reasoning goes beyond constraint-based reasoning and, hence, different forms of reasoning need to be supported by the toolboxes. To corroborate this claim we look at three potential application domains of QSTR, namely the areas of robot navigation, Geographic Information Systems (GIS), and computer-aided design. Our goal is to identify which kind of qualitative reasoning is required to solve the individual problems of spatial knowledge processing occurring in these domains and our conclusion will be that constraint-based satisfiability testing often only plays a minor role.

Based on this result, we organize the newly identified reasoning tasks into groups and discuss how well they are currently understood, how they need to be supported in QSTR toolboxes, and what kind of theoretical research is still required. We then provide a glimpse at our own QSTR toolbox SparQ which we are developing with the goal of providing an easy-to-use interface to a rich repository of qualitative calculi and reasoning methods. In particular, we describe to which extent SparQ already supports some of the newly identified reasoning tasks and sketch its future development.

While the focus of this chapter will be on different kinds of reasoning tasks where reasoning is interpreted in a rather broad sense, there are clearly other issues involved that would improve the dissemination of QSTR techniques and toolboxes, e.g., representational aspects and integration with other AI methodology. We will address some of these points in the final section of this text containing conclusions and an outlook.

The chapter is organized as follows. In Section 2 we look at the different kinds of reasoning tasks occurring in the previously mentioned application domains. In Section 3 we classify and discuss the newly identified reasoning tasks. Our own toolbox

SparQ will then be presented in Section 4, followed by conclusions and an outlook in Section 5.

## 2. THREE APPLICATION AREAS FOR QSTR

Three application domains which are often cited as natural application areas for qualitative spatial reasoning are robot navigation, Geographic Information Systems (GIS), and computer-aided design (see, among others Cohn & Hazarika, 2001; Cohn & Renz, 2007; Egenhofer & Mark, 1995; Bhatt, Dylla, & Hois, 2009). We will see that distinct spatial reasoning tasks can be identified and most of them appear throughout all of the three application areas.

### 2.1. QSTR and Mobile Robot Navigation

Being able to move through the environment and successfully reach a particular goal location is a fundamental ability for mobile robots as they are currently being developed for, e.g., service or autonomous exploration tasks. Navigation essentially is concerned with three questions (Levitt & Lawton, 1990): "Where am I?" "Where are other places relative to me?" and "How do I get to other places from here?" Two important problems distinguished in robotics are *self-localization* (determining one's position wrt. to an internal representation of the environment) and *map learning* (autonomously acquiring such an internal model of an initially unknown environment). In the following we look at these tasks individually. We also examine the emerging application field of language-based *human-robot interaction* where one would like to be able to communicate with robots using spatial concepts and natural language descriptions.

#### 2.1.1. Self-Localization

For goal-directed navigation, a robot needs to be able to localize itself within its own spatial representation of the environment, also termed its *map*. This task requires the robot to recognize locations in the map from observations made within the environment. Two principle approaches have been pursued: searching for a robot location within the map that would explain the robot's observation best (see, e.g., Fox, Burgard, & Thrun, 1999) or searching the map for the features observed (see, e.g., Castellanos, Neira, & Tardós, 2006). In the following we subscribe to the feature-based approach which makes self-localization a two-step process: First, the correct correspondences between objects currently perceived by the robot and objects in the map need to be established. The problem of finding the correct associations is often referred to as the *correspondence problem* or the *data association problem* (Bar-Shalom & Fortmann, 1988; Grimson, 1990; Neira & Tardós, 2001). Second, the location of the robot is determined based on its spatial relation with respect to the perceived objects.

Evaluating all potential correspondences between the objects observed and those stored in the map easily results in combinatorial explosion, so it can be beneficial to consider qualitative spatial relations among the objects to constrain data association, thereby enhancing efficiency (Wallgrün, 2010; Wolter, 2008). Qualitative relations constitute robust relations that are insensitive to measurement noise and, consequentially, can be utilized as hard constraints to restrict the search space of possible correspondences. An example for such a relation can be "left of" (Wolter, Freksa, & Latecki, 2008), or landmark panoramas (Schlieder, 1993) based on cyclic order. Exploiting qualitative constraints in robot self-localization comprises four tasks that are illustrated in Figure 1: First, the relations between all objects in the map are interpreted in terms of qualitative spatial relations (this only needs to be done once) and, in the second

*Figure 1. Four steps in exploiting qualitative relations in robot-self-localization*

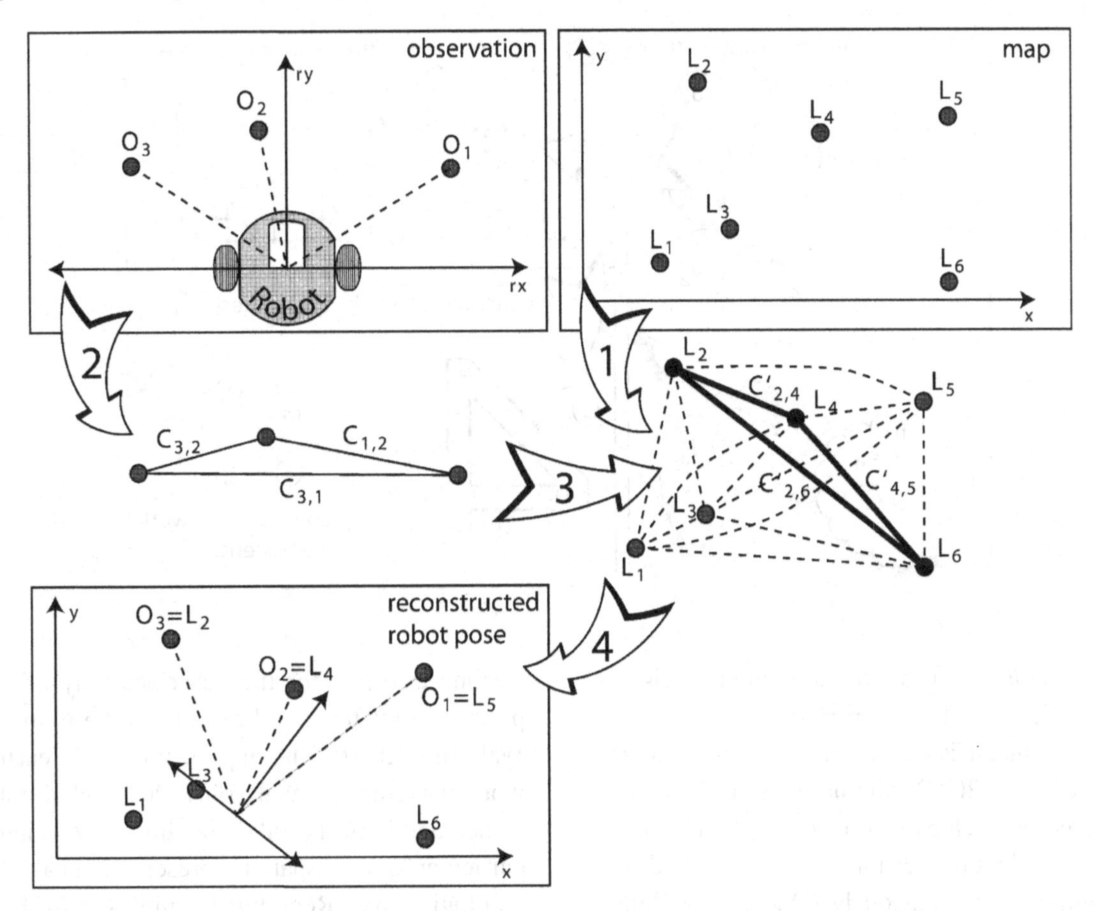


step, the same is done with the local observation. We obtain two qualitative constraint networks which are represented as graphs, one representing the map, and the other one representing the observation. In the third step the correspondence problem would be tackled by finding a subgraph of the map isomorphic to the one obtained from the observation such that both graphs share the same constraint labels. However, one has to take into account that we might perceive objects for the first time and as a result they will not be contained in the map yet. Hence, we actually are looking for the largest common subgraph of the constraint graphs generated from observation and map which, under general assumptions, yields the most likely matchings between observation and map.

### 2.1.2. Map Learning

The task of autonomously acquiring a map of the environment is called map learning, robot mapping, or the Simultaneous Localization and Mapping (SLAM) problem (Thrun, 2002; Leonard & Durrant-Whyte, 1991; Castellanos, et al., 2006). A significant part of map learning of course is localization as discussed above in order to allow the robot to register new parts of the environment at the right position with respect to the parts already mapped. The resulting map will only be correct if the data association decisions made are correct. However, one cannot assume that the correct associations are made in every localization performed during the mapping process. One approach to deal with errors in the

*Figure 2. Topological map learning using qualitative direction information and consistency checking*

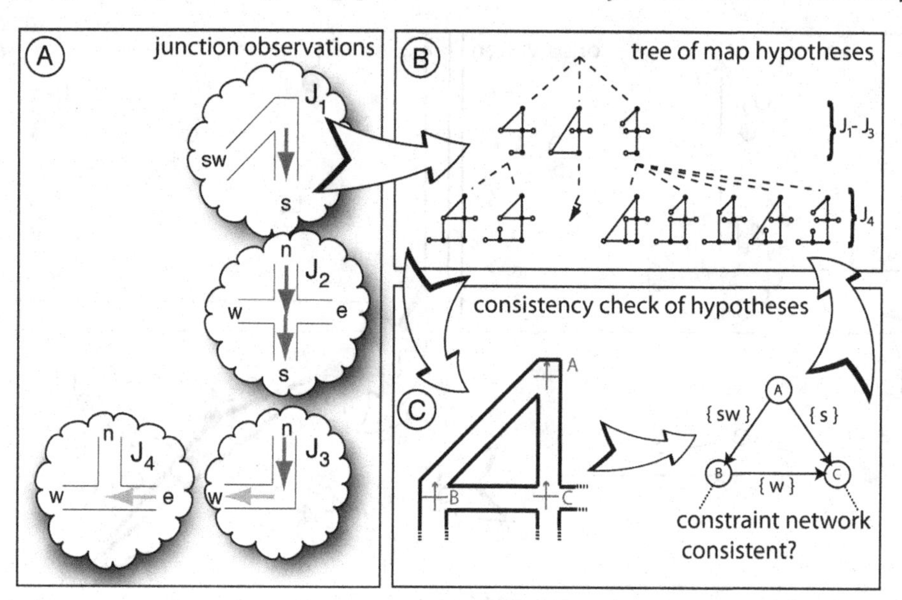


data associations is to retract previous decisions when they lead to a map representation that is spatially inconsistent (Hähnel, Burgard, Wegbreit, & Thrun, 2003). Alternatively, different map hypotheses, each based on a particular history of data association decisions, can be tracked and maintained simultaneously (Dudek, Freedman, & Hadjres, 1996; Kuipers, Modayil, Beeson, MacMahon, & Savelli, 2004). Whenever one of the map hypotheses becomes inconsistent, that is the perceived spatial relations holding between the objects cannot be satisfied for the data association decisions made, this hypothesis can be discarded. However, for both approaches it is crucial that the information on which the decision to discard a map hypothesis is based can be assumed to be perceivable reliably. For instance, in the approach tracking multiple hypotheses, we would want to make sure that we do not discard the correct hypothesis because a precise metric relation does not hold due to sensor noise. This is where map learning can benefit from employing qualitative relations and, as a result, QSTR approaches for deciding the consistency of a map hypothesis are valuable.

One example for the described way of applying QSTR for map learning can be found in Wallgrün (2009). The approach extends earlier work of Moratz and Wallgrün (2003) and Moratz, Nebel, and Freksa (2003) and aims at learning a particular kind of spatial representation called a topological map (Remolina & Kuipers, 2004, Kuipers, 2000) from coarse but reliably perceivable spatial relations (see Figure 2 for an illustration). A topological map is a graph-based representation in which the nodes stand for relevant places (e.g., junctions) and the edges connect adjacent places (e.g. they stand for hallways). The exploration history of the robot consists of junction observations and hallway traversal actions (Figure 2a). The perceived directions of leaving hallways are mapped to qualitative direction relations from a qualitative direction calculus which can then be treated as reliable information. Instead of maintaining a single map, multiple map hypotheses are tracked simultaneously as illustrated in Figure 2b. This results in a search tree of map hypotheses that represent different data association decisions made. Consistency checking based on the direction information contained in the individual hypotheses using standard QSTR techniques is then employed to discard invalid hypotheses (Figure 2c).

Approaches in which qualitative spatial relations are used as reliably perceivable constraints but for representations based on landmarks have for instance been discussed in Moratz (2009) and Steinhauer (2008).

### 2.1.3. Human-Robot Communication

One application researched in the field of robotics is to develop service robots which co-exist within a human society. Service robots are supposed to take orders from humans and, in some cases, report back to humans, or request more information to resolve ambiguities. In these scenarios, being able to communicate spatial information is a key capability. Among the multitude of modalities that can be employed in a human-robot interface, natural language is possibly the most desirable one. In order to interpret spatial information captured in natural language expressions, formal models of spatial relations and reference systems are required—the ability to handle relative spatial information is of great importance (Moratz & Tenbrink, 2006). In order to interpret relative spatial information it is necessary to change the frame of reference accordingly, e.g., "to the left" from the instructor's perspective translates "to the right" for an opposing robot. Such perspective changes can be realized with the help of the permutation operations (e.g., converse) defined in a qualitative calculus. We refer to these simple reasoning steps as *computing with relations*.

Considering the ability of a robot to communicate spatial information to a human, the use of qualitative relations is also advantageous. If we consider route descriptions that incrementally relate landmarks as, for example, "after turning right at the intersection the hardware store is to the left," constraint-based qualitative reasoning techniques become necessary to integrate information relative to path segments into a coherent whole. An example of using path integration of spatial knowledge for robot instruction can be found in Krieg-Brückner and Shi (2006). Ultimately, methods are required that allow a robot to find its way and recognize the goal position it has been requested to move to purely based on natural language expression. Thus, robot instruction involves a generalized form of self-localization that localizes the robot with respect to a location description (Wolter, et al., 2008).

## 2.2. QSTR and GIS

Another application area well-suited for qualitative representations and reasoning is that of Geographic Information Systems (GIS) which we approach in a general sense such as to comprise spatial data infrastructures, location-based service, etc. A typical GIS provides means to store, update, query, analyze, and visualize geospatial information (Burrough, 1986). A typical modern GIS stores spatial information quantitatively using either a vector-based approach or a raster-based approach (Winter, 1998). In the vector-based approach, different kind of geometries (line, point, polygon, etc.) can be used to describe the spatial extension of each object. There exist, however, several reasons why one would like to extend traditional GIS with the ability to directly store and process qualitative spatial relations. For instance, one could have one of the following situations:

- There is only qualitative information available, for instance innformation stemming from a sensor that can only distinguish certain qualities.
- Information is provided by a human—being able to use qualitative relations in queries or when feeding information to the system makes the interface more convenient and intuitive.
- Only imprecise information shall be provided about a location due to privacy concerns (Duckham & Kulik, 2005).

- Only the qualitative information can be assumed to be reliable, for instance when the information is extracted from a sketch map (Lovett, Dehghani, & Forbus, 2007).
- Only distinguishing categories that make a difference will increase the efficiency of an analysis or the spatial reasoning that needs to be performed.

Qualitative spatial representation and reasoning formalisms have always been of interest in geographic information science following the idea of a naive geography (Egenhofer & Mark, 1995) which is concerned with formal models of human common-sense reasoning about geographic space. While there exists a significant amount of theoretical research, for instance regarding consistency of topological relations in a multi-layer representation (Egenhofer, Clementini, & Felice, 1994; Belussi, Catania, & Podestà, 2005), very little of this work has found its way into existing GISs. Support for qualitative spatial representation and reasoning here is still mostly limited to realizing a set of topological predicates based on a topological formalism like the 9-intersection model (Egenhofer, 1989) or RCC-8 (Randell, Cui, & Cohn, 1992), e.g., relations like contains, overlaps, etc., as extensions of query languages such as SQL (Egenhofer, 1994; OpenGIS Consortium, 1999). When used for querying, the qualitative relations holding between objects are computed from the objects' geometries every time they are needed.

In the following we will look more closely at what kinds of demands for qualitative reasoning and representations methods arise from different subareas of the GIS domain. Although temporal aspects are also of great importance in GIS, we focus on aspects of spatial reasoning in our discussion. The identified tasks and approaches can in most cases be directly transferred to the temporal domain.

*Figure 3. Three steps in querying GIS databases qualitatively*

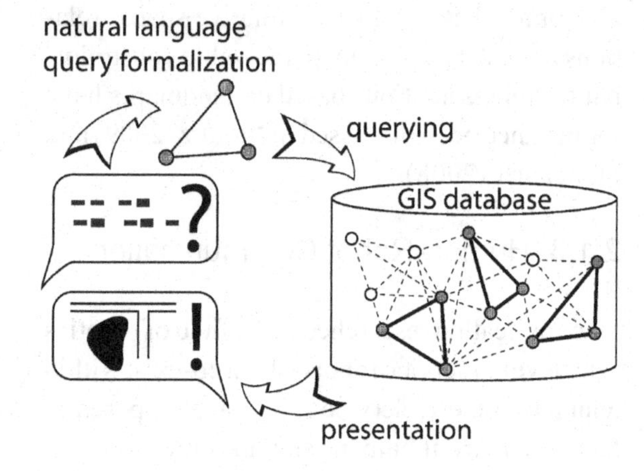


## 2.2.1. Query Processing

In many application scenarios, it is more natural for human users to pose queries in a qualitative way, e.g., by using a natural language interface (see Figure 3). A natural language query such as "give me all camping sites north of lake Constance which are directly at the lakeside but also close to a town" first has to be formalized using spatial relations from a qualitative calculus (cmp. Section 2.1.3). The result can be seen as a constraint network $Q$ with three objects $C$ (camping site), $L$ (lake), $T$ (town) and the constraints.

$C$(north_of, externally_connected_to,*)$L$

$C$(*, *, close_to) $T$

The constraints here are triples of relations from the three individual calculi used in the query: a cardinal direction calculus, a topological calculus based on RCC-8, and a proximity calculus. The '*' stands for the universal relations of the respective calculus. In an information system in which this kind of queries are common, it makes sense to store qualitative relations explicitly to avoid the additional costs of having to compute the qualitative information from the geometries every time and to provide special data structures in order to increase the efficiency of query processing. Hence, we can regard the spatial database as a large constraint network *D* in which the constraints consist of relations from several qualitative calculi. Query answering can then be seen as the subgraph isomorphism problem of finding all occurences of *Q* in *D*. This task is similar to what we discussed in the Section 2.1 regarding localization except that here we are looking for complete instances of *Q* rather than largest subgraphs of *Q* in *D*.

### 2.2.2. Similarity Assessment

The description in the previous section assumes that the result of a query is given in form of all instances that are subsumed by the query. However, often one would prefer to query by example and look for instances that are most similar to the query. For querying spatial configurations, similarity could involve several things: similarity between the concepts involved, similarity of object instance, or the similarity of the spatial relations holding between the objects. The problem of assessing the semantic similarity between concepts or objects has recently received increasing attention (Rodrguez & Egenhofer, 2004; Schwering, 2008; Janowicz, Raubal, Schwering, & Kuhn, 2008). With regard to qualitative spatial relations, one idea is to assess the similarity of two relations based on the notion of conceptual neighborhood (Freksa, 1991, 1992) by considering the distance between base relations in the conceptual neighborhood graph (Bruns & Egenhofer, 1996; Dylla & Wallgrün, 2007). The concrete conceptual neighborhood structure depends on the concrete set of continuous transformations we assume (Freksa, 1991; Dylla & Wallgrün, 2007) which in turn need to be grounded in spatial change over time (Galton, 2000). This approach can be extended to measure the similarity of complete spatial configurations which would allow to find the most similar spatial configuration to a given configuration or to generate similar configurations to a given one. As an overall goal, one would like to integrate techniques for assessing the different kinds of similarities (concept-concept, instance-instance, relation-relation) into a single general framework able to take all these aspects of similarity into account when processing a query.

### 2.2.3. Data Integration

The problem of data integration occurs in many GIS applications (Fonseca, Egenhofer, Agouris, & Câmara, 2002, Duckham & Worboys, 2005, Bittner, Donnelly, & Smith, 2009). Databases may need to be merged to create a new single knowledge base or data from different spatial data infrastructures should be combined on the fly in order to solve a particular task. Typically, the integration task comprises several subproblems:

- semantic alignment of the involved concepts
- identifying corresponding entities across different data sets
- determining conflicts between the different data sets
- resolving or managing these conflicts in a suitable way
- merging the data into a single representation

Focusing on the processing of qualitative knowledge required to solve these subproblems, we can identify several crucial issues: When combining information from different sources, we might be faced with the problem of having to merge qualitative information given in terms of different spatial calculi. To have a theoretical basis for this merging step, we need to know how the relations from different calculi are related with each other and how they constrain each other. In short: a combined calculus is needed to make sure that no information is lost and that all potential conflicts are discovered. It would be desirable if a suitable combined calculus could be constructed automatically based on a semantic description of the relations of the involved calculi. The result would again be the semantic descriptions of the relations of the combined calculus together with relevant operations like the composition. On the other hand, when we are combining information that is partially qualitative and partially quantitative, the quantitative information must first be transferred to the qualitative level before the real combination step can take place.

Automatically determining the correspondences between the databases to be merged poses the same problem we discussed in the localization scenario, namely finding a largest common subgraph between the databases which is isomorphic. This subgraph would then yield the correspondences between objects contained in both data sets and the objects which are only contained in one of them. However, unless the conceptual information available about the objects in the databases is very restrictive, it is unlikely that an automatic process will be able to always determine the correct correspondences. Hence, we imagine this will rather be a semi-automatic process in which a user verifies and corrects the result of the automatic matching.

Once the gaps on the qualitative level are filled and the correspondences are established, the information can be combined. Combining can be seen as the task of merging qualitative constraint networks. However, it is possible that the information to be merged is conflicting and, hence, simply taking the intersections over all constraints will result in an inconsistent constraint network. Discovering these conflicts is an application of standard constraint-based reasoning. However, in many applications one would like to also be able to resolve conflicts that occur by relaxing the constraints in the original data sets in a meaningful way (Dylla & Wallgrün, 2007; Condotta, Kaci, & Schwind, 2008). For instance, a common-sense approach would be to look for constraint networks which are most similar to the original networks but yield a consistent network when they are combined. As discussed in Section 2.2.2, a notion of similarity between constraint networks can be derived based on the distance of base relations in a conceptual neighborhood graph.

### 2.2.4. Spatial Analysis

GISs provide many different ways to analyze spatial data and processes including explanation and interpolation, simulation and prediction, and planning (Smith, Goodchild, & Longley, 2007). Performing these tasks on a qualitative level, it is possible to only consider the distinctions that make a difference. This increases the efficiency and simplifies the interpretation of the results by humans (Kuipers, 1994). The basic component that is needed is a way to describe potential transitions between qualitative configurations of more than two objects. As discussed in Section 2.2.2, conceptual neighborhood distance can be used to achieve this. The result is a generalized neighborhood graph as described by Ragni and Wölfl (2005) in which the nodes stand for consistent scenarios and the edges connect conceptually neighbored scenarios.

Given such a generalized neighborhood graph or a way to generate the adjacent scenarios for a given scenario, different possible temporal developments can be predicted and simulated straightforwardly. An example of this general approach is the work described in Cohn et al. (1997) about simulating phagocytosis and exocytosis in unicellular organisms using the RCC-8 relations.

In a similar way explanation of spatial processes can be realized via interpolation between a set of static snapshots which could explain what has happened in between. Interpolating between two spatial snapshots—which we again can imagine as constraint networks—would mean to find a sequence of scenarios which leads from the start scenario to the goal scenario. Given a generalized conceptual neighborhood graph, we can look for the shortest path connecting the snapshots as

*Figure 4. Quantification determines a model for a qualitative constraint network that can be used for visualization*

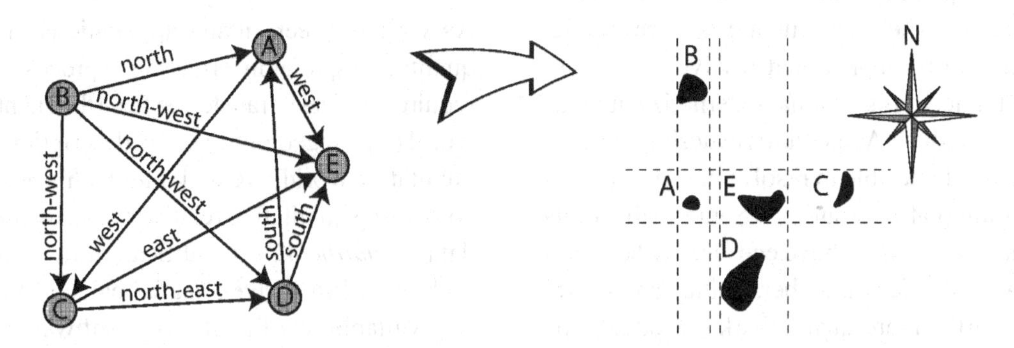


the "simplest" explanation of what could have occurred. The same approach can be employed for planning where the snapshots are replaced by start and goal scenarios (Ragni & Wölfl, 2006).

### 2.2.5. Visualization

A main task of a GIS is providing flexible ways to visualize the stored data and the intermediate steps during a spatial analysis (Hearnshaw & Unwin, 1994). For most kind of geometric data, visualization is unproblematic and research is more focused on how to adapt the visualization to meet the implicit demands of the user. For qualitative information the situation is more complicated but nevertheless we want to be able to produce visualizations even when parts or all information is given qualitatively. As an example application, let us consider a location-based system which accepts inputs about the user's location relative to some prominent buildings in the following form: "I am facing the cathedral and there is a fountain to my left and a street to my right." The location-based system is supposed to generate a you-are-here-map for the qualitatively described position of the user.

Applications of this kind require a way to derive new information from a mixture of quantitative and qualitative information and to generate a quantitative scene description (e.g., a drawing or a map) from a qualitative scene description or even from a mixed qualitative-quantitative scene description. A first step in this direction would be the ability to compute one exemplary quantitative solution for a qualitative scenario as shown in Figure 4. To deal with general constraint networks including disjunctions of base relations, one would then need to extend this approach, for instance by presenting one exemplary solution for each consistent qualitative scenario to the user or by providing ways to navigate through the solution space.

## 2.3. QSTR and Computer-Aided Design

Qualitative representation and reasoning can be important in the area of computer assistance in design processes, particularly by providing means to handle design constraints. Concrete tasks in computer-aided design that involve QSTR range from formal specification of design constraints to model checking and construction of solutions that are admissible with respect to the design constraints. Qualitative relations are valuable from on an early stage of engineering and architectural design processes, as they enable representation of uncertain knowledge which is common in early stages of a design (Schultz, Amor, Lobb, & Guesgen, 2009). Based on a formalization of design constraints, model-checking can be performed with (partially) existing designs; qualitative methods would be used in conjunction with a general logical formalism (Bhatt, et al., 2009). In situations where designs are not acceptable, methods can be applied that resolve conflicting constraint networks and that externalize qualitative knowledge. A qualitative design-support system would be able to resolve conflicts and to suggest alternative solutions. Some realizations of the ideas sketched above can already be found in the work of Richter, Weber, Bojduj, and Bertel (2011). Furthermore, qualitative knowledge helps to assess the complexity of building layouts from a wayfinder's point of view (Bojduj, Weber, Richter, & Bertel, 2008) which then can be used to design environments that ease wayfinding tasks.

Summing up, there are several QSTR reasoning tasks can provide assistance in design processes. For checking the consistency of a design with respect to design constraints, quantitative data has to be interpreted qualitatively (qualification) and constraint network have to be compared. Given that some design constraints are not met, relaxation of conflicting constraints helps to construct an admissible design on the qualitative level. By graphically externalizing the qualitative information (quantification), concrete design recommendations can be made in an easily comprehensible way.

## 3. QSTR SUPPORT FOR APPLICATIONS

In our inspection of the three application areas in the previous section, we identified a large potential for qualitative representation and reasoning approaches. However, several services required in these applications were not directly based on traditional constraint-based reasoning which has been the focus of theoretical research and development of reasoning software over the last two decades. In this section, we summarize and structure the identified services by dividing them into six groups.

### 3.1. Qualification

As we have seen, many applications in which qualitative spatial information is processed, first require that data is transferred from the quantitative world (e.g., a geometric scene description) to the qualitative world. We will refer to this process of computing qualitative relations from quantitative data as *qualification*. Qualification always occurs with regard to a given spatial calculus defining the available set of relations. A software module performing qualification for a particular calculus $C$ will be called a *qualifier for* $C$.

Typically, one would expect to obtain a consistent scenario as the result of qualification, i.e., the qualitative scene description would contain only base relations of $C$ which hold between the objects and the obtained constraint network is consistent. However, this task is challenging in two regards.

First, unavoidable rounding errors which occur in processing floating point numbers complicate the interpretation of data provided as floating point values. Floating point values discretize a continuous domain. As a consequence, for calculi which define exact relations like point coinciding with lines, it may be impossible to decide whether the data supplied is *meant* to be related by an exact relation. Thus, mapping floating point values to qualitative labels may introduce misinterpretations and, henceforth, the obtained constraint network may be inconsistent. It remains an open problem to efficiently determine a consistent qualitative constraint network only using atomic relations such that the constraint network optimally fits to the supplied data.

Second, any data obtained from sensors is affected by measurement noise. Thus, we cannot interpret the data as true information but we must also consider possible deviations of the values. As a consequence, it may not be possible to interpret object relationships in terms of base relations. Instead, we obtain a constraint network that includes (some) disjunctive relations. We illustrate the effects of measurement noise in an example

*Figure 5. Mapping noisy data to qualitative information: (a) probability distribution of measured point position, (b) cardinal direction relations, and (c) possible interpretation into qualitative information*

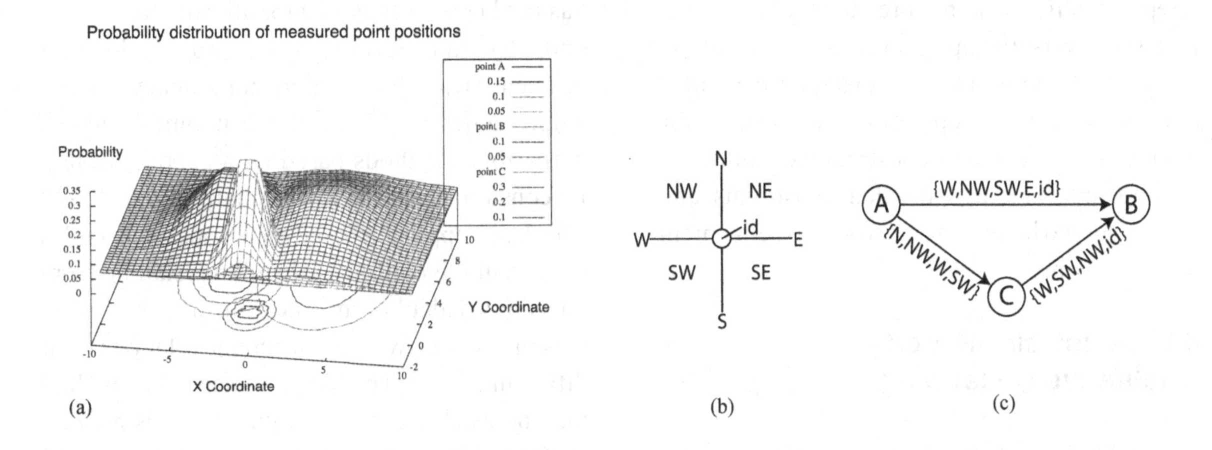


using the cardinal direction calculus (Frank, 1991; Ligozat, 1998) depicted in Figure 5. In the figure we can observe an actual challenge of qualifying data that is subject to noise: devising an efficient algorithm that enumerates all base relations that can hold between the objects. Difficulty arises from the need to evaluate all values from a continuous, hence, infinite set of values.

To our knowledge, these issues have not been tackled so far. If we do not consider noise in the input data, implementing a specific qualifier is rather straightforward. We note that no actual programming is required if the qualitative relations can be specified in a formal framework—a unified qualifier module can then match geometric scene descriptions to the formal specifications, identifying which relation holds. For example, for calculi over points in the plane or more generally in $n$-dimensional Euclidean space it is typically sufficient to check a set of criteria given in terms of (in)equality equations for each base relation (e.g., Euclidean distance of points or angles). In conclusion, providing a reasonable qualifier is not as trivial as it might look at first glance.

## 3.2. Manipulation, Retrieval, and Comparison

Qualitative relations are useful for formalizing queries in, for example, GIS applications. Technically, a query is given by a constraint network and one needs to compute a mapping from the variables in the query network to the variables in the database such that corresponding relations are identical. Reasoning plays an important role in making query answering efficient (Grimson, 1990). Efficient algorithms require specialized data structures. To avoid loosing time by setting up the data structures from a representation of constraint networks used in the application, it is helpful that a toolbox provides representations of constraint networks that suit efficient retrieval as well as the needs of an application. Thus, an application would not store all qualitative information itself, but it would rather utilize a constraint network representation that resides within the qualitative reasoner module used by the application. We note that the same reason holds for other qualitative reasoning tasks that involve specialized data structures. In conclusion, to avoid unnecessary setup of specialized data structures, we see the need that any qualitative reasoning toolbox provides qualitative constraint network representations that automatically update all specialized data structures. Naturally, providing a representation also requires the toolbox to offer a set of versatile operations for manipulation, access, and comparison of constraint networks. Examples of these operations are taking the intersection or union of constraint networks, accessing and changing individual constraints, and determining whether one network is a refinement of another one.

## 3.3. Constraint-Based Qualitative Reasoning

As qualitative relation networks are constraint networks over an infinite temporal or spatial domain, constraint-based reasoning is the typical approach to reasoning with qualitative information. The constraint-based reasoning tasks we identified are the following:

- Deciding consistency of a given network of qualitative relations
- Determining one or enumerating all consistent scenarios from a constraint network
- Removing redundancy from a constraint network, i.e., computing the minimal network (Dechter, Meiri, & Pearl, 1991)

Classically, these tasks are tackled by the algebraic closure algorithm using the composition and converse operation of a qualitative calculus. Although deciding consistency of qualitative calculi is NP-hard for almost for all calculi, this approach is very efficient (Renz, 2002). It is widely assumed that algebraic closure can be used to decide consistency of atomic constraint networks (see Renz & Nebel, 2007).

However, approaching consistency problems only by means of the algebraic closure algorithm has severe limitations. First and foremost, the assumption that algebraic closure can decide consistency of atomic network is not valid for relative orientation calculi that distinguish left- and right-hand side of arbitrary reference lines (Lücke, et al., 2008). The effectiveness of algebraic closure has not been investigated for all calculi yet. Second, algebraic closure may not provide the most efficient means for deciding consistency; for example, general SAT solvers can in some situations outperform methods based on algebraic closure for constraint networks (Westphal & Wölfl, 2009). Third, any approach based on the operation tables of a calculus is confined to handling relations from one single calculus only, i.e., it is not possible to reason about networks that contain relations from different calculi. The bipath-consistency method may be used as a work-around, but this method is often too weak for deciding consistency (Wölfl & Westphal, 2009).

Additionally, we treat elementary computations performed with qualitative relations under the label of constraint-based reasoning because these tasks can in principle be posed as constraint-satisfaction problems. For example, if one wants to determine the composition of two relations $r,s$, one can construct a network with three arbitrary variables $A,B,C$ and with constraints $r(A,B)$, $s(B,C)$, and the universal relation constraint between $A$ and $C$. After computing the minimal network the desired composition of $r$ and $s$ can be read off as the relation holding between $A$ and $C$. Of course, any qualitative reasoning toolbox would offer easier-to-use means that would neither require the user to set up constraint networks manually nor would the toolbox use costly CSP decision procedures if a simple relation lookup is sufficient.

## 3.4. Neighborhood-Based Reasoning

Under the term neighborhood-based reasoning we subsume all qualitative reasoning services which are based on the notion of conceptual neighborhood. Elementary operations we foresee here are the computation of the conceptual neighbors of a given relation and the distance of two base relations in the conceptual neighborhood graph which is defined by the length of the shortest path connecting them (Bruns & Egenhofer, 1996; Dylla & Wallgrün, 2007).

To facilitate these elementary services the conceptual neighbor relation or alternatively the conceptual neighborhood graph need to be specified as part of the calculus specification. However, the exact neighborhood structure depends on the concrete set of transformations (move, grow, shrink, change shape, etc.) that the related objects may perform (Freksa, 1991; Dylla & Wallgrün, 2007). Hence, instead of specifying a single neighborhood structure, one would like to specify several neighborhood structures and choose then the one that best suits the application at hand.

Based on the elementary neighborhood operations, one could then realize services for assessing the similarity or distance between constraint networks and for generating potential successor scenarios of a given network. The next step are operations that perform integration tasks (including conflict resolution) or are based on some kind of search through the generalized conceptual neighborhood graph (e.g., simulation, explanation, and planning as discussed in Section 2.2). Theoretical frameworks for relaxing a single inconsistent network or for merging several networks which contradict each other by considering scenarios which are at the same time consistent and closest the original network(s) have already been developed in (Dylla & Wallgrün, 2007; Condotta, et al., 2008). However, there is still a need for solutions that scale well to the large constraint networks occurring in potential application domains such as GIS.

## 3.5. Quantification

A symbolic qualitative scene description can be difficult to grasp for humans, particularly if many objects are involved. It is usually much easier to understand such a scene by looking at one particular drawing of it even though one has to be aware that this drawing is just one quantitative example among infinitely many ones subsumed by the qualitative description. Hence, often after doing some computation with qualitative relations one would want to visualize the result. This demand should be supported by QSTR toolboxes, at least by offering the service of computing one solution, i.e., quantitative example, for a given consistent scenario. Analogously to the qualification service, we call this process of computing a quantitative scene description from a qualitative scene description *quantification*. The process was already illustrated in Figure 4. Based on this service one could then visualize complete solution spaces by visualizing the individidual consistent scenarios comprised by a general constraint network. Unlike the quantification of cardinal direction relations as shown in Figure 4, which can be achieved by multiple sorting, quantification techniques for most qualitative calculi have not been studied yet. An universal quantification technique in the sense of composition-based reasoning applicable to all calculi would be most desirable. Also, good quantification methods would not compute some quantitative realization, but render a scene from which all qualitative relations can be easily read off (e.g., avoiding object distances visually too small) and support humans in understanding the image, for example by making use of preferred mental models (see Rauh, et al., 2005) whenever possible.

## 3.6. Geometric Reasoning with Relation Semantics

Applications may require us to handle qualitative relations from different calculi or to mix qualitative and quantitative information. So far there are few approaches to handle relations beyond those captured in a single calculus. Unfortunately, the relation algebraic approach taken by the bipath-consistency method is often too weak (Wölfl & Westphal, 2009). Therefore, we see the need to research additional means to address these application-relevant topics. One promising approach to tackle these unsolved reasoning problems in

*Figure 6. Methods provided by the SparQ toolbox*

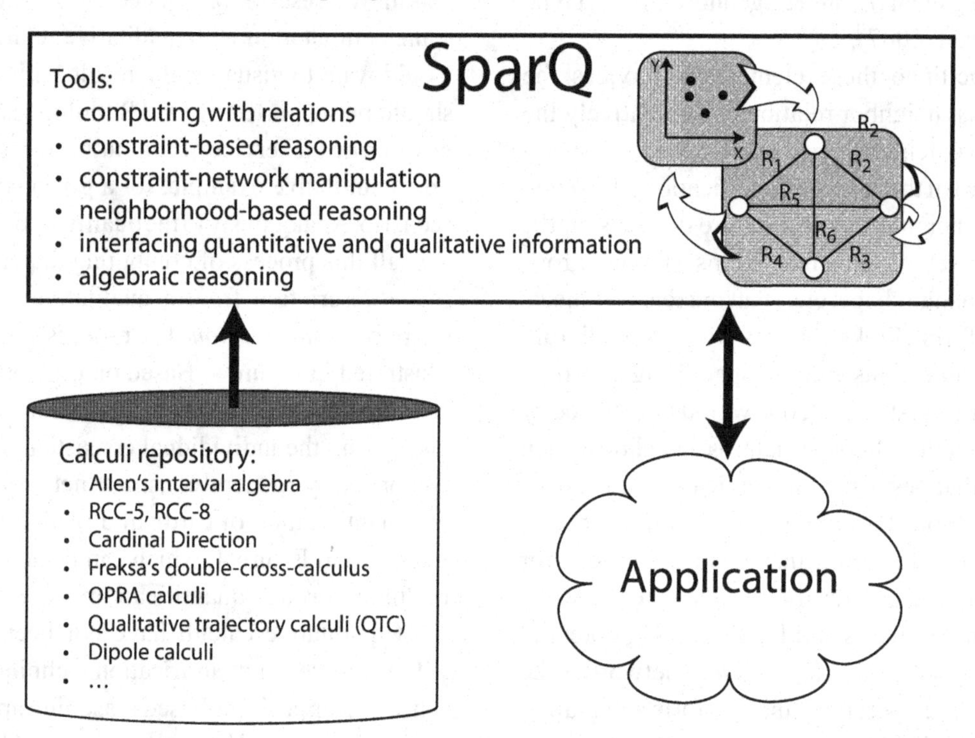


QSTR can be found in the field of real algebraic geometry (see Basu, Pollack, & Roy, 2006). In order to employ methods from real algebraic geometry, QSTR constraints must be written as systems of multivariate polynomials and reasoning tasks need to be posed as tests for solvability of the system of equations. Algebraic geometry is a domain-level method that allows us to perform general geometric reasoning tasks. Thus, we are not limited to reasoning about what can be modeled using one specific calculus as we are in classical constraint-based qualitative reasoning. Using algebraic geometry we can also, for instance, determine composition tables from a specification of a set of relations, i.e., geometric reasoning allows us to instantiate a qualitative calculus. In a first study we have evaluated the effectiveness of such an approach to computing operation tables (composition, converse) for qualitative constraint calculi (Wolter & Moshagen, 2008). Since the motivation of qualitative approaches is to only make distinctions necessary in the context of a given task, qualitative representations are highly task-dependent. Therefore, one ideally would like to only name qualitative relations useful for a specific task and reasoning methods would be instantiated automatically. Although this goal remains subject to further research, geometric reasoning using methods of real algebraic geometry is a promising approach.

## 4. THE SPARQ TOOLBOX

With our own spatial reasoning toolbox SparQ[2] we aim at providing a tool collection that connects qualitative reasoning to applications. We provide the toolbox as free software licensed under the GNU GPL license; it is available from http://www.sfbtr8.uni-bremen.de/project/r3/sparq/ and can be used in most POSIX-compliant operating systems. Our goal is to provide methods for all the different tasks we identified in the different application areas. Currently, we provide all standard

*Figure 7. Quantitative information derived from a map is stored in $DB_1$*

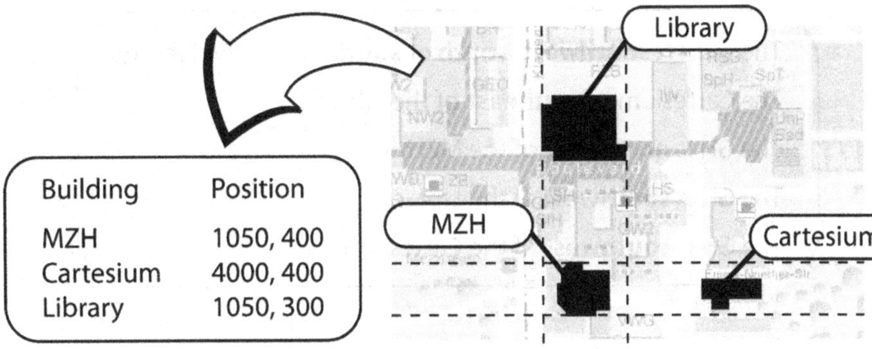

| Building | Position |
|---|---|
| MZH | 1050, 400 |
| Cartesium | 4000, 400 |
| Library | 1050, 300 |

constraint-based reasoning tools for binary and ternary calculi, means for connecting quantitative to qualitative data, tools for calculi analysis, and some manipulation of constraint-based knowledge bases—see Figure 6. Users can easily specify their own calculi or they can take advantage of the growing calculi repository that comes along with the toolbox. As heuristics are important to efficient reasoning, SparQ automatically computes reasoning heuristics for any calculus description provided—no manual work is required.

## 4.1. SparQ by Example

Let us consider a very simple example to illustrate how the different services provided by SparQ can be applied in the context of a GIS. The task in this example is to integrate two spatial knowledge bases of which one is a purely quantitative database and the other only provides qualitative information. After merging the two knowledge sources, the combined information shall be visualized for the user.

The two databases $DB_1$ and $DB_2$ are depicted in Figure 7 and Figure 8. They both contain information about the positions of buildings at the Bremen university campus. $DB_1$ contains positions within an Cartesian coordinate system extracted from a map. $DB_2$ contains qualitative direction information given in terms of relations from a qualitative spatial calculus. It could, for instance, be the result of a human writing down his knowledge about the buildings from memory. It also contains one object, the Glass Hall (GH), which is not contained in $DB_1$. The qualitative calculus we are using in this example is the cardinal direction calculus (Ligozat, 1998) which distinguishes nine base relations *n*, *nw*, *w*, *sw*, *s*, *se*, *e*, *ne*, and *eq* (for equal). Figure 9 shows the definition file of the cardinal direction calculus in SparQ. It specifies basic properties of the calculus such as its arity, base entities, base relations, and its identity relation and defines the converse and composition operations. Optionally, calculi definitions may contain an algebraic specification of the semantic of the base relations. Relations are defined by the zero sets of multivariate polynomials over the field of reals. SparQ offers a general method for interfacing qualitative and quantitative information using the algebraic specification. Identifying which relation holds between objects that are specified quantitatively (qualification), is performed by checking for each relation whether its algebraic specification is satisfied by the quantitative data. SparQ uses exact computations with rational numbers to avoid numerical problems. Of course, the algebraic approach is restricted to domains that can be formalized over a real-valued domain and whose relation can be modeled algebraically. We note that topological calculi like RCC-8 are defined for abstract domains and cannot be specified this way. However, to our knowledge, all other

*Figure 8. Qualitative information stemming from a human is stored in $DB_2$*

The MZH is **southwest, south** or **southeast** of the Library.
The Cartesium is **southeast** of the Library.
The GH is **northwest** of the MZH.
The GH is **southwest** of the Library.
The GH is **southwest** of the Cartesium.

*Figure 9. Definition of cardinal direction calculus in SparQ*

```
(def-calculus "Cardinal direction calculus (cardir)"
  :arity            :binary
  :basis-entity     :2d-point
  :base-relations (N NE E SE S SW W NW EQ)
  :identity-relation EQ

  :converse-operation
    ((N S) ; A (N) B => B (S) A
     (NE  SW)
     (E W)
     (SE  NW)
     ... )

  :composition-operation
    ((N N N) ; A (N) B, B (N) C => A (N) C
     (N S (N EQ S))
     (N E NE)
     (N W NW)
     ...)

  :algebraic-specification
    ((EQ ((1 ((ax 1))) = (1 ((bx 1))))  ;  EQ :<=> 1*ax^1 = 1*bx^1,
         ((1 ((ay 1))) = (1 ((by 1)))))  ;           1*ay^1 = 1*by^1
     (NW ((1 ((ax 1))) < (1 ((bx 1))))
         ((1 ((ay 1))) > (1 ((by 1)))))
     (W  ((1 ((ax 1))) < (1 ((bx 1))))
         ((1 ((ay 1))) = (1 ((by 1)))))
     ... )
```

*Box 1.*

```
let DB1 = ((MZH 1050 400) (CARTESIUM 4000 400) (LIBRARY 1050 300))     <ENTER>
```

and

```
let DB2 = ((MZH (sw s se) LIBRARY) (CARTESIUM se LIBRARY) (GH nw MZH)
           (GH sw LIBRARY) (GH sw CARTESIUM))                           <ENTER>
```

qualitative calculi documented in the literature can be formalized using polynomial equations.

Before we start with merging the information from $DB_1$ and $DB_2$, it is convenient to assign the information from both databases to variables inside SparQ for later use. To do this, the GIS software would send the commands in Box 1 to SparQ.

As we see, the quantitative scene description for $DB_1$ in SparQ is simple a list of tuples describing individual objects. The object tuples consist of an identifier (MZH, CARTESIUM, etc.) and the parameters to specify an object from the underlying domain (here points in the plane). The qualitative scene description for $DB_2$ is a list of relational tuples of the (*object* ×(*list−of−base−relations*)× *object*) describing the relations holding between the objects which might be unions of base relations like in the case of the MZH and the LIBRARY.

As a first step of merging the information from $DB_1$ and $DB_2$ we need to turn the quantitative information from $DB_1$ into qualitative information to make it comparable to the information in $DB_2$. Hence, our GIS software would send the following request to SparQ, asking it to perform a qualification using the cardinal direction calculus (abbreviated cardir in SparQ) and store the result for later use in the variable `DB1Qual`:

```
let DB1QUAL
   = qualify cardir all $DB1  <ENTER>
```

The parameter "all" has the effect that the resulting constraint network contains the relations holding between every pair of objects. Hence, the output of SparQ corresponding to the content now stored in `DB1Qual` is:

```
((MZH w CARTESIUM) (MZH s LIBRARY)
 (CARTESIUM se LIBRARY))
```

We now can merge the two constraint networks stored in `DB1Qual` and `DB2`. The intuitive way to do this is to merge the networks by taking the intersection of corresponding constraints. This can be done in SparQ using the refine command which is a subcommand of the constraint-reasoning module:

```
let DB3
    = constraint-reasoning cardir
      refine $DB1QUAL $DB2      <ENTER>
```

The result is:

```
((CARTESIUM se LIBRARY)
 (GH sw CARTESIUM) (GH sw LIBRARY)
 (GH nw MZH) (MZH w CARTESIUM)
 (MZH s LIBRARY))
```

However, intersecting both contraint networks is the strictest form of merging information and the result may very well be inconsistent if the networks contain conflicting information. Hence, our software could check whether the result of the

*Box 2.*

```
...
;; Checking GH->CARTESIUM:(sw) = GH->MZH:(nw) o MZH->CARTESIUM:(w) refining
to
GH->CARTESIUM:()
...
Not consistent.
```

merging is consistent or not. To do this, it uses the following SparQ command:

```
constraint-reasoning cardir
check-consistency check $DB3   <ENTER>
```

with the following result:

```
Not consistent.
```

By using the subcommand `check-consistency` we request SparQ to decide consistency of the specified constraint network using the appropriate decision method for this calculus. In this specific case, the computationally cheap algebraic closure algorithm suffices to decide consistency. For other calculi like e.g., RCC-8, one would need to perform a backtracking search to decide existence of a refined network that is algebraically closed and only contains relations known to be tractable (see Renz, 2002). Knowing that enforcing algebraic closure is suitable in our case, we could also invoke this tool directly resulting in Box 2.

This time we also get some additional information telling us where the algebraic closure algorithm failed: composing GH nw MZH and MZH w CARTESIUM yields GH nw CARTESIUM which contradicts the given information GH se CARTESIUM.

As we do not want to continue with an inconsistent database, we would like to relax the constraints in $DB_3$ until we end up with a consistent network. More precisely, we want to find a network that is as similar as possible to $DB_3$ but is consistent. Relaxation in this sense is realized within the neighborhood-reasoning module of SparQ because, as we previously mentioned, similarity of constraint networks can be defined based on the notion of conceptual neighborhood. The call to find a minimally relaxed network that is consistent is:

```
let DB4 = neighborhood-reasoning
          cardir relax $DB3   <ENTER>
```

yielding

```
((CARTESIUM se LIBRARY)
 (GH sw CARTESIUM) (GH sw LIBRARY)
 (GH nw MZH) (MZH sw CARTESIUM)
 (MZH s LIBRARY))
```

Comparing this $DB_4$ to $DB_3$, we see that only the relation between MZH and CARTESIUM has changed from west to southwest. The resulting network is indeed consistent:

```
constraint-reasoning cardir
   scenario-consistency check
   $DB4                           <ENTER>

Consistent.
```

Finally, we want to visualize the content of our merged database $DB_4$. Since $DB_4$ is already a scenario, our GIS software can directly call

*Figure 10. Resulting quantitative scene*

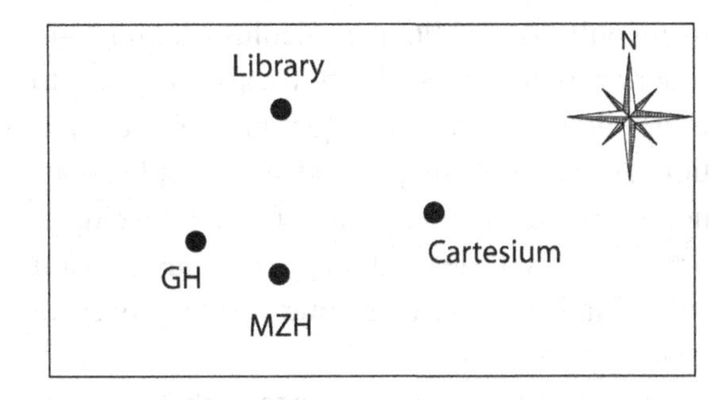


```
let DB4Quan
   = quantify cardir $DB4        <ENTER>
```

which yields a quantitative scene description like

```
((MZH 20 0) (CARTESIUM 100 20)
 (LIBRARY 20 100) (GH 0 10))
```

also depicted in Figure 10. If $DB_4$ would have been a non-atomic network, we could have first used

```
constraint-reasoning cardir
scenario-consistency all $DB4 <ENTER>
```

which yields a list of all consistent scenarios of $DB_4$ which then could be quantified individually.

## 4.2. SparQ Roadmap

Besides improving existing tools, we are working on long- and mid-term goals that require more research. We envisage the following three main directions:

**Algebraic geometry reasoning.** As discussed in Section 3.6, algebraic reasoning methods can provide alternative means to qualitative reasoning. This is particularly valuable in cases in which QSTR methods are not sufficient—for instance, when constraint-based reasoning using composition tables fails to decided consistency of constraint networks as, for example the case with relative position calculi (see,e.g., Lücke, et al., 2008). Second, algebraic geometry is calculi-independent, so qualitative reasoning tasks can be handled that involve relations from different calculi. For tasks involving multiple calculi we would obtain more effective means than, for example, the bipath-consistency (Gerivini & Renz, 2002; Westphal & Wölfl, 2008) method which is currently the only possibility of combining calculi without manually instantiating and analyzing a new, combined calculus.

**Universal method for mapping qualitative to quantitative information.** So far, only some specific methods for individual calculi are known that can map qualitative to quantitative information; for many calculi no method is known. This stands in contrast to the constraint-based reasoning methods in QSTR which are purely syntactically (they only make use of operation tables). However, interfacing of quantitative and qualitative knowledge builds on the semantics of qualitative relations. Therefore, we enhance calculi with a semantic specification using algebraic equations (this part is already contained in SparQ). We are currently developing algebraic reasoning techniques that provide us with a universal method capable of computing a quantitative scene for any (consistent) qualitative constraint network. Additionally, we will consider cognitive principles to generate scenes that humans would preferably reconstruct (cp. Rauh, et al., 2005), thereby easing the visual perception.

**Constraint-based querying.** We identified the need to being able to find parts in a constraint-network which are identical or similar to a given query network. Technically speaking, the task of detecting occurrences of constraint networks within a larger network as we discussed earlier is a form of subgraph isomorphy which in its general form is known to be NP-hard. Therefore, it is important to employ effective heuristics to solve this task. We will research means to compute these heuristics automatically and to make use of calculus operations.

## 5. CONCLUSION AND OUTLOOK

We argued that one issue impeding the dissemination of QSTR techniques in applications is a lack of software solutions which allow for an easy integration of QSTR methods by application developers. Existing toolboxes and theoretical research so far have focused on constraint-based reasoning and the consistency problem. By looking at three exemplary application domains we showed that classical constraint-based reasoning is only a small part of the reasoning that is required in these domains. Tasks that need to be carried out include mapping of quantitative data to qualitative and vice versa, efficient means for representing and retrieving qualitative knowledge, and neighborhood-reasoning. Existing toolboxes need to be extended to accommodate these demands. We discussed how well these additional reasoning tasks are currently understood theoretically and to which extent they are currently supported by the toolboxes. We then focused on our own QSTR toolbox SparQ and described what is currently already feasible in SparQ as well as our roadmap for the future towards offering all the discussed reasoning services in an easy-to-use way.

We also identified some important research questions. Currently, qualitative representations are not integrated with quantitative data, in particular it remains an open question which general approaches allow qualitative knowledge to be externalized diagrammatically. In general, integrating qualitative and quantitative approaches is important to systems which are classically based on quantitative data such as GIS. Moreover, qualitative representation and reasoning has so far been studied using one specific calculus at a time. Reasoning methods remain confined to using only one qualitative calculus at a time—in order to combine calculi a new calculus needs to be developed. However, as qualitative representations are per se task-dependent, many applications need to build on several calculi at the same time, or to utilize self-defined relations. Thus, general calculi-independent reasoning methods need to be developed.

We believe that developing tools that accomodate the practial needs arising in applications is key to overcoming the lack of successful QSTR applications. Ultimately, we envision that QSTR toolboxes will offer a variety of means for representing and manipulating spatial and temporal knowledge which are accessible through some kind of spatial programming language—similar to algebra toolboxes that offer a variety of mathematical tools today.

## ACKNOWLEDGMENT

We would like to thank Christian Freksa, Frank Dylla, Lutz Frommberger, Mehul Bhatt, Jae Hee Lee, Paolo Fogliaroni, and Giorgio de Felice for valuable discussions on the material presented here. This work was carried out in the framework of the SFB/TR 8 Spatial Cognition, project R3-[Q-Shape], and the IRTG GRK 1498 Semantic Integration of Geospatial Information. Financial support by the Deutsche Forschungsgemeinschaft is gratefully acknowledged.

## REFERENCES

Bar-Shalom, Y., & Fortmann, T. E. (1988). *Tracking and data association*. New York, NY: Academic Press.

Basu, S., Pollack, R., & Roy, M. F. (2006). *Algorithms in real algebraic geometry* (2nd ed.). London, UK: Springer.

Belussi, A., Catania, B., & Podestà, P. (2005). Towards topological consistency and similarity of multiresolution geographical maps. In *Proceedings of the 13th Annual ACM International Workshop on Geographic Information Systems,* (pp. 220–229). New York, NY: ACM.

Bhatt, M., Dylla, F., & Hois, J. (2009). Spatio-terminological inference for the design of ambient environments. In K. S. Hornsby, C. Claramunt, M. Denis, & G. Ligozat (Eds.), *Spatial Information Theory, 9th International Conference, COSIT 2009*. London, UK: Springer.

Bittner, T., Donnelly, M., & Smith, B. (2009). A spatio-temporal ontology for geographic information integration. *International Journal of Geographical Information Science, 23*(6), 765–798. doi:10.1080/13658810701776767

Bojduj, B., Weber, B., Richter, K. F., & Bertel, S. (2008). Computer aided architectural design: Wayfinding complexity analysis. In *Proceedings of the 12th International Conference on Computer Supported Collaborative Work in Design (CSCWD),* (pp. 919-924). CSCWD.

Bruns, H. T., & Egenhofer, M. J. (1996). Similarity of spatial scenes. In *Proceedings of the Seventh International Symposium on Spatial Data Handling,* (pp. 173-184). Taylor & Francis.

Burrough, P. A. (1986). *Principles of geographical information systems for land resources assessment*. Oxford, UK: Oxford University Press.

Castellanos, J., Neira, J., & Tardós, J. D. (2006). Map building and slam algorithms. In Ge, S. S., & Lewis, F. L. (Eds.), *Autonomous Mobile Robots: Sensing, Control, Decision-Making and Applications*. Taylor & Francis.

Cohn, A. G., Gotts, N. M., Randell, D. A., Cui, Z., Bennett, B., & Gooday, J. M. (1997). Exploiting temporal continuity in qualitative spatial calculi. In Golledge, R. G., & Egenhofer, M. J. (Eds.), *Spatial and Temporal Reasoning in Geographical Information Systems*. Elsevier.

Cohn, A. G., & Hazarika, S. M. (2001). Qualitative spatial representation and reasoning: An overview. *Fundamenta Informaticae, 46*, 1–29.

Cohn, A. G., & Renz, J. (2007). Qualitative spatial reasoning. In van Harmelen, F., Lifschitz, V., & Porter, B. (Eds.), *Handbook of Knowledge Representation* (pp. 551–596). Elsevier.

Condotta, J. F., Kaci, S., & Schwind, N. (2008). A framework for merging qualitative constraints networks. In D. Wilson & H. C. Lane (Eds.), *Proceedings of the Twenty-First International Florida Artificial Intelligence Research Society Conference,* (pp. 586-591). Coconut Grove, FL: AAAI Press.

Condotta, J. F., Ligozat, G., & Saade, M. (2006). A generic toolkit for n-ary qualitative temporal and spatial calculi. In *Proceedings of the 13th International Symposium on Temporal Representation and Reasoning (TIME'06),* (pp. 78 – 86). Budapest, Hungary: TIME.

Dechter, R., Meiri, I., & Pearl, J. (1991). Temporal constraint networks. *Artificial Intelligence, 49*(1-3), 61–95. doi:10.1016/0004-3702(91)90006-6

Duckham, M., & Kulik, L. (2005). A formal model of obfuscation and negotiation for location privacy. In Gellersen, H. W., Want, R., & Schmidt, A. (Eds.), *Pervasive* (*Vol. 3468*, pp. 152–170). Springer. doi:10.1007/11428572_10

Duckham, M., & Worboys, M. F. (2005). An algebraic approach to automated geospatial information fusion. *International Journal of Geographical Information Science, 19*(5), 537–557. doi:10.1080/13658810500032339

Dudek, G., Freedman, P., & Hadjres, S. (1996). Using multiple models for environmental mapping. *Journal of Robotic Systems*, *13*(8), 539–559. doi:10.1002/(SICI)1097-4563(199608)13:8<539::AID-ROB5>3.0.CO;2-O

Dylla, F., & Wallgrün, J. O. (2007). Qualitative spatial reasoning with conceptual neighborhoods for agent control. *Journal of Intelligent & Robotic Systems*, *48*(1), 55–78. doi:10.1007/s10846-006-9099-4

Egenhofer, M. J. (1989). A formal definition of binary topological relationships. In *Proceedings of the 3rd International Conference on Foundations of Data Organization and Algorithms*, (pp. 457–472). Springer.

Egenhofer, M. J. (1994). Spatial SQL: A query and presentation language. *IEEE Transactions on Knowledge and Data Engineering*, *6*(1), 86–95. doi:10.1109/69.273029

Egenhofer, M. J., Clementini, E., & Felice, P. D. (1994). Evaluating inconsistencies among multiple representations. In *Proceedings of the Sixth International Symposium on Spatial Data Handling,* (pp. 901–920). Spatial Data Handling.

Egenhofer, M. J., & Mark, D. M. (1995). Naive geography. In *Proceedings of COSIT'95,* (Vol. 988), (pp. 1-15). Springer.

Fonseca, F. T., Egenhofer, M. J., Agouris, P., & Câmara, G. (2002). Using ontologies for integrated geographic information systems. *Transactions on GIS*, *6*(3), 231–257. doi:10.1111/1467-9671.00109

Fox, D., Burgard, W., & Thrun, S. (1999). Markov localization for mobile robots in dynamic environments. *Journal of Artificial Intelligence Research*, *11*, 391–427.

Frank, A. (1991). Qualitative spatial reasoning about cardinal directions. In *Proceedings of the American Congress on Surveying and Mapping (ACSM-ASPRS),* (pp. 148–167). Baltimore, MD: ACSM.

Freksa, C. (1991). Conceptual neighborhood and its role in temporal and spatial reasoning. In Singh, M., & Travé-Massuyès, L. (Eds.), *Decision Support Systems and Qualitative Reasoning* (pp. 181–187). Amsterdam, The Netherlands: North-Holland.

Freksa, C. (1992). Temporal reasoning based on semi-intervals. *Artificial Intelligence*, *54*(1), 199–227. doi:10.1016/0004-3702(92)90090-K

Galton, A. (2000). *Qualitative spatial change*. Oxford, UK: Oxford University Press.

Gantner, Z., Westphal, M., & Wölfl, S. (2008). GQR–A fast reasoner for binary qualitative constraint calculi. In *Proceedings of the AAAI'08 Workshop on Spatial and Temporal Reasoning*. AAAI.

Gerivini, A., & Renz, J. (2002). Combining topological and size information for spatial reasoning. *Artificial Intelligence*, *137*(1–2), 1–42. doi:10.1016/S0004-3702(02)00193-5

Grimson, W. E. L. (1990). *Object recognition by computer: The role of geometric constraints*. Cambridge, MA: MIT Press.

Hähnel, D., Burgard, W., Wegbreit, B., & Thrun, S. (2003). Towards lazy data association in SLAM. In *Proceedings of the 11th International Symposium of Robotics Research (ISRR'03)*. ISRR.

Hearnshaw, H. M., & Unwin, D. J. (1994). *Visualization in geographical information systems*. Chichester, UK: John Wiley & Sons.

Janowicz, K., Raubal, M., Schwering, A., & Kuhn, W. (2008). Semantic similarity measurement and geospatial applications. *Transactions in GIS, 12*(6), 651–659. doi:10.1111/j.1467-9671.2008.01129.x

Krieg-Brückner, B., & Shi, H. (2006). Orientation calculi and route graphs: Towards semantic representations for route descriptions. In *Proceedings of Geographic Information Science - Fourth International Conference, GIScience,* (Vol. 4197), (pp. 234–250). Springer.

Kuipers, B. (1994). *Qualitative reasoning: Modeling and simulation with incomplete knowledge*. Cambridge, MA: MIT Press.

Kuipers, B. (2000). The spatial semantic hierarchy. *Artificial Intelligence, 119*, 191–233. doi:10.1016/S0004-3702(00)00017-5

Kuipers, B., Modayil, J., Beeson, P., MacMahon, M., & Savelli, F. (2004). Local metrical and global topological maps in the hybrid spatial semantic hierarchy. In *Proceedings of the IEEE International Conference on Robotics and Automation (ICRA-04)*. New Orleans, LA: IEEE Press.

Leonard, J. J., & Durrant-Whyte, H. F. (1991). Simultaneous map building and localization for an autonomous mobile robot. In *Proceedings of IEEE/RSJ International Workshop on Intelligent Robots and Systems,* (pp. 1442-1447). IEEE Press.

Levitt, T. S., & Lawton, D. T. (1990). Qualitative navigation for mobile robots. *Artificial Intelligence, 44*, 305–360. doi:10.1016/0004-3702(90)90027-W

Ligozat, G. (1998). Reasoning about cardinal directions. *Journal of Visual Languages and Computing, 9*, 23–44. doi:10.1006/jvlc.1997.9999

Ligozat, G., & Renz, J. (2004). What is a qualitative calculus? A general framework. In C. Zhang, H. W. Guesgen, & W. K. Yeap (Eds.), *PRICAI 2004: Trends in Artificial Intelligence — 8th Pacific Rim International Conference on Artificial Intelligence,* (pp. 53–64). Springer.

Lovett, A. M., Dehghani, M., & Forbus, K. D. (2007). Incremental learning of perceptual categories for open-domain sketch recognition. In M. M. Veloso (Ed.), *Proceedings of IJCAI* (pp. 447-452). IJCAI.

Lücke, D., Mossakowski, T., & Wolter, D. (2008). In Freksa, C., Newcombe, S. N., Gärdenfors, P., & Wölfl, S. (Eds.), *Qualitative reasoning about convex relations* (*Vol. 5248*, pp. 426–440). Spatial Cognition, VI: Springer.

Moratz, R. (2009). Ambiguous landmark problems in cognitive robotics: A benchmark for qualitative position calculi. In B. Nebel & S. Wölfl (Eds.), *Papers from the 2009 AAAI Spring Symposium Benchmarking of Qualitative Spatial and Temporal Reasoning Systems,* (pp. 17–22). Menlo Park, CA: AAAI Press.

Moratz, R., Nebel, B., & Freksa, C. (2003). Qualitative spatial reasoning about relative position: The tradeoff between strong formal properties and successful reasoning about route graphs. In C. Freksa, W. Brauer, C. Habel, & K. F. Wender (Eds.), *Spatial Cognition III,* (Vol. 2685), (pp. 385–400). Springer.

Moratz, R., & Tenbrink, T. (2006). Spatial reference in linguistic human-robot interaction: Iterative, empirically supported development of a model of projective relations. *Spatial Cognition and Computation, 6*(1), 63–106. doi:10.1207/s15427633scc0601_3

Moratz, R., & Wallgrün, J. O. (2003). Spatial reasoning about relative orientation and distance for robot exploration. In W. Kuhn, M. F. Worboys, & S. Timpf (Eds.), *Spatial Information Theory: Foundations of Geographic Information Science: Conference on Spatial Information Theory (COSIT),* (pp. 61-74). Springer.

Neira, J., & Tardós, J. D. (2001). Data association in stochastic mapping using the joint compability test. *IEEE Transactions on Robotics and Automation, 17*, 890–897. doi:10.1109/70.976019

OpenGIS Consortium. (1999). *OpenGIS simple features implementation specification for SQL rev. 1.1.* OpenGIS Project Document 99-049. OpenGIS.

Ragni, M., & Wölfl, S. (2005, Sep). Temporalizing spatial calculi—On generalized neighborhood graphs. In *Proceedings of the 28th German Conference on Artificial Intelligence (KI 2005).* Koblenz, Germany: KI.

Ragni, M., & Wölfl, S. (2006). Temporalizing cardinal directions: From constraint satisfaction to planning. In Doherty, P., Mylopoulos, J., & Welty, C. A. (Eds.), *KR* (pp. 472–480). AAAI Press.

Randell, D. A., Cui, Z., & Cohn, A. (1992). A spatial logic based on regions and connection. In B. Nebel, C. Rich, & W. Swartout (Eds.), *Principles of Knowledge Representation and Reasoning: Proceedings of the Third International Conference (KR'92),* (pp. 165–176). San Mateo, CA: Morgan Kaufmann.

Rauh, R., Hagen, C., Knauff, M., Kuß, T., Schlieder, C., & Strube, G. (2005). From preferred to alternative mental models in spatial reasoning. *Spatial Cognition and Computation, 5*, 239–269.

Remolina, E., & Kuipers, B. (2004). Towards a general theory of topological maps. *Artificial Intelligence, 152*(1), 47–104. doi:10.1016/S0004-3702(03)00114-0

Renz, J. (2002). *Qualitative spatial reasoning with topological information.* Berlin, Germany: Springer. doi:10.1007/3-540-70736-0

Renz, J. (2007). Qualitative spatial and temporal reasoning: Efficient algorithms for everyone. In *Proceedings of the 20th International Joint Conference on Artificial Intelligence (IJCAI-07),* (pp. 526-531). Hyderabad, India: IJCAI.

Renz, J., & Nebel, B. (2007). Qualitative spatial reasoning using constraint calculi. In Aiello, M., Pratt-Hartmann, I. E., & van Benthem, J. F. (Eds.), *Handbook of Spatial Logics* (pp. 161–215). Springer. doi:10.1007/978-1-4020-5587-4_4

Richter, K. F., Weber, B., Bojduj, B., & Bertel, S. (2009). Supporting the designer's and the user's perspectives in computer-aided architectural design. *Advanced Engineering Informatics, 24*(2).

Rodrìguez, M. A., & Egenhofer, M. J. (2004). Comparing geospatial entity classes: An asymmetric and context-dependent similarity measure. *International Journal of Geographical Information Science, 18*(3), 229–256. doi:10.1080/1365 8810310001629592

Schlieder, C. (1993). Representing visible locations for qualitative navigation. In Piera-Carrete, N., & Singh, M. (Eds.), *Qualitative Reasoning and Decision Technologies* (pp. 523–532). Springer.

Schultz, C. P. L., Amor, R., Lobb, B., & Guesgen, H. W. (2009). Qualitative design support for engineering and architecture. *Advanced Engineering Informatics, 23*(1), 68–80. doi:10.1016/j.aei.2008.07.003

Schwering, A. (2008). Approaches to semantic similarity measurement for geo-spatial data: A survey. *Transactions in GIS, 12*(1), 5–29. doi:10.1111/j.1467-9671.2008.01084.x

Smith, M. J., Goodchild, M. F., & Longley, P. A. (2007). *Geospatial analysis: A comprehensive guide to principles, techniques and software tools*. Troubador Publishing.

Steinhauer, H. J. (2008). Object configuration reconstruction from incomplete binary object relation descriptions. In Dengel, A. R., Berns, K., & Breul, T. M. (Eds.), *KI 2008: Advances in Artificial Intelligence* (pp. 348–355). Springer. doi:10.1007/978-3-540-85845-4_43

Thrun, S. (2002). *Robotic mapping: A survey*. Pittsburgh, PA: Carnegie Mellon University.

Wallgrün, J. O. (2009). Exploiting qualitative spatial constraints for multi-hypothesis topological map learning. In K. S. Hornsby, C. Claramunt, M. Denis, & G. Ligozat (Eds.), *Spatial Information Theory, 9th International Conference, COSIT 2009,* (Vol. 5756), (pp. 141-158). Springer.

Wallgrün, J. O. (2010). *Hierarchical Voronoi graphs–Spatial representation and reasoning for mobile robots*. London, UK: Springer.

Wallgrün, J. O., Frommberger, L., Wolter, D., Dylla, F., & Freksa, C. (2007). Qualitative spatial representation and reasoning in the SparQ-toolbox. In *Proceedings of Spatial Cognition V: Reasoning, Action, Interaction: International Conference Spatial Cognition 2006*. Bremen, Germany: Spatial Cognition.

Westphal, M., & Wölfl, S. (2008). Bipath consistency revisited. In M. Ghallab, C. Spyropoulos, N. Fakotakis, & N. Avouris (Eds.), *Proceedings of the 18th European Conference on Artificial Intelligence (ECAI 2008)*. Amsterdam, The Netherlands: IOS Press.

Westphal, M., & Wölfl, S. (2009). Qualitative CSP, finite CSP, and SAT: Comparing methods for qualitative constraint-based reasoning. In *Proceedings of IJCAI-09*. IJCAI.

Winter, S. (1998). Bridging vector and raster representation in GIS. In *Proceedings of the 6th ACM International Symposium on Advances in Geographic Information Systems,* (pp. 57–62). New York, NY: ACM.

Wölfl, S., & Westphal, M. (2009). On combinations of binary qualitative constraint calculi. In *Proceedings of IJCAI-09*. IJCAI.

Wolter, D. (2008). *Spatial representation and reasoning for robot mapping—A shape-based approach* (*Vol. 48*). Springer.

Wolter, D., Freksa, C., & Latecki, L. J. (2008). Towards a generalization of self-localization. In Jefferies, M. E., & Yeap, W. K. (Eds.), *Robot and Cognitive Approaches to Spatial Mapping*. London, UK: Springer. doi:10.1007/978-3-540-75388-9_7

Wolter, D., & Moshagen, L. (2008). Algebraic methods for analyzing qualitative spatio-temporal calculi. In *Proceedings of ECAI-2008 Workshop on Spatial and Temporal Reasoning*. ECAI.

## KEY TERMS AND DEFINITIONS

**Algebraic Closure:** Decision method for deciding consistency in qualitative constraint problems.

**Conceptual Neighborhood:** Qualitative relations are conceptually neighbored if the categories they represent are connected, e.g., "smaller" is neighbored with "same size," but not with "larger".

**Constraint-Based Reasoning:** Symbolic reasoning (e.g., deduction) with qualitative relations using the constraint-based semantics.

**Neighborhood-Based Reasoning:** Symbolic reasoning (e.g., deduction) with qualitative relations using conceptual neighborhoods.

**Qualitative Calculus:** Relation algebraic structure comprising qualitative relations and operations

**Qualitative Relation:** Relation (in the mathematical sense) between objects in a spatio-temporal domain that represents a meaningful category, e.g., "north of".

**SparQ:** A qualitative spatial reasoning toolbox.

## ENDNOTES

[1] A general, unspoken assumption underlying many QSTR calculi is that algebraic closure decides consistency for constraint networks involving base relations only (Renz, 2007); this is not the case in general though (Lücke, Mossakowski, & Wolter, 2008).

[2] **Spa**tial **R**easoning done **Q**ualtitatively

# Chapter 12
# On the Representation and Recognition of Temporal Patterns of Activities in Smart Environments

**Fulvio Mastrogiovanni**
*University of Genova, Italy*

**Antonello Scalmato**
*University of Genova, Italy*

**Antonio Sgorbissa**
*University of Genova, Italy*

**Renato Zaccaria**
*University of Genova, Italy*

## ABSTRACT

*This chapter introduces a framework for enabling context-aware behaviors in smart environment applications, with a special emphasis on smart homes and similar scenarios. In particular, an ontology-based architecture is described that allows system designers to specify non-trivial situations the system must be able to detect on the basis of available sensory data. Relevant situations may include activities and events that could be prolonged over long periods of time. Therefore, the ontology encodes temporal operators that, once applied to sensory information, allow the recognition and efficient correlation of different human activities and other events whose temporal relationships are contextually important. Special emphasis is devoted to actual representation and recognition of temporally distributed situations. The proof of the concept is validated through a thoroughly described example of system usage.*

DOI: 10.4018/978-1-61692-868-1.ch012

## 1. INTRODUCTION

Nowadays, the role that context-aware systems are going to play in our society is definitely clear: it is commonly accepted that rich and expressive context models must be designed and realized in order to improve the actual behaviour and to extend the capabilities offered by Ambient Intelligence (AmI in short) systems, such as smart homes, intelligent vehicles or even smart cities.

Although the very notion of "context" is particularly vanishing, the goal of a context-aware system is well defined. Referring to the work described in Dourish (2004), this goal can be resolved in the following question: *How computation can be made sensitive and responsive to the setting (both physical and social) in which it is harnessed and used?* Common examples are Personal Digital Assistants or Smart Phones that adaptively display information depending on both the surrounding environment and current user activities, such as a *to buy list* of goods which items are selectable or not depending on their availability in the store the user is currently visiting, or a *to do list* of activities which elements pop up depending on the current schedule and approaching deadlines.

In order to offer these kinds of services, human behaviour must be carefully detected and understood. The search for expressive and effective context models is heavily related to cognition modelling and understanding, especially in humans. As it has been shown by philosophers, psychologists, and cognitive scientists (refer to the work described in Dourish [2004] and Waldmann [2007] and the references therein), human *activity* does not necessarily follow long-term plans: on the contrary, it is very "situation dependent" and opportunistic, whereas long-term plans can usually be described as a dynamical sequence of short-term activities, each one set in a specific context. Early work in this field focused on "the big picture," which allows to consider contexts as *well-delimited* and *stable pieces of information*. On the other hand, it seems intuitive that:

1. Contexts are not relevant *per se*, but especially when related to other "pieces" of information that may originate as a consequence of user activity, specifically distributed over prolonged periods of time.
2. Contexts are not static and monolithic entities: on the contrary, they are based on many constituent parts (depending on activities and roles of the humans involved) and can contribute to other contexts with possibly significant temporal relationships.

To deal with these issues, different context models have been investigated, designed, and effectively used in real-world scenarios, with alternate success. On the basis of these considerations, in the work reported in Krummenacher and Strang (2007), a number of prerequisites are outlined, which are described as follows.

*Applicability*. The context model must conform to existing environments and different domains of human activity. This requires the definition of common infrastructures and context representation paradigms enforcing scalability and modularity.

*Comparability*. Proper metrics and classification procedures must be added to the context model in order to compare heterogeneous entities and to analyze sensory information. Furthermore, since context models are aimed at associating a "meaning" to a collection of sensory information, these metrics must span both numerical and symbolic domains.

*Traceability*. The model must be aware of how incoming data are manipulated before being handled by the model itself. This requires a tight integration between information processing and knowledge representation.

*History*. Knowledge of past events and activities must be considered in context definitions, along with their relationships with current situations. In particular, it is useful to define very expressive relationships among activities distributed over long periods of time using formalisms allowing to efficiently recognize temporal contexts.

*Quality*. Incoming information must be associated with meaningful metrics about quality and reliability.

*Satisfiability*. The context model must provide high levels of conformance between what is represented and inferred by the model itself and actual situations in the real world, which is a sort of *symbol grounding* problem (Harnad, 1990).

*Inference*. The context model must reason about abstract context representations in order to make sense of incoming sensory information in real-time.

From a theoretical perspective, a high-level symbolic framework for describing such a model represents a feasible solution, specifically when dealing with temporal patterns of data: as a matter of fact, symbolic approaches to context modelling received much attention in the past decade. From a practical perspective, these frameworks usually adopt formal *ontologies*, which constitute a representation of *what is relevant in a given domain*, therefore facing the *shared understanding* issue (Strang, Linnhoff-Popien, & Frank, 2003) that characterizes systems where human-environment interaction is important.

This paper proposes a temporal context model that is aimed at integrating the benefits of ontologies with temporal reasoning frameworks to enforce context-awareness in AmI systems. Specifically, the model allows the representation of non trivial patterns of interleaved events and human activities that must be searched for in sensory data (i.e., "symbolic features"), accounting for temporal patterns distributed over long periods of time. Sensory data are gathered from an AmI infrastructure that provides the ontology with information originating from distributed sources (Mastrogiovanni, Sgorbissa, & Zaccaria, 2007), which are functionally anchored to symbolic representations.

The paper is organized as follows. Section 2 discusses relevant literature. Next, the context model is introduced in its many facets in Section 3, specifically detailing how it is integrated with temporal reasoning operators. Section 4 discusses the associated context recognition process, whereas Section 5 details a specific example. Conclusion follows.

## 2. RELATED WORK

The problem of representing and effectively reasoning upon temporal relationships among detected events in smart environments and AmI scenarios in general has not been exhaustively addressed in AmI literature, specifically with respect to the principled integration of suitable formalisms to encode, maintain and process temporal information (Gottfried, Guesgen, & Hübner, 2006). As a matter of fact, different approaches adopt very different frameworks that are not widely accepted by the overall community (Allen, 1983; Morchen, 2006). Furthermore, given the current state of the art technology in temporal knowledge representation (Lutz, Wolter, & Zakharyashev, 2008), it is not currently possible to provide designers of AmI systems with guidelines and best practices to formally define and easily deploy smart environments (Rugnone, et al., 2007). This is due to the fact that it is not clear yet how to represent and manipulate detected temporal events occurring in a smart environment, as well as how to integrate this representation with events and human activities prolonged over extended periods of time.

As a consequence, during the past decade, research directions have been rather sparse and not well-focused on a holistic view of AmI systems. In particular, major stress has been dedicated either on infrastructural issues or the use of dedicated formal representation tools. Examples of the first class include the specific role played by information fusion in determining which sensing technology to adopt, the identification of suitable data formats to facilitate the representation of sensory information, and algorithms for the recognition of *a priori* defined sequences of events and activities originating from sensory data. On the other hand, formal representation tools include the Allen's Interval Algebra (Allen, 1983), the Time Point Algebra (Vilain & Kautz, 1989), the so-called Calendar Algebra (Bettini, Mascetti, & Sean Wang, 2007), and the Linear Temporal Logic (Emerson & Halpern, 1986).

Among the problems related to infrastructure, many researchers still debate on the interplay between the used technology for distributed sensing and how to represent this information in order to actually ground reasoning processes.

In practice, different approaches are pursued, which largely depend on both the authors' background and the particular "school of thought" they adhere to. On one hand, AmI architectures completely based on cameras information have been discussed (Takahashi, et al., 2007), which are mainly focused on information processing rather than on the principled integration of different sensory modalities. On the other hand, the work described in Mastrogiovanni, Sgorbissa, and Zaccaria (2007) and Monekosso and Remagnino (2007) stresses the importance of using sensors providing simple (i.e., binary) information, and the associated logic-based information fusion mechanisms. This paves the way for the introduction of more advanced techniques for assessing distributed knowledge. However, temporal knowledge is not explicitly maintained.

The Context Toolkit (Salber, Dey, & Abowd, 1999; Dey, 2001) is a widely used architecture for quickly deploying smart environments. In particular, it provides a formally defined modelling language that is based on three basic elements, namely context *widget*, context *interpreter* and context *aggregator*. Widgets correspond to real-world artefacts (i.e., distributed sensing devices and associated services) devoted to acquire contextual knowledge and to make it accessible for applications to use it in a way that is transparent to them. Interpreters correspond to modules meant at reasoning upon contextual knowledge: they receive different contexts in input and produce new contextual information. Finally, aggregators correspond to modules in charge of combining heterogeneous contextual knowledge to depict a broader view of their meaning. In spite of the powerful capabilities in managing distributed sources of information, the explicit use of temporal information is not addressed.

The Context Broker Architecture (CoBrA in short) and the associated ontology (Chen, Finin, & Joshi, 2003; Chen, Perich, Finin, & Joshi, 2004) originate from well-known requirements of distributed computing systems: (1) contextual knowledge must be shared in spite of the dynamic nature of distributed systems, thus dealing with temporally distributed situations; (2) intelligent autonomous agents must be provided with a well-defined declarative semantics allowing them to reason upon knowledge; (3) interoperability among different heterogeneous representations must be enforced. All these aspects are mediated by a *broker*, an entity in charge of: (1) maintaining a shared language used to model situations; (2) acquiring data from heterogeneous information sources; (3) establishing information delivery policies to share contextual knowledge. Unfortunately, very simple scenarios have been modeled (e.g., meeting rooms and similar environments), which do not clearly address how temporal situations are maintained within the system.

As it can be noticed, the stress is more on infrastructure and architecture for the efficient, scalable, and robust treatment of sensory data, rather than on integrating architectural aspects with formalisms allowing the processing of temporal relationships among the assessed events and human activities.

The explicit introduction of temporal reasoning in smart environments can be considered a 2-step process. The first step is to introduce a knowledge representation layer able to efficiently assess semantically relevant information originating from the underlying architecture over time, whereas the second step consists in integrating temporal reasoning techniques on the basis of the chosen representation formalism. In the specific case of smart environments, this is realized by encoding a suitable context model (and an associated context recognition process), and then by adding another representation layer that is devoted to extract temporally related patterns of data from the model itself.

Among the possible solutions, both probabilistic and logic-based frameworks have been adopted. As an example of probabilistic approaches dealing with temporal information, Markov networks have been used in Liao, Fox, and Kautz (2005) to represent events and human activities, specifically based on the notion of *location*: the system keeps track of the sequence of visited locations in order to infer human activities, which are described by chains in the network. Although the approach exhibits good computational performance, the expressivity is rather limited, since numerical information can be hardly provided with semantics (Harnad, 1990). This drawback (that is common to all the models based on Markov networks) is faced by purposively associating nodes in the network with specific labels, e.g., the name of a visited location, thereby being able to associate simple descriptions with detected paths. Nonetheless, major limits of the approach result in the limited significance that can be associated with labeled data, and in the inability to describe complex situations in a hierarchical fashion.

On the other hand, several approaches have been proposed that manage temporal knowledge using logic-based formalisms, such as ontologies. The importance of temporal relationships in activity recognition is formally and philosophically discussed in Chalmers (2004). Stemming from the work of Martin Heidegger, and adopting human activity as the inspiring conceptual paradigm, the author argues that situations (and in particular actual contexts situations are built of) must combine both temporal and subjective patterns of interaction with different artefacts as well as a representation of the subjective experience gained during the interaction itself. This forms the basis of the so-called Activity-based Computing paradigm (Muehlenbrock, Brdiczka, Snowdon, & Meunier, 2004; Mastrogiovanni, Sgorbissa, & Zaccaria, 2008): different properties of an entity are obtained by filling particular *activity roles* and *activity relationships* among different contextual elements. This perspective has major consequences on practical aspects of situation representation and interpretation: designers of context-aware ubiquitous systems do not provide computational representations with either meaning or conceptualization; on the contrary, they can limit themselves in influencing and constraining it. In spite of the appealing characteristics of the model, to date no practical implementation has been reported in literature.

The smart home architecture presented in Augusto, et al. (2008) and Aztiria, et al. (2008) adopts a rule-based system that exploits the ECA (Event–Condition–Action) model to determine a proper action, given a particular event and provided that the proper set of conditions hold. Each rule antecedent is constituted by an event type and an expression of literals, each one expressing a specific condition that must hold for the rule to fire. As soon as interesting events are detected over time, an algorithm iteratively checks whether the corresponding conditions hold: these may hold either at the same time or in different time instants. In the second case, temporal operators define the truth table of the full condition. However, two pitfalls must be accounted for: the former is the increased computational complexity that is associated with the rule verification algorithm, whereas the latter is related to the adopted "flat" model, that is not able to easily consider hierarchies of situations and structured events.

A formally defined language aimed at integrating definition and recognition of activities has been discussed in Mastrogiovanni, et al. (2008), which adopts an ontology to directly represent distributed sensory data in a hierarchical structure. In particular, a context model that is based on the three main base constructs of *predicate*, *context*, and *situation* is encoded within the ontology. These base constructs are composed using both relational and temporal operators that define the semantics associated with the whole structure. However, the temporal expressivity is rather limited to simple forms only, whereas the uncertainty associated to sensory data (and its impact over temporal relationships) is not properly addressed.

The work presented in Henricksen, Indulska, and Rakotonirainy (2002) describes a standard Entity-Relationship language where relationships between entities can be modified at run-time according to parameters related to both temporal characteristics and information uncertainty. Therefore, relationships can be either static or dynamic, thereby leading to situations that may exhibit different parallel representations. Unfortunately, it seems very difficult to provide an AmI system with a proper dynamics operating on relationships in order to reflect the true state of the environment. For this reason, the language has been applied to very simple *toy* scenarios.

The Event Calculus has been integrated within an ontology in Chen, et al. (2008), where a cognitive model based on the notion of *predicate* is introduced. Each predicate is directly related to a number of facts occurring in the real world, each one characterized by temporal information, such as the occurrence or the initial and final time instants. Predicates contribute to *axioms*, which encode general-purpose rules about events and activities. Unfortunately, the complexity of Event Calculus allows for an experimental evaluation that is limited to restricted scenarios only.

Adopting the terminology of the Allen's Algebra, the work presented in Jakkula and Cook (2007) describes an activity recognition system that is based on the pairwise checking of detected events and activities through temporal operators. Furthermore, this framework is extended to encompass machine learning algorithms that are used in order to predict future situations on the basis of current knowledge. Again, the checking process of temporal relationships is quite computationally expensive.

As a remark, the focus of these systems has been devoted to the effective representation of context models in intelligent systems. However, it is worth noting that, from one side, knowledge representation frameworks are seldom well integrated with the underlying infrastructure, whereas, on the other side, temporal reasoning mechanisms encoded so far are rather limited.

## 3. REPRESENTATION OF TEMPORAL CONTEXTS

The work described in this paper refers to standard knowledge representation systems, and in particular to *ontologies* described using Description Logics (DL in short), which are a formal conceptualization of a set of elements belonging to a specific domain and the relationships between those elements (Baader, et al., 2003). Conceptualized elements are called *concepts*. Within an ontology $\Sigma$, concepts are represented through *symbols*, and described using *descriptions*. Formally:

$$\Sigma = \{\sigma_k\}, \ \ k = 1,\ldots,|\sigma_k| \qquad (1)$$

Each symbol $\sigma_k$ in Equation 1 is unambiguously associated with a description $\mathcal{D}_k$ that allows to define it using (combinations of) other descriptions.

In $\mathcal{SHOIN}$ ontologies (Kutz, 2004), which are the target of this discussion, it is possible to assume the availability of common logic connectors, such as *definition* $\equiv$, *and* $\sqcap$, *or* $\sqcup$ and *not* $\neg$, whose meaning is intuitive (formal specification of both syntax and semantics are beyond the scope of this chapter). We collectively define them as *host* operators, as follows:

$$\mathcal{H} \doteq \{\equiv, \sqcap, \sqcup, \neg\}.$$

Symbols in $\mathcal{SHOIN}$ ontologies are always formalized using composite descriptions that use connectors in $\mathcal{H}$. Adopting an infix notation, descriptions can be thought as:

$$\mathcal{D}_k \equiv \mathcal{D}_{k,1} \Diamond \ldots \Diamond \mathcal{D}_{k,j} \Diamond \ldots \Diamond \mathcal{D}_{k,n}, \quad \Diamond \in \mathcal{H} \setminus \equiv$$

Specifically, each constituent description $\mathcal{D}_{k,j}$ is in the form:

- $\neg \mathcal{D}_k$, $\mathcal{D}_{k_1} \sqcap \mathcal{D}_{k_2}$, or $\mathcal{D}_{k_1} \sqcup \mathcal{D}_{k_2}$, which allow to iteratively compose *abstract* descriptions on the basis of simpler *low level* descriptions.
- $\exists r.\mathcal{D}_k$ or $\forall r.\mathcal{D}_k$, where *r* is a *role* that is filled either by other composite descriptions, or by numerical, ordered or non-ordered symbols whose semantics is grounded with respect to $\Sigma$: in this case, roles are the essential formal means by which to incorporate actual sensory data within the ontology.
- $\leq_n r.\mathcal{D}_k$ or $\geq_n r.\mathcal{D}_k$, which restrict the number of possible filling descriptions for the role *r*, respectively *at most* and *at least* *n* fillers.

Furthermore, a simple and efficient inference mechanism, called *subsumption* (and referred to as $\sqsubseteq$), is commonly assumed (Horrocks & Sattler, 2007; McGuinnes & Borgida, 1995). Subsumption can be considered a binary operator acting upon two descriptions $\mathcal{D}_1$ and $\mathcal{D}_2$. However, it is usually exploited in its *query* form subs?$[\mathcal{D}_1, \mathcal{D}_2]$ to return *true* if $\mathcal{D}_1$ is *more general* than $\mathcal{D}_2$, and *false* otherwise. Intuitively, subs?$[\mathcal{D}_1, \mathcal{D}_2]$ holds if and only if $\mathcal{D}_1$ holds whenever $\mathcal{D}_2$ holds. As a practical side effect, if we consider a description $\mathcal{D}_k$ as a collection of constituent descriptions $\mathcal{D}_{k,j}$, any aggregation of $\mathcal{D}_{k,j}$ subsumes $\mathcal{D}_k$ in principle.

According to this formalization, a *satisfied* symbol $\Sigma \models \sigma_k(\hat{\sigma}_l)$ is a grounded symbol (i.e., with no unspecified role) originating from the closure of roles in $\sigma_k$ through a proper *variable assignment* α: each role *r* in the definition of $\sigma_k$ is properly filled with the correct number and type of constituent descriptions. In a more formal perspective, given a collection of symbols $\hat{\sigma}_l$, each one grounded with respect to an object $\sigma_k$ described in the ontology $\Sigma$, and given a variable assignment α under a specific interpretation $\mathcal{I}$ at a given time instant $\tau$, then the proposed model for context assessment can be seen as a collection of satisfiability procedures:

$$(\Sigma, \mathcal{I}, \alpha) \models \sigma_k(\hat{\sigma}_l), \quad l = 1, \ldots |\hat{\sigma}_l| \qquad (2)$$

In particular, the proposed model for context assessment is based on a specific definition of the structure of $\Sigma$: part of the overall ontology is devoted to represent the *primitives* that build up the context model. Although the proposed model can manage contexts with many levels of nested symbols (thereby allowing to represent specific as well as more general activities, along with their relationships, see Figure 1), three primitives are used that are hierarchically organized in:

- *Predicate*, a concept that is aimed at explicitly representing information about sensory data, and referred to as $\mathcal{P}$. In particular, for each type of information that is represented within $\Sigma$, a specific child concept of $\mathcal{P}$ is modeled: as a consequence, a set of symbols $\sigma_k$ is defined such that $\{\sigma_k \mid \Sigma \models \mathcal{P}(\sigma_k)\}$[1]. A symbol $\sigma_k$ such that $\Sigma \models \mathcal{P}(\sigma_k)$ is defined with a description $\mathcal{D}_k$ that is based exclusively on numerical, ordered or non-ordered sensory data.
- Context, a concept which purpose is to aggregate descriptions of both predicates and

Figure 1. The proposed model for context assessment

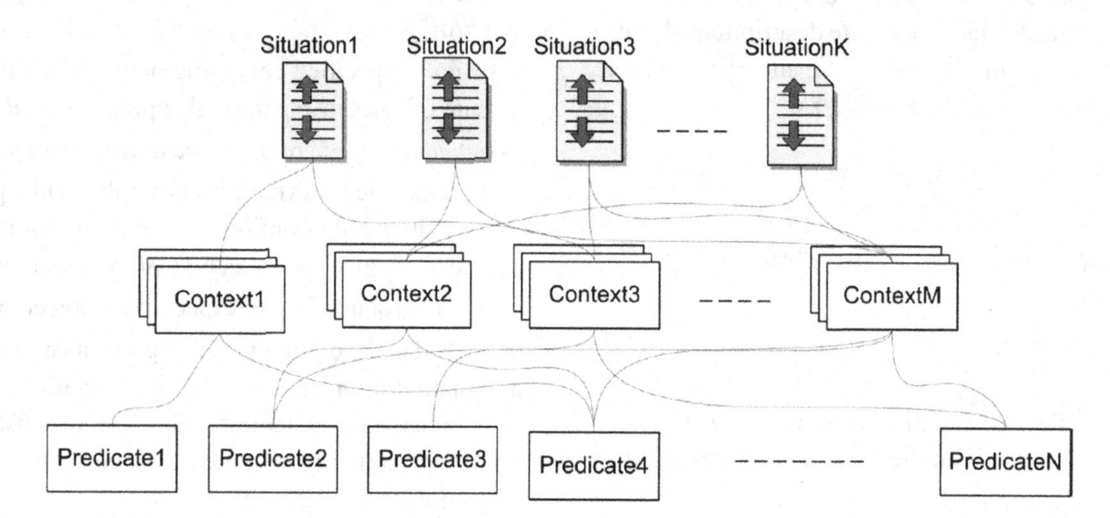


other contexts expressing information about the same entity (i.e., the same person, or the same object involved in a human-environment interaction), and referred to as $\mathcal{C}$. In particular, for each information aggregate that is to be represented, a child concept of Context is introduced in $\Sigma$. These are members of a set in the form $\{\sigma_k \mid \Sigma \vDash \mathcal{C}(\sigma_k)\}$, and correspond to descriptions based on both composite descriptions, and numerical, ordered and non-ordered sensory data. In our model, there are many Context layers, where the first is directly related to predicates.

- *Situation*, a concept that combines different contexts related to different entities to consider them *as a whole*, and is referred to as $\mathcal{S}$. Again, for each interesting situation, a child concept is introduced such that $\{\sigma_k \mid \Sigma \vDash \mathcal{S}(\sigma_k)\}$, which takes exclusively composite descriptions into account.

Since each symbol in the ontology either contributes to or ultimately represents real-world *events* the system can recognize, this structure over $\Sigma$ implicitly defines a computational process able to extract *Predicate* symbols from sensory data and to assess semantically relevant information from combinations of predicates into more complex descriptions, respectively *Context* and *Situation* descriptions. In principle, what we expect from the system is to be able to *generate* grounded descriptions $\hat{\mathcal{D}}_k$ from sensory data corresponding to those of symbols $\Sigma \vDash \mathcal{P}(\sigma_k)$, to iteratively *aggregate* them in order to satisfy symbols in $\Sigma \vDash \mathcal{C}(\sigma_k)$ and then to *combine* satisfied descriptions to check subsumption with respect to symbols in $\Sigma \vDash \mathcal{S}(\sigma_k)$. This process is described in detail in Section 3.

In order to take temporal dependencies among *Predicate*, *Context* and *Situation* symbols into account (thereby reflecting temporal relationships holding between the corresponding real-world events), the ontology is provided with a collection of temporal operators, which require to explicitly introduce time dependence, and to reformulate the context assessment satisfiability problem of Equation 2 for symbols in $\mathcal{P}$, $\mathcal{C}$ and $\mathcal{S}$. In particular, for a given time instant $\tau$, symbols $\sigma_k$, $k = 1, ..., |\mathcal{P}| + |\mathcal{C}| + |\mathcal{S}|$, are satisfied by $\hat{\sigma}_l$ in $\tau$ (and we write $\sigma_{k,\tau}$) if there is an interpretation $\mathcal{I}$ and a variable assignment $\alpha_\tau$ such that:

$$(\Sigma, \mathcal{I}, \alpha_\tau) \models \sigma_{k,\tau}(\hat{\sigma}_l), \quad l = 1, \ldots |\hat{\sigma}_l| \qquad (3)$$

This new formalization allows us to introduce a family of temporal operators, which can be roughly divided into two classes: the former:

$$\mathcal{T}_t \doteq \{\delta, \lambda\}$$

is aimed at monitoring the evolution of the single *truth value* of the term description, whereas the latter:

$$\mathcal{T}_r \doteq \{\prec_t, \succ_t, \{d\}, \{o\}, \{m\}, \Leftrightarrow, \{s\}, \{f\}\}$$

comprises the well-known operators formalized in the Allen's Interval Algebra, therefore being aimed at comparing pairwise different descriptions. Collectively, the set of temporal operators $\mathcal{T}$ is defined such that:

$$\mathcal{T} \doteq \mathcal{T}_t \cup \mathcal{T}_r.$$

Furthermore, time is modeled as an ordered sequence of time instants. In order to allow subsumption to reason upon temporal relationships, it is necessary to introduce a family of common mathematical operators:

$$\omega \in \{<, \leq, =, \geq, >\},$$

justified as *syntactic sugar*, and to use them to encode the previously introduced temporal operators into $\Sigma$.

Temporal relationships must be encoded within $\Sigma$. To this end, symbols such that $\Sigma \models \mathcal{P}(\sigma_k),$, $\Sigma \models \mathcal{C}(\sigma_k)$, and $\Sigma \models \mathcal{S}(\sigma_k)$, are characterized by descriptions $\mathcal{D}_k$ accounting for two specific roles, namely *starts_at* and *ends_at*, which are filled with instances of time instants and, considered together, specify the temporal interval when the corresponding grounded descriptions have been last satisfied by a given variable assignment. In particular, for a given symbol $\hat{\sigma}_l$, *starts_at* and *ends_at* are filled with two time instants $\tau_l^-$ and $\tau_l^+$ if, for each $\tau \in [\tau_l^-, \tau_l^+]$, $\alpha_\tau$ is such that $\hat{\sigma}_l$ is *true*. Operators in $\mathcal{T}_t$ are defined in the following paragraphs. Specifically, *starts_at* and *ends_at* are usually encoded in a specific symbol $\sigma_{PERIOD}$, which is usually associated with *Predicate*, *Context*, and *Situation* concepts.

*Change*: an unary operator, referred to as δ, which produces a description $\mathcal{D}_\delta \equiv \delta(\mathcal{D})$. Given $\mathcal{I}$, two time instants $\tau_1$ and $\tau_2$, where $\tau_1 < \tau_2$, and two variable assignments $\alpha_{\tau_1}$ and $\alpha_{\tau_2}$, $\delta_{\tau_2}(\hat{\mathcal{D}}_{\tau_2})$ is satisfied if and only if $\hat{\mathcal{D}}_{\tau_2} = \neg\hat{\mathcal{D}}_{\tau_1}$.

*Duration*: a family of binary operators, referred to as $\lambda_\omega$, which produces a description $\mathcal{D}_\lambda \equiv \lambda_\omega(\mathcal{D}_1, \mathcal{D}_2)$. Given $\mathcal{I}$, four time instants $\tau_1^-, \tau_1^+, \tau_2^-$ and $\tau_2^+$, and four variable assignments $\alpha_{\tau_1^-}, \alpha_{\tau_1^+}, \alpha_{\tau_2^-}$ and $\alpha_{\tau_2^+}$, $\alpha_{\tau_1^-} < \alpha_{\tau_1^+} < \alpha_{\tau_2^-} < \alpha_{\tau_2^+}$, for each $\tau$ such that $\alpha_{\tau_2^+} < \tau$, $\lambda_{\omega,\tau}(\hat{\mathcal{D}}_{1,\tau}, \hat{\mathcal{D}}_{2,\tau})$ is satisfied if and only if $(\tau_1^+ - \tau_1^-)\omega(\tau_2^+ - \tau_2^-)$ is *true*.

Next, operators in $\mathcal{T}_r$ are defined in the following paragraphs (see Figure 3).

*Before*[t]: a binary operator, referred to as $\prec_t$, which produces a description $\mathcal{D}_{\prec_t} \equiv \prec_t (\mathcal{D}_1, \mathcal{D}_2)$, i.e., when an events occurs *t* time instants before another one. Given $\mathcal{I}$ and a sequence of variable assignments $\{\alpha_\tau\}$, $(\hat{\mathcal{D}}_1 \prec_t \hat{\mathcal{D}}_2)$ is satisfied if and only if $\mathcal{D}_1, \mathcal{D}_2$ and $\tau_1^+ + t > \tau_2^-$ hold. When

*Figure 2. Operators table*

| Operator | Diagram | Definition |
|---|---|---|
| Before | 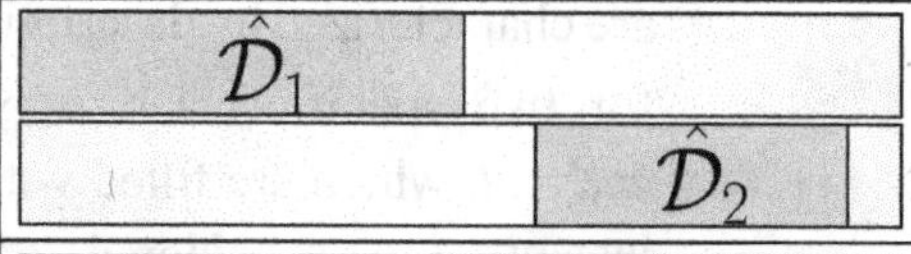 $\hat{\mathcal{D}}_1$ $\hat{\mathcal{D}}_2$ | $\hat{\mathcal{D}}_1 \prec_t \hat{\mathcal{D}}_2 \equiv \tau_1^+ + t < \tau_2^-$ |
| After | 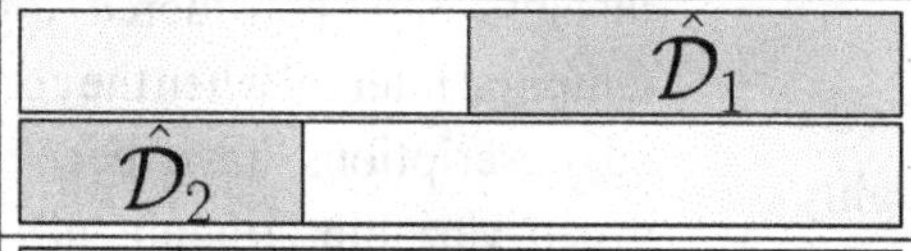 $\hat{\mathcal{D}}_1$ $\hat{\mathcal{D}}_2$ | $\hat{\mathcal{D}}_1 \succ_t \hat{\mathcal{D}}_2 \equiv \tau_1^- - t < \tau_2^+$ |
| During | 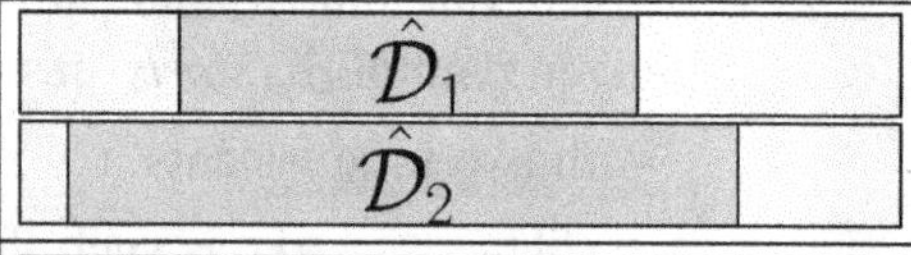 $\hat{\mathcal{D}}_1$ $\hat{\mathcal{D}}_2$ | $\hat{\mathcal{D}}_1\{d\}\hat{\mathcal{D}}_2 \equiv (\tau_1^- > \tau_2^-) \wedge (\tau_1^+ < \tau_2^+)$ |
| Overlaps | 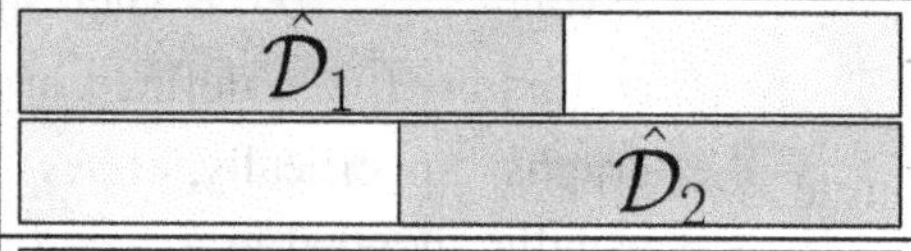 $\hat{\mathcal{D}}_1$ $\hat{\mathcal{D}}_2$ | $\hat{\mathcal{D}}_1\{o\}\hat{\mathcal{D}}_2 \equiv (\tau_1^- < \tau_2^-) \wedge (\tau_1^+ < \tau_2^-)$ |
| Meets | 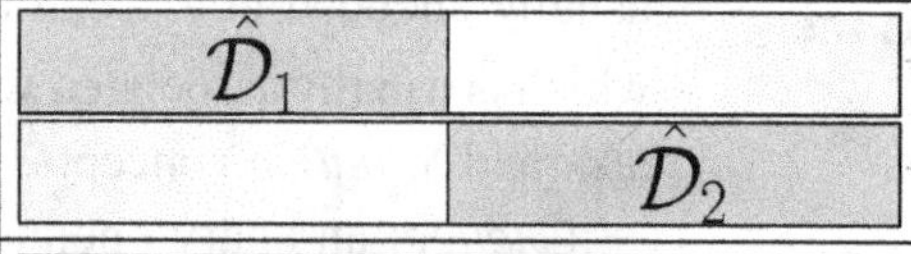 $\hat{\mathcal{D}}_1$ $\hat{\mathcal{D}}_2$ | $\hat{\mathcal{D}}_1\{m\}\hat{\mathcal{D}}_2 \equiv \tau_1^+ = \tau_2^-$ |
| Equals | 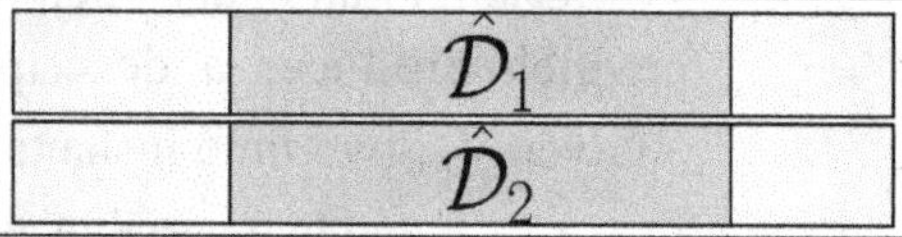 $\hat{\mathcal{D}}_1$ $\hat{\mathcal{D}}_2$ | $\hat{\mathcal{D}}_1 \circeq \hat{\mathcal{D}}_2 \equiv (\tau_1^- = \tau_2^-) \wedge (\tau_1^+ = \tau_2^+)$ |
| Starts | 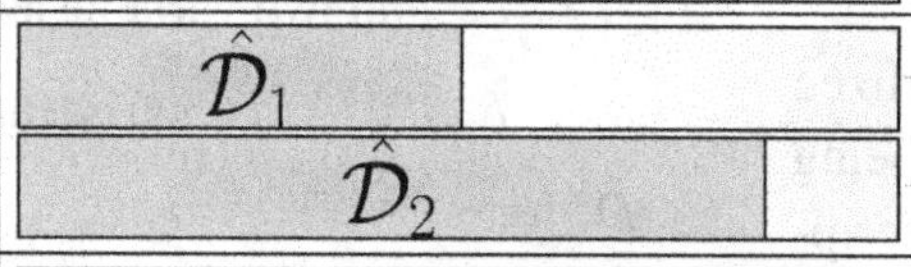 $\hat{\mathcal{D}}_1$ $\hat{\mathcal{D}}_2$ | $\hat{\mathcal{D}}_1\{s\}\hat{\mathcal{D}}_2 \equiv (\tau_1^- = \tau_2^-) \wedge (\tau_1^+ < \tau_2^+)$ |
| Finishes | 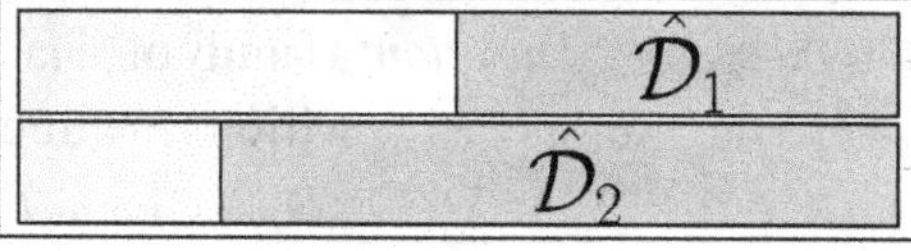 $\hat{\mathcal{D}}_1$ $\hat{\mathcal{D}}_2$ | $\hat{\mathcal{D}}_1\{f\}\hat{\mathcal{D}}_2 \equiv (\tau_1^- < \tau_2^-) \wedge (\tau_1^+ = \tau_2^+)$ |

$t$ is not specified there are no constraints over the period.

*After$^t$*: a binary operator, referred to as $\succ_t$, which produces a description $\mathcal{D}_{\succ_t} \equiv \succ_t (\mathcal{D}_1, \mathcal{D}_2)$, , i.e., the opposite of the previous case. Given $\mathcal{I}$ and a sequence of variable assignments $\{\alpha_\tau\}$, $(\hat{\mathcal{D}}_1 \succ_t \hat{\mathcal{D}}_2)$ is satisfied if and only if $\mathcal{D}_1, \mathcal{D}_2$ and $\tau_1^- - t < \tau_2^+$ holds. When $t$ is not specified there are no constraints over the period.

*During*: a binary operator, referred to as $\{d\}$, which produces a description $\mathcal{D}_d \equiv \{d\}(\mathcal{D}_1, \mathcal{D}_2)$, i.e., two events are parallel and one is entirely contained within the other one's span. Given $\mathcal{I}$ and a sequence of variable assignments $\{\alpha_\tau\}$, $\hat{\mathcal{D}}_1\{d\}\hat{\mathcal{D}}_2$ is satisfied if and only if $\mathcal{D}_1$, $\mathcal{D}_2$ and $(\tau_1^- > \tau_2^-) \wedge (\tau_1^+ < \tau_2^+)$ hold.

*Overlaps*: a binary operator, referred to as $\{o\}$, which produces a description $\mathcal{D}_o \equiv \{o\}(\mathcal{D}_1, \mathcal{D}_2)$, i.e., two events are partially parallel. Given $\mathcal{I}$ and a sequence of variable assignments $\{\alpha_\tau\}$, $\hat{\mathcal{D}}_1\{o\}\hat{\mathcal{D}}_2$ is satisfied if and only if $\mathcal{D}_1, \mathcal{D}_2$ and $(\tau_1^- < \tau_2^-) \wedge (\tau_1^+ < \tau_2^-)$ hold.

*Meets*: a binary operator, referred to as $\{m\}$, which produces a description $\mathcal{D}_m \equiv \{m\}(\mathcal{D}_1, \mathcal{D}_2)$, i.e., when one events exactly starts when the another one ends. Given $\mathcal{I}$ and a sequence of

*Figure 3. The context assessment process*

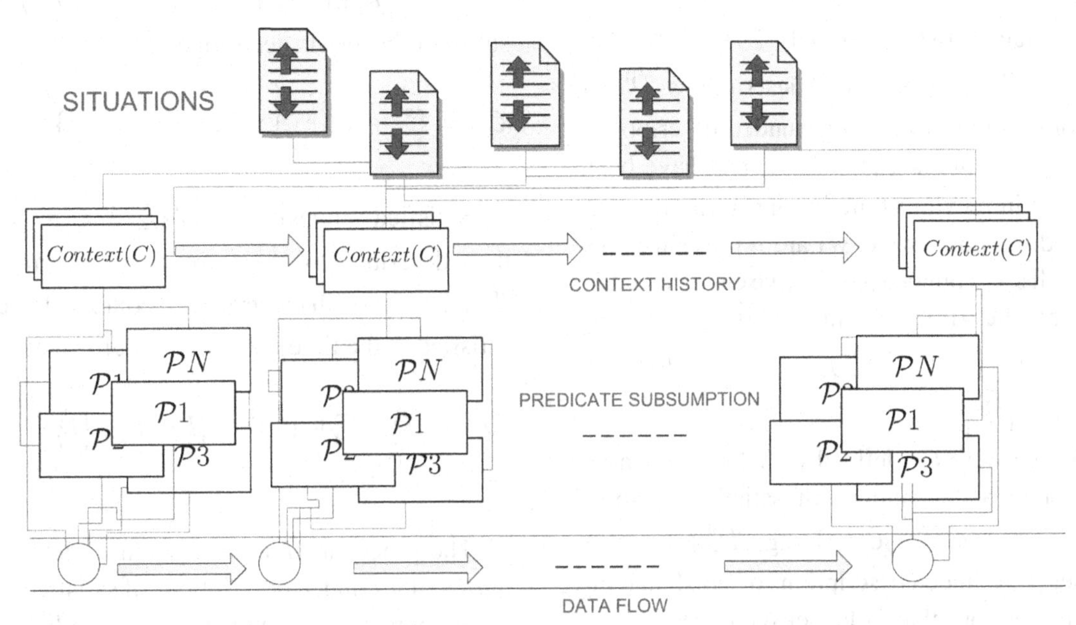


variable assignments $\{\alpha_\tau\}$, $\hat{\mathcal{D}}_1\{m\}\hat{\mathcal{D}}_2$ is satisfied if and only if $\mathcal{D}_1, \mathcal{D}_2$ and $\tau_1^{+} = \tau_2^{-}$ hold.

*Equals*: a binary operator, referred to as $\Leftrightarrow$, which produces a description $\mathcal{D}_{\Leftrightarrow} \equiv \Leftrightarrow(\mathcal{D}_1, \mathcal{D}_2)$, i.e., two events last exactly for the same period of time. Given $\mathcal{I}$ and a sequence of variable assignments $\{\alpha_\tau\}$, $\hat{\mathcal{D}}_1 \Leftrightarrow \hat{\mathcal{D}}_2$ is satisfied if and only if $\mathcal{D}_1, \mathcal{D}_2$ and $(\tau_1^{-} = \tau_2^{-}) \wedge (\tau_1^{+} = \tau_2^{+})$ hold.

*Starts*: a binary operator, referred to as $\{s\}$, which produces a description $\mathcal{D}_s \equiv \{s\}(\mathcal{D}_1, \mathcal{D}_2)$, i.e., two events start exactly at the same time. Given $\mathcal{I}$ and a sequence of variable assignments $\{\alpha_\tau\}$, $\hat{\mathcal{D}}_1\{s\}\hat{\mathcal{D}}_2$ is satisfied if and only if $\mathcal{D}_1, \mathcal{D}_2$ and $(\tau_1^{-} = \tau_2^{-}) \wedge (\tau_1^{+} < \tau_2^{+})$ hold.

*Finishes*: a binary operator, referred to as $\{f\}$, which produces a description $\mathcal{D}_s \equiv \{f\}(\mathcal{D}_1, \mathcal{D}_2)$, i.e., two events end exactly at the same time. Given $\mathcal{I}$ and a sequence of variable assignments $\{\alpha_\tau\}$, $\hat{\mathcal{D}}_1\{f\}\hat{\mathcal{D}}_2$ is satisfied if and only if $\mathcal{D}_1, \mathcal{D}_2$ and $(\tau_1^{-} < \tau_2^{-}) \wedge (\tau_1^{+} = \tau_2^{+})$ hold.

Collectively, operators in $\mathcal{T}$ are used during the context assessment phase to recognize temporal relationships between descriptions. In particular, grounded descriptions (originated from sensory data) are evaluated in order to establish temporal relationships by inspecting the values of the roles *starts_at* and *ends_at* through subsumption with respect to operators in $\mathcal{T}$. Obviously enough, the evaluation of temporal operators is deferred in time, since they involve many events to occur in sequence.

## 4. ASSESSMENT OF TEMPORAL CONTEXTS

Given an ontology-based context model defined as in the previous Section, temporal context assessment is realized by iteratively aggregating descriptions in order to satisfy elements in $\mathcal{C}$ and $\mathcal{S}$ (see Figure 3 on the bottom). Every time instant $\tau$, and as a consequence of a variable assignment $\alpha_\tau$ (i.e., when updated sensory data are available), a classification process is carried out over grounded symbols $\sum \models \mathcal{P}(\hat{\sigma}_l)$, thereby modifying their truth value. Satisfied symbols $\sum \models \mathcal{P}(\sigma_k)$ are then described by grounded descriptions $\hat{\mathcal{D}}_l^p$. It is worth noting that also grounded descriptions related to symbols $\sum \models \mathcal{P}(\sigma_k)$ that have been satisfied in previous time instants (within a predefined temporal window) are represented: the set of all the grounded predicative elements satisfied at the time instant $\tau$ is defined as $\hat{\mathcal{D}}_\tau^p \doteq \{\hat{\mathcal{D}}_l^p \mid \sum \models \mathcal{P}(\hat{\mathcal{D}}_l^p)\}$, where $l = 1,\ldots,\left|\hat{\mathcal{D}}_l^p\right|$.

A procedure $T$ is defined such that, given a set of grounded descriptions of satisfied symbols $\sum \models \mathcal{P}(\sigma_k)$ or $\sum \models \mathcal{C}(\sigma_k)$ (e.g., $\hat{\mathcal{D}}_\tau^p$), it returns the set of grounded descriptions of satisfied temporal operators that hold between them in $\tau$. Specifically, if the set of temporal relationships holding between grounded symbols $\sum \models \mathcal{P}(\hat{\sigma}_l)$ is defined as:

$$\hat{\mathcal{D}}_\tau^{t(p)} \doteq \{\hat{\mathcal{D}}_m^{t(p)} \mid \sum \models \bigcup_{\Upsilon \in \tau} \Upsilon(\hat{\mathcal{D}}_m^{t(p)})\}, \quad (4)$$

then $T$ is defined such that $\hat{\mathcal{D}}_\tau^{t(p)} = T(\hat{\mathcal{D}}_\tau^p)$. If we omit the dependency of temporal operator descriptions on those of predicates, we define the *history* of the system at the *Predicate* level by joining descriptions belonging to $\hat{\mathcal{D}}_\tau^p$ and $\hat{\mathcal{D}}_\tau^{t(p)}$, as:

$$\hat{\mathcal{D}}_{s,\tau}^{p\cup t(p)} = \hat{\mathcal{D}}_1^p \sqcap \ldots \sqcap \hat{\mathcal{D}}_{|\hat{\mathcal{D}}_l^p|}^p \sqcap \hat{\mathcal{D}}_1^t \sqcap \ldots \sqcap \hat{\mathcal{D}}_{|\hat{\mathcal{D}}_m^t|}^t \doteq \hat{\mathcal{D}}_{s,i}, \quad (5)$$

where $s$ stands for *satisfied*, and $i$ is an index (initialized to 0) whose meaning is related to the number of hierarchical *Context* levels that are represented within the ontology. At this point, a sequence of steps is recursively performed. The set $\mathcal{C}_{s,i}$ of $i$-th level symbols $\sum \models \mathcal{C}(\sigma_{k,i})$ that subsume *history* is determined as:

$$\mathcal{C}_{s,i} \doteq \{\sum \models \mathcal{C}(\sigma_{k,i}) : \text{subs?}[\sigma_{k,i}, \hat{\mathcal{D}}_{s,i}]\} \quad (6)$$

Satisfied $i$-th level symbols $\sum \models \mathcal{C}(\sigma_{k,i})$ are then described by their grounded descriptions $\hat{\mathcal{D}}_l^c$. The set of all the grounded context elements satisfied at the time instant $\tau$ is defined as:

$$\hat{\mathcal{D}}_\tau^c \doteq \{\hat{\mathcal{D}}_l^c \mid \sum \models \mathcal{C}(\hat{\mathcal{D}}_l^c)\}, l = 1,\ldots,\left|\hat{\mathcal{D}}_l^c\right|. \quad (7)$$

The procedure $T$ is used again to determine the set of grounded descriptions of satisfied temporal operators holding between grounded symbols $\sum \models \mathcal{C}(\hat{\sigma}_{k,i})$ at the time instant $\tau$ $\hat{\mathcal{D}}_\tau^{t(c)} = T(\hat{\mathcal{D}}_\tau^c)$, and therefore:

$$\hat{\mathcal{D}}_\tau^{t(c)} \doteq \{\hat{\mathcal{D}}_m^{t(c)} \mid \sum \models \bigcup_{\Upsilon \in \tau} \Upsilon(\hat{\mathcal{D}}_m^{t(c)})\}. \quad (8)$$

The *history* of the system at the $i$-th *Context* level is determined by joining descriptions belonging to $\hat{\mathcal{D}}_\tau^{t(c)}$ and $\hat{\mathcal{D}}_\tau^c$, as:

$$\hat{\mathcal{D}}_{s,\tau}^{c\cup t(c)} = \hat{\mathcal{D}}_1^c \sqcap \ldots \sqcap \hat{\mathcal{D}}_{|\hat{\mathcal{D}}_l^c|}^c \sqcap \hat{\mathcal{D}}_1^t \sqcap \ldots \sqcap \hat{\mathcal{D}}_{|\hat{\mathcal{D}}_m^t|}^t \doteq \hat{\mathcal{D}}_{s,i}. \quad (9)$$

The recursion over Equations 5-8 ends when there are no more ($i$+1)-th level symbols $\sum \models \mathcal{C}(\sigma_{k,i+1})$. As a final step, the set of *Situation* symbols $\sum \models \mathcal{S}(\sigma_k)$ that are satisfied at the time instant $\tau$, namely $\mathcal{S}_{s,\tau}$, is given by:

$$\mathcal{S}_{s,\tau} \doteq \{\sum \models \mathcal{S}(\sigma_k) : \text{subs?}[\sigma_k, \hat{\mathcal{D}}_{s,i}]\} \quad (10)$$

Once the set $\mathcal{S}_{s,\tau}$ is assessed, the system is said to be *aware* of modeled *events* occurring within the monitored environment at the time instant $\tau$. The architecture implements a 3-layer context-aware mechanism, each layer devoted to manage different aspects of context recognition:

- *Predicate layer*. A fast dynamically changing representation structure that, for efficiency reasons related to the complexity of inference mechanisms in DL-based ontologies (Horrocks & Sattler, 2007), is constrained to operate on a limited temporal window. However, its importance relies in that it follows *high frequency* variations in patterns of sensory data and the associated temporal relationships.
- *Context layer*. A multiple-resolution representation layer that allows to formally model contexts at different degrees of granularity. For this reason, it can cope with *middle* and *slow frequency* fluctuations in observed data thereby recognizing trends over long periods of time.
- *Situation layer*. An aggregation level that allows the evaluation of combined events, possibly spanned over time and only loosely coupled.

## 5. EXPERIMENTAL RESULTS AND DISCUSSION

During the past few years, many experiments have been performed in the Know-House environment (Mastrogiovanni, Sgorbissa, & Zaccaria, 2007) to validate both the temporal context model and the context assessment procedure. In this Section, an example is described with the purpose of clarifying the conceptual steps involved in representing temporal information and assessing temporal relationships between events and human activities as they are represented within the ontology. Specifically, in order to ground the discussion, we show how to encode and assess a sophisticated daily activity. The overall system is currently undergoing an experimental evaluation at Villa Basilea, an assisted-living facility located in Genoa (Italy), where a dedicated apartment has been provided with different kinds of sensors and smart appliances (see Figure 5). Specifically:

- Twelve Passive Infra Red (PIR) sensors located to monitor interesting areas of the apartment, such as the "bed area" in the bedroom or "table area" and "stove area" in the kitchen.
- Five integrated temperature, luminosity and humidity sensors, each one located in a different room.
- Five RFID antennas, which allow the system to track specific users in the apartment, each one located in a different room.
- Ten light switches to control lights state.
- Eleven contact sensors for detecting doors and windows state.
- Three smoke detectors located—respectively—in the kitchen, the bedroom and the living room.
- One smart TV, which is able to provide the system with information about its usage.
- Two pressure sensors, the first for the armchair in the living room and the second for detecting bed usage.
- Six cameras with integrated motion detection algorithms that allow the system to monitor wide apartment areas revealing "activities" therein.

As it has been described in Mastrogiovanni, Sgorbissa, and Zaccaria (2007), all collected sensory data are then processed on a centralized processing unit where both the ontology and the context assessment algorithms have been implemented.

### 5.1. An Example of System Usage

In this section, we focus on the following sequence of activities that must be detected by the context assessment process:

*Figure 5. The Villa Basilea set-up. Top: the living room; bottom left: the kitchen; bottom right: the bedroom.*

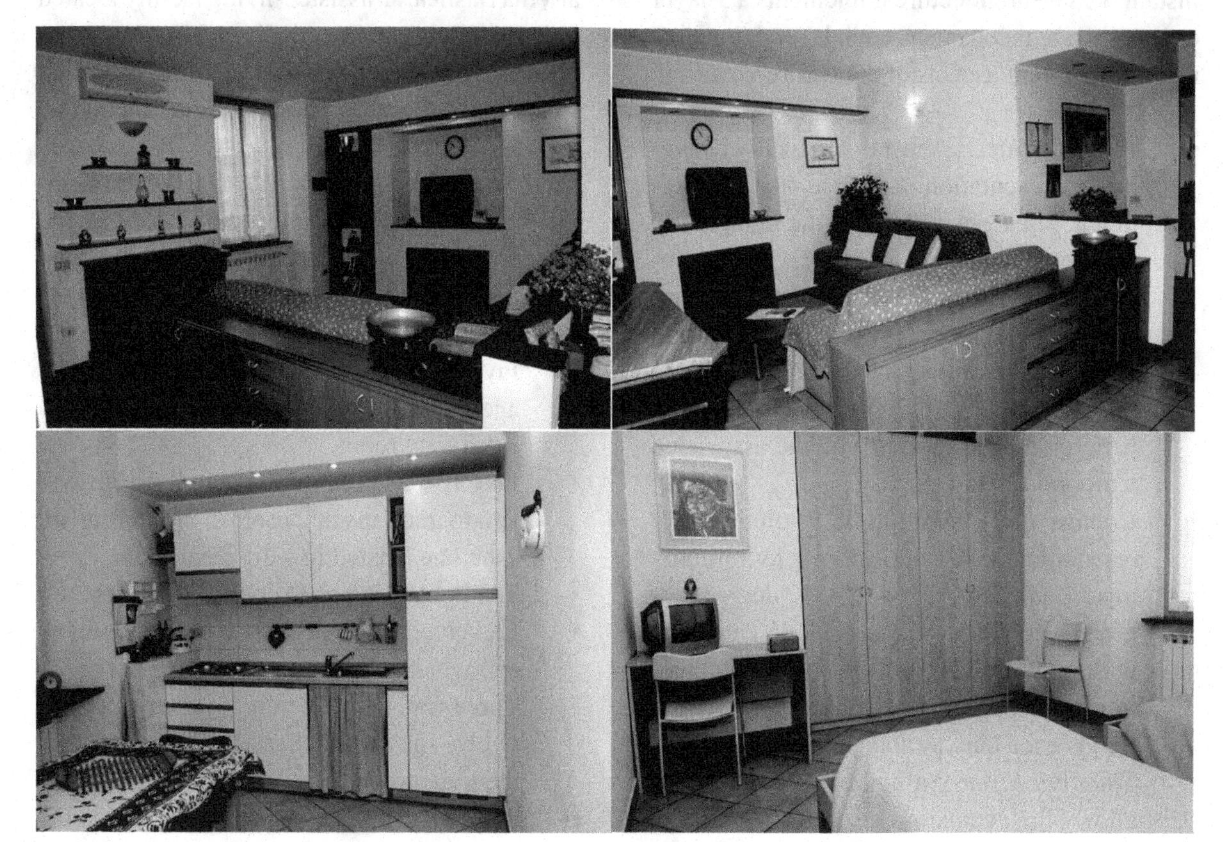

*"after having switched the light off, the user watches the TV while sitting on the armchair for about one hour; after that, within half an hour, he goes to bed."*

Specifically, in the following paragraphs, we focus only on issues related to the modeling phase and the associated context assessment process.

*Modeling.* First of all, it is important to notice that the previously introduced sequence of activities to be recognized must be modeled using a *Situation* concept, since it involves representation layers related to many entities: *user*, *TV*, and *bed*, just to name a few. Using the temporal operators in $\mathcal{T}$, this situation can be written using the composite formula:

$$NocturnalActivity \equiv TurnedOffKitchenLight \prec SittingOnChair \sqcap SittingOnChair\{d\}WatchingTV1hour \sqcap InBed \succ_{30min} WatchingTV1hour.$$

As it can be noticed, this definition is made up of three constituent descriptions, namely:

$$\mathcal{D}_1 \equiv TurnedOffKitchenLight \prec SittingOnChair,$$
$$\mathcal{D}_2 \equiv SittingOnChair\{d\}WatchingTV1hour,$$
$$\mathcal{D}_3 \equiv InBed \succ_{30min} WatchingTV1hour,$$

each one corresponding to a particular context. Then, each context is mapped to a number of predicates (see Figure 4 on the top). As previously described, Predicate concepts in $\sum$ directly represent sensory information. In the following paragraphs we exemplify how to model a particular contextual element, namely SittingOn-

*Figure 4. Top: a relevant sketch of the ontology; bottom: a variable assignment that satisfies the ontology*

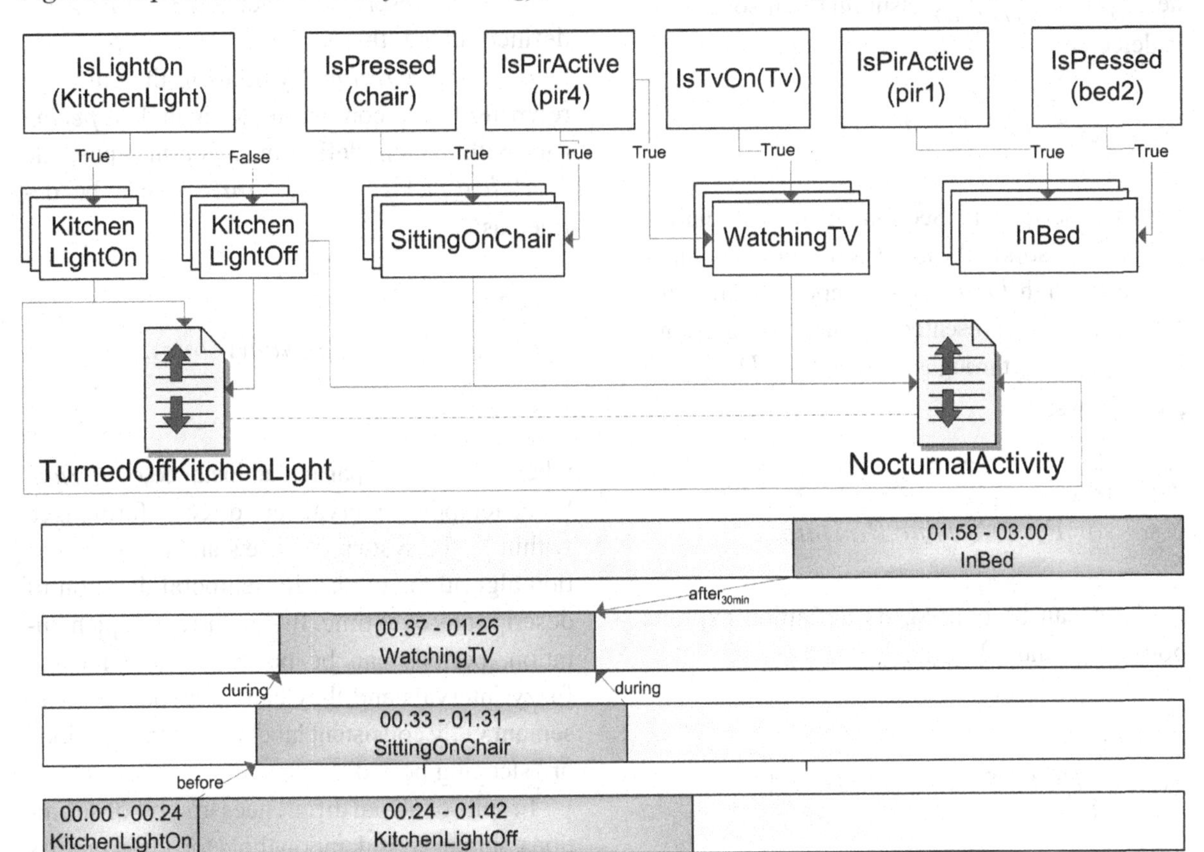


Chair. To this aim, we first specify the $PIR \sqsubseteq Sensor$ symbol $\sigma_{PIR}$, characterized by the description $\mathcal{D}_{PIR}$, as follows:

$$\mathcal{D}_{PIR} = \forall id.INTEGER \sqcap \forall description.STRING)\forall range.Area),$$

where *id* is the *PIR* identification number, *description* is aimed at providing system users with meaningful information about the sensor, whereas *range* is a role that is filled with instances of the *Area* concept in order to associate sensory data with labeled places within the environment. For instance, if we want to model a specific *PIR* sensor with *id* equal to "4" and detecting events in the *Kitchen* area (where the *chair* is located), we have:

$$\mathcal{D}_{PIR4} \equiv id(4) \sqcap description(\text{"}KitchenPIRSensor\text{"}) \sqcap range(Kitchen)$$

At the same time, we specify the $PIRData \sqsubseteq Data$ symbols $\sigma_{PIRData}$, that is characterized by the description $\mathcal{D}_{PIRData}$, as follows:

$$\mathcal{D}_{PIRData} = \forall Id.INTEGER \sqcap \forall value.INTEGER$$

where *id* specifies the *Data* type, whereas *value* is the actual sensor reading. For instance, if something is detected by *pir4*, this will be modeled within the ontology by the following grounded description $\hat{\mathcal{D}}_{PIRData4}$, assuming that something is detected:

$$\hat{\mathcal{D}}_{PIRData4} = Id(1) \sqcap value(1)$$

As described in Section 3, the association between sensors and sensory information is maintained through *Predicate* concepts. Specifically, *IsPirActive* is represented within $\sum$ using a symbol $\sigma_{IsPIRActive}$ through a description $\mathcal{D}_{IsPIRActive}$, as follows:

$$\mathcal{D}_{IsPirActive} = \forall sensor.Pir \sqcap \forall value.PirData.$$

As it can be noticed, its definition exploits both $\mathcal{D}_{PIR}$ and $\mathcal{D}_{PIRData}$:

$$\hat{\mathcal{D}}_{IsPIRActive4} = sensor(PIR4) \sqcap value(PirData4)$$

Similar considerations hold for all the other *Predicate* concepts, and in particular, for *Pressed*. Once both *IsPIRActive* and *IsPressed* are represented within the ontology, it is straightforward to introduce *SittingOnChair* using a symbol $\sigma_{SittingOnChair}$, that is described using the following description:

$$SittingOnChair \equiv Pressed(chair, chairData) \sqcap PirActive(PIR4, PirData4).$$

It is worth noticing that, in our current implementation, the system is able to dynamically create all the relevant *Predicate* instances on the basis of associated specifications for actual deployed sensors.

Temporal relationships in the *NocturnalActivity* formula are expressed using the $\sigma_{PERIOD}$ concept. As described in Section 3, *PERIOD* is defined using three roles, namely *starts_at*, *ends_at* and *duration*. Symbols in the ontology referring to the context model include a *period* role within their definitions. For instance, the $WatchingTV1hour \sqsubseteq Context$ can be defined as:

$$WatchingTV1hour \equiv WatchingTV \sqcap \forall period(1hour),$$

where *1hour* is a particular instance of *Period*. Since temporal intervals are directly formalized within $\sum$, the system can use standard subsumption algorithms to classify temporal duration of descriptions over time. In our current implementation, periods can be possibly defined using fuzzy intervals and they can be associated with semantically consistent labels, like "long period" or "sleeping period".

In spite of actual differences in symbol definitions, similar considerations hold for other contexts as well: first relevant *Predicates* are built, and then they are used to define *Contexts*. Contexts must be used to define more complex relationships, i.e., *Situations*.

It is now possible to define the description that has been previously labeled as $\mathcal{D}_2$, by combining *SittingOnChair* wirh *WatchingTV1hour* be means of the *during* temporal operator. In particular, assuming that $\tau_1^-$ and $\tau_1^+$ are—respectively—the initial and the final ends of the temporal interval when *SittingOnChair* holds, and that $\tau_2^-$ and $\tau_2^+$ are—respectively—the initial and the final ends of the temporal interval when *WaitingTV1hour* holds, then *SittingOnChair*{*d*}*WatchingTV1hour* is defined as follows:

$$\mathcal{D}_2 \equiv SittingOnChair \sqcap WatchingTV1hour \sqcap (\tau_1^- > \tau_2^+) \sqcap (\tau_1^+ < \tau_2^+)$$

If sensory data are such that the two contexts *SittingOnChair* and *WatchingTV1hour* hold, and if the two temporal intervals are such to satisfy the two relationships $(\tau_1^- > \tau_2^-)$ and $(\tau_1^+ > \tau_2^+)$, then the *during* temporal operator is said to be satisfied.

*Context recognition.* An example of sequence of variable assignments satisfying *NocturnalActivity* is given in Figure 4 on the bottom. According to the proposed model, context recognition is an iterative process that, every time instant $\tau$, determines the set of all the satisfied *Predicate* concepts $\hat{\mathcal{D}}_\tau^p$. On the basis of $\hat{\mathcal{D}}_\tau^p$, the set $\hat{\mathcal{D}}_\tau^{t(p)}$ of all the *relevant* temporal relationships among satisfied instances of *Predicate* is built. It is worth noticing that, in our current implementation, we do not exhaustively build all the *possible* relationships among satisfied *Predicate* concepts: on the contrary, we consider only those relationships appearing in definitions of either *Context* or *Situation* concepts. This mechanism can be easily extended to *Context* concepts satisfied in $\tau$ (see Equations 6-9).

If we carefully look at the definition of *NocturnalActivity*, it is possible to notice that *TurnOffKitchenLight* can be formalized into two ways, either using the derivative of *IsLightOn*, namely $\delta\{IsLightOn\}_\tau^{t\to f}$, or exploiting a sequence that represents the variation of the kitchen light from *on* to *off*, as *KitchenLightOn*$\{m\}$*KitchenLightOff*.

With the respect to our example, and starting from the *Context* level for the sake of brevity, we can see that at the time instant $\tau$=00.23, only one relevant *Context* is recognized, namely:

$$\hat{\mathcal{D}}_{00.23}^c = \{KitchenLightOn\}.$$

Since only one satisfied *Context* is represented within history, the corresponding set of temporal relationships is empty, and therefore:

$$\hat{\mathcal{D}}_{00.23}^{t(c)} = \{\}.$$

As a consequence, the overall history at the time instant $\tau$=00.23 is given by:

$$\hat{\mathcal{D}}_{s,00.23}^{c\cup t(c)} = \{KitchenLightOn\}.$$

When, at $\tau$=00.24, the lights are switched off, the Context *KitchenLightOff* is recognized, and therefore it becomes part of history:

$$\hat{\mathcal{D}}_{00.24}^c = \{KitchenLightOn, KitchenLightOff\}.$$

However, an interesting temporal relationships involving both *KitchenLightOn* and *KitchenLightOff* is detected, i.e.:

$$\hat{\mathcal{D}}_{00.24}^{t(c)} = \{TurnedOffKitchenLight\}.$$

The corresponding overall history at $\tau$=00.24 is updated as follows:

$$\hat{\mathcal{D}}_{s,00.23}^{c\cup t(c)} = \{KitchenLightOn, KitchenLightOff, TurnedOffKitchenLight\}.$$

As it is shown in Figure 4, the next interesting event occurs at the time instant $\tau$=00.40, when the TV is switched on. Analogously to what has been previously shown, history is updated as follows:

$$\hat{\mathcal{D}}_{00.40}^c = \{KitchenLightOn, KitchenLightOff, SittingOnChair, WatchingTV\},$$

$$\hat{\mathcal{D}}_{00.40}^{t(c)} = \{TurnedOffKitchenLight, \mathcal{D}_1\},$$

and then:

$$\hat{\mathcal{D}}_{s,00.40.}^{c\cup t(c)} = \{KitchenLightOn, KitchenLightOff, TurnedOffKitchenLight, SittingOnChair, WatchingTV, \mathcal{D}_1\}.$$

Obviously enough, the proper detection of *WatchingTV1hour* is postponed exactly of one hour (given its definition). Finally, at the time instant $\tau$=01.58, all the events described in *NocturnalActivity* are detected, since:

$$\hat{\mathcal{D}}^{c}_{01.58} = \{KitchenLightOn, KitchenLightOff, SittingOnChair, WatchingTV1hour, OnBed\},$$
$$\hat{\mathcal{D}}^{t(c)}_{01.58} = \{\mathcal{D}_1, \mathcal{D}_2, \mathcal{D}_3\},$$
$$\hat{\mathcal{D}}^{c \cup t(c)}_{s,01.58} = \{KitchenLightOn, KitchenLightOff, TurnedOffKitchenLight, SittingOnChair, WatchingTV1hour, OnBed, \mathcal{D}_1, \mathcal{D}_2, \mathcal{D}_3\}.$$

Finally:

$$\mathcal{S}_{s,01.58} \doteq \{\Sigma \models \mathcal{S}(\sigma_{NocturnalActivity}) : \text{subs?}[\sigma_{NocturnalActivity}, \hat{\mathcal{D}}_{s,01.58}]\}$$

As a practical example, at time instant 1.00pm, context history comprises three elements: *TurnedOffKitchenLight*, *WatchingTV*, and *SittingOnChair*. The overall sequence is detected at time instant 1.58, when *InBed* is detected. If we carefully look at the temporal order scheme, the two time instants *KitchenLightOn*$^+$ and *KitchenLightOff* are filled with the same numerical value (i.e., 00.24), and therefore *KitchenLightOn*$\{m\}$ *KitchenLightOff* is satisfied, thereby *satisfying TurnedOffKitchenLight* as well. The next event on the "timeline" is *SittingOnChair*, which starts at time instant 0.33; the following detected one is *WatchTV1hour*, and so on. In order for the overall *Situation* to be detected, time instants to be considered are only those directly expressed in temporal operators. As a major consequence, a possible instance of temporal relationships is:

$$TurnedOffKitchenLight^{+} < SittingOnChair^{-} \sqcap SittingOnChair^{-} < WatchingTV1hour^{-} \sqcap SittingOnChair^{+} > WatchingTV1hour^{+} + t < InBed^{-},$$

which, when actual temporal values are substituted, turns out to be:

$$0.24 < 0.33 \sqcap 0.33 < 0.37 \sqcap 1.39 > 1.38 \sqcap 1.38 + 0.30 > 1.58.$$

When this happens, the formula is said to be satisfied.

## 5.2. A Discussion about Context Assessment Complexity and System Performance

One of the major requirements of context assessment systems is to recognize a dangerous situation in real-time and to promptly react whenever the detected situation calls for an immediate action. As a consequence, performance issues are very important both in principle but also at a practical level. Furthermore, real-time requirements must be guaranteed at *system level*, i.e., both at the infrastructural and reasoning levels. With respect to real-time requirements at the infrastructural level, these have been addressed in previous work (Mastrogiovanni, Sgorbissa & Zaccaria, 2007), where a distributed, scalable and real-time architecture has been discussed that is at the basis of the current system implementation. However, the real challenge in any symbolic-based architecture is to guarantee real-time performance at the reasoning and knowledge representation levels.

The proposed system requires that information originating from distributed devices is represented and managed by means of an ontology, where reasoning processes occur that implement the described context assessment mechanism. As it has been described in Borgida (1996), low-order polynomial complexity in ontology-based inference can be obtained by imposing a monotonic increase of the number of represented concepts and individuals. This implies that named concepts and individuals cannot be removed from the ontology: the number of symbols is to be maintained constant.

This is in contrast with what is expected to happen in a real-world environment, where novel events, situations and human actions can originate new symbols (in particular, new individuals) in the ontology as time passes. In order to cope with this issue, the implemented system adopts a hybrid approach: the goal is to keep the number

*Figure 6. After system bootstrap, assuming 10 new symbols per hour, the blue line shows a generic increase rate for stored symbols in the ontology, whereas the red line shows the corresponding increase rate for the proposed system*

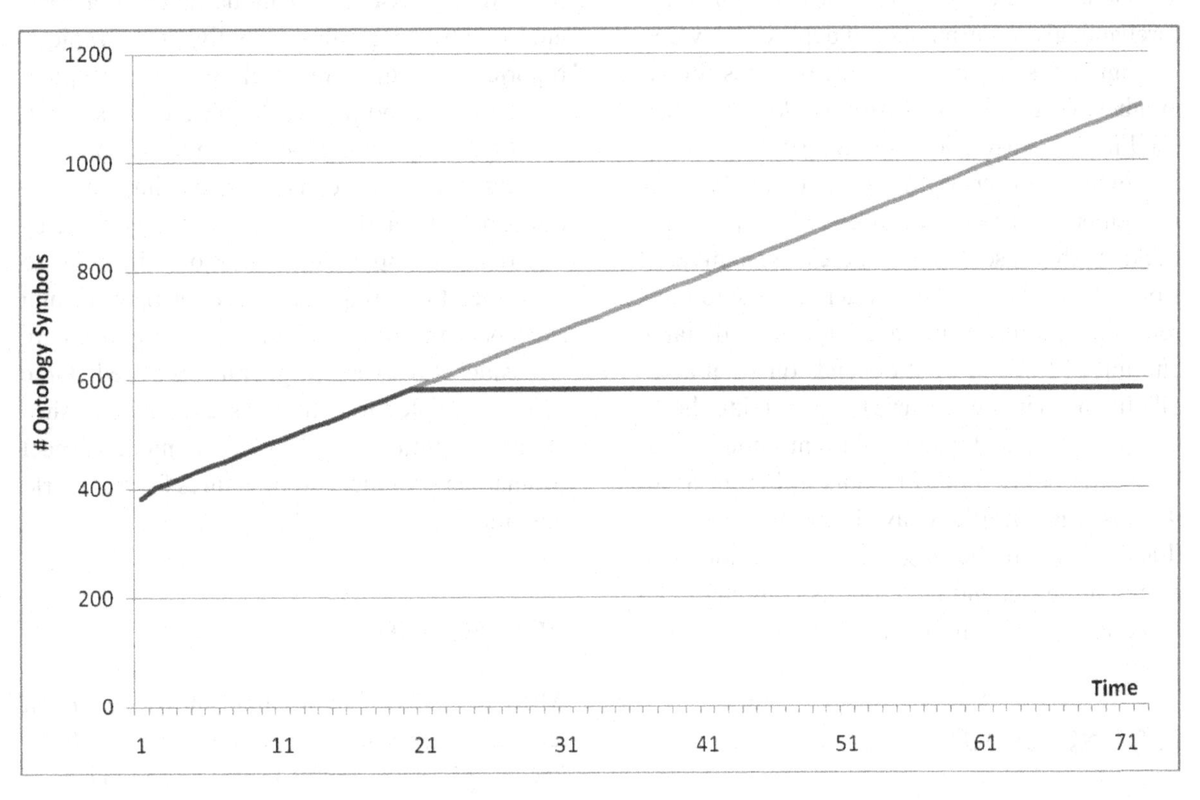


of concepts and individual constant over time, while being able to update relevant information in real-time.

Basically, two kinds of symbols must be dealt with: the former class comprises those symbols that are related to the context model, i.e., concepts and individuals related to *Predicates*, *Contexts*, and *Situations*, whereas the latter includes symbols that represent sensors and sensor data. With respect to the first class, detected instances of *Predicates*, *Contexts*, and *Situations* are represented using placeholder individuals that maintain information on a given number of their occurrences over time. Basically, the *same* individual is used to keep information about *many* actual instances. According to a formal perspective, this approach can be considered "semantically incoherent," since it is always assumed that a one-to-one mapping exists between instances and real-world entities; however, practice suggests that this "trick" does not impact on formal system properties. Obviously enough, the number of instances maintained within the corresponding individual affects the overall *history* length and, as a consequence, the temporal complexity of the situations that can be detected over time: the bigger this number, the longer the history of past events the system can reason upon. With respect to the second class, the number of needed symbols can be computed *in advance* with respect to the number of devices actually used: in this analysis, we consider a minimum of three concepts for each sensing device representing sensory data, the actual physical device and the related *Predicates*. Sensors measuring physical properties defined in a range (i.e., temperature) are characterized by discrete (fuzzy) intervals at the *Predicates* level: sensors and sensory data are represented with one corresponding individual.

Analogously to what happens for symbols in the context model, the number of symbols involved in grounding sensory data can be determined beforehand, given the number of deployed devices.

Figure 6 superimposes increase rates for the number of symbols stored in the ontology currently used in the real-world scenario of Villa Basilea. The blue line describes the rate associated with an implementation that does not exploit the proposed tricks. In this case, the ever-increasing number of stored symbols leads to a system unable to meet real-time requirements after an unpredictable amount of time, since it depends on what actually happens in the scenario). The red line shows the rate associated with the current implementation: after some time (21 hours in Figure 6) all the possible *Situations* have been detected: from this moment on, the system can be considered at a regime phase, and therefore its computational behavior can be carefully predicted.

## 6. CONCLUSION

In this chapter, an architecture for context assessment in smart environments has been proposed, with a particular emphasis on the knowledge representation and reasoning capabilities that are needed for real-time operation. In particular, the presented framework exploits an ontology and the associated subsumption inference process to reason upon sensory information that represents events and human actions the system must detect. The ontology is fed with sensory data originated from distributed devices by means of symbols that directly map data into semantically relevant information. These base symbols are then used as input to a hierarchical context model that is organized into three layers: *Predicates* are responsible for coupling sensory data with the relevant entities, *Contexts* are aimed at organizing *Predicates* in symbolic structures, which relate different information, *Situations* aggregate many Contexts to define more complex structures, which can include temporal relationships between events and human actions. Specific focus has been devoted to a context assessment model and the associated iterative algorithm. Finally, an example is reported with the aim of clarifying conceptual aspects related both to modeling and assessment.

Differently from what can be found in literature, a special attention is devoted to implementation aspects related to computational requirements and real-time operating conditions. In order to guarantee these requirements over time, formal aspects of the adopted logic-based approach are left aside. However, this guarantees a predictable behavior related to context assessment and situation recognition, which is a fundamental aspect of smart environment architectures for real world operation.

## REFERENCES


Allen, J. (1983). Maintaining knowledge about temporal intervals. *Communications of the ACM*, *26*(11), 832–843. doi:10.1145/182.358434

Augusto, J. C., Liu, J., McCullagh, P., Wang, H., & Yang, J.-B. (2008). Management of uncertainty and spatio-temporal aspects for monitoring and diagnosis in a smart home. *International Journal of Computational Intelligence Systems*, *1*(4), 361–378. doi:10.2991/ijcis.2008.1.4.8

Aztiria, A., Augusto, J. C., Izaguirre, A., & Cook, D. (2008). Learning accurate temporal relations from user actions in intelligent environments. In *Proceedings of the Symposium of Ubiquitous Computing and Ambient Intelligence*, (pp. 274-283). Salamanca, Spain. Ubiquitous Computing and Ambient Intelligence.

Baader, F., Calvanese, D., McGuinness, D., Nardi, D., & Patel-Schneider, P. (2003). *The description logic handbook*. New York, NY: Cambridge University Press.

Bettini, C., Mascetti, S., & Sean Wang, X. (2007). Supporting temporal reasoning by mapping calendar expressions to minimal periodic sets. *Journal of Artificial Intelligence Research, 28*(1), 299–348.

Borgida, A. (1996). On the relative expressiveness of description logics and predicate logics. *Artificial Intelligence, 82*(1-2), 353–367. doi:10.1016/0004-3702(96)00004-5

Chalmers, M. (2004). A historical view of context. *Computer Supported Cooperative Work, 13*(3-4), 223–247. doi:10.1007/s10606-004-2802-8

Chen, H., Finin, T., & Joshi, A. (2003). An ontology for context aware pervasive computing environments. In *Proceedings of the 18th International Joint Conferences on Artificial Intelligence (IJCAI-03).* Acapulco, Mexico: IJCAI.

Chen, H., Perich, F., Finin, T., & Joshi, A. (2004). SOUPA: Standard ontology for ubiquitous and pervasive applications. In *Proceedings of the 1st Annual International Conference on Mobile and Ubiquitous Systems (MobiQuitous2004).* Cambridge, MA: MobiQuitous.

Chen, L., Nugent, C., Mulvenna, M., Finlay, D., Hong, X., & Poland, M. (2008). Using event calculus for behaviour reasoning and assistance in a smart home. In *Proceedings of the International Conference On Smart Homes and Health Telematics (ICOST2008),* (pp. 81-89). Ames, IA: Springer.

Dey, A. (2001). Understanding and using context. *Personal and Ubiquitous Computing, 5*(1). doi:10.1007/s007790170019

Dourish, P. (2004). What we talk about when we talk about context. *Personal and Ubiquitous Computing, 8*(1), 19–30. doi:10.1007/s00779-003-0253-8

Emerson, A. E., & Halpern, J. (1986). Sometimes and not never revisited: On branching versus linear time temporal logic. *Journal of the ACM, 33*(1), 151–178. doi:10.1145/4904.4999

Gottfried, B., Guesgen, H. W., & Hübner, S. (2006). Spatiotemporal reasoning for smart homes. In *Designing Smart Homes* (*Vol. 4008*, pp. 16–34). Berlin, Germany: Springer. doi:10.1007/11788485_2

Harnad, S. (1990). The symbol grounding problem. *Physica, 42*, 335–346.

Henricksen, K., Indulska, J., & Rakotonirainy, A. (2002). Modelling context information in pervasive computing systems. In *Proceedings of the International Conference on Pervasive Computing (Pervasive 2002).* Zurich, Switzerland: Pervasive.

Horrocks, I., & Sattler, U. (2007). A tableau decision procedure for SHOIQ. *Journal of Automated Reasoning, 39*(3), 248–276. doi:10.1007/s10817-007-9079-9

Jakkula, V., & Cook, D. (2007). Anomaly detection using temporal data mining in a smart home environment. *Methods of Information in Medicine, 47*(1), 70–75.

Jakkula, V. R., & Cook, D. J. (2007). Using temporal relations in smart home data for activity prediction. In *Proceedings of the International Conference on Machine Learning (ICML) Workshop on the Induction of Process Models (IPM / ICML 2007).* Corvalis, OR: ICML.

Krummenacher, R., & Strang, T. (2007). Ontology-based context-modeling. In *Proceedings of the 3rd Workshop on Context Awareness for Proactive Systems (CAPS'07).* Guildford, UK: CAPS.

Kutz, O. L. (2004). E-connections of abstract description systems. *Artificial Intelligence, 156*(1), 1–73. doi:10.1016/j.artint.2004.02.002

Liao, L., Fox, D., & Kautz, H. (2005). Location-based activity recognition using relational Markov networks. In *Proceedings of the Advances in Neural Information Processing Systems (NIPS).* Edinburgh, UK: NIPS.

Lutz, C., Wolter, F., & Zakharyashev, M. (2008). Temporal description logics: A survey. In *Proceedings of the 15th International Symposium on Temporal Representation and Reasoning (TIME)*, (pp. 3-14). Montreal, Canada: TIME.

Mastrogiovanni, F., Scalmato, A., Sgorbissa, A., & Zaccaria, R. (2008). An integrated approach to context specification and recognition in smart homes. In *Smart Homes and Health Telematics* (pp. 26–33). Berlin, Germany: Springer. doi:10.1007/978-3-540-69916-3_4

Mastrogiovanni, F., Sgorbissa, A., & Zaccaria, R. (2007). Classification system for context representation and acquisition. In Augusto, J. C. (Ed.), *Advances in Ambient Intelligence*. IOS Press.

Mastrogiovanni, F., Sgorbissa, A., & Zaccaria, R. (2008). *Representing and reasoning upon contexts in artificial systems*. Paper presented at the 3rd Workshop on Artificial Intelligence Techniques for Ambient Intelligence (AITAmI-08), co-located with the 18th European Conference on Artificial Intelligence (ECAI 08). Patras, Greece.

McGuinness, D., & Borgida, A. (1995). Explaining subsumption in description logics. In *Proceedings of the 14th International Joint Conference on Artificial Intelligence (IJCAI-95)*. Montréal, Canada: IJCAI.

Monekosso, D. N., & Remagnino, P. (2007). Monitoring behavior with an array of sensors. *Computational Intelligence*, *23*(4), 420–438. doi:10.1111/j.1467-8640.2007.00314.x

Morchen, F. (2006). A better tool that Allen's relations for expressing temporal knowledge in interval data. In *Proceedings of the 12th ACM SIGKDD International Conference on Knowledge Discovery and Data Mining (KDD)*. Philadelphia, PA: ACM Press.

Muehlenbrock, M., Brdiczka, O., Snowdon, D., & Meunier, J. (2004). Learning to detect user activity and availability from a variety of sensor data. In *Proceedings of the 2004 IEEE International Conference on Pervasive Computing (PerCom04)*. Piscataway, NY: IEEE Press.

Rugnone, A., Nugent, C., Donnelly, M., Craig, D., Vicario, E., Paggetti, C., et al. (2007). HomeTL: A visual formalism, based on temporal logic, for the design of home based care. In *Proceedings of the 3rd Annual IEEE Conference on Automation Science and Engineering (CASE)*, (pp. 747-752). Scottsdale, AZ: IEEE Press.

Salber, D., Dey, A., & Abowd, G. (1999). The context toolkit: Aiding the development of context-enabled applications. In *Proceedings of the Conference on Human Factors in Computing Systems (CHI'99)*, (pp. 434-441). Pittsburgh, PA: CHI.

Strang, T., Linnhoff-Popien, C., & Frank, K. (2003). Applications of a context ontology language. In *Proceedings of the Internationall Conference on Software, Telecommunications and Computer Networks.* Dubrovnik, Croatia: Software, Telecommunications, and Computer Networks.

Strang, T., Linnhoff-Popien, C., & Frank, K. (2003). CoOL: A context ontology language to enable contextual interoperability. In *Proceedings of the 4th IFIP WG 6.1 International Conference on Distributed Applications and Interoperable Systems (DAIS2003).* Paris, France: DAIS.

Takahashi, H., Tokairin, Y., Yamanaka, K., Suganuma, T., Kinoshita, T., Sugawara, K., et al. (2007). uEyes: A ubiquitous care-support service based on multiple contexts coordination. In *Proceedings of the 2007 International Symposium on Applications and the Internet.* IEEE Computer Society.

Vilain, M., & Kautz, H. (1989). Constraint propagation algorithms for temporal reasoning: A revisited report. In *Readings in Qualitative Reasoning about Physical Systems* (pp. 373–381). Morgan Kaufmann Publishers Inc.

Waldmann, M. (2007). Combining versus analyzing multiple causes: How domain assumptions and task context affect integration rules. *Cognitive Science, 31*, 233–256.

## ENDNOTE

1 The two forms $\mathcal{P}(\sigma_k)$ and $\sigma_k \vee \mathcal{P}$ can be used indifferently.

# Chapter 13
# Topical and Spatio-Temporal Search over Distributed Online Databases

**Nikos Zotos**
*Patras University, Greece*

**Sofia Stamou**
*Patras University, Greece*

## ABSTRACT

*In this chapter, the authors propose a novel framework for the support of multi-faceted searches over distributed Web-accessible databases. Towards this goal, the authors introduce a method for analyzing and processing a sample of the database contents in order to deduce the topical, the geographic, and the temporal orientation of the entire database contents. To extract the database topics, the authors apply techniques leveraged from the NLP community. To identify the database geographic footprints, the authors first rely on geographic ontologies in order to extract toponyms from the database content samples and then employ geo-spatial similarity metrics to estimate the geographic coverage of the identified toponyms. Finally, to determine the time aspects associated with the database entities, the authors extract temporal expressions from the entities' contextual elements and utilize a time ontology against which the temporal similarity between the identified entities is estimated.*

DOI: 10.4018/978-1-61692-868-1.ch013

## INTRODUCTION

A significant fraction of the hidden Web content pertains to data stored in online databases. Previous studies have shown that the size of the hidden Web is much larger than that of the surface Web and that its quality is relatively high (cf. The Deep Web). Although online databases offer large volumes of qualitative content, typical Web users are generally deprived of these data for three main reasons: first, because search engines, i.e. the predominant medium for accessing the Web data, do not index the contents of online databases (Xu, et al., 1998); second, because information seekers are not aware of all the available online databases that could potentially serve their queries, and third, because the majority of users are either reluctant or incompetent to specify different queries for a single information need so that these conform to the query syntax and/or language that different databases support.

To overcome the above difficulties, researchers have proposed several approaches, the majority of which aim at tackling the following issues: (1) how to enable search engines index the hidden Web content (Ntoulas, et al., 2005), (2) how to aggregate the database contents into content summaries so as to facilitate database selection for search queries (Ipeirotis & Gravano, 2002; Ipeirotis & Gravano, 2008), and (3) how to translate queries into appropriate formats for each database (Sugiura & Etzioni, 2000). Despite the success of the above approaches, there are still open issues with respect to searching for information in online structured data sources. One such issue concerns the multi-faceted representation of the database contents so as to allow users query different databases across multiple dimensions.

Currently, databases organize their contents thematically via the use of concept hierarchies. However, this kind of data organization enables searching the database contents in a single dimension, i.e. by topic. Unfortunately, searching by topic cannot accommodate all user needs and search behaviors, since a significant fraction of search queries aim at retrieving spatio-temporal data about a subject of interest. For example, consider a news archive (database). Some users might want to search the database contents by topic (e.g. *economic crisis*), others might want to search the database contents by location (e.g. *job loses in France*), yet others might want to search the database contents by time constraints (e.g. *2008 economic crisis*). In this scenario, a monolithic topical organization of the database contents would hinder users from performing multi-dimensional searches, such as: *impact of the 2008 economic crisis in France*. Evidently, if we could organize the database contents across multiple dimensions, e.g. by topic [*Economy → economic crisis*], by location [*Regional→ Europe → France*], and by time [*21st century → 2008*], we would not only enable multi-faceted online searches, but we would also save a lot of time from information seekers since we would help them locate the most relevant (topical, spatial and temporal) data sources faster. That is, in our example query the documents indexed under all matching facets, i.e. *economic crisis*, *France* and *2008*, would be prioritized in the query results.

In addition to supporting multi-faceted searches over online databases, in many cases it is desirable that queries are simultaneously submitted to different databases that contain useful information. This is preferable in case the users are not aware of all the existing databases that could potentially serve their information needs, or in case the users do not want to bound their searchers to a particular source of information. In this scenario, the search should be distributed over different databases and the relevant documents should be merged in a single ranked list of retrieved results. To support distributed searches over online databases, we can build metasearchers, which provide a uniform interface for querying multiple databases at once. A metasearcher performs three main tasks: upon issuing a query it selects the databases that contain relevant information, it translates the query in a suitable form for every selected database and it retrieves, merges, and ranks the relevant results into a single list of documents.

In this article, we propose a novel framework for the support of multi-faceted searches over distributed Web-accessible databases. Towards this goal, we introduce a method for analyzing and processing a sample of the database contents in order to deduce the topical, the geographic, and the temporal orientation of the entire database contents. To extract the database topics, we apply techniques that we leverage from the NLP community. To identify the database geographic footprints, we first rely on geographic ontologies (e.g. Buscaldi & Roso, 2008) in order to extract toponyms from the database content samples and then we employ geo-spatial similarity metrics to estimate the geographic coverage of the identified toponyms. Finally, to determine the time aspects associated with the database entities we extract temporal expressions from the entities' contextual elements and we utilize a time ontology (e.g. OWL Time Ontology) against which we estimate the temporal similarity between the identified entities.

In brief, the contributions and contents of the article summarize to the following:

- A novel approach for representing the database contents into **multi-dimensional content summaries**. Although researchers have studied before the problem of building database content summaries, nevertheless existing works concentrate on how to represent the topical orientation of the database contents in the delivered summaries and ignore issues that pertain to multi-dimensional data representation. Our study is different from existing techniques in that we try to encapsulate both topical and spatio-temporal data aspects in the constructed database summaries.
- New **database selection algorithm** that exploits the multi-faceted database summaries to make database selection resilient to data multi-dimensionality. The novelty of our algorithm is that it estimates the suitability of every database in serving queries of different orientations adaptively and by employing various topical, spatial, and temporal similarity metrics between the query and the database contextual dimensions.

The remaining of the chapter presents our approach for the automatic identification and representation of the database contents into multidimensional summaries. Moreover, it discusses a number of similarity metrics that are employed for assisting the database selection process for distributed searches. In overall, this chapter introduces a theoretical framework for extracting useful information from the contents of online databases so as to enable distributed and multi-dimensional online searches.

## BACKGROUND

Related work falls in two main categories, namely database content summary construction and database selection for serving distributed searches. Building content summaries for the database records practically concerns the representation of the information stored in online databases into smaller pieces of representative information. In this respect, there have been several studies, the majority of which concentrate on the representation of the databases' topical content into the delivered summaries.

In Ipeirotis and Gravano (2002) a technique is introduced that automatically extracts content summaries for searchable text databases in the Web. This technique is based on a biased sample of documents extracted from the selected database using topically focused queries which are derived from a Yahoo!-like hierarchy of topics. The selection of the appropriate queries is based on the results of the earlier queries, thus focusing on the topics that are most representative of the database in question. The outcome of this work is that it produces content summaries of higher quality than other approaches and the database selection algorithm produces accurate results even for imperfect content summaries.

In Ipeirotis et al. (2001), the authors propose a method for automatic categorization of searchable Web databases into topic hierarchies using a combination of machine learning and database querying techniques. They introduce the use of query probing for database classification and use the number of documents matching each query to make classification decisions for the database topic instead of retrieving the actual documents from the database. They show through experiments that the proposed method is more accurate and efficient than the existing database classification methods.

The work of Xu et al. (1998) focuses on the database selection problem for bibliographic databases containing records with multiple text-based attributes. The authors designed three database selection techniques: the first one uses training queries and their result sizes to rank databases; the second adopts a set of statistical parameters that summarizes the content of the bibliographic databases. The third, which performs the best, combines the other two methods and derives the ranks of databases from the tuple frequencies of terms in the set of records sampled from each database using training queries.

In Callan and Conneli (2001) a new technique is proposed for acquiring accurate resource descriptions from text databases. The proposed method is based on the hypothesis that a sufficiently unbiased sample of documents can be constructed from the union of biased samples obtained by query-based sampling. The advantage of the proposed algorithm is that is does not require the cooperation of the resource providers or that resource providers use a particular search engine or representation technique. The authors used an extensive set of experimental results to demonstrate that accurate resource descriptions are created, that computation and communication costs are reasonable, and that the resource descriptions do enable accurate automatic database selection.

In Ipeirotis and Gravano (2008), a technique is described for automatically extracting high-quality content summaries from hidden-Web text databases. The proposed algorithm constructs these summaries from a biased sample of the documents in a database, extracted by adaptively probing the database using the topically focused queries sent to the database during a topic classification step. The authors introduce a method that exploits well-studied statistical properties of text collections in order to include in the content summary of a database accurate estimates the actual document frequency of words in the database. The experimental results showed a significant improvement in database selection quality over existing techniques, which are achieved just by exploiting the database classification information and without increasing the document-sample size.

Our approach builds upon existing works on database content summary construction but takes a step further in that content summaries do not pertain only to the topics covered in the database records but also represent the spatial and the temporal orientation of the database contents. Therefore, our study is perceived as a complement to existing techniques as we will describe next.

With respect to the database selection algorithms for distributed searches, the majority of the proposed approaches rely on statistical metadata about the contents of the databases and use content summaries for selecting the suitable database to answer user queries. Specifically, Meng et al. (1998) rely on content summaries for selecting the database that contains the most documents that relate to a user query. Their proposed query-document relevance values are determined via the cosine similarity metric. In a similar approach, Yu et al. (2001) order the databases that contain relevant information for a query according to their contents' similarity with the query terms. In another direction, Larkey et al. (2000) show that organizing documents by topic helps improve the database selection accuracy. Besides exploring database content summaries, researchers have proposed classifying the database contents into hierarchical structures so that user queries are directed to the appropriate categories of the hierarchy (Choi & Yoo, 2001; Fuhr, 1999). The database documents that are categorized under the query matching categories are those that relate to the query and the database containing most of the relevant documents are selected for serving the query search.

Our database selection algorithm explores the findings of other researchers and relies on database content summaries for deciding which database contains enough material to serve user queries. However, unlike existing works, our algorithm considers the multi-dimensional database summaries and places its selection policy upon the requirement that all query dimensions should be satisfied in the contents of the selected database. Overall, we consider our work as an expansion of existing techniques in the sense that our proposed distributed search approach tackles all dimensions of distributed data retrieval and not only the topical one. In the following sections, we describe in detail our proposed method for representing the database content dimensions into summaries and we present our multi-dimensional database selection algorithm.

## MULTI-DIMENSIONAL DATABASE CONTENT SUMMARIES

In this section, we describe our approach towards extracting multi-dimensional content summaries from searchable Web databases of text documents. A Web database is characterized as searchable when access to its contents is enabled via a Web-based search interface. The reason for concentrating on text is that 84% of all searchable databases on the Web are estimated to provide access to text documents (cf. The Deep Web).

The state-of-the-art database content summary extraction techniques rely on the statistical properties of the database textual contents in order to firstly detect the topics covered in the database and then extract documents that are representative of the database topical coverage. Unfortunately, topically-oriented database summaries are intrinsically limited in conveying the different aspects that the database contents cover, since they ignore the spatio-temporal orientation of the database documents. To fill this void, we introduce a novel method for representing the database contents into multi-dimensional content summaries. Our method exploits existing topical, geographic and time ontologies to adaptively send multi-dimensional queries to a database. The database documents retrieved for each of the queries constitute a representative sample of the database contents that share a common dimension (topical, spatial, or temporal) with the query. We then process the retrieved database samples across the dimensions considered in order to construct a content summary for each dimension, which we index into an appropriate data structure. Then, based on the content summaries of the different database dimensions, we estimate the representation ratio of every dimension in the database contents. Based on the above steps, we construct multi-dimensional database content summaries and we compute for each of the summaries a score that indicates how expressive the summary is for the entire database contents. Figure 1 schematically illustrates the architecture of our proposed approach towards capturing the dimensions of the database contents and encapsulating them in the constructed database summaries.

More specifically, given that the contents of the hidden Web databases cannot be accessed unless there is a query submitted to the database interface, the first step of our approach concentrates on the selection of queries that will be issued to the database in order to obtain a sufficient sample of documents for constructing the database summaries. The query selection process entails

*Figure 1. Representing the database contents into multidimensional summaries*

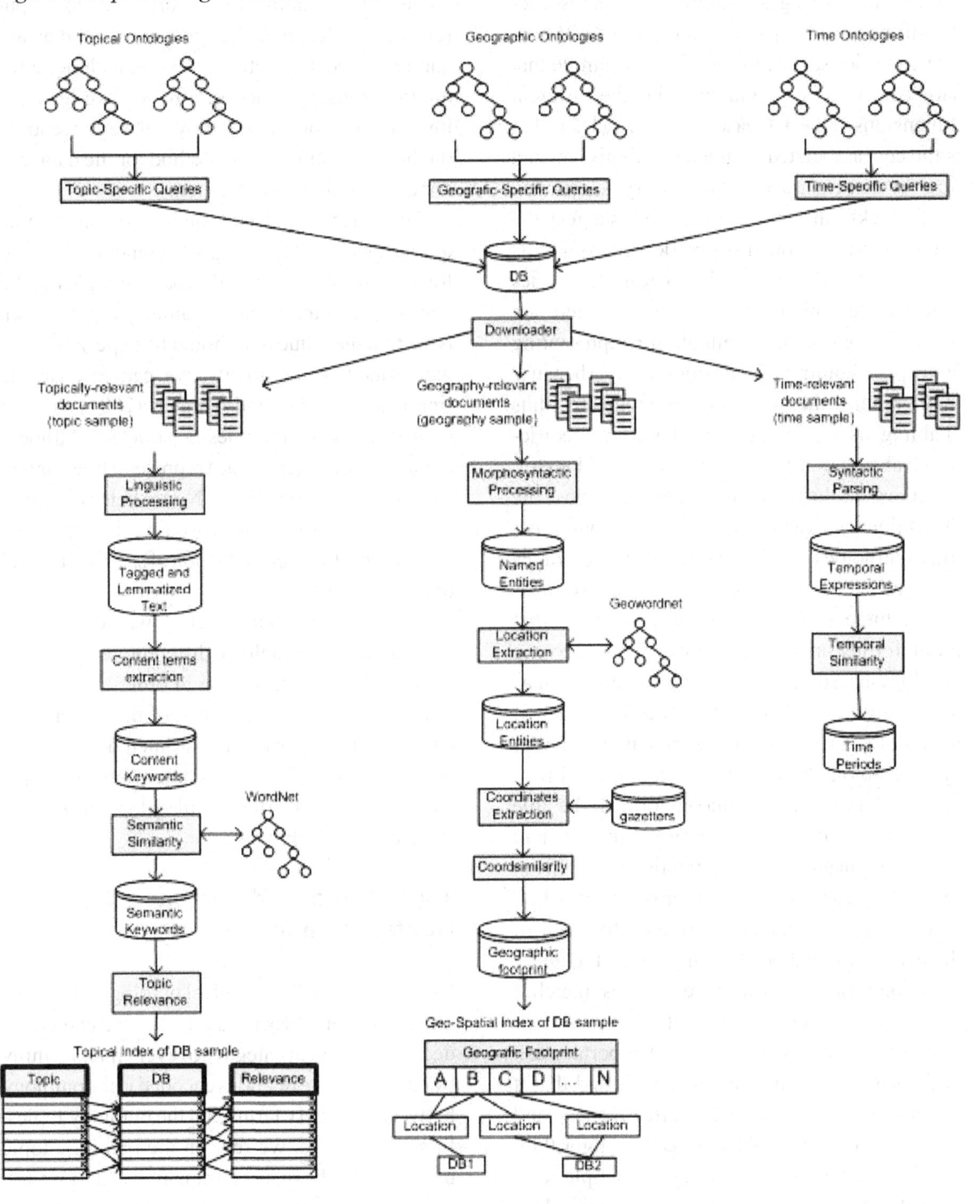

three main challenges, namely: (1) what resources will be used for picking our queries, (2) how many queries suffice for obtaining a sample that satisfactorily covers and specifies the different dimensions of the database contents, and (3) what is the cost associated with query submission and how we can ensure affordable query selections.

To tackle the above issues, we suggest the exploitation of domain-specific ontologies as the resources out of which our sample queries will emerge. This is not only because there are numerous ontologies available for representing concepts of multiple dimensions but also because they organize their contents hierarchically, thus enabling us to fine-tune the level of specificity or abstraction that our queries would entail. Therefore, as the figure illustrates we propose the utilization of existing topical, geographic, and time ontologies as the terminological resources from which to obtain our sample queries. Of course there still exist a number of issues that merit further investigation with respect to the ontology-based query selection process, such as how many queries should be picked from each of the ontologies, should the query matching nodes in the ontology be linked to each other and if so via which relation types and so forth. To be able to answer the above, we firstly need to experiment with different methods for extracting queries from the ontologies and based on the cross-examination of the sample documents retrieved for each of the examined methods to conclude on the query selection process that retrieves the best matches for every dimension considered.

Given that query selection is an important task in the summary construction process and that it has a critical impact on the effectiveness and efficiency of the database selection algorithm, it is imperative that we go beyond simple term extraction techniques in selecting our queries. This need is particularly pronounced for the geographic and the temporal queries that will be issued to the database contents and whose specification should adhere to real query formulation types. Therefore, a considerable amount of effort needs to be put towards the design and implementation of an accurate and cost-effective selection technique for multi-dimensional queries. However, we defer this investigation for a future study and we concentrate on the description of our method for the database content summaries extraction.

Having selected and submitted our sample queries, we rely on the top *k* documents retrieved for every query as the database samples to be considered for the database summary construction. Note that the value of *k* should be experimentally determined. Alternatively, we can rely on the findings of Callan and Conneli (2001) that for topical-focused summaries construction 300 documents suffice for creating a representative content summary of a database. Nevertheless, further investigation is needed for setting the value of *k* with respect to the construction of spatio-temporal database summaries.

After issuing our queries, we retrieve the documents that match the different query dimensions and we process them in order to construct a database summary for each of the dimensions considered. In particular, the methods we suggest for constructing multi-dimensional database summaries based on the sampled documents summarize to the following.

## Topical-Focused Database Content Summaries

Given that we rely on topical ontologies to determine our topical-focused queries, we can easily deduce the topical category of every query simply by examining the relations encoded in the ontology between the query terms and the ontology topics. In simple words, we rely on the ontology topic under which the query term is linked and we use it as the query topic. Upon issuing our topical-focused queries it is reasonable to assume that the documents retrieved for each of the queries somehow correlate to the respective query topics. For instance, if we submit the query *laptop* that is a specialization of the ontology topic *Computers* and we retrieve a number of documents in response to the query, then we assume that the contents of the top *k* retrieved documents also deal with the subject (i.e. topic) *Computers*. Therefore, we speculate that at least a portion of the database contents focus on the topic *Computers*. On the other hand, if upon issuing our previous query there are no documents retrieved from a given database, then we speculate that the contents of the database do not discuss the topic *Computers*.

Based on the above assumption (also supported in the work of Ipeirotis and Gravano [2008]), we can easily derive a number of topics that the database contents discuss. Depending on the number of documents retrieved for each of the topical queries, we can estimate the degree to which the database contents cover and specify the topic of the query. This can be estimated by applying the ***Coverage*** and ***Specificity*** metrics, reported in Ipeirotis and Gravano (2008). Specifically, *TopicalCoverage* indicates the absolute amount of information that the database documents contain about an ontology topic $T_i$ and it is given by:

$$TopicalCoverage\ (D,T_i) = \sum_{T_i=1}^{|D|} \left| d_1,T_i + .... + d_n,T_i \right| \quad (1)$$

where D is the database comprising *n* documents. On the other hand, *Specificity* indicates how focused are the database documents on topic $T_i$ and is given by:

$$Specificity\ (D,T_i) = \frac{Coverage(D,T_i)}{|D|} \quad (2)$$

Then, we rely on the set of topics with sufficient specificity and coverage (the respective threshold values need to be experimentally determined) and we process their retrieved documents in order to construct the database topical summary.

The main objective towards building our topical summaries is to associate every topical category identified for the database contents with a set of thematic terms that are expressive of the respective topics. In this respect, we analyze and linguistically process the top *k* documents retrieved for each of the considered topics in order to identify their thematic keywords, i.e. the terms that indicate the semantic orientation of the document contents. Linguistic processing concerns applying tokenization, Part-of-Speech tagging, stop word removal and lemmatization. Then, we explore the document terms that have been assigned the grammatical category tags: Noun and Proper Noun as the candidate document thematic terms. The reason for concentrating on the above grammatical categories for selecting the document thematic words is because according to the findings of Gliozzo et al. (2004) terms annotated with the above categories are the most informative of the semantic orientation of the text in which they appear.

Having selected the thematic terms that appear in each of the topical focused documents, we map them to their corresponding nodes in the WordNet lexical ontology (WordNet) in order to estimate the degree to which these semantically correlate to each other. For estimating the semantic correlation between pairs of terms, we rely on the Wu and Palmer similarity metric (1994) that computes the amount of semantic information that two terms share in common, given by:

$$Similarity\ (w_i,w_k) = \frac{2\ *\ depth\ \left(LCS\ (w_i,w_k)\right)}{depth(w_i) + depth(w_k)} \quad (3)$$

which combines the depth of word pairs ($w_i$, $w_k$) in WordNet graph and the depth of their Least Common Subsumer (LCS) in order to quantify the amount of semantic information that the two terms share. Based on the above, we extract from every topical focused document the set of thematic terms that are semantically similar to each other above a given threshold value. Those terms are deemed to be expressive of the document semantics. Next, we collect from all the documents that deal with the same topical category a set of thematic terms that are expressive of that topic's orientation. In other words, we pick from all the semantically similar thematic terms that appear in the topical focused documents the ones that are the most relevant to the topic semantics.

To select the thematic terms that are the most relevant to the query topic, we first remove duplicates from the thematic terms that have been extracted from the query retrieved pages and then we estimate the degree to which each of the remaining thematic terms relate to the topic's orientation. To account for that, we map thematic terms to their corresponding nodes in the topical ontologies (from which we extracted our topic-specific queries) and we estimate for each of the thematic terms a ***Relevance*** value that indicates the degree to which a term semantically relates to the query topic. To compute the *Relevance* between two ontology nodes (i.e. the node that represents the topical category *i* of the query and the node that represents a thematic term *j*), we firstly measure the distance between the two nodes (i,j) as:

$$Dist\ (i,j) = 1 - \frac{2 \bullet |common\ \ subsumers|}{|subsumers\ \ of\ i| + |subsumers\ \ of\ j|} \tag{4}$$

Given that the inverse distance of two concepts in the ontology indicates their semantic similarity (Budanitsky & Hirst, 2006), we can easily derive the degree of *Relevance* between the two concepts (i,j) as:

$$Relevance\ (i,j) = 1 - Dist\ (i,j) \tag{5}$$

Based on the above formula, we estimate the relevance values between the query topic and each of the thematic terms that have been determined for that topic. In the end, we sort the topic-specific thematic terms by relevance values and we retain the top *n* terms for representing that topic's semantic orientation. At this point we should note that the value of *n* needs to be experimentally fixed after experimenting with different thresholds. In addition, the process described above is applied in order to extract the most relevant thematic terms for each of the identified database topics. At the end of this process, we maintain the *n* thematic terms of the highest relevance values for the considered topics and we use them to construct the database topical summary. The latter essentially comprises the set of topics that the database contents discuss, their associated thematic terms, and the degree to which the latter relate to each of their corresponding topics. The above data is stored in an inverted topical index that constitutes the topical summary of the database contents. By applying the same process to all the different databases considered, we construct topical summaries for the contents of every database.

## Geography-Focused Database Content Summaries

So far, we have presented our method towards constructing topical focused summaries for the database contents. Topic-specific summaries can serve the database selection process when we deal with topic-sensitive queries. Nevertheless, in a practical setting the queries that online databases receive span multiple dimensions; the most common of which (besides topical) are geographic and temporal. Thus, if we want to design a database selection algorithm that is successful in selecting the databases against which multi-dimensional queries are searched, we need to account for multiple content dimensions in the constructed database summaries. In this section, we propose a method towards building geography-focused database summaries in order to represent the spatial orientation of the database contents.

The first step towards constructing location-specific database summaries is again to collect database geography-focused document samples. In this respect, we rely on geographic ontologies from which we pick a number of keywords for specifying the geography queries that will be submitted to the examined databases. In selecting our geography-sensitive queries, we again need to investigate different approaches in order to decide which nodes in the ontology graph will participate in the selection process. After picking our geography-specific queries, we submit them to the database and we retain the top *k* documents retrieved for each of the queries. As previously mentioned, several experimental iterations should be preformed before setting the value of *k*. Moreover, if the submission of a geography-focused query results into the retrieval of several matching documents from a database, we assume that the database contents do have some geographic orientation. On the other hand, in case the submission of a geography-focused query results into no matching documents from a database, then we assume that the database contents do not have a geographic orientation.

Based on the above, we can easily derive a number of location entities that the database contents discuss. Depending on the number of documents retrieved for each of the geographic queries, we can estimate the degree to which the database contents cover and specify the geographical area of the query. This can be estimated by applying the ***GeoCoverage*** and ***GeoFocus*** metrics. In particular, *GeoCoverage* indicates the amount of geographic information that the database documents contain about a location entity $L_e$ as given by:

$$GeoCoverage\ (D, L_e) = \sum_{L_e=1}^{|D|} \left| d_1, L_e + .... + d_n, L_e \right| \tag{6}$$

where D is the database comprising *n* documents. On the other hand, *GeoFocus* indicates how focused are the database documents on location $L_e$ and is given by:

$$GeoFocus\ (D, L_e) = \frac{Coverage\,(D, L_e)}{|D|} \tag{7}$$

We then explore the databases that do retrieve documents in response to geography-sensitive queries in order to construct their geography-focused content summaries. In this respect, we download the documents retrieved for a geographic query and we employ the vector space Geo-thematic model (Cai, 2002) to represent every document as a term vector associated with a geographic footprint. The term vector of a document contains the location entities that appear in its contextual elements, while the geographic footprint indicates the geographical coordinate space in which the document location entities span. To build the term vector of a document we start by processing its textual content in order to identify location entities. In this respect, we apply tokenization, Part-of-Speech tagging, and lemmatization to the document's content. Then, we rely on the lemmatized terms that are morphologically annotated as Proper Nouns and we look them up in GeoWordNet (Buscaldi & Roso, 2008). Named entities identified in GeoWordNet are characterized as location entities and are the ones that will be considered for building the term vector of the document.

The next step is to derive the location reference(s) of the identified location entities, in order to be able to infer the geographical area(s) that the document discusses. For deducing the location reference(s) of the identified geography entities, we map the location keywords of a document to their corresponding GeoWordNet nodes and we explore their geographic relations. This is done by investigating whether there are overlapping named entities in the definitions of location entities. For example, the location entity *Rhode Island*: defined as a state in New England and the location entity *Brown University*: defined as a university in Rhode Island, are deemed as geographically related since the name of the second location entity appears in the definition sentence of the first. Location entities that are found to be geographically related are grouped together under a common location reference. To verbalize the geographic reference of the document contents, we use the name of the location entity under which the document location entities are organized. On the other hand, in case the location entities in a document are not geographically related in GeoWordNet, we speculate that the document refers to many geographic areas and we use the names of all identified location entities to denote the geographic references of the document. Figure 2a shows an example of location entities that are geographically related, i.e. refer to the same geographic area, while Figure 2b shows an example of location entities that refer to distinct geographic areas. As the examples suggest, a document that contains the location entities of Figure 2a discusses a single geographic area, i.e. *Virginia*, while a document that contains the location entities of Figure 2b discusses multiple geographic areas. Therefore, the location reference of the document containing the entities of Figure 2a is *Virginia*, while the location references of the document containing the entities of Figure 2b are *Germany*, *Berkeley*, and *Brown University*.

Having extracted the location entities from the database documents and having also deduced the geographic area(s) to which every document refers, we now turn our attention on how to associate the geographic references in every document vector with their corresponding geographic footprints. In this respect, we rely on the geographic coordinates that GeoWordNet encodes for location entities and we estimate the spatial distance between the geography keywords in every document. Spatial distance is computed via the Map24 tool (Map 24). Then, we rely on the pair of location

*Figure 2. (a) example of location entities with a single geographic reference; (b) example of location entities with multiple geographic references*

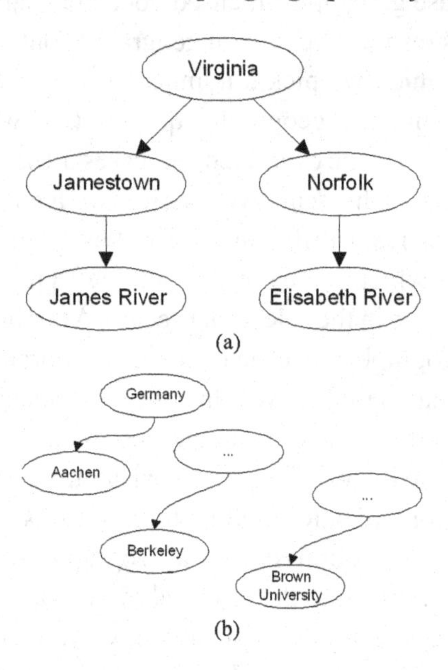


keywords in a document that share the maximum distance and use their geographic coordinates to specify the geographic footprint of the respective document. This way, in case a document has a single geographic reference (i.e. its location entities are geographically related) the geographic coordinates of that location reference will constitute the geographic footprint of the document. On the other hand, in case a document has multiple geographic references, the geographic coordinates of the most distant location references will be used as the document's geographic footprint.

Based on the above steps, we represent every geography specific document in the database as a set of location entities associated with the name of the geographic areas to which these entities span and the geographic footprint that indicates the areas' coordinates. Next, we group the database documents by geographic references (i.e. documents discussing the same geographic area are grouped together) and we further examine them in order to extract the geography terms and coordinates that are the most representative for every area considered. In this respect, we compute the geographic similarity between each of the considered geographic areas and their corresponding geography keywords. For our computations, we rely on GeoWordNet from which we derive the coordinates that correspond to the entity that represents the documents' geographic area, denoted as $(x, y) \in G$, and the coordinates that correspond to the entities that represent the documents' geography keywords, denotes as $(x', y') \in L$ and we measure the inverse of the Euclidian distance between coordinates as:

$$SimCoord\,(G, L) = \frac{1}{dist(G, L)} \tag{8}$$

Coordinates' similarity indicates the geographic proximity between the spatial area that the documents discuss and the geographic keywords that the documents contain. Based on the above values we sort the geography-specific keywords by geographic proximity to the area that they refer and we retain the top *n* keywords for representing that area's spatial orientation. Again, the value of *n* should be experimentally fixed to some threshold after several experimentations. In the end, we maintain the *n* geographic terms of the highest geographic similarity for the considered locations and we use them to construct the database geographic summary. The latter comprises the names of the geographic areas that the database contents discuss, the areas' geographic coordinates (i.e. footprints) and for every geographic area the location-specific keywords of similar coordinates with the area's geographic footprint. By applying the same process to all the different databases considered, we construct geography-focused summaries for the contents of every database.

## Temporal-Focused Database Content Summaries

A significant fraction of search queries that online databases receive, are time-sensitive in the sense that they intend the retrieval of documents whose contents refer to specific time periods. For instance, consider the query *[9/11 terrorist attack]* over a news archive. Evidently, the query aims at retrieving documents that are both topically and temporally similar to the query, i.e. documents discussing the terrorist attack that took place in a particular time interval, namely September 11, 2001. To answer our example query, database metasearchers would not only need to identify the databases that contain documents about terrorist attacks but also detect the databases that contain documents about the terrorist attack that took place at a specific time period. To account for that, we would need to construct database content summaries that represent not only the topics but also the time periods that are discussed in the database documents.

In this section, we introduce our approach towards constructing temporal-focused database content summaries so as to enable metasearchers serve time-sensitive queries. The most challenging task in characterizing the temporal aspects associated with the database contents is to be able to automatically identify the most important time intervals in the database documents. In the respect, we start by obtaining database samples that pertain to specific time periods. To acquire our samples, we rely on time ontologies from which we extract time-sensitive queries, which we submit over online databases. In case a time-sensitive query retrieves a significant number of documents from a database, we speculate that these documents discuss the time interval that the query represents and that the database from which the documents were retrieved does have a temporal focus. On the other hand, if there are no documents retrieved from a database in response to a time-sensitive query, we assume that the database contents have no temporal focus.

Based on the above, we derive the ***Temporal-Coverage*** of the database contents by considering the number of database documents that are retrieved in response to some time-specific query, as given by:

$$TemporalCoverage\ (D, C_t) = \sum_{t=1}^{|D|} |d_1, t + .... + d_n, t| \quad (9)$$

Based on the set of documents retrieved for each of the time-specific queries, we process them in order to construct the database temporal-focused summary. The main objective towards building our time-specific summaries is to associate every time interval identified for the database contents with a set of temporal expressions that describe the given time periods. A temporal expression is a sequence of tokens (words, numbers, and characters) that denote a point in time or duration. To identify temporal expressions in the contents of documents that are retrieved in response to time-sensitive queries, we proceed as follows. We rely on the top *k* documents retrieved for each of the time-specific queries we download their contents and morpho-syntactically process them. Morpho-syntactic processing concerns applying tokenization and temporal expression tagging (Mazur & Dale, 2007) in order to identify text chunks of temporal denotations. For each temporal expression *t* in a retrieved document, we compute $f(t)$ by measuring the number of documents sampled for a time-sensitive query that contain *t*. If a temporal expression has an $f(t)$ value above a given threshold (to be experimentally determined), it is deemed to be expressive of the sampled documents' temporal focus. Based on the above process, we extract from all the documents that are retrieved for a time-specific query, the most frequently occurring temporal expressions.

Our next step, is to estimate the similarity between the time period that the query represents and the time intervals that each of the frequently occurring temporal expressions denote in the database sample. To account for that, we start by mapping the time denotations of the query and the temporal expressions identified in the query matching documents to their corresponding nodes in the time ontology. Based on the ontology matching nodes, we derive the timestamp of the query and the temporal expressions. Then, based on the time specific query *q* and a temporal expression *e*, with a specific timestamp $\vec{t}$, we estimate the temporal similarity between the query and the time expression $S\left(\vec{q}, \vec{e} \mid \vec{t}\right)$ by quantifying the likelihood for the two time-specific expressions are grouped under a common ontology node O(t), given the timestamp $\vec{t}$, formally computed as:

$$S\left(\vec{q}, \vec{e} \mid \vec{t}\right) = \sum_{i \in O(t)} p(i \mid q, t)\, p(i \mid e, t) \quad (10)$$

Based on the above formula, we compute the probability that each temporal expression in the sampled documents refers to a similar time period with that of the query. Then, we retain the temporal expressions with similarity values above a threshold (to be experimentally determined) and we use them as the temporal denotations of the database contents. At the end of this process, we maintain a set of temporal expressions of the highest similarity for the query time intervals and we use them to construct the database temporal focused summaries.

## Estimating Multi-Dimensional Data Representation in the Database Contents

So far, we have presented our approach for building multi-dimensional content summaries for online databases. Specifically, we introduced three distinct yet complementary methods for representing the topical, spatial, and temporal orientations of the database contents. The derived representations constitute the respective database content summaries, where the latter comprise a set of domain-specific weighted keywords that have been assigned a suitable thematic, location or temporal ontology label.

Having built the database summaries, we essentially need to estimate the representation ratio of every dimension in the database contents. This is in order to quantify the degree to which a database is suitable for serving queries of different dimensions. To derive the degree to which the database contents discuss a given ontology topic, we rely on the *TopicalCoverage* metric (cf. eqn. 1), which informs us about the amount of information that the database contents communicate for each of the topics considered. In addition, when dealing with multiple databases and want to estimate the representation ratio of every database with respect to some topic, we normalize *TopicalCoverage* values by dividing by the total number of documents about a topic $T_i$ across all the considered databases. In a similar manner, we rely on the *GeoCoverage* metric (cf. eqn. 6) in order to quantify the amount of geographic information that the database contents convey and again we normalize *GeoCoverage* values as before, in order to capture the degree to which the contents in every database have a spatial orientation. Finally, we explore the *TemporalCoverage* metric (cf. eqn. 9) for quantifying the amount of time-specific information in the database contents and again we normalize *TemporalCoverage* values in order to capture the degree to which the contents in every database discuss time periods.

Based on the above computations, we can quantify the representation of every dimension within and across the database contents. Such quantification is useful to metasearchers that need to route user queries to the databases that are most likely to contain query relevant information. However, before deploying our database content representation metrics in a practical setting, we need to perform extensive experimentation and fine-tuning so as to validate our metrics' effectiveness.

## DATABASE SELECTION ALGORITHM

An important step in the distributed searching process is the determination of the databases that contain relevant documents with respect to some user query. Traditionally, database selection has relied on statistical database summaries, which merely contain the most frequently occurring database terms along with their associated term weight values (Meng, et al., 1998). In addition, traditional distributed online searching has assumed that the queries submitted over online databases are monolithic in nature, i.e. they pursue the retrieval of topically relevant database records. Another direction that researchers have proposed for database selection algorithms is to rely on document samples from the databases to make selection decisions (Si & Callan, 2005; Shokouhi, 2007; Ipeirotis & Gravano, 2008). However, such approaches are limited in scope and cannot serve all types of user queries. In addition, thematically focused database content summaries convey a limited amount of the information a database stores, since as previously mentioned topical content summaries are not informative of the spatial and temporal orientations to which the database topics span.

In this section, we propose a novel method for selecting the databases that are most probable to satisfy the search intention of a user query. Our approach relies on the intuition that search queries even when expressed as a flat list of keywords; they may have multiple semantic orientations. Therefore, if we are able to deduce the topical, the geographic, and the temporal aspects associated with the query terms, we can rely on the multi-dimensional database content summaries (previously computed) in order to determine which database contains records that relate to all the different query aspects. Eventually, by selecting the databases whose dimensions match the query pursuits we will be able to satisfy the user needs effectively.

In our work, we propose a database selection algorithm that upon query issuing, it identifies the query dimensions against the domain-specific ontologies and then it estimates the suitability of every database in serving the identified query orientations. For the first part of the algorithm, i.e. the identification of the query dimensions, we need to exploit the thematic, the geographic, and the temporal orientation of the query. In this respect, we propose mapping the query terms against the domain-specific ontology nodes. For query terms that match nodes in the thematic ontology, we rely on the topical category of the matching nodes and use it as the query topic. Moreover, if the query terms match nodes in the geographic ontology, we rely on the location entity under which the matching nodes are organized and use is as the concept that describes the query spatial orientation. Finally, if the query terms match nodes in the temporal ontology, we rely on the time denotations of the corresponding matching nodes and use them as the concepts that represent the temporal focus of the query. Note that in the case that a query matches nodes from a single ontology, we deem that the query intention has a single dimension; thematic, spatial, or temporal. Likewise, if a query matches nodes from two ontologies, we deem that its intention has two dimensions. Based on the above steps (schematically illustrated in Figure 3), we identify the dimensions of the user queries, which are represented as topical, geographic and/or temporal ontology concepts, respectively.

Having associated every query with all the possible search dimensions that it represents, our next step is to select from a set of available databases the ones that are the most likely to contain information relevant to all the identified query dimensions. In this respect, the database selection algorithm that we propose relies on the database content summaries and estimates the degree to

*Figure 3. Ontology-based query dimensions' identification*

**Input**: Query, Topical Ontology *TopicO*, Geographic Ontology *GeoO*, Temporal Ontology *TempoO*

**Output**: query dimensions

1: /*Identify the query dimensions*/
2: **Map** query terms q(t) to TopicO
3: **If** there is a matching node
4: Retrieve the matching node's topical label
5: Return topical label and go to Step8
6: **Else**
7: Go to Step8
8: **Map** q(t) t GeoO
9: **If** there is a matching node
10 Retrieve the matching node's location label
11: Return location label and go to Step14
12: **Else**
13: Go to Step14
14: **Map** q(t) to TempoO
15: **If** there is a matching node
16: Retrieve the matching node's temporal label
17: Return temporal label and go to Step20
18: **Else**
19: **Return** unknown query dimensions
20: **Return** the query dimensions (topical, geographic and/or temporal

which database summaries relate to the identified query dimensions. Recall that under our approach, the database content summaries for each of the examined dimensions are represented as follows. Topical-focused summaries comprise a set of ontology topics that describe the database contents and every topic is associated with a set of thematic terms extracted from the database-sampled documents. In addition, every thematic term is associated with a relevance value that indicates the degree to which the term relates to the corresponding topic. Geography-focused summaries comprise the names of the geographic areas that the database contents cover along with the areas' geographic coordinates. In addition, every geographic area is associated with a set of location entities that have been extracted from the database-sampled documents. Finally, temporal-focused summaries comprise a set of temporal expressions extracted from the database-sampled documents and which denote the time periods discussed in the database contents.

Based on the above representations of the databases multi-dimensional content summaries and by exploring the identified query dimensions, the proposed database selection algorithm operates in a straightforward manner, as shown in Figure 4.

*Figure 4. Database selection algorithm*

**Input**: Databases D, query q, query topic, query location, query time focus, D topical summary, D spatial summary, D temporal summary

**Output**: Database selection for answering q

```
1: /*Select a suitable database for q*/
2: For every database Di ∈ D
3: Map query topic to Di topical summary
4: If there is a mapping
5:    Select Di
6: Else
7:    Map query location to Di spatial summary
8:    If there is a mapping
9:       Select Di
10:   Else
11:      Map query time focus to Di temporal summary
12:      If there is a mapping
13:         Select Di
14:      Else
15:         Return Di is not suitable for answering q and go to Step 2 for Dj
16: Return the selected databases for answering q
```

It matches the concepts representing each of the detected query dimensions to the concepts in the corresponding dimensions that characterize the database contextual elements. If there are matchings found, the algorithm selects the databases the summaries of which match some query dimension and uses them as the data sources that can serve the query intention.

Before heading the query to the selected databases, the algorithm estimates the suitability of every selected database in serving the query orientation and orders them so that the contents of the most suitable database are prioritized in the query results. For quantifying the suitability of the selected databases, our algorithm relies on the combination of the following: (1) the representation ratio of the database contents to each of the identified query dimensions, and (2) the importance weights that the query matching terms have in their corresponding database content summaries.

Based on the above, the proposed database selection algorithm detects the databases that contain information relevant to all the identified query dimensions.

## FUTURE RESEARCH DIRECTIONS

In the previous sections, we described a novel approach for the representation of the database contents into multi-dimensional summaries. In particular, we have described how domain-specific ontologies can be utilized for deducing the thematic, the spatial, and the temporal orientations of the database contents. Moreover, we have introduced a method for the identification of the query dimensions as well as for the selection of the databases that can serve multi-dimensional queries. In this section, we summarize the main directions for future research.

One direction for future work is to examine how our content summary construction techniques can be extended to accommodate database updates. Considering that Web databases evolve over time, it is important that the database content summaries remain fresh so that they are able to serve all user queries. To account for that, we need to encapsulate into our summary construction techniques update algorithms that will be able to determine when the content summaries need to be modified.

Another area for future work is to investigate the query interface of different databases so as to deduce the syntax and the structure of the queries that various online databases support. Based on the identified query interface characteristics, we could implement rule-based query transformation algorithms that can be used to translate the user-typed query into a database-interpretable formulation. Upon translation, a metasearcher would be useful for directing the query to the selected databases and obtaining query-matching documents.

It would also be interesting to design and implement a multi-faceted retrieval algorithm that upon directing the user query to the selected databases it identifies the query relevant documents, aggregates them in a single results list and ranks them in terms of their relevance to the query orientations, i.e. topical, spatial and temporal. Above all, a challenging area for future investigation is how to integrate the above components and techniques into a single multi-faceted hidden Web retrieval framework that will be able to serve user queries effectively.

## CONCLUSION

In this chapter, we introduced a theoretical framework for extracting useful information from the contents of online databases so as to enable distributed and multi-dimensional online searches. In particular, we presented an ontology-based method for identifying the topical, the spatial, and the temporal orientation of the database contents and we defined a number of metrics for quantifying the degree to which the database contents are expressive of the above dimensions (i.e. thematic, geographic, and temporal). In addition, we introduced our approach for constructing multi-dimensional content summaries of online databases and we proposed a method for selecting the databases that are most likely to contain query relevant information. Unlike existing database content summary construction techniques that operate upon the databases' topical focus, our proposed method goes beyond thematic summaries and touches issues such as the spatial and the temporal representation of the database records into content summaries.

## REFERENCES


Budanitsky, A., & Hirst, G. (2006). Evaluating WordNet based measures of lexical semantic relatedness. *Computational Linguistics*, *32*(1), 13–44. doi:10.1162/coli.2006.32.1.13

Buscaldi, D., & Roso, P. (2008). Geo-WordNet: Automatic geo-referencing of WordNet. In *Proceedings of the 6th International Language Resources and Evaluation Conference (LREC)*. LREC.

Cai, G. (2002). GeoVSM: An integrated retrieval model for geographic information. *Geographic Information Science*. Retrieved from http://spatial.ist.psu.edu/cai/LNCS2478-GeoVSM.pdf.

Callan, J. P., & Conneli, M. (2001). Query-based sampling of text databases. *ACM Transactions on Information Systems*, *19*(2), 97–130. doi:10.1145/382979.383040

Choi, Y. S., & Yoo, S. I. (2001). Text database discovery on the Web: Neural net based approach. *Journal of Intelligent Information Systems*, *16*(1), 5–10. doi:10.1023/A:1008708725988

Complete Planet. (2000). *The deep Web: Surfacing hidden value*. Retrieved from http://www.completeplanet.com/Tutorials/ DeepWeb /index.asp.

Fuhr, N. (1999). A decision-theoretic approach to database selection in networked IR. *ACM Transactions on Information Systems*, *17*(3), 229–249. doi:10.1145/314516.314517

Gliozzo, A., Strapparava, C., & Dagan, I. (2004). Unsupervised and supervised exploitation of semantic domains in lexical disambiguation. *Computer Speech & Language*, *18*(3), 275–299. doi:10.1016/j.csl.2004.05.006

Ipeirotis, P., & Gravano, L. (2002). Distributed search over the hidden Web: Hierarchical database sampling and selection. In *Proceedings of the 28th International Conference on Very Large Databases*. Hong Kong, China: Very Large databases.

Ipeirotis, P., & Gravano, L. (2008). Classification-aware hidden-Web text database selection. *ACM Transactions on Information Systems*, *26*(2). doi:10.1145/1344411.1344412

Ipeirotis, P., Gravano, L., & Sahami, M. (2001). Probe, count and classify: Categorizing hidden-Web databases. In *Proceedings of the ACM SIGMOD International Conference on Management of Data*. ACM Press.

Larkey, L. S., Connell, M. E., & Callan, J. P. (2000). Collection selection and results merging with topically organized U.S. patents and TREC data. In *Proceedings of the ACM Conference on Information and Knowledge Management*, (pp. 282-289). ACM Press.

Map 24. (2010). *Website.* Retrieved from http://developer.navteq.com/site/global/zones/ms/downloads.jsp.

Mazur, P., & Dole, R. (2007). The Dante temporal expression tagger. In *Proceedings of the 3rd Language and Technology Conference*. Language and Technology.

Meng, W., Liu, K. L., Yu, C. T., Wang, X., Chang, Y., & Rishe, N. (1998). Determining text databases to search in the Internet. In *Proceedings of the 24th International Conference on Very Large Databases*, (pp. 14-15). Very Large Databases.

Ntoulas, A., Zerfos, P., & Cho, J. (2005). Downloading textual hidden Web content through keyword queries. In *Proceedings of the 5th ACM/IEEE-CS Joint Conference on Digital Libraries*. ACM Press.

OWL. (2010). *Time ontology in OWL*. Retrieved from http://www.w3.org/TR/owl-time/.

Shokouhi, M. (2007). Central-rank-based collection selection in uncooperative distributed information retrieval. In *Proceedings of the 29th European Conference on IR Research.* IR Research.

Si, L., & Callan, J. (2005). Modeling search engine effectiveness for federated search. In *Proceedings of the 28th International ACM SIGIR Conference on Research and Development in Information Retrieval*, (pp. 83-90). ACM Press.

Sugiura, A., & Etzioni, O. (2000). Query routing for Web search engines: Architecture and experiments. In *Proceedings of the 9th International World Wide Web Conference*. World Wide Web.

WordNet. (2010). *Website.* Retrieved from http://www.cogsci.princeton.edu/~wn/.

Wu, X., & Palmer, M. (1994). Web semantics and lexical selection. In *Proceedings of the 32nd ACL Meeting.* ACL.

Xu, J., Cao, Y., Lim, E., & Ng, W. (1998). Database selection techniques for routing bibliographic queries. In *Proceedings of the 3rd ACM International Conference on Digital Libraries*. ACM Press.

Yu, C. T., Meng, W., Wu, W., & Liu, K. L. (2001). Efficient and effective metasearch for text databases incorporating linkages among documents. In *Proceedings of the ACM SIGMOD International Conference on Management of Data*. ACM Press.

## KEY TERMS AND DEFINITIONS

**Database Selection:** An algorithm for finding among a set of available database the ones that contain information relevant to some user query.

**Geographic Ontology:** A mechanism to describe, manage and exchange toponyms (location names)

**Hidden Web:** The hidden Web refers to the World Wide Web content that is not part of the surface Web, which is indexed by standard search engines.

**Metasearcher:** A metasearcher is a search tool that sends user requests to several other databases (or search engines) and aggregates the results into a single list or displays them according to their source.

**Multi-Faceted Search:** an information seeking technique that allows users to search for different aspects by filtering available information.

**Temporal Ontology:** An easily understandable, flexible, formally defined and effective means of representing knowledge about time.

# Compilation of References


Abdelmoty, A., Smart, P., Jones, C., Fu, G., & Finch, D. (2005). A critical evaluation of ontology languages for geographic information retrieval on the Internet. *Journal of Visual Languages and Computing*, *16*(4), 331–358. doi:10.1016/j.jvlc.2004.11.001

Abraham, T., & Roddick, J. (1999). Survey of spatio-temporal databases. *GeoInformatica*, *3*(1), 61–99. doi:10.1023/A:1009800916313

ACE. (2007). *The ACE evaluation plan: Evaluation of the detection and recognition of ACE entities, values, temporal expressions, relations and events, ver. 1.9*. Retrieved from http://www.nist.gov/speech/tests/ace/2007/index.html.

Aiello, M., Pratt-Hartmann, I. E., & Benthem, J. F. V. (2007). *Handbook of spatial logics*. Secaucus, NJ: Springer-Verlag New York, Inc. doi:10.1007/978-1-4020-5587-4

Alboody, A., Sèdes, F., & Inglada, J. (2008). Post-classification and spatial reasoning: New approach to change detection for updating GIS database. In *Proceedings of the IEEE International Conference on Information and Communication Technologies: From Theory to Applications (ICTTA2008),* (pp. 1-7). Damascus, Syria. IEEE Press. Retrieved from http://ieeexplore.ieee.org/xpls/abs_all.jsp?arnumber=4530039.

Alboody, A., Sèdes, F., & Inglada, J. (2009b). Multi-level topological relations of the spatial reasoning system RCC-8. In *Proceedings of The First International Conference on Advances in Databases, Knowledge, and Data Applications (DBKDA 2009), IARIA Conferences - GlobeNet2009*, (pp. 13-21). IEEE Press.

Alboody, A., Inglada, J., & Sèdes, F. (2009a). Enriching the spatial reasoning system RCC8. *The SIGSPATIAL Special*, *1*(1), 14–20. doi:10.1145/1517463.1517464

Alchourrón, C. E., Gärdenfors, P., & Makinson, D. (1985). On the logic of theory change: Partial meet contraction and revision functions. *Journal of Symbolic Logic*, *50*(2), 510–530. doi:10.2307/2274239

Aliello, M., Pratt-Hartmann, I. E., & Van Benthem, J. (2007). *Handbook of spatial logics*. Spinger-Verlag. doi:10.1007/978-1-4020-5587-4

Allen, E., Edwards, G., & Bédard, Y. (1995). Qualitative causal modeling in temporal GIS. In *Proceedings of COSIT*, (pp 397–412). COSIT.

Allen, J. F., & Hayes, P. J. (1985). A common sense theory of time. In *Proceedings of IJCAI*. Los Altos, CA: Morgan Kaufmann.

Allen, J. F. (1983). Maintaining knowledge about temporal intervals. *Communications of the ACM*, *26*(11), 832–843. doi:10.1145/182.358434

Allen, J. F. (1984). Towards a general theory of action and time. *Artificial Intelligence*, *23*(2), 123–154. doi:10.1016/0004-3702(84)90008-0

Allen, J. F., & Ferguson, G. (1994). Actions and events in interval temporal logic. *Journal of Logic and Computation*, *4*(5), 531–579. doi:10.1093/logcom/4.5.531

Anderson, M., Meyer, N., & Olivier, P. (Eds.). (2002). *Diagrammatic representation and reasoning*. Springer-Verlag. doi:10.1007/978-1-4471-0109-3

André, E., Herzog, G., & Rist, T. (1989). *Natural language access to visual data: Dealing with space and movement*. Saarbrücken, Germany: German Research Center for Artificial Intelligence (DFKI).

Andréka, H., Németi, I., & Sain, I. (2001). Algebraic logic. In Gabbay, D. M., & Guenthner, F. (Eds.), *Handbook of Philosophical Logic* (2nd ed., *Vol. 2*, pp. 133–147). Dordrecht, The Netherlands: Kluwer.

Andronikos, T., Stefanidakis, M., & Papadakis, I. (2009). Adding temporal dimension to ontologies via OWL reification. In *Proceedings of Panhellenic Conference on Informatics*, (pp. 19-22). Panhellenic Conference.

Arpinal, B., Sheth, A., Ramakrishnan, C., Usery, L., Azami, M., & Kwan, M.-P. (2006). Geospatial ontology development and semantic analytics. *Transactions in GIS*, *10*(14), 551–575.

Artale, A., & Franconi, E. (2000). A survey of temporal extensions of description logics. *Annals of Mathematics and Artificial Intelligence*, *30*(1-4), 171–210. doi:10.1023/A:1016636131405

Asher, N., & Vieu, L. (1995). Toward a geometry of common sense: A semantics and a complete axiomatization for mereotopology. In *Proceedings of the International Joint Conference on Artificial Intelligence (IJCAI-95)*, (pp. 846–852). IJCAI.

Augusto, J. C., & Shapiro, D. (Eds.) (2007). Advances in ambient intelligence. *Frontiers in Artificial Intelligence and Applications* (Vol. 164). IOS.

Augusto, J. C., Liu, J., McCullagh, P., Wang, H., & Yang, J.-B. (2008). Management of uncertainty and spatio-temporal aspects for monitoring and diagnosis in a smart home. *International Journal of Computational Intelligence Systems*, *1*(4), 361–378. doi:10.2991/ijcis.2008.1.4.8

Augusto, J. C., & Nugent, C. D. (Eds.). (2006). *Designing smart homes, the role of artificial intelligence. (LNCS 4008)*. Springer.

Aztiria, A., Augusto, J. C., Izaguirre, A., & Cook, D. (2008). Learning accurate temporal relations from user actions in intelligent environments. In *Proceedings of the Symposium of Ubiquitous Computing and Ambient Intelligence*, (pp. 274-283). Salamanca, Spain. Ubiquitous Computing and Ambient Intelligence.

Baader, F., Calvanese, D., McGuinness, D., Nardi, D., & Patel-Schneider, P. (2003). *The description logic handbook*. New York, NY: Cambridge University Press.

Baader, F., Küsters, R., & Wolter, F. (2003). Extensions to description logics. In *The Description Logic Handbook: Theory, Implementation, and Applications* (pp. 219–261). New York, NY: Cambridge University Press.

Bailey-Kellog, C., & Zhao, F. (2003). Qualitative spatial reasoning: Extracting and reasoning with spatial aggregates. *AI Magazine*, *24*(4).

Balbiani, P., Condotta, J., & del Cerro, L. (1999). A new tractable subclass of the rectangle algebra. In *Proceedings of the Sixteenth International Joint Conference on Artificial Intelligence (IJCAI99)*, (pp. 442-447). IJCAI.

Balbiani, P., Condotta, J., & del Cerro, L. F. (1998). A model for reasoning about bidimsional temporal relations. In *Proceedings of KR98: Principles of Knowledge Representation and Reasoning* (pp. 124–130). Morgan Kaufmann.

Balbiani, P., Tinchev, T., & Vakarelov, D. (2008). Modal logics for region-based theories of space. *Fundamenta Informaticae*, *81*(1-3), 29–82.

Baratis, E., Petrakis, E. G., Batsakis, S., Maris, N., & Papadakis, N. (2009). TOQL: Temporal ontology querying language. In *Proceedings of the 11th International Symposium on Spatial and Temporal Databases (SSTD 2009)*, (pp. 338-354). SSTD.

Barr, W., Ashtari, M., Bilder, R., Degreef, G., & Lieberman, J. (1997). Brain morphometric comparison of first-episode schizophrenia and temporal lobe epilepsy. *The British Journal of Psychiatry*, *170*, 515–519. doi:10.1192/bjp.170.6.515

Bar-Shalom, Y., & Fortmann, T. E. (1988). *Tracking and data association*. New York, NY: Academic Press.

Basu, S., Pollack, R., & Roy, M. F. (2006). *Algorithms in real algebraic geometry* (2nd ed.). London, UK: Springer.

Bateman, J., & Farrar, S. (2005). *OntoSpace project report: Spatial ontology baseline deliverable D2 I1, version: 1.6. Technical Report*. Bremen, Germany: University of Bremen.

Beller, A. (1991). Spatio/temporal events in a GIS. In *Proceedings of GIS/LIS*, (pp. 766–775). ASPRS/ACSM.

Belussi, A., Catania, B., & Podestà, P. (2005). Towards topological consistency and similarity of multiresolution geographical maps. In *Proceedings of the 13th Annual ACM International Workshop on Geographic Information Systems,* (pp. 220–229). New York, NY: ACM.

Bennett, B. (1994). Spatial reasoning with propositional logic. In *Proceedings of the Fourth International Conference on Principles of Knowledge Representation and Reasoning (KR94),* (pp. 51-62). Morgan Kaufmann Publishers.

Bennett, B. (2002). Physical objects, identity and vagueness. In D. Fensel, D. McGuinness, & M.-A. Williams (Eds.), *Principles of Knowledge Representation and Reasoning: Proceedings of the Eighth International Conference (KR2002)*. San Francisco, CA: Morgan Kaufmann.

Bennett, B., Cohn, A. G., Torrini, P., & Hazarika, S. M. (2000). A foundation for region-based qualitative geometry. In *Proceedings of the European Conference on Artificial Intelligence (ECAI-2000)*, (pp. 204–208). ECAI.

Bennett, B. (1997). *Logical representations for automated reasoning about spatial relationships*. Leeds, UK: University of Leeds.

Bennett, B. (2001). A categorical axiomatisation of region-based geometry. *Fundamenta Informaticae, 46*(1-2), 145–158.

Bennett, B., Cohn, A. G., Wolter, F., & Zakharyaschev, M. (2002). Multi-dimensional modal logic as a framework for spatio-temporal reasoning. *Applied Intelligence, 17*(3), 239–251. doi:10.1023/A:1020083231504

Bennett, B., & Düntsch, I. (2007). Axioms, algebras and topology. In *Handbook of Spatial Logics* (pp. 99–159). London, UK: Springer. doi:10.1007/978-1-4020-5587-4_3

Bennett, B., & Galton, A. P. (2004). A unifying semantics for time and events. *Artificial Intelligence, 153*(1-2), 13–48. doi:10.1016/j.artint.2003.02.001

Bettini, C., Mascetti, S., & Sean Wang, X. (2007). Supporting temporal reasoning by mapping calendar expressions to minimal periodic sets. *Journal of Artificial Intelligence Research, 28*(1), 299–348.

Bhatt, M. (2008a). Dynamical spatial systems-A potential approach for the application of qualitative spatial calculi. In D. Wilson & H. C. Lane (Eds.), *FLAIRS Conference*, (pp. 580–585). AAAI Press.

Bhatt, M. (2008b). (Some) default and non-monotonic aspects of qualitative spatial reasoning. In *Proceedings of AAAI-08 Technical Reports, Workshop on Spatial and Temporal Reasoning*, (pp. 1–6). AAAI.

Bhatt, M. (2009a). Commonsense inference in dynamic spatial systems: Phenomenal and reasoning requirements. In *Proceedings of the 23rd International Workshop on Qualitative Reasoning (QR 09),* (pp. 1-6). Ljubljana, Slovenia: QR.

Bhatt, M. (2009b). Toward an experimental cognitive robotics framework: A position statement. In *Proceedings of the International Workshop on Hybrid Control of Autonomous Systems: Integrating Learning, Deliberation and Reactive Control (HYCAS 2009),* (pp. 7-12). Pasadena, CA: HYCAS.

Bhatt, M. (2010). Commonsense inference in dynamic spatial systems: Epistemological requirements. In *Proceedings of FLAIRS Conference: Special Track on Spatial and Temporal Reasoning*. AAAI Press.

Bhatt, M., & Flanagan, G. (2010). *Spatio-temporal abduction in the event calculus*. Unpublished.

Bhatt, M., & Freksa, C. (2010). Spatial computing for design: An artificial intelligence perspective. In *Proceedings of NSF International Workshop on Studying Visual and Spatial Reasoning for Design Creativity (SDC'10)*. SDC.

Bhatt, M., & Guesgen, H. (Eds.). (2009). *Spatial and temporal reasoning for ambient intelligence systems (STAMI 09)*. (SFB/TR 8 Spatial Cognition Report Series, No. 020-08/2009). STAMI.

Bhatt, M., Dylla, F., & Hois, J. (2009). Spatio-terminological inference for the design of ambient environments. In *Proceedings of the 9th International Conference on Spatial Information Theory (COSIT)*, (p. 505). Springer-Verlag.

Bhatt, M., Ichim, A., & Flanagan, G. (2010). DSIM: A tool for assisted spatial design. In *Proceedings of the 4th International Conference on Design Computing and Cognition (DCC'10)*. DCC.

Bhatt, M., & Dylla, F. (2009). A qualitative model of dynamic scene analysis and interpretation in ambient intelligence systems. *International Journal of Robotics and Automation*, *24*(3). doi:10.2316/Journal.206.2009.3.206-3274

Bhatt, M., & Loke, S. (2008). Modelling dynamic spatial systems in the situation calculus. *Spatial Cognition and Computation*, *8*(1), 86–130. doi:10.1080/13875860801926884

Biacino, L., & Gerla, G. (1991). Connection structures. *Notre Dame Journal of Formal Logic*, *32*(3), 242–247. doi:10.1305/ndjfl/1093635748

Birkhoff, G. (1967). *Lattice theory* (3rd ed.). New York, NY: American Mathematical Society.

Bitterlich, W., Sack, J. R., Sester, M., & Weibel, R. (2008). *08451 abstracts collection - Representation, analysis and visualization of moving objects.* Paper presented at the Representation, Analysis and Visualization of Moving Objects. Dagstuhl, Germany.

Bittner, T. (1999). *Rough location*. Unpublished Doctoral Dissertation. Vienna, Austria: Vienna Technical University.

Bittner, T. (2000). A qualitative formalization of built environments. In *Proceedings of the Conference on Database and Expert Systems Applications (DEXA-2000)*, (pp. 959–969). London, UK: Springer.

Bittner, T. (2002). Granularity in reference to spatio-temporal location and relations. In *Proceedings of the Florida Artificial Intelligence Research Society Conference (FLAIRS-15)*, (pp. 466–470). FLAIRS.

Bittner, T. (2009). Logical properties of foundational mereogeometrical relations in bio-ontologies. *Applied Ontology*, *4*.

Bittner, T., & Donnelly, M. (2007). A formal theory of qualitative size and distance relations between regions. In *Proceedings of the Workshop on Qualitative Reasoning (QR07)*. QR.

Bittner, T., & Smith, B. (2001). Vagueness and granular partitions. In *Proceedings of the Conference on Formal Ontology in Information Systems (FOIS-01)*, (pp. 309–320). FOIS.

Bittner, T., & Stell, J. G. (2000b). Rough sets in approximate spatial reasoning. In *Proceedings of the Conference on Rough Sets and Current Trends in Computing (RSCTC-2000)*, (pp. 445–453). Springer.

Bittner, T., & Stell, J. G. (2003). Stratified rough sets and vagueness. In *Proceedings of the Conference on Spatial Information Theory (COSIT-03)*, (pp. 270–286). Springer.

Bittner, T., & Winter, S. (1999). On ontology in image analysis. In *Selected Papers from the International Workshop on Integrated Spatial Databases, Digital Images and GIS*, (pp. 168–191). London, UK: Springer-Verlag.

Bittner, T. (2004). A mereological theory of frames of reference. *International Journal of Artificial Intelligence Tools*, *13*(1), 171–198. doi:10.1142/S0218213004001478

Bittner, T., Donnelly, M., & Smith, B. (2009). A spatio-temporal ontology for geographic information integration. *International Journal of Geographical Information Science*, *23*(6), 765–798. doi:10.1080/13658810701776767

Bittner, T., & Smith, B. (2003). *Foundations of geographic information science: A theory of granular partitions*. New York, NY: Taylor & Francis.

Bittner, T., & Stell, J. G. (1998). A boundary-sensitive approach to qualitative location. *Annals of Mathematics and Artificial Intelligence*, *24*(1-4), 93–114. doi:10.1023/A:1018945131135

Bittner, T., & Stell, J. G. (2000a). Approximate qualitative spatial reasoning. *Spatial Cognition and Computation*, *2*(4), 435–466. doi:10.1023/A:1015598320584

Bittner, T., & Stell, J. G. (2002). Vagueness and rough location. *GeoInformatica*, *6*(2), 99–121. doi:10.1023/A:1015291525685

Blyth, T. S. (2005). *Lattices and ordered algebraic structures*. London, UK: Springer.

Bobrow, D. G. (1984). Special volume on qualitative reasoning about physical systems. *Artificial Intelligence*, *24*(1-3). doi:10.1016/0004-3702(84)90036-5

Bogaert, P., Van de Weghe, N., Cohn, A. G., Witlox, F., & De Maeyer, P. (2006). *The qualitative trajectory calculus on networks.* Paper presented at the Spatial Cognition V Reasoning, Action, Interaction. Bremen, Germany.

Bogaert, P., Van der Zee, E., Maddens, R., Van de Weghe, N., & De Maeyer, P. (2008). *Cognitive and linguistic adequacy of the qualitative trajectory calculus*. Paper presented at the International Workshop on Moving Objects: From Natural to Formal Language. Park City, UT.

Bojduj, B., Weber, B., Richter, K. F., & Bertel, S. (2008). Computer aided architectural design: Wayfinding complexity analysis. In *Proceedings of the 12th International Conference on Computer Supported Collaborative Work in Design (CSCWD),* (pp. 919-924). CSCWD.

Borgida, A. (1996). On the relative expressiveness of description logics and predicate logics. *Artificial Intelligence*, *82*(1-2), 353–367. doi:10.1016/0004-3702(96)00004-5

Borgo, S. (2009). Euclidean and mereological qualitative space: A study of SCC and DCC. In *Proceedings of the Twenty-First International Joint Conference on Artificial Intelligence (IJCAI 2009)*, (pp. 708-713). IJCAI.

Borgo, S., & Masolo, C. (2009). Full mereogeometries. *The Review of Symbolic Logic*. Retrieved from http://citeseerx.ist.psu.edu/viewdoc/similar?doi=10.1.1.98.2266&type=ab.

Borgo, S., Guarino, N., & Masolo, C. (1996). A pointless theory of space based on strong connection and congruence. In *Proceedings of KR96: Principles of Knowledge Representation and Reasoning*, (pp. 220–229). KR.

Bota, M., & Swanson, L. (2008). Bams neuroanatomical ontology: Design and implementation. *Frontiers in Neuroinformatics*, *2*(2).

Brachman, R., & Levesque, H. (2004). *Knowledge representation and reasoning*. San Francisco, CA: Morgan Kaufmann Publishers Inc.

Breysse, O., & De Glas, M. (2007). A new approach to the concepts of boundary and contact: Toward an alternative to mereotopology. *Fundamenta Informaticae*, *78*(2), 217–238.

Bronzino, J., Morelli, R. A., & Goethe, J. (1989). Overseer: A prototype expert system for monitoring drug treatment in the psychiatric clinic. *IEEE Transactions on Bio-Medical Engineering*, *36*(5), 533–540. doi:10.1109/10.24255

Bruns, H. T., & Egenhofer, M. J. (1996). Similarity of spatial scenes. In *Proceedings of the Seventh International Symposium on Spatial Data Handling,* (pp. 173-184). Taylor & Francis.

Budanitsky, A., & Hirst, G. (2006). Evaluating WordNet based measures of lexical semantic relatedness. *Computational Linguistics*, *32*(1), 13–44. doi:10.1162/coli.2006.32.1.13

Burrough, A. (1996). Natural objects with indeterminate boundaries. In Burrough, A., & Frank, A. U. (Eds.), *Geographic Objects with Indeterminate Boundaries* (pp. 171–188). Taylor & Francis.

Burrough, A., & Frank, A. U. (1995). Concepts and paradigms in spatial information: Are current geographic information systems truly generic? *International Journal of Geographical Information Science*, *9*(2), 101–116. doi:10.1080/02693799508902028

Burrough, A., & Frank, A. U. (1996). *Geographic objects with indeterminate boundaries*. New York, NY: Taylor & Francis.

Burrough, P. A. (1986). *Principles of geographical information systems for land resources assessment*. Oxford, UK: Oxford University Press.

Buscaldi, D., & Roso, P. (2008). Geo-WordNet: Automatic geo-referencing of WordNet. In *Proceedings of the 6th International Language Resources and Evaluation Conference (LREC)*. LREC.

Cai, G. (2002). GeoVSM: An integrated retrieval model for geographic information. *Geographic Information Science*. Retrieved from http://spatial.ist.psu.edu/cai/LNCS2478-GeoVSM.pdf.

Callan, J. P., & Conneli, M. (2001). Query-based sampling of text databases. *ACM Transactions on Information Systems*, *19*(2), 97–130. doi:10.1145/382979.383040

Camiano, P. (2006). *Ontology learning and population from text: Algorithms, evaluation and applications*. London, UK: Springer.

Cardelli, L., & Gordon, A. D. (2000). Anytime, anywhere: Modal logics for mobile ambients. In *Proceedings of POPL*, (pp. 365–377). ACM.

Cardelli, L., & Gordon, A. D. (2006). Ambient logic. *Mathematical Structures in Computer Science*.

Casati, R., & Varzi, A. (1997). Spatial entities. In Stock, O. (Ed.), *Spaial and Temporal Reasoning* (pp. 73–96). Kluwer Academic Press. doi:10.1007/978-0-585-28322-7_3

Casati, R., & Varzi, A. C. (1994). *Holes and other superficialities*. Cambridge, MA: MIT Press.

Casati, R., & Varzi, A. C. (1996). The structure of spatial localization. *Philosophical Studies*, *82*, 205–239. doi:10.1007/BF00364776

Casati, R., & Varzi, A. C. (1999). *Parts and places: The structures of spatial representation*. Cambridge, MA: MIT Press.

Castellanos, J., Neira, J., & Tardós, J. D. (2006). Map building and slam algorithms. In Ge, S. S., & Lewis, F. L. (Eds.), *Autonomous Mobile Robots: Sensing, Control, Decision-Making and Applications*. Taylor & Francis.

Čech, E. (1966). *Topological spaces*. Berlin, Germany: Interscience.

Chalmers, M. (2004). A historical view of context. *Computer Supported Cooperative Work*, *13*(3-4), 223–247. doi:10.1007/s10606-004-2802-8

Chartland, G., & Lesniak, L. (1996). *Graphs & digraphs* (3rd ed). Wadsworth & Brooks/Cole.

Chaudet, H. (2004). STEEL: A spatio-temporal extended event language for tracking epidemic spread from outbreak reports. In *Proceedings of the CEUR Workshop on Formal Biomedical Knowledge Representation (KR-MED-04)*. KR-MED.

Chen, H., Finin, T., & Joshi, A. (2003). An ontology for context aware pervasive computing environments. In *Proceedings of the 18th International Joint Conferences on Artificial Intelligence (IJCAI-03)*. Acapulco, Mexico: IJCAI.

Chen, H., Fuller, S. S., Friedman, C., & Hersh, W. (Eds.). (2006). *Medical informatics, volume 8 of Integrated Series in Information Systems: Biomedical ontologies*, (pp. 211–236). Springer.

Chen, H., Perich, F., Finin, T., & Joshi, A. (2004). SOUPA: Standard ontology for ubiquitous and pervasive applications. In *Proceedings of the 1st Annual International Conference on Mobile and Ubiquitous Systems (MobiQuitous2004)*. Cambridge, MA: MobiQuitous.

Chen, J., Liu, D., Zhang, C., & Xie, Q. (2007a). Cardinal direction relations in 3D space. In *Proceedings of the Conference on Knowledge Science, Engineering and Management (KSEM-07)*, (pp. 623–629). Springer.

Chen, J., Liu, D., Zhang, C., & Xie, Q. (2007b). Combinative reasoning with RCC5 and cardinal direction relations. In *Proceedings of the Conference on Knowledge Science, Engineering and Management (KSEM-07)*, (pp. 92–102). Springer.

Chen, L., Nugent, C., Mulvenna, M., Finlay, D., Hong, X., & Poland, M. (2008). Using event calculus for behaviour reasoning and assistance in a smart home. In *Proceedings of the International Conference On Smart Homes and Health Telematics (ICOST2008)*, (pp. 81-89). Ames, IA: Springer.

Chen, J., Li, C., Li, Z., & Gold, C. (2001). A Voronoi-based 9-intersection model for spatial relations. *International Journal of Geographical Information Science*, *15*(3), 201–220. doi:10.1080/13658810151072831

Chen, J., Liu, D., Zhang, C., & Xie, Q. (2009). *Combinative reasoning with RCC5 and cardinal direction relations*. Berlin, Germany: Springer.

Choi, Y. S., & Yoo, S. I. (2001). Text database discovery on the Web: Neural net based approach. *Journal of Intelligent Information Systems*, *16*(1), 5–10. doi:10.1023/A:1008708725988

Chua, S., Lam, I., Tai, K., Cheung, C., Tang, W. N., & Chen, E. (2003). Brain morphological abnormality in schizophrenia is independent of country of origin. *Acta Psychiatrica Scandinavica*, *108*, 269–275. doi:10.1034/j.1600-0447.2003.00134.x

Claramunt, C., & Thériault, M. (1995). Managing time in GIS: An event-oriented approach. In *Proceedings of Temporal Databases* (pp. 23–42). Temporal Databases. doi:10.1007/978-1-4471-3033-8_2

Clarke, B. (1981). A calculus of individuals based on connection. *Notre Dame Journal of Formal Logic*, *22*(3), 204–218. doi:10.1305/ndjfl/1093883455

Clarke, B. (1985). Individuals and points. *Notre Dame Journal of Formal Logic*, *26*(1), 61–75. doi:10.1305/ndjfl/1093870761

Clementini, E., Di Felice, P., & Oosterom, P. (1993). A small set of formal topological relationships suitable for end user interaction. In *Proceedings of the Symposium on Spatial Databases (SSD93)*, (pp. 277–295). Springer.

Clementini, E., & Di Felice, P. (1997a). A global framework for qualitative shape description. *GeoInformatica*, *1*(1), 11–27. doi:10.1023/A:1009790715467

Clementini, E., & Di Felice, P. (1997b). Approximate topological relations. *International Journal of Approximate Reasoning*, *16*(2), 173–204. doi:10.1016/S0888-613X(96)00127-2

Clementini, E., & Di Felice, P. (1998). Topological invariants for lines. *IEEE Transactions on Knowledge and Data Engineering*, *10*(1), 38–54. doi:10.1109/69.667085

Cohn, A. G. (1993). Modal and non-modal qualitative spatial logics. In *Proceedings of the Workshop on Spatial and Temporal Reasoning at IJCAI-93*, (pp. 93–100). IJCAI.

Cohn, A. G. (1995). A hierarchical representation of qualitative shape based on connection and convexity. In *Proceedings of the Conference on Spatial Information Theory (COSIT-95)*, (pp. 311–326). Springer.

Cohn, A. G., & Gotts, N. M. (1996a). A mereological approach to representing spatial vagueness. In *Proceedings of KR96: Principles of Knowledge Representation and Reasoning*, (pp. 230–241). KR.

Cohn, A. G., & Varzi, A. C. (1998). Connection relations in mereotopology. In *Proceedings of the European Conference on Artificial Intelligence (ECAI-98)*, (pp. 150–154). ECAI.

Cohn, A. G., & Varzi, A. C. (1999). Modes of connection. In *Proceedings of the Conference on Spatial Information Theory (COSIT-99)*, (pp. 299–314). Springer.

Cohn, A. G., Bennett, B., Gooday, J. M., & Gotts, N. M. (1997a). RCC: A calculus for region based qualitative spatial reasoning. *GeoInformatica*, *1*, 275–316. doi:10.1023/A:1009712514511

Cohn, A. G., Bennett, B., Gooday, J. M., & Gotts, N. M. (1997b). Representing and reasoning with qualitative spatial relations about regions. In Stock, O. (Ed.), *Spatial and Temporal Reasoning* (pp. 97–134). Kluwer. doi:10.1007/978-0-585-28322-7_4

Cohn, A. G., Bennett, B., Gooday, J., & Gotts, N. M. (1997b). Qualitative spatial representation and reasoning with the region connection calculus. *GeoInformatica*, *1*(3), 275–316. doi:10.1023/A:1009712514511

Cohn, A. G., & Gotts, N. M. (1996b). The egg-yolk representation of regions with indeterminate boundaries. In Burrough, A., & Frank, A. U. (Eds.), *Geographic Objects with Indeterminate Boundaries* (pp. 171–188). Taylor & Francis.

Cohn, A. G., Gotts, N. M., Randell, D. A., Cui, Z., Bennett, B., & Gooday, J. M. (1997). Exploiting temporal continuity in qualitative spatial calculi. In Golledge, R. G., & Egenhofer, M. J. (Eds.), *Spatial and Temporal Reasoning in Geographical Information Systems*. Elsevier.

Cohn, A. G., & Hazarika, S. M. (2001). Qualitative spatial representation and reasoning: An overview. *Fundamenta Informaticae*, *46*(1-2), 1–29.

Cohn, A. G., Randell, D. A., & Cui, Z. (1994). Taxonomies of logically defined qualitative spatial relations. In Guarino, N., & Poli, R. (Eds.), *Formal Ontology in Conceptual Analysis and Knowledge Representation*. Dordrecht, The Netherlands: Kluwer. doi:10.1006/ijhc.1995.1077

Cohn, A. G., & Renz, J. (2007). Qualitative spatial reasoning. In van Harmelen, F., Lifschitz, V., & Porter, B. (Eds.), *Handbook of Knowledge Representation*. London, UK: Elsevier.

Cohn, A. G., & Renz, J. (2008). Qualitative spatial representation and reasoning. In *Handbook of Knowledge Representation: Foundations of Artificial Intelligence* (*Vol. 3*, pp. 551–596). London, UK: Elsevier.

Cohn, A. G., & Varzi, A. C. (2003). Mereotopological connection. *Journal of Symbolic Logic*, *32*(4), 357–390.

Cohn, A., Bennett, B., Gooday, J., & Gotts, N. (1997a). Representing and reasoning with qualitative spatial relations about regions. In Stock, O. (Ed.), *Spatial and Temporal Reasoning* (pp. 97–134). Dordrecht, The Netherlands: Kluwer Academic Publishers. doi:10.1007/978-0-585-28322-7_4

Collins, G. E. (1975). Lecture Notes in Computer Science: *Vol. 33. Quantifier elimination for real closed fields by cylindrical algebraic decomposition* (pp. 134–183). Berlin, Germany: Springer-Verlag.

Complete Planet. (2000). *The deep Web: Surfacing hidden value*. Retrieved from http://www.completeplanet.com/ Tutorials/ DeepWeb /index.asp.

Condotta, J. F., Kaci, S., & Schwind, N. (2008). A framework for merging qualitative constraints networks. In D. Wilson & H. C. Lane (Eds.), *Proceedings of the Twenty-First International Florida Artificial Intelligence Research Society Conference,* (pp. 586-591). Coconut Grove, FL: AAAI Press.

Condotta, J. F., Ligozat, G., & Saade, M. (2006). A generic toolkit for n-ary qualitative temporal and spatial calculi. In *Proceedings of the 13th International Symposium on Temporal Representation and Reasoning (TIME'06),* (pp. 78 – 86). Budapest, Hungary: TIME.

Costa, L., & Cesar, R. M. Jr. (2006). *Shape analysis and classification: Theory and practice*. Boca Raton, FL: CRC Press.

Couclelis, H. (2009). The abduction of geographic information science: Transporting spatial reasoning to the realm of purpose and design. In Hornsby, K. S., Claramunt, C., Denis, M., & Ligozat, G. (Eds.), *COSIT* (pp. 342–356). Springer. doi:10.1007/978-3-642-03832-7_21

Cristani, M., Cohn, A. G., & Bennett, B. (2000). *Spatial locations via morpho-mereology*. Paper presented at the Conference on Principles of Knowledge Representation and Reasoning (KR 2000). Breckinridge, CO.

Cristani, M. (1999). The complexity of reasoning about spatial congruence. *Journal of Artificial Intelligence Research, 11*, 361–390.

Cui, Z., Cohn, A. G., & Randell, D. A. (1992). Qualitative simulation based on a logical formalism of space and time. In *Proceedings of, AAAI-92*, 679–684.

Davis, E. (2009). Ontologies and representations of matter. In *Proceedings of the Twenty-Fourth AAAI Conference on Artificial Intelligence (AAAI-10)*. AAAI.

Davis, E. (1990). *Representations of commonsense knowledge*. San Mateo, CA: Morgan Kaufmann.

Davis, E. (2000). *Describing spatial transitions using mereotopological relations over histories. Technical Report #2000-809*. New York, NY: New York University.

Davis, E. (2001). Continuous shape transformations and metrics on regions. *Fundamenta Informaticae, 46*(1-2), 31–54.

Davis, E. (2006). The expressivity of quantifying over regions. *Journal of Logic and Computation, 16*(6), 891–916. doi:10.1093/logcom/exl020

Davis, E. (2008). Pouring liquids: A study in commonsense physical reasoning. *Artificial Intelligence, 172*(12-13), 1540–1578. doi:10.1016/j.artint.2008.04.003

Davis, E. (2009). How does a box work? A study in the qualitative dynamics of solid objects. *Artificial Intelligence, 175*(1), 299–345. doi:10.1016/j.artint.2010.04.006

Davis, E., Gotts, N. M., & Cohn, A. G. (1999). Constraint networks of topological relations and convexity. *Constraints, 4*(3), 241–280. doi:10.1023/A:1026401931919

Davis, E., & Morgenstern, L. (2004). Introduction: Progress in formal commonsense reasoning. *Artificial Intelligence, 153*(1-2), 1–12. doi:10.1016/j.artint.2003.09.001

de Berg, M., van Kreveld, M., Overmars, M., & Schwarzkopf, O. (1997). *Computational geometry*. Springer-Verlag.

de Kleer, J. (1977). Multiple representations of knowledge in a mechanics problem solver. In *Proceedings of the Fifth International Joint Conference on Artificial Intelligence (IJCAI-77)*, (pp. 299-304). IJCAI.

de Kleer, J., & Brown, J. S. (1985). A qualitative physics based on confluences. In Bobrow, D. (Ed.), *Qualitative Reasoning about Physical Systems* (pp. 7–83). Cambridge, MA: MIT Press.

de Laguna, T. (1922). Point, line, and surface, as sets of solids. *The Journal of Philosophy, 19*(17), 449–461. doi:10.2307/2939504

Dechter, R., Meiri, I., & Pearl, J. (1991). Temporal constraint networks. *Artificial Intelligence*, *49*(1-3), 61–95. doi:10.1016/0004-3702(91)90006-6

Degreef, G., Ashtari, M., Bogerts, B., Bilder, R. M., Jody, D. N., Alvir, J. M. J., & Lieberman, J. A. (1992). Volumes of ventricular system subdivisions measured from magnetic resonance images in first-episode schizophrenic patients. *Archives of General Psychiatry*, *49*(7), 531–537. doi:10.1001/archpsyc.1992.01820070025004

Delafontaine, M. (2008). *The qualitative trajectory calculus - From theory to practice*. Paper presented at the Representation, Analysis and Visualization of Moving Objects (Dagstuhl Seminar 08451). Zurich, Switzerland.

Delafontaine, M., & Van de Weghe, N. (2008). Towards an implementation of the qualitative trajectory calculus to analyze moving objects. In *Proceedings of the International Conference Spatial Cognition 2008, Poster Presentations*. Spatial Recognition.

Delafontaine, M., Van de Weghe, N., Bogaert, P., & De Maeyer, P. (2008). Qualitative relations between moving objects in a network changing its topological relations. *Information Sciences*, *178*(8), 1997–2006. doi:10.1016/j.ins.2007.11.027

Dellis, E., & Paliouras, G. (2007). *Management of large spatial ontology bases*. Berlin, Germany: Springer.

Deng, M., Cheng, T., Chen, X., & Li, Z. (2007). Multi-level topological relations between spatial regions based upon topological invariants. *International Journal of GeoInformatica*, *11*(2), 239–267. doi:10.1007/s10707-006-0004-x

Dey, A. (2001). Understanding and using context. *Personal and Ubiquitous Computing*, *5*(1). doi:10.1007/s007790170019

Dimov, G., & Vakarelov, D. (2005). Topological representations of precontact lattices. In *Proceedings of the Conference on Relational Methods in Computer Science (RelMiCS-5)*, (pp. 1–16). Springer.

Dimov, G., & Vakarelov, D. (2006a). Contact algebras and region-based theory of space: A proximity approach - I. *Fundamenta Informaticae*, *74*(2-3), 209–249.

Dimov, G., & Vakarelov, D. (2006b). Contact algebras and region-based theory of space: A proximity approach - II. *Fundamenta Informaticae*, *74*(2-3), 250–282.

Dong, T. (2008). A comment on RCC: From RCC to *RCC++*. *Journal of Philosophical Logic*, *37*(4), 319–352. doi:10.1007/s10992-007-9074-y

Donnelly, M. (2001). *An axiomatic theory of commonsense geometry*. Unpublished Doctoral Dissertation. Austin, TX: University of Texas.

Donnelly, M. (2003). Layered mereotopology. In *Proceedings of the Eighteenth International Joint Conference on Artificial Intelligence (IJCAI 2003)*, (pp. 1269-1274). IJCAI.

Donnelly, M. (2004). On parts and holes: The spatial structure of the human body. In *Proceedings of MedInfo, 2004*, 351–356.

Donnelly, M., Bittner, T., & Rosse, C. (2006). A formal theory for spatial representation and reasoning in biomedical ontologies. *Artificial Intelligence in Medicine*, *36*(1), 1–27. doi:10.1016/j.artmed.2005.07.004

Dornheim, C. (1998). Undecidability of plane polygonal mereotopology. In *Proceedings of KR98: Principles of Knowledge Representation and Reasoning*, (pp. 342–353). KR.

Dourish, P. (2004). What we talk about when we talk about context. *Personal and Ubiquitous Computing*, *8*(1), 19–30. doi:10.1007/s00779-003-0253-8

Drakengren, T., & Jonsson, P. (1997). Twenty one large tractable subclasses of Allen's algebra. *Artificial Intelligence Journal*, *93*, 297–319. doi:10.1016/S0004-3702(97)00021-0

Duckham, M., & Kulik, L. (2005). A formal model of obfuscation and negotiation for location privacy. In Gellersen, H. W., Want, R., & Schmidt, A. (Eds.), *Pervasive* (*Vol. 3468*, pp. 152–170). Springer. doi:10.1007/11428572_10

Duckham, M., & Worboys, M. F. (2005). An algebraic approach to automated geospatial information fusion. *International Journal of Geographical Information Science*, *19*(5), 537–557. doi:10.1080/13658810500032339

Dudek, G., Freedman, P., & Hadjres, S. (1996). Using multiple models for environmental mapping. *Journal of Robotic Systems*, *13*(8), 539–559. doi:10.1002/(SICI)1097-4563(199608)13:8<539::AID-ROB5>3.0.CO;2-O

Düntsch, I. (1999). *A tutorial on relation algebras and their application in spatial reasoning.*

Düntsch, I., & Winter, M. (2005b). Weak contact structures. In *Proceedings of the Conference on Relational Methods in Computer Science (RelMiCS-5)*, (pp. 73–82). Springer.

Düntsch, I., & Winter, M. (2008). The lattice of contact relations on a Boolean algebra. In *Proceedings of the Conference on Relational Methods in Computer Science (RelMiCS-10)*, (pp. 98–109). Springer.

Düntsch, I., MacCaull, W., Vakarelov, D., & Winter, M. (2006). Topological representations of contact lattices. In *Proceedings of the Conference on Relational Methods in Computer Science (RelMiCS-9)*, (pp. 135–147). Springer.

Düntsch, I. (1994). Rough relation algebras. *Fundamenta Informaticae*, *21*(4), 321–331.

Düntsch, I. (2005). Relation algebras and their application in temporal and spatial reasoning. *Artificial Intelligence Review*, *23*(4), 315–357. doi:10.1007/s10462-004-5899-8

Düntsch, I., & Winter. (2004a). Construction of Boolean contact algebras. *AI Communications*, *17*(4), 235–246.

Düntsch, I., MacCaull, W., Vakarelov, D., & Winter, M. (2008). Distributive contact lattices: Topological representations. *Journal of Logic and Algebraic Programming*, *76*(1), 18–34. doi:10.1016/j.jlap.2007.10.002

Düntsch, I., Orowska, E., & Wang, H. (2001a). Algebras of approximating regions. *Fundamenta Informaticae*, *46*(1-2), 71–82.

Düntsch, I., Schmidt, G., & Winter, M. (2001b). A necessary relation algebra for mereotopology. *Studia Logica*, *69*, 381–409. doi:10.1023/A:1013892110192

Düntsch, I., & Vakarelov, D. (2007). Region-based theory of discrete spaces: A proximity approach. *Annals of Mathematics and Artificial Intelligence*, *49*(1-4), 5–14. doi:10.1007/s10472-007-9064-3

Düntsch, I., Wang, H., & McCloskey, S. (1999). Relation algebras in qualitative spatial reasoning. *Fundamenta Informaticae*, *39*(3), 229–248.

Düntsch, I., & Winter, M. (2004b). Algebraization and representation of mereotopological structures. *Journal on Relational Methods in Computer Science*, *1*, 161–180.

Düntsch, I., & Winter, M. (2005a). A representation theorem for Boolean contact algebras. *Theoretical Computer Science*, *347*, 498–512. doi:10.1016/j.tcs.2005.06.030

Düntsch, I., & Winter, M. (2006). Rough relation algebras revisited. *Fundamenta Informaticae*, *74*(2-3), 283–300.

Dylla, F., & Moratz, R. (2004). Exploiting qualitative spatial neighborhoods in the situation calculus. In *Proceedings of Spatial Cognition* (pp. 304–322). Spatial Cognition. doi:10.1007/978-3-540-32255-9_18

Dylla, F., & Wallgrün, J. O. (2007). Qualitative spatial reasoning with conceptual neighborhoods for agent control. *Journal of Intelligent & Robotic Systems*, *48*(1), 55–78. doi:10.1007/s10846-006-9099-4

Efremovič, V. A. (1952). The geometry of proximity I. *New Series*, *31*, 189–200.

Egenhofer, M. J. (1989). A formal definition of binary topological relationships. In *Proceedings of the 3rd International Conference on Foundations of Data Organization and Algorithms*, (pp. 457–472). Springer.

Egenhofer, M. J. (1991). Reasoning about binary topological relations. In *Proceedings of the Symposium on Spatial Databases (SSD91)*, (pp. 141–160). Springer.

Egenhofer, M. J., & Al-Taha, K. K. (1992). *Reasoning about gradual changes of topological relationships*. Paper presented at the Theory and Methods of Spatio-Temporal Reasoning in Geographic Space. Pisa, Italy.

Egenhofer, M. J., & Mark, D. M. (1995). Naive geography. In *Proceedings of COSIT'95*, (Vol. 988), (pp. 1-15). Springer.

Egenhofer, M. J., & Mark, D. M. (1995b). Naive geography. In *Proceedings of the Conference on Spatial Information Theory (COSIT-95)*, (pp. 1–15). Springer.

Egenhofer, M. J., & Sharma, J. (1993). Topological relations between regions in R2 and Z2. In *Third International Symposium on Large Spatial Databases and Advances in Spatial Databases*, (pp. 316-336). Springer-Verlag.

Egenhofer, M. J., & Sharma, J. (1993b). Topological relations between regions in $R^2$ and $Z^2$. In *Proceedings of the Symposium on Spatial Databases (SSD93)*, (pp. 316–336). Springer.

Egenhofer, M. J., Clementini, E., & Felice, P. D. (1994). Evaluating inconsistencies among multiple representations. In *Proceedings of the Sixth International Symposium on Spatial Data Handling,* (pp. 901–920). Spatial Data Handling.

Egenhofer, M. J. (1989). A formal definition of binary topological relationships. In *Foundations of Data Organization and Algorithms: Interfaces and Formal Models* (pp. 457–472). Berlin, Germany: Springer-Verlag. doi:10.1007/3-540-51295-0_148

Egenhofer, M. J. (1993). A model for detailed binary topological relationships. *International Journal of Geomatica, 47*(3-4), 261–273.

Egenhofer, M. J. (1994). Deriving the composition of binary topological relations. *Journal of Visual Languages and Computing, 5*(2), 133–149. doi:10.1006/jvlc.1994.1007

Egenhofer, M. J. (1994). Spatial SQL: A query and presentation language. *IEEE Transactions on Knowledge and Data Engineering, 6*(1), 86–95. doi:10.1109/69.273029

Egenhofer, M. J., Clementini, E., & Di Felice, P. (1994). Topological relations between regions with holes. *International Journal of Geographical Information Science, 8*(2), 129–144. doi:10.1080/02693799408901990

Egenhofer, M. J., & Franzosa, R. (1991). Point-set topological spatial relations. *International Journal of Geographical Information Systems, 5*(2), 161–174. doi:10.1080/02693799108927841

Egenhofer, M. J., & Franzosa, R. (1995). On the equivalence of topological relations. *International Journal of Geographical Information Systems, 9*(2), 133–152. doi:10.1080/02693799508902030

Egenhofer, M. J., & Franzosa, R. D. (1991). Point-set topological spatial relations. *International Journal of Geographical Information Systems, 5*(2), 161–174. doi:10.1080/02693799108927841

Egenhofer, M. J., & Franzosa, R. D. (1995). On the equivalence of topological relations. *International Journal of Geographical Information Systems, 9*(2), 133–152. doi:10.1080/02693799508902030

Egenhofer, M. J., & Herring, J. (1990). *Categorizing binary topological relations between regions, lines and points in geographic databases. Technical Report.* Bangor, ME: University of Maine.

Egenhofer, M. J., & Herring, J. (1991). Categorizing binary topological relationships between regions, lines and points in geographic databases. In Egenhofer, M., & Herring, J. (Eds.), *A Framework for the Definition of Topological Relationships and an Approach to Spatial Reasoning within this Framework* (pp. 1–28). Santa Barbara, CA: Morgan Kaufmann.

Egenhofer, M. J., & Mark, D. M. (1995a). Modeling conceptual neighborhoods of topological line-region relations. *International Journal of Geographical Information Science, 9*(5), 555–565. doi:10.1080/02693799508902056

Egenhofer, M. J., & Sharma, J. (1993a). Assessing the consistency of complete and incomplete topological information. *Geographical Systems, 1*(1), 47–68.

Egenhofer, M., Clementini, E., & di Felis, P. (1994). Topological relations between regions with holes. *International Journal of Geographical Information Systems, 8*(2), 129–144. doi:10.1080/02693799408901990

Emerson, A. E., & Halpern, J. (1986). Sometimes and not never revisited: On branching versus linear time temporal logic. *Journal of the ACM, 33*(1), 151–178. doi:10.1145/4904.4999

Engelking, R. (1977). *General topology.* Warsaw, Poland: Polish Scientific Publishers.

Eschenbach, C. (1999). A predication calculus for qualitative spatial representations. In *Proceedings of the Spatial Information Theory: Cognitive and Computational Foundations of Geographic Information Science (COSIT99),* (pp. 157-172). Springer-Verlag.

Eschenbach, C. (2001). Viewing composition tables as axiomatic systems. In *Proceedings of the Conference on Formal Ontology in Information Systems (FOIS-01),* (pp. 93–104). FOIS.

Eschenbach, C. (2007). *A comparison of calculi of mereotopology.* Draft manuscript.

Eschenbach, C., & Heydrich, W. (1995). Classical mereology and restricted domains. *International Journal of Human-Computer Studies, 43*(5/6), 723–740. doi:10.1006/ijhc.1995.1071

Faltings, B. (1995). Qualitative spatial reasoning using algebraic topology. In *Proceedings of the Conference on Spatial Information Theory (COSIT-95)*, (pp. 17–30). Springer.

Fannon, D., Chitnis, X., Doku, V., Tennakoon, L., O'Ceallaigh, S., & Soni, W. (2000a). Features of structural brain abnormality detected in first-episode psychosis. *The American Journal of Psychiatry, 157*, 1829–1834. doi:10.1176/appi.ajp.157.11.1829

Fannon, D., Tennakoon, L., O'Ceallaigh, S., Doku, V., Soni, W., & Chitnis, X. (2000b). Third ventricle enlargement and developmental delay in first-episode psychosis: Preliminary findings. *The British Journal of Psychiatry, 177*, 354–359. doi:10.1192/bjp.177.4.354

Fatemi, S. H., & Folsom, T. D. (2009). The neurodevelopmental hypothesis of schizophrenia revisited. *Schizophrenia Bulletin, 35*(3), 528–548. doi:10.1093/schbul/sbn187

Ferguson, R. W., Bokor, J. L., Mappus, R. L., IV, & Feldman, A. (2003). Maintaining spatial relations in an incremental diagrammatic reasoner. In *Proceedings of COSIT*, (pp. 136–150). COSIT.

Fernyhough, J., Cohn, A. G., & Hogg, D. C. (2000). Constructing qualitative event models automatically from video input. *Image and Vision Computing, 18*(2), 81–103. doi:10.1016/S0262-8856(99)00023-2

Finger, J. (1987). *Exploiting constraints in design synthesis*. Unpublished Doctoral Dissertation. Palo Alto, CA: Stanford University.

First, M., Opler, L., Hamilton, R., Linder, J., Linfield, L., & Silver, J. (1993). Evaluation in a inpatient setting of DTREE, a computer-assisted diagnostic assessment procedure. *Comprehensive Psychiatry, 34*(3), 171–175. doi:10.1016/0010-440X(93)90043-4

Fleck, M. M. (1996). The topology of boundaries. *Artificial Intelligence, 80*, 1–27. doi:10.1016/0004-3702(94)00051-4

Fonseca, F. T., Egenhofer, M. J., Agouris, P., & Câmara, G. (2002). Using ontologies for integrated geographic information systems. *Transactions on GIS, 6*(3), 231–257. doi:10.1111/1467-9671.00109

Fonseca, F., Egenhofer, M. J., Davis, C., & Borges, K. (2000). Ontologies and knowledge sharing in urban GIS. *Computers, Environment and Urban Systems, 24*(3), 251–272. doi:10.1016/S0198-9715(00)00004-1

Forbus, K. (1980). Spatial and qualitative aspects of reasoning about motion. In *Proceedings of the First National Conference on Artificial Intelligence, (AAAI-80)*, (pp. 170-173). AAAI.

Forbus, K. D. (1981). Qualitative reasoning about physical processes. In *Proceedings of the Seventh International Joint Conference on Artificial Intelligence*. IJCAI.

Forbus, K. D. (1989). Introducing actions into qualitative simulation. In N. S. Sridharan (Ed.), *Proceedings of the Eleventh International Joint Conference on Artificial Intelligence*, (pp. 1273–1278). San Mateo, CA: Morgan Kaufmann.

Forbus, K. (1985). Qualitative process theory. In Bobrow, D. (Ed.), *Qualitative Reasoning about Physical Systems* (pp. 85–186). Cambridge, MA: MIT Press.

Forbus, K. D. (1984). Qualitative process theory. *Artificial Intelligence, 24*(1-3), 85–168. doi:10.1016/0004-3702(84)90038-9

Fox, D., Burgard, W., & Thrun, S. (1999). Markov localization for mobile robots in dynamic environments. *Journal of Artificial Intelligence Research, 11*, 391–427.

Frank, A. (1991). Qualitative spatial reasoning about cardinal directions. In *Proceedings of the American Congress on Surveying and Mapping (ACSM-ASPRS)*, (pp. 148–167). Baltimore, MD: ACSM.

Frank, A. U. (2005). *Practical geometry-the mathematics for geographic information systems*. Unpublished.

Frank, A. U., & Kuhn, W. (1986). Cell graphs: A provable correct method for the storage of geometry. In *Proceedings of the International Symposium on Spatial Data Handling*. International Symposium.

Frank, A. U. (1992). Qualitative spatial reasoning about distances and directions in geographic space. *Journal of Visual Languages and Computing, 3*, 343–371. doi:10.1016/1045-926X(92)90007-9

Frank, A. U. (1996). Qualitative spatial reasoning: Cardinal directions as an example. *International Journal of Geographical Information Systems, 10*(3), 269–290. doi:10.1080/02693799608902079

Freksa, C. (1992). Using orientation information for qualitative spatial reasoning. In *Theories and Methods of Spatio-Temporal Reasoning in Geographic Space*, (pp. 162–178). Berlin, Germany: Springer-Verlag.

Freksa, C. (1991). Conceptual neighborhood and its role in temporal and spatial reasoning. In Singh, M., & Travé-Massuyès, L. (Eds.), *Decision Support Systems and Qualitative Reasoning* (pp. 181–187). Amsterdam, The Netherlands: North-Holland.

Freksa, C. (1991). Qualitative spatial reasoning. In Mark, D., & Frank, A. (Eds.), *Cognitive and Linguistic Aspects of Geographic Space* (pp. 361–372). Dordrecht, The Netherlands: Kluwer.

Freksa, C. (1992). Temporal reasoning based on semi-intervals. *Artificial Intelligence, 54*(1), 199–227. doi:10.1016/0004-3702(92)90090-K

Freska, C. (1992). Using orientation information for qualitative spatial reasoning. In *Theories and Methods of Spatio-Temporal Reasoning in Geographic Space* (pp. 162–178). Springer-Verlag. doi:10.1007/3-540-55966-3_10

Fuhr, N. (1999). A decision-theoretic approach to database selection in networked IR. *ACM Transactions on Information Systems, 17*(3), 229–249. doi:10.1145/314516.314517

Gabelaia, D., Kontchakov, R., Kurucz, A., Wolter, F., & Zakharyaschev, M. (2005). Combining spatial and temporal logics: Expressiveness vs. complexity. *Journal of Artificial Intelligence Research, 23*, 167–243.

Gahegan, M. (1995). Proximity operators for qualitative spatial reasoning. In *Proceedings of the Conference on Spatial Information Theory (COSIT-95)*, (pp. 31–44). Springer.

Galata, A., Cohn, A. G., Magee, D., & Hogg, D. (2002). Modeling interaction using learnt qualitative spatio-temporal relations and variable lengths Markov models. In *Proceedings of the European Conference on Artificial Intelligence (ECAI-02)*, (pp. 741–745). ECAI.

Galton, A. (1996). Taking dimension seriously in qualitative spatial reasoning. In *Proceedings of ECAI*, (pp. 501–505). ECAI.

Galton, A. (1999). The mereotopology of discrete space. In *Proceedings of the Conference on Spatial Information Theory (COSIT-99)*, (pp. 251–266). Springer.

Galton, A. (2004). Multidimensional mereotopology. In *Proceedings of KR04: Principles of Knowledge Representation and Reasoning*, (pp. 45–54). KR.

Galton, A. P. (1993). Towards an integrated logic of space, time, and motion. In *Proceedings of the Thirteenth International Joint Conference on Artificial Intelligence, (IJCAI-93)*, (pp. 1550-1555). San Mateo, CA: Morgan Kaufmann.

Galton, A. P. (2000b). Continuous motion in discrete space. In *Proceedings of the Seventh International Conference on Principles of Knowledge Representation and Reasoning*, (pp. 26-37). Knowledge Representation and Reasoning.

Galton, A. (2000). *Qualitative spatial change*. Oxford, UK: Oxford University Press.

Galton, A. (2001). Dominance diagrams: A tool for qualitative reasoning about continuous systems. *Fundamenta Informaticae, 46*(1-2), 55–70.

Galton, A. (2003). *Foundations of geographic information science: On the ontological status of geographic boundaries*. Taylor & Francis.

Galton, A. (2006). Causal reasoning for alert generation in smart homes. In *Proceedings of Designing Smart Homes* (pp. 57–70). Designing Smart Homes. doi:10.1007/11788485_4

Galton, A. P. (1995). Towards a qualitative theory of motion. In *Proceedings of, COSIT-95*, 377–396.

Galton, A. P. (2000a). *Qualitative spatial change*. Oxford, UK: Oxford University Press.

Galton, A. P. (2003). A generalized topological view of motion in discrete space. *Theoretical Computer Science*, *305*, 111–134. doi:10.1016/S0304-3975(02)00701-6

Galton, A., & Hood, J. (2004). Qualitative interpolation for environmental knowledge representation. In de Mántaras, R. L., & Saitta, L. (Eds.), *ECAI* (pp. 1017–1018). IOS Press.

Gantner, Z., Westphal, M., & Wölfl, S. (2008). GQR–A fast reasoner for binary qualitative constraint calculi. In *Proceedings of the AAAI'08 Workshop on Spatial and Temporal Reasoning*. AAAI.

Gattaz, W. F., Rost, W., Kohlmeyer, K., Bauer, K., Hubner, C., & Gasser, T. (1988). CT scans and neuroleptic response in schizophrenia: A multidimensional approach. *Psychiatry Research*, *26*(3), 293–303. doi:10.1016/0165-1781(88)90124-2

Gerevini, A., & Renz, J. (2002). Combining topological and size constraints for spatial reasoning. *Artificial Intelligence*, *137*(1-2), 1–42. doi:10.1016/S0004-3702(02)00193-5

Gerivini, A., & Renz, J. (2002). Combining topological and size information for spatial reasoning. *Artificial Intelligence*, *137*(1–2), 1–42. doi:10.1016/S0004-3702(02)00193-5

Gerla, G., & Miranda, A. (2009). Inclusion and connection in Whiteheads point-free geometry. In M. Weber & W. Desmond (Eds.), *Handbook of Whiteheadian Process Thought*. Ontos Verlag.

Gerla, G. (1995). Pointless geometries. In Buekenhout, F. (Ed.), *Handbook of Incidence Geometry* (pp. 1015–1031). Elsevier. doi:10.1016/B978-044488355-1/50020-7

Giacomo, G. D., & Levesque, H. J. (1999). An incremental interpreter for high-level programs with sensing. In Levesque, H. J., & Pirri, F. (Eds.), *Logical Foundation for Cognitive Agents: Contributions in Honor of Ray Reiter* (pp. 86–102). Berlin, Germany: Springer. doi:10.1007/978-3-642-60211-5_8

Giunchiglia, E., Lee, J., Lifschitz, V., McCain, N., & Turner, H. (2004). Nonmonotonic causal theories. *Artificial Intelligence*, *153*(1-2), 49–104. doi:10.1016/j.artint.2002.12.001

Gliozzo, A., Strapparava, C., & Dagan, I. (2004). Unsupervised and supervised exploitation of semantic domains in lexical disambiguation. *Computer Speech & Language*, *18*(3), 275–299. doi:10.1016/j.csl.2004.05.006

Goldberg, D. E. (1989). *Genetic algorithms in search - Optimization and machine learning*. Kluwer Academic Publishers.

Gooday, J., & Cohn, A. (1996). Transition-based qualitative simulation. In *Proceeding of the 10th International Workshop on Qualitative Reasoning*, (pp. 74–82). AAAI Press.

Gooday, J., & Galton, A. (1997). The transition calculus: A high-level formalism for reasoning about action and change. *Journal of Experimental & Theoretical Artificial Intelligence*, *9*(1), 51–66. doi:10.1080/095281397147239

Gottfried, B., Guesgen, H. W., & Hübner, S. (2006). Spatiotemporal reasoning for smart homes. In *Designing Smart Homes* (*Vol. 4008*, pp. 16–34). Berlin, Germany: Springer. doi:10.1007/11788485_2

Gotts, N. M. (1994). How far can we C? Defining a doughnut using connection alone. In *Proceedings of KR94: Principles of Knowledge Representation and Reasoning*, (pp. 246–257). KR.

Gotts, N. M. (1996a). *An axiomatic approach to topology for spatial information systems*. Technical Report 96.24. Leeds, UK: University of Leeds.

Gotts, N. M. (1996b). Formalizing commonsense topology: The INCH calculus. In *Proceedings of the International Symposium on Artificial Intelligence and Mathematics*, (pp. 72–75). International Symposium.

Gotts, N. M. (1996c). *Using the RCC formalism to describe the topology of spherical regions*. Technical Report 96.24. Leeds, UK: University of Leeds.

Gotts, N. M., Gooday, J. M., & Cohn, A. G. (1996). A connection based approach to commonsense topological description and reasoning. *The Monist*, *79*(1), 51–75.

Graphisoft Inc. (2010). *ArchiCAD 13*. Retrieved from http://www.graphisoft.com/.

Grätzer, G. (1998). *General lattice theory* (2nd ed.). Birkhäuser.

Gray, H. (1918). *Anatomy of the human body*. Philadelphia, PA: Lea & Febiger.

Greferath, M., & Schmidt, S. E. (1998). *General lattice theory: Appendix E-projective lattice geometries* (2nd ed., pp. 539–553). Birkhäuser.

Gregersen, H., & Jensen, C. (1999). Temporal entity-relationship models-a survey. *IEEE Transactions on Knowledge and Data Engineering, 11*(3), 464–497. doi:10.1109/69.774104

Grenon, P. (2003). *BFO in a nutshell: A bi-categorical axiomatization of BFO and comparison with Dolce. Technical Report*. Leipzig, Germany: Leipzig University.

Grigni, M., Papadias, D., & Papadimitriou, C. (1995). Topological inference. In *Proceedings of the Fourteenth International Joint Conference on Artificial Intelligence (IJCAI95),* (pp. 901-906). IJCAI.

Grimson, W. E. L. (1990). *Object recognition by computer: The role of geometric constraints*. Cambridge, MA: MIT Press.

Gruszczyński, R., & Pietruszczak, A. (2008). Full development of Tarskis geometry of solids. *The Bulletin of Symbolic Logic, 14*(4), 481–540. doi:10.2178/bsl/1231081462

Grutter, R., & Bauer-Messmer, B. (2007). *Towards spatial reasoning in the semantic web: A hybrid knowledge representation system architecture* (pp. 349–364). Berlin, Germany: Springer.

Grzegorczyk, A. (1951). Undecidability of some topological theories. *Fundamenta Mathematicae, 38*, 109–127.

Grzegorczyk, A. (1955). The systems of Leśniewski in relation to contemporary logical research. *Studia Logic, 3*(1), 77–95. doi:10.1007/BF02067248

Grzegorczyk, A. (1960). Axiomatizability of geometry without points. *Synthese, 12*, 109–127. doi:10.1007/BF00485101

Gudmundsson, J., van Kreveld, M., & Speckmann, B. (2004). Efficient detection of motion patterns in spatio-temporal data sets. In *Proceedings of the 12th Annual ACM International Workshop on Geographic Information Systems*. ACM Press.

Guesgen, H. W. (2002). From the egg-yolk to the scrambled-egg theory. In *Proceedings of the Florida Artificial Intelligence Research Society Conference (FLAIRS-15)*. FLAIRS.

Güsgen, H. (1989). *Spatial reasoning based on Allen's temporal logic. Report ICSI TR89-049*. Berkeley, CA: International Computer Science Institute.

Gutierrez, C., Hurtado, C., & Vaisman, A. (2007). Introducing time into RDF. *IEEE Transactions on Knowledge and Data Engineering, 19*(2), 207–218. doi:10.1109/TKDE.2007.34

Guting, R. H., Bohlen, M. H., Erwig, M., Jensen, C. S., Lorentzos, N. A., & Schneider, M. (2000). A foundation for representing and querying moving objects. *ACM Transactions on Database Systems, 25*(1), 1–42. doi:10.1145/352958.352963

Gutting, R. (1994). An introduction to spatial database systems. *The VLDB Journal, 3*, 357–399. doi:10.1007/BF01231602

Hahmann, T., & Gruninger, M. (2009). Detecting physical defects: A practical 2D-study of cracks and holes. In *Proceedings of the AAAI-SS09: Benchmarking of Qualitative Spatial and Temporal Reasoning Systems,* (pp. 11–16). AAAI Press.

Hahmann, T., Gruninger, M., & Winter, M. (2009). Stonian p-ortholattices: A new approach to the mereotopology RT0. *Artificial Intelligence*. Retrieved from http://citeseerx.ist.psu.edu/viewdoc/summary?doi=10.1.1.149.8359.

Hähnel, D., Burgard, W., Wegbreit, B., & Thrun, S. (2003). Towards lazy data association in SLAM. In *Proceedings of the 11th International Symposium of Robotics Research (ISRR'03)*. ISRR.

Hall, N. (2000). Causation and the price of transitivity. *The Journal of Philosophy, 97*(4), 198–222. doi:10.2307/2678390

Hallot, P., & Billen, R. (2008). *Generalized life and motion configurations reasoning model*. Paper presented at the International Worshop on Moving Objects: From Natural to Formal Language. Park City, UT.

Halmos, P. R. (1963). *Lectures on Boolean algebras*. Van Nostrand Reinhold.

Harnad, S. (1990). The symbol grounding problem. *Physica, 42*, 335–346.

Harrison, P. J. (1999). The neuropathology of schizophrenia: A critical review of the data and their interpretation. *Brain, 122*(4), 593–624. doi:10.1093/brain/122.4.593

Harrison, P. J., & Owen, M. J. (2003). Genes for schizophrenia: Recent findings and their pathophysiological implications. *Lancet, 361*, 417–419. doi:10.1016/S0140-6736(03)12379-3

Hayes, P., & Welty, C. (2006). Defining n-ary relations on the semantic web. *W3C Working Group*. Retrieved from http://www.w3.org/TR/swbp--n-aryRelations/.

Hayes, P. (1979). The naive physics manifesto. In Michie, D. (Ed.), *Expert Systems in the Microelectronic Age* (pp. 242–270). Edinburgh, UK: Edinburgh University Press.

Hayes, P. J. (1978). The naive physics manifesto. In Michie, D. (Ed.), *Expert Systems in the Microelectronic Age* (pp. 242–270). Edinburgh, UK: Edinburgh University Press.

Hayes, P. J. (1985a). Naive physics I: Ontology of liquids. In Hobbs, J., & Moore, R. (Eds.), *Formal Theories of the Commonsense World* (pp. 71–108). Ablex Publishing.

Hayes, P. J. (1985b). The second naive physics manifesto. In Hobbs, J., & Moore, R. (Eds.), *Formal Theories of the Commonsense World* (pp. 567–585). Ablex Publishing.

Hazarika, S. M. (2005). *Qualitative spatial change: Space-time histories and continuity*. Unpublished Doctoral Dissertation. Leeds, UK: The University of Leeds.

Hazarika, S., & Cohn, A. G. (2011). *Qualitative spatial change in a mereotopology*. Unpublished.

Hazarika, J., & Roy, B. (2008). Semantic search of unstructured knowledge using qualitative analysis. *International Journal of Knowledge Management, 4*(2), 35–45. doi:10.4018/jkm.2008040103

Hearnshaw, H. M., & Unwin, D. J. (1994). *Visualization in geographical information systems*. Chichester, UK: John Wiley & Sons.

Henricksen, K., Indulska, J., & Rakotonirainy, A. (2002). Modelling context information in pervasive computing systems. In *Proceedings of the International Conference on Pervasive Computing (Pervasive 2002)*. Zurich, Switzerland: Pervasive.

Hernández, D., Clementini, E., & Di Felice, P. (1995). Qualitative distances. In *Proceedings of the Conference on Spatial Information Theory (COSIT-95)*, (pp. 45–58). Springer.

Hornsby, K., & Egenhofer, M. (2000). Identity-based change: A foundation for spatio-temporal knowledge representation. *International Journal of Geographical Information Science, 14*(3), 207–224. doi:10.1080/136588100240813

Horrocks, I., & Sattler, U. (2007). A tableau decision procedure for SHOIQ. *Journal of Automated Reasoning, 39*(3), 248–276. doi:10.1007/s10817-007-9079-9

Huntington, E. V. (1913). A set of postulates for abstract geometry, expressed in terms of the simple relation of inclusion. *Mathematische Annalen, 73*, 522–559. doi:10.1007/BF01455955

Husserl, E. (1913). *Logische untersuchungen: Zweiter band: Untersuchungen zur phänomenologie und theorie der erkenntnis (1. Teil)* (2nd ed.). Max Niemeyer.

Ibrahim, Z., & Tawfik, A. (2004). Spatio-temporal reasoning for vague regions. In *Proceedings of the Conference of the the Canadian Society for Computer Studies of Intelligence (Canadian AI)*, (pp. 308–321). Springer.

Ibrahim, Z., & Tawfik, A. (2007). An abstract theory and ontology of motion based on the regions connection calculus. In *Proceedings of the Abstraction, Reformulation, and Approximation,* (pp. 230-242). Abstraction Reformation and Approximation.

Imai Labo. (2001). *Program*. Retrieved from http://www.ise.chuo-u.ac.jp/ise-labs/imai-lab/program/program.html.

Inglada, J., & Michel, J. (2009). Qualitative spatial reasoning for high-resolution remote sensing image analysis. *IEEE Transactions on Geoscience and Remote Sensing, 47*(2), 599–612. doi:10.1109/TGRS.2008.2003435

Ipeirotis, P., & Gravano, L. (2002). Distributed search over the hidden Web: Hierarchical database sampling and selection. In *Proceedings of the 28th International Conference on Very Large Databases*. Hong Kong, China: Very Large databases.

Ipeirotis, P., Gravano, L., & Sahami, M. (2001). Probe, count and classify: Categorizing hidden-Web databases. In *Proceedings of the ACM SIGMOD International Conference on Management of Data*. ACM Press.

Ipeirotis, P., & Gravano, L. (2008). Classification-aware hidden-Web text database selection. *ACM Transactions on InformationSystems, 26*(2). doi:10.1145/1344411.1344412

Jakkula, V. R., & Cook, D. J. (2007). Using temporal relations in smart home data for activity prediction. In *Proceedings of the International Conference on Machine Learning (ICML) Workshop on the Induction of Process Models (IPM /ICML 2007).* Corvalis, OR: ICML.

Jakkula, V., & Cook, D. (2007). Anomaly detection using temporal data mining in a smart home environment. *Methods of Information in Medicine, 47*(1), 70–75.

James, A., Crow, T., Renowden, S., Wardell, A., Smith, D., & Anslow, P. (1999). Is the course of brain development in schizophrenia delayed? Evidence from onsets in adolescence. *Schizophrenia Research, 40*, 1–10. doi:10.1016/S0920-9964(99)00042-0

Janowicz, K., Raubal, M., Schwering, A., & Kuhn, W. (2008). Semantic similarity measurement and geospatial applications. *Transactions in GIS, 12*(6), 651–659. doi:10.1111/j.1467-9671.2008.01129.x

Johnstone, P. T. (1983). The point of pointless topology. *Bulletin of the American Mathematical Society, 8*(1), 41–53. doi:10.1090/S0273-0979-1983-15080-2

Jones, C., Abdelmoty, A., Finch, D., Fu, G., & Vaid, S. (2004). *The SPIRIT search engine: Architecture, ontologies and spatial indexing*. Berlin, Germany: Springer.

Joyce, E. M., & Roiser, J. P. (2007). Cognitive heterogeneity in schizophrenia. *Current Opinion in Psychiatry, 20*(3), 268–272.

Kalmbach, G. (1983). *Orthomodular lattices*. Academic Press.

Kandel, E. R., Schwartz, J. H., & Jessell, T. M. (2000). *Principles of neural science*. New York, NY: McGraw-Hill.

Katz, Y., & Grau, B. (2005). Representing qualitative spatial information in OWL-DL. In *Proceedings of International Workshop: OWL Experiences and Directions.* Galway, Ireland: OWL.

Kim, K.-Y., Chin, S., Kwon, O., & Ellis, R. D. (2009). Ontology-based modeling and integration of morphological characteristics of assembly joints for network-based collaborative assembly design. *Artificial Intelligence for Engineering Design, Analysis and Manufacturing, 23*, 71–88. doi:10.1017/S0890060409000110

Kim, K.-Y., Manley, D., & Yang, H. (2006). Ontology-based assembly design and information sharing for collaborative product development. *Computer Aided Design, 38*(12), 1233–1250. doi:10.1016/j.cad.2006.08.004

Kim, K.-Y., Yang, H.-J., & Kim, D.-W. (2008). Mereotopological assembly joint information representation for collaborative product design. *Robotics and Computer-integrated Manufacturing, 24*, 744–754. doi:10.1016/j.rcim.2008.03.010

Klein, M., & Fensel, D. (2001). Ontology versioning for the semantic web. In *Proceedings of International Semantic Web Working Symposioum (SWWS 2001),* (pp. 75-92). SWWS.

Knublauch, H., Fergerson, R. W., Noy, N. F., & Musen, M. A. (2004). The protégé owl plugin: An open development environment for Semantic Web applications. In *Proceedings of the 3rd International Semantic Web Conference (ISWC 2004)*, (pp. 229–243). Springer.

Kowalski, R., & Sergot, M. (1986). A logic-based calculus of events. *New Generation Computing, 4*(1), 67–95. doi:10.1007/BF03037383

Krieg-Brückner, B., & Shi, H. (2006). Orientation calculi and route graphs: Towards semantic representations for route descriptions. In *Proceedings of Geographic Information Science - Fourth International Conference, GIScience,* (Vol. 4197), (pp. 234–250). Springer.

Krokhin, A., Jeavons, P., & Jonsson, P. (2003). Reasoning about temporal relations: The tractable subalgebras of Allen's interval algebra. *Journal of the ACM, 50*(5), 591–640. doi:10.1145/876638.876639

Krummenacher, R., & Strang, T. (2007). Ontology-based context-modeling. In *Proceedings of the 3rd Workshop on Context Awareness for Proactive Systems (CAPS'07)*. Guildford, UK: CAPS.

Kuipers, B., Modayil, J., Beeson, P., MacMahon, M., & Savelli, F. (2004). Local metrical and global topological maps in the hybrid spatial semantic hierarchy. In *Proceedings of the IEEE International Conference on Robotics and Automation (ICRA-04)*. New Orleans, LA: IEEE Press.

Kuipers, B. (1986). Qualitative simulation. *Artificial Intelligence, 29*, 289–338. doi:10.1016/0004-3702(86)90073-1

Kuipers, B. (1994). *Qualitative reasoning: Modeling and simulation with incomplete knowledge*. Cambridge, MA: MIT Press.

Kuipers, B. (2000). The spatial semantic hierarchy. *Artificial Intelligence, 119*, 191–233. doi:10.1016/S0004-3702(00)00017-5

Kuipers, B. J. (1986). Qualitative simulation. *Artificial Intelligence, 29*(3), 289–338. doi:10.1016/0004-3702(86)90073-1

Kuipers, B. J., & Byun, Y.-T. (1991). A robot exploration and mapping strategy based on a semantic hierarchy of spatial representation. *Journal of Robots and Autonomous Systems, 8*, 47–63. doi:10.1016/0921-8890(91)90014-C

Kuipers, B. J., & Levitt, T. (1988). Navigation and mapping in large-scale space. *AI Magazine, 9*, 25–43.

Kumokawa, S., & Takahashi, K. (2007). Drawing a figure in a two-dimensional plane for a qualitative representation. In *Proceedings of the Conference on Spatial Information Theory (COSIT07)*, (pp. 337-353). Springer-Verlag.

Kumokawa, S., & Takahashi, K. (2008). Qualitative spatial representation based on connection patterns and convexity. In *Proceedings of the AAAI-08 Workshop on Spatial and Temporal Reasoning*, (pp. 57-62). AAAI.

Kurata, Y., & Egenhofer, M. J. (2009). Interpretation of behaviours from a viewpoint of topology. In Gottfried, B., & Aghajan, H. (Eds.), *Behaviour Monitoring and Interpretation-Ambient Intelligence and Smart Environments* (*Vol. 3*). Amsterdam, The Netherlands: IOS Press.

Kutz, O. L. (2004). E-connections of abstract description systems. *Artificial Intelligence, 156*(1), 1–73. doi:10.1016/j.artint.2004.02.002

Lancaster, J., Woldorff, M., Parsons, L., Liotti, M., Freitas, C., & Rainey, L. (2000). Automated Talairach atlas labels for functional brain mapping. *Human Brain Mapping, 10*(3), 120–131. doi:10.1002/1097-0193(200007)10:3<120::AID-HBM30>3.0.CO;2-8

Land Cover, C. O. R. I. N. E. (2000). *CLC2000*. Retrieved from http://terrestrial.eionet.europa.eu/CLC2000.

Larkey, L. S., Connell, M. E., & Callan, J. P. (2000). Collection selection and results merging with topically organized U.S. patents and TREC data. In *Proceedings of the ACM Conference on Information and Knowledge Management*, (pp. 282-289). ACM Press.

Laube, P. (2005). *Analysing point motion-spatio-temporal data mining of geospatial lifelines*. Zürich, Switzerland: Universität Zürich.

LaValle, S. (2006). *Planning algorithms*. Cambridge, UK: Cambridge University Press. doi:10.1017/CBO9780511546877

Lawrie, S. M., Hall, J., McIntosh, A. M., Cunningham-Owens, D. G., & Johnstone, E. C. (2008). Neuroimaging and molecular genetics of schizophrenia: Pathophysiological advances and therapeutic potential. *British Journal of Pharmacology, 153*, 120–124. doi:10.1038/sj.bjp.0707655

Lawrie, S. M., Whalley, H., Kestelman, J. N., Abukmeil, S. S., Byrne, M., & Hodges, A. (1999). Magnetic resonance imaging of brain in people at high risk of developing schizophrenia. *Lancet, 353*, 30–33. doi:10.1016/S0140-6736(98)06244-8

Leader, S. (1967). Local proximity spaces. *Mathematische Annalen, 169*.

Leonard, J. J., & Durrant-Whyte, H. F. (1991). Simultaneous map building and localization for an autonomous mobile robot. In *Proceedings of IEEE/RSJ International Workshop on Intelligent Robots and Systems*, (pp. 1442-1447). IEEE Press.

Leonard, H. S., & Goodman, N. (1940). The calculus of individuals and its uses. *Journal of Symbolic Logic, 5*(2), 45–55. doi:10.2307/2266169

Leśniewski, S. (1927). O podstawack matematyki. In *Prezeglad Filosoficzny* (pp. 30–34). Academic Publisher.

Levesque, H. J., Reiter, R., Lespérance, Y., Lin, F., & Scherl, R. B. (1997). Golog: A logic programming language for dynamic domains. *The Journal of Logic Programming, 31*(1-3), 59–83. doi:10.1016/S0743-1066(96)00121-5

Levesque, H., & Lakemeyer, G. (2007). Cognitive robotics. In Lifschitz, V., van Harmelen, F., & Porter, F. (Eds.), *Handbook of Knowledge Representation*. London, UK: Elsevier.

Levitt, T. S., & Lawton, D. T. (1990). Qualitative navigation for mobile robots. *Artificial Intelligence, 44*, 305–360. doi:10.1016/0004-3702(90)90027-W

Li, J., Ozsu, M., Szafron, D., & Oria, V. (1997). MOQL: A multimedia object query language. In *Proceedings of the 3rd International Workshop on Multimedia Information Systems,* (pp. 19-28). Multimedia Information Systems.

Liao, L., Fox, D., & Kautz, H. (2005). Location-based activity recognition using relational Markov networks. In *Proceedings of the Advances in Neural Information Processing Systems (NIPS).* Edinburgh, UK: NIPS.

Ligozat, G. (1996). A new proof of tractability for ORD-Horn relations. In *Proceedings of the Thirteenth National Conference on Artificial Intelligence (AAAI-96)*, (pp. 395-401). Menlo Park, CA: AAAI Press.

Ligozat, G. (2001). When tables tell it all: Qualitative spatial and temporal reasoning based on linear orderings. In *Proceedings of the Conference on Spatial Information Theory (COSIT-01)*, (pp. 60–75). Springer.

Ligozat, G. (2005). Categorical methods in qualitative reasoning: The case for weak representations. In *Proceedings of the Spatial Information Theory: Cognitive and Computational Foundations of Geographic Information Science (COSIT05),* (pp. 265-282). COSIT.

Ligozat, G., & Renz, J. (2004). What is a qualitative calculus? A general framework. In *Proceedings of PRICAI*, (pp. 53–64). PRICAI.

Ligozat, G. (1998). Reasoning about cardinal directions. *Journal of Visual Languages and Computing, 9*(1), 23–44. doi:10.1006/jvlc.1997.9999

Lin, F. (1995). Embracing causality in specifying the indirect effects of actions. In *Proceedings of IJCAI*, (pp. 1985–1993). IJCAI.

Li, S., & Nebel, B. (2007). Qualitative spatial representation and reasoning: A hierarchical approach. *The Computer Journal, 50*(4), 391–402. doi:10.1093/comjnl/bxl086

Li, S., & Ying, M. (2003). Region connection calculus: Its models and composition table. *Artificial Intelligence, 145*, 121–145. doi:10.1016/S0004-3702(02)00372-7

Li, S., & Ying, M. (2004). Generalized region connection calculus. *Artificial Intelligence, 160*, 1–34. doi:10.1016/j.artint.2004.05.012

Li, S., Ying, M., & Li, Y. (2005). On countable RCC models. *Fundamenta Informaticae, 64*(4), 329–351.

Liu, W., Li, S., & Renz, J. (2009). Combining RCC-8 with qualitative direction calculi: Algorithms and complexity. In *Proceedings of the Twenty-First International Joint Conference on Artificial Intelligence (IJCAI 2009)*, (pp. 854-869). IJCAI.

Liu, Y., & Hao, Z. (2005). The cardinal direction relations and the rectangle algebra. In *Proceedings of International Workshop on Machine Learning and Cybernetics,* (pp. 3115-3118). Machine Learning and Cybernetics.

Li, Z., Zhao, R., & Chen, J. (2002). A Voronoi-based spatial algebra for spatial relations. *Progress in Natural Science, 12*(7), 528–536.

Lobačevskij, N. I. (1834). *New principles of geometry with complete theory of parallels* (*Vol. 2*). Gostexizdat.

Lovett, A. M., Dehghani, M., & Forbus, K. D. (2007). Incremental learning of perceptual categories for open-domain sketch recognition. In M. M. Veloso (Ed.), *Proceedings of IJCAI* (pp. 447-452). IJCAI.

Lozano-Perez, T. (1983). Spatial planning: A configuration space approach. *IEEE Transactions on Computers, 32*(2), 108–120. doi:10.1109/TC.1983.1676196

Lücke, D., Mossakowski, T., & Wolter, D. (2008). In Freksa, C., Newcombe, S. N., Gärdenfors, P., & Wölfl, S. (Eds.), *Qualitative reasoning about convex relations* (*Vol. 5248*, pp. 426–440). Spatial Cognition, VI: Springer.

Luschei, E. C. (1962). *The logical systems of Leśniewski*. Amsterdam, The Netherlands: North-Holland Publisher.

Lutz, C., & Wolter, F. (2004). *Modal logics of topological relations*. Technical Report LTCS-04-05. Dresden, Germany: Dresden University of Technology. Aiello, I., Pratt-Hartmann, E., & van Benthem, J. F. (Eds). (2007). *Handbook of spatial logics*. Springer.

Lutz, C., Wolter, F., & Zakharyashev, M. (2008). Temporal description logics: A survey. In *Proceedings of the 15th International Symposium on Temporal Representation and Reasoning (TIME)*, (pp. 3-14). Montreal, Canada: TIME.

Makanin, G. (1977). The problem of solvability of equations in a free semigroup. *Matematicheskii Sbornik, 32*, 129–198. doi:10.1070/SM1977v032n02ABEH002376

Map24. (2010). *Website*. Retrieved from http://developer.navteq.com/site/global/zones/ms/downloads.jsp.

Mark, D., & Egenhofer, M. J. (1994). Modeling spatial relations between lines and regions: Combining formal mathematical models and human subjects testing. *Cartography and Geographic Information Systems, 21*(3), 195–212.

Martin, R. F., Mejino, J. L. V., Bowden, D. M., Brinkley, J., & Rosse, C. (2001). Foundational model of neuroanatomy: Implications for the human brain project. In *Proceedings of the American Medical Informatics Association Fall Symposium*, (pp. 438–442). Philadelphia, PA: Hanley & Belfus.

Masolo, C., & Vieu, L. (1999). Atomicity vs. infinite divisibility of space. In *Proceedings of the Conference on Spatial Information Theory (COSIT-99)*, (pp. 235–250). Springer.

Mastrogiovanni, F., Sgorbissa, A., & Zaccaria, R. (2008). *Representing and reasoning upon contexts in artificial systems*. Paper presented at the 3rd Workshop on Artificial Intelligence Techniques for Ambient Intelligence (AITAmI-08), co-located with the 18th European Conference on Artificial Intelligence (ECAI 08). Patras, Greece.

Mastrogiovanni, F., Scalmato, A., Sgorbissa, A., & Zaccaria, R. (2008). An integrated approach to context specification and recognition in smart homes. In *Smart Homes and Health Telematics* (pp. 26–33). Berlin, Germany: Springer. doi:10.1007/978-3-540-69916-3_4

Mastrogiovanni, F., Sgorbissa, A., & Zaccaria, R. (2007). Classification system for context representation and acquisition. In Augusto, J. C. (Ed.), *Advances in Ambient Intelligence*. IOS Press.

Mazur, P., & Dole, R. (2007). The Dante temporal expression tagger. In *Proceedings of the 3rd Language and Technology Conference*. Language and Technology.

McCarthy, J. (1977). Epistemological problems of artificial intelligence. In *Proceedings of IJCAI*, (pp. 1038–1044). IJCAI.

McCarthy, J. (1998). *Elaboration tolerance*. New York, NY: CommonSense.

McCarthy, J. (2008). The well-designed child. *Artificial Intelligence, 172*(18), 2003–2014. doi:10.1016/j.artint.2008.10.001

McCarthy, J., & Hayes, P. J. (1969). Some philosophical problems from the standpoint of artificial intelligence. In Meltzer, B., & Michie, D. (Eds.), *Machine Intelligence 4* (pp. 463–502). Edinburgh, UK: Edinburgh University Press.

McGuinness, D., & Borgida, A. (1995). Explaining subsumption in description logics. In *Proceedings of the 14th International Joint Conference on Artificial Intelligence (IJCAI-95)*. Montréal, Canada: IJCAI.

McKenney, M., Pauly, A., Praing, R., & Schneider, M. (2005). Dimension-refined topological predicates. In *Proceedings of the Conference on Advances in Geographic Information Systems (GIS-05)*, (pp. 240–249). ACM Press.

McKinsey, J. C. C., & Tarski, A. (1944). The algebra of topology. *The Annals of Mathematics, 45*(1), 141–191. doi:10.2307/1969080

Meng, W., Liu, K. L., Yu, C. T., Wang, X., Chang, Y., & Rishe, N. (1998). Determining text databases to search in the Internet. In *Proceedings of the 24th International Conference on Very Large Databases*, (pp. 14-15). Very Large Databases.

Menger, K. (1940). Topology without points. *Rice Institute Pamphlets, 27*(1), 80–107.

Monekosso, D. N., & Remagnino, P. (2007). Monitoring behavior with an array of sensors. *Computational Intelligence*, *23*(4), 420–438. doi:10.1111/j.1467-8640.2007.00314.x

Moratz, R. (2006). Representing relative direction as a binary relation of oriented points. In *Proceedings of ECAI*, (pp. 407–411). ECAI.

Moratz, R. (2009). Ambiguous landmark problems in cognitive robotics: A benchmark for qualitative position calculi. In B. Nebel & S. Wölfl (Eds.), *Papers from the 2009 AAAI Spring Symposium Benchmarking of Qualitative Spatial and Temporal Reasoning Systems,* (pp. 17–22). Menlo Park, CA: AAAI Press.

Moratz, R., & Wallgrün, J. O. (2003). Spatial reasoning about relative orientation and distance for robot exploration. In W. Kuhn, M. F. Worboys, & S. Timpf (Eds.), *Spatial Information Theory: Foundations of Geographic Information Science: Conference on Spatial Information Theory (COSIT),* (pp. 61-74). Springer.

Moratz, R., Nebel, B., & Freksa, C. (2003). Qualitative spatial reasoning about relative position: The tradeoff between strong formal properties and successful reasoning about route graphs. In C. Freksa, W. Brauer, C. Habel, & K. F. Wender (Eds.), *Spatial Cognition III,* (Vol. 2685), (pp. 385–400). Springer.

Moratz, R., Renz, J., & Wolter, D. (2000). Qualitative spatial reasoning about line segments. In *Proceedings of ECAI*, (pp. 234–238). ECAI.

Moratz, R., & Tenbrink, T. (2006). Spatial reference in linguistic human-robot interaction: Iterative, empirically supported development of a model of projective relations. *Spatial Cognition and Computation*, *6*(1), 63–106. doi:10.1207/s15427633scc0601_3

Morchen, F. (2006). A better tool that Allen's relations for expressing temporal knowledge in interval data. In *Proceedings of the 12th ACM SIGKDD International Conference on Knowledge Discovery and Data Mining (KDD).* Philadelphia, PA: ACM Press.

Mormann, T. (2001). *Holes in the region connection calculus*. Preprint presented at RelMiCS-6.

Mormann, T. (1998). Continuous lattices and Whiteheadian theory of space. *Logic and Logical Philosophy*, *6*, 35–54.

Muehlenbrock, M., Brdiczka, O., Snowdon, D., & Meunier, J. (2004). Learning to detect user activity and availability from a variety of sensor data. In *Proceedings of the 2004 IEEE International Conference on Pervasive Computing (PerCom04).* Piscataway, NY: IEEE Press.

Mueller, E. T. (2006). *Commonsense reasoning*. San Francisco, CA: Morgan Kaufmann Publishers Inc.

Mueller, E. T. (2009). Automating commonsense reasoning using the event calculus. *Communications of the ACM*, *52*(1), 113–117. doi:10.1145/1435417.1435443

Muller, P. (1998a). A qualitative theory of motion based on spatio-temporal primitives. In *Proceedings of KR98: Principles of Knowledge Representation and Reasoning*, (pp. 131–143). KR.

Muller, P. (1998b). *Éléments d'une théorie du mouvement pour la modélisation du raisonnement spatio-temporel de sens commun.* Doctoral Dissertation. Toulouse, France: Université Paul Sabatier.

Muller, P. (1998b). Space-time as a primitive for space and motion. In *Proceedings of the Conference on Formal Ontology in Information Systems (FOIS-98),* (pp. 3–15). FOIS.

Muller, P. (2002). Topological spatiotemporal reasoning and representation. *Computational Intelligence*, *18*(3), 420–450. doi:10.1111/1467-8640.00196

Munkres, J. R. (2000). *Topology* (2nd ed.). Prentice Hall.

Museros, L., & Escrig, M. T. (2004). A qualitative theory for shape representation and matching. In *Proceedings of the Eighteenth International Workshop on Qualitative Reasoning*. Qualitative Reasoning.

Naimpally, S. A., & Warrack, B. D. (1970). *Proximity spaces*. Cambridge University Press.

National Institute of Health. (2009). *National institute of mental health.* Retrieved from http://www.nimh.nih.gov.

Navarrete, I. S. G. (2006). Spatial reasoning with rectangular cardinal direction relations. In *Proceedings of the Workshop on Spatial and Temporal Reasoning at ECAI-06*, (pp. 1–9). ECAI.

Nebel, B., & Bürckert, H. J. (1995). Reasoning about temporal relations: A maximal tractable subclass of Allen's algebra. *Journal of the ACM, 42*(1), 43–66. doi:10.1145/200836.200848

Nedas, K., Egenhofer, M. J., & Wilmsen, D. (2007). Metric details of topological line-line relations. *International Journal of Geographical Information Science, 21*(1), 21–48. doi:10.1080/13658810600852164

Neira, J., & Tardós, J. D. (2001). Data association in stochastic mapping using the joint compability test. *IEEE Transactions on Robotics and Automation, 17*, 890–897. doi:10.1109/70.976019

Nicod, J. (1924). *Geometry in the sensible world.* Unpublished Doctoral Thesis. Paris, France: Sorbonne.

NIMA. (2000). *The big idea framework.* Washington, DC: National Imagery and Mapping Agency.

Noyon, V., Claramunt, C., & Devogele, T. (2007). A relative representation of trajectories in geographical spaces. *GeoInformatica, 11*(4), 479–496. doi:10.1007/s10707-007-0023-2

Ntoulas, A., Zerfos, P., & Cho, J. (2005). Downloading textual hidden Web content through keyword queries. In *Proceedings of the 5th ACM/IEEE-CS Joint Conference on Digital Libraries*. ACM Press.

Nuechterlein, K. H., & Dawson, M. E. (1984). A heuristic vulnerability/stress model of schizophrenic episodes. *Schizophrenia Bulletin, 10*, 300–312.

Ochiai, N. (2004). *Introduction to graph theory: Application for plane graph.* Nihon-Hyouron-sha.

OpenGIS Consortium. (1999). *OpenGIS simple features implementation specification for SQL rev. 1.1.* OpenGIS Project Document 99-049. OpenGIS.

OWL. (2010). *Time ontology in OWL.* Retrieved from http://www.w3.org/TR/owl-time/.

Ozsoyoglu, G., & Snodgrass, R. (1995). Temporal and real-time databases: A survey. *IEEE Transactions on Knowledge and Data Engineering, 7*(4), 513–532. doi:10.1109/69.404027

Padmanabhan, R., & Rudeanu, S. (2008). *Axioms for lattices and Boolean algebras.* World Scientific. doi:10.1142/9789812834553

Papadakis, N., & Plexousakis, D. (2003). Actions with duration and constraints: The ramification problem in temporal databases. *International Journal of Artificial Intelligence Tools, 12*(3), 315–353. doi:10.1142/S0218213003001265

Parent, A., & Carpenter, M. (1996). *Carpenter's human neuroanatomy.* Baltimore, MD: Williams & Wilkins.

Pawlak, Z. (1991). *Rough sets: Theoretical aspects of reasoning about data.* Dordrecht, The Netherlands: Kluwer.

Petrakis, E. G. (2002). Fast retrieval by spatial structure in image databases. *Journal of Visual Languages and Computing, 13*(5), 545–569. doi:10.1006/jvlc.2002.0233

Petrakis, E. G. (2002a). Design and evaluation of spatial similarity approaches for image retrieval. *Image and Vision Computing, 20*(1), 59–76. doi:10.1016/S0262-8856(01)00077-4

Peuquet, D. J. (2001). Making space for time: Issues in space-time data representation. *GeoInformatica, 5*(1), 11–32. doi:10.1023/A:1011455820644

Philipose, M., Fishkin, K. P., Perkowitz, M., Patterson, D. J., Fox, D., Kautz, H., & Hahnel, D. (2004). Inferring activities from interactions with objects. *IEEE Pervasive Computing / IEEE Computer Society and IEEE Communications Society, 3*(4), 50–57. doi:10.1109/MPRV.2004.7

Piaget, J., & Inhelder, B. (1967). *The child's conception of space.* New York, NY: Basic Books.

Pierce, C. S. (1935). *The collected papers of Charles Sanders Peirce.* Cambridge, MA: Harvard University Press.

Plandowski, W. (1999). Satisfiability of word equations with constants is in PSPACE. In *Proceedings of the Annual Symposium on Foundations of Computer Science (FOCS '99),* (pp. 495-500). Los Alamitos, CA: IEEE Computer Society Press.

Poole, D., Goebel, R., & Aleliunas, R. (1987). Theorist: A logical reasoning system for defaults and diagnosis. In Cercone, N., & McCalla, G. (Eds.), *The Knowledge Frontier* (pp. 331–352). New York, NY: Springer. doi:10.1007/978-1-4612-4792-0_13

Pratt, I. (1999). Qualitative spatial representation languages with convexity. *Journal of Spatial Cognition and Computation, 1*, 181–204. doi:10.1023/A:1010037123582

Pratt, I., & Schoop, D. (1997). *A complete axiom system for polygonal mereotopology of the real plane. UMCS-97-2-2, Technical Report*. Manchester, UK: University of Manchester.

Priestley, H. A. (1970). Representation of distributive lattices by means of ordered stone spaces. *Bulletin of the London Mathematical Society, 2*(2), 186–190. doi:10.1112/blms/2.2.186

R3-[Q-Shape]. (2003). *SFB/TR 8 spatial cognition*. Berlin, Germany: Project R3-[Q-Shape]: Reasoning about Paths, Shapes, and Configurations.

Ragni, M., & Wölfl, S. (2005, Sep). Temporalizing spatial calculi—On generalized neighborhood graphs. In *Proceedings of the 28th German Conference on Artificial Intelligence (KI 2005)*. Koblenz, Germany: KI.

Ragni, M., & Wölfl, S. (2006). Temporalizing cardinal directions: From constraint satisfaction to planning. In Doherty, P., Mylopoulos, J., & Welty, C. A. (Eds.), *KR* (pp. 472–480). AAAI Press.

Ramos, C., Augusto, J. C., & Shapiro, D. (2008). Ambient intelligence: The next step for artificial intelligence. *IEEE Intelligent Systems, 23*(2), 15–18. doi:10.1109/MIS.2008.19

Randell, D. A., & Cohn, A. G. (1989). Modelling topological and metrical properites of physical processes. In *Proceedings of the First International Conference on Principles of Knowledge Representation and Reasoning, (KR-89),* (pp. 55-66). KR.

Randell, D. A., Cohn, A. G., & Cui, Z. (1992b). Computing transivity tables: A challenge for automated theorem provers. In *Proceedings of the 11th International Conference on Automated Deduction: Automated Deduction,* (pp. 786-790). Automated Deduction.

Randell, D. A., Cui, Z., & Cohn, A. (1992). A spatial logic based on regions and connection. In *Proceedings of KR'92: Principles of Knowledge Representation and Reasoning,* (pp. 165–176). San Mateo, CA: Morgan Kaufmann.

Randell, D. A., Cui, Z., & Cohn, A. G. (1992). A spatial logic based on regions and connection. In B. Nebel, C. Rich, & W. Swartout (Eds.), *Principles of Knowledge Representation and Reasoning: Proceedings of the Third International Conference* (pp. 165-176). Springer.

Randell, D., & Witkowski, M. (2004). Tracking regions using conceptual neighbourhoods. In *Proceedings of the Workshop on Spatial and Temporal Reasoning,* (pp. 63–71). ECAI.

Randell, D., Cui, Z., & Cohn, A. G. (1992). A spatial logic based on regions and connection. In *Proceedings of the Third International Conference on Principles of Knowledge Representation and Reasoning (KR92),* (pp. 165-176). Morgan Kaufmann Publishers.

Rauh, R., Hagen, C., Knauff, M., Kuß, T., Schlieder, C., & Strube, G. (2005). From preferred to alternative mental models in spatial reasoning. *Spatial Cognition and Computation, 5*, 239–269.

Razzouk, D. (2001). *Construção de uma base de conhecimento de um sistema de apoio a decisao*. PhD Thesis. São Paulo, Brazil: UNIFESP.

Rector, A., Rogers, J., & Pole, P. (1996). The GALEN high level ontology. In *Medical Informatics Europe 96* (Part A), (pp. 174–178). IOS Press.

Reiter, R. (2001). *Knowledge in action: Logical foundations for describing and implementing dynamical systems*. Cambridge, MA: MIT Press.

Remolina, E., & Kuipers, B. J. (2004). Towards a general theory of topological maps. *Artificial Intelligence, 152*, 47–104. doi:10.1016/S0004-3702(03)00114-0

Renz, J. (1999). Maximal tractable fragments of the region connection calculus: A complete analysis. In *Proceedings of the International Joint Conference on Artificial Intelligence (IJCAI-99)*, (pp. 448–454). IJCAI.

Renz, J. (2007). Qualitative spatial and temporal reasoning: Efficient algorithms for everyone. In *Proceedings of the 20th International Joint Conference on Artificial Intelligence (IJCAI-07),* (pp. 526-531). Hyderabad, India: IJCAI.

Renz, J., & Li, J. J. (2008). Automated complexity proofs for qualitative spatial and temporal calculi. In *Proceedings of KR08: Principles of Knowledge Representation and Reasoning*, (pp. 715–723). KR.

Renz, J., & Ligozat, G. (2004). What is a qualitative calculus? A general framework. In *Proceedings of the Pacific Rim International Conference on Artificial Intelligence (PRICAI-04)*, (pp. 53–64). Springer.

Renz, J., & Mitra, D. (2004). Qualitative direction calculi with arbitrary granularity. In *Proceedings of the Pacific Rim International Conference on Artificial Intelligence (PRICAI-04)*, (pp. 65–74). PRICAI.

Renz, J., & Nebel, B. (1998). Efficient methods for qualitative spatial reasoning. In *Proceedings of the European Conference on Artificial Intelligence (ECAI-98)*, (pp. 562–566). ECAI.

Renz, J., & Nebel, B. (2007). *Qualitative spatial reasoning using constraint calculi*. Retrieved from http://users.cecs.anu.edu.au/~jrenz/papers/renz-nebel-los.pdf.

Renz, J. (2002). *Qualitative spatial reasoning with topological information*. Berlin, Germany: Springer. doi:10.1007/3-540-70736-0

Renz, J. (2002). *Qualitative spatial reasoning with topological information*. Springer-Verlag. doi:10.1007/3-540-70736-0

Renz, J., & Ligozat, G. (2005). Weak composition for qualitative spatial and temporal reasoning. In *Proceedings of Principles and Practice of Constraint Programming (CP-05)* (pp. 534–548). Springer. doi:10.1007/11564751_40

Renz, J., & Nebel, B. (1999). On the complexity of qualitative spatial reasoning: A maximal tractable fragment of the region connection calculus. *Artificial Intelligence*, *108*(1-2), 69–123. doi:10.1016/S0004-3702(99)00002-8

Renz, J., & Nebel, B. (2001). Efficient methods for qualitative spatial reasoning. *Journal of Artificial Intelligence Research*, *5*, 289–318.

Renz, J., & Nebel, B. (2007). Qualitative spatial reasoning using constraint calculi. In Aiello, M., Pratt-Hartmann, I. E., & van Benthem, J. F. (Eds.), *Handbook of Spatial Logics* (pp. 161–215). Springer. doi:10.1007/978-1-4020-5587-4_4

Rescher, N. (2005). *Epistemic logic: A survey of the logic of knowledge*. Pittsburgh, PA: University of Pittsburgh Press.

Richter, K. F., Weber, B., Bojduj, B., & Bertel, S. (2009). Supporting the designer's and the user's perspectives in computer-aided architectural design. *Advanced Engineering Informatics*, *24*(2).

Robinson, R. M. (1959). Binary relations as primitive notions in elementary geometry. In Henkin, L., Suppes, P., & Tarski, A. (Eds.), *The Axiomatic Method with Special Reference to Geometry and Physics* (pp. 68–85). Amsterdam, The Netherlands: North-Holland. doi:10.1016/S0049-237X(09)70020-5

Rodrìguez, M. A., & Egenhofer, M. J. (2004). Comparing geospatial entity classes: An asymmetric and context-dependent similarity measure. *International Journal of Geographical Information Science*, *18*(3), 229–256. doi:10.1080/13658810310001629592

Roeper, P. (1997). Region-based topology. *Journal of Philosophical Logic*, *26*(3), 251–309. doi:10.1023/A:1017904631349

Rogers, J., & Rector, A. (2000). GALENS model of parts and wholes: Experience and comparisons. In *Proceedings of the Symposium of the American Medical Informatics Association (AMIA-2000)*, (pp. 714–718). Hanley & Belfus.

Rosse, C., & Mejino, J. (2003). A reference ontology for biomedical informatics: The foundational model of anatomy. *Journal of Biomedical Informatics*, *36*(6), 478–500. doi:10.1016/j.jbi.2003.11.007

Roy, A. J., & Stell, J. G. (2002). A qualitative account of discrete space. In *Proceedings of the Conference on Geographic Information Science (GIScience-02)*, (pp. 276–290). Springer.

Rugnone, A., Nugent, C., Donnelly, M., Craig, D., Vicario, E., Paggetti, C., et al. (2007). HomeTL: A visual formalism, based on temporal logic, for the design of home based care. In *Proceedings of the 3rd Annual IEEE Conference on Automation Science and Engineering (CASE)*, (pp. 747-752). Scottsdale, AZ: IEEE Press.

Salber, D., Dey, A., & Abowd, G. (1999). The context toolkit: Aiding the development of context-enabled applications. In *Proceedings of the Conference on Human Factors in Computing Systems (CHI'99)*, (pp. 434-441). Pittsburgh, PA: CHI.

Salustri, F. A. (2002). Mereotopology for product modeling. *Journal of Desert Research, 2*(1).

Sandewall, E. (1994). *Features and fluents: The representation of knowledge about dynamical systems*. New York, NY: Oxford University Press, Inc.

Santos, P., & Cabalar, P. (2008). The space within fisherman's folly: Playing with a puzzle in mereotopology. *Spatial Cognition and Computation, 8*(1-2), 47–64. doi:10.1080/13875860801944804

Santos, P., Thomaz, C., Santos, D., Freire, R., Sato, J., & Louza, M. (2009). Exploring the knowledge contained in neuroimages: Statistical discriminant analysis and automatic segmentation of the most significant changes. *Artificial Intelligence in Medicine, 49*(2), 105–115. doi:10.1016/j.artmed.2010.03.003

Schlieder, C. (1993). Representing visible locations for qualitative navigation. In Piera-Carrete, N., & Singh, M. (Eds.), *Qualitative Reasoning and Decision Technologies* (pp. 523–532). Springer.

Schlieder, C. (1996). Qualitative shape representation. In Frank, A. (Ed.), *Spatial Conceptual Models for Geographic Objects with Undetermined Boundaries* (pp. 123–140). London, UK: Taylor & Francis.

Schmidtke, H. R., & Woo, W. (2007). A size-based qualitative approach to the representation of spatial granularity. In *Proceedings of the Twentieth International Joint Conference on Artificial Intelligence (IJCAI 2007)*, (pp. 563-568). IJCAI.

Schmolze, J. G. (1996). A topological account of the space occupied by physical objects. *The Monist, 79*(1), 128–140.

Schockaert, S., De Cock, M., & Kerre, E. (2008). Modelling nearness and cardinal directions between fuzzy regions. In *Proceedings of the Conference on Fuzzy Systems (FUZZ 08)*, (pp. 1548–1555). FUZZ.

Schockaert, S., De Cock, M., & Kerre, E. (2009). Spatial reasoning in a fuzzy region connection calculus. *Artificial Intelligence, 173*, 258–298. doi:10.1016/j.artint.2008.10.009

Schultz, C. P. L., Amor, R., Lobb, B., & Guesgen, H. W. (2009). Qualitative design support for engineering and architecture. *Advanced Engineering Informatics, 23*(1), 68–80. doi:10.1016/j.aei.2008.07.003

Schultz, C. P. L., Clephane, T. R., Guesgen, H. W., & Amor, R. (2006). Utilization of qualitative spatial reasoning in geographic information systems. In Riedl, A., Kainz, W., & Elmes, G. A. (Eds.), *Progress in Spatial Data Handling, Part 2* (pp. 27–42). Berlin, Germany: Springer. doi:10.1007/3-540-35589-8_3

Schulz, S., & Hahn, U. (2001a). Mereotopological reasoning about parts and (w)holes in bio-ontologies. In *Proceedings of the Conference on Formal Ontology in Information Systems (FOIS-01)*, (pp. 210–221). FOIS.

Schulz, S., & Hahn, U. (2001b). Parts, locations, and holes-formal reasoning about anatomical structures. In *Proceedings of the Conference on Artificial Intelligence in Medicine in Europe (AIME-01)*. Springer.

Schulz, S., Daumke, P., Smith, B., & Hahn, U. (2005). How to distinguish parthood from location in bio-ontologies. In *Proceedings of the Symposium of the American Medical Informatics Association (AMIA-05)*, (pp. 669–673). AMIA.

Schwering, A. (2008). Approaches to semantic similarity measurement for geo-spatial data: A survey. *Transactions in GIS, 12*(1), 5–29. doi:10.1111/j.1467-9671.2008.01084.x

Shanahan, M. (1989). Prediction is deduction but explanation is abduction. In *Proceedings of IJCAI*, (pp. 1055–1060). IJCAI.

Shanahan, M. (1993). Explanation in the situation calculus. In *Proceedings of IJCAI*, (pp. 160–165). IJCAI.

Shanahan, M. (1995). Default reasoning about spatial occupancy. *Artificial Intelligence, 74*(1), 147–163. doi:10.1016/0004-3702(94)00071-8

Shanahan, M. (1997). *Solving the frame problem: A mathematical investigation of the common sense law of inertia*. Cambridge, MA: MIT Press.

Sheth, A., Arpinar, I., Perry, M., & Hakimpour, F. (2009). Geospatial and temporal semantic analytics. In Karimi, H. A. (Ed.), *Handbook of Research in Geoinformatics*. Hershey, PA: IGI Global.

Shokouhi, M. (2007). Central-rank-based collection selection in uncooperative distributed information retrieval. In *Proceedings of the 29th European Conference on IR Research*. IR Research.

Si, L., & Callan, J. (2005). Modeling search engine effectiveness for federated search. In *Proceedings of the 28th International ACM SIGIR Conference on Research and Development in Information Retrieval*, (pp. 83-90). ACM Press.

Simons, P. (1987). *Parts-a study in ontology*. Clarendon Press.

Skiadopoulos, S., & Koubarakis, M. (2004). Composing cardinal direction relations. *Artificial Intelligence*, *152*(2), 143–171. doi:10.1016/S0004-3702(03)00137-1

Skiadopoulos, S., & Koubarakis, M. (2005). On the consistency of cardinal directions constraints. *Artificial Intelligence*, *163*, 91–135. doi:10.1016/j.artint.2004.10.010

Sloman, A. (2008). The well-designed young mathematician. *Artificial Intelligence*, *172*(18), 2015–2034. doi:10.1016/j.artint.2008.09.004

Smith, B., & Varzi, A. (1997). Fiat and bona fide boundaries: Towards and ontology of spatially extended objects. In *Proceedings of the Conference on Spatial Information Theory (COSIT-97)*, (pp. 103–119). Springer.

Smith, B. (1996). Mereotopology: A theory of parts and boundaries. *Data & Knowledge Engineering*, *20*(3), 287–303. doi:10.1016/S0169-023X(96)00015-8

Smith, B., & Casati, R. (1994). Naive physics: An essay in ontology. *Philosophical Psychology*, *7*(2), 225–244.

Smith, B., & Ceusters, W. (2007). Ontology as the core discipline of biomedical informatics: Legacies of the past and recommendations for the future direction of research. In Crnkovic, G., & Stuart, S. (Eds.), *Computing, Philosophy, and Cognitive Science* (pp. 104–122). Newcastle, UK: Cambridge Scholars Press.

Smith, B., Ceusters, W., Klagges, B., Kohler, J., Kumar, A., & Lomax, J. (2005). Relations in biomedical ontologies. *Genome Biology*, *6*(5), 1–15. doi:10.1186/gb-2005-6-5-r46

Smith, B., & Varzi, A. (2000). Fiat and bona fide boundaries. *Philosophy and Phenomenological Research*, *60*(2), 401–420. doi:10.2307/2653492

Smith, M. J., Goodchild, M. F., & Longley, P. A. (2007). *Geospatial analysis: A comprehensive guide to principles, techniques and software tools*. Troubador Publishing.

Smith, T., & Park, K. (1992). Algebraic approach to spatial reasoning. *International Journal of Geographical Information Science*, *6*(3), 177–192. doi:10.1080/02693799208901904

Spitzer, R. L., & Endicott, J. (1968). Diagno: Computerized program for psychiatric diagnosis utilizing the differential diagnostic procedure. *Archives of General Psychiatry*, *18*, 747–756. doi:10.1001/archpsyc.1968.01740060106013

Steen, R. G., Mull, C., McClure, R., Hamer, R. M., & Lieberman, J. A. (2006). Brain volume in first-episode schizophrenia. *The British Journal of Psychiatry*, *188*, 510–518. doi:10.1192/bjp.188.6.510

Steinhauer, H. J. (2008). Object configuration reconstruction from incomplete binary object relation descriptions. In Dengel, A. R., Berns, K., & Breul, T. M. (Eds.), *KI 2008: Advances in Artificial Intelligence* (pp. 348–355). Springer. doi:10.1007/978-3-540-85845-4_43

Stell, J. G., & Worboys, M. F. (1997). The algebraic structure of sets of regions. In *Proceedings of the Conference on Spatial Information Theory (COSIT-97)*, (pp. 163–174). Springer.

Stell, J. G. (2000). Boolean connection algebras: A new approach to the region-connection calculus. *Artificial Intelligence*, *122*, 111–136. doi:10.1016/S0004-3702(00)00045-X

Stell, J. G. (2003). *Foundations of geographic information science: Granularity in change over time* (pp. 101–122). Taylor & Francis.

Stephenson, K. (2005). *Introduction to circle packing-the theory of discrete analytic functions*. Cambridge University Press.

Stock, O. (1997). *Spatial and temporal reasoning*. Dordrecht, The Netherlands: Kluwer Academic Publishers. doi:10.1007/978-0-585-28322-7

Stone, M. H. (1937). Topological representation of distributive lattices and Brouwerian logics. *Časopis pro Pěstování Matematiky a Fysiky, 67*, 1–25.

Stone, M. H. (1936). The theory of representations for Boolean algebra. *Transactions of the American Society, 40*(1), 37–111.

Strang, T., Linnhoff-Popien, C., & Frank, K. (2003). Applications of a context ontology language. In *Proceedings of the Internationall Conference on Software, Telecommunications and Computer Networks*. Dubrovnik, Croatia: Software, Telecommunications, and Computer Networks.

Strang, T., Linnhoff-Popien, C., & Frank, K. (2003). CoOL: A context ontology language to enable contextual interoperability. In *Proceedings of the 4th IFIP WG 6.1 International Conference on Distributed Applications and Interoperable Systems (DAIS2003)*. Paris, France: DAIS.

Streitz, N. A., Kameas, A., & Mavrommati, I. (Eds.). (2007). *The disappearing computer, interaction design, system infrastructures and applications for smart environments. (LNCS 4500)*. Springer.

Sugiura, A., & Etzioni, O. (2000). Query routing for Web search engines: Architecture and experiments. In *Proceedings of the 9th International World Wide Web Conference*. World Wide Web.

Takahashi, H., Tokairin, Y., Yamanaka, K., Suganuma, T., Kinoshita, T., Sugawara, K., et al. (2007). uEyes: A ubiquitous care-support service based on multiple contexts coordination. In *Proceedings of the 2007 International Symposium on Applications and the Internet*. IEEE Computer Society.

Takahashi, K., & Sumitomo, T. (2005). A framework for qualitative spatial reasoning based on connection patterns of regions. In *Proceedings of the IJCAI-05 Workshop on Spatial and Temporal Reasoning*, (pp. 57-62). IJCAI.

Takahashi, K., & Sumitomo, T. (2007). The qualitative treatment of spatial data. *International Journal of Artificial Intelligence Tools, 16*(4), 661–682. doi:10.1142/S0218213007003497

Takahashi, K., Sumitomo, T., & Takeuti, I. (2008). On embedding a qualitative representation in a two-dimensional plane. *Spatial Cognition and Computation, 8*(1-2), 4–26. doi:10.1080/13875860801944887

Tan, H.-Y., Callicott, J. H., & Weinberger, D. R. (2008). Intermediate phenotypes in schizophrenia genetics redux: Is it a no brainer? *Molecular Psychiatry, 13*, 233–238. doi:10.1038/sj.mp.4002145

Tarski, A. (1935). Zur grundlegung der Booleschen algebra I. *Fundamenta Mathematicae, 24*, 177–198.

Tarski, A. (1956a). Foundations of the geometry of solids. In Tarski, A. (Ed.), *Logics, Semantics, Metamathematics: Papers from 1923-1938 by Alfred Tarski*. Clarendon Press.

Tarski, A. (1956b). On the foundation of Boolean algebra. In Tarski, A. (Ed.), *Logics, Semantics, Metamathematics: Papers from 1923-1938 by Alfred Tarski*. Clarendon Press.

Tarski, A. (1959). What is elementary geometry? In Henkin, L., Suppes, P., & Tarski, A. (Eds.), *The Axiomatic Method with Special Reference to Geometry and Physics* (pp. 16–29). North-Holland.

Thielscher, M. (1997). Ramification and causality. *Artificial Intelligence, 89*(1-2), 317–364. doi:10.1016/S0004-3702(96)00033-1

Thielscher, M. (1998). Introduction to the fluent calculus. *Electronic Transactions in Artificial Intelligence, 2*, 179–192.

Thielscher, M. (2005). Flux: A logic programming method for reasoning agents. *Theory and Practice of Logic Programming, 5*(4-5), 533–565. doi:10.1017/S1471068405002358

Thomaz, C. E., Boardman, J. P., Counsell, S., Hill, D. L. G., Hajnal, J. V., & Edwards, A. D. (2007a). A multivariate statistical analysis of the developing human brain in preterm infants. *Image and Vision Computing, 25*(6), 981–994. doi:10.1016/j.imavis.2006.07.011

Thomaz, C. E., Duran, F. L. S., Busatto, G. F., Gillies, D. F., & Rueckert, D. (2007b). Multivariate statistical differences of MRI samples of the human brain. *Journal of Mathematical Imaging and Vision, 29*(2-3), 95–106. doi:10.1007/s10851-007-0033-6

Thrun, S. (1998). Learning metric-topological maps for indoor mobile robot navigation. *Artificial Intelligence, 99*, 21–71. doi:10.1016/S0004-3702(97)00078-7

Thrun, S. (2002). *Robotic mapping: A survey*. Pittsburgh, PA: Carnegie Mellon University.

Timpf, S. (1999). Abstraction, levels of detail, and hierarchies in map series. In *Proceedings of the Spatial Information Theory: Cognitive and Computational Foundations of Geographic Information Science (COSIT99)*, (pp. 125-139). Springer-Verlag.

Urquhart, A. (1978). A topological representation theory for lattices. *Algebra Universalis, 8*, 45–58. doi:10.1007/BF02485369

Vakarelov, D., Düntsch, I., & Bennett, B. (2001). A note on proximity spaces and connection based mereology. In *Proceedings of the Conference on Formal Ontology in Inf. Systems (FOIS-01)*, (pp. 139–150). FOIS.

Vakarelov, D. (2007). Region-based theory of space: Algebras of regions, representation theory, and logics. In Gabbay, D., Goncharov, S., & Zakharyaschev, M. (Eds.), *Mathematical Problems from Applied Logic II* (pp. 267–348). Springer. doi:10.1007/978-0-387-69245-6_6

Vakarelov, D., Dimov, G., Düntsch, I., & Bennett, B. (2002). A proximity approach to some region-based theories of space. *Journal of Applied Non-classical Logics, 12*(3-4), 527–559. doi:10.3166/jancl.12.527-559

Van Beek, P. (1992). Reasoning about qualitative temporal information. *Artificial Intelligence, 58*, 297–326. doi:10.1016/0004-3702(92)90011-L

Van de Weghe, N., & De Maeyer, P. (2005). Conceptual neighbourhood diagrams for representing moving objects. In *Proceedings of the Perspectives in Conceptual Modeling*, (pp. 228-238). Perspectives in Conceptual Modeling.

Van de Weghe, N., De Tré, G., Kuijpers, B., & De Maeyer, P. (2005). *The double-cross and the generalization concept as a basis for representing and comparing shapes of polylines.* Paper presented at the First International Workshop on Semantic-Based Geographical Information Systems (SeBGIS'05). Agia Napa, Cyprus.

Van de Weghe, N., Kuijpers, B., Bogaert, P., & De Maeyer, P. (2005, 2005). *A qualitative trajectory calculus and the composition of its relations.* In *Proceedings of the 1st International Conference on Geospatial Semantics (GeoS)*. GeoS.

Van de Weghe, N. (2004). *Representing and reasoning about moving objects: A qualitative approach*. Ghent, Belgium: Ghent University.

Van de Weghe, N., Cohn, A. G., De Maeyer, P., & Witlox, F. (2005). Representing moving objects in computer-based expert systems: The overtake event example. *Expert Systems with Applications, 29*(4), 977–983. doi:10.1016/j.eswa.2005.06.022

Van de Weghe, N., Cohn, A. G., De Tré, G., & De Maeyer, P. (2006). A qualitative trajectory calculus as a basis for representing moving objects in Geographical Information Systems. *Control and Cybernetics, 35*(1), 97–119.

Van Harmelen, F., Lifschitz, V., & Porter, B. (Eds.). (2007). *Handbook of knowledge representation (foundations of artificial intelligence)*. Elsevier Science.

Varzi, A. C. (1998). Basic problems of mereotopology. In *Proceedings of the Conference on Formal Ontology in Information Systems (FOIS-98)*, (pp. 29–38). FOIS.

Varzi, A. (1997). Boundaries, continuity, and contact. *Nous (Detroit, Mich.), 31*(1), 26–58. doi:10.1111/0029-4624.00034

Varzi, A. C. (1994). On the boundary between mereology and topology. In Casati, R., Smith, B., & White, G. (Eds.), *Philosophy and Cognitive Science* (pp. 423–442). Holder-Pichler-Tempsky.

Varzi, A. C. (1996). Reasoning about space: The hole story. *Logic and Logical Philosophy, 4*, 3–39.

Varzi, A. C. (1996a). Parts, wholes, and part-whole relations: The prospects of mereotopology. *Data & Knowledge Engineering, 20*(3), 259–286. doi:10.1016/S0169-023X(96)00017-1

Varzi, A. C. (1996b). Reasoning about space: The hole story. *Logic and Logical Philosophy, 4*, 3–39.

Varzi, A. C. (2008). Boundary. In *The Stanford Encyclopedia of Philosophy*. Palo Alto, CA: Stanford University Press.

Varzi, A. C. (2009). Mereology. In *The Stanford Encyclopedia of Philosophy*. Palo Alto, CA: Stanford University Press.

Verhagen, M., Mani, I., Sauri, R., Knippen, R., Jang, S. B., Littman, J., et al. (2005). Automating temporal annotation with TARSQI. In *Proceedings of the Association for Computational Linguistics (ACL-05)*, (pp. 81–84). ACL.

Vieu, L. (1997). Spatial representation and reasoning in artificial intelligence. In Stock, O. (Ed.), *Spatial and Temporal Reasoning* (pp. 5–41). Dordrecht, The Netherlands: Kluwer. doi:10.1007/978-0-585-28322-7_1

Vilain, M., & Kautz, H. (1986). Constraint propagation algorithms for temporal reasoning. In *Proceedings of the Fifth National Conference on Artificial Intelligence (AAAI)*, (pp. 377-382). AAAI.

Vilain, M., & Kautz, H. (1989). Constraint propagation algorithms for temporal reasoning: A revisited report. In *Readings in Qualitative Reasoning about Physical Systems* (pp. 373–381). Morgan Kaufmann Publishers Inc.

Waldmann, M. (2007). Combining versus analyzing multiple causes: How domain assumptions and task context affect integration rules. *Cognitive Science*, *31*, 233–256.

Wallgrün, J. O. (2009). Exploiting qualitative spatial constraints for multi-hypothesis topological map learning. In K. S. Hornsby, C. Claramunt, M. Denis, & G. Ligozat (Eds.), *Spatial Information Theory, 9th International Conference, COSIT 2009*, (Vol. 5756), (pp. 141-158). Springer.

Wallgrün, J. O., Frommberger, L., Wolter, D., Dylla, F., & Freksa, C. (2007). Qualitative spatial representation and reasoning in the SparQ-toolbox. In *Proceedings of Spatial Cognition V: Reasoning, Action, Interaction: International Conference Spatial Cognition 2006*. Bremen, Germany: Spatial Cognition.

Wallgrün, J. O. (2010). *Hierarchical Voronoi graphs–Spatial representation and reasoning for mobile robots*. London, UK: Springer.

Wallman, H. (1938). Lattices and topological spaces. *The Annals of Mathematics*, *39*(2), 112–126. doi:10.2307/1968717

Wang, X., Zhang, D., Gu, T., & Pung, H. (2004). Ontology based context modeling and reasoning using OWL. In *Proceedings of the Second IEEE Conference on Pervasive Computing and Communications Workshops*. Orlando, FL: IEEE Press.

Wang, S. S., & Liu, D. Y. (2006). Qualitative spatial relation database for semantic web. In Mizoguchi, R., Shi, Z., & Giunchiglia, F. (Eds.), *The Semantic Web* (pp. 387–399). Berlin, Germany: Springer-Verlag. doi:10.1007/11836025_39

Wehrung, F. (1998). *General lattice theory: Appendix E-projective lattice geometries* (2nd ed.). Birkhäuser.

Weidenbach, C. (2001). SPASS: Combining superposition, sorts, and splitting. In Robinson, A., & Voronkov, A. (Eds.), *Handbook of Automated Reasoning* (*Vol. 2*, pp. 1965–2013). Amsterdam, The Netherlands: Elsevier.

Weld, D. S., & de Kleer, J. (1989). *Readings in qualitative reasoning about physical systems*. San Mateo, CA: Morgan Kaufmann Publishers.

Welty, C., & Fikes, R. (2006). A reusable ontology for fluents in OWL. In *Proceedings of International Conference on Formal Ontology in Information Systems (FOIS-2006)*, (pp. 226-236). FOIS.

Westphal, M., & Wölfl, S. (2008). Bipath consistency revisited. In M. Ghallab, C. Spyropoulos, N. Fakotakis, & N. Avouris (Eds.), *Proceedings of the 18th European Conference on Artificial Intelligence (ECAI 2008)*. Amsterdam, The Netherlands: IOS Press.

Westphal, M., & Wölfl, S. (2009). Qualitative CSP, finite CSP, and SAT: Comparing methods for qualitative constraint-based reasoning. In *Proceedings of IJCAI-09*. IJCAI.

Whitehead, A. N. (1920). *Concept of nature*. Cambridge University Press.

Whitehead, A. N. (1929). *Process and reality*. MacMillan.

Wikipedia. (2009). *Region connection calculus*. Retrieved from http://en.wikipedia.org/wiki/Region_Connection_Calculus.

Williams, B. (1985). Qualitative analysis of MOS circuits. In Bobrow, D. (Ed.), *Qualitative Reasoning about Physical Systems* (pp. 281–346). Cambridge, MA: MIT Press.

Williams, R. (1979). Circle packings, plane tessellations, and networks. In *The Geometrical Foundation of Natural Structure: A Source Book of Design* (pp. 34–47). New York, NY: Dover.

Winter, M., Hahmann, T., & Gruninger, M. (2009). On the skeleton of Stonian p-ortholattices. In *Proceedings of the Conference on Relational Methods in Computer Science (RelMiCS-11)*, (pp. 351–365). Springer.

Winter, S. (1998). Bridging vector and raster representation in GIS. In *Proceedings of the 6th ACM International Symposium on Advances in Geographic Information Systems,* (pp. 57–62). New York, NY: ACM.

Winter, S., & Frank, A. U. (2000). Topology in raster and vector representation. *GeoInformatica, 4,* 35–65. doi:10.1023/A:1009828425380

Wölfl, S., & Westphal, M. (2009). On combinations of binary qualitative constraint calculi. In *Proceedings of IJCAI-09.* IJCAI.

Wolter, D., & Moshagen, L. (2008). Algebraic methods for analyzing qualitative spatio-temporal calculi. In *Proceedings of ECAI-2008 Workshop on Spatial and Temporal Reasoning.* ECAI.

Wolter, F., & Zakharyaschev, M. (2000). Spatial representation and reasoning in RCC-8 with Boolean region terms. In *Proceedings of the European Conference on Artificial Intelligence (ECAI-2000)*, (pp. 244–248). ECAI.

Wolter, F., & Zakharyaschev, M. (2000). Spatio-temporal representation and reasoning based on RCC-8. In *Proceedings of the Seventh International Conference on Principles of Knowledge Representation and Reasoning (KR2000),* (pp. 3-14). Morgan Kaufmann Publishers.

Wolter, D. (2008). *Spatial representation and reasoning for robot mapping—A shape-based approach* (*Vol. 48*). Springer.

Wolter, D., Freksa, C., & Latecki, L. J. (2008). Towards a generalization of self-localization. In Jefferies, M. E., & Yeap, W. K. (Eds.), *Robot and Cognitive Approaches to Spatial Mapping.* London, UK: Springer. doi:10.1007/978-3-540-75388-9_7

Wolter, F., & Zakharyaschev, M. (2002). Qualitative spatiotemporal representation and reasoning: A computational perspective. In Lakemeyer, G., & Nebel, B. (Eds.), *Exploring Artificial Intelligence in the New Millennium* (pp. 175–215). Morgan Kaufmann.

Worboys, M. (1998). Modelling changes and events in dynamic spatial systems with reference to socio-economic units. In *Proceedings of ESF GISDATA Conference on Modelling Change in Socio-Economic Units.* Taylor and Francis.

Worboys, M., & Hornby, K. (2004). From objects to events: GEM, the geospatial event model. In *Proceedings of International Conference on GIScience 2004,* (pp. 327-344). Springer Verlag.

Worboys, M. F. (2005). Event-oriented approaches to geographic phenomena. *International Journal of Geographical Information Science, 19*(1), 1–28. doi:10.1080/13658810412331280167

WordNet. (2010). *Website.* Retrieved from http://www.cogsci.princeton.edu/~wn/.

Wu, X., & Palmer, M. (1994). Web semantics and lexical selection. In *Proceedings of the 32nd ACL Meeting.* ACL.

Xia, L., & Li, S. (2006). On mimimal models of the region connection calculus. *Fundamenta Informaticae, 69*(4), 427–446.

Xu, J., Cao, Y., Lim, E., & Ng, W. (1998). Database selection techniques for routing bibliographic queries. In *Proceedings of the 3rd ACM International Conference on Digital Libraries.* ACM Press.

Yang, B., & Salustri, F. (1999). Function modeling based on interactions of mass, energy and information. In *Proceedings of the Florida Artificial Intelligence Research Society Conference (FLAIRS-12)*, (pp. 384–388). FLAIRS.

Youngblood, G. M., & Cook, D. J. (2007). Data mining for hierarchical model creation. *IEEE Transactions on Systems, Man, and Cybernetics. Part C, 37*(4), 561–572.

Yu, C. T., Meng, W., Wu, W., & Liu, K. L. (2001). Efficient and effective metasearch for text databases incorporating linkages among documents. In *Proceedings of the ACM SIGMOD International Conference on Management of Data.* ACM Press.

Yuan, M., Mark, D. M., Egenhofer, M. J., & Peuquet, D. J. (2004). *Extensions to geographic representations in a research agenda for geographic information science*. Boca Raton, FL: CRC Press.

Zimmermann, K., & Freksa, C. (1996). Qualitative spatial reasoning using orientation, distance, and path knowledge. *Applied Intelligence*, *6*(1), 49–58. doi:10.1007/BF00117601

# About the Contributors

**Shyamanta M. Hazarika** is a Professor of Computer Science and Engineering at Tezpur University. He completed his BE from Assam Engineering College, Guwhati, M.Tech in Robotics from IIT Kanpur, and PhD from University of Leeds, England. He has been a Full Professor for Cognitive Systems and NeuroInformatics at the Cognitive Systems Group, University of Bremen, Germany, for Winter 2009-2010. His work has focused primarily in knowledge representation and reasoning and rehabilitation robotics with an aim towards development of intelligent assistive systems.

* * *

**Ahed Alboody** was born at Lattakia in Syria, on August 28, 1978. He received the B.Sc degree in Electrical Engineering (Electronics) and diploma of higher studies in Computer Science and Automatic Control from Tishreen University in Syria, in 2002 and 2003, respectively. From 2002 to 2005, he was an Assistant Professor at the faculty of Electrical and Electronics Engineering in Tishreen University. In 2006, he received the M.S degree in Master 2 Recherche Micro-Ondes, Electro- Magnétisme et Opto-Electronique (MEMO 2) from the École Nationale Supérieure d'Electrotechnique, d'Electronique, d'Informatique, d'Hydraulique et des Télécommunications (ENSEEIHT) and the Institut National Polytechnique de Toulouse (INPT) at Toulouse in France. From 2006 to 2009, he was a Ph.D student in Informatics, Hypermedia, and Image at the University of Paul Sabatier-Toulouse III at Toulouse in France. His research interests include qualitative spatial reasoning, topological models, topological relations, spatial databases, Geographic Information System (GIS), and satellite image processing. A. Alboody is a member of Association for Computing Machinery (ACM), ACM Sigspatial Group, and the Technical Program Committees of the Second International Conference on Advances in Databases, Knowledge, and Data Applications (DBKDA 2010).

**Robert Amor** is an Associate Professor in the Department of Computer Science at the University of Auckland. He has been researching in the field of Construction IT for over twenty years in positions around New Zealand and also for five years as a Research Scientist at the Building Research Establishment (BRE Ltd). Robert is the coordinator of the CIB's (International Council for Research and Innovation in Building and Construction) working group on Construction IT (W78, http://w78.civil.auc.dk/). Robert has been involved with international standards development for the representation of buildings for over a decade and is currently a board member of the Australasian chapter of the International Alliance for Interoperability (IAI, http://www.buildingsmart.com/). Robert has published extensively in the field of Construction IT with 4 edited books, 1 book chapter, 13 refereed journal papers, 44 refereed conference papers, 47 abstract refereed conference papers, and 36 other works.

**Sotiris Batsakis** received a diploma in Computer Engineering and Informatics from the University of Patras, Greece, and a Master's degree in Electronic and Computer Engineering from the Technical University of Crete, Greece. He is currently working toward a Ph.D. degree at the Technical University of Crete. His research interests include Web information retrieval, semantic Web, spatial and temporal representation and reasoning.

**Mehul Bhatt** is an Alexander von Humboldt Postdoctoral Fellow based at the SFB/TR 8 Spatial Cognition, University of Bremen. His academic career also includes research experiences at the Data Engineering and Knowledge Management Group, La Trobe University, Australia (PhD), at the Knowledge Representation and Reasoning Group, University of New South Wales, Australia (Research Scholar), and at the Spatial Information Research Center (SIRC), University of Otago, New Zealand (Guest Researcher). His interests and publications encompass the areas of spatio-temporal reasoning, commonsense and non-monotonic reasoning as applicable to space and time, cognitive robotics, applied ontology, and parallel and distributed systems. Mehul Bhatt has been an organizer / editor of specialized workshops / publications in the area of spatial and temporal reasoning and its application in several areas of emerging interest.

**Seyed Hossein Chavoshi** is a Ph.D. Researcher in Geographical Information Science. He received a Master's degree in Geospatial Information Systems at the University of Tehran (Iran). As a researcher, he is active in a variety of research fields including moving objects (spatio-temporal modelling), 3D GIS, Web GIS, Mobile GIS, agent-based simulation, and disaster management. In 2009, he joined the CartoGIS Cluster at the Department of Geography of Ghent University (Belgium) and started his current Ph.D. research. This work aims at the development, evaluation, and application of a conceptual model for representing, reasoning about, and querying evolutions of objects in multi-dimensional space and time.

**Anthony G. Cohn** holds a Personal Chair at the University of Leeds (United Kingdom) and leads a research group working on Knowledge Representation and Reasoning with a particular focus on qualitative spatial/spatio-temporal reasoning. His research interests range from theoretical work on spatial calculi (including the Region Connection Calculus) and spatial ontologies, to cognitive vision, modelling spatial information in the hippocampus, and theory and applications in geographical information science. He has been Chairman/President of the UK AI Society SSAISB, the European Coordinating Committee on AI (ECCAI), KR Inc, the IJCAI Board of Trustees, and is Editor-in-Chief of the AAAI Press, *Spatial Cognition and Computation*, and *Artificial Intelligence*. He was elected a founding Fellow of ECCAI, and is also a Fellow of AAAI, AISB, the BCS, and the IET.

**Ernest Davis** is a Professor of Computer Science at New York University. His research interest is to study the problem of representing commonsense knowledge: that is, the problem of taking the basic knowledge about the real world that is common to all humans, expressing it in a form that is systematic enough to be used by a computer program, and providing the program with techniques for effectively using that knowledge. His work has focused primarily on spatial and physical reasoning, but he has also looked at reasoning about knowledge, belief, plans, and goals, and their interaction with physical reasoning.

**Matthias Delafontaine** is a Ph.D. Researcher in Geographical Information Science. He holds a Master of Science degree in Geography with a specialization in Cartography and Geographical Information Systems. In 2006, he started working on both fundamental and applied research projects as a scientific staff member at the Department of Geography of Ghent University (Belgium). In 2007, he received a Research Grant from the Research Foundation – Flanders and started his current research, which focuses on the implementation of information systems for the retrieval and extraction of information from moving objects. He joined the CartoGIS Cluster research team in 2008. An important part of his work has contributed to the extension and implementation of the Qualitative Trajectory Calculus (QTC).

**Danilo dos Santos** M.Sc. at FEI in 2009 and is currently a PhD student.

**Rodolpho Freire** M.Sc. at FEI in 2009 and is currently a PhD student.

**Michael Grüninger** is a Professor at the Department of Mechanical and Industrial Engineering of University of Toronto (Ontario, Canada). His research focus is in the design and formal characterization of ontologies and their application to problems in manufacturing and enterprise engineering. Previously, he has held research positions at the Institute for Systems Research at the University of Maryland College Park and at the National Institute for Standards and Technology (NIST) in the USA. Michael received his Ph.D. and M.Sc. in Computer Science at the University of Toronto and his B.Sc. in Computer Science at the University of Alberta. His current research focuses on the design and formal characterization of ontologies and their application to problems in manufacturing and enterprise engineering. He is the project leader for the Process Specification Language project at NIST. He is also the project leader for ISO 18629 (Process Specification Language) within the International Standards Organization (ISO), and he was the project editor for project ISO 24707 (Common Logic).

**Hans Guesgen** is a Professor of Computer Science in the School of Engineering and Advanced Technology at Massey University in Palmerston North, New Zealand. He holds a diploma in Computer Science and Mathematics of the University of Bonn, a Doctorate in Computer Science of the University of Kaiserslautern, and a Higher Doctorate (Habilitation) in Computer Science of the University of Hamburg, Germany. He worked as a research scientist at the German National Research Center of Computer Science (GMD) at Sankt Augustin from 1983 to 1992. During this period he held a one-year post-doctoral fellowship at the International Computer Science Institute in Berkeley, California. In 1992, he joined the Computer Science Department of the University of Auckland, where he worked until moving to Massey University in 2007. His research interests include ambient intelligence and spatio-temporal reasoning.

**Torsten Hahmann** is a PhD student at the Department of Computer Science of University of Toronto (Ontaria, Canada). A native of Germany, he completed, in 2006, his B.Sc. in Software Systems Engineering at the Hasso-Plattner-Institute (HPI) Potsdam, Germany. He has been involved with research on service oriented architectures as part of the PESOA (Process Family Engineering in Service-Oriented Applications) and the ASG (Adaptive Service Grid, part of the FP6 of the EU) projects. For his graduate studies at the University of Toronto, Torsten's research has been focused on first-order representations of region-based space, so-called mereotopological ontologies, receiving his M.Sc. in Computer Science in 2008. Besides a focus on algebraic and topological representations of mereotopologies, he is interested in real-world applications of such mereotopological ontologies as well in building repositories of first-order ontologies for his ongoing research.

**Jordi Inglada** received the Telecommunications Engineer degree in 1997 from both Universitat Politècnica de Catalunya and Ecole Nationale Supérieure des Télécommunications de Bretagne and the PhD degree in Signal Processing and Telecommunications in 2000 from Université de Rennes 1. He has been since working at Centre National d'Etudes Spatiales, the French Space Agency, in Toulouse, France, in the field of remote sensing image processing. He is in charge for the development of image processing algorithms for the operational exploitation of earth observation images, mainly in the fields of image registration, change detection, and object recognition.

**Florent Launay** focused his research on constraint satisfaction problem in time and interval algebras during his undergraduate and graduate studies at Florida Institute of Technology. After defending his graduate thesis, Florent continued his research with a new interest towards minimal culprit detection in inconsistent interval systems and maximal tractable interval sub-algebra. Florent Launay currently works as a test engineer at Microsoft Corporation and lives with his wife and son in Redmond, Washington.

**Mário Louzã** is a MD graduate at São Paulo University Medical School (1987), Ph.D. in Psychiatry by Universität Würzburg (1988), Postdoctorate by Deutscher Akademischer Austauschdienst (1991), Postdoctorate by Deutscher Akademischer Austauschdienst (1994) at the Zentralinstitut für Seelische Gesundheit. Currently he is an Attending Physician at the Institut of Psychiatry, University of São Paulo Medical School, Coordinator of the Schizophrenia Research Program (PROJESQ), and Professor of Post-Graduation at the Department of Psychiatry of the São Paulo University Medical School.

**Fulvio Mastrogiovanni** received the M.S. degree in Computer Science Engineering and the Ph.D. degree in Robotics from the University of Genova, Italy. He is currently a Postdoctoral Associate with the Department of Communication, Computer, and System Sciences, University of Genova, where he works on designing artificial and biologically inspired cognitive systems, with a special focus on knowledge representation and acquisition, as well as reasoning, self-acquired knowledge self-awareness.

**Euripides Petrakis** received a Bachelors degree in Physics from the National University of Athens in 1985 and a Ph.D degree in Computer Science from the University of Crete in 1993. Between 1996 and 1998, he was a Visiting Researcher at the Department of Computer Science of York University, Toronto, Canada, and at GMD/IPSI Institute, Darmstadt, Germany. He joined the Technical University of Crete (TUC) in January 1998, where he is serving as Associate Professor at the Computer Science division of the Department of Electronic and Computer Engineering, and Director of the Intelligent Systems Laboratory. He has published on the processing and analysis of image content, image indexing, image database and medical information systems. He is currently involved in research on modern aspects of information retrieval, multimedia information systems, Web information systems, Semantic Web, and information extraction from text. He is a member of the IEEE.

**Paulo Sallet** is a MD graduate from the Federal University of Santa Maria and has a Ph.D. in Psychiatry from the University of São Paulo (2002), during which he spent one year at the University of Würzburg – Germany (1999-2000). He is currently a Medical Assistant at the Institute of Hospital das Clínicas, Faculty of Medicine, University of São Paulo, and works as a Doctor in a Psychiatric Emergency at the Psychiatric Department II, Franco da Rocha, and at a private psychiatric clinic – Clínica

Sallet. He has experience in psychiatry, with emphasis on psychosis, acting mainly on the following topics: schizophrenia, psychopharmacology, neuroimaging, classification of psychosis, binge eating, and psychiatric disorders associated with bariatric.

**Paulo Santos** received his PhD degree in Electrical Engineering from Imperial College, London, in 2003. He was a research assistant at the School of Computing, University of Leeds, from mid-2003 to 2005, where he was par t of a team of researchers that conceived and developed a system that was awarded the British Machine Intelligence Price in 2004. Currently Paulo is an Associate Professor at FEI, Sao Paulo, Brazil, in the ðeld of Artiðcial Intelligence and Robotics. His research interests include spatial reasoning, cognitive vision, medical image interpretation, and intelligent robotics.

**Antonello Scalmato** received the M.S. degree in Computer Science from the University of Genova, Italy. He is currently a Ph.D. student with the Department of Communication, Computer, and System Sciences, University of Genova. His research topics are related to Robotics and Ambient Intelligence, with a special focus on knowledge representation and intelligent autonomous agents.

**Carl Schultz** is a PhD student at the Department of Computer Science, the University of Auckland. He received the Bachelor of Engineering degree in Software Engineering with First Class Honours from the University of Auckland in 2006. The focus of his research is applied qualitative spatial and temporal reasoning. He is a recipient of the Bright Future Top Achiever Doctoral Scholarship.

**Florence Sèdes** (IEEE member) is a Professor in Computer Science at Paul Sabatier University (Université des Sciences, Toulouse, France). She received her PhD degree in Computer Science in 1987. She is currently heading the Generalised Information Systems group at the IRIT (Institut de Recherché en Informatique de Toulouse, CNRS/UPS, France). She also is the director of the Information-Interaction-Intelligence National Research Network (GDR CNRS i3). She is member of the French National Council of Universities, for Computer Science.

**Antonio Sgorbissa** received the M.S. degree in Electronics Engineering and the Ph.D. degree in Robotics from the University of Genova, Italy. Currently, he is Assistant Professor in Computer Science with the Faculty of Engineering and of the Department of Humanities, University of Genova, and he leads the Mobile Robotics "Laboratorium," Department of Communication, Computer, and System Sciences. His main research interests are related to intelligent systems, with a special focus on robotics, distributed systems, reasoning, and ambient intelligence.

**Sofia Stamou** is a Lecturer at the Department of Archives and Library Science of the Ionian University and Adjunct Lecturer at the Computer Engineering and Informatics Department of Patras University. Her area of expertise is text analysis and language processing with an emphasis on semantic analysis of textual data. Her research interests include Web searching, personalization, ontologies, text mining, and data organization. She received her Ph.D. and M.Sc. degrees from the Computer Engineering and Informatics Department of Patras University in 2002 and 2006, respectively, and her B.A. in Philosophy from the University of Ioannina in 1999. She has served as a program committee member in several conferences that relate to the areas of expertise and she has published the results of her research in several international conferences and journals.

**Kazuko Takahashi** received the degrees of B.S. and Dr. of Engineering from Kyoto University in 1982 and 1994, respectively. She was a researcher at the Central Research Laboratory and Advanced Technology R&D Center of Mitsubishi Electric Corporation from 1982 to 2000. In 2000, she joined the School of Science, Kwansei Gakuin University, as an Associate Professor. Since 2006, she has been a Professor at School of Science and Technology, Kwansei Gakuin University. She is interested in knowledge representation and reasoning systems, especially on temporal spatial reasoning. She is a member of the Institute of Electronics, Information and Communication Engineers (IEICE), Information Processing Society of Japan (IPSJ), Japan Society for Software Science and Technology (JSSST), and the Japanese Society for Artificial Intelligence (JSAI).

**Carlos Thomaz** is currently an Associate Professor at the Department of Electrical Engineering, at FEI, Sao Paulo, Brazil. He has a Ph. D. in Statistical Pattern Recognition in 2004 from the Department of Computing at Imperial College, London, where he was a Research Associate from December 2003 to January 2005. Carlos's general interests are in computer vision, statistical pattern recognition, medical image computing, and machine learning, whereas his specific research interests are in limited-sample-size problems in pattern recognition.

**Jan Oliver Wallgrün** studied Informatics at the University of Hamburg, Germany, and received his PhD from the University of Bremen, Germany, in 2008 for his work on spatial representations and reasoning for mobile robot navigation employing hierarchical Voronoi graphs. He is currently working as a Post-Doctoral Researcher at the University of Bremen in the DFG-funded International Research Training Group on "Semantic Integration of Geospatial Information." His main research interests are qualitative spatial reasoning and abstract spatial representations, and their application for robot navigation and geographic information systems.

**Nico Van de Weghe** is Professor in Geographical Information Science. In 2004, he obtained a Ph.D. degree in Geography at the Department of Geography of Ghent University (Belgium), where he was appointed as a full-time Lecturer since 2006. In 2008, he became a Leading Member of the CartoGIS Cluster, an academic team combining research and education in cartography and Geographical Information Systems and Science. Van de Weghe is specialized in geographical information science, with a focus on research related to modelling, representing and reasoning about moving objects. Particular emphasis is placed on the use of qualitative descriptions as to be consistent with human cognition, perception, and communication. Although the theoretical foundation of his work, recent evolutions in geographical information technology have triggered the aim for implementing and valorising his results in applications.

**Diedrich Wolter** studied informatics at the University of Hamburg, Germany, and received his Doctoral degree from the University of Bremen, Germany, in 2006 for his work on robot self-localization and mapping using shape-based spatial representations. He is currently principal investigator of the DFG-funded project R3-[Q-Shape] "Qualitative Reasoning about Paths, Shapes, and Configurations" in which primarily qualitative methods are researched that allow an intelligent agent to solve complex spatial tasks. His research interests are spatial reasoning, knowledge representation, and reasoning techniques for intelligent agents.

**Renato Zaccaria** received the M.S. degree in Electrical Engineering from the University of Genova, Italy. He started working on Robotics in the '70s in one of the earlier Italian research groups, which was characterized by a strong interdisciplinary approach. He is currently a Full Professor in Computer Science within the Department of Communication, Computer, and System Sciences, University of Genova, and he is the Local Coordinator of the European Master on Advanced Robotica (EMARO study programme). In 2000, he founded the company "Genova Robotics," whose present R&D activity is strongly linked to academic research. His current research interests mainly include Service Robotica and Ambient Intelligence. Prof. Zaccaria has been awarded the title "Commendatore della Repubblica" because of his activity in technology transfer in Robotics.

**Nikos Zotos** is a Ph.D. candidate at the Computer Engineering and Informatics Department of Patras University. His area of expertise is online database selection, text mining, personalized search, text extraction, and data organization. He received his Diploma and M.Sc. degrees from the Computer Engineering and Informatics Department of Patras University in 2005 and 2007, respectively. He has published the results of his research in international conferences and journals.

# Index

## R



## S



## T



## V



## W